Lecture Notes in Information Systems and Organisation

Volume 53

Lecture Notes in Information Systems and Organization—LNISO—is a series of scientific books that explore the current scenario of information systems, in particular IS and organization. The focus on the relationship between IT, IS and organization is the common thread of this collection, which aspires to provide scholars across the world with a point of reference and comparison in the study and research of information systems and organization. LNISO is the publication forum for the community of scholars investigating behavioral and design aspects of IS and organization. The series offers an integrated publication platform for high-quality conferences, symposia and workshops in this field. Materials are published upon a strictly controlled double blind peer review evaluation made by selected reviewers.

LNISO is abstracted/indexed in Scopus

More information about this series at https://link.springer.com/bookseries/11237

Evgeny Zaramenskikh · Alena Fedorova
Editors

Digitalization of Society, Economics and Management

A Digital Strategy Based on Post-pandemic Developments

Springer

Editors
Evgeny Zaramenskikh
Higher School of Economics
National Research University
Moscow, Russia

Alena Fedorova
HR Management and Psychology
Ural Federal University
Yekaterinburg, Russia

ISSN 2195-4968 ISSN 2195-4976 (electronic)
Lecture Notes in Information Systems and Organisation
ISBN 978-3-030-94251-9 ISBN 978-3-030-94252-6 (eBook)
https://doi.org/10.1007/978-3-030-94252-6

This Springer imprint is published by the registered company Springer Nature Switzerland AG
The registered company address is: Gewerbestrasse 11, 6330 Cham, Switzerland

Foreword by Jan vom Brocke

Building the digital world is one of the most challenging and rewarding endeavors of our times.[1] It is rewarding, since digitalization affords new action possibilities in all facets of today's life and work.[2] It is challenging, at the same time, it is a socio-technical endeavor of design in highly complex and dynamic environments—it is a journey through space and time.[3] In this regard, the rich collection of articles presented in this book, cover this journey very well, and many exciting "places" are visited, including the construction industry, innovation hubs, hospitals, water supply, higher education, pharmacies, and private households, to name but a few.

A research paradigm that serves to help building the digital world is Design Science Research (DSR).[4] DSR is a research paradigm that enables us to make innovative solutions to real-world problems. DSR is inherently socio-technical, as the real world is socio-technical and it also is inherently work in the intersection of academia and practice, as scientifically grounded solutions to real-world problems are developed in many iterations of design and evaluation. I see that many of the fine contributions in this book show the potential to making such contributions of societal value. The DSR approach can be used to tie together the various exciting contributions to make important solutions to building the digital world.

What is fascinating is the way digital technologies are changing the way things can be (and are) done. In this regard, building the digital world very much means

[1] Becker, J., vom Brocke, J., Heddier, M., Seidel, S. (2015), In Search of Information Systems (Grand) Challenges: A Community of Inquirers Perspective. Business & Information Systems Engineering (BISE), 6(1), 39–43.

[2] Dremel, C., Herterich, M., Wulf, J., vom Brocke, J. (2020). Actualizing Big Data Analytics Affordances: A Revelatory Case Study. Information & Management (I&M), 57(1), 103–121.

[3] vom Brocke, J., Winter, R., Hevner, A., Maedche, A. (2020), Accumulation and Evolution of Design Knowledge in Design Science Research—A Journey Through Time and Space, in: Journals of the Association for Information Systems (JAIS), 2020, 21(3), 520–544.

[4] An Introduction together with a collection of cases is provided by vom Brocke J., Hevner A., Maedche A. (2020) Introduction to Design Science Research. In: vom Brocke J., Hevner A., Maedche A. (eds) Design Science Research. Cases, Cham. https://doi.org/10.1007/978-3-030-46781-4_1.

to discover new ways to do things. In other words: we innovate processes.[5] Such processes are more efficient, but they are also more environmentally friendly[6] or more healthy, as recent studies show.[7] In this book, processes of diverse areas are covered, in which digital technology, such as Bid Data Analytics, Data Mining, Process Mining, and Dynamic Computation Planning, is used to improve, e.g., learning processes, water supply processes, medical processes, supply processes, telecommunication processes, decision processes, and construction processes, to name but a few.

I would like to applaud the editors of this book, Evgeny Zaramenskikh and Alena Fedorova, for their vision and strength in organizing this impressive collection of contributions on such an important matter both for academia and practice as well as society. I would also like to express my appreciation to all authors, for their high-quality work on building the digital world. It is fascinating to see the many important contributions the Russian Chapter of the Association for Information Systems has accomplished over the past years. I feel very privileged that I have been provided the opportunity to be part of this movement.

I wish the readers rich insights and much pleasure with the reading.

Vaduz, Liechtenstein Prof. Dr. Jan vom Brocke

[5] J. vom Brocke & J. Mendling, Rosemann (Eds.). (2021). Digital Transformation—Strategy, Processes and Execution—Business Process Management Cases (Vol. 2). Berlin et al.: Springer.

[6] Seidel, S., Recker, J., & vom Brocke, J. (2012). Green Business Process Management. In J. vom Brocke, S. Seidel & J. Recker (Eds.), Green Business Process Management – Towards the Sustainable Enterprise (pp. 3–14). Heidelberg, Germany: Springer.

[7] Hacker, J., vom Brocke, J., Handali, J., Otto, M., Schneider, J. (2020), Virtually in this Together—How Web-Conferencing Systems Enabled a New Virtual Togetherness During the COVID-19 Crisis, in: European Journal of Information Systems (EJIS), 29(5): 563–584.

Foreword by Marco de Marco

In the current era known as Industry 4.0., a central theme emerged which shapes the entire society from different perspectives. This requires further attention from the academic world. Specifically, our focus as scholars should be given to the digital transformation.

Therefore, in the today's digital age many questions arise that need important investigations and analyses to better understand the *state of art* of this unique phenomenon that influence our daily life at the individual, organizational as well as at the institutional level.

The today's digital revolution has changed the past rules and features. It presents new challenges and opportunities for the majority of actor. Many well-known and established standards should be reviewed with the lens of innovative assumptions and aspects.

In other words, previous methods and techniques that were validated and consistent in the pre-digital period have to be reconsidered in this actual setting addressed by the digital trend. Thus, what does it mean digital transformation?

On the one hand, digital identifies changes driven by information technologies (IT) that allow different methods and approaches related to data management. On the other hand, transformation underlines as well a change toward an evolutionary set of elements related to peculiar aspects, domains, and targets. Consequently, we are living an important shift worldwide no matter if at the individual or organizational level.

In a certain sense, we have to adapt and transform ourselves to build the digital world. Thriving on the digitalization, businesses, people, governments need to handle this disruptive threat formulating new techniques, tools, and strategies which help the development of this transformation.

In pursuing this necessary goal, crucial insights, perspectives and questions are growing in the scientific community. For instance, the implementation of new business models revolutionized the traditional way of doing business.

In the meantime, alternative organizational structures and managerial concepts emerged. Hence, the exploitation of digital technologies brings and overall rethinking of a huge number of elements such as processes, products, supply chain, and sales channels.

In fact, innovative techniques redefine not only the processes and products of various activities but also the interactions with customers. Following the higher technology connectivity and its speed, we face also changes in consumer behaviors.

In other words, nowadays, new digital frameworks have come out to adequate the business development of different kinds of organizations. Thus, a set of strategies and tolls are designed to respond to the dimensions of the digital transformation.

In this unique scenario, data analytics, cloud storage, augmented reality, Internet of things, open data, machine learning, artificial intelligence are some of the main examples and fundamental players of our complex architecture.

Given this, industries, sectors, organizations are rethinking the standard modes seeking disruptive approaches.

Digital transformation implies the integration of new digital technologies even in terms of innovative culture that influences the working system. The latter is clearly highlighted with the COVID-19 pandemic that in many cases represents a global compulsory test. Despite the current pandemic opens asleep discussion on a bunch of topics related to the digital setting, as for instance, the remote or smart working. Indeed, many scholars already dealt with the role of the digital work setting from different sides such as employment, human resources management, etc.[8]

In addition, the teaching and learning perspective is moving forward focusing on the digital skills and capabilities to achieve excellent results on the education system.

Moreover, further investigations are required in the digital governmental services as in the interesting field of platform that aggregate different services to improve the citizens security and the overall safety.[9] However, also the communication sphere asks for adequate infrastructures to fit this transformation.

In other terms, digital transformation affects the economic, social, regulatory, technical backdrop but also it influences the psychological as well as the behavioral perspective.

These are only few examples that our society should consider for the present and close future development. In line with this, the digital transformation required a holistic approach. A large reflection of interest at the individual, company, and at government level.

All these players have to better exploit the digital setting recognizing its value, importance, opportunities, and challenges.

This is a significant course change for various disciplines as well as for different fields of research. In this book, a broader view is presented, looking at several domains

[8] For example, Menshikova M., Fedorova A. and Gatti M. *Introducing Smart-Working in the Conditions of Digital Business Transformation: Analysis of an Employee's Experience* (Springer, LNISO, volume 40, 2020).

[9] For example, Zaramenskikh E., Lyubarskaya M. *Integration of Digital Services Within the Framework of the Implementation of "Government as a Platform"(GaaP)* (Springer, Digital Transformation and New Challenges: Digitalization of Society, Economics, Management and Education, volume 40, 2020).

that deeply study the digital dimension to contribute to the current knowledge about building a digital world.

Roma, Italy
Prof. Marco de Marco

Contents

The Role of Big Data Technologies in Geographically Distributed Medical Organizations' IT Service Architecture

Alissa Dubgorn and Alena Ershova

Abstract The paper presents an analysis of how big data technologies can be applied to the business activities of geographically distributed medical organizations. Characteristics of geographically distributed medical organizations are analyzed in the context of information requirements and opportunities of big data matching these requirements. A case study is presented, describing a Russian geographically distributed organization's functional structure and enterprise architecture model presenting, how IT applications and big data technologies interact when realizing analytics IT services.

Keywords Medical organizations · Geographically distributed medical organizations · IT service architecture · Big data in health care

1 Introduction

The introduction of digital technologies into the activities of modern organizations is an urgent issue for most areas of activity. The field of medicine and health care is no exception—the evolving concepts of value-based medicine, personalized and predictive medicine, as well as end-to-end digital technologies open up great opportunities for the complex digitalization of medical institutions. The implementation of projects within the framework of the state programs "Healthcare Development," "Information Society," "Digital Economy of the Russian Federation" is aimed, inter alia, at the formation of a single digital space in the field of medicine and health care. Since 2011, a program has been implemented to create a Unified State Information System in the Healthcare Sector, designed to unite the existing state information systems in the healthcare sector—information systems of medical institutions, Federal and territorial compulsory medical insurance funds, health care of the constituent entities of the Russian Federation, pharmaceutical organizations. At the same time, the issue of integrating medical and economic data within the framework of a single

A. Dubgorn (✉) · A. Ershova
Peter the Great St. Petersburg Polytechnic University, Polytechnicheskaya str.29, St. Petersburg 195251, Russia

E. Zaramenskikh and A. Fedorova (eds.), *Digitalization of Society, Economics and Management*, Lecture Notes in Information Systems and Organisation 53,
https://doi.org/10.1007/978-3-030-94252-6_1

information space is relevant not only for the state but also for commercial medical institutions interacting, in addition to the above-mentioned healthcare entities, with medical insurance funds.

Over the past ten years, the number of medical information systems developed on the Russian market has approached a hundred, projects for the implementation of such systems have been successfully completed in many medical organizations, however, the challenges of digital transformation and the need to create a unified information space in the field of medicine and health care form new requirements for information and technological support of both the processes of providing medical care and the processes of managing medical organizations. At the same time, the issue of the development of the management system and its information technology support becomes especially relevant for geographically distributed organizations due to the need to ensure the quality and compatibility of data from various sources for the purpose of their comprehensive analysis, the formation of corporate reporting and compliance with legal requirements.

Reforming the activities of medical organizations, caused by the need to introduce end-to-end digital technologies, including technologies for collecting, storing, and processing big data, poses an urgent task to develop architectural models for the activities of geographically distributed organizations, taking into account the possibilities of digital technologies.

2 Materials and Methods

The object of the research is represented by geographically distributed medical organizations, situated in Russian Federation. The first part of the Results paragraph describes types and forms of medical organizations in Russian Federation according to the type of ownership and geographical factor.

The second part of the Results paragraph represents the review of the possibilities of applying Big Data technologies in medical organizations focusing on those topical for geographically distributed organizations, which basically means there are several clinics located in different regions. Here, the method of analysis of literary sources is used, including scientific articles, monographs, reports of consulting and research companies.

The last part of the Results paragraph represents the Case of a Russian geographically distributed medical organization, where IT service architecture, based on Big Data opportunities, is modeled. The main research methods used in this part of research are:

- The enterprise architecture (EA) approach [1], which allows modeling the business, information and technology domains of an enterprise in order to analyze the interdependencies of the domain's object and to realize organization development projects based on the results of such analysis. The TOGAF EA framework and ArchiMate EA modeling language represent the methodological basis EA approach.

- The method of modeling IT service architecture is presented in Dubgorn [2]. This method involves the implementation of the following steps:
  - Formation of a functional model of the organization.
  - Determine the needs of business functions in IT services.
  - Analysis of the capabilities of information systems and digital technologies.
  - Formulation of the main task of the IT service (naming the IT service).
  - Adding the identified IT service into the overall service architecture.

3 Results

3.1 Toward Geographically Distributed Medical Organizations in Russian Federation

All modern medical organizations in Russian Federation can be conditionally divided into two groups: localized and geographically distributed.

The term "localized" means that a given company is located in a relatively small area with uniform environmental conditions for all its divisions and with the possibility of organizing its control and management activities through unified channels [3].

The structure of complex geographically distributed organizations corresponds to the network model. The development of networks covering several medical organizations has become one of the notable trends in recent times. The economic growth of the past decade has given a powerful impetus to phenomena such as corporate network clinics and private medical networks not directly associated with corporations.

It should be noted that the phrase "network of medical clinics" refers to a group of enterprises, which, regardless of the organizational and legal form of its individual units and regardless of the details of the management system, is united by the presence of common material and technological resources. In other words, within the network, there is a fairly free, although not always strictly formalized exchange of personnel, funds, and information. Commercial networks usually have a common composition of owners, although franchise schemes have also appeared recently. In public institutions, the elements of the network structure can be presented as an option in the form of regulatory, methodological, and administrative links between organizational units. As in other industries, the network model in health care can reduce administrative costs, form service delivery standards, gain economies of scale in procurement, etc. [4].

Networks of medical organizations are usually represented by the following organizational models:

- A large (multidisciplinary) healthcare facility located in several buildings, possibly geographically distant from each other.
- A network of branches with separate legal entities.
- Close cooperation of several "friendly" healthcare facilities, roughly equivalent in capacity, but possibly with different specializations.

Let us list some features of each of the above cases.

Large (multidisciplinary) healthcare facility at geographically close or remote sites.

- One legal entity.
- The structure includes several components of the same type, such as Hospital, Paraclinic, Polyclinic (it should be noted that they are not always explicitly present in the organizational structure of medical facilities).
- The collection of statistical data on various aspects of activities is carried out both in the context of the building (territory, site) and throughout the healthcare facility as a whole.
- Unified database of patients, electronic medical records. It is possible to maintain several paper outpatient records for one patient (in different buildings), but for management, it is important to combine the history of visits/cases of patient care, the transition to a single electronic medical record.
- Transfer of patients from departments of one building to departments of another is possible. It is considered a hospital transfer. But more often the movement of patients occurs within the same building/territory.
- A unified register of services is being formed. Financial statements are generated from the organization as a whole.
- Material supply is carried out through the central warehouse (according to the accessories—pharmacy, medical equipment, catering, etc.).

A number of "friendly" healthcare facilities

Such forms of cooperation are often found in the work of departmental institutions that have not only a contingent of the same affiliation, but also a certain degree of freedom in such areas of mutual cooperation as the exchange of information, the direction of patient flows, etc. An example is departmental health facilities with differing sets of patient care options. For example, one has the capacity of an immunological laboratory, the other has tomography and angiography, and at the same time contracts are concluded for the mutual service of patients in the amount of services that are not available at this healthcare facility. Private clinics can also informally unite into similar structures to optimize their activities, provide an expanded range of services, etc.

Branch network

It is formed on the basis of/with the separation of the head institution, either multidisciplinary or specialized. Branches can be both separate legal entities and as part of the head medical institution (usually with a close territorial location).

- Branches are registered, as a rule, as separate legal entities.
- Among the individual linear, located on the periphery of the branches, there can be found both consisting of only one component (as a rule, it is a Polyclinic), and complex. The central healthcare facility is a large complex multidisciplinary medical institution (see especially above) or specialized.
- The collection of statistical data is carried out separately for each branch. At the head office, it is also necessary to analyze the aggregated statistics for the entire network. Much attention is paid to the design of patients transferred from the branches to the Center (completeness, correctness, timeliness of documentation, the quality of medical measures is assessed at all levels of the network).
- The exchange of initial data is necessary to ensure the continuity and correct continuation of treatment.
- Transfers of patients to another healthcare facility are issued with an extract and accompanied by all the necessary documentation. It is possible to provide additional data, analyze the correspondence of information in the outgoing and receiving healthcare facilities (the coincidence of diagnoses, assessment of the quality of medical care at the previous stage, etc.).
- Service registers are formed separately. The center receives summary information about the financial performance of each health facility in the network.
- Material supply is carried out through the central warehouses of each legal entity (centralized purchases are possible with transfer to the warehouses of branches) [5].

Based on the analysis [6–8] the following principles of a geographically distributed medical organization's management were considered:

Centralized control system;

Functional subordination to the relevant departments the parent company in priority over the administrative subordination to the management of the branch;

- Transparency;
- Office of Exceptions;
- Single information space;
- Standardization of process management;
- Uniform standards for the implementation of activities;
- Accounting and adaptation to local (economic, cultural, etc.) peculiarities of the branch location.

All of the above principles should be taken into account when considering the possibilities of using certain digital technologies in the activities of geographically distributed medical organizations.

3.2 Big Data Opportunities for Medical Organizations

In the field of health care, one can single out such areas of application of Big Data as solving problems of personalized medicine, forecasting epidemics, combating existing diseases, treating, and preventing diseases, improving treatment methods based on a huge statistical base [9]. The main purpose of using Big Data in health care is aimed at processing biomedical data, data analysis, visualization, and obtaining results.

Big data can be classified into three main groups:

- transactional data—data from invoices, payment orders, storage records, delivery records, orders, and expense data;
- clinical data—data collected from medical information systems, industrial equipment, real-time data from sensors and wearable technologies, medical mobile applications as well as weblogs that track user behavior on the Internet;
- social data—data coming from social services such as Facebook, Twitter, VK, and YouTube that provide insight into patient behavior and moods [10].

Presenting the results of an in-depth study of the possibilities of Big Data technology for use in the medical field, the following should be highlighted:

- carrying out comprehensive diagnostics allows solving the problems of diagnosing rare diseases, preventing epidemics;
- processing of the data collection results obtained using signals from medical gadgets. New medical devices allow collecting information about a patient and sending it to one data warehouse;
- information support for emergency assistance, which allows timely diagnosis of critical conditions, prevention of lethal effects of the environment;
- medical assistance using telemedicine technologies. This allows for remote examination, promptly prescribing the trajectory of treatment;
- introduction of comprehensive prevention, which allows for comprehensive treatment of patients receiving a range of drugs. In the event of an operation, it becomes necessary to process an array of data on the patient's life processes;
- supporting patient safety in intensive care and intensive care units using analytical systems to predict surgical risk;
- reducing costs with the help of value that drives better patient outcomes for long-term savings;
- the intelligence of electronic health records (EHR) [11].

Big data processing technologies allow you to answer 4 types of questions [12]:

- Descriptive (descriptive analytics)—"what happened?" The purpose of such an analysis is to compose an objective and maximally accurate description of the current situation, to turn huge amounts of data into accessible, understandable, and easily perceived information. Most organizations today are at this initial stage of analytics and even here are experiencing enormous difficulties due to data shortages.

- Diagnostic—"why did this happen?" The purpose of diagnostic analytics is to identify predictors of the development of the current situation. Such analytics still implies a retrospective analysis, but it still allows us to understand the reasons for certain trends, shortcomings and outline ways to improve.
- Predictive (predictive analytics)—"what happens next?" The purpose of predictive analytics is to predict the onset of certain events, to model development scenarios. Competent predictive analytics systems can predict changes in patient flows, simulate clinical scenarios and the time a patient is in a particular stage of medical care, simulate the epidemiological situation, predict morbidity, outcomes, mortality [13].
- Prescriptive (prescriptive analytics)—"what to do?" The goal is to build a trajectory of change to obtain the desired result. Prescriptive analytics is the highest level of data manipulation. It allows, based on the model, to determine what needs to be changed in order to reach the desired result, in what time frame and with what resources. As you move along the hierarchy of analytics, the complexity of the analysis increases, but the value of its result also progressively increases.

If we talk about geographically distributed medical organizations in the context of the relevance of the use of big data technologies to support their main (medical), as well as managerial and auxiliary processes [14, 15], the following conclusions can be drawn:

- Big data technologies as support of telemedicine processes play a big role due to the opportunity of providing medical services in remote regions, as well as connecting top specialists from the specific medical center to medical consultations and manipulations realized in other centers situated in different regions.
- Big data technologies as a resource for potential market analysis—this helps with identifying geographic markets with a high potential for growth, which is especially important for commercial medical organizations.
- When a potential market is found, there is a need in effective marketing activities, which big data allows due to collecting and systemizing information about consumers, patients, physician needs, and preferences.
- The larger the geographically distributed medical organization is, the more data it collects not only about patients but also about management processes. Analyzing this data helps improve management decisions, e.g., on drugs & materials logistics, patient flow processes, HR management (especially the processes of continuous training of medical specialists), etc.
- The research activities of geographically distributed medical organizations are seen as one of the main directions of big data technologies application, because of the ability to analyze medical data represented from different regions of the Russian Federation. This makes it possible to find non-trivial patterns, interdependencies, trends, etc., and form new standards and treatment protocols based on the analysis results.

3.3 Case Study: IT Service Architecture for Big Data Usage

The formal structure of the Case organization is represented by several legal entities united under a single brand and functionally managed by a single body—the management company.

The organization has faced the challenge of reorganizing its IT architecture in response to strong growth over the past few years. At the same time, growth occurs both through the construction and opening of new medical centers in different regions of RF "from scratch" and the acquisition of existing (operating) organizations. The management model has undergone significant changes since it became necessary to create a unified management center that could act as a developer of operating standards, as well as a body for strategic and current control of activities carried out in geographically distributed business units. This need was reflected in the creation of a management company.

Tasks faced by the medical organization at the time of the decision on the need to apply big data technologies are:

- The need to integrate disparate information systems used by "acquired" healthcare organizations with systems used in the management organization;
- The need to improve systems that support management functions, taking into account the increasing number and specifics of individual business units;
- The need for analysis of real-time data produced by supporting functions of the organization (engineering, procurement, and logistics, etc.);
- The need to introduce digital services to attract new customers, increase the loyalty of existing customers, increase competitiveness due to a large number of commercial medical organizations with a similar profile of activity.

In accordance with the method of developing the architecture of IT services [2] as a first step, a functional model of the case organization was developed. The result is represented in Fig. 1.

The next step in the application of the method for developing the architecture of IT services for the presented organization was the identification of information needs of business functions. In the process of a dialogue between a business analyst and a manager/representative of each of the functions presented in the model, as well as studying the documentation existing within the framework of the function being performed, a list of information needs was developed. Next, an analysis was made of the capabilities of big data technologies in relation to meeting the identified information needs. Table 1 represents the results of this analysis.

Based on the aggregated information from Table 1 the high-level architecture model [16] was designed, describing data flows from IT applications to the big data engine, as well as analytics results flow back to IT applications, used by business functions. The architecture model is presented in Fig. 2.

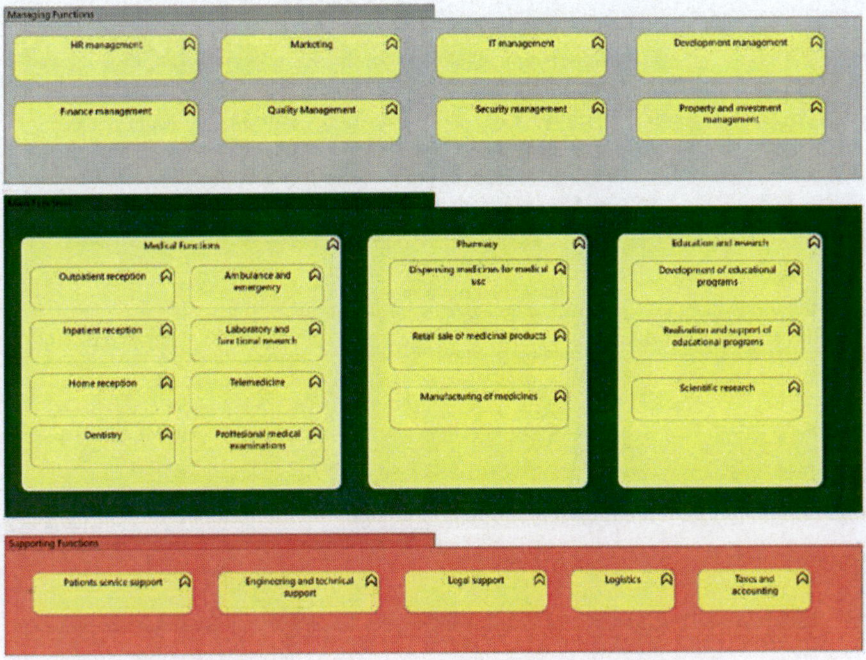

Fig. 1 Functional model of a geographically distributed medical organization

4 Conclusion

The use of digital technologies is becoming an increasingly relevant and demanded task for medical organizations. This is due, among other things, to the increasing availability of such technologies. Geographically distributed medical organizations face a number of management and scientific tasks, the solution of which using big data technologies may be more effective and efficient.

Enterprise architecture approach can be applied to analyze, how to build big data technologies into the complex architecture of a medical organization. The next step of research is to model a detailed IT service architecture of a geographically distributed medical organization with the use of digital technologies opportunities.

Table 1 Ways of applying technologies at different levels

Function	Information requirement of the function	Opportunities of using big data technologies
Development management	Collection and processing of data on market share in the context of segments of medical services and individual business units	Collection of data from social networks and Web, integration of data from different sources (incl. MIS and CRM), intelligent analysis of data
Marketing	Collection and processing of data on market opportunities and consumer behavior	
Quality Management	Collection and processing of data on the quality of medical services	Collection and processing of data (from patients) from various sources about the quality of medical services
HR Management	Collection and processing of personnel data (incl. job seekers) Collection and processing of data on the need for staff training	Building analytical reports in the required sections. Automatic selection of suitable applicants among job seekers according to the specified parameters, taking into account the analysis of data on past interviews with applicants. Automatic staff training scheduling based on real-time analysis
All medical functions	Collection and processing of data on best medical practices	Selection of best practices for specific cases based on analysis of existing data
Laboratory and functional research	Preparation, storage, and processing of medical images. Registration and analysis (interpretation) of the obtained laboratory data	Collection and processing of unstructured data from different laboratory and radiation diagnostics

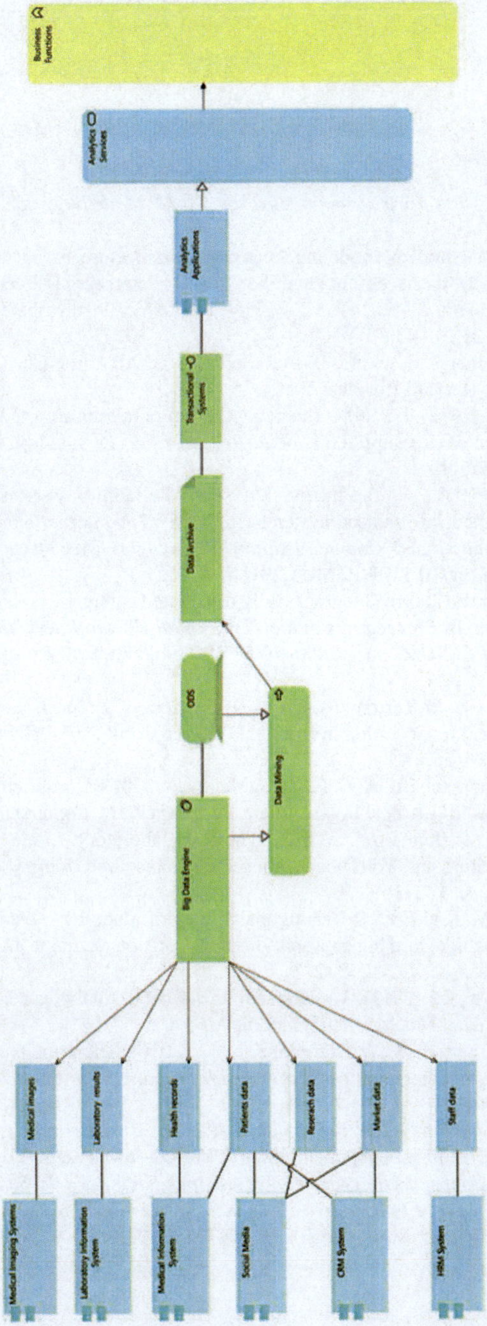

Fig. 2 Enterprise architecture model for using big data technologies in medical organizations

Acknowledgements The reported study was funded by RFBR according to the research project No. 20–010–00955.

References

1. Lankhorst, M. (2017). *Enterprise architecture at work: Modelling, communication and analysis*. Springer.
2. Dubgorn, A. (2020). Method of modeling enterprise architecture based on organization's functional structure. Ph.D. thesis, def. in Peter the Great St. Petersburg Polytechnic University.
3. Savinykh, V., & Bulgakov, S. (2014). Managing geographically distributed organizations. *Economic Consultant, 21*, 38–43.
4. Porter, M. E., & Teisberg, E. O. (2006). Redefining health care: Creating value-based competition on results. Harvard Business Press.
5. Chao, C., & Cheng, B. (2012). Factors influencing the future relationship of hospital procurement staff with medical device suppliers. *Social Behavior and Personality: An International Journal, 40*(6), 945–957.
6. Akimova, G., Solovyev, A., & Tarkhanov, I. (2018). Reliability assessment method for geographically distributed information systems. In *IEEE 12th International Conference on Application of Information and Communication Technologies (AICT)* (pp. 1–4). Almaty, Kazakhstan. https://doi.org/10.1109/ICAICT.2018.8747055.
7. Espinosa, J., & Armour, F. (2008). Geographically distributed enterprise architecting: Towards a theoretical framework. In *Proceedings of the 41st Annual Hawaii International Conference on System Sciences (HICSS 2008)* (pp. 400–400). Waikoloa. https://doi.org/10.1109/HICSS.2008.183.
8. Dubgorn, A., Svetunkov, S., & Borremans, A. (2020). Features of the functioning of a geographically distributed medical organization in Russia. E3S Web Conf., 217. 06014. https://doi.org/10.1051/e3sconf/202021706014.
9. Ilin, I., Iliashenko, V., von Schmit, A. C. F. M., & Makov, K. (2019). Requirements for big data processing technologies for medical organizations. In *33rd IBIMA Conference proceedings*.
10. Giglietto, F., Rossi, L., & Bennato, D. (2012). The open laboratory: Limits and possibilities of using Facebook, Twitter, and YouTube as a research data source. *Journal of Technology in Human Services, 30*(3–4), 145–159.
11. Wu, P.-Y., Cheng, C.-W., Kaddi, C. D., Venugopalan, J., Hoffman, R., & Wang, M. D. (2016). Omic and electronic health record big data analytics for precision medicine. *IEEE Transactions on Biomedical Engineering, 64*(2), 263–273.
12. Zikopoulos, P., & Eaton, C. (2011). Understanding big data: Analytics for enterprise class hadoop and streaming data. McGraw-Hill Osborne Media.
13. Zaramenskikh, E. P., Isaev, E. A., & Korovkina, N. L. (2016). The principles of information processing in electronic medical monitoring system. *Mathematical Biology and Bioinformatics, 11*(2), 288–298.
14. Ilin, I., Levina, A., Lepekhin, A., & Kalyazina, S. (2018). Business requirements to the IT architecture: A case of a healthcare organization. In V. Murgul & M. Pasetti (Eds.), *International Scientific Conference Energy Management of Municipal Facilities and Sustainable Energy Technologies EMMFT 2018. EMMFT-2018. Advances in Intelligent Systems and Computing* (Vol. 983. Cham: Springer. https://doi.org/10.1007/978-3-030-19868-8_29.

15. Ilin, I. V., Iliashenko, O. Y., & Iliashenko, V. M. (2019). Architectural approach to the digital transformation of the modern medical organization. In *Proceedings of the 33rd International Business Information Management Association Conference, IBIMA 2019: Education Excellence and Innovation Management through Vision 2020* (pp. 5058–5067).
16. Gorton, I., & Klein, J. (2014). Distribution, data, deployment: Software architecture convergence in big data systems. *IEEE Software, 32*(3), 78–85.

Key Indicators, Innovations, Trends, and Main Factors Influencing Transformation of the Building Construction Industry in Russia

Anton Vasiliev and Sergey Bruskin

Abstract Construction is already one of the largest industry sectors which includes enterprises and organizations aimed at the production of finished construction products for various purposes (residential, industrial, cultural, domestic, and other purposes). Steady growth comes with some underlying challenges in productivity, profitability, performance, labor, rising cost of building materials, site safety issues, and an overwhelming number of technological solutions, digitalization, and sustainability which could derail the industry's development. Companies must therefore address these challenges head-on and re-imagine their business processes.

Keywords Digital transformation · Cloud technologies · Augmented reality · Construction industry

1 Introduction

The level of technological conditions, depreciation level of the fixed assets as well as the composition of production assets of the main enterprises in Russia today is significantly worse than in the major part of foreign companies. The impact of COVID-19 on the market is also taking shape.

There was not enough time for preparation for the online mode in terms of software usage, reconstruction of the business processes, and even models. The situation created new conditions for the back offices. Manufacturers of building construction firms were forced to create lines with decreased fixed costs because of the inability to pay and control the process without employees being at work. From the economical point of view, the demand for construction materials after the pandemic remains at the last year level because developers were not able to deliver construction in time

A. Vasiliev (✉)
Russian Presidential Academy of National Economy and Public Administration Under the President of the Russian Federation, Moscow, Russian Federation

S. Bruskin
HSE University, 100100 Myasnitskaya 20, Moscow, Russian Federation
e-mail: sbruskin@hse.ru

E. Zaramenskikh and A. Fedorova (eds.), *Digitalization of Society, Economics and Management*, Lecture Notes in Information Systems and Organisation 53,
https://doi.org/10.1007/978-3-030-94252-6_2

within the fixed schedule. The importance of traditional jobs as a secure source of income has decreased.

The research points out how the pandemic changes the underlying assumptions and directions of the building materials and construction industry. The solution to the product changes and effective results lies in the updated rules and smart regulations, appropriate state programs as well as corresponding requirements to the industry standards.

The study presents the importance of innovations for industry development. The solutions that drive sustainability in the industry are advanced construction machinery, IT software with artificial intelligence, data analytics, cloud capabilities, local prefabrication plants, usage of common platforms such as building information modeling (BIM) in projects, the shift of value-chain from sequential to innovative business models with the logic of value networks, interconnected and performed simultaneously.

The research findings presents the extent of the fourth industrial revolution to the construction industry and the correlation between the industry development and transformation of socio-economic processes in Russia in the transition to a new economic order.

The worldwide COVID-19 pandemic changed businesses putting economies at high risk. As of today, countries all over the world are still struggling with the COVID-19 outbreak while its compound implications have not yet been fully unfolded [1]. The global GDP is expected to fall −6% in a single-lockdown scenario and −7.6% if a second wave occurs. The projected trends have an even more significant effect for the countries of Organization for Economic Cooperation and Development (OECD), forecasting a −7.5% loss in a single-lockdown scenario that drops to −9.3% in a double-lockdown situation [2]. Stagnation, unlike the economic crisis, does not have a mechanism for the resumption of economic growth within it. Therefore, a mechanism for economic recovery should be introduced at the state level and should take decisive measures for structural reforms. The tool must consist of planned systematic incorporated measures. The planning should not be adapted to the market economy (for example, the Chinese planning experience). In current economic conditions there are more and more confirmations of the macroeconomic postulate that the main drivers of economic growth are investments in fixed assets, not just investments, but long-term investments in cardinal technological renewal [3].

The purpose of the research is to provide a clear view of the situation in the Russian building construction industry and detect the recommended solutions and measures for future industry development. The present article focuses on the main trends and factors influencing the digital transformation of the building construction industry in Russia in the post-corona time. More specifically, the following questions related to the accelerated transformation of organizations in the context of the COVID-19 pandemic are intended to be answered: what are the indicators? What are the main global innovative trends that will make a huge impact on future industry formation? Where does Russia stay in terms of Industry 4.0 compared to other countries and why? What is the technological order of the socio-economic system of Russia, the level of the technological state, and the assets composition of the enterprises in Russia?

Which rules and state support tools could be implemented based on the experience of other countries in order to facilitate industry growth in Russia by the transfer of the technical base to the modern level? What are the main factors accelerating digital transformation of construction industry?

The disposition of the article is organized as follows. The next section discusses the main innovative trends, the assumption of the technological base, gives an overview of the context and background of the research problem with an expansion of the arguments the authors set to achieve objectives. Following that, the rules and state regulations, industry standards are described. Finally, the paper ends with some concluding remarks and guidelines for global main factors affecting the transformation of the construction industry as a producer of fixed assets in all sectors of the world economy. It should be noted that current research analyzes factors stimulating supply and demand. The critical discussion deliberates the complex procedure necessary to be implemented, implications on managerial practices, and limitations of the research topic.

The problem is considered based on some historical indication on the subject and international successful practices. The evidence of the process of digital transformation is shown through the paper supporting by examples from the business cases and theoretical explanations.

The article is unique in terms of the complexity of managerial, technological, and regulative aspects taking into account answering research questions that provide opportunity to understand and estimate the current state of the industry related to in-depth composite analysis.

2 Related Work

The purpose of the current fragment is to establish a theoretical framework of the research topic, to define key terminology, terms, and model which will support the study, and to limit the subject area. The section continues to disclose the topic of innovations, unfolding the features which drive the phenomenon or inhibit it. The industrial revolution is a moment of sharp qualitative transition from one technological order to another, accompanied by a zero increase in labor productivity in the core of the existing technological order with an increase in labor productivity in the economic spheres associated with a new fundamental innovation. Pandemic changed the digital transformation with the long-term macroeconomic consequences and new opportunities for disruptive innovations [4]. Thus, European countries present 30% growth in technological innovations annually whereas Russia steadily stays on the same innovations level [5]. Consequently, further efforts should be done in order to stay competitive and defend local market from foreign entrants, imported materials, and supplied substitutes [6]. Therefore, it will influence partially dependent economies of former Soviet Republics, including the Commonwealth of Independent States' (CIS) members with over 275 million citizens. Such socio-economic system is a set of used resources (material, intangible, labor, organizational, and managerial) and industrial relations, capable of performing, exchanging, distributing, and redistributing, partially or completely, useful products (services) of certain types [7]. The interdependence of technological orders with innovations sets the hierarchical relationship between the components of the innovation environment: values, institutions, maturity of industries, infrastructure [8]. Hence the mentioned technological structure is united by a key factor in the growth of labor productivity—fundamental innovation.

The architecture incorporates the trends of technology, functionality, and artistic needs of society forming into a general trend of design and construction, which is rapidly occupying a leading position in the market. Then, like any large system, the style becomes "bureaucratic", acquires decorative features. All the promising possibilities of a technical and design property transform to the extreme decoration of the object. It leads to the destruction of the constructive foundations of the style. It should be noted that the transition from style to style, from innovation to innovation occurs over a significant period of time. During this period, there are usually several styles balanced in demand—for example, eclecticism and modernism, classicism and baroque. There are two axioms: the exhaustion of evolutionary improvements of the existing fundamental innovation (both due to the direct potential for growth in labor productivity, and due to economies of scale—in the diffusion of innovations) and the asynchrony of the time frames for the existence and start of technological order and industrial revolutions. The industrial revolution inevitably completes one technological order and makes the transition to the next technological order. The transition criteria are the objective conditions for the massive rejection of fundamental innovation in favor of another.

Construction project management software is updating faster and faster improved with more features. A major part of the project management and IT solutions are bundling scheduling, project management, and time for better quality service. However, the technological advancements aren't limited just to software. Drone usage is becoming more popular with construction companies as drones themselves become cheaper. For instance Group of Companies PIK, the largest real estate and home-builder company in Russia, engaged in residential construction, uses drones at the construction sites for territory checks and control. Aerial photography is useful for getting photographs and video of the landscape [9]. They are increasing safety around the construction site and can add more information to survey data. Industrial Exoskeleton allows the user to be able to lift power tools as if they don't weigh anything [10]. Mobile technologies, Building Information Modeling (BIM), Virtual Reality (VR) and wearables, Augmented Reality (AR) and Mixed Reality (MR), 3D printing such as Apis Cor's 3D printed house in 24 h, robots such as bricklayers also facilitate to the reduction of costs for the process in general, including monthly rent, electricity, gas, water consumption, service invoices, and providing features that work best for house owners (video cameras, automatic light, doors, smart gadgets). Robots are stably helping businesses to supplement different functions that humans do on job sites. Construction companies prefer automation to manual labor because it saves time, improves the quality of buildings (demolish them), cheaper for bringing down concrete structures at the end of their life cycle in case of demolition. As an example graphene was originally an expensive building material, the mass usage started after the price drop.

More and more buildings and plants are incorporating green technology into the construction process [11]. Green construction is a way of building projects in an environmentally responsible and resource-efficient way from planning to design, to construction, maintenance, and demolition. These methods aren't that different from the classic building methods since the economy, utility, and durability are all important facets of the process. Along with green construction methods, there is an increase in research into green construction projects. There are carbon scrubbing building facades, bricks made of recycled cigarette butts, thermally driven air conditioners, and asphalt that will heal itself.

The construction industry counts for about 20% of global emissions. However, with crumbling buildings and an expanding population, there is a need for growth by constructing environmentally friendly buildings and focusing on their longevity.

Despite huge potential for innovations within the industry the standards that limit the performance of construction industry players are very old and have to be updated on a frequent basis. New requirements for the construction of residential and infrastructure facilities in terms of the quality of building materials should be implemented.

During the last decade, Moscow created many programs supporting small and medium enterprises such as financial incentives in the form of free credit for new businesses. However, the bureaucracy is still a big problem for firms willing to receive it. Many European countries and US regions have deducted taxes for different industries—Russia just offers it for agricultural industry or in a particular location such as special economic zones. Furthermore, best foreign practices present us the long-term credits with a low rate of 3–5% a year.

Other identified growth opportunities might be investments in employees capability in operating advanced construction machinery and IT software; shift of business model to the benefits of a more systematic operation and transparent collaborations with other project participants; establishment of local prefabrication plants as solutions that drive sustainability; formation of vertically integration with large companies, small and medium-sized enterprises (SMEs), start-up businesses through common platforms.

3 Research Methodology

The methodology is an application of the procedure for answering the research question. The contexts vary in accordance with a research question, researcher‘s motivation and style, degree of creativity, supervision, and own professional skills and qualities which investigator received before starting the analysis [12].

The authors use qualitative method. The qualitative method allows the immersion to the depth of events, detailed analysis. It provides the description of contradictory behaviors and opinions, gives the opportunity to avoid pre-judgments.

The data is collected through case studies and interviews. In the early phases of discovering new ideas or theories, the information is gathered through secondary literature sources. In comparison with other methods, case studies seek to investigate phenomenon in context, rather than independently [13]. The case study analysis is based on longitudinal examination of an event to identify causation and consequences in order to build the principles. The purposive sample was elected for the interviews.

The right balance of validity and reliability shows whether the conclusion completed enough and the reasoning is justified. The rationales for it are:

1. Authenticity—convincing the reader that the researcher has a deep understanding of what happened in the organization. It may be supported by facts and information received from the interviews.
2. Plausibility—requires the research to link into some ongoing concern among other researchers. The support by references shows clear evidence of it.
3. Criticality—stimulate the reader to question their taken-for-granted assumptions, and thus offer something novel. This indicator should be observed with the highest level of accuracy because often academic papers failed for being too much criticized. It could not follow the aim of the research, just in case if we will take critical theory.

The phenomenology as a chosen philosophy reduces possible errors which could decrease quality and interpretability [14]. The random error in the investigation will not have an impact on the entire sample. Research ethics relates to the formulation of research topic, design, collecting, analyzing data, and writing the research findings [15]. In other words, the approach should be methodologically sound and morally defensible to all participants. The authors adhere deontological view. According to it, the ends concluded by the investigator can never justify the use of research which is unethical. The conduct of current research is guided by ethical guidelines.

4 Results

Modern main factors influencing the construction industry as a producer of fixed assets in all sectors of the world economy today can be divided into factors driving demand and supply.

The factors stimulating demand:

- Incomes of consumers of finished construction products, as a factor that quantitatively determines effective demand (1). There are four components here: first, the growth of GDP per capita as a stimulus for private consumption (1.1); secondly, the quantitative growth of the solvent population due to demography, migration (1.2); thirdly, the expected future profitability in a specific area of the economy, as an incentive for its quantitative and qualitative development and, as a consequence, to an increase in demand for fixed assets in this area of the economy (special industrial design and technological solutions for buildings and structures in which production will be located, their embodiment in finished construction products) (1.3); fourthly, consumer expectations as a mechanism to stimulate final consumption (including by reducing the habit to save budget) (1.4).

- The level of physical (2.1) and moral (2.2) depreciation of fixed assets (2). It is obvious that an increase in the degree of wear and tear stimulates the pace of construction production, its quantitative and qualitative growth. In the obsolescence category, we include Consumer Tastes or Preferences. Indeed, the growth and development of needs, for example, in the field of housing, create prerequisites for stimulating the quantitative and qualitative growth of construction products, including stimulating the use of innovative technologies and materials.
- Global climate change (3). In the scientific world, there are discussions about global climate change and its consequences for the world economy. Quite contradictory points of view are expressed: a number of scientists speak of global warming as a consequence of an increase in CO_2 concentration; another group of scientists speaks of a possible cooling in the Northern Hemisphere and a decrease in precipitation based on data on the slowing down of thermocline circulation in the oceans [16, 17].
- The constructive role of the state as a producer of a strategic vector of economic development, its transformation (4).

The factors that simulate the supply (5–7):

- Profitability of production. This factor is complex and, if prices remain unchanged, it includes all the possibilities to reduce the cost of finished construction products (5):
- Changes in the regulatory framework (5.1). For example, the optional nature of SNIPs (building codes and regulations)—from July 1, 2010, amendments to the legislation came into force regulating the activities of builders within the framework of self-regulatory organizations—"Technical Regulations on the Safety of Buildings and Structures" (No. 384-FZ dated December 30, 2009 d.) replaced the outdated SNiPs and GOSTs, allowed the introduction of new design and technical solutions, new materials. So, again as an example, the use of prestressed reinforced concrete beams reduces the consumption of cement in their production by 20–30%, and fittings by 50%!
- The growth of labor productivity is also achieved by the integrated implementation of innovations (organizational, technical, technological, product, etc.) (5.2).
- The development of engineering and transport infrastructure, in particular, leads to a decrease in logistics costs within the framework of construction production, supply of raw materials, materials, structures to the construction site (5.3).
- Prices for resources (5.4).
- Taxes and subsidies (5.5).
- Decrease in the degree of competition in the construction sector due to the greater specialization of finished construction products (production processes),

Table 1 The degree of the interrelation of the main factors influencing the global construction industry with Industry 4.0

Factor	The degree of interrelation (the darker the color, the higher the manifestation)[1]
1. Incomes of consumers of finished construction products as a factor that quantitatively determines effective demand	
1.1. GDP per capita growth	0,6
1.2. Quantitative growth of the solvent population	0,3
1.3. The expected income in a specific area of the economy	0,9
1.4. Consumer expectations (demand)	0,3
2. The level of physical and obsolescence of fixed assets	
2.1. The level of physical wear and tear of fixed assets	0,3
2.2. Obsolescence of fixed assets	0,9
3. Global climate change	0,3
4. The effective role of the state	0,9
5. Profitability of construction production	
5.1. Changes in the regulatory framework	0,6
5.2. Labor productivity growth	0,9
5.3. Infrastructure development	0,6
5.4. Resource prices	0,3
5.5. Taxes and subsidies	0,6
6. Reducing the degree of competition in the construction industry	0,6
7. Consumer expectations (offer)	0,6

the processes of vertical and horizontal integration of the construction industry enterprises, and growth in demand (6).

- Consumer expectations as potential market growth in the future (7).

The study pays significant attention to the place and role of Industry 4.0. in the generation and maintenance of the transformation processes of the construction industry. Why are we linking the transformation of the construction industry to the 4th industrial revolution? The answer is obvious: any economy, even less material, and energy-intensive needs fixed assets. Their presence and reproduction are at the same time the award and duty of the construction industry.

Let us determine the degree of interconnection of the main factors influencing the global construction industry with Industry 4.0. The results of the assessment carried out by the author are presented in Table 1 (the essential content of each factor corresponds to the numbering proposed by the authors earlier in the text).

If qualitatively interpret (1) –0,53; (2) –0,6; (3) –0,3; (4) –0,9; (5) –0,6; (6) –0,6; (7) –0,6, average correlation is 0,59. It confirms the thesis of the high relationship between the transformation of the construction industry and the 4th industrial revolution. There are megatrends and the corresponding factors of influence on the structure of the world economy.

The National Intelligence Council of the United States, with the support of the Atlantic Council of the United States (ACUS), issued an analytical report, "Global Trends 2030: Alternative Worlds," several years ago, which highlighted four megatrends that will change the world in the near future. These include [18]:

1. Personal empowerment will lead to the growth of the middle class, the growth of education, the development of medicine, communication, and production technologies.
2. The distribution of world influence will entail a transition to a multipolar world, in which several coalitions of countries will be formed with a leading country at the head.
3. Reduction of the "demographic arc of instability" (in the part of the "third world"—from Algeria to Pakistan), aging of the Earth's population, migration, urbanization.
4. Deficiency of food, water, and energy resources due to the growth of the world's population and the growth of needs (including, as a result of the increase in the middle class). Hence an obvious conclusion that the classification of the main factors of influence proposed in Table 1 is absolutely interconnected and takes into account the megatrends of the world order in the coming decades.

Within the framework of Industry 4.0: firstly, the sectoral structure of the economy is changing: in terms of the volume of contribution to GDP, sectors of the economy associated with knowledge and its bearer—human, the quality of life; secondly, the quality of the fixed assets of already existing sectors of the economy is changing (for example, the emergence of "smart factories" will require structural changes in enclosing structures, buildings: the absence or minimal presence of a person changes the requirements for illumination of workplaces, the temperature regime of premises, their layout, places to support human life—change houses, canteens, etc.). As a result, there is a need for a significant increase in the production of the construction industry.

Initially, Industry 4.0 in Germany was developed as part of the national high-tech development plan approved by the government in 2010. The plan includes 8 global projects, in addition to "Industry 4.0" they include:

- energy efficient cities with a neutral balance of CO_2 emissions;
- renewable biomaterials as an alternative to oil;
- "smart restructuring" of energy supply;
- healthcare (personalized medicine; improving health through prevention and optimized diets, an active lifestyle in old age);

[1] Experts assessment.

- sustainable mobility (transport, infrastructure, logistics);
- Internet services for business;
- secure personal identification [19].

On the basis of the "German ICT Strategy: Digital Germany 2015," the German strategy "Industry 4.0" was proposed in April 2013. The document was declarative in nature and defined the vector of development as "… the development of smart production and the creation of cyber-physical systems, in order to increase the competitiveness of the German manufacturing industry and, subsequently, Germany's occupation of a leading position in a new round of the industrial revolution" [19, 20].

The existing need for detailing the Industry 4.0 strategy was largely satisfied in 2016 (March) by the Digital Strategy until 2025 (developed by the Federal Ministry of Economics and Technology, Germany), which systematizes measures for the development of digitalization in Germany. For the period up to 2025, 10 steps have been proposed: building a gigabit fiber network, opening an innovative era of entrepreneurship, transparency of the political structure, promoting intelligent interaction, strengthening information security of software and hardware, digital transformation of small and medium-sized enterprises, helping German companies to apply the Industry 4.0 strategy ", Expanding R&D opportunities, strengthening digital education and training, creating federal digital institutions [20].

From the idea of classical macroeconomics—non-intervention of the state, reliance on the "invisible hand of the market", there is a transition to the idea of a new industrial policy within the framework of neoinstitutionalism—to "smart regulation" (smart regulation).

The rationale for this trend is the reduction of low-skilled workers/workers/employees of the lower and middle management involved in the production process in favor of intellectual workers. The main benefit from the transfer of production to third-world countries with cheap labor is disappearing.

On the background of the reduction in high-tech production, the damage to the environment, the benefits are more and more obvious, both from a decrease in the value-added chain and from the multiplier effect of industrial production. The more means of labor are produced, the greater the production of goods and services (including those with high added value) in many areas of the economy (computerization services, digitalization, communications, etc.).

The industry creates the highest job multiplier in the economy (1: 4.6), that is, one industrial job creates 4.6 other jobs. Industry 4.0 (digital industry) creates even more related specialties and jobs, increasing the multiplier to 1:16 [20].

Hence there is a concern of the US authorities with the return of industrial production to the country (the process was started by Barack Obama with the Advanced Manufacturing Partnership Program (AMP, 2011), Donald Trump proclaimed reindustrialization and set the goal of increasing the number of jobs in industrial production by 5 million).

It is logical that Germany also does not stay away from the general trend. On the basis of the Industry 4.0 strategy in 2019, the Minister of Economy presented the draft National Industrial Strategy until 2030. It clearly states that, within the framework of Industry 4.0, innovative technologies and digitalization should be integrated into traditional industries.

The concept of "industrial Internet" (digital interconnection of equipment, digital technologies, artificial intelligence) appears in the strategy. The goal is to increase the share of manufacturing in Germany's gross added value to 25% by 2030 (currently 23%). The main provisions of the National Industrial Strategy of Germany until 2030 will become the common objectives of industrial policy in all EU countries.

In general, according to UNCTAD data for 2019, no less than 100 countries of the world have adopted official industrial development strategies. The problem lies in the difference in the basic conditions for the implementation of national industrial development strategies in different countries. Even within the European Union, the author of the "National Industrial Strategy until 2030" notes German Minister of Economy and Energy Peter Altmeier: "in many countries the de-industrialization process is still in full swing." And it immediately indicates a common benchmark for the EU countries—20% (the share of manufacturing in the creation of gross value added) on average in the European Union.

Peter Altmeier, evaluating the best practices of Industry 4.0, talks about China and its state program Made in China 2025, which is based on the ideas of Industry 4.0 and creatively rethinking it in order to adapt to the Chinese realities. The basic "groundwork" for the implementation of the "Made in China 2025" program:

- Possibility to stimulate the economy due to the growth of domestic demand (according to the indicator "Share of household expenditures in GDP", China is on the level of Gabon, Algeria, Oman—35–38%, sharply lagging behind the advanced economies).
- Huge domestic market (due to population size).
- A significant number of small and medium-sized enterprises in all industries have a low-efficient production base but are ready and willing to produce innovative high-tech products. Now they are mainly engaged in the assembly of finished products and units, and these are processes that create minimal added value.
- Significant human capital.
- Low non-purposeful component of development due to the planned economy of China, which is based on a significant public sector in the industry. In the field of telecommunications, shipbuilding, aviation, railways, the share of the public sector is 83%; in electronics—45%.

The main goal of the program is to develop smart manufacturing in China.

2015–2020 were devoted to the introduction of digital network technologies in manufacturing industries. The second stage—until 2025, will be focused on the integration of network technologies, intellectualization of production processes. The result is the integration of the processes of informatization and industrialization, the growth of the country's production capital, the improvement of the environment, and the growth of product quality.

What are the principles behind the Made in China 2025 program?

- Innovativeness of production, goods, business processes.

- Artificial intelligence in production processes.
- Support and develop industrial enterprises.
- Environmental safety of all processes and innovations.

It is important to create the infrastructure of "Industry 4.0" in China. Large data centers are being built, the mechanics and software of cloud technologies, artificial intelligence, and the Internet of Things (IoT) industry are developing. Provinces in China have entered into competition under the program. Shandong Province aims to become a leader in construction volume and digital infrastructure development by 2023. Guangzhou has published "22 regulations" on the development of the digital economy, accelerated city-building based on the digital economy, and innovation.

The Chinese experience of strategic planning of industrial policy for Russia is less interesting than the German experience, because of two points:

1. We cannot stimulate economic growth at the expense of domestic consumption, because unlike China, the share of final consumption expenditures in the structure of Russia's GDP, for example, in the third quarter of 2019 amounted to 67.7%.
2. We do not have the problem of avoiding the "middle-income trap", which is very acute now in China.

Another specific problem of the Russian economy during the transition to Industry 4.0—at the moment we have a very low share of investments in GDP, especially in fixed assets—17% in 2019. The share of investments in human capital is also low—14%.

5 Discussion

A number of authors note that the innovation environment needs to be updated in terms of adding the role of human capital (a complex characteristic, including the quality of education, science, competence, knowledge). In general, the fourth industrial revolution is often going in line, as a concept, with the knowledge economy, considering it the basis of the knowledge society/information society. It should, nevertheless, define the key differences between the two concepts. The technological order is a wider concept since uses all the results of knowledge: information and innovation (knowledge that is transformed into solving problems of the real sector).

Huge amounts of scientific investigations have been done in order to explore the research topic. However, there were no papers that tried to set the relationship between major factors influencing the transformation of construction industry today or an analysis of changes in a retrospective view.

The data is created for CEOs and managers of Russian construction companies as well as government representatives in order to assist them in accepting the right managerial decision. The recommendation for the future research goes into different directions: investigating the larger sample in terms of size of the companies, regional redistribution, the influence of pandemic on digital transformation in different industries, detailed comparative analysis of construction industry in countries with the highest and the lowest industry indicators.

The analysis does not present a new view of observable data, just reinterprets it in a "new way" of viewing what is genuinely discoverable and potentially exist but usually is not seen. Furthermore, there is too much data for analysis and the information captured by the researchers could not cover the whole field of study. Limitations of the study also lie in the distinct position of researchers restricting the information flows and confining the access to the depth of facts. The qualitative study discovers the reality of the event, the reason, and consequences but not a statistical representation of those events that could be useful to support findings by numerical data capturing a larger sample. The authors also should recognize the limitations in judging the interests of external audiences. Future research could use the model of different research scenarios such as changing time period, using different measures, units of analysis, and other data sources.

6 Conclusion

Summing up it should be noted that in developed countries global structural changes continue to occur against the background of moderate rates of economic growth due to the development of technologies and the creative destruction provided by the competitive environment. Creative destruction presupposes deliberate losses from the liquidation of the fixed assets before the onset of acceptable levels of moral and physical deterioration, which allows accelerating the pace of the fixed assets renewal, adapting them to the needs of Industry 4.0.

Crises and post-corona market conditions foster structural change. The global trend in the development of the information and communication technologies sector has led around the world to a decrease in the share of education in the structure of GDP due to the transfer of some of the educational functions to information systems.

The need for a significant increase in the production of the construction industry is observed in countries that have begun to live in the framework of a new technological order earlier than others, in countries where the active phase of the fourth industrial revolution is already underway.

The fourth industrial revolution, which is beginning in Russia, is becoming the main driver of the transformation of the construction industry. So far, unfortunately, it should be noted that the construction industry is not ready for growth and transformation. Moreover, the main regulatory and legislative documents do not create an institutional field for both Industry 4.0 and the construction industry. A good example is the study of the "Strategy for the development of the building materials industry for the period up to 2020 and further prospects until 2030 (approved by the order of the Government of the Russian Federation of May 10, 2016, No. 868-r)".

Obviously, fundamental changes are needed in the institutional plan, stimulating the development of fixed assets of the economy, identifying "growth points," their state support, and stimulating the flow of private capital, including public–private partnership.

References

1. Soto-Acosta, P. (2020). COVID-19 Pandemic: Shifting digital transformation to a high-speed gear. *Information Systems Management, 37*(4), 260–266. https://doi.org/10.1080/10580530.2020.1814461.
2. OECD. (2020a). Economic outlook.
3. Aganbegyan, A. G. (2020). What the regions can do to overcome stagnation and rekindle significant socioeconomic growth. *Regional Research of Russia, 10*, 291–300. https://doi.org/10.1134/S2079970520030016.
4. Nagel, L. (2020). The influence of the COVID-19 pandemic on the digital transformation of work. *International Journal of Sociology and Social Policy, 40*(9/10), 861–875. https://doi.org/10.1108/IJSSP-07-2020-0323.
5. Asaul, V., & Pesotskaya, E. (2019). Innovative technologies in construction: International experience and problems of incorporation in Russia. *IOP Conference Series: Materials Science and Engineering, 497*(012004). https://doi.org/10.1088/1757-899X/497/1/012004.
6. New York, July 02. (2020). (GLOBE NEWSWIRE)–Reportlinker.com announces the release of the report "Business Model Innovations in the Building Construction Industry". https://www.reportlinker.com/p05917932/?utm_source=GNW.
7. Chistov, L. M. (2008). Innovative approach as an optimization in the theory of effective management of socio-economic systems. SPb: Asteron.
8. National Report on Innovations in Russia. (2015). State Fund of Foundations Institute for the Development of the Russian Federation. Official site. https://www.rvc.ru/upload/iblock/b70/NROI_RVC.pdf.
9. Yi, W., & Sutrisna, M. (2020). Drone scheduling for construction site surveillance. *Computer-Aided Civil and Infrastructure Engineering, 36*. https://doi.org/10.1111/mice.12593.
10. Geregey, A., & Glukhov, D., & Efimov, A. (2020). Industrial exoskeletons. Normative and methodological regulation. *Russian Journal of Occupational Health and Industrial Ecology*, 598–598. https://doi.org/10.31089/1026-9428-2019-59-9-598-599.
11. Qamar, M. Z., Ali, W., Qamar, O., & Noor, M. (2021). Green technology and its implications worldwide.
12. Easterby-Smith, M., Thorpe, R., & Jackson, P. R. (2008). Management research (3rd edn). London: SAGE Publication Ltd.
13. de Vries, K. (2020). Case study methodology. https://doi.org/10.4324/9780429432774-2.
14. Laletas, S., & Grové, C. (2020). Phenomenology. https://doi.org/10.4324/9780429285646-16.
15. Sixsmith, J., & Sixsmith, A. (2021). Doing research ethically. https://doi.org/10.1007/978-3-030-34390-3_26.
16. Tyunyaev, A.A. (2016). Metaphysics of the earth's climate (p. 496). M: White Alves.
17. Matishov, G. G. (2016). Climate and large marine ecosystems of the arctic. In G. G. Matishov, P. R. Makarevich & D. V. Moiseev (Eds.), Dokl. at the RAS presidium on May 24 (pp. 88–93). Rostov on Don: Publishing house of the SSC RAS.
18. Global Trends. (2030). Alternative Worlds. National Intelligence Council of the United States, Atlantic Council of the United States (ACUS). ISBN: 978–1–929667–21–5. http://www.dni.gov/nic/globaltrends.
19. Structural Changes in the Russian Economy and Structural Policy. (2018). Analytical report. In Y. Simachev Y., Akindinova N., Yakovlev A., and others; under the supervision of Yasin E.G.-M: National Research University Higher School of Economics.
20. Golovienchik, G. G., & Yuan W. (2020). Digital transformation of China's industry: Experience for the EAEU–Minsk: Ed. center of BSU (p. 166).

Explaining the IT Value Through the Information Support of Decision-Making

Yuri Zelenkov

Abstract The issue of how IT impact the performance of an organization is still not fully explained. Many researchers believe that this effect is based on the automation of business processes and the replacement of unskilled routine labor. However, this does not explain the expected impact of digital transformation, since it offers completely new models. Relying on the achievements of organization theory, we suggest that the impact of IT on performance is realized through the quality of decision-making. We analyze the role of information processing in decision-making, identify the sources of inefficiency, which can be associated with incorrect assessment, lack or excess of information. Next, we revise the organization's design strategies and classify the information systems according to their information processing capabilities. The proposed approach can explain the way how IT impact is created and manifested both for traditional enterprise information systems and for new digital technologies.

Keywords IT value · Organization design · Decision-making · Information processing

1 Introduction

Many studies conducted since the 1980s consistently show that the impact of IT investment on labor productivity and economic growth is significant and positive at both the firm- and country-levels [1]. The explanation of IT value from economics point of view is the following. At the firm level, the performance of IT investments can be explained by complementary investments in organizational capital such as decentralized decision-making, quality management, personnel training, and business process redesign [2]. It leads to an increase in labor productivity, which stimulates the IT use sector, which, in turn, leads to a rise in demand and encourages the development of the IT industry. As a result, all this has a positive effect on economic growth [3].

Y. Zelenkov (✉)
HSE University, 100100 Myasnitskaya 20, Moscow, Russian Federation
e-mail: yzelenkov@hse.ru

E. Zaramenskikh and A. Fedorova (eds.), *Digitalization of Society, Economics and Management*, Lecture Notes in Information Systems and Organisation 53,
https://doi.org/10.1007/978-3-030-94252-6_3

A lot of authors have empirically investigated the impact of IT investments on organizational performance. Some results confirm the presence of a positive relationship [4]; other authors do not detect such a dependence [5]. Although most researchers and practitioners are confident that there is a positive IT effect, the mechanism for creating this effect remains poorly understood [6, 7].

Many researchers believe that this effect is based on the automation of business processes and the replacement of unskilled routine labor [8, 9]. However, this does not explain the expected impact of digital transformation, since it does not come down to improving processes, but offers completely new business models.

In this paper, we consider the mechanism for creating and manifesting the value of IT through information support for decision-making [10]. The theory of organization has proved that the optimization of decision-making is the reason and meaning of the existence of an organization [11], determines its structure [12], and performance [13].

The work is structured as follows. After reviewing the literature in Sect. 3, we present a decision-making framework that extends the well-known models [12, 14, 15] by highlighting information processing. A glance through the prism of information support allows us to identify potential sources of ineffective decisions that are associated with incorrect assessment, lack or excess of information.

In Sect. 4, we look at organizational design strategies in terms of increasing its information effectiveness. These strategies are aimed at providing effective decisions and, therefore, obviously affect all other metrics of the organization's performance (finance, HR, etc.). To do this, we use the Galbraith model [16], which we revise following the latest achievements in management, organization theory, and information systems.

In Sect. 5, we analyze various types of information systems in terms of information processing. We consider two dimensions: the complexity of the work performed and the number of employees interacting in solving problems. This analysis allows you to determine the expected effect of each type of information system.

The contribution of our work has two components. Firstly, a theoretical model is proposed that explains the mechanism of the influence of IT as an information processing tool on organizational performance. The mediator of this influence is decision-making. Secondly, the proposed models can be of practical importance, since they allow you to identify the causes of ineffective decisions and enable choosing the best tools (both managerial and IT) to eliminate these problems.

2 Literature Review

2.1 IT Value

David [17] was the first who note that the impact of IT on an economy is best described through the concept of "general-purpose technology" (GPT). The main contribution of GPT to improving efficiency is the creation of a foundation for new technologies, working methods, etc. [3]. Next, Milgrom and Roberts [18] showed that investments in IT should be complemented by simultaneous investments in other assets, such as changes in work processes and a portfolio of products and services, which is accompanied by a change in personnel qualification requirements [2].

Dedrick et al. [1], reviewing empirical research of the IT impact on productivity, highlighted that IT is not merely a tool for automating existing processes but is, more importantly, an enabler of organizational changes that can lead to additional productivity gains. Enterprise information systems substitute low- and middle-skilled workers while creating more demand for high-skilled workers.

Melville et al. [8] presented a model of IT business value based on the resource-based view of the firm and designed to combine various strands of research into a single framework. According to their model, IT impacts organizational performance via business processes. Other organizational resources such as workplace practices moderate or mediate IT in the attainment of organizational performance impacts. The external environment also plays a role in IT business value generation.

Summing up these and many other works, Kohli and Grover [6] noted that IT creates value only under certain conditions, it must be a part of a business value creating process when all organizational factors operating synergistically. Next, IT value could manifest itself in many ways: in the form of productivity similar to other types of capital, process improvements (cycle time), profitability (return on assets), or consumer surplus. Mediating factors that allow transforming IT resources in the value are complementary resources, organizational capabilities, and IT strategy alignment. However, the authors noted that, despite significant progress in IT value understanding, many issues remain unexplored, in particular topics on information and knowledge sharing and creating.

More recent empirical studies have provided additional evidence of the relationship between IT investment and business value. However, some researchers obtained contradictory results. In particular, Tambe and Hitt [4] found a significant difference between large and medium-sized firms. IT returns are substantially lower in medium-sized firms than in Fortune 500 companies, but they materialize faster in midsize firms. The second important finding of work [4] is that the measured marginal product of IT investment is higher from 2000 to 2006 than in any previous period. It can be explained by the fact that unlike the 1990s, when proprietary information systems prevailed, the 2000s are characterized by more standardized information systems with the rapid adoption of ERP and web technologies. However, contrary to early studies, the results of Chae et al. analysis [5] showed no significant link between IT capability and firm performance from 2001 to 2007. Analysis of 303 empirical studies [19] shows that primarily this contradiction is a consequence of methodological issues. There is no single widely adopted methodology, and the results of various authors depend on the model used (mainly it is regression), selected variables, and measurements. However, the scientific community and practitioners consider the impact of IT on firm performance as proven.

To conclude this part of the review, we refer to Mithas and Rust's remark [7] that there are three strategic paths from IT to firm performance. IT can be used to

(1) reduce costs by improving productivity and efficiency; (2) increase revenues; or (3) reduce costs and increase revenues simultaneously. However, despite significant progress in the literature, little is known about how these strategies jointly moderate the relationship between IT investments and firm performance.

From our point of view, the critical issue in ensuring overall performance is effective decision-making, which is based on the ability to provide the right information to the right people at the right time. So, information processing capability is vital to effective management, and it should be viewed as the primary function of an enterprise information system founding its value.

2.2 Information Management Capability

According to the definition of Mithas et al. [20]: *Information management capability is an ability to provide data and information to users with the appropriate level of accuracy, timeliness, reliability, security, confidentiality, connectivity, and access and the ability to tailor these in response to changing business needs and directions.*

As noted in the previous section, the research literature highlights the importance of information management aspects of IT capability. However, to the best of our knowledge, just a few studies examined the link between information management and firm performance before the 2010s. Nunamaker and Briggs [21] discussing Information Systems (IS) as an academic discipline argue that the crucial function of IS is informing the decision-makers. Thereby IS reduces the risk of decision and creates value for stakeholders affected by the decision.

Mithas et al. [20] confirmed these assumptions empirically. Authors found that information management capability plays an essential role in developing other firm capabilities, namely, for customer management, process management, and performance management. These capabilities enhance all aspects of the firm performance (customers, finance, human resources, etc.). Moreover, according to the authors, information management capability has a direct and most significant impact on the financial performance of the firm.

Few more recent works have empirically studied particular aspects of the impact of information management on performance. Liu et al. [22] found that IT capabilities affect firm performance through absorptive capacity and supply chain agility. Absorptive capacity refers to a firm's ability to value, assimilate, and apply new knowledge received from external sources. Information management has positive relationship with process management, which in turn has a positive effect on operational performance [9]. Besides, the effect of information management capabilities on firm performance was confirmed not only for the US but also for other countries, for example, Spain [23], India [24], and Brazil [25].

In the 2010s, new IT (such as big data, artificial intelligence, and blockchain) fundamentally reshaped business models, business processes, products, and services. Over previous decades, the prevailing notion of an IT strategy considered it as a functional level strategy, which should correspond to the firm's chosen business.

However, now it is necessary to view the IT strategy not as a subordinate of the business strategy, but as a digital transformation strategy [26]. Therefore, starting in 2010, many researchers pay attention to the impact of new IT on firm performance. For example, authors of [27] found that big data is associated with an average of three to seven percent improvement in the productivity of firms in information technology-intensive or highly competitive industries.

Data-Driven Decision-Making (DDD) became the new best practice since new opportunities to collect and leverage data have led many managers to change how they make decisions—relying less on intuition and more on data. Paper [28] reports that the use of DDD in US manufacturing nearly tripled (from 11 to 30% of plants) between 2005 and 2010.

Recent improvements in artificial intelligence (AI) can also help to reduce the cost of decision-making, as modern machine learning models make predictions that often exceed human capabilities, especially using large datasets. Thus, humans will delegate some decisions to algorithms [29]. According to [1], information systems replace low and medium-skilled workers; that is, routine mental tasks. According to the most radical point of view, AI aims to substitute, supplement, and amplify practically almost all the tasks currently performed by humans, and in fact, for the first time becomes a serious competitor for them [30]. Regardless of whether this assumption will turn out to be true, some of the decisions are already made by algorithms, i.e., for the first time, humanity is confronted with non-human actors.

To summarize this part of the review, we can note that according to the view presented in [21], the enterprise IS does not consist solely of IT artifacts (hardware and software). The information system is a balanced combination of people, data, procedures, policies, standards, equipment, software, etc. [31]. By extrapolating this approach, we can consider the entire organization as an information processing system facing uncertainty [32]. All aspects of the organization's activities require effective decision-making; very often, these decisions must be taken in uncertainty. Therefore, the effectiveness of the use of information to reduce uncertainty in decision-making underlies all other aspects of measuring effectiveness (processes, customers, finances, etc.). Empirical results show that the information system capabilities primarily positively affect the performance of decision-making [33]. Decision-making performance mediates the effect on business process performance and firm performance. Thus, considering digital technologies from this angle, we in particular can argue that their popularity is primarily due to the potential to improve decision-making.

2.3 Data, Information, Knowledge and Decision-Making

The objective of this part of the literature review is to provide a current understanding of the decision-making process and the role of data, information, and knowledge in it. The main results regarding the decision-making process were obtained back in the 1970s. The main results regarding the transformation of data to information and knowledge were obtained back in 1990s. Here, we review the key concepts of both directions.

Davenport and Prusak [34] defined the data as objective facts about some events. In their view, data are simple sequences of signs and symbols that do not matter and simply exist. However, this definition was clarified later by Choo [35], who indicated that actual events that exist independently of the observer generate signals, i.e., sensory phenomena that are perceived by subject. An observer usually draws attention to a small number of signals that he senses as data. The selection and transformation of signals depend both on their physical nature and the observer's ability to adequately perceive them, and on the observer's previous experience (for example, on his expectations that this signal may indicate). An observer selects and recognizes signals following a specific structure that already exists in his mental model of the world, isomorphic, as he believes, to the current situation.

Data, therefore, is a more or less subjective set of facts and messages. In the context of an organization, data is usually stored as structured records of various transactions. Any transaction can be described using data, but they do not say anything, for example, about the reasons, goals, and quality of its implementation.

The subject interprets the data following his goals. In this process of giving data meaning, they are transformed into information, which, therefore, is even more subjective. Information is always processed in a specific context and influences the behavior of the subject [36]. We can say that the value of information depends on the degree of uncertainty reduction of the situation in which the subject makes the decision. In an organization, information is distributed through various networks, which can be both technical (for example, e-mail) and purely social (informal communication), and multiple combinations of them are also possible [37].

According to the definition of [34], knowledge is a mixture of accumulated experience, values, contextual information, and expert opinions that allow us to evaluate and absorb new skills and new information. Knowledge is entirely subjective since its carrier is an individual [36]. However, knowledge can also exist at the organization level, not only in the form of documents but also in the form of routines, norms, and procedures.

The knowledge allows us to transform data into information: evaluate its relevance taking into account a specific context, highlight critical components, remove apparent errors, and create a more compact representation. Knowledge allows us to make decisions, recognize and identify events, analyze the situation, and adapt to it, plan and control actions. Knowledge forms those mental structures that a person considers isomorphic to the current situation. Knowledge, unlike information, presupposes the presence of opinions and beliefs and implies action [36]. Besides, information, since it has contextual value, must effect a change in knowledge [32].

Managers frequently plan, solve problems, and make decisions based upon incomplete and sometimes inaccurate information. There are two general theories regarding management decision-making. One is the process theory, in which decision-making is viewed as a three-phase process [12, 14]. The first phase is an intelligence phase, in which a decision-maker understands the problem. The second is a conception phase, in which a decision-maker develops alternative solutions. The last is the choice phase, in which a decision-maker chooses best alternative. Simon [12] also points out that decision-making process is not always rational and that decision-makers often possess incomplete and imperfect information.

The "garbage can" model is an alternative way of discovering order in decision-making that complements the process approach. The central idea of the garbage can model is the substitution of a temporal order by the dynamic, open process subjected to interferences, feedback loops, and dead-ends [15].

Information use is critical in both the process and garbage can models of decision-making. Saunders and Jones [10] proposed a general model relating information acquisition to the decision-making process. The model consists of three major components: decisional, information acquisition, and contextual. The decisional component reflects an integration of the Mintzberg et al. model [14] of unstructured decision processes with "garbage can" concepts. The information acquisition component focuses on the role of information sources (internal and external) and media (informal communications both scheduled and unscheduled, documents, computer systems, etc.) in channeling information to the decision-maker. The contextual component of the model focuses on factors that impinge directly upon the selection of source and medium. These factors include the perceived importance of the decision, a number of problems the decision-maker is working on simultaneously, time pressures, the organization's information environment, interaction patterns, etc.

Based on the above definition of information and knowledge, we can deduce two consequences of this model that are significant for the further presentation of our work. First, if the decision-maker has sufficient knowledge of a certain problem, his need for information is lower. It may even happen that his previous experience in solving such problems is exceptionally high; in this case, he does not need information at all. This way of decision-making is often interpreted as an intuitive style [38]. Patton [39] identified three sources of intuition used by decision-makers: (1) general experience, which coincides with the way described above; and two others: (2) innate response—the instinct that brings subconscious but adequate reactions; and (3) focused learning that originates from deliberate efforts to attain intuitive responses.

The second consequence is the fact that the information search process routinizes, as it is limited to the number of problems solved simultaneously, established interaction patterns, available sources and media, and other contextual factors. Thus, this issue is closely linked with information processing efficiency.

To summarize this part of the discussion, we should note that knowledge management is a critical element in decision-making. As IT radically changes the way of information access and processing, it facilitates the creation of knowledge in organizations and society [40]. Perhaps this is the most important aspect of the creation and manifestation of IT value today, superior to the effect of automation of routine processes.

3 Knowledge-Based Decision-Making Process

An underlying assumption in the theory of organization is that organizations are open social systems that must deal with external and internal sources of uncertainty. Since organizations must deal with uncertainty, a critical task of the organization is information processing. Information processing refers to the gathering, interpreting, and synthesis of information in the context of organizational decision-making [32].

Based on the results presented in the previous section, we propose a decision-making model that takes into account information processing (Fig. 1). For simplicity, it is represented using the Mintzberg et al. [14] process approach. Still, it implicitly suggests that, according to the "garbage can" model, there are feedback loops and recursive relationships between the phases and also dead-ends, interferences.

Simon [12] noted that "different representations of the problem will produce different proposals for solutions." Moreover, as certain solutions become familiar, they are more likely to shape the problem understanding itself [13]. Thus, according to the proposed model, at each stage, the decision-maker (DM) evaluates (explicitly or implicitly) the sufficiency of his knowledge. As a result of this assessment, he or she has two scenarios:

- If DM feels that his or her knowledge and experience are enough, he or she proceeds to the next stage. This way of action implements an intuitive decision-making style. However, the intuitive decisions are not necessarily optimal, since, as noted above, familiar solutions may distort the understanding of the problem. The decision-maker is too self-confident in this case.
- If a DM believes that his experience is not enough, he or she creates an information request to collect the data that can reduce uncertainty in a given context.

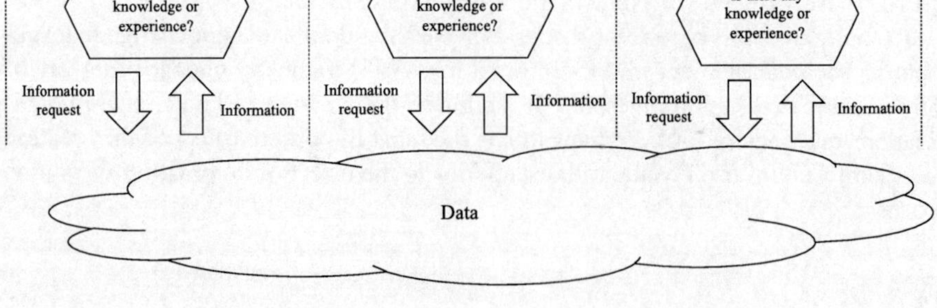

Fig. 1 Knowledge-based decision-making process

In this case, the search, processing, and provision of information (i.e., information processing) are of particular importance. These are functions that are usually considered as functions of an information system. However, these functions do not have to be implemented necessarily using IT; information processing can be performed using search in the paper archive or informal communication. A potential source of failure in this scenario is the routine procedures of information processing. As the context is continually changing, outdated procedures may return distorted, incomplete, and untimely data. It is the reason why many managers criticize their enterprise information systems [41, 42].

So, the performance of decision-making (i.e., quality of solutions or reasoning in general) depends on the quantity and quality of information that DM can receive. Note that the performance of DM correlates positively with the amount of information he or she receives—up to a certain point [43]. If further information is provided beyond this point, the performance will rapidly decline since extra information does not integrate into the decision-making process. Information overload will be the result in that case. Thus, we identified three potential sources for making wrong decisions:

- incorrect assessment of knowledge and competencies, in particular, by ignoring relevant information.
- inefficient information processing, i.e., distortion, incompleteness, or untimely presentation of information.
- information overload.

The central information processing problem is an optimal task allocation, i.e., organizational structure, given the costs of knowledge acquisition and communication [13]. This point of view is consistent with Milgrom and Roberts [11], who argue that two main functions of an organization are.

- coordination upon reaching an agreement between its participants, i.e., allocation of tasks, rights, and responsibilities.
- motivation to comply with the agreement reached.

To perform these functions, organization should know how its different components are functioning, about the quality of outputs, and conditions in external technological and market domains. However, information processing requires additional investments in systems, which increases costs, but is not directly related to the increase in the consumer value of products or services. Thus, the cost of information processing is a constraint that limited information capabilities of the organization. A trade-off between the amount of information necessary for the management and its cost is the main problem of organizational design.

4 Organizational Design from Information Processing View

Since the pioneering works of H. Simon in the 1940s, information processing was a central concept in organizational research related to knowledge acquisition and communication among decision-makers. According to Galbraith [16] and Tushman and Nadler [32], the role of the organizational structure is to increase the organization's information processing capacity to deal with internal complexity and environmental uncertainty.

In the review of research literature in organizational structures, information processing, and decision-making, Joseph and Gaba [13] conclude that existing research is divided into two directions: aggregation and constraint. The aggregation view reflects how different types of structures enable individuals to interact to make collective decisions. The constraint view reflects how the context established by the organizational structure enables or constrains individual decision-making.

In his seminal work, Galbraith [16] identified four organizational design strategies for information processing. Two of them aim at reducing the information necessary for management; the other two increase the organization's ability to process information. Here we propose a revision of the Galbraith model [16], taking into account the achievements in management over the 45 years that have passed since the publication of his work (Fig. 2).

Two strategies that allow reducing information that is processed are *Creation of Slack Resources* and *Creation of Self-Contained Tasks*. The next two strategies (*Investment in Information Systems* and *Creation of Knowledge Management System*) adapt the organization to process the growing amount of information from internal or external sources.

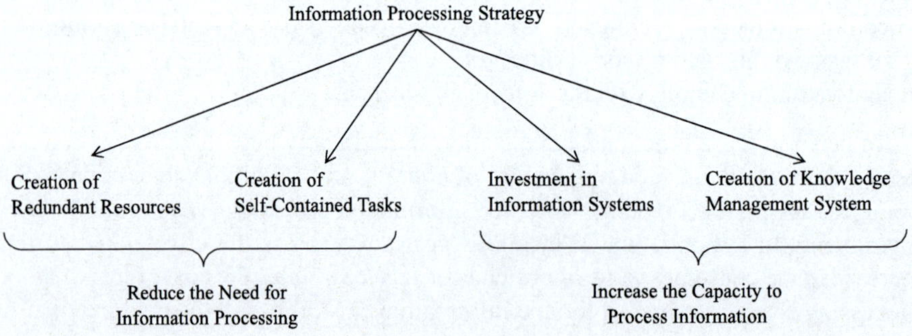

Fig. 2 Organizational information processing strategies, revised Galbraith [16] model

4.1 *Creation of Redundant Resources*

Galbraith [16] notes that Creation of a Slack Resources is a regular practice in solving job scheduling problems when completion dates can be extended until the number of exceptions that occur is within the existing information processing capabilities of the organization. However, from three popular managerial techniques, namely Theory of Constraints (TOC), Just in Time (JIT), and Lean Manufacturing (LM), these resources are losses.

For example, the purchasing manager to create the purchasing plan for the next period should know the manufacturing plan for this period. If the probability of changes in the manufacturing schedule is very high, he or she extends the list and quantity of purchased items to compensate for these variations. Obviously that a significant part of purchased items will not be claimed that leads to unnecessary stocks, freeze money, etc. It is an example of how uncertainty in one subdivision of the organization impacts the decision in another subdivision. In fact, the purchasing manager reduces the uncertainty by extra stocks.

Galbraith [16] notes that the strategy of using slack resources has its costs and whether slack resources are used to reduce information or not depends on the relative cost of the other alternatives. But we should add that this strategy appears spontaneously when available information does not allow reducing uncertainty, see example in [44]. All managerial approaches listed above (TOC, JIT, and LM) aim to reduce uncertainty and, therefore, to reduce the extra resources. In the Theory of Constraints, such excess resources are considered as buffers. TOC justifies that a buffer is needed only before the least productive node of the production chain since it determines the throughput of the entire line. So, we rename this strategy as *Creation of Redundant Resources*, bearing in mind that this strategy *contraries to the desire of management, arises from a lack of information, and leads to inefficiency of organizations in general.*

4.2 *Creation of Self-Contained Tasks*

The second strategy to reduce the amount of information processed is the *Creation of Self-Contained Tasks.* It is the decomposition of the system into loosely coupled modules grouped around similar products or services. Such a module should have all the necessary resources to ensure the entire value chain, and after that, it can be considered as a "black box" that hides internal information flows. Galbraith [16] notes that this approach shifts the basis of the authority structure from one based on input, resource, skill, or occupational categories to one based on output or geographical categories. We can add that it is today the main direction in the design of the organization not only at the enterprise level as Galbraith noted but also at the level of small teams (e.g., flexible manufacturing cells, agile project teams, etc.). This approach effectively solves the coupling problem described above, but it is not always easy to implement. For example, it is impractical to split the IT team responsible for corporate data centers according to the business lines. The second problem is that organizations can lose economies of scale. Third, small autonomous teams can solve only small problems. If it becomes necessary to combine several teams for a more complex task, the processing of information may require more effort than in the case of non-autonomous groups, e.g., see discussion of scaling agile methods on the enterprise level in [45].

4.3 Investment in Information Systems

Galbraith [16] argues that the organization can invest in a mechanism that allows it to process information acquired during task performance without overloading the hierarchical communication channels. He calls such a tool as a *Vertical Information System*. The author notes that the effect of such systems is achieved by the formalization of a decision-making language that simplifies information processing in the authority hierarchy. The accounting system is an example of such a language.

However, providing more information, more often, may simply overload the decision-makers. It should be noted that modern information systems (based on IT) can solve the problem of information overload. First, "classical" enterprise resource management systems offer an optimized model of processes, which reduces the complexity of choosing an operating model at a strategic level. Secondly, these systems prescribe to workers certain actions that are rigidly integrated into the software and thereby reduce the uncertainty at the operational level. Thirdly, such systems provide a wide range of reports consolidating and transmitting information on the levels of management; this reduces uncertainty at the middle and higher levels. All this shapes the value of IT, which was considered by most researchers, e.g. [1, 4, 6–8, 19, 46].

New IT, often referred to as technology enabling digital transformation, opens up new ways to reduce information overload. First of all, it is the analysis of large volumes of data and the transfer of decision-making to algorithms [28].

So, this strategy that we renamed as an *Investment in Information Systems* potentially can provide improvement of information capabilities without information overload.

4.4 Creation of Knowledge Management Systems

The last strategy that Galbraith [16] identifies as a *Creation of Lateral Relationships* was most strongly redeveloped in the years since the publication of his work. According to the author, this strategy moves the decision-making down in the level to where the information exists but does so without reorganizing into self-contained groups. It is achieved through lateral relationships. However, since these informal processes do not always arise spontaneously out of the needs of the task, they should be designed. In the 1970s researchers identified a few types of lateral relationships, e.g., direct contacts, liaison and integration roles, task forces, etc. [16, 32]. According to modern understanding, all these issues are related to the field of Knowledge Management (KM).

Paper [47] identifies four generations in the development of KM as a research discipline. In the first stage (1960–1980), concept of knowledge as a tool that impacts the performance of the organization has emerged. In the second stage (1990s), knowledge was viewed as a process. The third generation of research (2000s) had linked knowledge management to the success of organizations in general. In the current period (2010s), KM role is identified more as a social process than a management system that should be designed.

Thus, the modern knowledge management system in the broad sense is the technology and managerial methods that support the development of social capital, i.e., corporate culture motivating and stimulating the information exchange. Technologically, the knowledge management system can be based both on traditional communication systems [37] and on social networks. Note that the paradigm of social networks exactly corresponds to the model of social capital [48], which is defined through structural (horizontal relationships on the work level), cognitive (shared codes and language), and relational components (trust, norms, and obligations). In other words, we can say that the purpose of the knowledge management system is not to provide all the necessary knowledge to a specific employee but to quickly find in the organization or even outside it someone who has the competencies required. *Not to know everything, but to know who knows.*

Therefore, following the presented concepts, this information design strategy can be defined as the *Creation of a Knowledge Management System*. We can assume that it can be the most attractive strategy of organization design in the near future. However, it requires significant changes in a corporate culture that can become an insurmountable barrier for many organizations.

Table 1 presents all of the organization's design strategies in terms of information processing, their benefits, and limitations. As we can see, the first strategy—Creation of Redundant Resources—is viewed as the worst choice in any circumstances; and last—Creation of Knowledge Management System—as potentially the best one. However, in reality, any organization combines all four strategies that can exist at different levels of the hierarchy or in different vertical sub-systems.

5 Information Processing Capabilities of Information Systems

We have established above that effective information support for decision-making is the key to the performance of an organization in all other senses. Organizational design strategies that enhance an organization's ability to process information must

Table 1 Organizational information processing strategies

Strategy	Benefits	Limitations
Creation of redundant resources	In general, this strategy does not produce any benefits. According to TOC, the creation of redundant resources (buffers) is justified only in front of the least productive nodes of the job chain to guarantee their stable load	This strategy arises from a lack of information and leads to the inefficiency of organizations in general
Creation of self-contained tasks	The moving of the decision-making down in the level to where the tasks processed, and the information exists. The organization consists of a set of "black boxes" that hide internal complexity. There is no information exchange between "black boxes" and, therefore, no need for coordination and synchronization	It is complicated to implement such a system in practice fully. Small autonomous teams can solve only small problems. If it becomes necessary to combine several teams for a more complex task, the processing of information may require more effort than in the case of non-autonomous groups
Investment in information systems	The simplifying information processing in the authority hierarchy by the formalization of a decision-making language. It can be realized without IT	May lead to information overload. However, IT-based applications can reduce this overload due to (1) process and rules standardization and (2) implementation of algorithms that make a decision
Creation of knowledge management System	The moving of the decision-making down in the level to where the tasks processed and the information exists. Establishing a context that supports information and knowledge exchange between workers and groups	It requires significant changes in a corporate culture that can become an insurmountable barrier for many organizations

rely on Information Systems (IS). Currently, there are a significant number of classes of IS that ensure the satisfaction of the various needs of individuals, organizations, and humanity as a whole. Therefore, it is essential to assess information processing capabilities for each class of IS. This should help to align IT and business in choosing the best organizational design.

The results of an empirical study [49] show that IT-related practices have a significant impact on the information processing and knowledge management (KM), financial results, and competitiveness of the company, mainly if they are supported by appropriate actions in the field of HR.

A comparison of KM processes and core IT was conducted in [37]. Authors noted the role of technologies such as data mining (knowledge creation), databases (knowledge storage), forums (knowledge transfer), and expert and workflow systems (knowledge use). In [50], the list of KM processes and associated IT systems has been significantly expanded to take into account recent technologies.

Hayes [51] noted that key IT that is associated with information processing and knowledge management could be classified into three main groups: integration systems that provide storage and retrieval (document management, data mining, directories, expert systems, workflow systems, etc.); interactive systems that support the interaction of people, the distribution, creation, and use of knowledge (e-mail, forums, social networks, blogs, and other Web 2.0 systems); and platforms (groupware, intranet, and enterprise 2.0) that offer general principles for building infrastructure.

Davenport [52] proposed a classification of organizational technologies that support the activities of various classes of employees. He considered two dimensions—the complexity of the work performed (from performing routine procedures to expert activity) and the level of independence from other employees (from an individual activity to large group interaction). Wiig [53] proposed a more detailed classification of work complexity—from routines to actions in a completely unpredictable situation. Based on the integration of the approaches of these researchers, it is possible to construct a classification of information systems that are used to support various types of activities related to information processing (Fig. 3).

The transactional class includes ERP systems that automate the performance of routine procedures and require the employee to know only their duties. The general process, the purpose of data, and their further use may not be known to him or her.

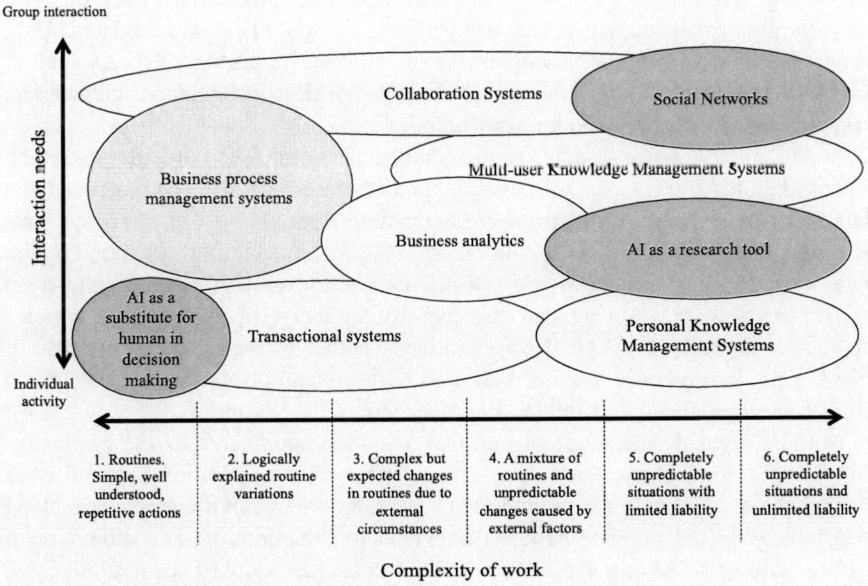

Fig. 3 Classification of information systems

Business process management systems (BPMS) support small and medium group collaboration within rigidly defined models; changing a process requires, at a minimum, modifying its description in the system.

Collaboration systems (e-mail, messengers, forums, and social networks) do not impose any restrictions on the processes. It can also be noted that the degree of data formalization decreases as one moves up the axis "Interaction needs."

Personal knowledge management systems include any tools that allow an employee to save his existing digital objects and the connections between them—from merely storing documents in a file system, to mind maps, etc. Search for objects in such systems, as a rule, is carried out using classifiers created by the user (for example, by the structure of the file system folders). Effectiveness of personal information management is determined, firstly, by the motivation of the employee, and secondly, by his ability to manage information [54].

Multi-user knowledge management systems should provide tools for working with metadata (data about data); advanced search tools; the ability to analyze the relationships that arise between elements of the system (users, documents, etc.). Traditionally, such systems were built as centralized repositories, often assuming the existence of a certain structure for saving and searching for knowledge. However, the modern view implies that knowledge cannot be controlled in this way, it is only necessary to provide the user with flexible tools for organizing their personalized networks of communication and knowledge, similar to how it is done in social networks such as Facebook. Therefore, the use of enterprise social networks (ESN) is today the main trend in the technological support of knowledge management [55].

The first studies of enterprise social networks [56] showed that the introduction of this class of systems has a positive effect on the individual productivity of employees, while the quality of processes is enhanced, and innovation activity is stimulated. Also, Leonardi [57] noted another essential role of ESN; they contribute to the spread of not only knowledge itself, but also meta-knowledge (knowledge about knowledge: "who knows what" and "who knows whom").

Business intelligence systems in their traditional form (i.e., On-Line Analytical Processing/OLAP) are designed to execute predefined queries that return generalized data sets. Recently, their functions are expanding through the use of AI systems. The use of artificial intelligence/data mining systems, especially those based on big data, is more like a scientific activity—hypotheses formulation and testing them against existing data. But we can also identify another class of AI-based systems that automate decision-making (for example, whether a given message is spam or whether this borrower is a scam) based on patterns and pre-trained models. Such models are implemented as routine functions and replace humans.

Note that outside the scope of our analysis, such approaches as the Internet of things (IoT), blockchain, etc. IoT is a metasystem that is a combination of smart devices that self-learn in the production process and interact with people in making decisions. From this point of view, IoT integrates the functions of both automation of routine processes (AI as a substitute for man) and AI as a tool of accumulating and analyzing data. Blockchain is a new technology for trusting data management that opens up new opportunities for communities, but its influence on decision-making is much less pronounced. We can compare it with database technologies, which are technical components of information systems.

To summarize the above, each type of information system has its own niche both in terms of the complexity of the supported processes and in terms of the employees involved in them. Obviously, one information system cannot satisfy all the needs of an organization. Therefore, the set of systems must comply with the organization's information design strategy.

6 Conclusion

In the presented work, we examined the mechanism for creating and manifesting the impact of IT on the performance of an organization. Many researchers note that this effect is mainly due to the automation of processes and the implementation of best practices. Still, we believe that this is not true, especially with the advent of new technologies that enable digital transformation.

In our opinion, which is based on organization theory, the effect of IT is created through effective information support for decision-making. This approach allows us to identify the consequences of a lack and excess of information that equally lead to ineffective solutions.

Since information processing is the essential function of the organization, we revised the design strategies identified by Galbraith [16], taking into account the achievements in theory and practice since the publication of his work. As a result, we identified a lack of information as the cause of redundant resources.

We also presented an analysis of information processing capabilities for different types of information systems, which should help in aligning IT and business in choosing the optimal organization design strategy.

References

1. Dedrick, J., Gurbaxani, V., & Kraemer, K. (2003). Information technology and economic performance: A critical review of the empirical evidence. *ACM Computing Surveys (CSUR), 35*(1), 1–28.
2. Bresnahan, T. F., Brynjolfsson, E., & Hitt, L. M. (2002). Information technology, workplace organization, and the demand for skilled labor: Firm-level evidence. *The Quarterly Journal of Economics, 117*(1), 339–376.
3. Brynjolfsson, E., & Saunders, A. (2009). *Wired for innovation: How information technology is reshaping the economy*. MIT Press.
4. Tambe, P., & Hitt, L. M. (2012). The productivity of information technology investments: new evidence from it labor data. *Information Systems Research, 23:3*(1), 599–617.
5. Chae, H. C., Koh, C. E., & Prybutok, V. (2014). Information technology capability and firm performance: Contradictory findings and their possible causes. *MIS Quarterly, 38*(1), 305–326.
6. Kohli, R., & Grover, V. (2008). Business value of IT: An essay on expanding research directions to keep up with the times. *Journal of the Association for Information System, 9*(1), 23–39.

7. Mithas, S., & Rust, R. (2016). How information technology strategy and investments influence firm performance: Conjecture and empirical evidence. *MIS Quarterly, 40*(1), 223–245.
8. Melville, N., Kraemer, K., & Gurbaxani, V. (2004). Review: Information technology and organizational performance: An integrative model of IT business value. *MIS Quarterly, 28*(2), 283–322.
9. Prajogo, D., Toy, J., Bhattacharya, A., Oke, A., & Cheng, T. (2018). The relationships between information management, process management and operational performance: Internal and external contexts. *International Journal of Production Economics, 199*, 95–103.
10. Saunders, C., & Jones, J. W. (1990). Temporal sequences in information acquisition for decision making: A focus on source and medium. *Academy of Management Review, 15*(1), 29–46.
11. Milgrom, P., & Roberts, J. (1992). *Economics*. Prentice-Hall.
12. Simon, H. A. (1977). *The new science of management decision*. Prentice-Hall.
13. Joseph, J., & Gaba, V. (2020). Organizational structure, information processing, and decision-making: A retrospective and road map for research. *Academy of Management Annals, 14*(1), 267–302.
14. Mintzberg, H., Raisinghani, D., & Theoret, A. (1976). The structure of unstructured decision processes. *Administrative Science Quarterly, 21*(2), 246–275.
15. Cohen, M. D., & Olsen, J. P. (1972). A garbage can model of organizational choice. *Administrative Science Quarterly, 17*(1), 1–25.
16. Galbraith, J. R. (1974). Organizational design: An information processing view. *Interfaces, 4*(3), 28–36.
17. David, P. A. (1990). The dynamo and the computer: An historical perspective on the modern productivity paradox. *The American Economic Review, 80*, 355–361.
18. Milgrom, P., & Roberts, J. (1990). The economics of modern manufacturing: Technology, strategy, and organization. *The American Economic Review, 80*, 511–528.
19. Sabherwal, R., & Jeyaraj, A. (2015). Information technology impacts on firm performance: An extension of kohli and devaraj (2003). *MIS Quarterly, 39*(4), 809–836.
20. Mithas, S., Ramasubbu, N., & Sambamurthy, V. (2011). How information management capability influences firm performance. *MIS Quarterly, 35*(1), 237–256.
21. Nunamaker, Jr, J. F., & Briggs, R. O. (2011). Toward a broader vision for information systems. *ACM Transactions on Management Information System, 2:4*(20).
22. Liu, H., Ke, W., Wei, K. K., & Hua, Z. (2013). The impact of IT capabilities on firm performance: The mediating roles of absorptive capacity and supply chain agility. *Decision Support Systems, 54*(3), 1452–1462.
23. Devece, C., Palacios, D., & Martinez-Simarro, D. (2017). Effect of information management capability on organizational performance. *Service Business, 11*, 563–580.
24. Kathuria, A., Saldanha, T., Khuntia, J., & Rojas, M. (2016). How information management capability affects innovation capability and firm performance under turbulence: Evidence from india. In *Proceedings of the ICIS*.
25. Brinkhues, R. A., da Silva, J., da Silva Freitas, J., Maçada, A., & Dolci, P. (2019). IT ambidexterity, organizational agility and information management capability: A brazilian case. In *Proceedings of the 25 ACIS*.
26. Bharadwaj, A., El Sawy, O., Pavlou, P., & Venkatraman, N. (2013). Digital business strategy: Toward a next generation of insights. *MIS Quarterly, 37*(2), 471–482.
27. Müller, O., Fay, M., & vom Brocke, J. (2018). The effect of big data and analytics on firm performance: An econometric analysis considering industry characteristics. *Journal of Management Information Systems, 35*(2), 488–509.
28. Brynjolfsson, E., & McElheran, K. (2016). The rapid adoption of data-driven decision-making. *The American Economic Review, 106*(5), 133–139.
29. Agrawal, A., Gans, J. S., & Goldfarb, A. (2019). Exploring the impact of artificial intelligence: Prediction versus judgment. *Information Economics and Policy, 47*, 1–6.
30. Makridakis, S. (2017). The forthcoming artificial intelligence (AI) revolution: Its impact on society and firms. *Futures, 90*, 46–60.

31. Lyytinen, K., & Newman, M. (2008). Explaining information systems change: A punctuated socio-technical change model. *European Journal of Information Systems, 17*(6), 589–613.
32. Tushman, M., & Nadler, D. (1978). Information processing as an integrating concept in organizational design. *The Academy of Management Review, 3*(3), 613–624.
33. Aydiner, A. S., Tatoglu, E., Bayraktar, E., & Zaim, S. (2019). Information system capabilities and firm performance: Opening the black box through decision-making performance and business-process performance. *International Journal of Information Management, 47*, 168–182.
34. Davenport, T. H., & Prusak, L. (1998). *Working knowledge: How organizations manage that they know*. Harvard Business Press.
35. Choo, C. W. (2006). *The knowing organization: How organizations use information to construct meaning*. Create Knowledge and Make Decisions. Oxford University Press.
36. Nonaka, I., & Takeuchi, H. (1995). *The knowledge- creating company: How japanese companies create the dynamics of innovation*. Oxford University Press.
37. Alavi, M., & Leidner, D. E. (2001). Knowledge management and knowledge management systems: Conceptual foundations and research issues. *MIS Quarterly, 25*(1), 107–136.
38. Bierman, D. J., Destrebecqz, A., & Cleeremans, A. (2005). Intuitive decision making in complex situations: Somatic markers in an artificial grammar learning task. *Cognitive, Affective, and Behavioral Neuroscience, 5*(3), 297–305.
39. Patton, J. R. (2003). Intuition in decisions. *Management Decision, 41*(10), 989–996.
40. Huarng, K. H., Mas-Tur, A., & Moreno, F. C. (2018). Innovation, knowledge, judgment, and decision-making as virtuous cycles. *Journal of Business Research, 88*, 278–281.
41. Zelenkov, Y. (2018). Agility of enterprise information systems: A conceptual model, design principles and quantitative measurement. *Business Informatics, 2*, 30–44.
42. Zelenkov, Y. (2015). Critical regular components of IT strategy: Decision making model and efficiency measurement. *Journal of Management Analytics, 2*(2), 95–110.
43. Eppler, M., & Mengis, J. (2004). The concept of information overload: A review of literature from organization science, accounting, marketing, mis, and related disciplines. *The Information Society, 20*(5), 325–344.
44. Zelenkov, Y. (2017). Information efficiency, information design and information system of an organization. *Business Informatics, 2*, 25–32.
45. Leffingwell, D. (2007). *Scaling software agility: Best practices for large enterprises*. Addison-Wesley.
46. Zelenkov, Y. (2015). Business and IT alignment in turbulent business environment. LNBIP. In W. Abramowicz (Ed.), *BIS 2015 Workshops* (Vol. 228, pp. 101–112). Springer.
47. Gaviria-Marin, M., Merigó, J. M., & Baier-Fuentes, H. (2019). Knowledge management: A global examination based on bibliometric analysis. *Technological Forecasting and Social Change, 140*, 194–220.
48. Nahapiet, J., & Ghoshal, S. (1998). Social capital, intellectual capital, and the organizational advantage. *Academy of Management Review, 23*(2), 242–266.
49. Andreeva, T., & Kianto, A. (2012). Does knowledge management really matter? linking knowledge management practices, competitiveness and economic performance. *Journal of Knowledge Management, 16*(4), 617–636.
50. Ragab, M., & Arisha, A. (2013). Knowledge management and measurement: A critical review. *Journal of Knowledge Management, 17*(6), 873–901.
51. Hayes, N. (2011). Information technology and the possibilities for knowledge sharing. In M. Easterby-Smith & M. Lyles (Eds.), *Handbook of organizational learning and knowledge management*, pp. 83--95. Wiley.
52. Davenport, T. H. (2005). *Thinking for a living: How to get better performances and results from knowledge workers*. Harvard Business School Press.
53. Wiig, K. (2004). *People-focused knowledge management: How effective decision-making leads to corporate success*. Elsevier.
54. Hwang, Y., Kettinger, W. J., & Mun, Y. Y. (2015). Personal information management effectiveness of knowledge workers: Conceptual development and empirical validation. *European Journal of Information Systems, 24*(6), 588–606.

55. Von Krogh, G. (2012). How does social software change knowledge management? toward a strategic research agenda. *The Journal of Strategic Information Systems, 21*(2), 154–164.
56. Kuegler, M., Smolnik, S., & Kane, G. (2015). What's in IT for employees? understanding the relationship between use and performance in enterprise social software. *The Journal of Strategic Information Systems 24*(2), 90–112.
57. Leonardi, P. (2015). Ambient awareness and knowledge acquisition: Using social media to learn "who knows what" and "who knows whom." *MIS Quarterly, 39*(4), 747–762.

Innovation Hub and Its IT Support: Architecture Model

Igor Ilin, Anastasia Levina, and Victoria Iliashenko

Abstract The paper proposes to consider the concepts of an innovation ecosystem and a digital platform for an innovation hub. The analysis of world experience in terms of innovative hubs contributing to the accelerated implementation of innovations is presented. The basic requirements for the digital platform were formed. The purpose of this paper is to form a reference model of an industry innovation hub for the accelerated implementation of digital technologies and a reference model of a digital platform for an industry innovation hub. The methodological basis of the paper is the analysis of open sources.

Keywords Digital technologies · Innovation hubs · Innovations ecosystems · Reference model · IT-architecture

1 Introduction

The basic conditions for the introduction of new developments are government support, funding, technology, a strong scientific and technological base, as well as an appropriate culture of innovation development. Today, in working with innovations, the key role is played by a properly built and most transparent process within the company, which will contribute to the achievement of the set results. The need for innovation is driven by the challenge of economic development. Thus, importantly the basis for the stability of the progressive development is to ensure continuous generation of innovative projects. If earlier almost all companies that worked with innovations tried to find as many projects as possible, cover the entire market, collect a wide funnel of solutions, today this trend is sharply transformed into a point search for technologies that are already ready for implementation in business [1]. The main goal of this approach is to find a solution that can be quickly assessed, determine a future customer for it within the company, and launch it into a separate dedicated project for yourself or in cooperation with partners in the market [2]. The creation of

I. Ilin · A. Levina · V. Iliashenko (✉)
Peter the Great St.Petersburg Polytechnic University, Polytechnicheskaya 29, St. Petersburg 195251, Russia

E. Zaramenskikh and A. Fedorova (eds.), *Digitalization of Society, Economics and Management*, Lecture Notes in Information Systems and Organisation 53,
https://doi.org/10.1007/978-3-030-94252-6_4

ecosystems and innovation hubs for the dissemination of digital innovations seems to be an expedient form of organizing the interaction of the participants in the innovation process, which will allow achieving a synergistic effect from the integrated efforts of the participants and will contribute to the accelerated digital transformation of the state. Innovation hubs are becoming popular with executives looking to support local economies and boost employment. But for the effective development of innovations special conditions are needed [3, 4].

Innovation hubs are increasingly becoming an integral part of urban planning as planners seek to revitalize economic and employment opportunities by creating an environment conducive to innovation. The scale of this environment can range from company departments or individual buildings with multiple tenants (often called incubators) to entire geographic regions called clusters. For the most part, as defined by the Massachusetts Institute of Technology, these are "dense networks of interconnected technology companies, customers and suppliers." Such an element of the innovation infrastructure will make it possible to create new products in an end-to-end cycle: from seed to a startup with its subsequent implementation. An innovative hub is believed to provide an attractive work environment and first-class infrastructure in terms of network connectivity [5].

The purpose of this paper is to form a reference model of an industry innovation hub for the accelerated implementation of digital technologies and a reference model of a digital platform for an industry innovation hub.

As a result of the research, the authors of the article want to get a generalized understanding of the interaction between the innovation hub and the digital platform of industry solutions.

2 Overview of Innovation Ecosystems and Hubs

The purpose of the innovation ecosystem is, first, to create a network community in which conditions favorable for the intensive dissemination of knowledge and the sharing of resources are provided. Under such conditions, a high intensity of interaction will be ensured through trusting relationships, contributing to the dissemination of knowledge and other resources [6].

Analysis of information about the established, generally recognized, and effectively operating global innovation ecosystems and hubs made it possible to formulate the main goals of creating an innovation ecosystem (Fig. 1) [7].

As for the characteristics of an innovation ecosystem, it can be considered as a complex system that has the following characteristics [8]:

- Self-organization—the ability of a system to create "order" without the participation of an external or internal leader when changes occur spontaneously or because of local interactions.

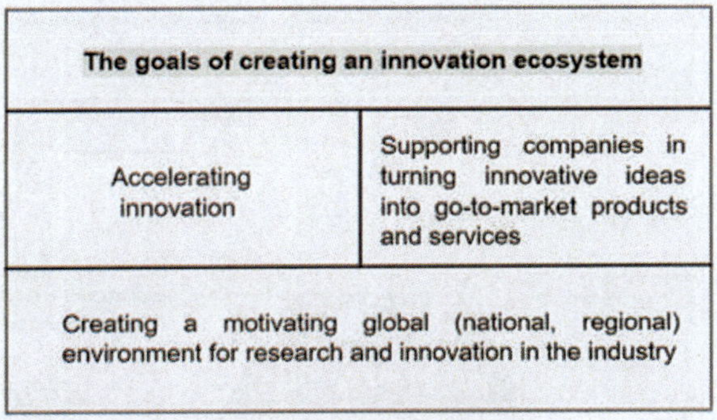

Fig. 1 Key goals of creating an innovation ecosystem

- Emergence is the property of a system to have characteristics that its elements cannot have individually—cooperation between companies leads to a result that they cannot create alone.
- Co-evolution is a process of mutual changes during the development of interrelated subjects.
- Adaptability—adaptation to changing conditions through internal changes.

Thus, it is possible to form the structure of the innovation ecosystem (Fig. 2). It is assumed that participants in the innovation ecosystem implement the entire cycle of innovation implementation.

2.1 World Experience in Creating Innovative Hubs

The USA, Singapore, Finland, Japan, and Israel are the most striking examples of the implementation of their innovative capabilities. The main global trends in innovation can be identified in four areas, presented in Table 1 below [2].

Cyber-Physical Security

In 2020, the City of New York opened a new cyber security technology hub in Manhattan. The project is being implemented in close and unique collaboration with the Israeli firm Jerusalem Venture Partners. The partnership, funded by $ 100 million, including $ 30 million from New York City authorities, will partner with companies that can offer cutting-edge cyber security solutions [9, 10].

Among other things, they will work on solutions not only for large corporations but also for small and medium-sized businesses, whose representatives often cannot afford expensive developments that guarantee high protection efficiency.

Medicine Industry

The modern pharmaceutical industry is unthinkable without innovations, including digital ones, and global pharmaceutical giants play an important role in their search,

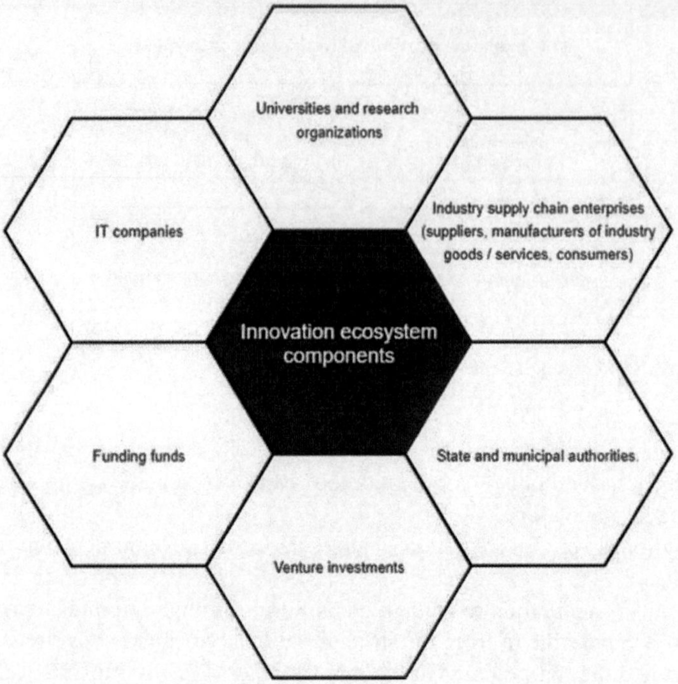

Fig. 2 Detailed structure of the innovation ecosystem

Table 1 Key trends in innovation

Name	Description
System crisis venture investing	• Reduction of investments at the initial stages of innovative projects • Increasing the distance between entrepreneur and venture capitalist fund • Increased competition between foundations and business angels
Strengthening the role states as customer innovation Edge Analytics	Asian, Israeli, and Finnish models are built entirely on state participation
Crisis of the existing system of intellectual property protection	• Monopolization of certain segments (biotechnology and IT) and oligopoly on others (music) • Creation of barriers to technological development in individual regions by large corporations
Democratizing the innovation process	• Expansion of investment in terms of geographic expansion and involvement of more people in this process • Starting entrepreneurship while still at university

support, and then implementation. Among them is the international biopharmaceutical company AstraZeneca, operating in more than 100 countries around the world and known for its drugs in the field of cardiology, oncology, nephrology and metabolism, and respiratory diseases. As part of supporting innovation, the company has deployed a global health innovation hub system or Health Innovation Hubs. In Russia, such a hub iDream was opened in 2018 in cooperation with the Skolkovo Foundation; today the company has eight hubs in emerging markets, including Singapore, India, and China [11].

Ecosystems for the development of innovation generally work to improve the health system. Thanks to the cooperation of all partners, from business to government agencies, we can all solve problems of the state, industry, and patients faster and more efficiently. We can say that health care of the future will become patient-centered. The industry has already formed a clear trend toward the transition from quantity to quality, from a fragmented approach to the development of innovation and the integration of all players. Digital technologies are the core of the new system. Building a fully integrated ecosystem of patient data is essential to advance science and technology and build the most efficient healthcare systems.

Enel Company Experience

Enel has created a global network of ten innovation hubs. Innovation hubs are in Brazil (Rio de Janeiro), Chile (Santiago), Israel (Tel Aviv), Italy (Milan, Catania, Pisa), Russia (Moscow), Spain (Madrid), and the USA (Boston, San Francisco) to find startups with great potential in terms of technologies and business models relevant to Enel's operations.

Since 2015, when Enel introduced the Open Innovation approach, focusing on development from external sources, the company has received about 10,000 cooperation proposals, 6,500 of which were sent by startups. In total, about 650 projects have been implemented during this time, of which about 250 are startups. Thanks to Enel, over 50 startups have been scaled to a global level. Among the many areas of such cooperation, the most significant are energy storage, big data, energy management, smart homes, electric transport, the Internet of things, preventive maintenance of equipment, artificial intelligence, intelligent technologies, and robotics [12, 13].

French Innovation Hub

A French innovation hub has already been set up in New York and Tokyo, and Moscow has become the third capital in the world to support the expansion of French Tech outside of France. In Russia, the French Tech community began to form in 2014, together with the arrival of new innovative companies: AT Internet, Blablacar, Cegid, Criteo, Generix, and others. The creation of such a community has three goals: facilitating the exchange of experience between members, popularizing French projects among large companies, increasing the attractiveness of the French Tech label among members of the Tech community, investors, and Russian media [14].

Financial and Technical Hubs

One of the world's largest financial and technical hubs is located in California's Silicon Valley. Projects like Affirm, Stripe, Lending Club, Prosper, SoFi, Square, and many more have formed the Silicon Valley Unicorn Club. This is a unique place where any innovative project is put to the test. Customers are spoiled for technology because they get the opportunity to be the first to try any technology solution. Nevertheless, even though the top ten US startup accelerators are located in California, there is one snag—it is not a fact that a project that has become successful in Silicon Valley will become successful beyond its borders [15].

New York is becoming another center of innovation. This is where the comprehensive guidelines for walking the digital currency Bitcoin and accepting this cryptocurrency to pay parking bills took shape. New York has become a promising region for established investors and companies hunting for innovative fintech startups. Potential investors include Bain Capital Ventures, JPMorgan Chase, FinTech Innovation Lab, New York Digital Health Accelerator, and NYC Seed.

London is still considered one of the world's financial-technical centers. Unicorns such as Klarna, iZettle, Adyen, Funding Circle, TransferWise, and POWA Technologies came from Europe as proof of the significant role of the European market in the global fintech arena. In Q2 2014, European startups raised over $2.8 billion from venture capitalists [16].

India, Singapore, and Hong Kong are fueling Asian fintech, making it globally competitive. Leading financial group DBS, with some 280 subsidiaries operating in 18 global markets, announced at the end of last year that it will invest $7.1 million in initiatives that can support the startup ecosystem in Singapore. Japanese internet giant Rakuten has launched a $100 million fintech fund. The fund will focus on fintech projects that are either in the early or mid-stage of their development [17, 18].

3 Results

3.1 Ideality Diagram of an Innovation Ecosystem

Within the framework of this paper, the authors introduce the concept of the ideality of the innovation ecosystem, based on the best world practices described in paragraph 2. Figure 3 shows a diagram of the ideality of the innovation ecosystem in the Spider Diagram format. This diagram reflects the key properties of the ecosystem using angles. Each of the lines of development of the ecosystem has its beginning and end, and the entire path of the ecosystem from inception to "ideal state" along a specific line can be taken as 100%. Analyzing the existing stage of ecosystem development for each line, the expert can give each line a quantitative expert assessment [19].

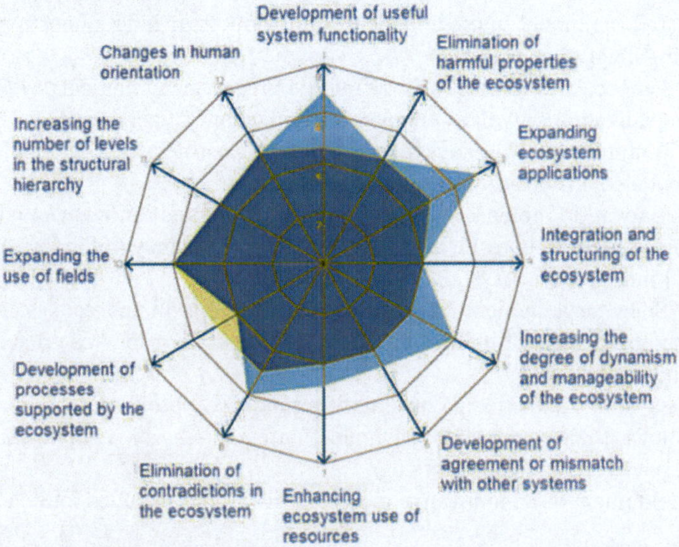

Fig. 3 Ideality diagram of an innovation ecosystem

3.2 *A Reference Model for an Industry Innovation Hub for Accelerating Digital Adoption*

In Fig. 4, the authors propose a general reference model for an industry innovation hub. When we talk about the common center of the so-called congestion of the flow of companies, people, we should focus on three key components of our ecosystem: community, data, and digital platform.

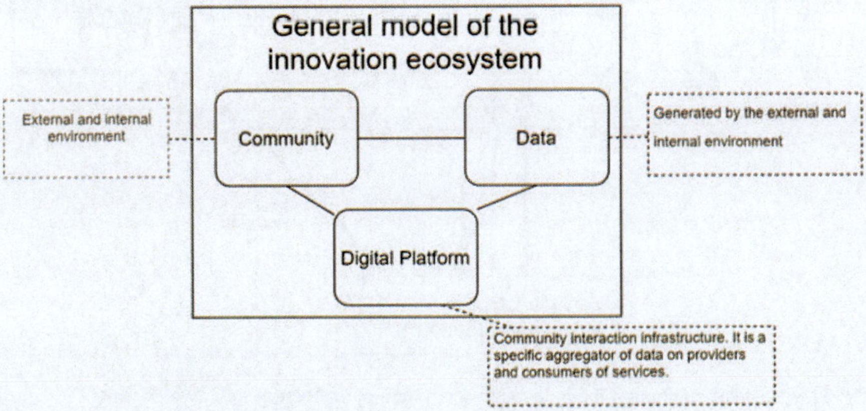

Fig. 4 General reference model of the innovation ecosystem

If we detail the model into components and show their interconnection, we get the following diagram in Fig. 5:

Block "Science, Universities"—is the main source of technological developments for commercialization as well as engineering and technical personnel.

Block "Venture capital"—plays in the ecosystem the role of a provider of not only financing but also business competencies for startups.

Block "Innovation projects/Startups"—are implemented innovative and technological projects. The main result and indicator of the efficiency of the functioning of the national innovation ecosystem and all its elements.

Block "State Development Institutions"—close gaps in the ecosystem (especially at the initial stage of development) and concentrate resources on accelerated breakthrough areas.

"Business" block is the main consumer for innovative projects.

Block "Infrastructure (including Digital Platform)"—is of a supporting nature (general services and industry services).

The development of an innovative project is linear and includes four steps:

- Basic research
- Applied research
- Product development
- Product distribution.

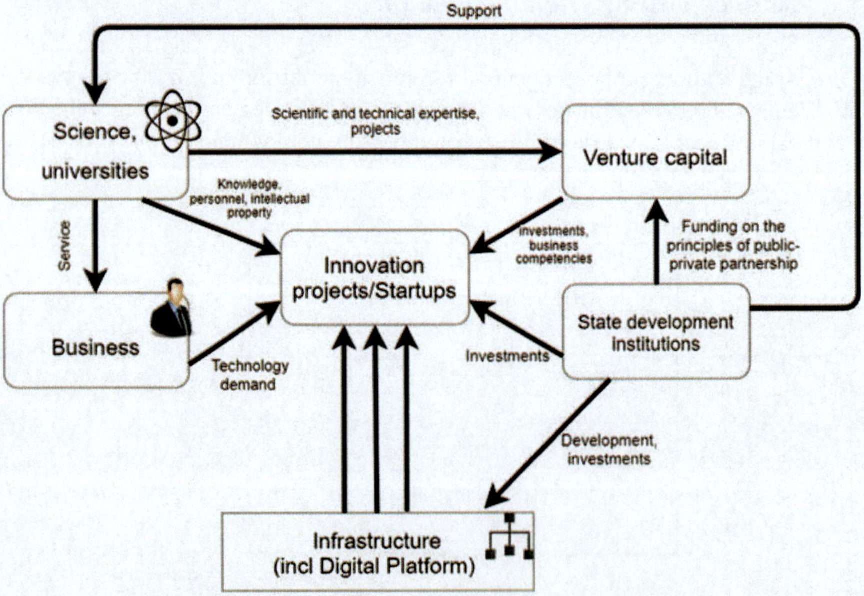

Fig. 5 Scheme of combining the innovation ecosystem components

Moreover, we can talk about the discrete nature of the innovative project, which allows us to identify five main steps. Figure 6 proposes a reference model for an innovation ecosystem based on a discrete definition of an innovation project.

At each stage of its development, an innovative project can only participate in generalized competitions, the conditions for participation in which it meets at the time of participation. If we consider the innovation ecosystem from the point of view of a startup, it turns out that there is no single ecosystem, but a set of ecosystems for each stage of development. At the same time, if we consider the situation from the point of view of external beneficiaries of successfully implemented projects (investors, government, and corporations), then the entire ecosystem works as one global super competition, the winners of which are successful projects, due to which the existence of the entire ecosystem pays off. This circumstance is also well modeled within the framework of the proposed approach since a sequence of several generalized competitions is also a generalized competition in accordance with our definition.

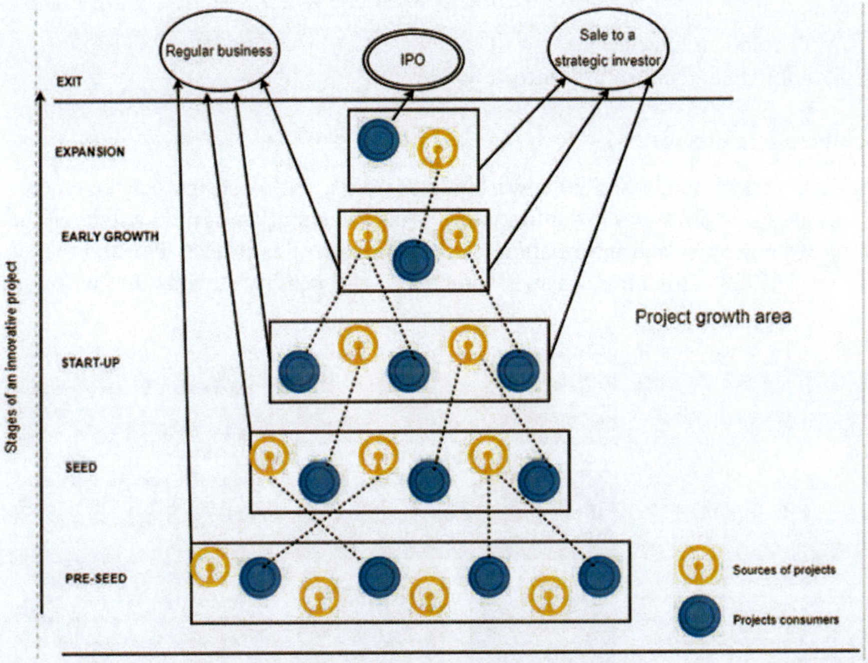

Fig. 6 A reference model for an innovation ecosystem based on a discrete definition of an innovation project

3.3 *Innovation Hub Architecture*

General Architecture of the Innovation Hub

Figure 7 shows the overall architecture of the innovation hub. The innovation hub architecture defines the overall structure and functions of systems (business and IT) across the entire ecosystem (including partners and other organizations that form the so-called "real-time enterprise") and provides a common framework, standards, and guidelines for architecture the level of individual projects. The shared vision provided by the enterprise architecture creates the possibility of a unified design of systems that are adequate in terms of meeting the needs of the organization, and capable of interoperability and integration where necessary [20].

Four architectures are considered as the main levels (layers) of enterprise architecture [21]:

- Business architecture (business architecture).
- Data architecture.
- Application architecture.
- Technological architecture (infrastructure).

Business Architecture

Business architecture describes how a business works. The most significant elements in this area are "processes and information," "organization," and "productivity." The element "processes and information" is most important as it describes and classifies the business structures, business processes, and activity streams that make up

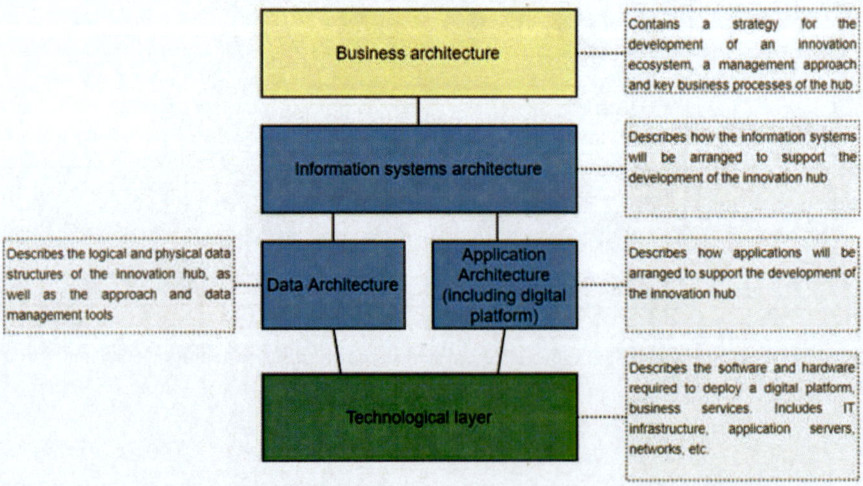

Fig. 7 General architecture of the innovation hub

the organization's business model. The element "organization" describes the organizational structure and methods of work, the products, and services that the business produces, the business units, their location, etc. The element "performance" describes the indicators that measure the efficiency of the enterprise (productivity, business risks, etc.).

Data Architecture

Data architecture describes the data used by an enterprise. It is customary to distinguish four key groups of data architecture requirements [22]:

- Requirements for the data structure.
- Requirements for data transfer.
- Requirements for data management.
- Requirements for data security.

The data structure, in turn, consists of classifiers and data characteristics. Four types of data are distinguished: master data, metadata, transactional, and historical data.

When integrating and replacing software applications, it becomes necessary to transfer data. The requirements for data migration shape the data architecture. Also, at this architectural level, the data transformation and cleaning systems needed to represent data in a format that meets the requirements and constraints of the target application should be defined. It is this element of the data architecture that is responsible for data quality.

Data management requirements describe the resources that an enterprise must carry out data transformations. First, these are:

- structure—organizational structure and standardization bodies for data transformation management;
- people—the skills and roles required to transform data;
- data management systems throughout their life cycles.

Data security requirements can be defined as maintaining data integrity, confidentiality, and availability properties. This element of the data architecture describes the requirements for different categories of data.

Application Architecture

Application architecture (application architecture) describes the applications that automate the organization's activities (business architecture) and process information flows (data architecture). First, the application architecture is described through classes and types of applications without being tied to specific solutions and technologies. Application classes are stable and do not change too much over time, while implementation technologies for dedicated application classes can change rapidly [23].

Technological Architecture

A technology architecture describes the physical implementation of an enterprise IT infrastructure and relies on the requirements derived from the application architecture description. There are various ways to categorize technologies. According to Gartner, the technology architecture has six elements [24]:

- data services (DBMS, data warehouses, etc.);
- application services (mail, collaboration systems, development tools, etc.);
- middleware (application servers and other integration tools);
- computing infrastructure (server and user equipment, storage systems, etc.);
- network services (local and global network infrastructure and access technologies);
- security services.

After analyzing the methods of modeling the architecture of an enterprise, explaining in detail each of its components, the authors of the paper propose a model of the upper level of the architecture of an innovation hub that promotes the introduction of innovations considering the integration of a digital platform (Fig. 8).

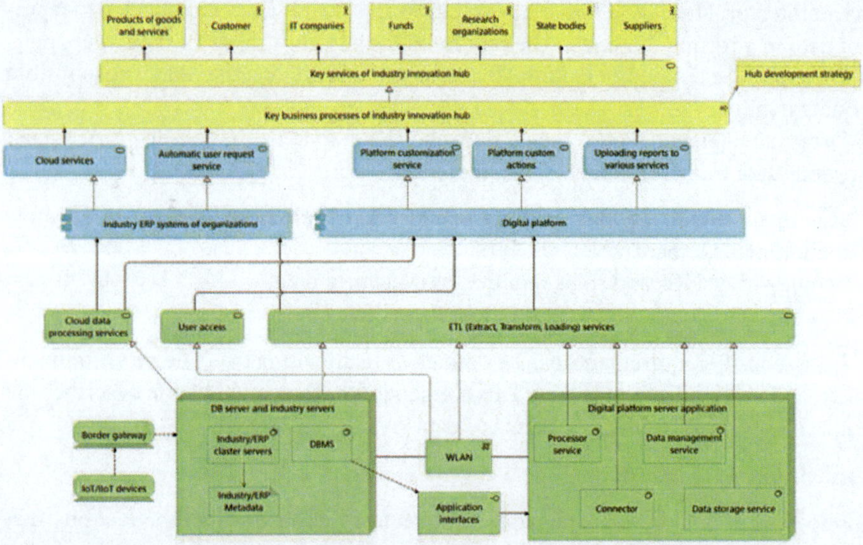

Fig. 8 Top-level architecture of the innovation hub

3.4 *Digital Platform of the Industry Innovation Hub*

Requirements for the Digital Platform of the Innovation Hub

The construction of a digital platform is based on the principles of ontological models. The architecture of the digital platform provides for the principles of constructing the BEOM (Business Entity Ontological Model) matrix for both individual enterprises and the industry as a whole:

- Structured solutions for industry challenges.
- Data on stakeholder interaction.
- Description of objects of activity (for example, digital twins).
- Organization of relationships (relationships) for all participants in the ecosystem.
- Geo-referencing for objects and processes.
- Structured data storage for analysis of temporary changes as well as the ability to monitor processes online.

Digital Platforms can associate needs with resources (product service providers to consumers, etc.) through different interaction formats: people-to-people, people-to machines, machines-with-machines "(machines-to machines). The concept of a digital platform includes both the technological structure itself and the platform business model and ecosystem. The platform as a business model is a model of providing through a technological platform for direct interaction and the implementation of transactions between entities using new methods and forms of interaction, value creation, and pricing.

The development process of digital platforms can be divided into three blocks:

- Structures and stages of formation of digital platforms.
- Platform Business Aspects.
- Challenges and opportunities for integration into ecosystems.

The interaction of these blocks leads to an understanding of the value of using digital platforms in innovative hubs.

The digital platform of the innovation hub allows:

- perform scenario calculations of the development of the technological direction;
- map value chains, providing market participants with a holistic picture of economic ties;
- design optimal "Supplier–Consumer" relationships;
- identify promising areas of development (growth drivers) for the creation of new businesses, products, and services;
- to formulate justifications for investment projects for the production and launch of products and services on promising markets.

To achieve economies of scale and focused market launch of new products, the digital platform helps organize the structured work of a team of experts to develop the supplier/consumer network and identify and develop technologies that are priority for the entire supply chain.

Using a digital platform allows you to reduce the risks of investment projects, attracting a network of international partners to create a new product for target foreign markets. The digital platform is formed in two stages (Fig. 9). The first stage includes building a model of the value chain and includes two sub-stages, the second stage is aimed at Building digital models of market supply (value proposition) in promising areas (growth drivers) and consists of four sub-stages.

After analyzing the world experiences of countries and companies in the creation and implementation of innovative hubs, the authors of this paper propose to form a map of requirements for a digital platform. The authors identified seven key requirements required to implement the digital platform of industry innovation hubs (Fig. 10):

- General functional system requirements
- Reliability requirements
- Performance and hardware requirements
- Security requirements
- Requirements for the modes of functioning, diagnosis, and monitoring of the system
- System interface requirements
- Requirements for the composition of information, volumes, methods of its organization, and life cycle.

If we talk about the general requirements for a digital platform, the following several points can be distinguished:

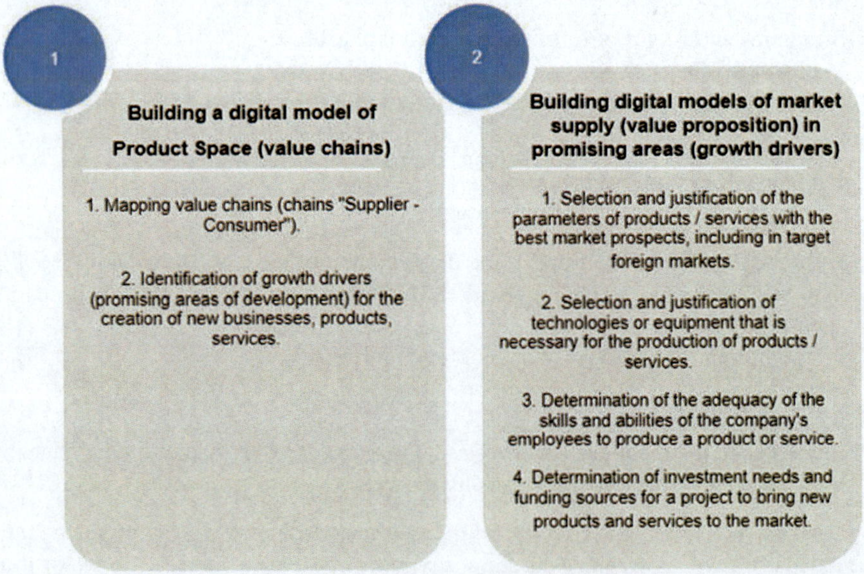

Fig. 9 Stages of creating a digital platform for an innovation ecosystem

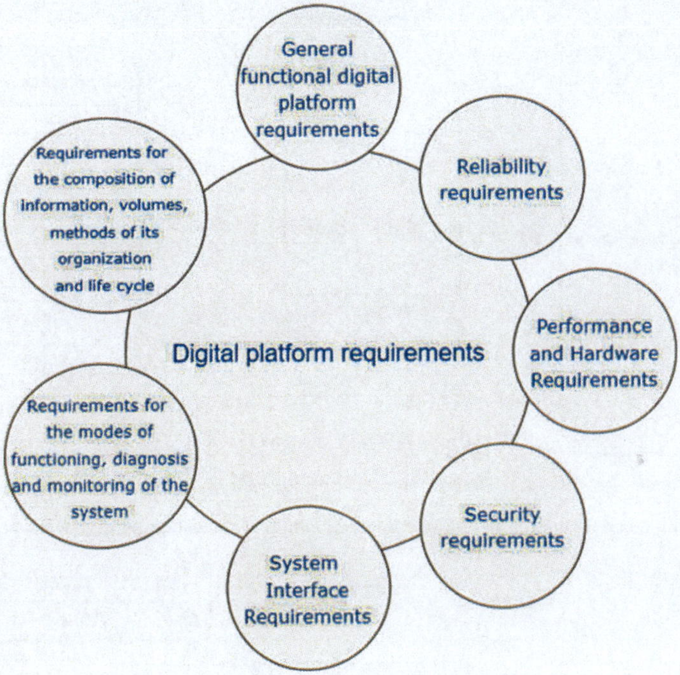

Fig. 10 Digital Platform Requirements Map

1. Automated loading of data from information systems-sources in the established format.
2. Integration of all platform participants.
3. Support for the platform in real time and considering the workload of its attendance.
4. Availability of high-level technical characteristics and sufficient capacity for multi-channel user work.

A Reference Model for an Industry Innovation Hub for Accelerating Digital Adoption

Figure 11 presents a digital platform reference model showing the influences and interconnections of key participants in the innovation hub.

Digital Platform Architecture

Based on the description of digital platforms and the formation of a system of requirements for them, it is possible to analyze the architecture of the digital platform (Fig. 12).

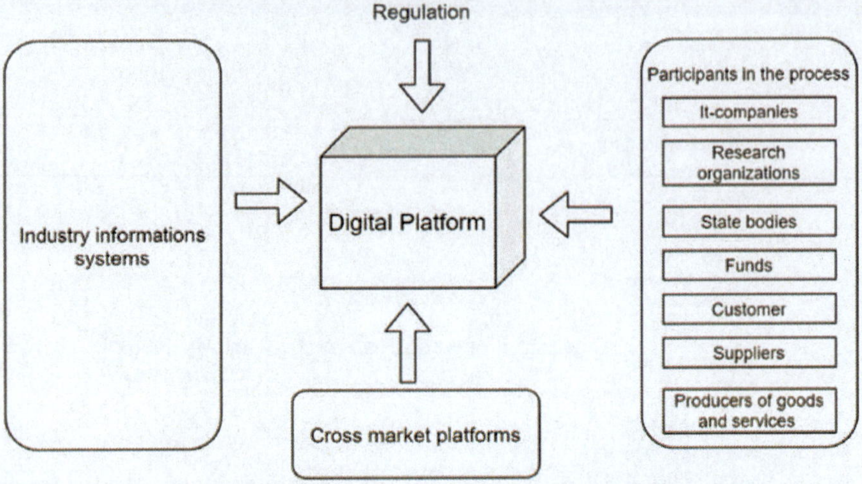

Fig. 11 A reference model for an industry innovation hub for accelerating digital adoption

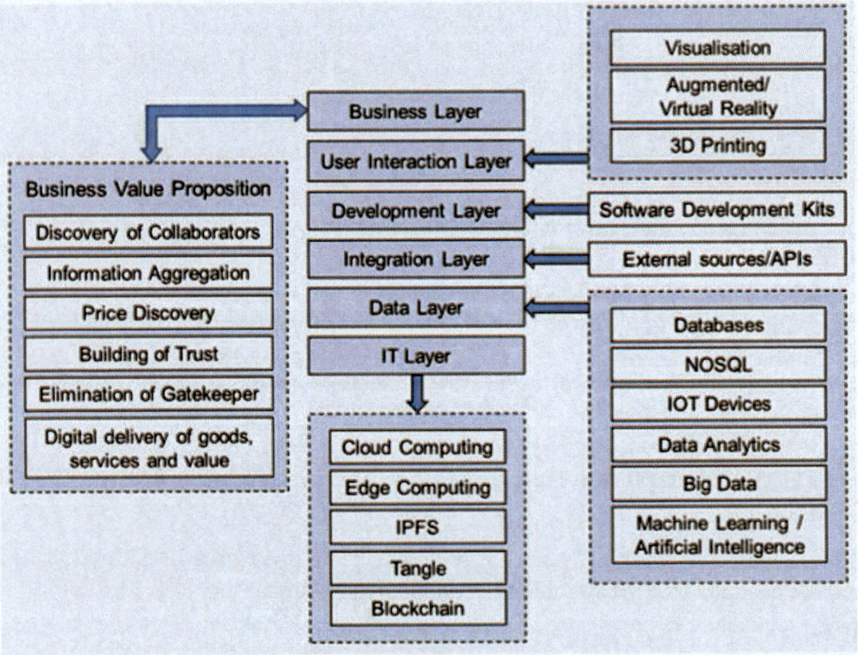

Fig. 12 Digital Platform Architecture

4 Discussion

The results of such studies will serve as a basis for identifying end-to-end technologies for the key sectors of the economy discussed in this paper. Based on this, it is proposed to build reference models of industry innovation hubs, depending on the specifics of the industry, to provide an effective digital environment for individual industries. This will allow technology to develop in accordance with the requirements of stakeholders in a particular area. In the future, the authors plan to come to the development-specific industry solutions of the innovation hub model. It is also planned to develop an integrated architecture of the digital platform and formulate requirements for its services.

5 Conclusion

In this paper, the key concepts of an innovation ecosystem and a digital platform for an innovation center are presented. The analysis of the world experience in creating innovative hubs that contribute to the accelerated implementation of innovations is carried out. The authors suggested the ideality diagram of an innovation ecosystem, which reflects the key properties of the ecosystem using angles.

The basic requirements for the digital platform were formed in map view. Stages of creating a digital platform for an innovation ecosystem were described.

Reference models of the industry innovation hub were formed for the accelerated implementation of digital technologies. Moreover, a reference model for an innovation ecosystem based on a discrete definition of an innovation project was proposed. Also, the authors suggested the reference model of the digital platform for the industry innovation hub.

One of the research results is the formation of the general architecture of the industry innovation hub. The high-level architecture of the innovation hub using the ArchiMate modeling language was proposed. Based on the description of digital platforms and the formation of a system of requirements for them the architecture of the digital platform was proposed.

Acknowledgements The reported study was funded by RSCF according to the research project № 19-18-00452.

References

1. Maydanova, S., & Ilin, I. (2019). Strategic approach to global company digital transformation. In *Proceedings of the 33rd International Business Information Management Association Conference, IBIMA 2019: Education Excellence and Innovation Management through Vision 2020* (pp. 8818–8833).
2. Factors and models of formation and development innovative ecosystems. https://www.hse.ru/data/2012/05/31/1250851792 Accessed 02 Feb 2021.
3. Zaramenskikh, E., & Lyubarskaya, M. (2020). Integration of digital services within the framework of the implementation of "government as a platform" (GaaP) model on the example of a social fund. *Lecture Notes in Information Systems and Organisation, 40*, 1–10.
4. Digital business: 3 requirements to make it real. https://inform.tmforum.org/features-and-analysis/2017/01/digital-business-3-requirements-make-real/. Accessed 02 Feb 2021.
5. Iliinsky, A., Afanasiev, M., & Metkin, D. (2019). Digital technologies of investment analysis of projects for the development of oil fields of unallocated subsoil reserve fund. In *IOP Conference Series: Materials Science and Engineering*. https://doi.org/10.1088/1757-899X/497/1/012028.
6. Approaches to defining and typing digital platforms. https://files.data-economy.ru/digital_platforms_project.pdf. Accessed 03 Feb 2021.
7. Ilin, I. V., Levina, A. I., & Dubgorn, A. S. (2020). Digital enterprise: Models of interaction in the digital environment. Nauka I business: puti razvitia.
8. Gribanov, Yu. I. (2018). The main models of industrial digital platforms development. *Russian Journal of Innovation Economics, 2*, (April–June).
9. New York and Israel have opened a new technology hub. https://news.myseldon.com/ru/news/index/223161834. Accessed 03 Feb 2021.
10. New York and Israel have opened a new technology hub. https://shofar.fm/2020/02/04/nu-iork-i-izrail-otkryli-novyi-tehnologicheskii-hab/. Accessed 03 Feb 2021.
11. Ghicavii, V., et al. (2018). The role of scientific research in the field of medicines and the development of the pharmaceutical industry. *Moldovan Medical Journal, 61*(3), 53–56.
12. Enel has created a global network of 10 innovation hubs. https://news.myseldon.com/ru/news/index/220630190. Accessed 03 Feb 2021.
13. How Enel is looking for new technologies in the energy market https://generation-startup.ru/media-center/smi/53099/. Accessed 03 Feb 2021.
14. The role of hubs in the development of innovations. https://www.bytemag.ru/press/detail.php?ID=25846. Accessed 03 Feb 2021.
15. 7 Silicon Valley tech startups in 2019. https://zen.yandex.ru/media/id/5d02575dc0305700afaa0c49/7-tehnologicheskih-startapov-silikonovoi-doliny-v-2019-godu-5d03deec9415b00db99b9a73. Accessed 04 Feb 2021.
16. Why London is the financial capital of the world. https://www.talk-business.co.uk/2018/11/01/why-london-is-the-financial-capital-of-the-world/. Accessed 04 Feb 2021.
17. Cambodia Fintech Startup Report, Fintech Startup Map and Infographic. https://fintechnews.sg/31533/studies/fintech-adoption-ey-global/. Accessed 04 Feb 2021.
18. FinTech in 2020: Five Global Trends to Watch. https://newsroom.mastercard.com/wp-content/uploads/2020/01/Start-Path-_-CB-Insights-2020-Trends-Report_FINAL.pdf. Accessed 04 Feb 2021.
19. Karpunina, E. K., Okunkova, E. A., Sazanova, E. V., & Gubernatorova, N. N. (2020). The ecosystem of the digital economy: a new approach to the study of structural features and content. In *Lecture Notes in Networks and Systems* (Vol. 129, pp. 497–508). LNNS.
20. Ilin, I. V., Iliashenko, O. Y., & Iliashenko, V. M. (2019). Architectural approach to the digital transformation of the modern medical organization. In *Proceedings of the 33rd International Business Information Management Association Conference, IBIMA 2019: Education Excellence and Innovation Management through Vision 2020* (pp. 5058–5067).
21. Ilin, I., Levina, A., & Iliashenko, O. (2018). Enterprise architecture analysis for energy efficiency of saint-petersburg underground. *Advances in Intelligent Systems and Computing, 692*, 1214–1223. https://doi.org/10.1007/978-3-319-70987-1_130

22. Levina, A. I., Dubgorn, A. S., & Iliashenko, O. Y. (2018). Internet of things within the service architecture of intelligent transport systems. In *Proceedings 2017 European Conference on Electrical Engineering and Computer Science, EECS 2017* (pp. 351–355). https://doi.org/10.1109/EECS.2017.72
23. IT-director book. https://book4cio.ru. Accessed 06 Feb 2021.
24. Ilin, I. V., Bolobonov, D. D., & Frolov, A. K. (2019). Innovative business model as a factor in the successful implementation of IIoT in logistics enterprises. In *Proceedings of the 33rd International Business Information Management Association Conference, IBIMA 2019: Education Excellence and Innovation Management through Vision 2020* (pp. 5092–5102).

Smart Hospital Medical Equipment: Integration into the Enterprise Architecture

Roman Marchenko and Alexandra Borremans

Abstract Digitalization is actively affecting various areas of our lives and health care is no exception. The concepts of e-health, Smart Hospital, and the principles of value-based and personalized medicine are increasingly becoming the object of research and approbation in organizations around the world. This article will consider the opportunities for medical organizations that follow the trends in the modern digital technologies development. Moreover, Smart Infrastructure will be presented as part of a comprehensive architectural Smart Hospital solution.

Keywords Smart hospital · Enterprise architecture · e-Health · Medical equipment · Infrastructure · Digital technologies

1 Introduction

Every year the level of computerization and digitalization of various industries increases, the idea of digital transformation covers the whole world. This leads to the fact that most developed countries, including Russia, pay great attention to such terms as digitalization and digital transformation for in-depth study of a new field of scientific and technological progress.

Currently, the number of new technologies and their capabilities is growing exponentially. In the course of a new technological revolution that has affected various business areas, huge amounts of data, cloud computing services, machine learning methods and solutions based on artificial intelligence, as well as the Internet of Things, are being combined, allowing users to obtain and analyze information at a relatively low cost. The technological boom could not but affect the healthcare system: today, healthcare automation is one of the most important and complex tasks around the world, requiring huge investments and having a large number of questions and problems.

R. Marchenko · A. Borremans (✉)
Peter the Great St.Petersburg Polytechnic University, Polytechnicheskaya 29, 195351 St. Petersburg, Russia

E. Zaramenskikh and A. Fedorova (eds.), *Digitalization of Society, Economics and Management*, Lecture Notes in Information Systems and Organisation 53,
https://doi.org/10.1007/978-3-030-94252-6_5

The integration of medical equipment into a network has already changed the way we work in health care. By 2020, the widespread introduction of high-tech methods in medicine will lead to the implementation of the concept of a "Smart hospital".

It is estimated that the Smart hospital market will be worth $63 billion by 2024. The concept is based on the optimization and automation of processes in the information and communication and technological environment of interconnected objects (the Internet of Things). The goal of this environment is to improve existing procedures for providing modern medical care and to open up new opportunities for medicine.

Ten key principles of e-health are:

- Efficiency.
- Improving the quality.
- Attention to personal data.
- Expanding the patient's capabilities.
- Improving the relationship between the patient and the medical organization.
- Continuing education and professional development through information technology.
- Implementation of secure data exchange.
- Expansion of the healthcare system.
- Ethical standards.
- Accessibility for all.

In connection with the above, the main purpose of the article is to analyze the architecture of the medical organization and the integration of digital services into the technological infrastructure of the organization.

The objectives of the study are:

- Description of the architectural approach to the development of a medical organization.
- Analysis of the main top-level business processes in a medical organization.
- Analysis of services in a digital medical organization.
- Modeling of the technological layer of the architecture of a typical medical organization.

2 An Overview of the Concept of "Smart Hospital"

Smart hospitals are institutions that optimize, redesign, or build new clinical processes, management systems, and possibly even infrastructure [1]. They are supported by an underlying digital network that brings together interconnected assets to provide valuable service or information not previously available to provide better patient care [2]. Smart hospitals are built on technologies that allow you to automate clinical, management, and support processes, including communication and interaction with patients. As a rule, such technologies include:

- systems for remote monitoring of vital functions of patients by integrating personal devices with information systems of medical centers for remote monitoring of vital signs, telemedicine technologies, "hospital to home" technologies;
- identification systems (wristbands, labels, badges, etc.) and location monitoring, biometric scanners, and patient flow management system;
- "smart building", which implies the management of the state of the environment inside the medical center (temperature, humidity, etc.), a system for monitoring the condition and repair needs in real time, access control, etc.
- high-power network equipment;
- network medical equipment (wearable and implantable devices; stationary and mobile medical and diagnostic equipment);
- integrated information system of the institution (administrative information system, pharmacy and warehouse information system with automated replenishment of medicines and consumables with predictive analysis of the required level of stock, information system of blood transfusion stations, laboratories, imaging, pathoanatomical, and pathomorphological services, biobank, sterilization control, etc.);
- electronic medical records of patients, scientific and clinical research data.

Due to digitalization, patient expectations are increasing: they are increasingly using advanced technologies and devices; therefore, the hospital also needs to implement technologies in hospital wards and on an outpatient basis.

Advantages of the "Smart Hospital" concept:

- Interaction with patients. Devices such as touch-screen monitors or tablets can enable patients and their families to improve the patient–doctor relationship. Thanks to the "smart" functions, it will be possible to learn more information about the treatment process, the state of health; while in the hospital room, the patient will have the opportunity to view their medical records, find out the results of tests, and find out and make a daily treatment schedule.
- Optimization of the workflow. Through the use of mobile and information technologies, you can improve workflow efficiency, increase productivity when tracking and identifying bottlenecks, and service slowdowns. Smart apps will improve hospital navigation for both patients and visitors, as well as for staff. Messaging and routing features can provide step-by-step directions and arrival times to make navigating major hospitals easier and less stressful for visitors.
- Notice to patients. This function can significantly reduce no-show patients and, thereby, reduce the loss of the hospital. Push notifications generated by this software can be sent to patients in your preferred language, informing them about the time of ingestion and accurate hospital room, her address, and to notify of changes in schedule or location.
- Tracking resources of the hospital. Internet of Things (IoT) technologies are widely used in many industries for efficient resource tracking. Hospitals and care centers can use IoT applications to correctly track required assets, their distribution, and location.

- Using data analysis. Smartphones and smart clothes track huge amounts of biometric data that can be used by caregivers to get more detailed information about both individual patients and population groups. The findings could improve the quality of patient care, as well as accelerate research aimed at saving lives.

Problems of creating and integrating a "smart" hospital system:

- Conflict of priorities. Health organizations must provide high-quality care, maintain patient safety (including the security of patient data), prevent infections, ensure financial productivity, comply with regulatory standards, and maintain patient satisfaction. All these tasks, as a rule, should be solved with the help of limited resources.
- The process of becoming a smart hospital takes time. Smart solutions can be implemented one by one, rather than in a single step. At the same time, newer solutions should be integrated with previously implemented ones. Interoperability and cybersecurity are imperative, as hospital devices, systems, and networks must interact with each other in a way that allows data to be analyzed, and that the data is protected and inaccessible to hackers.
- Unstructured data. Unstructured data and legacy systems must be integrated to provide holistic analysis and access to all collected medical data.
- Training and adaptation of personnel. All medical personnel should be trained to effectively use intelligent systems and devices to support their workflow and provide semi-automated data flow management [3].

3 Principles of Value-Based Personalized Medicine

Personalized medicine is the adaptation of treatment to the individual characteristics of each patient. This approach is based on scientific advances in understanding how a person's unique molecular genetic profile makes them susceptible to certain diseases. These same studies increase our ability to predict which medical treatments will be safe and effective for each patient, and which will not.

Personalized medicine is the adaptation of treatment to the individual characteristics of each patient. This approach is based on scientific advances in understanding how a person's unique molecular genetic profile makes them susceptible to certain diseases. These same studies increase our ability to predict which medical treatments will be safe and effective for each patient, and which will not.

Personalized medicine is a multi-faceted approach to the treatment of patients, which not only allows for more accurate diagnosis and treatment of diseases but also makes it possible to detect diseases at an earlier stage when they are easier to cure. The full implementation of personalized medicine includes:

- Risk assessment. Genetic testing to identify a predisposition to the disease.
- Prevention. Lifestyle changes and therapeutic intervention to prevent the disease.
- Detection. Early detection of the disease at the molecular level.

- Diagnosis. Accurate diagnosis of diseases allows you to develop an individual treatment strategy.
- Treatment. Improved results through targeted treatment and reduced side effects.
- Management. Active monitoring of therapeutic responses and disease progression.

Personalized medicine has a major impact on how medicines are researched and developed; how patients are diagnosed and treated; and how health care directs its resources to maximize patient benefits.

4 Materials and Methods

To apply the concept of "Smart Hospital", IT is necessary to use IT support, and the requirements for the technological infrastructure to ensure the implementation of processes are set. The methodology of an integrated management system for medical organizations is needed. The use of an architectural approach is the optimal solution for the formation of this methodology [4].

The enterprise architecture is a single whole of such elements of the management system as business processes, functional and organizational structures, material and cash flows, information systems and applications, data, document management, and technological infrastructure objects.

There are different methods (standards) for architecture development:

- Rational Unified Process (RUP). The software development and implementation process are iterative in this approach, with each new iteration adding functionality to the software architecture.
- UN/CEFACT Modeling Methodology (UMM). This methodology is a methodology for building business processes and information models.
- Enterprise Architecture Description Standard IEEE1471-2000 (IEEE Computer Society 2000). The standard is a theoretical framework for defining, analyzing, and describing system architectures. IEEE 1471 focuses on software systems for information and complex systems.
- The standard describes the architecture TOGAF (The Open Group Architecture Framework). The method was positioned by the developers as a "tool for developing information system architectures".
- Architecture Capability Framework. It examines the organization, processes, skills, roles, and responsibilities required to create and use architecture functions within an enterprise.
- An Architecture Development Method (ADM) provides a "way of working" for architects [5].

5 Architectural Approach to the Development of a Medical Organization

The concept of architecture is inextricably linked to the concept of the system. For example, when studying the design of information systems, the architecture of the system is determined by the class and structure of information systems. The concept of enterprise architecture is based on the principles of a systematic approach.

Enterprise architecture is typically used as a tool for managing the day-to-day operations and future development of a company (Fig. 1 shows a representation).

An enterprise management approach or standard is a structured set of methods and process steps for creating and maintaining enterprise architecture [6]. Methods usually define the different stages of the architecture lifecycle, what results should be obtained at each stage, and how they are tested. This chapter will look at the TOGAF standard mentioned earlier.

The TOGAF (The Open Group Architecture Framework) architecture description standard describes the structure and method of developing enterprise architectures.

Within a medical organization, TOGAF will have the following main components:

- Architecture Capability Framework, mentioned earlier.
- ADM, which is considered the core of TOGAF and consists of a step-by-step cyclical approach to the development of the overall enterprise architecture (Fig. 2 shows the approach).

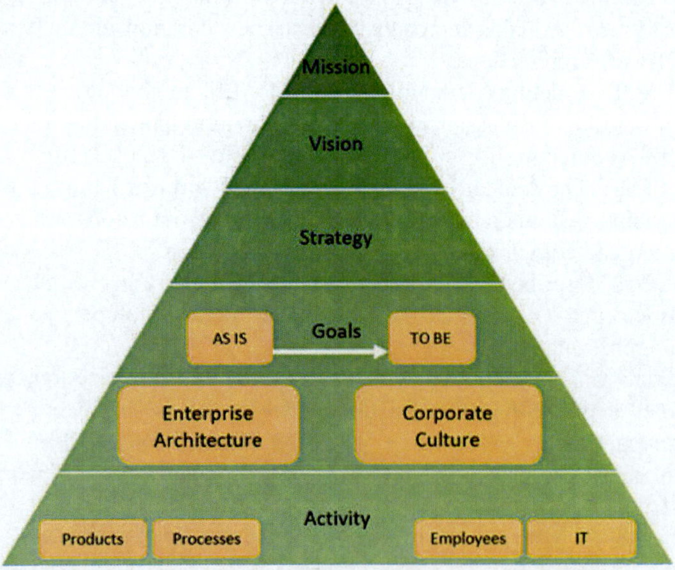

Fig. 1 Enterprise architecture as a management tool

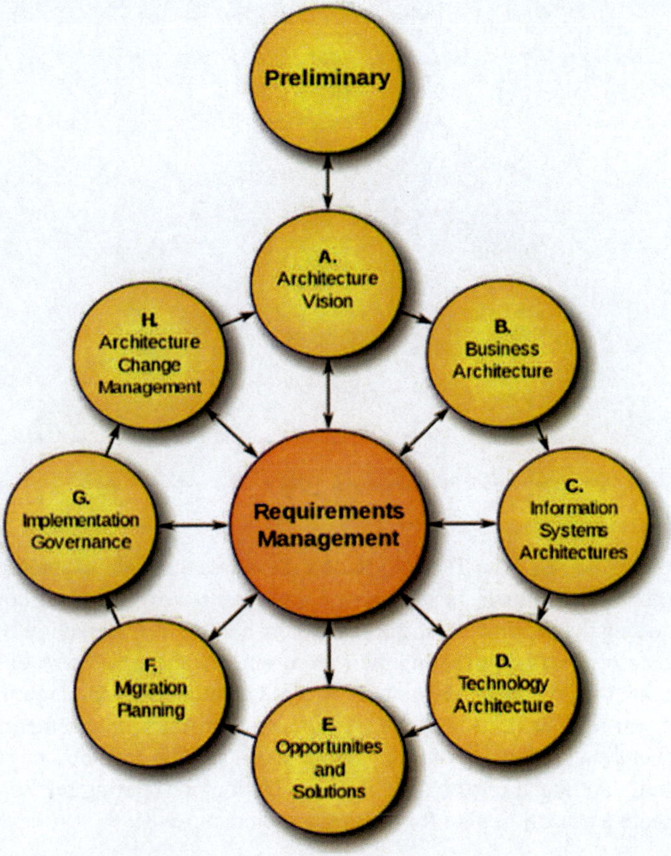

Fig. 2 Architecture development method (ADM), TOGAF

- Architecture Content Framework, which examines the overall enterprise architecture, consisting of four closely interrelated architectures (Fig. 3 shows the layers):
  - business architecture;
  - data architecture;
  - application architecture;
  - technological architecture.

To date, TOGAF is one of the most conceptually appropriate methodologies and corporate architecture framework used by leading global organizations to improve business performance [7]. This methodology allows to identify different elements of the enterprise architecture at different levels of abstraction and gives architecture developers the opportunity to choose architectural models, examples, and experience

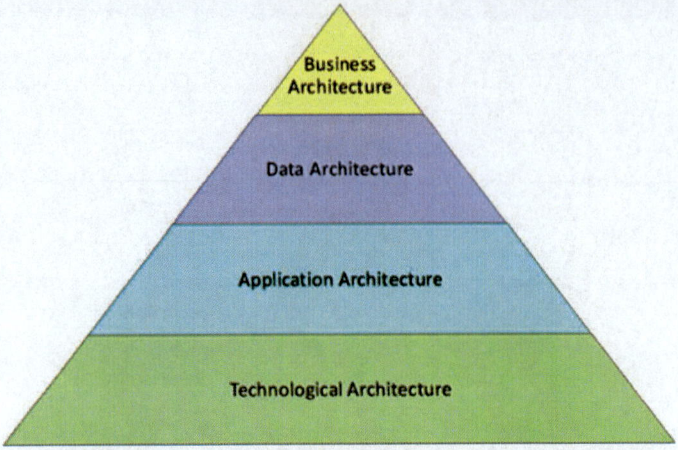

Fig. 3 Enterprise architecture model (TOGAF standard)

from different industries. The TOGAF standard ensures the openness and compatibility of the developed models. In addition to the ability to create a holistic conceptual picture describing the activities of the organization, continuous interaction with business representatives, and considering their requirements, the developers of TOGAF actively interact with the developers of the ArchiMate modeling language. The standard allows you to consider the architecture "as is", to form requirements for the target architecture with the help of motivational expansion, to develop a target model of the corporate architecture of a medical organization considering medical and IT trends, to create a transition plan for the target architecture [8].

6 Results

In the previous sections of the article, the concept of a "Smart Hospital" was analyzed and the principles of value-based personalized medicine were defined. Using the given reference model of the enterprise architecture, in the following sections of the study, the authors will present their vision regarding the reference model of the architecture of a medical organization based on the identified main business processes.

The top-level digital medical organization processes consists of several processes:

- admission to the hospital;
- being in the operating room;
- stay in the hospital;
- discharge from a hospital.

Table 1 Admission to the hospital services

Service	Description
Real-time patient queue management	Staff can use a personal computer or mobile device to call the next patient in the queue. LED indicators to display the numbers of issued e-tickets in the queue and the waiting time in real time. Patients can see the information on the display. Medical institutions can also use the display queue to represent the appropriate medical information
Information services at the reception	The registration cost dashboard with information on doctors, their schedule, a description of the services of the medical center, the cost of the paid services, when patients receiving plaintive appeals, and reviews about the work of the center
Patient appointment service	Patients are recorded via the web or mobile interface, as well as through the information desks in the medical center
SMS notifications of patients about appointments to the medical center	When making an appointment, the patient is offered an SMS notification service, with which he can confirm the appointment, get information about it, and, if necessary, cancel it
Tracking the KPI of registration employees	The system monitors and evaluates key performance indicators based on the data obtained on the results of employees' work
Online view of the current queue in the branches of the medical center	The system calculates and predicts the approximate time depending on the patient's treatment category and the average doctor's appointment time, distributing the flow of patients in the queue

6.1 Admission to the Hospital

The admission of a patient to a medical institution is a process that is often neglected, but this does not make the process any less important. It is this process that allows the patient to "enter" the system of the medical institution. And how smoothly and conveniently this happens affects the further results of the institution's activities and the client's satisfaction with these results. In Table 1, admission services are presented.

6.2 Hospitalization

The use of services in the hospital removes the burden on the hospital staff from filling out a huge number of papers manually, gives a complete picture of what is happening in the hospital, reduces the likelihood of staff errors, stores all data in one place, eliminating losses, and automates business processes occurring in the hospital. In Table 2, hospitalization services are described.

6.3 The Operating Room

One of the areas where advanced technologies have been introduced for a long time is operational activities. Speaking about technologies and IT services from the point of view of a Smart hospital, the services presented in Table 3 can be highlighted.

6.4 Discharge from a Hospital

Moreover, an important process in working with patients is his/her discharge from the ward and subsequent monitoring of his/her condition. Both medical and non-medical personnel are involved in the discharge process. Smart hospital services presented in Table 4 will simplify and optimize the work of all participants in the process.

Thus, all the services listed in this chapter can be represented as a model (see Fig. 4). It displays the upper level processes and functions of the hospital, and the Smart Hospital services described above are marked at the intersection.

7 Creating a Service Architecture that Supports Smart Hospital Operations

When modeling the activities of medical organizations, there are a number of specific features of this industry that affect the choice of approach to identifying processes: a patient-oriented approach, a pronounced matrix management system based on functional and administrative subordination, an individual trajectory of patient treatment, a high degree of regulation of medical care processes and related processes, including certain requirements for document management in health care.

The functional model of the enterprise is one of the key elements of the business architecture. It provides an understanding of the business structure as the basis for the formation of end-to-end and functional processes, provides input information for the formation of the organizational structure, and can also serve as a basis for subsequent feature-oriented automation [10].

The main business processes are service-oriented processes designed to create an enterprise and generate revenue.

Management processes are processes that cover the entire set of management functions at the level of each process and the business system as a whole.

Table 2 Hospitalization services

Service	Description
Thermal imaging sensors	Used to detect pathologies that are difficult to diagnose in other ways, including the detection of malignant tumors
Infrared sensors	Can be used, for example, to determine whether your hands have been washed
Sensors for monitoring patient movement	Provides healthcare professionals with the most important information about the patient's condition
Sensors with AI for remote monitoring of required health indicators	Allows to remotely monitor such indicators as temperature, respiratory rate, sweating, pulse rate, heart rate, and pressure
Sensors for monitoring the level of saline in the dropper	Allows to carry out continuous monitoring of the level of saline solution to monitor the patient's condition and rapid response
RFID tags for identifying and tracking patients, staff, and medicines	Using the label on the package, you can simplify inventory, track the product, and protect yourself from counterfeit goods The patient's wristband label may contain information about the patient's identity, his placement in medical institutions, the data on the title page of the inpatient card, information about the allergic history, drug intolerance, the diagnosis, and the attending physician
Telepresence robots: multifunctional, portable, and audiovisual robotic systems	Such systems virtually connect patients and doctors, for example, in cases where the doctor is not physically able to be near or there is a risk of infection
Patients telemetry	Allows to collect data about the physical condition of the patient and analyze the data obtained
The location of the patient; The location of the staff; Tracking drug flows	The real-time location system automatically identifies and tracks the location of objects or people in real time using tags and sensors
Assessment of the hygienic condition of surfaces (wards and equipment); Conducting diagnostic and functional tests in the ward; Equipment monitoring	Allows to pre-evaluate and, in some cases, remotely check the ward and its equipment for errors, contamination, or malfunctions
Predicting the outcome of the disease	Based on the obtained data, it allows the system to search for patterns and make forecasts for diseases and their outcome, keeping in mind the patient's indicators
Telemedicine/telepresence	Telemedicine is the remote provision of medical services

(continued)

Table 2 (continued)

Service	Description
Predictive diagnostics	Diagnosis based on the analysis of the results of genetic studies. It allows you to predict the development of diseases even without visible symptoms, which reduces the risk of complications and deaths
Access to the electronic patient card (MIS)	Prompt access to the patient's card, which allows you to immediately use the available information, check it for veracity, and can notice the risks that have appeared [9]
Access to the patient's daily schedule	The system makes a request to the available information on the patient and shows the patient's daily schedule, consisting of activities aimed at recovery and discharge
Creating a schedule for taking medications	The system makes a request to the available information on the availability of medicines and generates a schedule for taking medicines. The schedule is formed based on the recommended method of use from the manufacturer of the drug
Transfer of data from bedside devices	Bedside devices are equipped with special sensors that send the data obtained by the analysis directly to the doctor for further observation

Auxiliary-processes designed to support the execution of key business processes and their specific functions.

The structure can be represented using a set of applications that implement key information technology services. This set of applications includes:

- electronic medical record;
- system for the provision of outpatient care;
- the system of providing inpatient care;
- clinical monitoring system;
- anesthetic monitoring system;
- accounting system;
- personnel management system;
- Pharmacy POS system;
- laboratory medical information systems.

For example, we can consider in more detail the application "hospital care system" (Fig. 5 shows an example).

At the same time, according to the upper level of processes, it is necessary to create a technological architecture for each process using the necessary services (Fig. 6 shows an example).

Table 3 Services in the operating room

Service	Description
Access to the electronic patient card (MIS)	Prompt access to the patient's card, which allows you to immediately use the available information, check it for veracity, and can notice the risks that have appeared
Interaction with a Robot-assisted surgical system	The implementation of medical procedures
Patient telemetry	Allows you to collect data about the physical condition of the patient and analyze the data obtained
Voice recognition	The voice recognition system is used in cases where the patient has problems with hand motor skills, is unable to press buttons or the screen, or is unable to move
Integration with other services	If there is a production need or the patient's desire and capabilities, it is possible to integrate with services to increase convenience and efficiency
Telemedicine/telepresence	Provides hardware at the point of delivery of medical services, designed primarily for collecting primary data from patients, including using diagnostic equipment

Table 4 Discharge from hospital services

Service	Description
Real-Time Locating System (RTLS)	The real-time location system automatically identifies and tracks the location of objects or people in real time using tags and sensors
Instant notification system for patient discharge	At discharge, creates an appropriate notification that is sent to specific doctors
Notifications to non-medical staff about changing the bed, about the need for cleaning when the patient is discharged, about the release of the ward	From time to time or under certain conditions, the program sends a notification to further the work of the employees
Automatic generation of reports according to the statement	Automatic creation of the discharge epicrisis, conclusions, prescriptions, data on the course of treatment and prescribed drugs, recommendations after discharge, etc

8 Trends in Digital Infrastructure Solutions for the Implementation of the Smart Hospital Concept

The modern market offers more and more solutions to ensure the Smart Hospital operation. These devices are becoming useful not only for the internal processes

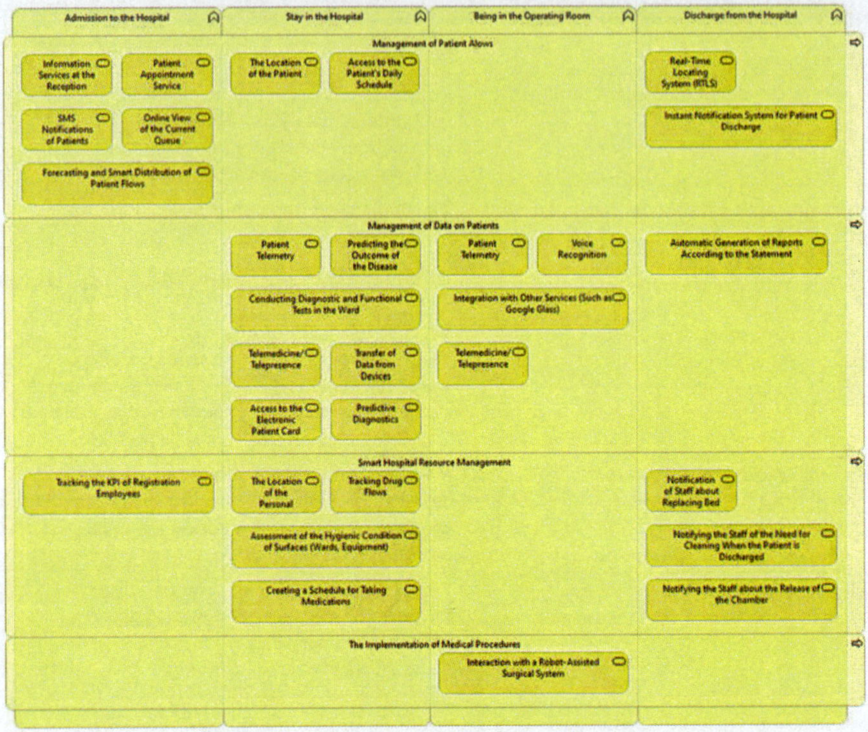

Fig. 4 The upper level of the processes of digital medical organization

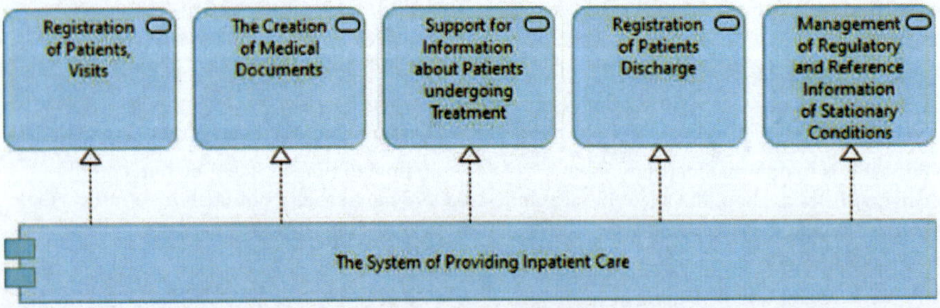

Fig. 5 Component of the application "System of inpatient care"

of staff but also for simplifying the interaction with the user and increasing his/her level of satisfaction with the services provided, for example, systems and devices for managing the flow of patients. The variety of devices on the market allows medical organizations to choose the best option for them from a number of all kinds of steles, telemedicine stands, tracking bracelets, and much more.

Let's consider a few examples of such devices.

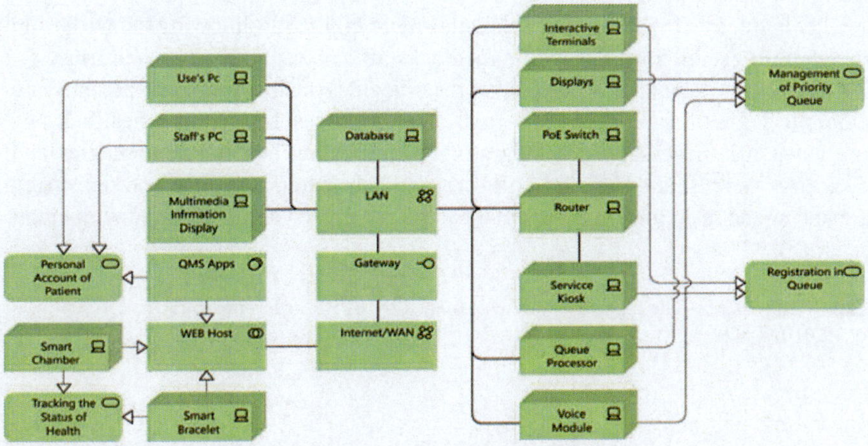

Fig. 6 Technological architecture of admission to a medical institution

An interactive information stand allows patients to view on-site information about the clinic, schedule doctors, make appointments, receive certificates and coupons for electronic queues, pay for paid services, and so on. This allows us to make the process of patient admission much more transparent and faster, and also to strengthen control over queues in order to avoid conflict situations.

Services that help implement an infrastructure solution:

- patient appointment service;
- real-time patient queue management;
- information services at the reception [11].

Smart watches with the help of sensors, and sensors allow you to monitor the patient's condition and location. The device screen allows you to display health data for a more accurate patient survey and self-monitoring of the patient's health. All information about the patient's health is sent and stored on the hospital's servers and is available for viewing by the doctor.

Services that help implement an infrastructure solution:

- Sensors with AI for remote monitoring of required health indicators;
- RFID tags for patient identification and tracking [12].

9 Conclusion

In today's world, with an extremely fast pace of life, electronic healthcare systems and smart hospital projects have become an absolutely necessary and important issue. Smart Hospital will allow people to save time and take better care of them. In addition, it will help doctors organize their schedules more efficiently, allowing them to avoid long waiting lists in hospitals, while medical staff can easily manage their time.

Another significant advantage is that the e-health system allows both patients and doctors to get all the necessary information about the state of human health at any time when it is necessary. By integrating with existing hospital technologies and developing new Smart Hospital software, we help caregivers focus on delivering care and spend less time on things that can be automated and performed with smart systems.

Acknowledgements The reported study was funded by RFBR according to the research project No. 19-010-00579.

References

1. Holzinger, A., Röcker C., & Ziefle, M. (2015). From smart health to smart hospitals. *Smart Health* (pp. 1–20). Cham: Springer.
2. Borremans, A., Dubgorn, A., Levina, A. I., & Lepekhin A. A. (2019). Development of requirements for the management system of a medical organization in the context of digital transformation.
3. KILIÇ, T. (2016). Digital hospital; An example of best practice. *International Journal of Health Services Research and Policy, 1.2*, 52–58.
4. Ilin, I. V., Iliashenko, O. Y., & Iliashenko, V. M. (2019). Architectural approach to the digital transformation of the modern medical organization. In *Proceedings of the 33d International Business Information Management Association Conference, IBIMA 2019: Innovation Management and Education Excellence through Vision 2020* (pp. 5058–5067).
5. Greefhorst, D., Koning, H., & Van Vliet, H. (2006). The many faces of architectural descriptions. *Information Systems Frontiers, 8*(2), 103–113.
6. Kudryavtsev, D., Zaramenskikh, E., & Arzumanyan, M. (2018). The simplified enterprise architecture management methodology for teaching purposes. *Lecture Notes in Business Information Processing, 332*, 76–90.
7. Qurratuaini, H. (2018) "Designing enterprise architecture based on TOGAF 9.1.
8. Ilin, I., Levina, A., Lepekhin, A., & Kalyazina, S. (2019). Business requirements to the IT architecture: A case of a healthcare organization. *Advances in Intelligent Systems and Computing, 983*, 287–294.
9. Zaramenskikh, E. P., Isaev, E. A., & Korovkina, N. L. (2016). The principles of information processing in electronic medical monitoring system. *Mathematical Biology and Bioinformatics, 11*(2), 288–298.
10. Dubgorn, A. S., Ilin, I. V., Levina, A., & Borremans, A. D. (2019). Reference model of healthcare company functional structure. In *Proceedings of the 33d International Business Information Management Association Conference, IBIMA 2019: Innovation Management and Education Excellence through Vision 2020* (pp. 5129–5137).
11. Haghighi, S. M., & Torabi, S. A. (2018). A novel mixed sustainability-resilience framework for evaluating hospital information systems. *International Journal of Medical Informatics, 118*, 16–28.
12. Foster, K. R., & Torous, J. (2019). The opportunity and obstacles for smartwatches and wearable sensors. *IEEE Pulse, 10*(1), 22–25.

Value-Based Concept in the Architecture Model of a Water Supply Company

Dmitry Serov, Igor Ilin, and Sofia Kalyazina

Abstract The article analyzes the activities of a water supply company, builds an existing model of enterprise architecture, gives suggestions for reengineering the model, and builds a target model of enterprise architecture. When building the target model, the goals of achieving maximum value for the end consumer were taken into account simultaneously with the achievement of maximum results of the enterprise's efficiency. This work required significant changes and modernization at the application level and the technological level. As a result, a unified system of automated active monitoring and control of the water supply system is being formed.

Keywords Resource-supplying organization · Model of the enterprise architecture · Value-oriented approach · Water supply and sewerage enterprise

1 Introduction

Water is an important natural resource; the availability and quality of which directly affect the functioning of various sectors of the national economy. Stabilization and development of the country's water supply and sewerage system are components of ensuring sustainable economic growth and improving the living standards of the population. Effective management of water resources is necessary to maintain the quality and availability of water, and in a broader sense—to form optimal social, economic, and environmental health [1]. In this case, the changing conditions of the environment and climate should be taken into account. It is also important that the water sector operates in a complex interplay between water resources, socio-economic, and ecological systems.

D. Serov
State Unitary Enterprise "Vodokanal of St. Petersburg", St. Petersburg, Russia

I. Ilin · S. Kalyazina (✉)
Peter the Great St. Petersburg Polytechnic University, St. Petersburg, Russia
e-mail: kalyazina_se@spbstu.ru

E. Zaramenskikh and A. Fedorova (eds.), *Digitalization of Society, Economics and Management*, Lecture Notes in Information Systems and Organisation 53,
https://doi.org/10.1007/978-3-030-94252-6_6

Optimization of investment and operational activities and the management system of water supply and sewerage enterprises require the correct definition of criteria and quality indicators, standardization, and implementation of modern information and analytical systems.

In accordance with the federal legislation of the Russian Federation [2], water supply includes "water treatment, transportation, and supply of drinking or industrial water to subscribers using centralized or non-centralized cold and hot water supply systems".

The expanded water supply chain includes such technological stages as water intake from water supply sources and supply to treatment plants, water treatment (drinking water preparation), transportation of treated water to the consumer (through water supply networks using booster pumping stations), and transfer purified water to the consumer.

Water management aims to meet the increasing demands of different consumers. For example, the main values of the end consumer are the provision of water in the required volume, with the necessary pressure, with the proper quality, 24/7, at commensurate tariffs and with an understandable calculation, as well as general quality service for the subscriber. In this case, it is required to consider the values of the consumer taking into account the existing contradictions between them [3–5].

The article examines the case of a water supply organization, which set the task of implementing the value approach. A personalized, value-based approach to working with consumers requires the preliminary collection and analysis of consumption data, the design of a personalized value proposition [6]. The implementation of this approach requires the use of modern information and communication and digital technologies. Building a value proposition model requires reengineering the enterprise architecture. In this regard, the article discusses the necessary changes that need to be made during the transformation.

2 Materials and Methods

In this article, the following approaches are used as a methodological basis for the study:

1. An architectural approach. Enterprise architecture is considered as an integrated approach to the integration of heterogeneous elements (business processes, functional structure, organizational structure, information systems and technologies, digital technologies, production technologies, and assets) into an effective business system [7–10].
2. Service-oriented approach as a means of harmonization (coordination) of requirements and capabilities of business and IT elements of a single system [11–13].

When building an enterprise architecture, the following levels are distinguished: the business level (describes the activities of the enterprise and its development), the application level (describes applications, data, and their relationships), and the technological level (describes the hardware and system software) [14].

In this article, a water supply organization was investigated. Based on the results of considering the current activities of the organization, a model of the enterprise architecture AS-IS was built and a TO-BE model was proposed.

An architectural approach to water supply/water use management provides a number of advantages and allows to optimize the whole process. Additional opportunities are provided by the use of modern key digital technologies. The construction of specialized platforms using these technologies makes it possible to take into account a number of factors affecting water use [14].

3 Results

At the beginning, an analysis of the architecture of the resource-supplying organization was carried out in order to build an AS-IS model.

When analyzing the current activities of the company, the following main business processes were identified:

- Water supply (water supply control, water intake, and purification) includes “water treatment, transportation and supply of drinking or industrial water to subscribers using centralized or non-centralized cold and hot water supply systems” [2].
- Water consumption (use of water associated with its withdrawal from localization sites with partial or complete irretrievable consumption or with return to water intake sources in a changed (contaminated) state), assessment and rationalization of consumption, accounting, setting standards, and quality assessment
- Quality control
- Collecting data from measuring devices
- Analysis, aggregation, and further use of data collected from measuring devices
- Automatic billing for water users
- Management of technological facilities—monitoring the parameters of the water supply network; water quality control; dispatch control; control and management of automation objects, and engineering centers of water supply zones
- Risk management—identification of losses and unaccounted expenses; prevention of failures at peak loads; support of staff work in emergency; and emergency situations.

The Business level is shown in Fig. 1.

The resource-supplying organization under study uses the following application level services:

Fig. 1 The business level

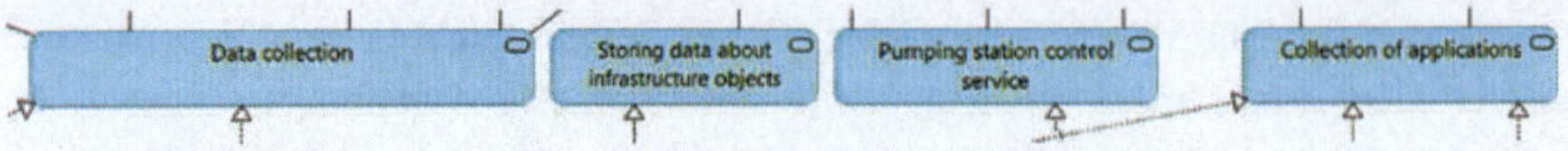

Fig. 2 Application level services

- Data collection service—designed to collect data on water quality indicators obtained from an automated water quality control system, data on meter readings, charges, etc., received from the Information system of the center for settlements with subscribers, as well as to transmit the received data for further use in the company's business processes.
- Storing data about infrastructure objects—designed for backup, storage, synchronization of technological information at all levels without data loss and with the formation and storage of archives.
- Pumping station control service—designed to collect information about the parameters of pumping stations to calculate the water balance.
- Collection of applications—designed to collect information about received applications on the Hotline, information on the work schedules of repair teams, schedules and plans for work and maintenance, as well as for transferring the received data for further use in the company's business processes.

Application level services are shown in Fig. 2.
Further, the applied information systems and their functions were analyzed:

- Automated water quality control system—designed for continuous measurements of water quality indicators, water quality monitoring for solving problems of environmental monitoring, and control of technological processes [15].
- Information system of the center for settlements with subscribers—maintains a unified database of clients and their requests, permits, contracts with clients, meter readings, charges, invoices, payments, accounts receivable, allows to analyze the interest of potential subscribers in the company's services; plan the volume of water supply (wastewater disposal) services; efficiently manage accounts receivable; ensure timely and reliable accounting and reporting; and increase revenue collection [16].
- GIS—a geographic information system that contains information about networks, buildings, structures, and property rights. It provides information exchange with government authorities, makes it possible to determine the location of network objects, coordinate the boundaries of land plots, control the executive documentation of contractors, and allows you to organize prompt access to the necessary information in real time for all departments and services of the enterprise [17].
- Hotline—an information system that allows a company to quickly analyze the quality of services; to efficiently process citizens' appeals about emergencies; control the elimination of emergency situations; coordinate the work of operational units and emergency teams in real time.
- Integrated Dispatch Management System—designed for automatic collection, processing, accumulation, display, and analysis of technological information from

automated process control systems of all technological objects of the enterprise [18].
- Maintenance and repair information system—designed to optimize and control processes related to the repair and maintenance of hardware, units of the enterprise [19].
- An information system designed for planning, organizing, and optimizing the work of teams and their visits (denoted as IST in the model).
- Accounting system—designed to maintain the accounting of the organization [20].
- Meteorological automated information system (designated as MAIS in the model)—consists of automated observation posts in different areas of the city as part of a rain gauge and a meteorological complex. The installed meteorological systems automatically measure atmospheric pressure, wind speed and direction, air temperature, and humidity and regularly transmit information to the resource-supplying organization and meteorological services. It allows you to quickly regulate the filling of sewer networks during rains, to accurately calculate the volume of surface runoff for specific territories, and to prevent flooding of city areas with the highest intensity of atmospheric precipitation. The data received from MAIS helps to improve the performance of not only the sewage system but also all municipal services in the city [21].

Application components of the application level are shown in Fig. 3.

At the technological level, the following main services are distinguished:

- Collecting water quality data—designed to collect information from peripheral devices, water analyzers on biological, physical, chemical, organoleptic, radiological parameters of water, and transfer the collected data to the Automated water quality control system.
- Collection and transmission of data—designed to collect information from water meters and pumping stations on water consumption by consumers and transfer the collected data to the Information System of the center for settlements with subscribers.
- Consumption data transmission—performs a similar function, collecting data from automatic flow meters.
- Transmission of data on precipitation and climatic parameters of the environment—designed to collect data from meteorological sensors and regularly transmit the collected data to the MAIS.

Services of the technological level are shown in Fig. 4.

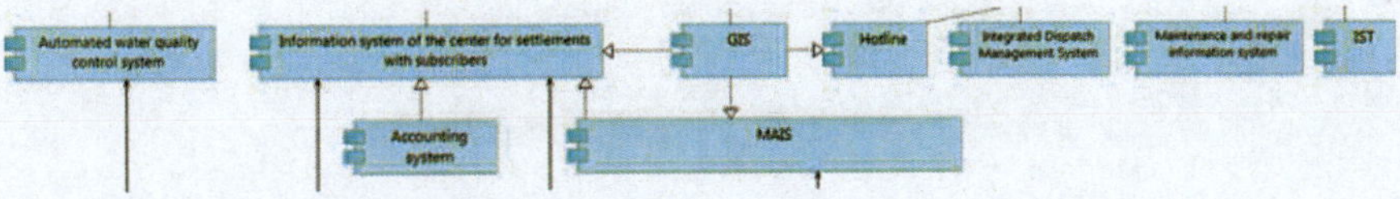

Fig. 3 Application components of the application level

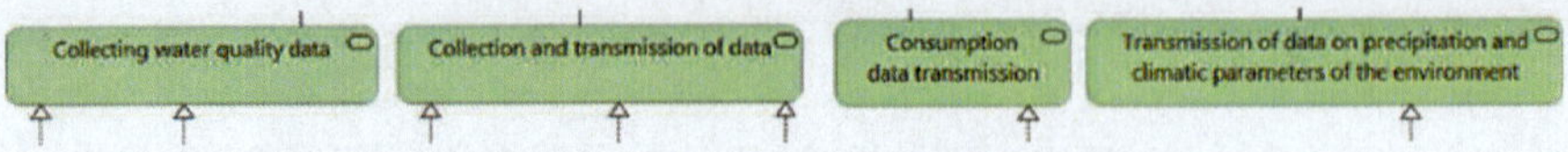

Fig. 4 Services of the technological level

These services receive information from the following basic pieces of equipment:

- Analyzers;
- Disinfectants;
- Pressure Sensors;
- Water meters with remote data transmission;
- Pumping stations;
- Low-error electromagnetic flowmeters;
- Meteorological sensors.

Equipment of the technological level is shown in Fig. 5.

The resulting overall enterprise architecture model in the AS-IS state is shown in Fig. 6.

The development of the considered system should be aimed at creating a unified system of automated active monitoring of the state of the water supply system and control of technological objects of the water supply system; immediate informing of personnel and the formation of recommendations on actions in emergency situations.

The main task is to implement a value-oriented approach, in which the tools of value-oriented water supply management are especially important: water balance, hydraulic modeling, balance of income and expenses, and water-chemical balance.

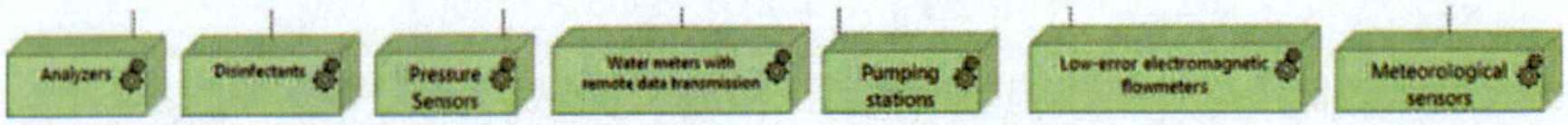

Fig. 5 Equipment of the technological level

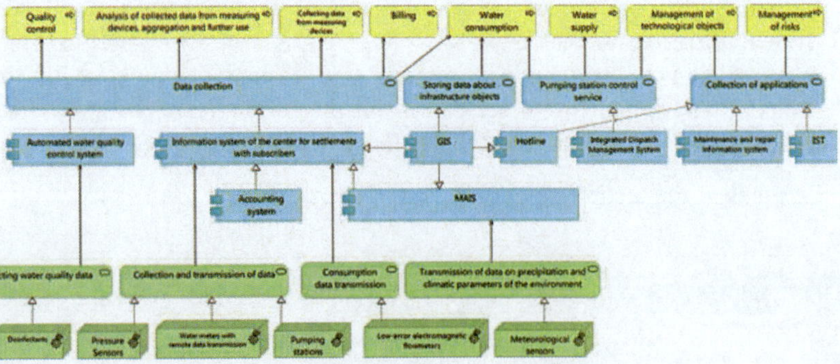

Fig. 6 AS-IS model of the enterprise architecture

This task requires the introduction of significant changes at the level of information systems—both the addition of new information systems and the modernization of existing ones. In addition, modernization of equipment at the technological level is required.

The main proposed changes are as follows:

1. Modernization of information systems and equipment.
2. In the AS-IS state, local control of the equipment takes place. The task was set to move to a single management. For this purpose, it is planned to introduce a monitoring and control subsystem.
3. It is planned to introduce CRM, which will carry out information exchange with other systems.
4. It is planned to introduce a measurement and accounting subsystem.
5. Modernization of the outdated Integrated Dispatch Management System.

The monitoring and control subsystem should ensure the solution of the following tasks:

- implementation of centralized management of technological objects and centralized control of technological parameters, operating modes, and equipment condition directly from engineering centers and a water supply control center;
- active monitoring of technological water supply facilities to support the work of personnel in emergency situations, identify, early warning and inform personnel about problem situations and formulate recommendations for personnel to prevent them or eliminate negative consequences for the process of water supply to consumers;
- information interaction with the duty units and external structures;
- information support and coordination of actions in the elimination of abnormal, emergency situations.
- In addition, the monitoring and control subsystem should provide:
- automated analysis of incoming telemetric information from objects of the water supply system and control points on the water supply network;
- automated construction of an assessment of the severity and forecast of further development of the accident;
- automated recording of the actions taken to eliminate the situation.

The measurement and accounting subsystem should provide means for receiving, storing, processing, and analyzing data from instrumentation and automation in order to provide information about the state of the water supply network.

The subsystem should assess the mismatch between the volumes of water supplied to the water supply network and consumed (received) by subscribers, identify time intervals with unusual values of supply and consumption volumes, and also carry out other calculations to assess inconsistencies caused by unaccounted water costs and losses, as well as assess probable causes and places of their occurrence, within the area defined by the nearest key points. When such cases are detected, the subsystem should automatically generate notifications to inform users. The subsystem should record water quality according to the Automated water quality control system. The subsystem should record the consumed energy resources according to the data of the automated system for commercial metering of electricity.

To ensure monitoring of the water supply network, the subsystem must track the statuses of instrumentation and communication equipment during the entire period of operation. The results of the analytical work of the Measurement and accounting subsystem in terms of control of unaccounted water consumption and losses, forecasting water consumption, operational monitoring of the state of the water supply network should also be displayed in the Visualization and decision support subsystem.

Configuration data for the Measurement and Accounting Subsystem is integrated data, including data on water supply and consumption facilities, water supply networks and inputs, lines, metering devices, subscribers, their statuses, and location from the GIS and the Information system of the center for settlements with subscribers.

The Integrated Dispatch Management System, interrogating water quality devices on the network, requires modernization. It is planned to add functionality for automatic tracking of exceeding the values of water quality indicators, to include the addition of information on laboratory control and informing personnel about exceeding the values of indicators.

The final proposed TO-BE model is shown in Fig. 7.

The following requirements are imposed on a unified information system in this model:

1. Functional.

    1.1 Business Requirements:

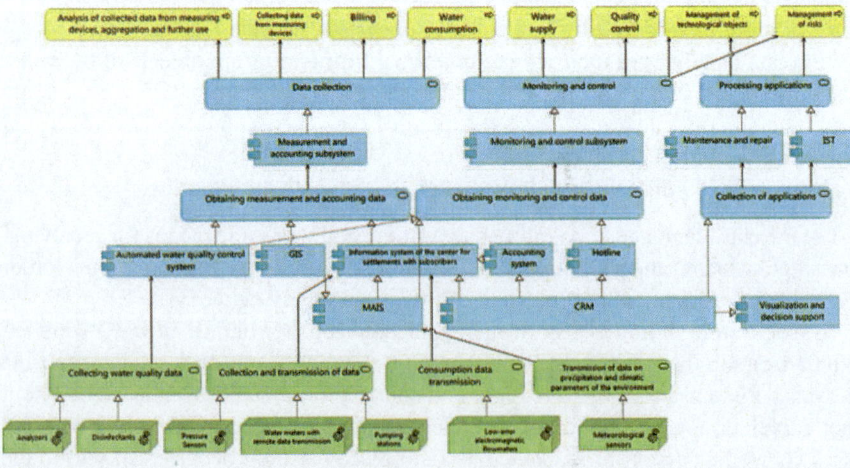

Fig. 7 TO-BE model of the enterprise architecture

- Measurement, accounting, monitoring, and management of water supply;
- Increased efficiency;
- Elimination of losses;
- Increased user satisfaction;
- Identification of theft;
- Leveling of non-standard peak loads.

1.2 User Requirements:

- Accuracy of charges;
- Automatic invoicing without the influence of the human factor;
- Application for mobile devices;
- Notifications;
- Consistently high water quality.

1.3 Requirements for the Collection and Processing of Data:

- Monitoring of unaccounted water costs and losses;
- Forecasting of water consumption;
- Data analysis.

2. Non-Functional.

2.1 Business Rules:

- Possibility of transition to unmanned (automated) production based on means of remote monitoring, control, and video recording;
- The maximum possible use of automation systems already implemented at the enterprise, if there is a technical possibility of their effective integration.

2.2 System Requirements:

- System of sensors connected to the IoT;
- Installation of flow meters;
- Support for Big Data operation;
- Preferred use of communication channels based on wire technologies;
- Use of a single hardware and software platform and software;
- Possibility of using servers and stations of automatic control systems of the software complex based on open-source operating systems.

2.3 Requirements for Design and Usability:

- Use of the Russian language in interfaces;
- Interfaces for monitoring, billing, troubleshooting, and data storage;
- Interface of administrator, operator, and consumer;

2.4 Requirements for Safety and Reliability:

- Protection against unauthorized access;
- User identification;
- Checking the user's authority when working with the system;
- Differentiation of user access at the level of tasks and information arrays;
- Data backup.

2.5 Requirements for Destination Indicators:

- Mandatory preliminary selection of "key points" (automated metering stations).

2.6 Other Requirements and Restrictions:

- Flexible interfaces for adjacent enterprise systems;
- Data synchronization with adjacent systems;
- Adaptation to the business processes of the enterprise;
- Integration with a video surveillance system for technological water supply facilities;
- Replication of the solution.

4 Discussion and Conclusion

As part of further research, a more detailed consideration of the direct implementation and deployment of the proposed model of the enterprise architecture with the calculation of the results achieved is expected.

The article deals with the case of a resource-supplying organization that has set the task of implementing a value-based approach to activities. In the course of the research, a model of the AS-IS enterprise architecture was built, an analysis was made of what functional areas should be automated, what changes should be made to the enterprise information systems, what services and for what purpose should be added. As a result, a target enterprise architecture model TO-BE was built, and the requirements for a unified information system in this model were identified.

The implementation of a value-oriented approach in building a model of the enterprise architecture for a resource-supplying organization makes it possible to increase the efficiency of decision-making on the management of the water supply system by aggregating all possible information from both related services, and about the state of the network and equipment. Active automated monitoring and control become possible. The quality of planning of production processes is improved. All this increases the efficiency of the organization and contributes to more complete satisfaction of the needs of the end consumer and the delivery of value to the consumer without contradicting the goals of achieving the main performance indicators of the organization itself.

References

1. Loucks, D. P., & van Beek, E. (2017). Water resources planning and management: An overview. In *Water Resource Systems Planning and Management*. Cham: Springer.
2. Federal Law of the Russian Federation dated 7.12.2011. No. 416–FZ "On water supply and sewerage".
3. Norton, M., & Lane, A. (2012). 'New water architecture': An integrated water management model. *Proceedings of the Institution of Civil Engineers-Management, Procurement and Law, 165*(3), 159–171.
4. Fatimah, H. A., Hermadi, I., & Nurhadryani, Y. (2019). Enterprise architecture approachment for designing it master plan based on ERP for water utility company. *Jurnal Aplikasi Manajemen, 17*(2), 336–344.
5. Rodríguez, A., & Cisneros, A. (2014). Challenges and benefits of an open ICT architecture for urban water management. *Procedia Engineering, 89*, 1073–1079.
6. Klamer, A. (2017). *Doing the Right Thing: A Value Based Economy* (p. 266). Ubiquity Press.
7. Lankhorst, M. (2017). *Enterprise Architecture at Work: Modelling, Communication and Analysis*. Springer.
8. Zaychenko, I. M., Ilin, I. V., & Lyovina, A. I. (2019). Enterprise architecture as a means of digital transformation of mining enterprises in the arctic. *In Innovation Management and Education Excellence through Vision, 2020*, 4652–4659.
9. Anisiforov, A., Dubgorn, A., & Lepekhin, A. (2019). Organizational and economic changes in the development of enterprise architecture. In *E3S Web of Conferences* (Vol. 110, p. 02051). EDP Sciences.
10. Kudryavtsev, D., Zaramenskikh, E., & Arzumanyan, M. (2018). The simplified enterprise architecture management methodology for teaching purposes. *Lecture Notes in Business Information Processing, 332*, 76–90.
11. Papazoglou, M. P., & Van Den Heuvel, W.-J. (2007). Service oriented architectures: Approaches, technologies and research issues. *The VLDB Journal, 16*, 389–415. https://doi.org/10.1007/s00778-007-0044-3.
12. Clement, S. J., McKee, D. W., & Xu, J. (2017). Service-oriented reference architecture for smart cities. In *2017 IEEE Symposium on Service-Oriented System Engineering (SOSE)* (pp. 81–85). IEEE.
13. Borremans, A. D., Zaychenko, I. M., & Iliashenko, O. Y. (2018). Digital economy. IT strategy of the company development. In *MATEC Web of Conferences* (Vol. 170, p. 01034). EDP Sciences (2018).
14. Ilin, I., Levina, A., Borremans, A., & Kalyazina, S. (2019). Enterprise architecture modeling in digital transformation Era. In *Energy Management of Municipal Transportation Facilities and Transport* (pp. 124–142). Cham: Springer.
15. Cerdá, V., Avivar, J., Ferrer, L., & Leal, L. O. (2013). Automatic water and wastewater quality monitoring systems. In *Smart Sensors for Real-Time Water Quality Monitoring* (pp. 105–123). Berlin, Heidelberg: Springer.
16. New Zealand (Ed.). (2014). Watercare services limited: Review of service performance. Controller and auditor-general.
17. National Geographic. https://www.nationalgeographic.org/encyclopedia/geographic-information-system-gis/.
18. OT. https://www.ot.ru/en/solutions/au-dispatcher-process-control/.
19. Snap-on. https://www.snapon.com/EN/UK/Diagnostics/Diagnostics/Platforms/Information-System/Snap-on-Information-System-Maintenance-Repair-Data.
20. Debitoor. https://debitoor.com/dictionary/accounting-system.
21. Nitu, R., & Wong, K. (2010). CIMO survey on national summaries of methods and instruments for solid precipitation measurement at automatic weather stations (Vol. 425).

Strategic Integration of Alignment Models for the IT-Business Misalignment Detection and Redress

Natalia Aseeva, Eduard Babkin, Pavel Malyzhenkov, and Maurizio Masi

Abstract The information technologies era exaggerates the link between IT and business. One power eventually affects another. The current IT-business misalignment diagnostics methodologies are able to identify an issue (like SAM, SAMM, etc.), but they do not formulate a particular algorithm to eliminate the misalignment. Therefore, the goal of this study is represented with the way of eliminating the gap between IT and business via a SAM, TOGAF, and BISMAM combination. This model integration represents eminent advantages through the ability to solve misalignment issues using the proposed model. This is the novelty of this research. The core of this approach is an Enterprise Architecture discipline which divides a company into architectural levels. It guarantees a comprehensive view on the issue. Moreover, the most appropriate methodologies of IT-business accordance were evaluated for the future integration. The results were demonstrated through the model usage on the organization example.

Keywords IT-business misalignment · Enterprise architecture · Symptoms collection · Misalignment redress

N. Aseeva · E. Babkin · P. Malyzhenkov (✉)
National Research University Higher School of Economics, Bolshaya Pecherskaya Str., 25/12, 603155 Nizhni Novgorod, Russia
e-mail: pmalyzhenkov@hse.ru

N. Aseeva
e-mail: naseeva@hse.ru

E. Babkin
e-mail: eababkin@hse.ru

M. Masi
Department of Economics, Engineering, Society and Business Organization, University of Tuscia, Via del Paradiso, 47, 01100 Viterbo, Italy

E. Zaramenskikh and A. Fedorova (eds.), *Digitalization of Society, Economics and Management*, Lecture Notes in Information Systems and Organisation 53,
https://doi.org/10.1007/978-3-030-94252-6_7

1 Introduction

The postindustrial era has made the IT-systems usage a crucial factor of competitiveness, as digitalization of business processes and mapping of information into an understandable format assists management in making decisions which are now based on more than just personal experience and intuition but also on data sources [1]. Nevertheless, information technologies may lead to negative results that can make a company lose its competitive position [2]. On the other hand, if certain resources were contributed to the achievement of an IT-business alignment state then it will give some advantage [3]: rising profit, ROI increase in IT projects, strengthening of competitive position.

The issue of IT-business alignment is widely covered in the current literature. The importance of accordance of IT and business was described in [4–8]. This evidence of the IT-business alignment benefit for the business shows that this aspect is vital to the companies [9, 10]. Moreover, IT-business alignment issue has been staying in the top of priorities for a long time until now [11, 12] (Fig. 1). This fact emphasizes the need to contribute to this topic from both research and practical points of view.

Deepening the IT-business misalignment literature it's possible to find the way of detection misalignment symptoms [14–16]. It is sufficiently appropriate but symptoms bank is not comprehensive and there is no obvious way of symptoms elimination. That is why, this study envisages the algorithm of IT-business misalignment redress. The novelty of this research is proposed model integration which is able to provide specific artifacts and set of actions to get an IT-business alignment state.

Most current research investigates [9, 13–15] IT-business alignment/misalignment in the terms of detection but they are not targeted on a specific set of actions to solve this issue. We introduce one set of such actions and demonstrate the benefits of integrated model application in the case of one company operating in electronic trade sector. So, the algorithm presented in this research in a form of a guideline of the specific IT-business misalignment symptoms eliminating via set of corrective

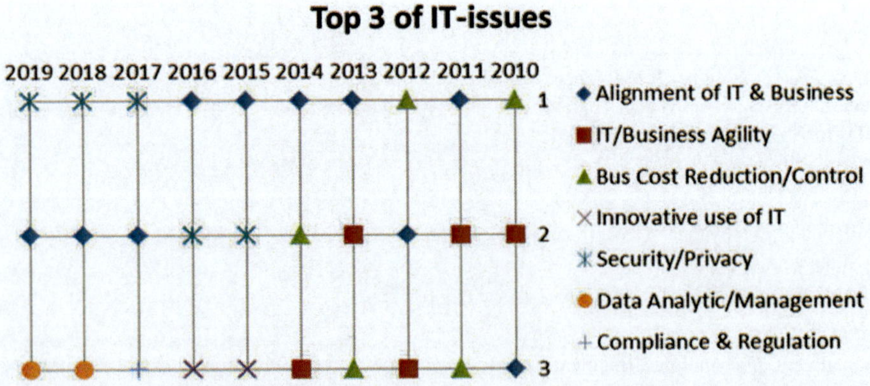

Fig. 1 Top of IT-issues (according to [12])

actions is proposed. It can be used by business analytics for a construction of aligned enterprise architecture.

In order to see misalignment symptoms it is necessary to diagnose and redress them via an enterprise architecture approach. So, the present research seeks for a way of detection and leveling of IT-business misalignment via usage of advantages of current IT-business alignment methodologies.

The paper is structured as follows: Sect. 2 describes the theoretical background of the research, Sect. 3 presents our approach to the integration of the models on the base of a concrete business case in the sector of electronic trade, Sect. 4 is dedicated to the conclusions and future directions of the research.

2 Theoretical Background and a Tools Overview

2.1 IT-Business Misalignment Definition

The current literature provides a definition of IT-business alignment [17–19] which makes it possible to formulate an IT-business misalignment definition:

1. The extent to which the IT strategy does not support/is not supported by the business strategy;
2. The extent to which the IT mission, goals, and plan are not available.

Therefore, synchronization should be established between business and IT artifacts. IT-business misalignment may be viewed in terms of the following dimensions:

1. Intellectual (strategic) dimension: the level of mutual assistance between business and IT plans/strategies. Misalignment indicates that the organization has no documented plans;
2. A structural one is the level of structural conformity of IT and acceptance of law decisions, relationships in the field of reporting, centralization/IT decentralization, and deployment of IT personnel;
3. A social one is a social status and understanding among business units and their commitment of mission, goals, and plans of business and IT;
4. A cultural one emphasizes the cultural relevance between business and IT as a precondition for everyone to plan information systems.

In this study, achieving alignment between IT and business is examined precisely from the point of view of intelligent measurement through the use of discipline in enterprise architecture and the search for symptoms.

To place the present contribution in a proper context this section outlines some related works and important concepts. In this study, we will focus mainly on the intellectual aspect of IT-business discrepancy, since most of the developed methods are aimed specifically at it. Moreover, the intellectual dimension is more measurable than the structural one due to the documented nature of this IT-business alignment. But the other dimension should not be neglected.

The Enterprise Architecture approach provides the business and IT specialists with complete and ready-made recommendations for adjustment in order to achieve targeted business results that take into account the corresponding failures in the business. Thus, the architecture of the enterprise represents the basis for applying methodologies to avoid IT-business misalignment in the direction of matching all architectural levels to each other.

It should also be noted that the researchers mostly study the IT-business misalignment in statics, although dynamics is also important.

In this research, compliance achievement will include a tremendous work with methodologies based on IT-business misalignment in the intellectual dimension via enterprise architecture highlighting the organization's architectural levels to align each of them through symptom identification.

For now, there is a sufficiently thorough definition of the concept of IT-business misalignment, the selected dimension (intellectual) and the enterprise architecture based approach. These theoretical findings help to select proper methods to achieve an IT-business alignment state on the base of high-leveled alignment models and to establish the relationship between them on the basis of the overlapping shortcomings of each of them.

2.2 SAM

In 1991, the Strategic Alignment Model (SAM) [20] was proposed which differentiates the external and internal forces of IT and business (Fig. 2).

There are four domains of alignment:

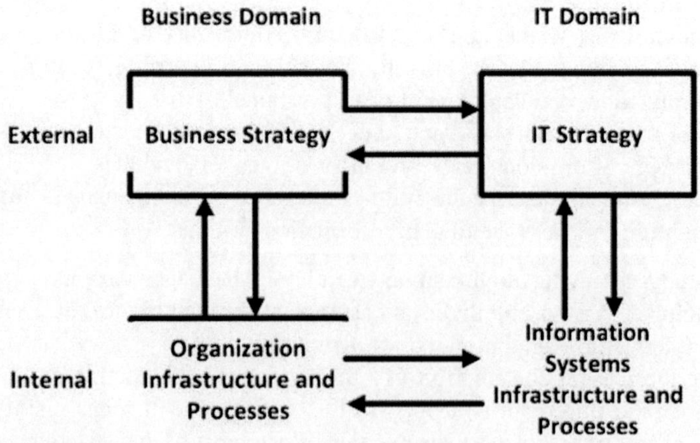

Fig. 2 Strategic Alignment Model (according to [20])

1. Business strategy (business domain) is the company's place in the external competitive environment: positioning, a competitive advantage condition, and a key success factor;
2. Organizational infrastructure and processes (business domain): organizational structure and business processes;
3. IT strategy (IT domain) is the company's place in the IT market—technologies that can form new business initiatives; information system attributes that can help support the current or create a new business strategy; diversification of available IT resources to support the business;
4. IT-infrastructure and processes (IT domain): an information system architecture, a set of applications, IT processes and, in addition, decisions that affect the time required by IT professionals to manage the corporate technical infrastructure.

Thus, there are two ways of domain integration:

1. A strategic one is business strategy + IT strategy, which means IT strategy usage to support or formulate the business strategy;
2. A functional one is organizational structure + process and IT-infrastructure to display the consistency of the requirements and expectations of employees and the capabilities of the IT department.

Moreover, SAM includes cross-domain relations called alignment perspectives (Fig. 3). It should be emphasized that at least three of four domains have to be aligned to achieve IT-business alignment.

It should also be noted that the effectiveness of the SAM model was called into question and this sounds reasonable, but this study just shows how it can be successfully used together with other models.

Despite the overall theoretical importance, this model is a conceptual one and does not propose an algorithm of achieving an IT-business alignment state.

2.3 *BISMAM*

The Business and Information Systems Misalignment model (BISMAM) [22] uses the terminology of medical sciences (misalignment = disease). In order to eliminate IT-business misalignment the model establishes the nomenclature and semantics of misalignment, divided into three aspects: organ system, symptom, etiology. A three-step algorithm is used:

1. Identification of inconsistencies: compare the AS-IS state of the organization with the symptoms (Figs. 4 and 5)
2. Correction of symptoms via therapy (Figs. 6 and 7).
3. Prevention of the non-compliance: use the collection of preventive measures (Figs. 8 and 9) to prevent reoccurrence of the same situation (Figs. 10 and 11).

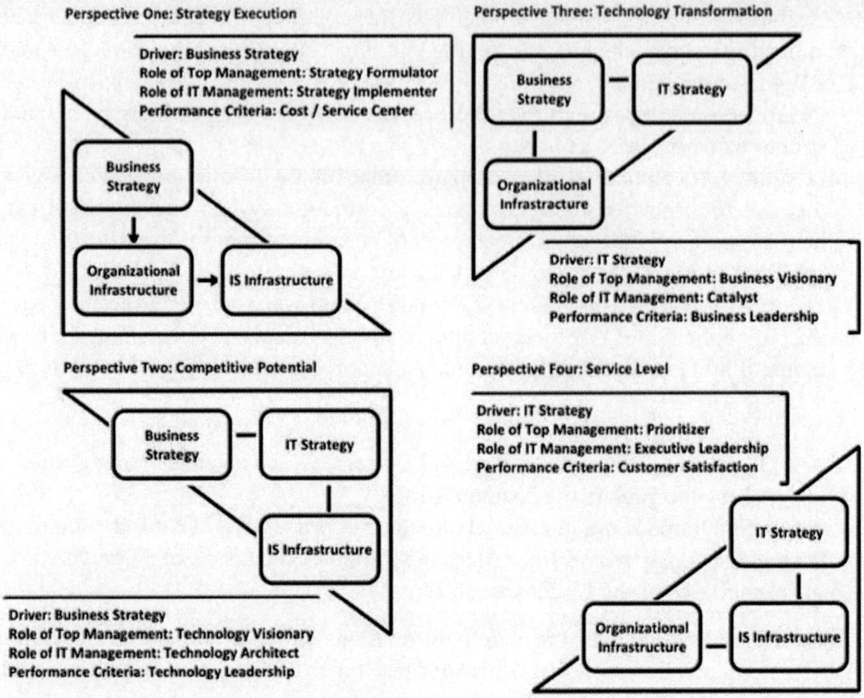

Fig. 3 Alignment perspectives (according to [20])

Code	Classification Scheme Record
S.01	I am not aware of the organization's mission.
S.02	I am not aware of the organization's strategy and goals.
S.03	I do not know who the ultimate responsible for a business process is.
S.04	I do not know with whom I should speak to obtain knowledge about business processes.
S.05	I do not know what my responsibilities are.
S.06	I do not know what the expectations about my work are.
S.07	I do not know to whom I should report within the context of different activities.
S.08	I am not aware of the process contribution towards the organization goals.
S.09	I am not aware of my contribution towards the organization goals.
S.10	I do not know with whom I should speak to obtain the semantics of informational entities.
S.11	I do not know who the ultimate responsible for a business informational entity is.
S.12	I find that same entity has different semantic according to the interlocutor.
S.13	I find that different concepts and names are used to refer to same entity.
S.14	I do not have the required information to support day-to-day activities.
S.15	I do not have the required information to support decision-making.

Fig. 4 Symptoms library (1/2) (according to [22])

Code	Classification Scheme Record
S.16	I find information outdated.
S.17	I do not know with whom I should speak to obtain information and help about an application.
S.18	I do not know who the ultimate responsible for an application is.
S.19	I need to repeat the login in different applications.
S.20	I spend time configuring and updating users' profiles in several applications.
S.21	I need to develop and use end user computing applications.
S.22	I cannot develop/innovate certain types of business and products.
S.23	I spend time reintroducing the same information over different applications.
S.24	I need to use different applications during the day to perform my business activities.
S.25	I spend time executing manual validations that could be automatic.
S.26	I need to repeat the same application task several times to perform a business activity.
S.27	I do not understand how to use and interpret the same concept in different applications.
S.28	I need to run queries on different applications to get a full picture over an entity.
S.29	I find information consistency problems.
S.30	I find information integrity problems.
S.31	I spend time to correct data to ensure consistency between information replicas.
S.32	I have no confidence on application's information.
S.33	I find information entities with required fields not filled.
S.34	I spent time synchronizing data between applications.
S.35	I need to keep competencies on several different technology, operating systems and DBMS.
S.36	I can't comply with the business level of service.
S.37	I have frequent periods where applications are unavailable.
S.38	I find that batch processes are not completed during the non-working period.
S.39	I spent extra resources and costs with new developments facing information volume increase.
S.40	I have found unprotected confidential information.
S.41	I have found that users have access to information not required for their business activities.

Fig. 5 Symptoms library (2/2) (according to [22])

Code	Description
T.01	Define and communicate organization's mission, strategy and goals.
T.02	Define and assign business processes ownership and responsibility.
T.03	Define and assign business roles, responsibilities and reporting lines.
T.04	Define business process goals and link it to organizational goals.
T.05	Define and assign information entities ownership and responsibility.
T.06	Define and assign application ownership and responsibility.
T.07	Develop a data dictionary and promote dictionary rules and standards.
T.08	Perform business process improvement
T.09	Implement a management information system.
T.10	Develop application interfaces.
T.11	Implement a single-sign-on solution.
T.12	Implement an identity and access management solution.

Fig. 6 Therapy library (1/2) (according to [22])

This generalized approach resembles the methods of systemic thinking and analysis: the methods are universal for situations and can be used in organizations engaged in various subject areas.

On the figures above OA, BA, IA, AA and TA mean Organizational, Business, Information, Application, and Technology Architecture. Despite the architectural and system approach, this model neglects the driving forces of alignment and has no documented artifacts which help to resolve the IT-business misalignment issue.

Code	Description
T.13	Implement data integrity, data consistency and data quality controls.
T.14	Perform database consolidation and migrate data.
T.15	Implement a workflow system.
T.16	Implement a load balancing solution.
T.17	Upgrade application and database server's capacity.
T.18	Implement a failover solution.
T.19	Define levels of service and performance indicators.
T.20	Reprioritize the project portfolio.
T.21	Implement encryption mechanisms to secure confidential information
T.22	Implement an enterprise information integration layer.
T.23	Provide training on specific applications functionality.
T.24	Review users' profiles and access rights.
T.25	Consolidate and standardize platforms and technologies.

Fig. 7 Therapy library (2/2) (according to [22])

Code	Description
P.01	Organization's mission, strategy and goals shall be defined and published.
P.02	Business processes shall have an owner responsible for process update, control, quality and improvement.
P.03	Business roles and responsibilities shall be defined and assigned, and lines of reporting shall be established to different roles.
P.04	Business process goals shall be defined and linked to organizational goals, and roles operational goals shall be defined and linked to business process goals.
P.05	Information entities shall have an owner responsible for ensuring quality and accuracy, and for defining security requirements.
P.06	Information architecture with all relevant business information entities shall be identified, including concepts, semantic and alias.
P.07	Information shall have a means of being communicated to the appropriate audience using standard applications and tools.
P.08	Applications shall have an owner responsible for ensuring documentation, new developments and maintenance prioritization, availability and performance requirements.
P.09	User identification, authentication and authorizations should be managed centrally.
P.10	New business and new products launching shall be preceded by the identification of application's functionalities gaps and required developments shall be performed.
P.11	Each business process shall be supported by a minimum number of applications and each business activity shall be supported by one application.
P.12	Applications shall support efficient automatism for repeated tasks and for sequential tasks without input required.
P.13	Each information entity shall be managed by only one application that provide the services to access and update the entities it manages.
P.14	Applications shall provide data quality controls.
P.15	Technology standards shall be defined and followed by all projects.
P.16	IT service levels shall be defined, and availability/performance monitored.

Fig. 8 Prophylaxis library (according to [22])

Code	Description
P.17	High availability infrastructure shall be provided for high critical processes with demanding performance and availability requirements.
P.18	Applications shall be scalable to support business volume increase.
P.19	Information security mechanisms shall be implemented according to sensitive information, according to security requirements.
P.20	Information access shall be provided on a need-to-know basis, using least privilege rule.

Fig. 9 Prophylaxis library (according to [22])

Organ System	Symptom/Sign	Therapy	Prophylaxis
OA	S.01, S.02	T.01	P.01
BA	S.03, S.04	T.02	P.02
OA-BA	S.05, S.06, S.07	T.03	P.03
OA-BA	S.08, S.09	T.04	P.04
IA	S.10, S.11	T.05	P.05
IA	S.12, S.13	T.07	P.05, P.06
BA-IA	S.14, S.15, S.16	T.09, T.10	P.06, P.07
AA	S.17, S.18	T.06	P.08

Fig. 10 Proposed solution (prophylaxis and therapy) (1/2) (according to [22])

Organ System	Symptom/Sign	Therapy	Prophylaxis
BA-AA	S.19, S.20	T.11, T.12	P.09
BA-AA	S.21, S.22	T.20	P.10
BA-AA	S.23, S.24	T.10, T.15	P.11
BA-AA	S.25, S.26		P.11, P.12
IA-AA	S.27, S.28	T.14	P.13
IA-AA	S.29, S.30, S.31, S.32, S.33	T.13, T.22	P.13, P.14
TA	S.34	T.22	P.15
AA-TA	S.35	T.25	P.13
AA-TA	S.36, S.37, S.38	T.16, T.17, T.18	P.16, P.17
IA-TA	S.39		P.18
IA-TA	S.40, S.41	T.21, T.24	P.19, P.20

Fig. 11 Proposed solution (prophylaxis and therapy) (2/2) (according to [22])

2.4 *Luftman's Symptoms*

The BISMAM symptom base covers many of the possible manifestations of IT-business misalignment; however, it does not cover all its aspects.

Therefore, the symptom bank was expanded with a collection of Lufthman's symptoms [23]. These are precisely the symptoms that are associated with similar BISMAM symptoms in terms of expressing IT-business misalignment of the same aspect, which means that they can be "cured" with the same treatment and prevention measures. The symptoms of Luftman are presented in Fig. 12. They extend the bank of BISMAM and improve the indicators collection.

3 Integration of Models

Now it is time to add some novelty to all mentioned models and approaches (Fig. 13).

Our approach is based on the searching for similar notions in analyzed models and making generalization of the concepts. The final result in this phase may be represented as a catalogue of actions and further as a software program.

The first integration of SAM and TOGAF was done in [24] (Fig. 13) demonstrating that it leads to overlapping the drawbacks of one another: one (SAM) takes

LF1	Lack of understanding between IT and business representatives	LF6	Redundancy of developed systems
LF2	Lack of vision / strategy	LF7	Lack of system competencies (key IT capabilities that create competitive advantage)
LF3	Lack of effective communication channels between IT and users	LF8	Difficulties in integrating systems
LF4	Continuous conflicts between business and IT	LF9	Dissatisfied users/complaints
LF5	Performance degradation		

Fig. 12 Luftman's symptoms (according to [23])

SAM integration domains		Business Domains		IT Domains			
		Business Strategy	Organizational Infrastructure and Processes	IT Strategy	IS Infrastructure and Processes		
TOGAF	**Architecture domains**	Business Architecture		IS Architecture	Application Architecture	Data Architecture	Technology Architecture
	ADM phases	Phase A	Phase B	Phase C	Phase C (Applications)	Phase C (Data)	Phase D
	Artifacts	*Stakeholder *Map Matrix Value Chain *Diagram *Driver/ Goal/Objective Catalog	*Driver/ Goal/ Objective Catalog *Role Catalog *Business Service/Function Catalog *Process/Event/ Control/Product Catalog *Contract/Measure Catalog *Business Interaction Matrix *Business Footprint Diagram *Functional Decomposition Diagram *Goal/Objective/ Service Diagram *Business Use-Case Diagram *Organization Decomposition Diagram *Process Flow Diagram	*IT Strategy	*Application Portfolio Catalog *Application/ Function Matrix *Application Interaction Matrix *Application Use-Case Diagram *Process/ Application Realization Diagram *Software Distribution Diagram	*Data Entity/ Data Component Catalog *Data Entity/ Business Function Matrix *Application/Data Matrix	*Technology Standards Catalog *Technology Portfolio Catalog *Application/ Technology Matrix *Platform De-composition Diagram *Processing Diagram

Fig. 13 SAM and TOGAF [21] integration (according to [24])

into account the perspective of IT-business alignment; another proposes some artifacts, which should be developed according to the chosen perspective. We will go deeper than the SAM + TOGAF integration and propose the dynamic measure for prophilaxy. Though these approaches contain different terminology, it was possible to align it partially. The IT-business alignment by means of terminology alignment constitutes a new promising branch of further research. Firstly, BISMAM and the Luftman's symptoms indicate where something is misaligned. That is why the BISMAM symptoms were associated with the Luftman's ones (column 1, 3 of Fig. 12).

The principle of association means that each Luftman's symptom is of a nature similar to the selected BISMAM one. This rule is convenient because similar symptoms cover a misalignment issue wider. Secondly, these symptoms were embedded into the artifacts of ADM phases on the SAM basis. Thus, if we find a symptom, this will enable us to understand what artifact should be developed and what therapy/prophylaxis should be used (column 2, 4 of Fig. 12).

Thirdly, there will be an example of usage of the integration of these models.

The principle of association means that each Luftman's symptom is of a nature similar to the selected BISMAM one. This rule is convenient because similar symptoms cover a misalignment issue wider. Secondly, these symptoms were embedded into the artifacts of ADM phases on the SAM basis. Thus, if we find a symptom, this will enable us to understand what artifact should be developed and what therapy/prophylaxis should be used (column 2, 4 of Fig. 12).

Thirdly, there will be an example of usage of the integration of these models (Fig. 14).

If an individual desires to use this model integration, he/she should perform the following sequence of acts in order to avoid IT-business misalignment symptoms and balance the IT and the business sphere of such individual's organization.

1. Define what IT-business alignment perspectives prevail in the organization and select those that must be supported (SAM, Fig. 2);
2. Identify IT-business misalignment symptoms (BISMAM, Luftman) via interview and analysis of stakeholders (Figs. 6, 7 and 10);
3. Conduct therapy and prophylaxis via elaboration of artifacts within the ADM model (TOGAF) which should be taken into account according to the symptoms (Fig. 11) in the order defined by alignment perspectives.

Now we demonstrate some cases of the derived algorithm application. It represents more than just a detection tool, but the tool that proposes a specific set of actions:

Example 1 (Fig. 13):

- Identified symptoms of non-compliance: S1, S2, S3, LF2
- SAM Perspective: Strategy Execution
- ADM phase sequence: A, B, C, D
- Treatment. T1: define the mission, goals, strategies, and allocate them to employees (Principal Catalog, Driver/Goal/Objective Catalog); T2: Identify and appoint owners and responsible business processes (Role Catalog, Process Flow)

Symptom	Artifact	Symptom	Artifact
S.01	Principle Catalogue	S.22	Application/ Technology Matrix
S.02 /LF2	Driver/Goal/Objective Catalogue	S.23/LF6	Data Dissemination Diagram
S.03	Role Catalogue, Process Flow	S.24/LF6	Application/Data Matrix, Application/Function Matrix
S.04	Role Catalogue, Process Flow	S.25/LF7	Application Use-Case Diagram
S.05	Actor/Role Matrix	S.26/LF7	Application Use-Case Diagram
S.06	Actor/Role Matrix	S.27	Role/Application Matrix
S.07	Organization Decomposition Diagram	S.28	Application/ Data Matrix, Application/ Function Matrix
S.08/ LF1	Goal/Objective/Service Diagram	S.29/LF8	Logical Data Diagram, Data Dissemination Diagram
S.09/LF1	Goal/Objective/Service Diagram, Process Flow Diagram	S.30/LF8	Conceptual Data Diagram Logical Data Diagram, Data Dissemination Diagram
S.10/LF4/ LF9	Role/Application Matrix, Application/ Organization Matrix	S.31/LF8	Conceptual Data Diagram, Logical Data Diagram, Data Dissemination Diagram
S.11/LF4/ LF9	Role/Application Matrix	S.32/LF8	Application/ Data Matrix
S.12/LF1	Role/Application Matrix	S.33/LF8	Data Entity/Data Component Catalogue
S.13/LF1	Conceptual Data Diagram	S.34	Application/ Technology Matrix
S.14	Data Dissemination Diagram	S.35	Technology Portfolio Catalog
S.15	Data Dissemination Diagram	S.36/LF5	Technology Standards Catalogue Application/ Technology Matrix
S.16	Interface Catalog	S.37/LF5	Environments and Locations Diagram
S.17/LF3	Role/Application Matrix	S.38/LF5	Technology Standards Catalog, Application/ Technology Matrix
S.18/LF3	Role/Application Matrix	S.39/ LF5	Application/ Technology Matrix
S.19/LF8	Application Interaction Matrix	S.40	Data Dissemination Diagram, Data Entity/ Business Function Matrix
S.20/LF8	Data Entity/ Data Component Catalogue	S.41	Data Entity/ Business Function
S.21	Application/ Technology Matrix, Technology Standards Catalog, Application/ Function Matrix		

Fig. 14 BISMAM and the Luftman's symptoms linked with TOGAF artifacts in terms of ADM

- Prevention. P1: Identify and communicate the mission, strategy, and goals of the organization; P2: Identify and designate owners and responsible business processes.

This example is presented in Fig. 15.

In Fig. 15 AA, DA and TA mean Application, Data, and Technology architecture. Another example has alternative SAM perspective, so the tabular structure representation should be the same but with another order of SAM domains, architectural domains, and ADM phases.

Example 2:

- Identified symptoms of non-compliance: S7, S8, S9, LF1
- SAM Perspective: Competitive Potential
- ADM phase sequence: C, A, B, D

(SAM) perspective	Strategy Execution							
(SAM) Domains	Business strategy	Organizational Infrastructure and Processes	IT strategy	IS Infrastructure and Processes			Treatment (BISMAM)	Prophylaxis (BISMAM)
Architecture domain	Business Architecture		IS Architecture	AA	DA	TA		
ADM Phases (TOGAF)	A	B	C	(Application)	(Data)			
Symptoms (BISMAM+ Luftman)								
S.01	Principle Catalog						T1	P1
S.02/LF2		Driver/Goal/ Objective Catalog						
S.03		Role Catalog Process Catalog					T2	P2

Fig. 15 Example of model integration

- Decision. T3: Define and assign business roles, responsibilities, and reporting lines (Organization Decomposition Diagram); T4: Define the goals of business processes and associate them with the goals of the organization (Goal/Objective/Service Diagram, Process Flow Diagram)
- Prevention. P3: Define and assign business roles, responsibilities, and reporting lines; P4: Define the goals of business processes and their relationship with organizational goals.

In an analyzed company, there exists the prospect of an IT-business alignment—technological potential. As a rule, a business formulates what it needs in order to attract users and make the product more competitive, and IT already decides how to do this in the shortest possible time.

According to the TOGAF-ADM development model and integration with SAM: the phase sequence will be as follows: CABD.

1. SAM: Business strategy (TOGAF ADM: A)
   1. S.01 (Principle Catalog)
      - T.1 Define and communicate the mission, strategy, and goals of the organization
      - Recommendation: to declare the mission, strategy, and goals of the organization periodically—once a year the general director of the company comes to motivate employees—let him mention the organization's guidelines and they should be placed on the information stand (Principle Catalog).
   2. SAM: IT-infrastructure (TOGAF ADM: C (Application))
   3. LF.04 (Actor/Role Matrix)
      - T.5 Identify and designate owners and responsible information entities
      - Recommendation: misunderstanding may arise due to the fact that it is not clear who is responsible for what, in order to clarify this, there must be a document (Actor/Role Matrix), with which you can determine who can be contacted.. SAM: IT-infrastructure (TOGAF ADM: C (Data))
   4. LF.06 (Data Dissemination Diagram)
      - T9 Implement information systems management
      - Recommendation: create a data distribution diagram to determine which data to send to which application. All these recommendations were accepted by the organization as the base for IT-business alignment realizations.

To recap the integration, this set of acts has several advantages:

1. It considers the architectural levels, which guarantees that there will be no improvement of one aspect of the organization that leads to degradation in another one;

2. It offers not just the identification of an IT-business misalignment state, but also some advice as to what to do and what artifacts to elaborate;
3. The set of actions is more specific due to the extended symptom diagnostics and the choice of an alignment perspective.

To sum up, this new algorithm has no analogues and provides great assistance in making an organization more IT-business aligned. That is the crucial novelty of the research. This research can also be continued on the field of models validation [25–28], using the approach adopted in [29].

4 Conclusions

All in all, the result of this research is the novel algorithm of an Enterprise Architecture based approach to the IT-business misalignment detection and redress with an extended symptoms collection. There were defined misalignment symptoms and the diagnostics method.

The goal of the research is the search for a way of detection and leveling of IT-business misalignment via usage of advantages of current IT-business alignment methodologies. To emphasize, the novelty of the research is a proposed algorithm of IT-business misalignment redress.

The search for a way of detection and leveling of IT-business misalignment via usage of advantages of current IT-business alignment methodologies was successful. It was presented as the linkage between BISMAM and the Luftman's symptoms and the artifacts of ADM phases of the TOGAF methodology which takes into account strategic alignment perspectives of the SAM-methodology.

Moreover, there was the demonstration of model usage to solve misalignment issues of one IT-company. Thus, it shows how an integrated model is effective on the real case.

Notwithstanding the multiple linkages to get an integrated model, there can be some further study directions:

1. A computer automation of the algorithm;
2. Extension of the IT-business misalignment symptom library collection;
3. Extension of the IT-business misalignment therapy library collection.
4. A comparison analysis with other known methods.
5. A realization of a concrete artifact realizing the overall approach of misalignment symptoms detection and a targeted prophylaxis.

References

1. Mendelson, E. (2016). Exposed: Desire and disobedience in the digital age. In Workshop on Enterprise and Organizational Modeling and Simulation (pp. 214–232). Cham: Springer.
2. Legner, C., et al. (2017). Digitalization: Opportunity and challenge for the business and information systems engineering community. *Business & Information Systems Engineering, 59*(4), 301–308.
3. Chi, M., Huang, R., & George, J. F. (2020). Collaboration in demand-driven supply chain: Based on a perspective of governance and IT-business strategic alignment. *International Journal of Information Management, 102062.*
4. Al-Surmi, A., Cao, G., & Duan, Y. (2020). The impact of aligning business, IT, and marketing strategies on firm performance. *Industrial Marketing Management, 84*, 39–49.
5. Schlosser, F., Wagner, H. T., & Coltman, T. (2012). Reconsidering the dimensions of business-IT alignment. In *2012 45th Hawaii International Conference on System Sciences* (pp. 5053–5061). IEEE. Khaiata, M., & Zualkernan, I. A. (2009). A simple instrument to measure IT-business alignment maturity. *Information Systems Management, 26*(2), 138–152.
6. Sledgianowski, D., & Luftman, J. (2005). IT-business strategic alignment maturity: A case study. *Journal of Cases on Information Technology (JCIT), 7*(2), 102–120.
7. Nickels, D. W. (2004). IT-Business Alignment: What we know that we still don't know. In *Proceedings of the 7th Annual Conference of the Southern Association for Information Systems* (Vol. 79, pp. 79–84).
8. Hu, Q., & Huang, C. D. (2006). Using the balanced scorecard to achieve sustained IT-business alignment: A case study. *Communications of the Association for Information Systems, 17*(1).
9. Sharma, S., & Behl, R. (2020). Strategic alignment of information technology in public and private organizations in india: A comparative study. *Global Business Review*, 0972150919893839.
10. Gerow, J. E., Grover, V., Thatcher, J., & Roth, P. L. (2014). Looking Toward the Future of IT–Business Strategic Alignment through the Past. *Mis Quarterly, 38*(4), 1159–1186.
11. Luftman, J. (2003). Assessing IT/business alignment. *Information Systems Management, 20*(4), 9–15.
12. The Global IT Trends Survey (2019). Retrieved from http://www.globaliim.com/
13. Őri, D. (2015). Towards detecting misalignment symptoms: An alignment perspective-driven architecture-matching framework.
14. Őri, D. (2017). Misalignment symptom detection with XML-based enterprise architecture model analysis. In *CEUR Workshop Proceedings* (Vol. 1859, pp. 153–157).
15. Őri, D., & Szabó, Z. (2017). Pattern-based analysis of business-IT mismatches in EA models: Insights from a case study. In *2017 IEEE 21st International Enterprise Distributed Object Computing Workshop (EDOCW)* (pp. 92–99). IEEE.
16. Szabó, Z., & Öri, D. (2017). Information strategy challenges in the digital era how enterprise architecture management can support strategic IS planning. In *2017 11th International Conference on Software, Knowledge, Information Management and Applications (SKIMA)* (pp. 1–8). IEEE.
17. Al Ghazi, A., Li, M., Cui, T., Fosso, S., & Shen, J. (2017). Exploration of the misalignment between business and it strategic objectives in public-sector organisations: An empirical study in Saudi Arabia. In *Workshop on E-Business* (pp. 15–28). Cham: Springer.
18. Reich, B. H., & Benbasat, I. (1996). Measuring the linkage between business and information technology objectives. *MIS Quarterly*, 55–81.
19. Jacobs, J. (2002). Gartner's collaboration glossary. Gartner Report.
20. Henderson, J. C., & Venkatraman, H. (1999). Strategic alignment: Leveraging information technology for transforming organizations. *IBM Systems Journal, 38*(2.3), 472–484.
21. Harrison, R. (2018). Togaf (r) 9 Foundation study guide. Van Haren.
22. Carvalho, R., & Sousa, P. (2008). Business and Information Systems Misalignment Model (BISMAM): An holistic model leveraged on misalignment and medical sciences approaches. *Proceedings of BUSITAL, 8*, 105.

23. Luftman, J. N. (2003). *Competing in the Information Age: Align in the Sand*. Oxford University Press.
24. Ivanova, M., & Malyzhenkov, P. (2018). The intellectual dimension of IT-business alignment problem: Alloy application. In *Workshop on Enterprise and Organizational Modeling and Simulation* (pp. 153–168). Cham: Springer.
25. The Standish Group (2015) Chaos Report : http://www.standishgroup.com/.
26. "Why Doesn't the FEA Work".https://www.ech-bpm.ch/sites/default/files/articles/why_doesnt_the_federal_enterprise_architecture_work.pdf .
27. Zelenkov, Y. (2015). Business and IT alignment in turbulent business environment. In *International Conference on Business Information Systems* (pp. 101–112). Cham: Springer.
28. Renaud, A., Walsh, I., & Kalika, M. (2016). Is SAM still alive? a bibliometric and interpretive mapping of the strategic alignment research field. *The Journal of Strategic Information Systems, 25*(2), 75–103.
29. Babkin, E., Malyzhenkov, P. V., Ivanova, M., & Ponomarev, N. (2019). A methodology for automatic formal verification of enterprise architecture. . *International Journal of Information System Modeling and Design., 10*(1), 1–19. https://doi.org/10.4018/IJISMD.2019010101,ISSN:1947-8186

Supply Chain Design Approach Based on Composite Simulation Models

Natalia Lychkina, Gleb Zakhodyakin, and Yulia Morozova

Abstract Strategic transformation and logistic integration in supply chain management requires systematic strategic supply chain modeling, and modern simulation provides such opportunities for analysis and synthesis of efficient and integrated supply chains. Authors suggest a method of constructing an analysis of conceptual supply chain models. The following base levels of the supply chain representation are considered: object-based, configuration/network-based, process-based, and logistics coordination levels. A general simulation model of integrative supply chain is proposed based on technologies of hybrid process and agent-based simulation modeling. Literature review on simulation modeling application for integrative and collaborative supply chains is presented. Iterative simulation and optimization procedures for complex analysis and optimization of supply chains are proposed. The suggested approaches and techniques were tested in the case of strategic transformation of supply chain. Authors present and interpret the results of supply chain optimization и simulation modeling for a set of scenarios of logistic processes transformation and inventory management policies, inter-organizational coordination mechanisms, and related technological solutions.

Keywords Simulation modeling · Supply chain · Design approach · Composite models

N. Lychkina · G. Zakhodyakin · Y. Morozova (✉)
HSE University, 100100 Myasnitskaya 20, Moscow, Russian Federation
e-mail: yumorozova@hse.ru

N. Lychkina
e-mail: nlychkina@hse.ru

G. Zakhodyakin
e-mail: gzakhodiakin@hse.ru

E. Zaramenskikh and A. Fedorova (eds.), *Digitalization of Society, Economics and Management*, Lecture Notes in Information Systems and Organisation 53,
https://doi.org/10.1007/978-3-030-94252-6_8

1 Introduction

In the practice of supply chain management (SCM), a wide range of tasks are traditionally solved through modeling [41], among them: supply chain structure, process redesign, supplier selection, facilities/ capacity planning, supply chain integration, information sharing, bullwhip effect, reverse logistics, replenishment control policies, supply chain optimization, cost reduction, system performance, inventory planning/management, planning & forecasting demand, production planning & scheduling, distribution & transportation planning, dispatching rules. In real SC transformation projects, the range of tasks to be solved is determined by project purposes and can be significantly expanded. That will require more process details and analysis of specific phenomena of the functioning of complex and dynamic SC.

In the practice of improving logistics activities in the SC, numerous logistics technologies are being implemented (S&OP, VMI, CPFR, etc.), based on the principles of logistics integration and integrated planning mechanisms in SCM. A common task in the implementation of modern logistics concepts and technologies based on integration, embedded in the content of the holistic concept of the SC, is to ensure a synergistic effect in the SC. This is achieved by integrating and synchronizing logistics processes in the SC, combining the logistics capacities of the SC participants, effective inter-organizational coordination, improving planning and implementing integrated planning mechanisms, using a wide range of organizational and technological solutions focused on the use of modern IT technologies and creating a single information space for SCM [39]. Integration of different types provides a synergistic effect in the SC, which cannot be obtained by local optimization to detriment of system efficiency or solving specific problems in the functional areas of logistics. In practice, this is always a project of strategic development and transformation of the existing SC, including new principles of the organization of SCM, improving the mechanisms of inter-organizational interaction of participants and integrated planning, a reengineering project that ensures the integration and synchronization of logistics processes in the SC, creating an IT infrastructure that supports the implementation of logistics concepts. Without testing these numerous management decisions through modeling, it is impossible to obtain options for organizing the SC that provide a synergistic effect. It is necessary to form the best option for implementing transformations in the SC. This requires systematic strategic SC modeling, and modern simulation provides such opportunities for analysis and synthesis of efficient and integrated SC.

The article explores the possibilities of using hybrid simulation for integrated SC.

2 Background

Literature offers different qualitative and quantitative supply chain modeling methods: analytical methods, simulation and modeling (S&M), physical experiments, heuristics, etc. Depending on the goals, various combinations of optimization, computer simulation, heuristics, and statistics are used.

Several studies performed benchmarking of the applicability of different simulation paradigms for supply chain examination. Tako and Robinson [41] studied the application of discrete event simulation (DES) and system dynamics (SD) as decision-making support systems in the field of logistics and supply chain management taking account of the nature of addressed tasks and the level of management. In particular, the authors showed that SD is the leader in bullwhip effect analysis tasks, with the same application frequency as DES in studying information sharing and return flows. DES is used more often than SD for studying SC structures and tactical and operational tasks. The authors' shared view is that both DES and SD may be actively used to achieve SC strategic planning goals.

The status and prospects of supply chain simulation were analyzed in a review by Oliveira, Lima and Montevechi [31], which discussed the most popular application of mono methods (DES, SD, ABMS) in scientific publications and determined the prospects of hybrid simulation modeling. Kersten and Saeed [20] have reached similar conclusions. The authors examined the application of various simulation methods for the description of core processes in a supply chain (as per SCOR reference process model) and pointed out the fragmented nature of the well-known models, since only a few studies examine more than one SC process. It proved that simulation tools were more often used for improvement and reengineering of individual processes rather than for complex analysis of synergies in the performance of integrated supply chains.

ABMS, DES and SD paradigms have essentially different points of view on the modeling of the structure and dynamics of a supply chain for different representations [26]. DES best works for describing network configurations and core processes in a supply chain and is wildly used in case studies [7, 11, 13, 29, 42–45]. Modeling by core processes (Plan, Source, Make and Deliver) and subprocesses in a supply chain is based on a reference process model using SCOR recommendations. Barnett and Miller [4] described the architectural components used to implement the distributed supply chain modeling tool (e-SCOR), and e-SCOR applications that demonstrate how businesses are modeled and analyzed to determine the validity of alternative, virtual business models. Herrmann et al. [19] described a new supply chain modeling framework that follows the SCOR model. The development and application of e-SCOR technique are presented in Chatfield et al. [9, 15, 30, 33, 40].

Application of SD in studying supply chains and engineering activities helps to study fluctuations in supply chains, the bullwhip effect; show complex interaction in managing material, finance and information flows when making managerial decisions. Several studies address adaptive SC modeling using SD methods [1, 6, 12,

23]. Angerhofer and Angelides [1] suggested a system dynamics model of collaborative supply chains highlighting such model components as agents, interconnections system (topology), interrelations system (cooperation levels), processes, supporting technology and business strategy. Langroodi and Amiri [23] investigated supplier–buyer relationships in each level of five-level multi-product supply chain depending on the operational costs and in conditions of non-stationary demand. Crowe et al. [12] studied disruptions of supplies in three echelon food retail supply chain. Therefore, system dynamics best fits the object-based approach to SC decomposition. SD and DES reproduce (emulate) the actual performance of logistics infrastructure at various levels of aggregation of SC objects or processes.

Behdani [5] evaluated paradigms for modeling supply chains as complex socio-technical systems. At micro-level author highlighted such systemic properties of supply chains as numerousness and heterogeneity, local interactions, nestedness, adaptiveness. At macro-level supply chains have such properties as emergence, self-organization, co-evolution, path dependency. Author concluded that agent-based modeling and simulation (ABMS) covers these properties most of all.

The dynamics of collaborative supply chains and behavior of supply chain partners were studied in Baratt [3, 16, 24]. ABMS methodology was proposed to address the lack of methodologies supporting collaborative supply chain planning. It was shown in review [37] that capabilities of the ABMS method in exploring complex cooperation between supply chain partners related to organizational and technological changes in a supply chain, information and knowledge sharing have been understudied. Hernández et al. [18] considered the technologies of multi-agent systems as a powerful modeling tool for all kinds of complexities that arise in the process of planning supply chains during negotiations in the context of cooperation. In paper [26] author concluded that ABMS best works for representing processes and occurrences of inter-organizational coordination within a supply chain. Arvitrida et al. [2] examined competition and collaboration in supply chains using ABMS. The proposed model could assess supply chain revenue and supply chain service level depending on collaboration strategy including duration of collaboration between supplier and manufacturer and manufacturers' number of sourcing and competition behavior.

Ponte et al. [35] used agent-based model of the four-echelon supply chain to prove that decision-making process requires evolving "from a reductionist approach (where the overall strategy is the sum of individual strategies) to a holistic approach (where global optimization is sought through collaboration)". Additionally, authors applied the theory of constraints to define an appropriate framework and the Drum–Buffer–Rope method to integrate supply chain processes and synchronize decisions.

Long [25] confirmed that inter-organizational collaborative simulation requires covering the knowledge of agent, flow and process to qualifiedly represent the supply chain network operation. For this purpose, author proposed a multi-methodological collaborative simulation framework, in which a multi-agent system is adopted to represent the inter-organizational structure of a supply chain network; the three flows of material, information and time are enabled to represent the operational mechanisms; and the processes are used to represent the micro behaviors of agents.

Compensatory combination of SC simulation paradigms was addressed in several studies [14, 21, 27, 28, 36]. Hennies et al. [17] offered the mesoscopic approach for modeling supply chains that combines discrete impulse-like flows with piecewise constant flow rates. Palma-Mendoza [32] built a hybrid SC model, using different modeling paradigms at different levels of representation (SD was used for aggregated model and DES for more detailed model). Castilho et al. [8] proposed a hierarchically integrated set of models consisting of a system dynamic model to support strategic decisions, an analytical-optimization model to support tactical decisions, and a discrete event model to support decisions at the operational level. Various combinations of agents and processes in hybrid SC models are discussed in Chatfield [10, 22, 25, 34].

However, literature analysis has shown that the presented supply chain models are fragmentary and do not cover a broad class of SC design and strategic transformation tasks sufficiently. The current task is to create a general supply chain simulation model that can be applied in supply chain transformation projects.

3 Proposed Approach

The integrated nature of activity within a supply chain and systemic representation of its issues require the concurrent achievement of a number of goals focused on integration and the systemic representation of a supply chain: the alignment and optimization of key business processes by adding more value (a supply chain as a set of interacting processes), management of interrelated material, finance and information flows, and inter-organizational coordination or collaborative interaction and cooperation of supply chain participants. Description of a supply chain as an integral whole from the viewpoint of a systemic approach calls for studying the aggregate of multiple interrelated structures, flows, processes, participants and coordination mechanisms. The conceptualization, structuring and detailing of objects and processes in a supply chain may be performed from any angle of vision depending on the addressed tasks. In real tasks of supply chain analysis and synthesis, configuration and supply chain development analysis, these representations may overlap and complete each other. It is also necessary to address the static and dynamic descriptions of a supply chain in conceptual modeling, in addition to structural descriptions.

Comprehensive SCM challenges require a combined use of different modeling methods. A description of a supply chain, as shown above, should combine representation methods for network structures, processes, flows, cooperation and inter-organizational coordination and many other occurrences or phenomena in the description of dynamic supply chains are considered: object-based, configuration/network-based, process-based, and logistics coordination levels. Composite simulation models allow combining simulation approaches for creating more adequate supply chain models.

This defines a compensatory (composite) combination of simulation paradigms in high-level SC models based on the above proposed conceptual model. DES and

SD are used to describe SC logistic processes and some properties of adaptive SC (SD). The iterative optimization simulation design procedures developed by applying heuristics are more efficient in management consulting and are usually tested on solutions for network structure optimization and SC logistics process modeling.

Process and system dynamic simulation models can be more detailed depending on addressable tasks of supply chain analysis and synthesis. Agent-based modeling is used to model inter-organizational coordination between supply chain partners.

The general methodology for constructing conceptual SC models is based on the description of the network structure and configuration of the supply chain and the process approach to the decomposition of the SC and includes the following descriptions and stages of forming a simulation model, in which the following parameters are specified:

- Setting the forecast characteristics of demand.
- Network structure of the logistics system. Structure of input and output material flows.
- Description of the spatial structure of the system with reference to the map of the territory. Location of intermediate storage and transshipment points.
- Description of material flows or the structure of dynamic logistics objects that are moved and stored in the system, volume-time characteristics of material flows, rules for processing cargo flows, models for combining and separating material flows in network nodes.
- Detailed processes based on the SCOR model. Algorithms, time characteristics, and the cost of performing operations in network nodes. Logistics processes are asynchronous and are defined in the SC model as a description of parallel and interconnected processes.
- Description of supply chain management strategies. Inventory control and management policies related to the nodes of the network structure of the CPU.
- Characteristics of transport channels (participants in the transport process, type of transport, routes, tariffs, etc.). Transport policies and parameters.
- Description of the mechanisms used for interaction and inter-organizational coordination of supply chain participants.
- Creating output characteristics and performance indicators of the modeled logistics system.

The network configuration of the supply chain can be refined in a series of studies, based on the use of optimization models. The selected configuration is embedded in the description of the SC structure, and is supplemented with policies, as well as a detailed description of processes and material flows based on the object and process approach to SC decomposition.

The SCOR reference model is basic for the process model. The SCOR reference model consists of processes at three hierarchical levels that help integrate the supply chain from supplier to customer. At the first level, the SCOR models distinguish five main types of processes (Plan, Source, Make, Deliver, and Return), which are defined for the top level of the description of all supply chain operations. The SCOR reference model defines the structure and content of the supply chain model through these five different management processes. All SC entities, such as the supplier, manufacturer, distributor, and seller in the supply chain, can be described using these five processes. At levels 2 and 3, these processes can be detailed.

However, the SCOR model is a static tool that does not include any capabilities for dynamic SC analysis and active reengineering of business processes using quantitative methods for analyzing SC performance indicators and dynamic parameters.

The integration of simulation modeling and the SCOR reference model of operations provides advantages for the formation of a common simulation methodology for solving a wide range of supply chain management tasks.

The e-SCOR technique offers and supports a common methodology and hierarchical structure for modeling processes in supply chains, based on the conceptual structure of the SCOR reference model, the building blocks of which combine standard processes from the SCOR model and simulation models of multiple processes in supply chains, performed at various levels of detail, most often implemented using the DES process simulation technique (as well as ABMS), which provide not only improvement, but also synchronization of processes in the SC. When modeling the supply chain, a quantitative analysis of the efficiency of business processes is carried out, which allows you to analyze the order lead time, delivery accuracy and delivery speed, and other indicators defined in the SCOR recommendations, as well as to identify bottlenecks in the processes, and problems with the synchronization of processes in the SC.

The scenario study of collaborative supply chains and defining strategies for inter-organizational interaction and cooperation of supply chain participants using ABMS is based on the reference model of the maturity of inter-organizational relations "4C", in which [24] levels and models of maturity of inter-organizational interaction of SC counterparties: communication, coordination, collaboration, and cooperation, corresponding to the integration of processes, information exchange, joint decision-making based on trust, the formation of a community of equal partners demonstrating commitment to common strategic goals). The conceptual foundations for building a multi-agent SC model are presented in the paper [38].

Key phases of the iterative optimization and simulation design procedure of supply chain include:

- a preliminary synthesis of the SC structure through optimization;
- a detailed simulation of SC processes and scenario analysis of simulation results;
- SC optimization (reducing multiple scenarios with the optimization function built into the simulator);
- SC engineering and scenario analysis using heuristics and simulation considering additional risk factors (stress testing).

The effective modeling constructs of developing supply chains build on the principles of a composite combination of system dynamic, process-based, and agent-based simulation models. Composite dynamic SC models function based on a single model and information framework, thus enabling to arrange information sharing processes and interaction mechanisms between the model-based system representations. The top level of a model layer represents the logistics infrastructure of a supply chain and the business environment where economic agents manifest their individual behavior and which predefines decision-making rules, agents' experience, knowledge, and cooperation strategies. In turn, the model layer, which describes behavior and interaction between agents, launches the processes of self-organization, cooperation strategy, and new organizational forms that define overall supply chain performance and management. Such an approach to building multi-model complexes based on composite simulation models allows studying the dynamics and development of a supply chain by using interconnection of model strata in the examined organizational system [26].

4 Case-Study

To illustrate the applicability of the approach presented in this paper we consider a supply chain design case for an online home appliances retailer operating on Russian market. Currently the company operates in Moscow region only but is considering expansion into new regions within Central and Povolzhsky Federal Districts. The key questions the supply chain model should answer are:

- How many distribution centers (DC) are required to serve the demand?
- Where should they be located?
- What is the service zone for each DC?
- What transportation mode should be used for each leg of the distribution network?
- What storage and handling capacity is required?
- What cyclic and safety stock should be kept in each DC?
- What will be the cost of the whole distribution network? What will be the profit?

4.1 Conceptual Modeling

In this section we describe a conceptual model of the supply chain according to the proposed methodology.

Demand Characteristics

To estimate demand historical order data is used: the average number of orders per month and the average items per order. These numbers are be scaled based on population data to new regions. Historic data shows high variability of the order size that can be described by Poisson distribution.

To be competitive on a crowded online retail market the company must ensure that the order fulfillment time is within 2 days.

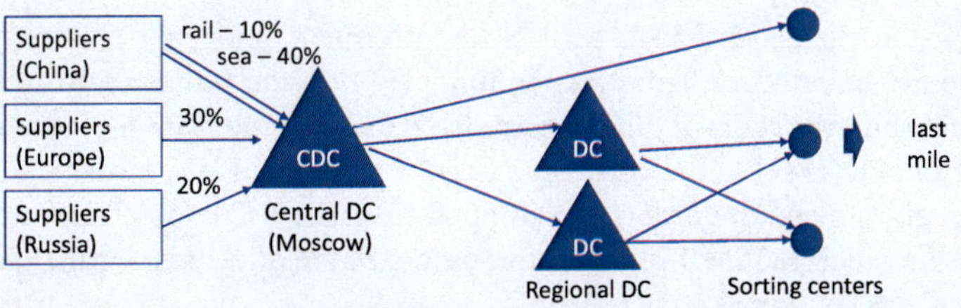

Fig. 1 Network structure of the logistics system

Network Structure of the Logistics System Structure of Material Flows

Currently the goods are delivered from the central warehouse to customer locations and self-pickup points operated by the logistics service providers. Local sorting centers will be established in major cities to split the material flow into different logistics channels in the last mile (Fig. 1). These sorting centers are considered as demand endpoints in this case study, so the demand forecast is aggregated by sorting center.

To guarantee the order fulfillment time below 2 days the company must establish regional warehouses (distribution centers) to hold the stock close to the customers. Considering the processing time at the fulfillment, sorting and last-mile stages, the transportation should not take more than 1 day. This converts to approximately 500 km distance limit for the leg between a DC and a sorting center.

The regional DCs are supplied from the central DC located near Moscow. This allows to consolidate orders to suppliers and simplifies importing operations. This DC is also servicing orders from Moscow region. Some of the newly added regions can be served from here as well.

Most goods sold by the company originate from China. Currently 80% of such goods are shipped via sea and 20% via rail in standard containers. The sea route terminates in Finland from where the goods are transported with trucks to the Moscow DC. The rail route flows through a multi-modal terminal near Moscow. Approximately 30% of goods are shipped by European suppliers. The remaining 20% of goods come from local suppliers.

The company sells multiple product categories. Since they all share the same distribution network and are assumed to have similar demand patterns in regions, the products were aggregated into one category. The average number of items per pallet is 20.

Supply Chain Processes and Inventory Control Policies

The supply chain operates according to the Source Stocked Product and Deliver Stocked Product process as described in the SCOR model. The end customers (consumers) cannot be incorporated into the model directly. Instead, they are aggregated to nearest sorting center. Such aggregated demand points are represented as customers in the model. The customer's order fulfillment time requirements are translated to the Expected Lead Time for the modeled demand points (sorting centers). Each sorting center is ordering the consolidated daily demand for a given city.

The regional DCs serve the sorting centers' orders on a FIFO basis. Due to strict lead time requirements the orders are shipped from the DC daily. The regional DC must maintain stock required to fulfill the orders of the allocated sorting centers. A simple Min/Max (S, s) policy is used.

The regional DCs are supplied from the central DC, which also is also using the Min/Max policy. The central DC sources the goods from the suppliers according to the breakdown shown in Fig. 1. Supply constraints can be ignored for the purpose of this case study.

Characteristics of the Transport Channels

Delivery from DCs to sorting centers uses trucks of different capacities (20, 5 and 1.5 ton). The shipments must be made daily to keep the order fulfillment time within the limit. The choice of a truck for a particular route is based on the daily demand. The transportation rate is 60 Rubles per km per a 20-ton truck (50 and 40 Rubles for smaller trucks).

Delivery from Central DC to regional DCs and from Local Suppliers to DCs employs 20- and 5-ton trucks with the same rates. Delivery from European distributor is also using 20-ton trucks.

Shipments from China come via rail and sea routes. For these routes, flat rates of 200 and 150 Rubles per pallet are used. The delivery via sea route takes much longer compared to the rail route (70 days vs 20 days on average).

The Choice of the Performance Indicators

The economic KPIs such as profit and total cost are commonly used to compare the alternative supply chain networks. The choice of the main KPI, will it be profit or cost, determines the ability of the model to support commercial decisions in addition to logistics decisions. For example, what market coverage or what service level is profitable to maintain. In our case demand is fixed, so there is no difference between profit- and cost-based network design.

But cost alone is not enough to guide the final decision. In our case the second most important KPI is the service level, which is defined as the proportion of orders that are delivered within the lead time expected by the end customer (Expected Lead Time, or ELT Service Level). In addition, we can use the aggregated order lead times for all orders to explore the problematic areas of the distribution network.

The choice of a right transportation mode for a route requires also to consider the vehicle capacity utilization metric.

Finally, when setting the inventory control parameters, the dynamic inventory levels, or aggregated metrics, such as demand lost due to out-of-stock or late orders, must be considered.

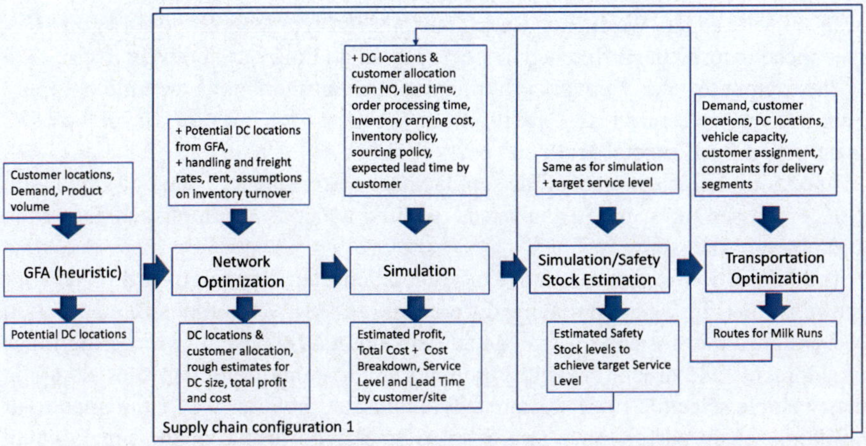

Fig. 2 Phases of the supply chain design

4.2 Model Implementation

To implement the proposed conceptual model, we use the Anylogistix software (ALX). The final supply chain design is obtained via a series of experiments using analytical, heuristic or simulation-based approaches (Fig. 2).

The preliminary synthesis of the supply chain structure involves two phases: the Greenfield Analysis (GFA) and the Network Optimization.

The GFA experiment in Anylogistix employs the Center of Gravity method to find the best locations for DCs servicing the demand based on an extremely limited amount of data: customer locations, demand, and product volume/weight characteristics only. The required number of DCs must also be provided. The outputs of the GFA experiment are the proposed DC locations, the groups of customers serviced from each DC, and a distribution of demand according to specified distance bands. We found that minimum 3 regional DCs in addition to the Central DC are required to deliver orders on time.

The second phase is Network optimization which is implemented in ALX as an uncapacitated facility location-allocation model solved by CPLEX solver. This experiment input uses potential DC locations to choose from and cost data that includes handling and freight rates and inventory holding cost. The basic model in ALX accounts only for a pre-specified safety stock level and for a seasonal inventory that can appear in a multi-period model. The space required to hold cyclic stock is not considered. However, one can define custom constraints, that can estimate this space and properly account for the corresponding storage cost in the objective function. This requires an assumption on the inventory turnover rate for each DC (1 turn per month in our case).

We specified the DC locations proposed by the GFA experiment as candidate locations. In our case the proposed locations were appropriate, so no more alternative locations were added. We did not use any customer assignments proposed by the GFA since these ignored the difference in storage and handling rates between DCs.

The output of the Network Optimization experiment is a complete supply chain network structure (Fig. 3) with rough estimates for inventory levels and DC capacities, as well as total profit and cost (Table 1).

To obtain a better estimate of the supply chain performance, a detailed simulation of SC processes and scenario analysis is required which is accomplished during the third phase of the study.

The simulation requires a much more detailed data compared to the Network Optimization (Fig. 2). Most notable differences are the use of order size distribution for each customer instead of aggregated demand, lead times and processing times for shipments and orders, inventory policy specifications, sourcing rules, shipping rules, vehicle selection rules. As a result, simulation provides a dynamic picture of the supply chain performance at a detailed level. The results of the supply chain simulation (Fig. 4) suggest that the baseline structure obtained from the Network Optimization experiment cannot provide the required service level for all customers.

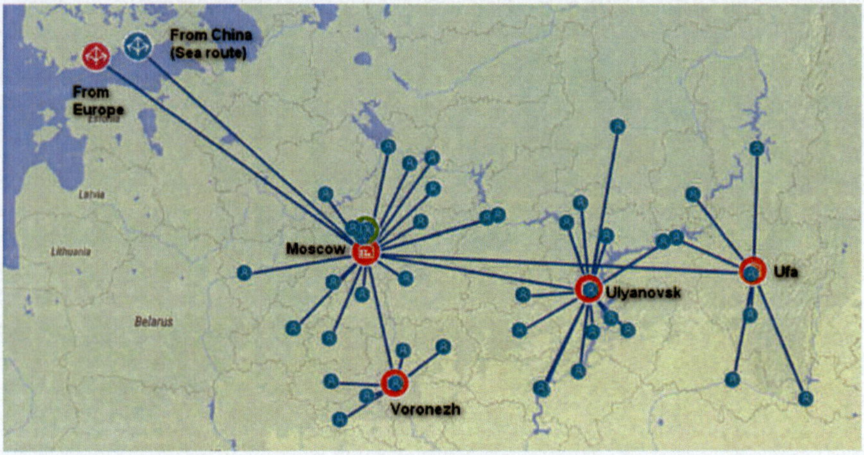

Fig. 3 Supply chain structure from Network Optimization

Table 1 Supply chain cost estimates from Network Optimization

	Amount. million Rubles
Revenue	6 161
DC rent cost	6.7
Transportation cost	48
Supply cost	4 005
Outbound processing cost	2.9
Inventory holding cost	3.3
Profit	2 095

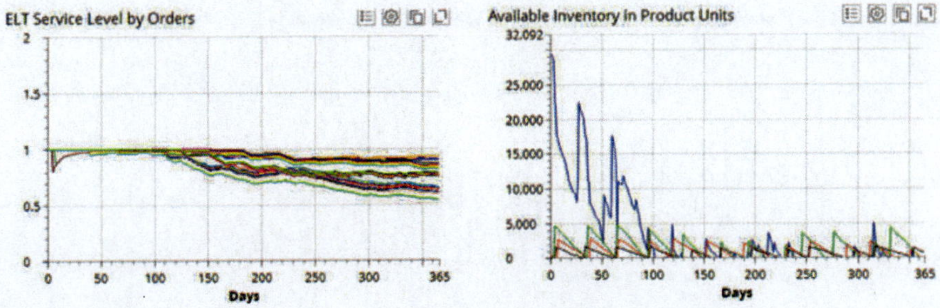

Fig. 4 Service level and available inventory from simulation experiment

This is caused by an insufficient safety stock level at the central DC. Combined with a long lead time to suppliers, this leads to long periods of out-of-stock.

The third phase of the supply chain design involves experiments with the model aimed at improvement of the supply chain performance. In our study we employed simulation-based optimization to estimate the safety stock levels for all DCs (Safety stock estimation experiment in ALX). Next, we considered introduction of milk-run routes for some customers to improve the vehicle capacity utilization. The routes were obtained from the Transportation optimization experiment in ALX. The results are provided in Table 2 and Fig. 5. The Facility Cost estimate from NO is quite close to the results from the simulation. Otherwise, an update for inventory turnover and re-run of the network optimization would be necessary. This could potentially change the customer assignments and require a further re-run of the simulation model as well. The improved supply chain designs updated with safety stock policies and milk runs have worse performance compared to the baseline due to higher inventory carrying cost, however the baseline is certainly unacceptable in terms of customer service.

Table 2 Supply chain KPIs from network optimization and simulation experiments

KPI	Baseline (estimate from NO)	Baseline (estimate from Simulation)	+ Safety stock optimization	+ Milk Runs
Facility cost	6.7	7.0	6.2	6.3
Inventory carrying cost	3.3	11.4	31.4	29.7
Sourcing	4 005	3 517	3 769	3 913
Outbound processing cost	2.9	2.8	2.9	3.0
Transportation cost	48.3	153.7	201.4	165.8
Revenue	6 161	6 015	6 105	6 258
Profit	2 095	2 322	2 094	2 141

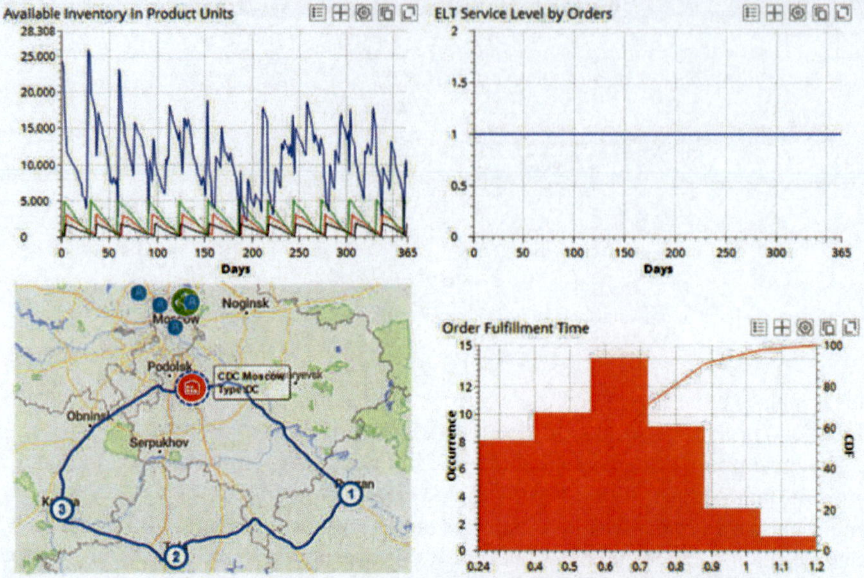

Fig. 5 Service and inventory levels after safety stock optimization and introducing milk runs

The fourth phase of supply chain design involves scenario analysis and simulation considering additional risk factors. In the supply chain under study the most prominent risk factor is a long (70 days on average) supplier lead time for the sea route. To estimate the possible impact, we simulated a temporary increase in demand by 100% for a short period (days 59–89) using Risk analysis experiment in ALX. Figure 6 shows the simulated results for the baseline supply chain design (40% of goods are sourced via the sea route) compared to an alternative design where all import from China is switched to the rail route, that is just 20 days on average. Our results show that the alternative design is robust to changes in demand. There is a trade-off however: the transportation cost has increased from 165 Million Rubles to 170 Million Rubles due to higher freight rates for the rail route. The bulk of

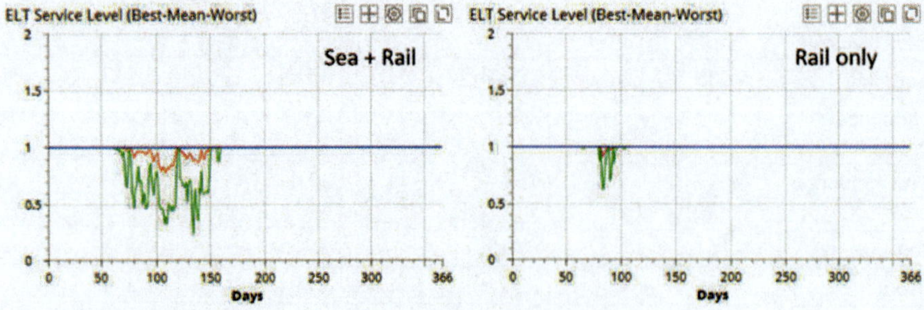

Fig. 6 Supply chain response to a short-term spike in demand

transportation cost is however related to DC-DC and last-mile routes, so the relative change is only 3% despite the 30% difference in freight rates for sea and rail routes.

5 Conclusion

The authors proposed a method of constructing and analysis of conceptual supply chain models, which is based on multilayered representations of supply chain structures and processes that describe strategic planning and development of the supply chain and logistics infrastructure. The following base levels of the supply chain representation were considered: object-based, configuration/network-based, process-based, and logistics coordination levels.

The proposed approach was tested and the set of scenario studies based on iterative simulation and optimization design procedures and simulation modeling was carried out.

The study has shown that efficient system and simulation solutions in supply chain management rest on the following:

- principles of managerial integration and balanced strategic, tactical and operational decisions, and principles of alignment of models of different levels;
- systemic representation and simulation of the logistics and supply chain as a basis for creating a single model framework;
- composite system dynamic and agent-based supply chain models based on integral SCM paradigm, which allows describing network structure, logistic processes, performance of a supply chain, and its measurable characteristics, as well as the behavior of supply chain agents, their cooperation strategies and logistics technologies based on collaboration.

Composite simulation models include descriptions of transforming supply chains development (by using SD and DES constructs) and descriptions representing inter-organizational coordination processes of supply chain agents based on ABMS.

Such modeling constructs help to study the structural and dynamic aspects of SC, solve the tasks of long-term development and efficient transformation of supply chains, evaluate inventory and transportation management policies, achieving overall supply chain efficiency and synergies, align strategic managerial decisions at inter-organizational levels, and search for efficient long-term cooperation strategies between supply chain participants.

References

1. Angerhofer, B. J., & Angelides, M. C. (2006). A model and a performance measurement system for collaborative supply chains. *Decision Support Systems, 42*, 283–301.
2. Arvitrida, N. I., Robinson, S., & Tako, A. A. (2015). How do competition and collaboration affect supply chain performance? An agent-based modeling approach. In *Proceedings of the 2015 Winter Simulation Conference* (pp. 218–229).
3. Baratt, M. (2004). Understanding the meaning of collaboration in the supply chain. *Supply chain management: An International Journal, 9*(1), 30–42.
4. Barnett, M. W. & Miller, C. J. (2000). Analysis of the virtual enterprise using distributed supply chain modeling and simulation: An application of e-SCOR. In *2000 Winter Simulation Conference (WSC)* (Vol. 1, pp. 352–355).
5. Behdani, B. (2012). Evaluation of paradigms for modeling supply chains as complex socio-technical systems. In *Proceedings of the 2012 Winter Simulation Conference* (pp. 3794–3808).
6. Bhattacharjee, S., & Cruz, J. (2015). Economic sustainability of closed loop supply chains: A holistic model for decision and policy analysis. *Decision Support Systems, 77*, 67–86.
7. Cannella, S., Lopez-Campos, M., Dominguez, R., Ashayeri, J., & Miranda, P. A. (2015). A simulation model of a coordinated decentralized supply chain. In *International Transactions in Operational Research* (Vol. 22, no.4, pp. 735–756).
8. Castilho, J. A., Lang, T. E., & Peterson, D. K., Volovoi, V. (2015). Quantifying variability impacts upon supply chain performance. In *Proceedings of the 2015 Winter Simulation Conference* (pp. 1892–1903).
9. Chatfield, D. C., Harrison, T. P., & Hayya, J. C. (2006). SISCO: An object-oriented supply chain simulation system. *Decision Support Systems, 42*(1), 422–434.
10. Chatfield, D. C., Hayya, J. C., & Harrison, T. P. (2007). A multi-formalism architecture for agent-based, order-centric supply chain simulation. *Simulation Modelling Practice and Theory, 15*(2), 153–174.
11. Cigolini, R., Pero, M., Rossi, T., & Sianesi, A. (2014). Linking supply chain configuration to supply chain perfrmance: A discrete event simulation model. *Simulation Modelling Practice and Theory, 40*, 1–11.
12. Crowe, J., Mesabbah, M., & Arisha, A. (2015). Understanding the dynamic behaviour of three echelon retail supply chain disruptions. In *Proceedings of the 2015 Winter Simulation Conference* (pp. 1948–1959).
13. Cui, Y., Shi, J., & Wang, Z. (2015). Discrete event logistics systems (DELS) simulation modeling incorporating two-step remaining useful life (RUL) estimation. *Computers in Industry, 72*, 68–81.
14. Fayez, M. S., Rabelo, L., & Mollaghasemi, M. (2005). Ontologies for supply chain simulation modeling. In *Proceedings of the 2005 Winter Simulation Conference* (pp. 2364–2370). Orlando, FL: IEEE.
15. Fredrik, P. (2011). SCOR template-A simulation based dynamic supply chain analysis tool. *International Journal of Production Economics, 131*(1), 288–294.
16. Fugate, B., Sahin, F., & Menzer, J. T. (2006). Supply chain management coordination mechanisms. *Journal of Business Logistics, 27*(2), 129–161.
17. Hennies, T., Reggelin, T., Tolujew, J., & Piccut, P.-A. (2014). Mesoscopic supply chain simulation. *Journal of Computational Science, 5*, 463–470.
18. Hernández, J. E., Alemany, M. M. E., Lario, F. C., & Poler, R. (2009). A supply chain agent-based modelling methodology that supports a collaborative planning process. *Innovar: Revista de Ciencias Administrativas y Sociales, 19* (34), 99–120.
19. Herrmann, J. W., Lin, E., & Pundoor, G. (2003). Supply chain simulation modeling using the supply chain operations reference model. In *Proceedings of the ASME 2003 Design Engineering Technical Conference*, Chicago, Illinois, USA.
20. Kersten W., & Saeed, M. A. (2014). A SCOR based analysis of simulation in supply chain management. In *Proceedings 28th European Conference on Modeling and Simulation.* Brescia, Italy.

21. Kim, W. S. (2009). Effects of a trust mechanisms on complex adaptive supply networks: An agent-based social simulation study. *Journal of Artificial Societies and Social Simulation, 12*(4), 2.
22. Krejci, C. (2015). Hybrid simulation modeling for humanitarian relief chain coordination. *Journal of Humanitarian Logistics and Supply Chain Management, 5*(3), 325–347.
23. Langroodi, R. R. P., & Amiri, M. (2016). A system dynamics modeling approach for a multi-level, multi-product, multi-region supply chain under demand uncertainty. *Expert Systems with Applications, 51*, 231–244.
24. Lejeune, M. A., & Yakova, N. (2005). On characterizing the 4 C's in supply chain management. *Journal of Operations Management, 23*(1), 81–100.
25. Long, Q. (2016). A multi-methodological collaborative simulation for inter-organizational supply chain networks. *Knowledge-Based Systems, 96*, 84–95.
26. Lychkina, N. (2016). Synergetics and development processes in socio-economic systems: Search for effective modeling constructs. *Business Informatics, 1*, 66–79.
27. Lychkina N. N. (2018). Strategic development and dynamic models of supply chains: search for effective model constructions, lecture notes in networks and systems. In *Proceedings of SAI Intelligent Systems Conference (IntelliSys)* (Vol. 2, no. 2, pp. 175–185). London: Springer.
28. Lychkina, N. N. (2018). Simulation of dynamic supply chains. *Logistics and Supply Chain Management, 6*(89), 137–152.
29. Mohd, R., Kaanodiya, K. K., & Sachin, K. V. (2017). Modeling of supply chain dynamics: A lingo based three-tier distribution approach. *International Journal of Education & Applied Sciences Research, 4*(1), 24–32.
30. Ntabe, E. N., LeBela, L., Munsona, A. D., & Santa-Eulalia, L. A. (2015). A systematic literature review of the supply chain operations reference (SCOR) model application with special attention to environmental issues. *International Journal of Production Economics, 169*, 310–332.
31. Oliveira, J. B., Lima, R. S., & Montevechi, J. A. B. (2016). Perspectives and relationships in supply chain simulation: a systematic literature review. *Simulation Modelling Practice and Theory, 62*, 166–191.
32. Palma-Mendoza, J. A. (2017). Hybrid DES/SD simulation conceptual framework for supply chain analysis. *International Journal of Data Science; Geneva, 2*(3), 246–259.
33. Persson, F. (2011). SCOR template–a simulation based dynamic supply chain analysis tool. *International Journal of Production Economics, 131*(1), 288–294.
34. Persson, F., Bartoll, C., Ganovic, A., Lidberg, M., Nilsson, M., Wibaeus, J., & Winge, F. (2012). Supply chain dynamics in the scor model–a simulation modeling approach. In *Proceedings of the 2012 Winter Simulation Conference* (pp.1–12). Berlin.
35. Ponte, B., Costas, J., Puche, J., de la Fuente, D., & Pinoa, R. (2016). Holism versus reductionism in supply chain management: An economic analysis. *Decision Support Systems, 86*, 83–94.
36. Rabelo, L., Eskandari, H., Shaalan, T., & Helal, M. (2007). Value chain analysis using hybrid simulation and AHP. *International Journal of Production Economics, 105*(2), 536–547.
37. Santa-Eulalia, L. A., Halladjian, G., D'Amours, S., & Frayret, J. M. (2011). Integrated methodological frameworks for modeling agent-based advanced supply chain planning systems: A systematic literature review. *Journal of Industrial Engineering and Management, 4*(4), 624–668.
38. Sergeyev, V., Lychkina, N. N. (2019). Agent-based modelling and simulation of inter-organizational integration and coordination of supply chain participants. In *2019 IEEE 21st Conference on Business Informatics (CBI)* (Vol. 2, pp. 436–444). IEEE Computer Society.
39. Sergeyev, V. (2014). *Supply chain management: Bachelor's and master's degree*. Uright.
40. Šitova, I., & Pečerska, J. (2017). A concept of simulation-based sc performance analysis using SCOR metrics. *Information Technology and Management Science, 20*, 85–89.
41. Tako, A. A., & Robinson, S. (2012). The application of discrete event simulation and system dynamics in the logistics and supply chain context. *Decision Support Systems, 52*, 802–815.
42. Windisch, J., Väätäinen, K., Anttila, P., Nivala, M., Laitila, J., Asikainen, A., & Sikanen, L. (2015). Discrete-event simulation of an information-based raw material allocation process for increasing the efficiency of an energy wood supply chain. *Applied Energy, 149*, 315–325.

43. Yoo, T., Cho, H., & Yücesan, E. (2010). Hybrid algorithm for discrete event simulation based supply chain optimization. *Expert Systems with Applications, 37*(3), 2354–2361.
44. Zengin, A. (2011). Modeling discrete event scalable network systems. *Information Sciences, 181*(5), 1028–1043.
45. Zengin, A., Sarjoughian, H., & Ekiz, H. (2013). Discrete event modeling of swarm intelligence based routing in network systems. *Information Sciences, 222*(10), 81–98.

Digital Products Design Pattern for Digital Platform

Evgeny Zaramenskikh and Maria Guseva

Abstract The article presents the possibility of application of modeling patterns when creating digital products. The research examines various aspects of digital products and constructs an appropriate modeling pattern based on the ArchiMate language. The study also demonstrates an example of its usage. The application of the digital product modeling pattern is illustrated by the example of the experience of a large Russian marketplace company operating in a highly competitive market in big Russian cities.

Keywords Design pattern · Digital product · Enterprise architecture

1 Introduction

The concept of a digital product has already become an important part of the definition of the digital economy, which some researchers comprehend as part of economic output derived solely or primarily from digital technologies with a business model based on digital goods or services [1].

In a rapidly changing global economic environment companies worldwide need easy-to-use tools for design, development and further implementation of the digital products. An architectural approach can be effectively applied for this purpose.

Digital products are offered to consumers in various business models because the very fact of their offering to the target audience allows solving the quite typical for digital enterprises problem of transition to the revenue growth from the audience growth [2].

Many companies start to design, develop and sell digital products within the framework of other business models. However, the presentation of digital products on the foundation of the enterprise digital platform looks especially perspective.

The appeal comes from the nature of the digital platform. The owner of the digital platform acts in the role of the "club owner" and receives commissions for the

E. Zaramenskikh (✉) · M. Guseva
HSE University, 100100 Myasnitskaya 20, Moscow, Russian Federation

E. Zaramenskikh and A. Fedorova (eds.), *Digitalization of Society, Economics and Management*, Lecture Notes in Information Systems and Organisation 53,
https://doi.org/10.1007/978-3-030-94252-6_9

transaction costs reduction when platform users are interacting. At the same time, the cost of creating an additional transaction for the platform owner is zero.

Such phenomenon makes a digital platform similar to a digital product, the classical understanding of which assumes zero costs for a creation of an additional copy and for the delivery of the product to the consumer.

Quah [3] understood a digital product as “a sequence of bits, a sequence of zeros and ones that have economic value”, additionally emphasizing on non-competitive access and unlimited scalability as the main characteristics of a digital product. The key characteristics of a digital product are arranged in such a way that the product can be effectively used within the frameworks of the digital platform as a business model.

The highest expenses in the digital product lifecycle are in the design and development phases. However, there is a reason to believe that the usage of modeling patterns will not only reduce these costs, but also make the product more transparent, manageable at all stages of the life cycle, as well as highly demanded among the target audience.

Despite the fact that a significant share of consumers consider digital products to be less valuable than physical products [4], there is a significant demand for digital products in the markets of developed and developing countries, especially among millennials [5].

The high demand for the digital products is confirmed by different studies, according to which the value received by consumers of digital products significantly exceeds the financial costs of purchasing them. Thus, according to research findings of Brynjolfsson [6], users of streaming platforms paid $120–$240 per year for access to Netflix, Hulu and HBO. However, survey participants agreed to reject access to streaming platforms only for an amount that exceeded their annual cost of access in 5–10 times.

Even higher is the value of digital products that do not have convenient offline substitutes and are regularly used by humans in daily life or when performing work functions. First of all it concerns search products, e-mail and electronic geographic maps.

It is important to understand that the reasons for buying a digital product usually are closely related to the digital platform where they are sold. The value of a digital product directly depends on the environment and conditions where the digital product can be used [7].

Thus, designing and developing a digital product in isolation from the components of the digital platform and in isolation from the architecture of the enterprise in general reduces the likelihood of getting a final product highly demanded by consumers. The usage of an architectural approach in combination with conceptual ontological modeling allows avoiding this problem.

2 Related Work

One of the options for applying conceptual ontological modeling was proposed by the author in his early work, where three levels of abstraction were considered that underlie the conceptual ontological modeling of enterprise architecture [8].

At the moment, research on the application of patterns mainly covers the issues of modeling enterprise services [9]. Nevertheless, the ArchiMate language has a Product element that includes a set of related services. In this regard, it seems possible to adapt distinct elements of service patterns in order to simulate digital products.

Directly related to the modeling of digital products and their corresponding value is research on consumer trust in relation to the architectural approach. The authors demonstrate the possibilities of modeling consumer trust using modeling patterns formed on the ArchiMate language (for example, the Trust Composition Pattern, The Intention Belief Pattern, etc.).The work demonstrates a high degree of adaptability and applicability of ArchiMate in modeling, including fairly abstract economic and social concepts in conjunction with the traditional concept of enterprise architecture [10].

A number of works indirectly consider the conceptual ontological modeling of products in the context of data modeling of a digital platform [11] and modeling of the consumers' economic behavior [12].

3 Digital Product Pattern

3.1 A Development of the Digital Product Pattern

Previously the author proposed a metamodel for modeling enterprise architecture. This metamodel was based on the ArchiMate language and included the various elements of the business layer, application layer, technology layer, motivation expansion and strategic expansion, and the links between them. Based on the metamodel a digital service modeling pattern was proposed. This pattern can be taken as a basis for creating a pattern for a digital product.

The previously developed digital service modeling pattern has some superfluity in case of its complete transfer as the basis of the digital product pattern. Pattern objects related to technological architecture may not be described within the generated pattern.

Figure 1 shows a pattern for modeling digital services with two areas marked.

One of them includes the elements of the pattern, which will be taken as a basis for the formation of a pattern for modeling a digital product. The second one includes elements of the pattern that will not be used within the framework of the pattern being formed.

The ArchiMate language contains a Product element that can be adapted to modeling digital products. Accordingly, within the framework of this article, a digital

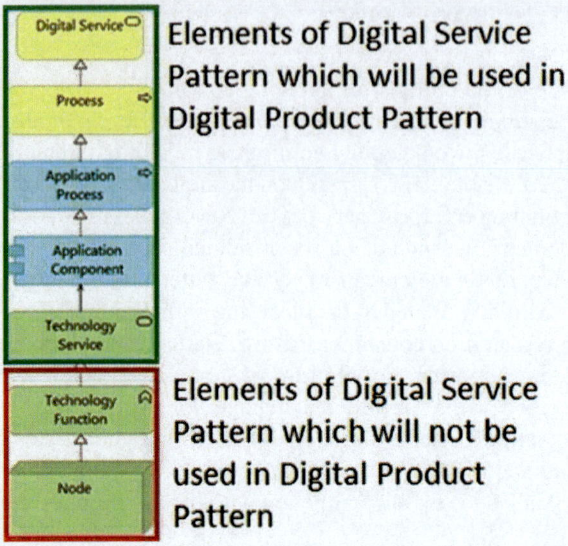

Fig. 1 Author's pattern for modeling digital services as a basis for developing a pattern for modeling digital products

product will be understood as "coherent collection of digital services and/or passive structure elements accompanied by a contract/set of agreements, which is offered as a whole to customers". Furthermore, basing on the presented definition, we will form a fragment of the developed pattern that reveals the content of the concept of "digital product" and will present it in Fig. 2.

The element Contract shown in Fig. 2 is also included in the ArchiMate notation and is defined as «formal or informal specification of an agreement between a provider and a consumer that specifies the rights and obligations associated with a product and establishes functional and non-functional parameters for interaction».

Contracts modeling in the context of enterprise architecture is discussed in detail in [13] and [14]. The authors note that effective modeling of contracts based on the ArchiMate language seems to be unrealizable without appropriate ontological extensions. However, within the framework of this study, additional detailing of the

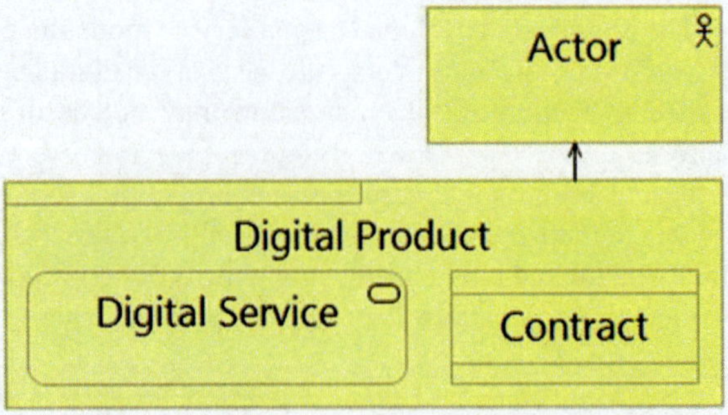

Fig. 2 A fragment of the developed pattern revealing the definition of the "digital product" concept

content of the element Contract is not required. Although in some cases it can be decomposed for ease of visualization.

Afterward, the element Value has to be defined. Some researchers believe that the concept of Value can have an association relationship both with elements of the ArchiMate core and with elements of motivation expansion. In fact, in the context of digital product modeling, the object Value becomes a kind of bridge between the business layer and the elements of motivation expansion.

Nonetheless, addition of a Value element is not a limit. To ensure the connection of a digital product not only with the architecture of the enterprise, but also with its strategic goals, the element Goal can be added to the pattern.

Figure 3 displays a BSVC Metamodel snippet illustrating the relationship of the Value element [15].

In case of need of a wider or more detailed modeling of the Value, the Value Pattern Language based on ArchiMate can be used [16]. Researchers have also noted an increasing interest in value modeling as part of an architectural approach in order to align the strategic objectives of an enterprise with its architecture. The authors offer several patterns (including Value Event Pattern, Value Subject Pattern, etc.). Based on it various types of value and their relationship with other objects of enterprise architecture can be modeled.

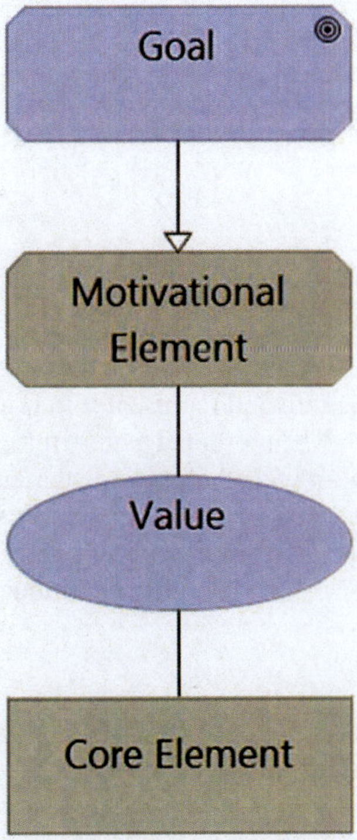

Fig. 3 A snippet of a BSVC metamodel, illustrating the relationship of the Value element

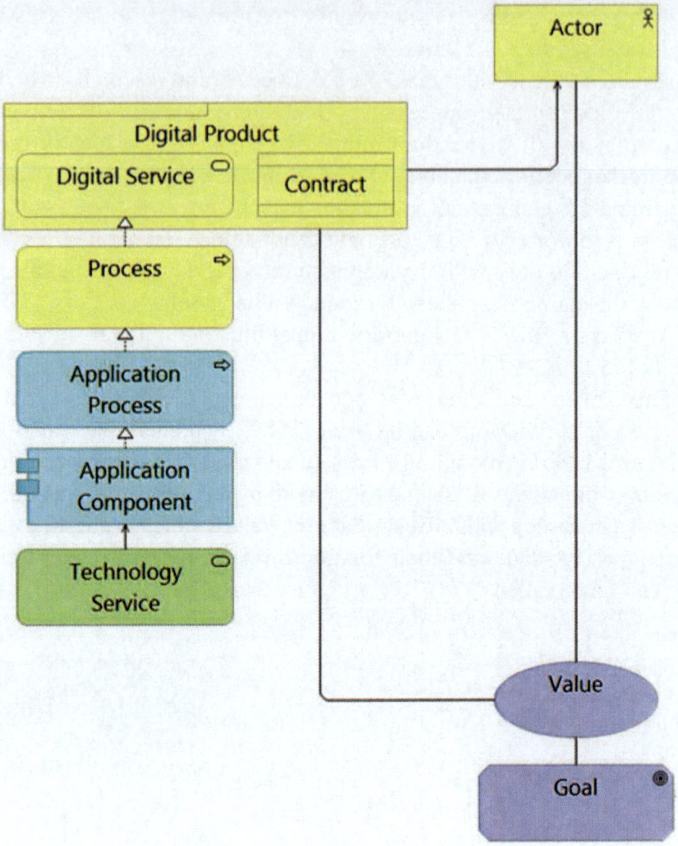

Fig. 4 Author's pattern of digital product modeling

Now, collecting all the information presented earlier, we will form a digital product pattern and represent it in Fig. 4.

The presented pattern makes it possible to trace the connection of a digital product both with the goals of the enterprise (and, accordingly, can be extended by other elements of expanding motivation), and with that segment of the enterprise architecture that ensures the value creation and delivery to the consumer within the framework of the modeled digital product.

3.2 *Modeling of a Digital Product Based on a Pattern*

The application of the digital product modeling pattern will be demonstrated on the example of a real Russian company under the conditional name LLC "Marketplace".

LLC "Marketplace" operates in a hyper-competitive market, and in some product categories the company is forced to compete with international marketplaces such as Amazon and AliExpress.

The main categories of counterparties that carry out transactions on the digital platform LLC "Marketplace" are buyers of goods, sellers and partner delivery companies. As of the beginning of 2021, the company has more than 3 million active buyers, more than 12,000 active sellers and cooperates with several hundred delivery companies operating in the largest cities in Russia.

Taking into account the hyper-competitive market environment the company's management is currently focusing on improving the customer experience and considering various options for using digital products as sources of competitive advantage.

During the analysis of the company's activities, a set of digital products recommended for implementation was formed, one of which was Premium Subscription for Consumers. The implementation of this digital product is expected to increase sales by 15% within two years of product launch.

The company's analysts predict that the closed sale model included in the product for premium subscribers will increase sales of low-demand items by providing additional discounts on them. It is expected that about 15% of sellers selling their goods through the digital platform of LLC "Marketplace" will eventually take part in closed sales at least once a quarter.

Analysts estimate that Premium Subscription for Consumers will prove to be a highly sought-after product with 500,000 active users within two years of product launch.

This digital product is also planned to be used as part of the company's advertising strategy. The Premium Subscription is expected to be played out among the company's social media subscribers. An option of launching an advertising campaign to promote the product on the popular Russian platforms Odnoklassniki and VKontakte is considered.

The Premium Subscription for Consumers is also planned to be used as compensation for consumers who have received negative customer experiences due to the fault of LLC "Marketplace". The company is currently offering its customers a 20% discount on their next purchase, but the premium status is expected to be more in demand and less costly for the enterprise in case of an incident.

Premium Subscription digital product will be sold to one category Actors—consumers. Consumers who purchase a Premium Subscription will receive 5% Bonus Points on each purchase they make. In 15 days from the date of purchase, Bonus Points can be used to pay up to 99% of the cost of a new purchase. Currently Bonus Points are credited only for certain categories of purchases for 1% of its value.

Consumers will also get the opportunity to participate in special closed sales where only premium subscribers will have access to.

At these sales low-demanded goods with big discount (up to 90%) and popular goods with a relatively small discount (10–30%) are planned to be offered for sale.

Consumers who purchase a premium subscription will be able to enjoy free shipping regardless of the purchase amount. At the moment, free shipping is carried out only if the purchase price exceeds 1000 rubles. Otherwise, the cost of delivery varies from 99 to 500 rubles. At the same time, Consumers will be able to indicate a convenient delivery time. Ordinary buyers can choose only the desired delivery day, but not the exact delivery time.

Sellers are secondary clients of the digital product Premium Subscription for Consumers, who will receive a free opportunity to offer their products for participation in a closed sale. The participation in closed sale aimed to significantly increase sales, rise customer loyalty to a particular seller and provide an opportunity to sell unclaimed products.

Thus, a digital product Premium Subscription for Consumers can be represented as a combination of the following components:

- Service of Special Sales for Premium Subscribers;
- Bonus Points as a Service;
- Shipping Service;
- Commercial Agreement;
- Premium Status;
- Discount Sales for Premium Subscribers (only for Sellers).

Relating to the strategy planned the digital product Premium Subscription for Consumers is going to be used on the already existing digital platform of LLC "Marketplace". Nowadays various digital services are available to users of this digital platform. However, only a number of Application Processes of the digital platform will be used within the analyzed digital product: Sending Notifications about Special Sales, Shipment Management, Bonus Points Accounting, Personalized Catalog, Making Payments.

The indicated Application Process platforms are implemented through the corresponding components including Mobile Application, Marketplace Website, Payment System.

Consumers and Sellers are expected to use both personal computers and smartphones and/or tablets to access the services that are part of the digital product Premium Subscription for Consumers.

Figure 5 demonstrates an example of a model of a digital product for LLC "Marketplace" formed on the basis of the pattern proposed by the author earlier.

4 Conclusion

The example given in the article demonstrates the application of the digital product modeling pattern based on the ArchiMate modeling language, which is further used to build a digital product model. The presented pattern allows coverage of the relationship of a digital product with elements of enterprise architecture, as well as determination of its impact on the achievement of enterprise goals.

As part of this study:

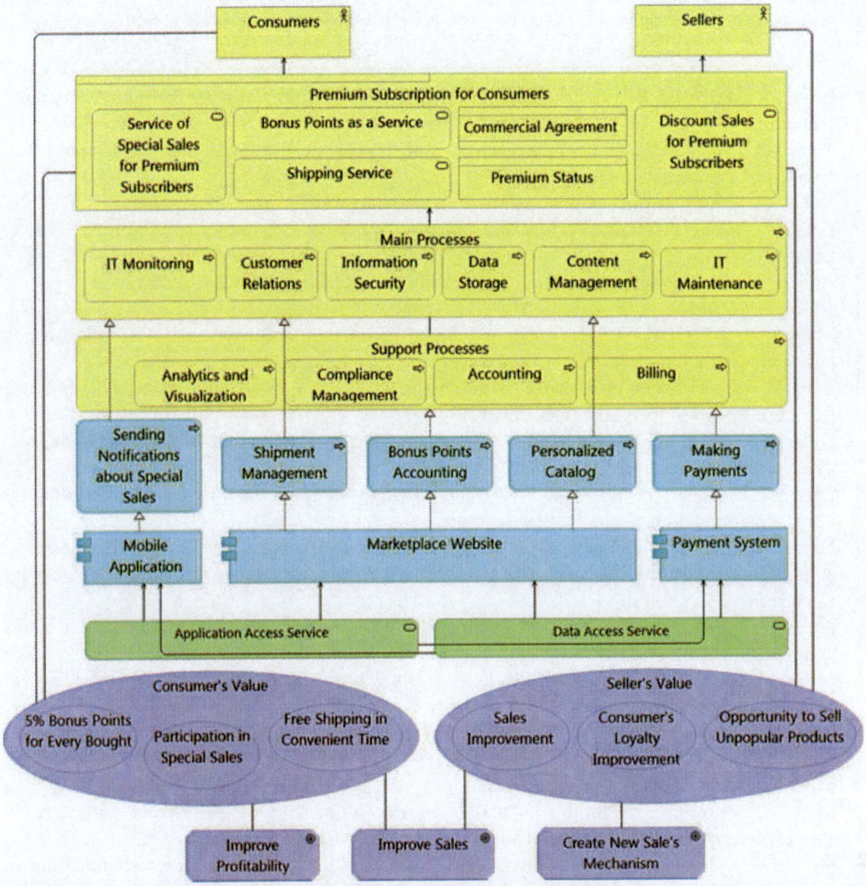

Fig. 5 Example of a model of a digital product for LLC "Marketplace"

- A practical example of a digital product pattern development is demonstrated.
- The case of a big Russian company LLC "Marketplace" and its digital platform is presented.
- An example of the application of the modeling pattern for the development of a digital product, which will be offered to users of the digital platform in the future, is presented.

References

1. Bukht, R., & Heeks, R. (2018). Defining, conceptualising and measuring the digital economy. *International Organisations Research Journal, 13*, 143–172.
2. Teece, D. J., & Linden G. (2017). Business models, value capture, and the digital enterprise. *Journal of Organization Design, 6*.
3. Quah, D. (2003). Digital goods and the new economy. CEP discussion paper: CEPDP0563 (563). Centre for Economic Performance, London School of Economics and Political Science, London, UK.
4. Atasoy, O., & Morewedge, C. K. (2018). Digital goods are valued less than physical goods. *Journal of Consumer Research, 44*(6), 1343–1357.
5. Manurung, S. P. (2018). Virtual goods and digital goods: indonesian millennial attitude towards online shopping intention (ATOSI). *Advanced Science Letters, 24*, 7172–7174.
6. Brynjolfsson, E., & Collis, A. (2019). How should we measure the digital economy? In Harvard Business Review, November–December.
7. Hamari, J., & Keronen, L. (2017). Why do people buy virtual goods: A meta-analysis. *Computers in Human Behavior, 71*, 59–69.
8. Zaramenskikh, E., & Oleynik, A. (2021). Design patterns for digital platforms/digital transformation and new challenges. Springer.
9. Nardi, J. C., de Almeida Falbo, R., & etc. (2014). An ontological analysis of service modeling at archimate's business layer. In *2014 IEEE 18th International Enterprise Distributed Object Computing Conference*.
10. Amaral, G., Sales, T. P., Guizzardi, G., Almeida, J. P. A., & etc. (2020). Modeling trust in enterprise architecture: A pattern language for archimate. In J. Grabis & D. Bork (Eds.), The Practice of Enterprise Modeling. PoEM 2020. *Lecture Notes in Business Information Processing* (vol 400). Cham: Springer.
11. Landolfi, G., et al. (2018). An ontology based semantic data model supporting a maas digital platform. in *2018 International Conference on Intelligent Systems (IS)* (pp. 896–904). Funchal: Madeira.
12. Vajda, J., Merrell, E., & Snith, B. (2019). Toward an ontology of commercial exchange. In *Proceedings of the Joint Ontology Workshops (JOWO)*. Graz.
13. Griffo, C., Almeida, J. P. A., Guizzardi, G., & etc. (2019). Service contract modeling in enterprise architecture: An ontology-based approach. In Information Systems.
14. Griffo, C., Almeida, J. P. A., Guizzardi G., & etc. (2017). From an ontology of service contracts to contract modeling in enterprise architecture. In *IEEE 21st International Enterprise Distributed Object Computing Conference (EDOC)* (pp. 40–49).
15. Azevedo, C. L. B., Iacob, M. E., Almeida, J. P. A., & etc. (2015). Modeling resources and capabilities in enterprise architecture: A well-founded ontology-based proposal for ArchiMate. *Information Systems, 54*, 235–262.
16. Sales, T. P., Roelens, B., Poels, G., & etc. (2019). A pattern language for value modeling in archiMate. In *International Conference on Advanced Information Systems Engineering (CAiSE 2019)* (pp. 230–245).

Providing Fault Tolerance of Cluster Computing Systems Based on Fault-Tolerant Dynamic Computation Planning

Evgeniy Tourouta, Mikhail Gorodnichev, Ksenia Polyantseva, and Marina Moseva

Abstract A cluster computing system is an array of computing nodes united by a certain communication environment, which, from the user's point of view, is a single computing resource. The nodes of a cluster computing system can be servers, workstations, and personal computers. Such computing systems are used to solve complex and responsible tasks in various spheres of life of modern society and must have high reliability. This paper is devoted to the organization of fault-tolerant functioning of cluster computing systems based on dynamic fault-tolerant computing planning. The proposed approach is considered on the example of a computer system corresponding to the following model. A cluster computing system contains N nodes, i.e., computing modules intended for solving applied problems, and the main computing module intended for organizing the system operation. We believe that all computing modules are identical and are single-processor, operate in multi-program mode and have the same amount of RAM. We know the set W = {Uj, j = 1, …, L} of mutually independent tasks designed to be performed by a given system.

Keywords Fault tolerance · Dispatching · Cluster computing systems · Computing planning

1 Introduction

One of the promising approaches to the construction of highly reliable computing systems is the organization of their work based on the methods of rational fault-tolerant planning of calculations in the system. The use of such methods allows at the failure of a certain number of computational modules to be executed not failed computing modules of all required tasks to achieve the necessary system reliability while taking into account constraints on the resources of each computer module and requirements for specific quality indicators of functioning of the system. In this case,

E. Tourouta · M. Gorodnichev (✉) · K. Polyantseva · M. Moseva
Moscow Technical University of Communications and Informatics, Aviamotornaya St. 8A, 111024 Moscow, Russia
e-mail: m.g.gorodnichev@mtuci.ru

E. Zaramenskikh and A. Fedorova (eds.), *Digitalization of Society, Economics and Management*, Lecture Notes in Information Systems and Organisation 53,
https://doi.org/10.1007/978-3-030-94252-6_10

the natural redundancy of the resources of each computing module (in memory and processor time), characteristic of multiprocessor computing systems, is used, which allows you not to resort to reserving the computing module or significantly reduce the number of required backup computing modules.

The methods of fault-tolerant computing planning are based on two well-known principles used in computing planning without taking into account the failures of computing modules.

1. Static planning: for a given set of tasks, plans for the distribution of these tasks across computing modules (both for the case of failure-free operation of all computing modules, and for the cases of failures of a certain number of them) They are built using certain algorithms until the computational process is activated, and then these plans are implemented, possibly repeatedly, in the process of functioning of computing systems. The development of such methods is discussed in [1–3].
2. Dynamic scheduling (dispatching): The decision to assign the tasks that make up this complex to be performed in certain computing modules is made during the computational process, for which dynamic planning algorithms are used that correspond to a certain dispatching strategy.

2 Cluster Computing System Operating Modes

2.1 *Batch Processing Mode*

The task of the set W in a clustered computing system is implemented in the form of several sessions: during each k-th session performs a batch of tasks, pre-formed tasks from the set W and the list given $A_k = \{U_r, r = 1, \ldots, L_r\}$. A batch of tasks that need to be completed in a given session, in particular, may include the entire set of tasks W. The list of tasks of this package, ordered according to one or another principle, together with the program codes for solving them, is loaded into the memory of the main computing module, and the program codes for solving all problems are also loaded into the memory of each computing module.

2.2 *Online Processing Mode*

Program codes for solving all problems of the known set W are loaded into the memory of each computing module. The execution of these tasks is initiated by requests received at the input of the system from its users (clients) K_1,.., K_j,.., K_F. Each user K_j generates a stream of Z_j requests z_j, each of which initiates the solution of the problem U_j. There are two typical modes of receiving applications for the input of the computer system: (a) applications z_j are received at the input of the computer system at discrete time points with a given period T_j; (b) applications z_j are received at random times with a given intensity λ_j. From the streams Z_j, j = 1,.., F, a total stream F is formed, whose requests form a queue Q at the input of the cluster computing system (ordered according to a previously accepted principle).

When the cluster computing system is functioning, the D manager, implemented in the main computing module, looks at: in batch mode-the list of A_k (ordered in a certain way); in the online processing mode—queue Q, and selects from the list or queue application z_j in accordance with a pre-accepted principle (for example, from the list A_k—the application with the lowest sequential number in this list, from the queue Q, the application with the earliest time of receipt in the queue) and assigns the corresponding task U_j to this or that computing module according to the accepted dispatching strategy for this multiprocessor computing system.

3 Dispatching Procedure

The development of the dispatching strategy and the procedure that implements it is based on the application of a particular criterion for the effectiveness of this procedure and taking into account certain resources of the computing module that make up the system.

The criterion for the effectiveness of the dispatching procedure is the criterion for the quality of the functioning of the computer system achieved by using this procedure. As a rule, the main goal of developing a dispatching procedure is to reduce the value of the indicator that characterizes the time of task execution in the system, which determines the choice of the following criteria for the effectiveness of this procedure:

- for a batch processing computing system-the total execution time of all tasks in a given batch—T;
- for a computer system of operational processing—the average time T^ of staying in the application system for solving a problem from a given set W (i.e., the average response time of the system to the receipt of any request zj).

This time is determined on the basis of the evaluation time T_j stay in the system with specific applications of the z_j, the components of which are the waiting time ω of the requests in the queue and time of service, i.e., time τ_j runs the program to solve this problem in one of the computing modules of the system (from start to finish). The time τ_j depends on the application service discipline in a single computing module, which is considered to be single-processor and operates in multi-program mode in accordance with any discipline of dispatching calculations in a single computing module adopted for all modules of a given computing system [4].

This time is defined as

$$T^{\wedge} = 1/L \sum_{j^L=1} T_j \tag{1}$$

where T_j is the time spent in the system of a specific application z_j to solve the problem U_j, i.e., the time interval from the moment t_j^n of receipt of this application in the system to the moment t_j^3 of completion of the task U_j. Components time T_j is the waiting time of the requests in the queue and the service time, i.e., the time τ_j the execution of the program solves this problem in one computational module of the system from start to finish. The time τ_j depends on the accepted application service discipline in a single computing module, which is considered to be single-processor and operates in multi-program mode in accordance with any task dispatching discipline adopted for all computing modules of a given computing system.

The main critical resource of the system is the processor time of each computing module. To evaluate this resource, the concept of processor load is used. The amount of load G characterizes the fraction of time during which the processor is busy performing the tasks assigned to it, and, at the same time, the probability that at any time the processor is busy performing a task (not idle) [4].

When the computing module is running in single-program mode, its processor time is fully used to solve only one task (from start to finish). During this period, the computing module is busy, i.e., its processor load $G = 1$, and only after the completion of this task, when the load takes the value $G = 0$, can any other task be assigned to perform in this computing module.

When working computer module in the multi-program mode, it performs some set of tasks sharing a CPU time of this computer module in accordance with one or another discipline of scheduling for a single processor [4] and a load value computing module in a given time varies in the process of performing multiple assigned tasks within $G_{min} = 0$ (in this computational module is not running any task) to $G_{max} = 1$ (in this computing module executes a set of tasks, creating the maximum load). When $G = 1$, it is not possible to assign new tasks to this computing module.

The specific value of the processor load at some arbitrary point in time depends both on the composition of the set of tasks performed by it (which changes during the operation of the computing system), and on the accepted discipline of dispatching for one computing module, and does not lend itself to a priori evaluation.

There are theoretical definitions of the concept of loading for cases when the processor performs tasks:

1. in accordance with requests received at fixed times with a given period [3];
2. in accordance with a random flow of applications with a given intensity [4].

However, when dispatching calculations during the operation of the computing system, the use of analytical expressions to evaluate the load of the computing module is not possible.

4 Fault Tolerance of the System

The proposed approach to developing procedures dispatching to ensure the required level of fault tolerance systems ("fault-tolerant scheduling"), considers the example cluster computing system for batch processing, for which the quality criterion of the operation is the total time T_A of all tasks in a given package A.

The failure of such a system is considered an event that leads to exceeding the required value $T^0{}_A$ of the T_A time (i.e., $T_A > T^0{}_A$). Suppose that for a cluster computing system of this type, assuming that there are no failures, the computing module has adopted a dispatching strategy based on the following principles.

The selection of a task from a given A_k package to assign it to a particular computing module is carried out in accordance with some accepted principle (for example, in ascending order of the number of tasks in the package).

The choice of the computational module to perform selected from the list of A_k task minimum computational module: once the selected package from the A_k, the task is assigned for execution in the computing module, characterized by minimal (from all modules of this cluster computing system) load at the time of adoption of the decision on the appointment [5].

Choosing another task from the package, the definition of the load of each computing module at the moment and a decision on the appointment of the selected task in a specific module, is the Manager D at certain points of time t_r, which is one of the objectives of the implementation strategy scheduling.

It should be taken into account: During the operation of the system, the load of each computing module continuously changes due to the completion of certain tasks in it and the assignment of new tasks to this computing module.

After assigning a new task to a computing module at time t_r, which is already in the process of solving previously assigned tasks, the load of this computing module (the minimum at time t_r) increases, and after completing any tasks in this computing module, even one, the load of the module decreases. Therefore, the load of each computing module at any given moment cannot be determined in advance, and the assignment of a task at some point t_r in the computing module that is least loaded at the moment may lead to an overload of this module (i.e., exceeding a certain allowed load) at the nearest next moment.

Perhaps, when describing the process of solving problems in a cluster computing system, it is advisable to use the concept of the state of the computing module M_i at some point in time t, which is determined by the load value $G_i(t)$ of this module.

Information about the states of all computing modules is stored in the memory of the main computing module and is updated at certain points in time.

We believe that the computing modules of a cluster computing system can allow sudden failures with a known intensity, independent of each other.

When addressing the reliability of the structural state of a computer system, consisting of N computing modules, represented by the vector $s_k = \sigma, \ldots., \sigma_N$, where $\sigma_i = 0$, if i-th computing module is working, $\sigma_i = 1$, if the i-th computing module refused; i = 1, …, N; k = 1, …, 2^N. Is called the initial state $s^0 = 0, \ldots, 0$ (all computational modules are operational); distorted—any state s_ν corresponding to the failure of any module (i.e., $s_\nu \neq s^0$).

Let us assume that in the absence of failures of computing modules (i.e., for the s^0 state), by applying some dispatching strategy for cluster computing systems, the required value $T^0{}_A$ of the time T_A is achieved. Failures of the computing module cause the system to transition to a certain distorted state s_ν, which corresponds to $N_\nu < N$ functional modules. In general, a decrease in the number of functional computing modules leads to an increase in time T_A, so that for distorted states of the computing system, $T_A(s_\nu) > T_A^0$, where $T_A(s_\nu)$ is the execution time of a given batch of tasks in a system that is in a distorted state s_ν. The transition of the computing system to such a state s_ν is a failure.

For many applications of cluster computing system in the event of failure of the computing module may be increased (within specified limits) time T_A compared to the value $T^0{}_A$, which is required in the absence of failures all modules (the principle of permissible degradation). At the same time, based on the specifics of a particular application of a cluster computing system and the requirements of users, the maximum allowed time $T^*{}_A$ is set, the system performs the specified task package, where $T^*{}_A > T^0{}_A$. Next, we consider this particular case and the failure of the computing system is considered an event that causes the system to transition to such a distorted state s_ν, which corresponds to the execution time of a given task package $T_A(s_\nu) > T_A^*$.

The health domain of a system is the set $S = \{s_r\}$ of its health states, i.e., such states s_r, for each of which the system's execution time of a given task package $T_A(s_r)$ satisfies the requirement $T_A^* \geq T_A(s_r) \geq T_A^0$. The health domain S of a fault-tolerant system includes, in addition to the initial state s^0, a certain set of S^ω distorted states s_ν that satisfy the requirement $T_A(s_\nu) \leq T_A^*$ and, therefore, are healthy. Accordingly, the probability P(T) of a fault-tolerant system running for time T is defined as the probability that any state s_k that the system may find itself in during this time belongs to the health domain S, i.e., the state of the fault-tolerant system:

$$P_T = P^{S^0}(T) + \sum_{S_\nu \in S^\omega} P^{S_\nu}(T) \tag{2}$$

where $P^{S^0}(T)$, $P^{S_\nu}(T)$ are the probabilities of the system staying in the state s^0 and in the state s_ν during the time interval T;

S^ω—the set of distorted states s_ν that are operable, i.e. for which $T_A(s_\nu) \leq T_A^*$ is valid.

If the requirement is $T_A(s_\nu) \leq T_A^*$ satisfy all such distorted states s_ν for which the number k of failed computing modules is within $1 \leq k \leq d$, then the probability of failure-free operation of the system during the time interval T, taking into account that for the initial state s^0, the number of failed computing modules $k = 0$, is defined as

$$P(T) = \sum_{k=0}^{d} C_N^k p^k (1-p)^{N-k} \tag{3}$$

where $p = p(T)$ is the probability of failure of any computing module during time T, defined as $p(T) = (1 - e^{-\lambda T})$, λ is the known failure rate of computing modules.

Suppose it is necessary to develop a dispatching procedure that provides the required level of fault tolerance for a given cluster computing system, which can be set by the required value of the probability of failure-free operation P (T) for a given time T or by the maximum allowable number d of failed computing modules available in the system at any time during the interval T. This procedure should, with a given probability P(T), ensure the execution time of a given task package $T_A \leq T_A^0$ in the absence of failures of all computing modules and $T_A \leq T_A^*$ in the case of failures of no more than a given number d of any modules.

When developing the dispatching procedure, assuming possible failures of computing modules, we will take into account the unequal value of the tasks performed in terms of their importance for the user of the cluster computing system. We introduce the parameter b_j—the weight of the task U_j, the value of which is determined by the amount of losses, i.e., damage to the user, which is a consequence of the system's failure to perform this task (a more important task corresponds to greater losses, i.e., greater weight).

The procedure for dispatching calculations in a computer system, taking into account possible failures of a computer, is based on the following principles.

For the initial state s^0, dispatching can be performed using any strategy aimed at minimizing the execution time of a given task package and allowing for the time $T^0{}_A$. In particular, the task selection from the pack for a purpose in one or another computing module can be performed in accordance with the increase in the number of tasks in the batch, and assigns the selected task to a specific computational engine—the principle of a minimum current load on the modules.

For distorted states s_ν, corresponding to failures of any computing modules, the number of which does not exceed d, dispatching is performed taking into account the weight of the tasks, so that the most important tasks, i.e. the tasks with the highest weight, are performed first.

The choice of a task from this package A to assign it to a particular computing module is carried out in accordance with the principle of "the task with the highest weight is the first". To do this, the list of tasks in package A is ordered according to the decreasing weights of tasks b_j (at the beginning of the list—the tasks with the highest weight) and the task is selected in the order of the tasks in the list.

In order to ensure that the requirement $T_A(s_\nu) \leq T_A^*$ is met, non-compliance is allowed ("discarding") some tasks that, under this principle, will be the least important tasks. You can set a requirement that the total weight of the discarded tasks does not exceed the allowed value.

The choice of the computing module to perform the task selected from list A in it is carried out in accordance with the principle "the selected task is assigned in the computing module with the minimum current load".

If in the initial state s^0, a strategy that does not take into account the weight of the tasks does not allow you to fulfill the requirement $T_A \leq T_A^0$, then to fulfill it, you should also apply a strategy that takes into account the importance of the tasks and is used for distorted states.

5 Conclusion

The use of this strategy allows for the operation of a cluster computing system in conditions of possible failures of computing modules to provide the required level of fault tolerance of the system, set by the required probability of failure-free operation of the computing system (or the maximum allowable number d of failed computing modules) at the specified values $T^0{}_A$ and $T^*{}_A$.

This strategy can be applied to clustered computing systems operational processing when the criterion of quality of functioning of cluster computing systems is the average time T^ of the system response on receipt of any application and z_j must satisfy the requirements of $T^\wedge(s^0) \leq T_A^{\wedge 0}$ and $T^\wedge(s_\nu) \leq T_A^{\wedge *}$ a given probability.

References

1. Tourouta, E. N. (1992). Kompleks metodov obespecheniya otkazoustoichivosti mnogoprotsessornih system na osnove ratsional'nogo pereraspredeleniya zadach [A set of methods for ensuring fault tolerance of multiprocessor systems based on the rational redistribution of tasks]. In *Proceedings of the Fifth Meeting on Distributed Computing Systems and Networks (CDS-92)*.
2. Tourouta, E. N. (1994). The methods for ensuring fault-tolerance of distributed control systems. In *Proceedings of IFAC Symposium SAFEPROCESS' 94*, 2. Helsinki, Finland.
3. Stollings, V. (2002). Operatsionnye sistemy [Operating systems].
4. Mayorov, S. A. (1978). Osnovy teorii vychislitel'nykh system [Fundamentals of the theory of computing systems].
5. Denning, P. J. (1976). Fault tolerant operating systems. *ACM Computing Surveys, 8*(4), 359–389.

Research of Correlation Dependencies in Russian Household Data Using Data Mining Methods

Vasily Usachev, Veronika Brus, Lilia Voronova, and Elena Tarasenko

Abstract The article is devoted to the study of big data using modern Data Mining tools. For the analysis, the authors use survey data from the Russian Monitoring of the Economic Situation and Health of the Population at the Higher School of Economics (RLMS HSE) "conducted by the National Research University Higher School of Economics and Demoscope LLC with the participation of the University of North Carolina Population Center at Chapel Hill and the Federal Institute of Sociology Research Sociological Center of the Russian Academy of Sciences. The set under study contains data from surveys of households and individuals. For the study, we took household data for 2019 and 2009, each containing more than a thousand attributes included in 12 information groups. For data preprocessing, the Python language and the PyCharm development environment were used. For basic analysis, we used the IBM SPSS Statistics 26 program, as well as the Cloudera CDH tools (Hue and Impala) from the Apache Hadoop distribution, which contains a set of modules for processing big data and machine learning. Automation of the search for dependencies for Pearson's correlation coefficients was carried out, comparison and visualization of detailed dependencies of the influence of the status of a settlement and the region of family residence on the availability of centralized utilities at the beginning and end of a ten-year period was carried out.

Keywords Data mining · RLMS HSE · Apache hadoop

V. Usachev · V. Brus · L. Voronova (✉)
Moscow Technical University of Communications and Informatics, Aviamotornaya St. 8A, 111024 Moscow, Russia
e-mail: voronova.lilia@ya.ru

V. Brus
e-mail: veronika-brus@yandex.ru

E. Tarasenko
HSE University, 100100 Myasnitskaya 20, Moscow, Russian Federation
e-mail: etarasenko@hse.ru

E. Zaramenskikh and A. Fedorova (eds.), *Digitalization of Society, Economics and Management*, Lecture Notes in Information Systems and Organisation 53,
https://doi.org/10.1007/978-3-030-94252-6_11

1 Introduction

Big data is widely used in various spheres of life. They have become the engine of the development of the digital economy in the world. The most active technologies Big Data and Data Mining are used in the economy, IT-spheres, in industry [1–3].

Big data processing methods are being introduced into healthcare and social sphere. These methods allow for deep analytical research and find hidden patterns in the data and non-obvious correlation dependencies between different characteristics.

At the Department of Intelligent Systems in Control and Automation of the Moscow Technical University of Communications and Informatics, scientific research in the field of Big Data is carried out within the framework of master's and postgraduate works [4–6]. The article presents the results of research using modern software tools. It describes the search for correlation dependencies in the survey data of the Russian Monitoring of the Economic Situation and Health of the Population of the National Research University Higher School of Economics (RLMS HSE) [7] using tools for Big Data analytics Hue and Impala, automating the search for high-level dependencies for Pearson correlation coefficients, comparing the impact of point and region of residence of the family for the availability of centralized utilities at the beginning and end of the ten-year period.

2 Data Mining Methods and Tools

Big Data is a series of approaches, tools and methods for processing structured and unstructured data of huge volumes and significant diversity to obtain human-perceived results that are effective in conditions of continuous growth of information and its distribution across numerous computing nodes [8]. Today, there are many tools for processing big data. The most well-known and powerful Big Data processing tool is Cloudera CDH, an Apache Hadoop distribution that contains a set of modules for big data processing and machine learning [9]:

- basic (HDFS, MapReduce, Yarn, and Hadoop Common);
- tools for managing data flows (Flume, Sqoop);
- distributed and streaming processing frameworks, as well as message brokers (Spark, Kafka);
- DBMS for Big Data analytics (HBase, Hive, Impala);
- a set of libraries for running cloud services.

HBase is a NoSQL-type DBMS that allows you to process huge amounts of data: billions of rows and millions of columns. The tool is open source. It runs on top of the distributed HDFS file system and provides a fault-tolerant way to store large amounts of sparse data [10]. HBase is a distributed, column-oriented, key-value multiversion database. The data is organized into tables indexed by a primary key (RowKey). An unlimited set of attributes can be stored for each RowKey. The columns are organized into groups of columns (Column Family), which usually combine columns with the same usage and storage pattern into one Column Family.

Attributes that belong to the same column group and correspond to the same key are physically stored as a sorted list.

HBase supports the following operations: Put-allows you to add a new record to the database; Get - allows you to get data on the RowKey, Column Family and version of the record, the last two attributes are optional; Scan-allows you to read records in turn, Delete-allows you to mark a certain one. The remote version is ready for deletion, and the physical deletion will occur only when performing a high-priority merge operation (Major Compaction) You can work with HBase using the console, using the Hbase Shell, or in the Native Api application.

Hive is a database management system based on the Hadoop platform. Allows you to read, write, and manage large data sets located in distributed storage and queried using the SQL syntax [11].

Hive provides tools for providing easy access to data using SQL; a mechanism for superimposing structure on various data formats; accessing files stored by HDFS or on other systems; executing queries via Apache Spark or MapReduce. Hive SQL can be extended with user-defined functions (UDF), user-defined aggregate functions (UDAFs), and user-defined table functions (UDTFs).

Hive works with various data formats, such as CSV/TSV, Apache Parquet, Apache ORC, etc., is designed for traditional data processing and is not suitable for online data processing.

Impala is a tool for parallel processing of large volumes of data using SQL queries that must be stored in HDFS or HBase. Impala provides support for: the most common SQL-92 functions and includes its own specific commands in HiveQL; the HDFS, HBase, and S3 file systems; common data access interfaces (JDBC, ODBC), and the Impala Query user interface.

The Impala architecture includes: a client interfaces such as HUE, ODBC and JDBC clients, Impala Shell, SQL App; metadata storage (United metadata); Query Planner (Query Planner); Query Coordinator (Query Exec Engine); query results storage HDFS or HBase [12]. Impala provides: a typical SQL interface; the ability to query large amounts of data in Apache Hadoop; distributed queries in a cluster environment, for easy scaling and use cost-effective equipment; the ability to share data files between different components without copying, exporting, or importing steps; the ability to read and write Hive tables, providing analytics of the data created by Hive.

3 Problem Statement and Data Set Description

This article describes how to search for correlations in the survey data of the Russian monitoring of economic situation and public health HSE (RLMS HSE)", conducted by the National research University "Higher school of Economics" and OOO "Demoscope" with the participation of the population Center University of North Carolina at chapel hill and the Institute of sociology of the Federal research sociological center of RAS [7].

The set is positioned as the only representative socio-economic survey of households in Russia, which has a significant panel component. Allows you to track the daily life of the same people/households over a long time, which opens up opportunities for not only static, but also retrospective analysis.

The monitoring program includes interrelated questionnaires for all households, for all adults (over 14 years old), for children, as well as data on the social infrastructure of localities. The content structure of the questionnaires used in the survey meets the standard accepted in the world practice, which allows for comparisons between countries. The household (family) is the primary unit that ensures the population's production, and the main decisions are made not individually, but within the household, taking into account the interests of its other members. The survey has been conducted since 1994.

When analyzing the information in the set, the following tasks were set: to find high values of correlation coefficients between attributes, to compare correlated attributes in two files, to find similarities; to use the Hue and Impala tools to find real, frequently occurring attribute values and describe the resulting dependencies; to investigate the presence of these correlations in families who participated in the survey of the current and previous year.

For research undertaken two sets of household data for 2019 and 2009. Files contain 1040 1001 and attributes, respectively, which are included in eleven groups of information: identifiers families in previous waves of the survey, information about family members and their belonging to the household, about the village; on the various appliances and other major purchases, the duration of their use; availability of land and subsistence farming, the harvest and sale or transfer to relatives; about spending on food, appliances, insurance, loans, etc.; about volunteer activities and assistance to older family members; about financial and physical assistance provided to the family; about the resale of household property, receiving interest on the deposit; about medical care.

Each attribute is a question of the questionnaire and has no intuitive designations, only codes of questions asked. Source files are in *sav* format and can be opened with IBM SPSS Statistics 26. When you open the file, two tabs appear that contain data and variable descriptions. Examples of data and descriptions of attributes are shown in Figs. 1 and 2.

For the convenience of further research, the files were translated from the highly specialized *sav* format to *csv*, using the file format change function in IBM SPSS Statistics 26. The built-in function performs only data transformation, and the variable description must be processed manually, selecting and transferring the necessary attributes to Excel.

For the initial analysis of attributes, the Python language and the PyCharm development environment were used [12]. To analyze the data, the files were loaded into DataFrame objects using the to_csv function. The fullness of the attributes was checked using the count () and describe () functions. Attributes describing up to 20 family members in terms of their household membership were immediately

wc9.8.1b	wc9.9a	wc9.9b	wc9.9.1a	wc9.9.1b	wc9.13a	wc9.13b	wc9.14a	wc9.14b	wc9.15a	wc9.15b	wc9.101a
1	2	.	2	.	2	.	1	0	1	99999997	2
.	2	.	2	.	2	.	2	.	1	5	2
.	2	.	2	.	2	.	2	.	1	99999997	2
.	2	.	2	.	2	.	2	.	1	99999997	2
.	2	.	2	.	2	.	2	.	1	99999997	2
.	2	.	2	.	2	.	2	.	1	99999997	2
5	2	.	1	3	2	.	1	9	1	99999997	1
.	2	.	2	.	2	.	2	.	1	99999997	2
99999997	2	.	1	99999997	2	.	2	.	1	24	2
2	2	.	2	.	2	.	2	.	1	12	1
5	2	.	2	.	2	.	2	.	1	99999997	2
6	2	.	2	.	2	.	1	4	2	.	2
20	2	.	2	.	2	.	2	.	1	20	2
.	2	.	2	.	2	.	2	.	1	99999997	1
.	2	.	2	.	2	.	2	.	1	3	2
5	2	.	2	.	2	.	2	.	1	99999997	2
.	2	.	2	.	2	.	2	.	1	99999997	2
.	2	.	1	1	2	.	2	.	1	99999997	2
.	2	.	1	4	2	.	2	.	1	99999997	1
.	2	.	1	99999997	2	.	2	.	1	99999997	1
.	2	.	2	.	2	.	1	3	2	.	2

Fig. 1 Data block from the dataset [1]

Имя	Тип	Ширина	Десятич...	Метка	Значения
wc9.8b	Числовой	2	0	Сколько лет мотоциклу, мотороллеру, моторной ...	{99999997, ЗАТРУДНЯЮСЬ ОТВЕТИТЬ}...
wc9.8.1a	Числовой	1	0	У Вас есть взрослый велосипед?	{1, Да}...
wc9.8.1b	Числовой	2	0	Сколько лет взрослому велосипеду?	{99999997, ЗАТРУДНЯЮСЬ ОТВЕТИТЬ}...
wc9.9a	Числовой	1	0	У Вас есть трактор или минитрактор?	{1, Да}...
wc9.9b	Числовой	2	0	Сколько лет трактору или минитрактору?	{99999997, ЗАТРУДНЯЮСЬ ОТВЕТИТЬ}...
wc9.9.1a	Числовой	1	0	У Вас есть газонокосилка?	{1, Да}...
wc9.9.1b	Числовой	2	0	Сколько лет газонокосилке?	{99999997, ЗАТРУДНЯЮСЬ ОТВЕТИТЬ}...
wc9.13a	Числовой	1	0	У Вас есть кондиционер воздуха?	{1, Да}...
wc9.13b	Числовой	2	0	Сколько лет кондиционеру воздуха?	{99999997, ЗАТРУДНЯЮСЬ ОТВЕТИТЬ}...
wc9.14a	Числовой	1	0	У Вас есть спутниковая антенна?	{1, Да}...
wc9.14b	Числовой	2	0	Сколько лет спутниковой антенне	{99999997, ЗАТРУДНЯЮСЬ ОТВЕТИТЬ}...
wc9.15a	Числовой	1	0	У Вас есть кабельное телевидение?	{1, Да}...
wc9.15b	Числовой	2	0	Сколько лет кабельному телевидению?	{99999997, ЗАТРУДНЯЮСЬ ОТВЕТИТЬ}...
wc9.101a	Числовой	1	0	У Вас есть дача или другой дом, часть дома, с...	{1, Да}...
wc9.101b	Числовой	3	0	Сколько лет даче или другому дому, части дом...	{99999997, ЗАТРУДНЯЮСЬ ОТВЕТИТЬ}...
wc9.12a	Числовой	1	0	У Вас есть другая квартира или часть квартиры?	{1, Да}...
wc9.12b	Числовой	3	0	Сколько лет квартире или части квартиры?	{99999997, ЗАТРУДНЯЮСЬ ОТВЕТИТЬ}...
wd1	Числовой	1	0	В течение последних 12 месяцев у Вашей семь...	{1, Да}...
wd2	Числовой	1	0	В настоящее время у Вашей семьи есть в поль...	{1, Да}...
wd3	Числовой	7	2	Сколько всего соток земли у Вашей семьи в на...	{99999997,00, ЗАТРУДНЯЮСЬ ОТВЕТИТЬ}...
wd4	Числовой	1	U	Кому принадлежит эта земля?	{1, Вся земля - собственность Вашей семьи}...
wd5	Числовой	1	0	В последние 12 месяцев Ваша семья платила з...	{1, Да}...
wd6	Числовой	11	2	Сколько всего рублей Вы заплатили за пользов...	{99999997,00, ЗАТРУДНЯЮСЬ ОТВЕТИТЬ}...
wd7	Числовой	1	0	В течение последних 12 месяцев Ваша семья в...	{1, Да}...
wd8.1a	Числовой	1	0	За последние 12 месяцев Ваша семья собрала...	{1, Да}...
wd8.1b	Числовой	9	2	Сколько всего килограмм собрали? Картофеля	{99999997,00, ЗАТРУДНЯЮСЬ ОТВЕТИТЬ}...
wd8.1c	Числовой	9	2	Сколько килограмм потребили в семье в натура...	{99999997,00, ЗАТРУДНЯЮСЬ ОТВЕТИТЬ}...
wd8.1d	Числовой	9	2	Сколько килограмм отдали бесплатно родствен...	{99999997,00, ЗАТРУДНЯЮСЬ ОТВЕТИТЬ}...
wd8.1e	Числовой	9	2	Сколько килограмм продали в натуральном или...	{99999997,00, ЗАТРУДНЯЮСЬ ОТВЕТИТЬ}...
wd8.2a	Числовой	1	0	За последние 12 месяцев Ваша семья собрала...	{1, Да}...

Fig. 2 Example of the description of the attributes of the set under consideration

excluded from the original data sets. Family identifiers in previous questionnaires are also excluded. These attributes are uninformative and have a low percentage of occupancy. Thus, it was possible to reduce the number of considered attributes to 750 in both sets.

4 Research of Upper-Level Dependencies

To find correlations, the data was applied to the built-in IBM SPSS Statistics function *corr* with the parameter *method* = '*pearson*', which allows you to calculate the Pearson coefficients. The total number of obtained correlation coefficients was 750 × 750 = 562,500. The high dimensionality of the data requires an automatic search for correlation coefficients that are similar in attributes. Examples of the obtained values are shown in Fig. 3.

To select attributes that are highly correlated, a loop is created in which the correlation value from the current row is compared with the threshold values of 0.6 and –0.6. If the value is greater, the row containing the correlated attributes and the correlation value is written to a new list. A prerequisite is the inequality of correlated attributes, because the correlation coefficient of an attribute with itself always gives 1. This operation is performed for both files.

From the resulting lists, you must exclude rows where the same attribute names appear, because there is no need to process the same correlation twice. To do this, an empty list is created and a loop is created, during which each row is compared with the rows of the new list, and then the elements containing the attribute names are cross-compared. If no equality is satisfied for a string, it is included in the list. Thus, the number of processed values was reduced by another half. An example of the obtained values is shown in Fig. 4.

The next step is to compare the correlated attributes in both files. The same attributes in different files are called differently, so a special processing technique was applied. Examples are shown in Fig. 5. In the end, we selected 493 correlations. To search for dependencies, abbreviations were processed by creating files with attribute descriptions and uploading them to the Cloudera VM along with the found correlations, followed by connections by attribute names.

When detailing the correlations found, it was revealed that a simple correlation analysis is not suitable for this data set, since large number of attributes have more than half of the omissions, which results in high correlation coefficients. If you exclude

Fig. 3 Examples of the obtained correlation coefficients

	0	1	2
0	WREDID_H	we13.5b	1.000000
1	WREDID_H	wf12.6bb	0.666093
2	WID_H	VID_H	0.951525
3	WID_H	wa3	0.675999
4	WID_H	wd8.14d	0.664800
5	WID_H	we13.5b	1.000000
6	VID_H	WID_H	0.951525
7	VID_H	wd8.14d	0.664800
8	VID_H	we13.5b	-1.000000
9	w_origsm	wd14.4d	-0.631189

	0	1	2
0	WREDID_H	wel3.5b	1.000000
1	WREDID_H	wf12.6bb	0.666093
2	WID_H	VID_H	0.951525
3	WID_H	wa3	0.675999
4	WID_H	wd8.14d	0.664800
5	WID_H	wel3.5b	1.000000
6	VID_H	wd8.14d	0.664800
7	VID_H	wel3.5b	-1.000000
8	w_origsm	wd14.4d	-0.631189
9	w_origsm	wf9.8b	-0.763756

Fig. 4 The selected correlation coefficients

	0	1	2	3	4	5
0	WREDID_H	wel3.5b	1.000000	VREDID_H	vel3.5b	-1.000000
1	WID_H	wel3.5b	1.000000	VID_H	vel3.5b	-1.000000
2	VID_H	wel3.5b	-1.000000	VID_H	vel3.5b	-1.000000
3	w_origsm	wf12.7b	1.000000	v_origsm	vf12.7b	0.716185
4	region	site	0.945859	region	site	0.949563
5	psu	wf12.6bb	-0.946288	psu	vf12.6bb	0.841403
6	status	wel3.5b	1.000000	status	vel3.5b	1.000000
7	popul	wel3.5b	-1.000000	popul	vel3.5b	-1.000000
8	site	wel3.5b	-1.000000	site	vel3.5b	-1.000000
9	wa3	wel3.5b	1.000000	va3	vel3.5b	1.000000

Fig. 5 Correlations observed in both data sets

missing values in all attributes, the data set is reduced to 6 rows, which cannot be considered a big data set. In this regard, the attribute-by-attribute exclusion of omissions and the search for correlations with fully filled attributes were performed. As a result, it was found that there is no correlation between the attributes.

The data set with households does not contain clearly influencing values, so it was decided to check whether there are dependencies in different files using visualizations.

5 Selection and Visualization of the Detailed Dependencies

We examined the impact of the status of the locality and the region of family residence on the availability of centralized public services in the period with a gap of 10 years. The analyzed attributes are shown in Table 1.

According to the *region* attribute, four regions were selected for analysis: the Tver Region, Rzhev and Rzhevsky District, the Republic of Kabardino-Balkaria,

Table 1 The analyzed attributes

Selection attribute		Description
2019	2009	
status	status	Type of settlement
region	region	Region code
wc7.1	mc7.1	Do you have central heating in your house from a thermal power plant, a boiler room?
wc7.2	mc7.2	Do you have a centralized water supply in your house?
wc7.7	mc7.7	Do you have a gas main in your house, not a gas cylinder?
wc7.5	mc7.5	Do you have a centralized sewer system in your house?

Zalukokoazhe and Zolsky District, the Saratov Region, Volsk and Volsky District, and the Moscow Region. For these regions, the *status* attribute, which describes the categories of localities, has values such as regional center, city,village.

Attributes describing the presence of centralized utilities take the values yes (1) or no (2). To reduce the captions in the figures, all the values obtained were numbered according to Table 2.

The dependence of the availability of central heating on the region and the status of the settlement for both samples are shown in Fig. 6.

It can be seen that the lack of central heating prevails in the regional villages, while the majority of settlements in the Moscow region are equipped with central

Table 2 Group captions in the figures

Name of the region	Group number
Tver region, Rzhev and Rzhevsky district, city	1
Tver region, Rzhev and Rzhevsky district, village	2
KBR, Zalukokoazhe and Zolsky district, urban settlement	3
KBR, Zalukokoazhe and Zolsky district, village	4
Saratov region, Volsk and Volsky district, city	5
Saratov region, Volsk and Volsk district, village	6
Saratov region, Volsk and Volsky district, urban settlement	7
Moscow region, city	8
Moscow region, urban settlement	9
Moscow region, village	10

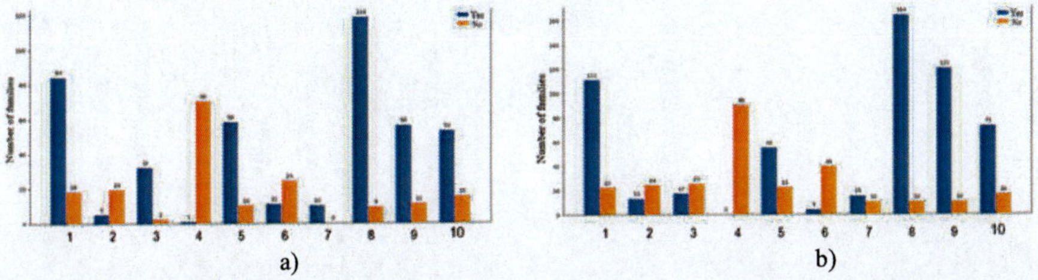

Fig. 6 Dependence of the availability of central heating on the settlement: **a** in 2009, **b** in 2019

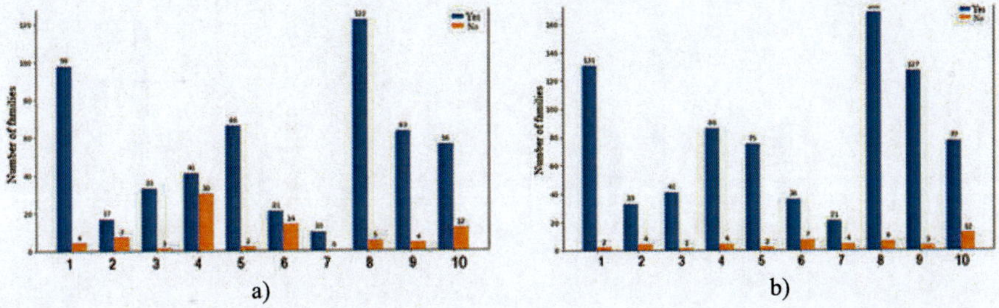

Fig. 7 Dependence of the availability of water supply on the settlement: **a** in 2009, **b** in 2019

heating. This trend continues in both samples. For urban-type settlements (PGTS), there is an increase in the number of families that are not equipped with central heating. This trend may be explained by the wider coverage of different localities and the participation of more families in the survey.

The dependence of the availability of centralized water supply on the region and the status of the settlement for both samples are shown in Fig. 7.

Both graphs show that most families from any locality have a centralized water supply. At the same time, there has been a steady decrease in the number of families without centralized water supply in the sample 2019 compared with the sample of 2009.

Most of the identified types of settlements in various regions are equipped with main gas. From sample to sample, there is a decrease in the number of families without gas supplies in villages.

The dependence of the availability of main gas on the region and the status of the locality for both samples is shown in Fig. 8.

The dependence of the presence of a centralized sewage system on the region and the status of the settlement for both samples are shown in Fig. 9.

Over time, in some settlements, there is an increase in the number of families with centralized sewage systems. At the same time, the villages of the non-central part of Russia are not equipped with centralized sewage systems.

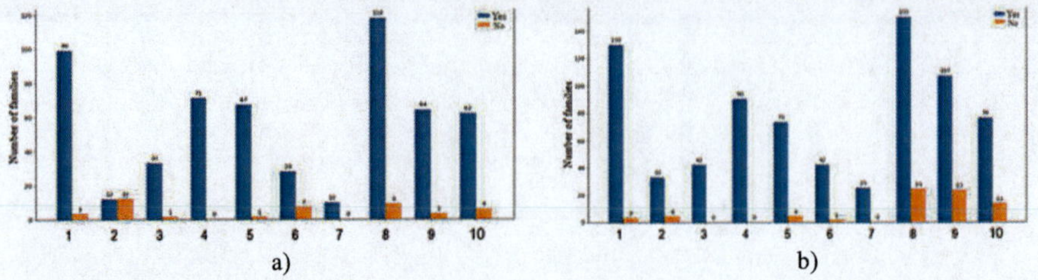

Fig. 8 The dependence of the presence of the main gas pipeline in the village: **a** in 2009; **b** in 2019

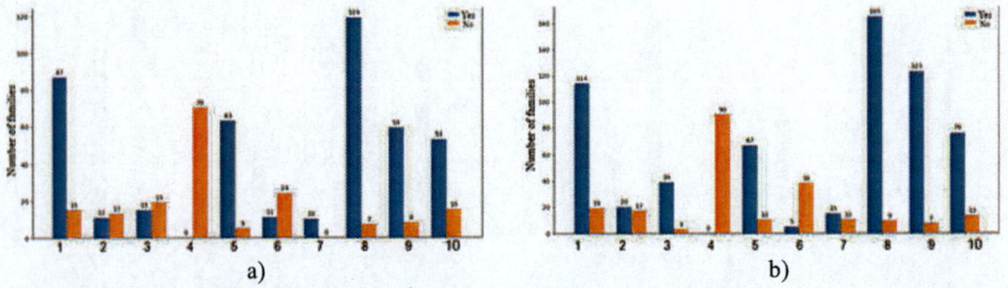

Fig. 9 Dependence of the availability of centralized sewerage system on the settlement: **a** in 2009, **b** in 2019

6 Conclusion

The search for correlations for the survey data of the Russian Monitoring of the economic situation and health of the population was carried out. The conclusion is made about the weak detection of hidden correlations in this set, due to the large number of omissions of values in the attributes.

A retrospective analysis of the data on the impact of the status of the locality and the region of residence of the family on the availability of centralized public services in the period with a gap of 10 years was carried out, which showed a certain improvement in the studied indicators for the specified period.

References

1. Sivarajah, U., Kamal, M. M., Irani, Z., & Weerakkody, V. (2017). Critical analysis of Big Data challenges and analytical methods. *Journal of Business Research, 70*, 263–286.
2. Yi, X., Liu, F., Liu, J., & Jin, H. (2014). Building a network highway for big data: Architecture and challenges. *IEEE Network, 28*, 5–13.
3. Gandomi, A., & Haider, M. (2015). Beyond the hype: Big data concepts, methods, and analytics. *International Journal of Information Management, 35*(2), 137–144.
4. Yue, W., Voronova, L. I., & Voronov, V. I. (2020). Design and implementation of a remote monitoring human health system. *Systems of Signals Generating and Processing in the Field*

of on Board Communications (pp. 1–7). Moscow: Russia. https://doi.org/10.1109/IEEECONF48371.2020.9078574
5. Usachev, V. A., Voronova, L. I., Voronov, V. I., Zharov, I. A., & Strelnikov, V. G. (2019). Neural network using to analyze the results of environmental monitoring of water. *Systems of Signals Generating and Processing in the Field of on Board Communications* (pp. 1–6). Moscow: Russia. https://doi.org/10.1109/SOSG.2019.8706733
6. Voronova, L. I., Tolmachev, R. V., & Usachev, A. V. A. (2018). Resource development to prevent riots at mass events. *Systems of Signals Generating and Processing in the Field of on Board Communications* (pp. 1–5). Moscow. https://doi.org/10.1109/SOSG.2018.8350580
7. Russian Monitoring of the Economic Situation and Health of the National Research University Higher School of Economics (RLMS HSE) "conducted by the National Research University Higher School of Economics and Demoscope LLC with the participation of the Population Center of the University of North Carolina at Chapel Hill and the Institute of Sociology Federal Scientific Research Sociological Center of the Russian Academy of Sciences. (RLMS HSE survey sites. http://www.cpc.unc.edu/projects/rlms, http://www.hse.ru/rlms).
8. Big Data—New Theory and Practice | Open systems. DBMS | Publishing house "Open systems"—[Electronic resource]. Access mode. http://www.osp.ru/os/2011/10/13010990/. Date of access 02.02.2021.
9. What is Cloudera: Architecture, history, use—[Electronic resource]. Access mode: https://www.bigdataschool.ru/wiki/cloudera. Date of application: 02.02.2021Apache HBase–[Электронный ресурс].—Режим доступа: https://hbase.apache.org/. Дата обращения: 03.02.2021.
10. https://hive.com/.
11. https://impala.apache.org/.
12. Scientific & Data Science Tools—Features | PyCharm. https://www.jetbrains.com/pycharm/features/scientific_tools.html. Дата обращения: 15.05.2020.

Agency of Interactive Environment in Shaping Users' Behaviour Through Actor–Network Theory

Kristina Boychenko, Irina Boychenko, and Galina Platunina

Abstract The paper defines the role of interactive space in social relationships using Actor–network theory as a methodological tool. It examines interactive space from Actor–network theory perspective, as one of the actors in a heterogeneous network consisting of human and non-human components with their own agency. This methodology allows to consider interactive space as an active participant of social relationship, communicating with other participants of society using non-verbal means of communication. Applying Actor–network theory allows to understand the rules of communication between users and the space, evaluates responsiveness to the system signals and defines participants' stages of involvement into this communication. A full-scale interactive prototype was designed and built as a proof-of-concept to analyse the influence of interactive space on human behaviour and space perception, examining this communication in real time and assessing human responsiveness to different types of signals from the space (light/sound/motion).

Keywords Interactive space · Behaviour · Communication · Socio-Technological · Actor–Network theory

1 Introduction

The proof-of-concept used in this research incorporates creating a prototype as a part of the experiment as a programme with an inquiry-driven approach, in which prototype is a part of experiments meant to explore and open new design

K. Boychenko
The University of Queensland, Brisbane, QLD 4072, Australia

I. Boychenko · G. Platunina (✉)
Moscow Technical University of Communication and Informatics, st. Aviamotornaya 8a, Moscow 111024, Russia
e-mail: g.p.platunina@mtuci.ru

I. Boychenko
e-mail: 1k.boychenko@uqconnect.edu.au

E. Zaramenskikh and A. Fedorova (eds.), *Digitalization of Society, Economics and Management*, Lecture Notes in Information Systems and Organisation 53,
https://doi.org/10.1007/978-3-030-94252-6_12

spaces [1]. The prototype interactive development is the programme, followed up by experiments—interactive communication between users and space, human and non-human components. The programme of this type of Research through Design (RtD) includes obtaining knowledge, developing observations and survey of the prototype construction and other research-related activities. Experiments introduced prototype operation related activities are developed, conducted, consolidated and processed, contributing to generation of the new knowledge. This RtD approach allows to take application of obtained knowledge beyond the created prototype and applies it in different conditions, contributing to design practice [2].

2 Methodology

Actor–Network Theory is applied as a set of prisms, through which interactive space is considered in order to obtain a different perspective and different properties are brought into the foreground for viewing. In later chapters the different views afforded by the techniques described here are used to explain features of how interactive features are used in design and to move towards a design of an interactive space.

Within the context of this research Actor–network theory (ANT) describes general forms of social, epistemological or ontological order. Society is comprised of actor-networks, therefore ANT to a large extent relies on communication and social relationships between human and non-human actors, considering the world around us as an agglomeration of actor-networks. Therefore, ANT can be described by social processes, activities, and various forms. of relationship and communication that create networks. These processes and relationships are integrated into behaviour of network components, combining being, perceiving and acting. ANT here describes the actors, their interactions and relationships, what they do, how their associations are transformed, maintained or dismantled, and how it influences other actors and relationships within network [3].

Within this research ANT is used as a set of prisms, through which interactive space is considered in order to obtain a different perspective and different properties are brought into the foreground for examination. Different views afforded by the techniques described here are used to explain features of how interactive features are used in design and to move towards a design of an interactive space. Each prism or a frame allows to consider various communication aspects and actors' conditions in order to understand in what ways they influence each other. In this manner ANT considers interactive space in order to obtain different perspectives and what properties are brought into the foreground for viewing. In later chapters the different views afforded by the techniques described above will explain how interactive features are used in design and move towards the creation of an interactive space.

The research relies on the prototype as proof-of-concept not only for the reasons of describing its' specifications, design process and interactive behaviour, but to a large extent because it allows to apply Actor–network theory as a research tool. This approach allows to consider various aspects of communication between user and interactive space from different perspectives, considering various means of space communication effecting humans' perception and a variety of factors defining it. A proof-of-concept provides ground for qualitative and qualitative analysis that can be later translated into development of interactive space communication tools, techniques and methods. By reviewing different scenarios through the lens of obtained information, assumption about a different actor-network can be made, in order to predict its' actor's behaviour and contribute to design quality.

2.1 The Prototype Behaviour

The prototype was developed in collaboration of School of Architecture and School of Music. The prototype can be described as an audio-visual, immersive and interactive experience. From spatial point of view, the prototype is a 10-m diameter dome-like structure that moves, breathes and sings in response to human activity. The dome constituted robotic components inside and was equipped with LED lights and speakers. This tangible and emotional experience with its' own behaviour and various interactive components offers sensation of changing sounds and the spectacles of light produced by the life like creature. Several robotic objects within the dome have also been fashioned to resemble blossoming flowers to tie in with the theme of the festival. As a proof-of-concept for the study, the prototype communicates with visitors using audio, visual and kinetic stimuli.

The prototype setup allowed the space inside of the prototype to be fully enclosed yet inviting, with an entrance on one side of the structure, and the exit on the opposite side. While providing a shelter and creating its' own immersive environment inside, with its' ambient sound and changing colourful light, the light fabric cover was transmitting diffused light from the LED light inside, evoking curiosity among the people passing by, inviting them to approach and investigate the space (Fig. 1).

Inside the dome, ambient sound (4 large subwoofer speakers) and floor LED strips were creating unique and changing immersive environment. Sound and light were synced, creating a soundscape pattern that would define the prototype behaviour. Several robotic objects resembling blossoms were hanging from the internal ends of

Fig. 1 in.bloom exterior

the rods. The blossoms were equipped with independent speakers, LEDs and motors, demonstrating their individual behaviour and responding to the visitors' proximity by means of ultrasonic sensors.

The prototype continuously communicates with visitors in real time, responding to their presence, creating immersive experience and encouraging visitors to continue communicating with it and discover more about its' behaviour.

The prototype creates interactive environment that triggers various senses have proven to be immersive and stimulate further communication. Using unique space qualities and tangible means of interactive space design visitors can be guided through space and get engaged into various activities as part of communication with the space. Visitors would approach the prototype to explore the space and its' behaviour, being non-verbally offered to understand the rules of communication with the space and to act in a certain way to continue this communication. During this process they can be brought through different modes of space cognition requiring their active or passive participation in this real-time communication.

Communication between visitors and the prototype begins before they even come in, the prototype invites them with its light and sound perceived from the outside. Observations show that people, especially students that were passing by, tend to be curious about light effects and would be willing to come in and investigate.

When the visitors respond to the invitation positively and step into the prototype area, they get immersed into the space, where the LEDs light is reflected from the white fabric surface and its' pattern and changing rhythm follows the soundscape ambience (Fig. 2).

Then the visitors start noticing the objects (blossoms) hanging from the end of the rods, they begin wondering what these are and what they do. Shortly it becomes evident to most of the visitors that each of the robotic blossoms demonstrates different behaviour. The robotic blossoms perceive visitors with embedded pair of ultrasonic sensors and if the visitors are willing to interact with the blossoms, they need to figure out how to be perceived by them. Each blossom has its own communication manner, its own sound effect and light, which makes each object unique. When the visitors' approach, the blossoms light gets brighter and sound gets louder. Finally,

Fig. 2 in.bloom prototype, interior

the blossoms open their petals (individual motors are placed above the blossoms) as an expression of the final stage of communication with visitors.

According to Callon,[1] ANT allows to focus the research on features of a socio-technical system that are relevant for the analysis. It consists of four connected overlapping stages that define how firm the networks can be.

- Interessment
- Enrolment
- Points of Passage
- Trial of Strength [4].

Status quo is represented by a firm actor-network. This research tool can be used to define how stable networks became or find the reasons why certain connections within it fail.

The interessment stage refers to actors being introduced to the network. Within the framework of this research this step was considered as a moment when the visitors (new actors) decide to explore the prototype and see the activity inside, the invitation by an interactive prototype. Each actor of the network has a unique experience of discovering this new situation, therefore each connection within this network is unique and exists only in this moment.

Enrolment stage happens when actors choose to follow the rules of the network and play their role in it, they commit to the program of the interaction. Applied to this research, this stage includes establishment of communication between interactive space and users, when users discover the signal from the space and learn how to interpret them, when the space and visitors begin to interact, the exploration mode of the visitors discovering the space and getting familiar with its components and their communication means.

Points of passage stand for an emerging type of actors that attempt to represent another network participant or the network itself. Attempt of more than one actor to become a point of passage causes a conflict within the network. This conflict is solved by achieving the final stage—the trial of strength, when the actors accept their roles and act accordingly. This process is unavoidable in an actor-network and can be traced in the interactive space prototype when the actors overestimate their influence in signals altercation and try to cause effects that don't depend on their actions. Despite the ability to directly communicate with robotic blossoms of the prototype, visitors can't control the ambient light and sound. With trial and error, they understand their roles in the network and bring the network to equilibrium when they understand the rules of communication and interact effectively with other agents of the network: human and non-human.

[1] Michel Callon, is a professor of sociology at the École des mines de Paris and member of the Centre de sociologie de l'innovation, an influential author in the field of Science and Technology Studies and one of the leading proponents of actor–network theory with Bruno Latour Suggested distinguishing between actors and intermediaries.

Therefore, ANT offers a way to understand relationships between space and users (non-human and human actors) avoiding defined outcomes and protocol that would occur if the agency was granted only to human components [5].

2.2 The Prototype Communication Means

The in.bloom prototype uses different means of communication with visitors:

- Sound—volume, rhythm and tone of the soundscape
- Vision—intensity and colour of light,
- Motion—tangible change of the structure shape.

The prototype has two main levels of communication with visitors: ambient sound/light of the dome itself (subwoofer speakers, floor LED stripes) and individual sound/light effects for each blossom.

Ambient (or general) sound and light communication means were creating immersive environment of the prototype, articulating its attitude and declaring prototype as an active participant of social relationship, with its' own agency of behaving in a certain way.

Individual sound and light are represented by the robotic blossoms. Each blossom was equipped with its own set of LEDs, a speaker, a motor and ultrasonic sensors, the light and sound within the object would react to the presence of a visitor within close proximity and the petals would open up if the visitors would spend enough at the spot where the sensors would perceive them (Fig. 3).

As a person approached, the motor would open the petals and the LED saturation would increase; however, it would not light up unless there was audio produced from its speaker. The overall effect of this was that the object was singing out and glowing bright to the person as they approached [6].

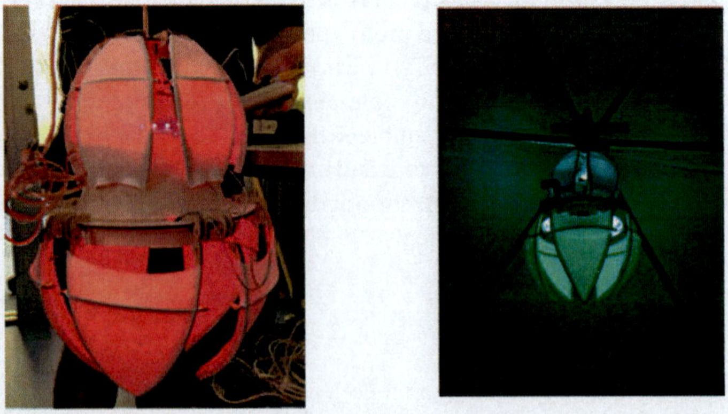

Fig. 3 Robotic blossoms

2.3 Analysis

To estimate the influence of interactive space on visitors' space perception, visitors of the prototype were asked a series of open-end questions in a survey. These visitors interacted with the in.bloom prototype and described their experience. A survey is one of the most common ways of quantitative analysis and it allows to understand communication between users and interactive space in real time. The survey was examining participants' opinion about interaction with the prototype and shows factors and means of perception and motivation of the participants' actions.

The survey participants were invited to explore interactive nature of the prototype, experience various means of spatial communication (sound/light/motion), find the triggers of the prototype components that enable response to the visitor's presence, and evaluate their interaction with the prototype. The aim of the survey was to quantify interactive qualities of prototypes' behaviour, considering its kinetic, light and sound properties. The survey was conducted on an aggregate basis of the score translated in the table through three-point scale. The results of the individual survey were systemized according to the Delphi expert method that allows quantitative expression of the respondents' opinion and statistically evaluates their opinion consistency. Survey results are summarized in Table 1 and represented in the following diagrams. (Figs. 4, 5 and 6).

3 Conclusion

Considering Actor–network theory, design acts as a mediator of social relationships, space itself constitutes, recreates and modifies social relationships by inviting, regrouping and reconnecting the users in a different manner. Interactive space creates a cognitive environment by itself, where users get immersed and connected, and gain social or functional enjoyment. Through interactive space, users get linked through communication with the same space and its agency, participating in a dialogue with the space, exploring its responsiveness and committing to the rules of this communication [7].

By applying ANT to the prototype strategy both visitors and the space become a part of a social interaction where they influence each other. The way visitors perceive the space is shaped by its' interactive properties and can change depending on the character of this communication.

Interactive design allows coming across non-human components, like objects in space and various environments, that mediate interaction with other humans, while ANT proposes a network of heterogeneous components, which influence each other in order to create a balance, resulting in harmony of social collaboration, afford movement through it and bring comfort to its' human components. This way designed space is not merely the mode of connection that cannot be explained by other economic, social or political means, but has its' own diffusion, objectivity and

Table 1 Results of the prototype survey

Question	Average score
1. How difficult was it to understand that the prototype was interactive?	2,55
2. To what degree was the prototype attractive upon entering it?	2,55
3. How appealing was the design and component configuration of the pavilion?	2,82
4. How effective is communication method by means of: – robotic blossoms motion – light – sound	2,55 2,64 2,73
5. The difficulty of understanding the behaviour of: – robotic blossoms motion – light changing – sound changing	2,55 2,18 2,55
6. The degree of responsiveness: – of robotic blossoms – light – sound	2,73 2,64 2,27
6. Willingness to follow the various cues from space: – robotic blossoms – light – sound	2,18 2,82 2,73
7. To what extent should the components of the prototype be changed to improve: – its' functionality – its' perception	2,02 2,45
8. the general effectiveness of the project	2,82
On an aggregate basis: – mean score – coefficient of variation of standard (mean-square) deviation, %	2,45 12,6

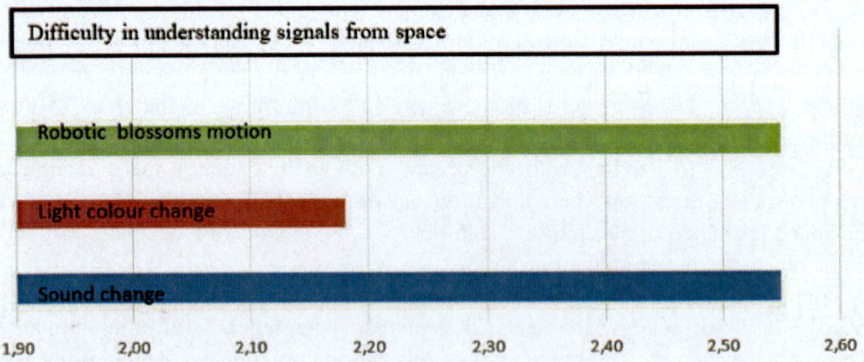

Fig. 4 Difficulty understanding signals from space chart

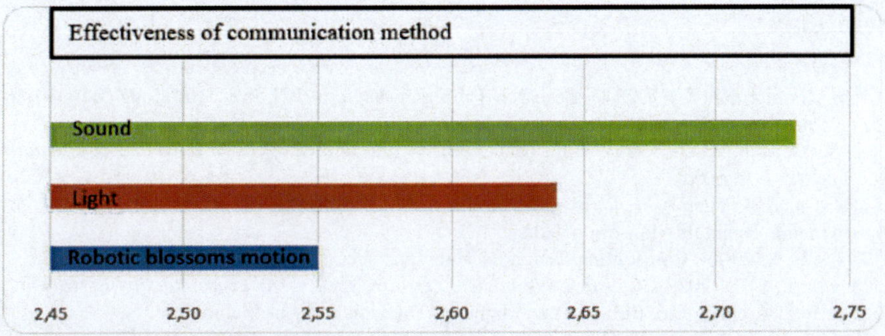

Fig. 5 Effectiveness of communication method chart

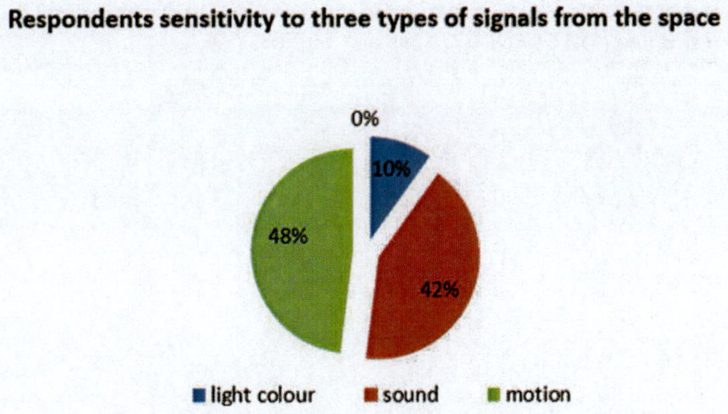

Fig. 6 Respondents' preference of different signal types responsiveness

solidity. Together with ethic, technical, cultural and artistic ties, the space contributes to social durability.

Interactive space can be considered as participant of social relationships through understanding of its communication with users, assessment of their assembling into groups and seeking participation of others, attribution of their actions meaning, evaluation of information exchange and willingness to be engaged in a dialogue with the space. The space can consider from two perspectives: either through its intrinsic materiality (or tangibility), or through its symbolic or aesthetic performance (defining it as social and subjective). ANT allows to shift from this modernist consideration, suggesting understanding space as a matter absorbed into meaning, making it both tangible and alive.

ANT allows to consider built context as a variable, that can move, change and evolve in real time, consisting of many dimensions itself, impacting performance of architecture and influencing its behaviour if it is interactive.

References

1. John Zimmerman, J. F. (2014). Research Through Design in HCI. In J. S. Kellogg (Ed.), *Ways of Knowing in HCI* (pp. 167–189). Springer.
2. Stappers, P. J., & Giaccardy, E. (2017). Research through design. *Encyclopedia of Human-Computer Interaction.*
3. David, J., & Krieger, A. B. (2014). Interpreting networks hermeneutics, actor-network theory & new media. Bielefeld: transcript Verlag.
4. Kraal, B. J. (2006). Considering design for automatic speech. Canberra, ACT, Australia.
5. Mewburn, I. B. (2009). *Constructing bodies: Gesture, speech and representation at work in.* Faculty of Architecture, Building and Planning, The University of Melbourne.
6. Boychenko, K. J. R. (2020). Interactive space as a signal processing device. In *2020 Systems of Signal Synchronization, Generating and Processing in Telecommunications (SYNCHROINFO* (pp. 1–6). Svetlogorsk: IEEE.
7. Kristina Boychenko, I. V. (2019). Interactive built space as the new means of information communication. In *2019 Systems of Signal Synchronization, Generating and Processing in Telecommunications (SYNCHROINFO).* Yaroslavl: IEEE.

A Practical Study of Process Mining from Event Logs Using Machine Learning and Petry Net Models

Valeria Nikitina and Peter Panfilov

Abstract This practical study is aimed at finding the value of synergy between the process mining and machine learning concepts using python programming. The paper introduces an analysis of an event log data with annual performance results for the purchase process. The purpose was to understand the whole process derived from data, indicate deviations from the standard sequence of events and visualize the process in Petri nets. For this purpose, the input data such as event log is transformed so that the use of process mining open source library is possible. For in-depth analysis the machine learning algorithms such as CatBoost were applied to find out how this sort of data can be used and how the machine learning problem such as regression problem can be solved.

Keywords Business process intelligence · Machine learning · Data mining · Process mining · Petry net

1 Introduction

Digital transformation of businesses and enterprises involves redesign of business processes along with certain enterprise architectures, infrastructures and systems with the aim of improving performance. Information and communication technology (ICT) and information systems (IS) drive this transformation since they form the digital core of todays' business processes [1]. Leveraging the transformative power of ICT/IS requires support from business process management that provides basis for modeling, analyzing and improving internal processes. Business process management systems (BMPS) are comprising modeling, mining and runtime subsystems. A business process modeling relies on advances in ICT/IS and is extensively used to identify existing processes in an organization for analysis to improve quality and efficiency of processes. In the time of redesigning and reengineering the deployed process models, process mining subsystems are gaining more and more attention.

V. Nikitina · P. Panfilov (✉)
HSE University, Myasnitskaya 20, Moscow 101000, Russian Federation
e-mail: ppanfilov@hse.ru

E. Zaramenskikh and A. Fedorova (eds.), *Digitalization of Society, Economics and Management*, Lecture Notes in Information Systems and Organisation 53,
https://doi.org/10.1007/978-3-030-94252-6_13

Sophisticated process mining techniques and data mining/machine learning software tools facilitate business transformation through innovative approaches to process management enhancement and automation. These integrated approaches combine power of mining system and the functional analysis of the modeling system with optimization techniques.

The concept of process mining has been introduced and developed in the late1990s. It is part of business process intelligence and represents the combination of process modeling, data mining and Big Data analysis techniques.

Process mining stands for extracting meaningful knowledge from large event logs that nowadays cannot be modeled and analyzed manually because of the size and complexity of the data. The necessary attributes are use case (a process instance or some identifier that groups specific activities), an activity, which reflects real events that happened in the company workflow process, and a timestamp that helps to identify the sequence of events. A unique sequence of events composes a trace. Additional attributes can be a resource that performs an activity, such as device or user, the user's name, cost, department, category and others.

Event log can be analyzed using three types of process mining techniques, namely: process discovery, conformance checking, and enhancement [2]. The first technique helps to construct a model in some notation which visualizes the whole process. It requires an event log itself and some algorithms such as an alpha-algorithm which is most often used due to simplicity. The second technique allows for checking whether the created model matches the real process and to find alignments. For conformance check it is obligatory to use an event log and process model as inputs. Finally, enhancement technique provides an improvement to move from «as-is» to «to-be» process using repair or extension type of enhancement [2] or some other possible recommendations.

In our study, we are looking for solution to optimization problem of a business process on the basis of analysis of peculiarities of different use cases and discovery of inherent bottlenecks. The starting point is the Process Mining Manifesto that helps to classify the steps and to make the whole analysis complete and including all necessary important parts [3].

In this paper, we describe an integrated approach to the process mining, analysis and timing optimization for the process redesigning work using process models that are discovered from their corresponding event logs. The analyzer is used to discover a process model from a process log dataset and to validate the discovered process model. We describe the detailed description of the system architecture with its functional integration of process mining, analysis and optimization. And more precisely, we define functional algorithms for extracting the structural constructs as well as for visualizing the structure and machine learning algorithms for optimizing timing behavior of those discovered process models. As experimental validation, we apply the proposed approach and analyzer to a purchasing process event log.

2 Related Works

Number of business process analysis tools were proposed that perform multiple functions of process discovery, analysis, simulation, modeling and reengineering. The authors of van der Aalst [4] discussed some of the process analysis tools and pointed out the importance of the comparison between designed and redesigned processes by using the process analysis and simulation tools. They also proposed a system based on the theory of the information control net modeling methodology. In paper [5], the Yasper tool for the process modeling, analysis and simulation is presented which is based on the use of Petri net modeling methodology. Another example of the use of Petry net-based methodology for process modeling and analysis are presented in papers [6] and [7]. An interesting combination of process mining and fuzzy methods is proposed in Wang et al. [8], where, an extraction of event logs from data is accomplished by using the System Entity Structure method, process discovery techniques are used for discovery of a transition system, and fuzzy methods help to generate a Fuzzy-DEVS model from the transition system. There is a plugin in the process mining framework (ProM) environment for inferring a Fuzzy-DEVS model from an event log dataset, and a SimStudio tool for simulation. Strategies based on exhaustive search, genetic algorithms and a greedy heuristic are proposed in Arriagada-Benitez [9] that use event data to automatically derive a process model from a configurable process model that represents the process in a specific branch. The strategies were tested on business-like event logs recorded in a real case scenario from a set of Dutch municipalities.

3 Process Mining and Analysis Functionality

3.1 Comprehensive Analysis of Event Log Data

The purpose was to receive a clear understanding of the process and to know whether we can apply process mining techniques. In accordance with the first guiding principle event data should be treated as first-class citizens [10]: it should be measured in terms of quality. Our event log has the third level pursuant to «Maturity levels for event logs» due to incompleteness of events in some use cases because data collecting stopped at a specific point in time. Since process mining requires the quality from 5 to 3 level it allows to follow other principles and continue the work.

3.2 Questions to Answer

Before the start, it was necessary to define issues which are interesting to explore and extract significant value and can help us to respond to the 11th challenge [10] and to improve comprehensibility for the company. Questions to answer here are as follows:

- Which are the most frequent and rarest activities and use cases?
- How strong are deviations are how many and what variants does the process have?
- What features determine the duration of events?

3.3 Support of Control Flow Constructs

For correct and clear understanding, the process should be visualized in a unified notation that maintains by all mainstream languages such as sequence, parallel routing, choice, and loops [10]. In our case while working with Python we mostly use Petri nets that have only places, transitions, and arcs as graphical elements and BPMN notation with much more composed notation elements.

4 Integrated System Implementation and Experimentation

4.1 Purchasing Process Data Description and Analysis

The data used in our study for process mining purposes describes the whole purchasing process mostly starting from issuing an invoice by supplier to completing delivery and closing the debt. The steps of the purchasing process are as follows:

1. Invoice issued by supplier;
2. Purchase order created;
3. Order unlocked;
4. Item accepted;
5. Invoice registered;
6. Debt repaid;
7. Delivery completed;
8. Debt closed.

Most process traces in the sample event log file start from steps such as *Invoice issued by supplier*, *Purchase order created* and *Purchasing request created*, while only few of them start from such rare activities as *Currency changed*, *Item accepted,* or *Price changed* (Fig. 1).

For this sample data set, events were recorded during the whole year period from January 1, 2015 to December 31, 2015. In total, the log file contains 282,391 events, which makes up 30,582 use cases and 26 possible activities. The maximum and minimum events per use case are 158 and 2, correspondingly. The longest use case lasted for 304 days 23 h 46 min and 27 s ecand the shortest one – for 0 days 00 h 00 min and 47 s. Thus, the mean duration of the use case is about 48 days 22 h 00 min

```
In [45]: from pm4py.algo.filtering.log.start_activities import start_activities_filter
         log_start = start_activities_filter.get_start_activities(log)
         filtered_log = start_activities_filter.apply(log, ["S1"])

In [46]: log_start

Out[46]: {'Invoice issued by supplier': 14862,
          'Purchase order created': 2987,
          'Purchasing request created': 12520,
          'Order unlocked': 160,
          'Application approved': 15,
          'Approval for order changed': 26,
          'Application rejected': 1,
          'Supplier changed': 5,
          'Currency changed': 3,
          'Item accepted': 2,
          'Price changed': 1}
```

Fig. 1 Starting steps of the process traces in the event log file

and 45.358838 s. We have 2558 traces and 1699 of them are traces with 1 frequency (single occurrence).

Table 1 shows the excerpt from the experimental data set that represents the main trace of the purchasing process that happens 6814 times and includes all the steps listed above for the use case No. 300450002891900010.

Tables 2 and 3 provide statistical data for purchasing process traces such as number of occurrences (frequencies) as per activity and per trace. From these, one can see that the *Order unlocked* step represents a most frequent activity even though this is not the most frequent start step. The rarest activities are *Supplier changed*, *Order confirmation received* and *Order line blocked* steps with single occurrence frequency.

4.2 Process Discovery and Filtering Implementation

The implementation of the first technique of process mining was done using the Python library pm4py [11]. The process graph was visualized using the Heuristics Miner algorithm that provides a way to handle the process with noise (Fig. 2).

The process graph (Fig. 3) is constructed in Petri net or place/transition (PT) net notation. Numbers and colors show the frequency of events and transitions, so the darker the positions the more often they occurred. The graph has many transitions and cycles to reflect the whole purchasing process. For example, we have cycles formed by *Application approved* and *Purchasing request created* steps (13,675 times), as well as cycles by *Application approved* and *Application rejected* steps (106 times), thus all of the rejected applications were approved afterwards. The process has many variants to follow after *Order unlocked*, *Approval for order changed*, *Price changed*, *Item accepted*, and *Debt repaid* steps (Fig. 3).

Table 1 An example of event log file for the purchasing process

	Case_Key	Event	Eventtime	User_Name	Purchases	Subdivision	Category	Supplier
0	300,450,002,891,900,010	Invoice issued by supplier	2015–01-03T12:01:00	User 96	MAT 000,000,001,500,000,379	JSC Leader""	MATGRP 235	Supplier 0,011,008,074
1	300,450,002,891,900,010	Purchase order created	2015–01-05T10:17:33	User 248	MAT 000,000,001,500,000,379	JSC Leader""	MATGRP 235	Supplier 0,011,008,074
2	300,450,002,891,900,010	Unlocked order	2015–01-05T10:21:37	User 248	MAT 000,000,001,500,000,379	JSC Leader""	MATGRP 235	Supplier 0,011,008,074
3	300,450,002,891,900,010	Item accepted	2015–01-05T10:28:09	User 215	MAT 000,000,001,500,000,379	JSC Leader""	MATGRP 235	Supplier 0,011,008,074
4	300,450,002,891,900,010	Invoice registered	2015–02-03T17:31:01	User 96	MAT 000,000,001,500,000,379	JSC Leader""	MATGRP 235	Supplier 0,011,008,074
5	300,450,002,891,900,010	Debt repaid	2015–02-03T17:31:01	User 96	MAT 000,000,001,500,000,379	JSC Leader""	MATGRP 235	Supplier 0,011,008,074
6	300,450,002,891,900,010	Delivery completed	2015–02-03T17:31:05	User 96	MAT 000,000,001,500,000,379	JSC Leader""	MATGRP 235	Supplier 0,011,008,074
7	300,450,002,891,900,010	Debt closed	2015–02-19T23:31:40	User 13	MAT 000,000,001,500,000,379	JSC Leader""	MATGRP 235	Supplier 0,011,008,074
8	300,450,002,891,900,020	Invoice issued by supplier	2015–01-03T12:01:00	User 96	MAT 000,000,001,500,000,380	JSC Leader""	MATGRP 235	Supplier 0,011,008,074
9	300,450,002,891,900,020	Purchase order created	2015–01-05T10:17:33	User 248	MAT 000,000,001,500,000,380	JSC Leader""	MATGRP 235	Supplier 0,011,008,074

Table 2 Number of occurrences (frequency) per trace

Trace	Frequency	%
Invoice issued by supplier; Purchase order created; Order unlocked; Item accepted; Invoice registered; Debt repaid; Delivery completed; Debt closed	6814	22,28
Invoice issued by supplier; Purchase order created; Order unlocked; Item accepted; Debt repaid; Invoice registered; Delivery completed; Debt closed	4175	13,65
Purchasing request created; Application approved; Purchase order created; Order unlocked; Invoice issued by supplier; Item accepted; Invoice registered; Debt repaid; Delivery completed; Debt closed	1913	6,25
Purchasing request created; Application approved; Purchase order created; Order unlocked; Invoice issued by supplier; Item accepted; Debt repaid; Invoice registered; Delivery completed; Debt closed	1519	4,97
Currency changed; Purchase order created; Order unlocked; Item accepted	1	0,003
Application approved; Purchase order created; Approval for order changed; Order unlocked; Invoice issued by supplier; Invoice issued by supplier; Item accepted; Debt repaid; Invoice registered; Delivery completed; Debt closed; Debt closed	1	0,003

4.3 *Machine Learning-Based Solution for Process Time Prediction Problem*

To apply the machine learning technique to the purchasing process data, an event log file needed to be changed. The idea behind the ML application to process mining problem was to predict the time duration of each state depending on suppliers and other attributes. For example, suppose the purchased goods are accepted, an important question to answer here would be, for example: How much time will pass before the invoice registration happens? Then it would be also important to evaluate quality metrics as R-squared and MSE on the test results.

Activities/steps in an event log were shifted per use case, so the new log structure contains not only current activity, but also the previous activity. The start activity with NaN value for previous activity was deleted. A new column was calculated as the difference between timestamps and added to the log (Table 4).

The training data for the machine learning model consists of CASE_KEY, EVENT, PREVIOUS_EVENT, USER_NAME, CATEGORY, and SUPPLIER features, and the DURATION is considered a target variable (Fig. 4).

The ensemble learning technique such as Gradient boosting was applied to our modified process data. In particular, a CatBoost algorithm developed by Yandex engineers and researchers [12] was used for gradient boosting on decision trees. An important advantage of using CatBoost library with our data set is that it supports categorical features, which were defined for «cat_features» as categorical_features_indices (Fig. 5).

Table 3 Number of occurrences (frequency) per activity

Activity	Frequency
Order unlocked	34,301
Item accepted	32,935
Invoice registered	31,296
Invoice issued by supplier	30,667
Purchase order created	30,579
Delivery completed	29,026
Debt repaid	27,125
Debt closed	26,852
Purchasing request created	13,675
Application approved	13,209
Approval for order changed	6537
Price changed	2643
Deliver cancelled	1653
Quantity changed	673
Invoice reversed	213
Order line deleted	200
Currency changed	183
Supply cancelled	183
Warehouse changed	145
Application rejected	106
Order rejected	76
Delivery flag changed	68
Order line restored	24
Supplier changed	19
Order confirmation updated	1
Order confirmation received	1
Order line blocked	1

Fig. 2 An example of Heuristic Miner application to the process graph visualization

To predict duration, CatBoost Regressor model was used with large number of iterations, that is 5000 which corresponds to the number of trees that can be built in the model, and an «Iter» type detector to avoid overfitting. It is recommended to use the depth value from 4 to 10, so we chose the depth value 10 to ensure better results (Fig. 6).

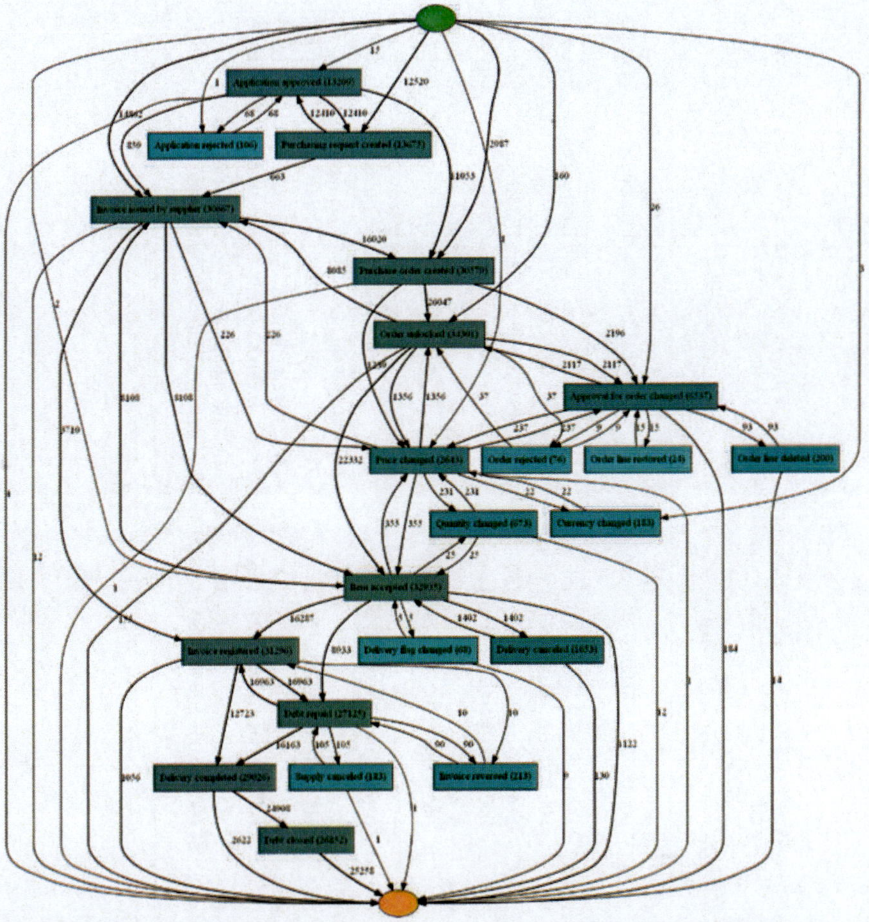

Fig. 3 The whole purchasing process derived by Python library pm4py from event log

The model training process stopped after about half of iterations and the best one was the 2562nd iteration (Fig. 7).

As Fig. 8 shows, the results of CatBoost feature importance ranking indicate that previous activity (PREVIOUS_EVENT feature) has the most impact on duration, and an activity (EVENT) takes only fourth place after user (USER_NAME) that perform that activity and supplier (SUPPLIER).

Different metrics can be calculated for the results of process mining using machine learning techniques as it is shown in Fig. 9. The following metrics were obtained for the process mining results on sample log data of purchasing process. Mean squared error is about 401,487,808 and the RMSE is about 20,037. The duration is explained by the parameters included in the model by 52.32% (R2 metrics).

Table 4 New structure of the event log

	Case_Key	Event	Eventtime	User_Name	Purchases	Subdivision	Category	Supplier	Previous_Event	Duration
1	300,450,002,891,900,010	Purchase order created	2015–01-05 T10:17:33	User 248	MAT 000,000,001,500,000,379	JSC Leader""	MATGRP 235	Supplier 0,011,008,074	Invoice issued by supplier	1 days 22:16:33
2	300,450,002,891,900,010	Unlocked order	2015–01-05 T10:21:37	User 248	MAT 000,000,001,500,000,379	JSC Leader""	MATGRP 235	Supplier 0,011,008,074	Purchase order created	0 days 00:04:04
3	300,450,002,891,900,010	Item accepted	2015–01-05 T10:28:09	User 215	MAT 000,000,001,500,000,379	JSC Leader""	MATGRP 235	Supplier 0,011,008,074	Unlocked Order	0 days 00:06:32
4	300,450,002,891,900,010	Invoice registered	2015–02-03 T17:31:01	User 96	MAT 000,000,001,500,000,379	JSC Leader""	MATGRP 235	Supplier 0,011,008,074	Item accepted	29 days 07:02:52
5	300,450,002,891,900,010	Debt repaid	2015–02-03 T17:31:01	User 96	MAT 000,000,001,500,000,379	JSC Leader""	MATGRP 235	Supplier 0,011,008,074	Invoice registered	0 days 00:00:00
6	300,450,002,891,900,010	Delivery completed	2015–02-03 T17:31:05	User 96	MAT 000,000,001,500,000,379	JSC Leader""	MATGRP 235	Supplier 0,011,008,074	Debt repaid	0 days 00:00:04
7	300,450,002,891,900,010	Debt closed	2015–02-19 T23:31:40	User 13	MAT 000,000,001,500,000,379	JSC Leader""	MATGRP 235	Supplier 0,011,008,074	Delivery completed	16 days 06:00:35
9	300,450,002,891,900,020	Purchase order created	2015–01-05 T10:17:33	User 248	MAT 000,000,001,500,000,380	JSC Leader""	MATGRP 235	Supplier 0,011,008,074	Invoice issued by supplier	1 days 22:16:33

```
In [29]: plt.figure(figsize = (10, 4))
         n, bins, patches = plt.hist(y, 100, alpha=0.75)
         plt.title('Histogram of duration')
         plt.show();
```

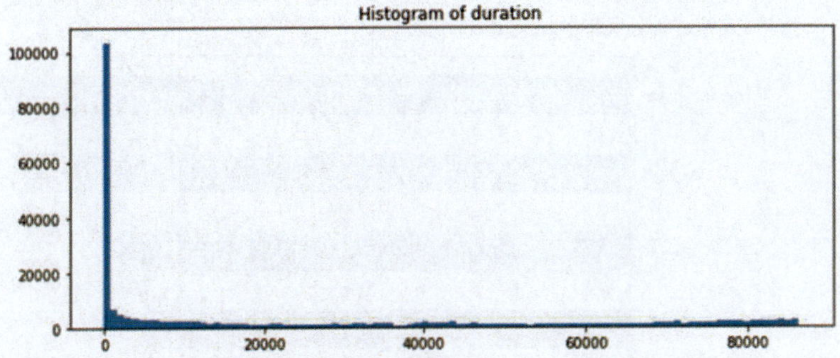

Fig. 4 A code fragment and diagram of the histogram of duration parameter

```
In [23]: categorical_features_indices = np.where(X.dtypes != np.float)[0]
         categorical_features_indices

Out[23]: array([0, 1, 2, 3, 4, 5], dtype=int64)
```

Fig. 5 A code fragment illustrating the categorical_features_indicies use in CatBoost library

```
In [39]: model =  CatBoostRegressor(iterations=5000,
                                    learning_rate=0.03,
                                    depth=10,
                                    eval_metric='RMSE',
                                    random_seed = 23,
                                    bagging_temperature = 0.2,
                                    od_type='Iter',
                                    metric_period = 75,
                                    od_wait=100)
         model.fit(X_train, y_train,
                   eval_set=(X_test, y_test),
                   cat_features=categorical_features_indices,
                   plot=True,
                   use_best_model=True)
```

Fig. 6 A code fragment for the CatBoostRegressor model

```
2025:   learn: 18102.3240949   test: 20054.0845298   best: 20053.8547001 (2023)   total: 6m 50s   remaining: 10m 2s
2100:   learn: 18040.3306352   test: 20051.7700849   best: 20051.7700849 (2100)   total: 7m 5s    remaining: 9m 46s
2175:   learn: 17982.5727073   test: 20049.1712323   best: 20049.1712323 (2175)   total: 7m 19s   remaining: 9m 30s
2250:   learn: 17917.7878731   test: 20045.8612355   best: 20045.7212727 (2249)   total: 7m 34s   remaining: 9m 14s
2325:   learn: 17851.2727461   test: 20042.9641440   best: 20042.9641440 (2325)   total: 7m 48s   remaining: 8m 59s
2400:   learn: 17790.9552924   test: 20041.9642750   best: 20041.5621200 (2391)   total: 8m 3s    remaining: 8m 43s
2475:   learn: 17731.7614483   test: 20040.3819432   best: 20040.2624589 (2474)   total: 8m 18s   remaining: 8m 28s
2550:   learn: 17672.8520073   test: 20037.6565197   best: 20037.6565197 (2550)   total: 8m 32s   remaining: 8m 12s
2625:   learn: 17623.5884483   test: 20038.0950825   best: 20037.1606797 (2562)   total: 8m 47s   remaining: 7m 56s
Stopped by overfitting detector  (100 iterations wait)

bestTest = 20037.16068
bestIteration = 2562
```

Fig. 7 Machine learning model training process (iterations)

```
In [40]: fea_imp = pd.DataFrame({'imp': model.feature_importances_, 'col': X.columns})
         fea_imp = fea_imp.sort_values(['imp', 'col'], ascending=[True, False]).iloc[-30:]
         fea_imp.plot(kind='barh', x='col', y='imp', figsize=(10, 7), legend=None)
         plt.title('CatBoost - Feature Importance')
         plt.ylabel('Features')
         plt.xlabel('Importance');
```

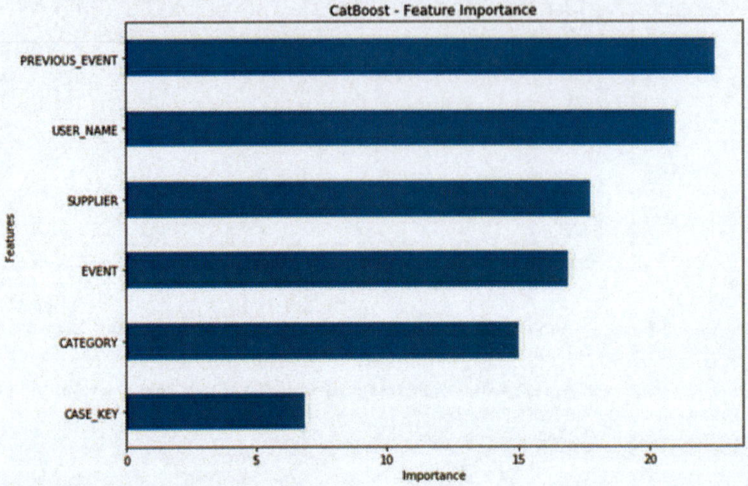

Fig. 8 Feature importance analysis

```
In [58]: print('MSE for model:', metrics.mean_squared_error(y_test, predictions3))

         MSE for model: 401487808.1024255

In [59]: print('RMSE for model:', np.sqrt(metrics.mean_squared_error(y_test, predictions3)))

         RMSE for model: 20037.160679657823

In [60]: print('R2 for model:', metrics.r2_score(y_test, predictions3))

         R2 for model: 0.5232000708753206
```

Fig. 9 Metrics

5 Conclusion and Future Work

The work is focused on the analysis and understanding of the business process data derived from event log using python libraries. In order to deal with process mining, libraries pm4py and GraphViz were used. Pm4py library functions help to filter and explore the data while using GraphViz is for visualization purpose. CatBoost helps to solve the regression problem, but the results were not so impressive. Metrics on the test performance are not good enough so the model improvements should be enforced.

Thereby the future research will be directed toward improving metrics and models as well as finding possible ways to use machine learning techniques. As to the process mining side the analysis will go deep into the bottlenecks and problems of the process and propose possible recommendations. The second type of process mining—conformance checking will be useful to find alignments and then to apply the third type—enhancement for process optimization.

Acknowledgements This research was partially supported by the RFBR (Grant No 20–07–00958) and the Program of Project Group Competition of the HSE University.

References

1. Ramirez, R., Melville, N., & Lawler, E. (2010). Information technology infrastructure, organizational process redesign, and business value: An empirical analysis. *Decision Support Systems, 49*(4), 417–429.
2. vom Brocke, J., & Mendling, J. (Eds). (2018). Business process management cases. Digital innovation and business transformation in practice (1st ed, p.626). Berlin: Springer.
3. van der Aalst, W. (2015). Process mining: Data science in action. 2nd edn (p. 477). Springer Science+Business Media, Netherlands.
4. Jansen-Vullers, M., & Netjes, M. (2006). Business process simulation—a tool survey. In *Proceedings of the Workshop and Tutorial on Practical Use of Coloured Petry Nets and the CPN Tools.*
5. van Hee, K. M., Oanea, O., Post, R., Somers, L. J., & van Werf, J. M. E. M. (2006). Yasper: A tool for workflow modeling and analysis. In *Proceedings of the 6th International Conference on Application of Concurrency to System Design* (pp. 279–282).
6. Wynn, M., Dumas, M., & Fidge, C. J. (2007). Business process simulation for operational decision support. In *Proceedings of the 3rd International Workshop on Business Process Intelligence (BPI 07) in conjunction with Business Process Management Conference.*
7. Verbeek, H. M., Basten, T., & van der Aalst, W. M. P. (2001). Diagnosing workflow processes using woflan. *The Computer Journal*, 246–279.
8. Wang, Y., Zacharewicz, G., Traore, M. K., & Chen, D. (2018). An integrative approach to simulation model discovery: Combining system theory, process mining and fuzzy logic. *Journal of Intelligent & Fuzzy Systems, 34*, 477–490.
9. Arriagada-Benitez, M., Sepulveda, M., Munoz-Gama, J., & Buijs, J. C. A. M. (2017). Strategies to automatically derive a process model from a configurable process model based on event data. *Applied Sciences, 7*, 1023–1051.
10. van der Aalst, W. et al. (2012). Process mining manifesto. In F. Daniel, K. Barkaoui, S. Dustdar (Eds.), *Business Process Management Workshops. BPM 2011. Lecture Notes in Business Information Processing* (Vol. 99). Berlin, Heidelberg: Springer.
11. State-of-the-art-process mining in Python Homepage. https://pm4py.fit.fraunhofer.de/. Accessed 11 May 2020.
12. CatBoost Homepage. https://catboost.ai/. Accessed 11 May 2020.

Management of Distributed Medical Information Systems

Elena Kukharenko and Alexey Yankevskiy

Abstract The article deals with the problem of managing medical information systems, including the example of quality control of the provision of medical services using isotope-containing medical materials. A digitalization of economics leads to a strong transformation of business routines of companies in wide variety of industry branches. The transition from paper media to electronic document management systems all over the world is associated with a complex of methodological and organizational and technical tasks to ensure the availability and reliability of data, regulatory support for the interactions of all participants in the process of collecting, transferring, processing and storing information, as well as the formation of an archive of data of former periods. The mathematical model allows at the practical level to carry out multi-parameter monitoring and control in the main critical areas. The use of a qualitative assessment in parallel with a quantitative one allows the managing staff of the administration of a medical institution to obtain a more complete assessment of the situation in controlling the circulation of isotope-containing materials in the provision of medical services to the population.

Keywords Medical information system · Information technology · Management

1 Introduction

A digitalization of economics leads to a strong transformation of business routines of companies in wide variety of industry branches [1]. The transition from paper media to electronic document management systems all over the world is associated with a complex of methodological and organizational and technical tasks to ensure the

E. Kukharenko (✉)
Moscow Technical University of Communications and Informatics, Aviamotornaya St. 8A, 111024 Moscow, Russia
e-mail: e.g.kukharenko@mtuci.ru

A. Yankevskiy
Peoples Friendship University of Russia, Miklukho-Maclay St. 6, 117198 Moscow, Russia

E. Zaramenskikh and A. Fedorova (eds.), *Digitalization of Society, Economics and Management*, Lecture Notes in Information Systems and Organisation 53,
https://doi.org/10.1007/978-3-030-94252-6_14

availability and reliability of data, regulatory support for the interactions of all participants in the process of collecting, transferring, processing and storing information. as well as the formation of an archive of data of former periods [2, 3]. For example, collection and storage of large volumes of medical information on a local computer does not make sense or because of the high requirements for reliability and safety imposed by the legislation of the country for this class of information in connection with which cloud storage technologies are used to store access to it. Consider the basic principles of building geographically distributed info-communication medical systems:

- Confidentiality and security of patient data.
- Information service providers.
- Regulatory support, security policy and control.
- Infrastructure for information exchange.
- Construction options.
- Geographic locations of data storage.
- Data access models.
- Ensuring data integrity.
- Geographically distributed multi-user environment.
- Incidents in the system and algorithms for responding to them.
- Data protection (monitoring, encryption, deletion).
- Confidentiality and security of patient data.

2 Regulation

The formation of a systemic approach to the functioning of medical information systems was laid by the laws adopted by the US government in 1996 and the Health Information Technology for Economic and Clinical Health (HITECH) Act and in 2003 the Health Information Portability and Accountability Act (HIPAA) in 1996 and the Health Information Technology for Economic and Clinical Health (HITECH) Act. They require organizations involved in the work with health information to implement a set of measures to ensure confidentiality and security, as well as inform patients when the privacy and security of their personal data is at risk. HIPAA covers medical organizations: medical institutions, insurance companies, and medical settlement centers. The HITECH Act has extended the HIPAA Privacy Rule and Security Rule standards to business partners. Business partners provide processing and administration, data analysis and management services. A cloud provider where PHI is considered a business partner. In January 2013, the OCR published the final Modifications to the HIPAA Privacy, Security, Enforcement, and Breach Notification Rules Under the Health Information Technology for Economic and Clinical Health Act and the Genetic Information Nondiscrimination Act, as well as the Other Modifications to the HIPAA Rules. They are changing the definition of a business partner, improving the security and privacy of PHI, placing direct responsibility on business partners, changing the damage threshold in the Breach Notification Rule, and clarifying the content of the business partner agreement. An important point–OCR jurisdiction extends to business partners and their subcontractors. The definition of a business partner has been changed in the Omnibus Rules. Business partner subcontractors are considered to be acting on their behalf, i.e. they are persons to whom a business partner has delegated the performance of a function covered by HIPAA.

2.1 Information Service Providers

Cloud service providers are uniquely placed among the business partners trusted by EPHI. When EPHI is stored in the cloud, consumers disclose it to a cloud provider who become a business partner and is HIPAA and HITECH compliant. Organizations are allowed to share EPHI information in the course of treatment, payment, and healthcare operations without patient consent. When exchanging, only the required minimum EPHI should be opened. Medical organizations can share EPHIs with each other and with business partners. When disclosing this information to a business partner, healthcare organizations must ensure that the business partner will adequately protect the information provided by the BAA. BAA is a Service Level Agreement containing HIPAA and HITECH compliance clauses. Medical organizations are required to enter into BAAs with business partners to whom they provide EPHI. Business Partners must enter into a BAA with their subcontractors to whom they share this information. Business partners must enter into BAAs with subcontractors. Healthcare organizations are not required to enter into separate agreements with subcontractors to provide PHI. By clearly defining the roles and responsibilities of the healthcare organization, business partner and subcontractor in the BAA, the responsibility of each party to the agreement can be reduced and the processes for reporting leaks are simplified. Agreements between healthcare organizations and business partners must adhere to the Security Rule when reporting unprotected PHI leaks to the organization, and ensure that their subcontractors comply with business partner level PHI restrictions and conditions. If the healthcare organization is aware of the business partner's activities that violate the BAA, then it must take appropriate action to correct the leak or stop the violation, and otherwise terminate the BAA. The BAA states that a business partner must comply with the Privacy Rule applicable to a healthcare organization. Even without a BAA, business partners and subcontractors are directly responsible for their actions, but agreements help define important commitments.

2.2 Unconditional Commitment

OCR emphasizes that the privacy and security of PHI should be held accountable by all who are trusted with it. Formulating these rules, OCR explains that it wants to "avoid a situation where the privacy and security of PHI is not ensured just because the work is performed by a subcontractor and not by a business partner directly associated with a healthcare organization." Cloud service providers are directly responsible and must carefully monitor data. To avoid violations, it is necessary to constantly monitor client access to data, to ensure proper authentication procedures. This will reduce the risk of vulnerabilities, increase the chances of detecting and fixing violations before they cause damage, and also facilitate interaction with other business partners, medical organizations and the ministry in the event of a PHI leak.

2.3 Civil Monetary Penalties (CMP)

This new liability can be very costly for business partners, with penalties of up to $1.5 million per year for violation. However, OCR clarifies that this is a ceiling for one type of violation. When imposing fines, the ministry takes into account many factors and can change the amount of the fine if it is inadequate for the violation. Cloud services are specific to each consumer, especially private clouds customized to a specific client. Therefore, the cloud services provided can be an important factor in determining the amount of penalties. For example, some consumers may use software as a service (SaaS), thereby giving the cloud provider control of most of their data, including PHI. Consumers can also use open clouds. In both cases, efficient data management results in cost savings. However, such services can become a source of leaks, damaging many people in a short period of time, while a consumer using infrastructure as a service (IaaS) or a private cloud can better control leaks. Regardless of the cloud service model, the Omnibus Rules change from "history of violations" to "previous noncompliance" allows the ministry to take into account the good faith efforts of the cloud service provider, its business partners, and healthcare organizations to eliminate or mitigate leaks. Cloud providers are unlikely to have a "history of violations," and a proactive approach to compliance can be an effective way to reduce penalties.

2.4 Leaks

HHS defines an EPHI leak as "inappropriate use or disclosure… compromising the security or privacy of protected health information and posing a significant risk of financial, reputational or other harm to an individual." Since 2009, major EPHI leaks affecting medical records of 500 or more people have compromised the data of almost 21 million people. The share of business partners in large leaks was 21%. More and more information is stored electronically (including in the cloud), these statistics will inevitably change. Migration to the cloud spawns new methods of attacking EPHI. These attacks now threaten off-site EPHI, where those to whom it was originally trusted have less control. Regardless of the reason for the leak, violations of HIPAA are subject to criminal and civil penalties at both the state and federal levels.

2.5 Leak Notification

Business partners are directly responsible for leaks of PHI under their control and must report them to healthcare providers (as well as subcontractors with an agreement with business partners). Business partners who have access to, use, or disclose PHI must notify the healthcare organization if this information is leaked. After receiving the notification of the leak, the medical organization is fully responsible for notifying the affected persons, the ministry, the media and other organizations. However, OCR permits BAA parties to determine who will be responsible for the notification. OCR provides healthcare organizations and business partners with the ability to determine who will take responsibility for the notification, as well as set requirements for how, when and to whom the notification should be sent. A healthcare organization is more suited to this role than cloud providers, who may be subcontractors and located far from affected individuals. However, the cloud provider may be more able to collect information that the healthcare organization needs to include in the notification because it stores the EPHI. Therefore, the business partner must provide the healthcare organization with all available information that the organization must include in the notification. If this information cannot be provided at the time the leak is discovered, the business partner can first notify their business partner or healthcare organization of the leak and then send additional information. In addition, the regulations require the medical organization to be informed of all the facts regarding the leak, so the business partner must provide this information, even if it becomes available after sending the notification to the victims.

2.6 HIPAA Compliance: Cloud Specific Issues

Moving data to the cloud poses a number of challenges that complicate HIPAA compliance for healthcare organizations, business partners, and cloud providers themselves. These are control, access, availability, shared multi-tenant environments, incident preparedness and response, and data protection, all of which are covered in the remainder of this article. While there are many benefits to storing EPHI in the cloud, customers and cloud service providers should be aware of how each of these issues impacts HIPAA and HITECH compliance.

2.7 Control Over Data

By entrusting cloud providers with storing their data, consumers are relinquishing direct control over that data from the application layer. Due to the change in control when moving EPHI to the cloud, the consumer and supplier must clearly define in the BAA who takes responsibility for the privacy and security of the data.

3 Customer Control

The cloud service provider offers processing, storage, networking, and other resources to enable the consumer to deploy and run any software. The consumer controls the operating systems, storage systems, deployed applications, and possibly some of the networking components, and therefore must take on more responsibility.

3.1 Application and Infrastructure

Cloud computing service level models provide consumers with different levels of control, often offering appropriate security tradeoffs. Consumers and suppliers must balance their organizations and determine the risk they are willing to take in losing control of their data.

3.2 Deployment Models

Cloud deployment models themselves affect data control regardless of the application or infrastructure tier. In the open cloud model, infrastructure is publicly available, and control is lost when data is deployed. At the other end, there is a private cloud infrastructure available to only one consumer. A public cloud is available to a specific community, and a hybrid cloud combines open and private cloud models. To provide the highest level of control, and therefore the greatest confidentiality and security of EPHI, it is necessary to use a private cloud model. However, open clouds can also be used to store EPHI. The open cloud makes EPHI more vulnerable. A number of vendors specifically separate a portion of their cloud services to host EPHI-related data. However, many vendors do not, so such services can be costly to consumers. Consumers must choose the degree of risk they are willing to take when hosting data in open, private or hybrid clouds. Regardless of where consumers host their data, cloud service providers must ensure the privacy and security of EPHI in accordance with HIPAA and HITECH requirements, given the level of control they have over that data.

3.3 Geographic Location of the Data

Cloud services allow you to store data in multiple locations, which is useful in emergency situations. Storing data off-site or in multiple locations ensures that critical business operations are not interrupted. However, consumers who don't know where their data is located lose control of EPHI at a different level. They need to know where the data is in order to understand which laws, rules and regulations must be followed. In some cases, the geographic location of EPHI may lead to problems with international legislation that is contrary to HIPAA and HITECH.

4 Access to Data

Given that the consumer loses control over the data at several levels, the question arises who has access to it and how to control access. The growing number of actors involved means more people are able to access EPHI in the cloud, increasing the risks of data security breaches. Cloud service providers and consumers must work together to ensure security by managing the granting and modification of access rights. It all starts with determining the right of a user or a computer system to carry out a certain activity.

4.1 Granting Access Rights for Personnel

It is the user's responsibility to determine who should have access to the data stored in the cloud, and the cloud provider enforces the user's decisions. All employees who may have access to EPHI must go through the clearance process. Customers, cloud providers, and those the providers work with should create job descriptions that clearly describe the responsibilities assigned to each employee and oversee compliance with them. All employees with access to EPHI must receive unique usernames and receive training to maintain the confidentiality of their registration information. Each user is granted access in accordance with his assigned role, and if necessary, the access rights must be immediately changed or revoked.

4.2 Authentication

According to HIPAA, procedures must be in place to ensure that only registered individuals have access to EPHI. This could be an authorization system using a unique username and password or other data. A number of cloud service providers offer integration with consumer authentication systems using LDAP mechanisms or single sign-on (SSO) technologies. However, these methods can themselves become a source of security threats.

4.3 Audit of Access

The Security Rule requires regular review of information system activity reports to identify any inappropriate EPHI disclosure. In addition, hardware, software, and/or procedural mechanisms must be used to record and study activity in information systems containing or using EPHI. The HITECH Act requires additional EPHI leak monitoring. Audit is a particular concern of HIPAA and HITECH because it is dependent on incident response, reporting procedures and ultimately the ability to stop and mitigate leaks.4) Integrity. The integrity of EPHI depends on who has access to the data. Suppliers and consumers have a responsibility not only to determine who has access to the EPHI stored in the cloud, but also to maintain the integrity of the data and protect it from tampering.

4.4 Common Multi-User Environment

Open cloud services are cost-effective because such infrastructure often includes shared multi-tenant environments, whereby consumers share components and resources with other consumers that they do not know.

4.5 Data Availability

One of the Security Rule is the availability of EPHI, especially in case of emergency or other incidents. One of the benefits of moving EPHI to the cloud is the ability to improve data availability in a variety of ways. Cloud services that store redundant data in multiple locations are better at handling disasters.

5 Preparedness and Response to Incidents

Incident response is a key issue in HIPAA and HITECH compliance. Regardless of the number of actions taken, not all incidents can be prevented.

5.1 Preparedness for Incidents

Before an incident occurs, customers and suppliers must develop specific policies and procedures, such as an emergency plan. They must perform proactive monitoring of threats and vulnerabilities. Cloud service providers must communicate these vulnerabilities to customers so that they can determine the acceptability of risks or fix vulnerabilities. In addition to locating EPHI and assessing risk, consumers must back up their data. A backup EPHI must be created and maintained. Cloud services provide the ability to back up data externally. Consumers and cloud providers must control access to EPHI and ensure that only authenticated authorized users get it. Cloud service providers and consumers must continually test for vulnerabilities and adjust their policies and procedures accordingly.

5.2 *Incident Response*

The cloud provider must respond to incidents and is responsible for verifying and analyzing incidents, isolating consequences, collecting data, storing, resolving problems and restoring normal operations. Based on the results of the investigation, he must isolate the consequences of the incident to ensure the confidentiality, integrity and availability of EPHI. Customers should determine how an incident will be verified and how information will be collected to analyze it.

6 Data Protection

Transferred data and backups must be protected in different ways. Security measures must be taken by cloud service providers and include: monitoring, encryption, key management, and data deletion.

6.1 *Monitoring Data Leaks*

By handing over control of data to a cloud provider, consumers are forced to rely on the processes that the provider uses to monitor data leaks on their systems. Such as firewalls, network intrusion detection, monitoring server logs and end user access. Cloud service providers must perform regular checks to ensure that they are operational. If a leak or vulnerability is discovered, the cloud provider must inform the consumer.

6.2 *Encryption*

Organizations can encrypt data to make it unusable, unreadable, or indecipherable by unauthorized persons.

6.3 Key Management

Encryption key management schemes are another way to protect data. Consumers can use this tool on their own or through a cloud service provider. Those who already use key management schemes must address the issues of securing key vaults, limiting access to vaults, and their backup and recovery.

6.4 Data Deletion

The Security Rule requires healthcare organizations and business partners to "implement policies and procedures for the permanent disposal of electronic health information and/or the hardware or electronic media on which it is stored." Therefore, cloud service providers must ensure that the EPHI is correctly deleted and cannot be re-created at the request of consumers, including from backups.

The use of geographically distributed medical information systems of electronic document management using cloud technologies of various types allows doctors to collect more information to study patient histories. Various systems for the exchange of information about the patient's health constantly perform operations to exchange information, which creates risks and vulnerabilities for such systems.

Medical staff are no longer the only owners and custodians of confidential information about a patient's health, medical history and prescribed procedures and drugs and treatment plan. For example, employees of telecommunications companies or system integrators who manage the storage of data also have access to this information and, thus, are responsible for its safety.

Analysis of statistical data and the practice of operating the currently geographically distributed information and communication systems in the field of treatment of cancer patients in cities with a population of one million allows us to formulate the management task for this class of systems—the level of a metropolis—in a balanced way.

From the point of view of management of complexes of systems, it is most clearly and more convenient from the point of view of information presentation, when the features describing control objects have a qualitative characteristic.

This is due to the fact that the quality parameter is more stable and unchanged over time.

It is not characterized by the uncertainties inherent in quantitative parameters, possible incompleteness of information about the object, various subjective quantitative inaccuracies, etc.

In the case of a study of multidimensional control systems of the scale of a megalopolis, it becomes necessary to compare (compare) the systems and objects from them according to several common features.

In particular, in some cases, some of the parameters of objects lend themselves to quantitative assessment, and some cannot be expressed numerically.

7 Formulation of the Control Problem

Based on the above data and a balanced analysis of the parameters affecting the system in the use of medical information systems for the provision of medical services to cancer patients, the following management task is formulated: multi-parameter control of the quality of services provided to the population in the field of health care using isotope-containing radioactive materials.

Construction and analysis of a mathematical model for the development of medical information systems for the treatment of cancer patients.

Based on the formulated problem, we will construct a mathematical model using the optimized quantitative parameters. Limitations imposed on the system:

External:

- Federal Legislation (Constitution).
- Regional level legislation.
- City legislation.

Internal:

- The current level of development of technologies in medicine.
- The patient's health status.

Using the "black box" principle, we will graphically represent the economic and mathematical model of the control problem with corrective feedback (Fig. 1).

$$N' = F[N] = F[H; T; G], \quad (1)$$

where:

H—A set of parameters describing the availability of employees with the proper qualifications for the process of providing services.

T —A set of parameters describing the logistics of the service delivery process.

G —A set of parameters describing the environmental component of the service delivery process.

Figure 2 shows a graphical representation of the mathematical model with detailing from the general view (Formula 1) to detailing by parameters.

where:

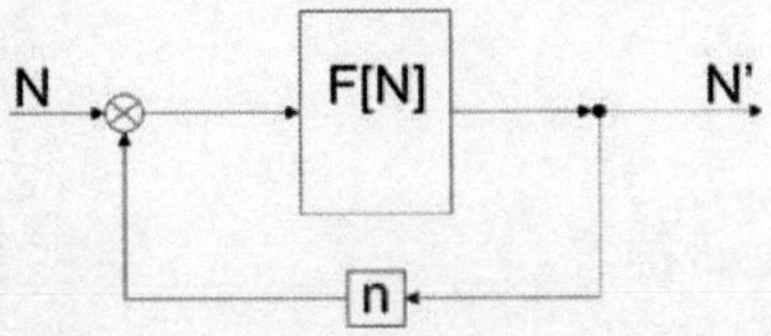

Fig. 1 General mathematical model of the system. Where N is a set of input parameters, N 'is a set of output parameters, n—corrective action. In general, the functional is as follows:

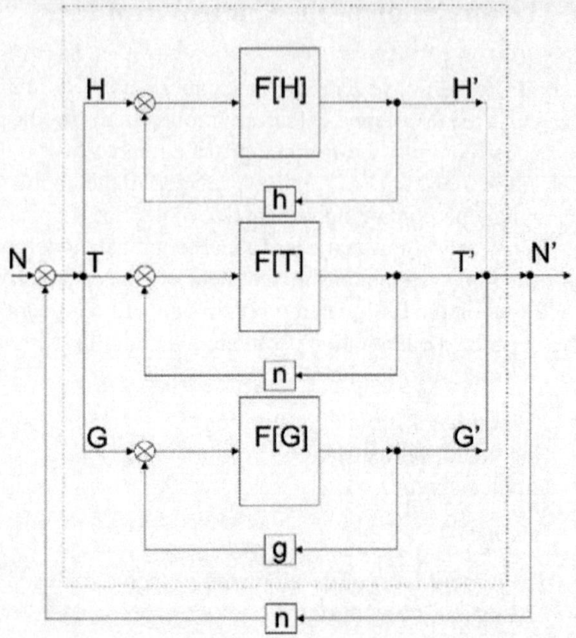

Fig. 2 A mathematical model with a representation by parameters

H is a set of input parameters according to the level of training of human resources (Formula 2).

H' is a set of output parameters by the level of training of human resources,

h —Corrective action on the level of training of human resources,

T is a set of parameters for the provision of services (Formula 3).

T' is a set of output parameters for the provision of services, t is the corrective action for the provision of services.

G is a set of parameters associated with the circulation of isotopic materials (Formula 4).

G 'is a set of output parameters associated with the circulation of isotopic materials.

g is the corrective action associated with the circulation of isotopic materials.

Let us write the set for each of the parameters in the form of functionals:

$$H' = F[H] = F[E, S, P, O], \tag{2}$$

where:

E —personnel training;

S —personnel certification;

P —practical experience;

O —staffing with proper qualifications.

$$T' = F[T] = F\left[Eqm,\ Eqit,\ Est,\ Sec\right], \tag{3}$$

where:

Eqm is a set of measures for the software and hardware of the process of providing medical services;

Eqit is a set of measures for software and hardware exchange of information between participants in the process;

Est —a set of measures for archiving and data storage hardware and software;

Sec is a set of measures for information security software and hardware and information protection.

$$G' = F[G] = F[M,\ St,\ U,\ Ut], \tag{4}$$

where:

M —a set of measures for the transportation of isotopic materials;

St —a set of measures for the storage of isotopic materials;

U —a set of measures to ensure the normal use of isotopic materials;

Ut —a set of measures to ensure the utilization and disposal of isotopic materials.

Final functional is as follows:

$$N' = F[N] = F[H;\ T;\ G] = F\left[E,\ S,\ P,\ O;\ Eqm,\ Eqit,\ Est,\ Sec;\ M,\ St,\ U,\ Ut\right] \tag{5}$$

Thus, the final functional is a set of vector matrices for each of the optimized parameters. The area where the optimal values are found is graphically represented as a three-dimensional figure. The volume of this figure is calculated using a double integral. In the absence and/or loss of a part of the statistical values of previous periods, genetic algorithms for multicriteria optimization (GAMO) with Cauchy and Pareto optimization are used to find the missing parameter values. Analysis of the proposed mathematical model makes it possible to provide the following control functions: in terms of the time of the event, from the point of view of the object of control.

Control functions in terms of the time of the event (point of time, PoT) can be illustrated at high level as it is presented in Fig. 3.

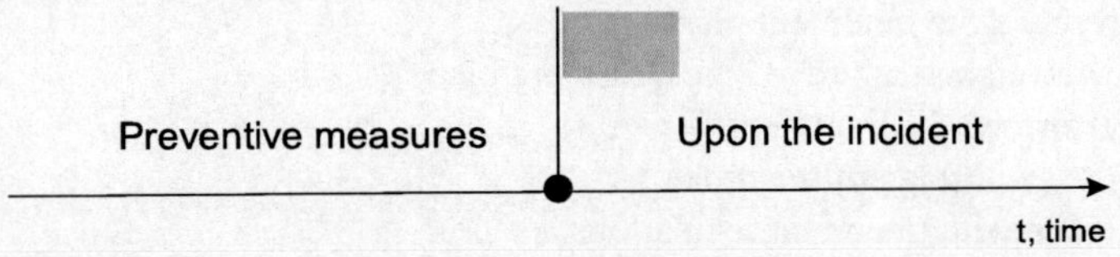

Fig. 3 Control function in terms of the time of the event

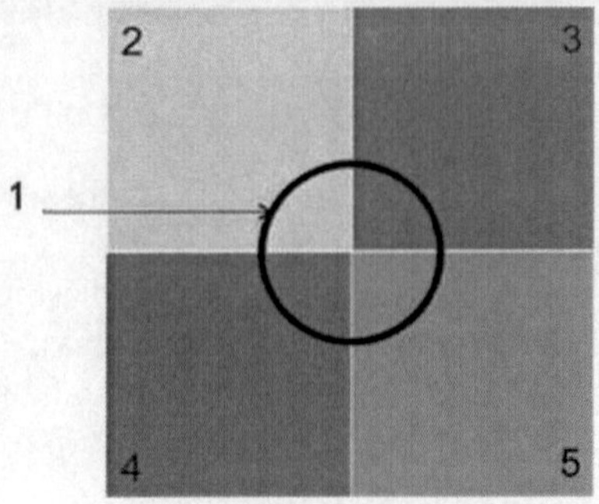

Fig. 4 Control function from the prospective of the controlled object. Here 1 —is Patient (ID); 2 —Medical and scientific staff; 3 —Clinic; 4 —Equipment; and 5—Interaction

The Flag sign in Fig. 3 denotes the time of the incident (events outside the controlled parameters). All functions can be split into two groups: Preventive measures such as monitoring of the current activities of organization and checking the current activities of organizations for compliance with regulations and upon the incident actions such as investigation of incidents and the development of recommendations for the prevention of incidents.

Control functions from the point of object (PoO) prospective are represented by the diagram in Fig. 4.

Patient (ID is a unique patient number in the electronic medical document management system):

- Electronic medical history,
- Survey results,
- Treatment plan,
- Results of stages of treatment.

Medical and scientific staff:

- Training,
- Personnel certification,
- Control over the planning and execution of works,
- Provision of institutions with personnel with proper qualifications.

Clinic:

- Which clinic examined,
- Who conducted the survey,
- Who prepared the treatment plan,
- Who reviewed and approved the treatment plan,
- Who performed the treatment,
- Results at each stage of treatment,
- Compliance with treatment regulations.

Equipment:

- What equipment was used,

- What materials were used,
- Who is the supplier of the equipment,
- Who is the supplier of the materials,
- How the materials were disposed of.

Interaction:

- Organizations, participants in the treatment process,
- Organizations for the material support of the medical process,
- Organizations participating in the electronic exchange of information,
- Organizations, participants in the process of archiving and storing information.

8 Methodology of Conversion of Quantitative Indicators into Qualitative Indicators and Their Following Assessment

The result of building a mathematical model by quantitative parameters is the final functional (Formula 5). On the basis of which it is necessary to translate quantitative values into their qualitative analogs of quality gradations. The mathematical apparatus considered below allows you to convert quantitative values into precise fractional numbers, in some cases, in order to level errors and distortions associated with incomplete information, they can be rounded to the nearest integer. Since we use a relative system for assessing the quality of the services provided and statistical data from 2017 were chosen as zero, the total number of quality levels (Q) varies in the range from –10 to + 10 a total of 20. Let's find the length of the quality interval:

$$Dq = Q - -1 \quad (6)$$

Using the linear dependence of the translation of the quantitative value of the attribute Xj of the final function (Formula 7) into its qualitative analog Qj:

$$Qj = (Xj - Xmin) / (Xmax + Xmin/Dq) + 1 \quad (7)$$

The qualitative parameters obtained as a result of translation are relative analogs of the quantitative data preceding them. Thus, Fig. 3 obtained as a result of the calculations should be considered quality level 3. From the point of view of the control function for monitoring and analyzing the interaction of a set of different systems, it is necessary to determine an integral qualitative assessment of their functioning across the entire set of the above-mentioned features.

Consider three options for determining this integral quality indicator:

Method 1. Determination of the reference quality (if possible), as is done for measuring physical quantities. Subsequently, the comparison of the obtained quality parameter with the reference one.

Method 2. The quality of the object at the current stage in comparison with its state at the previous stages.

Method 3. Determination of the quality level in comparison with other objects of the same class.

If objects are compared only on one basis, then it is easy to assign a rating – who is the best, that has a higher rating.

However, in the case of managing infocommunication systems of the megalopolis level, it is more difficult to determine the ratings, since they are characterized by several features of a different nature. In this case, for each feature that characterizes the object, it is proposed to establish the upper and lower limit of the quantitative values of each feature or index. One of the simplest indices is economic indicators or the number of patients served.

For example, to integrate a new entity (enterprise or organization) into the existing system for each indicator involved in assessing the "suitability" of the organization set objective upper and lower quantitative boundaries. The method proposed above is at the testing stage in the structures for the provision of medical services to cancer patients in Moscow to determine the integral quality indicator, the suitability of the structure's components for effective functioning and integration.

9 Development of a Roadmap for the Management and Development of Territorial Distributed Medical Information Systems

From the point of view of the current functioning and development of medical information systems used in the treatment of cancer patients, we distinguish the following levels:

- operational;
- knowledge level;
- tactical level;
- strategic level.

A feature of the functioning of this class of systems is that it is not a separate legally formalized enterprise or organization, but combines parts of municipal, commercial and state structures with a bidirectional exchange of information.

From the point of view of the municipality, the roadmap for maintenance and development should have the following subsystems.

At the operational level:

executive management support systems.

- Executive Support Systems (ESS).

At the strategic level:

management information systems.

- Management Information Systems (MIS).

  decision support systems.

- Decision Support Systems (DSS).

  At the tactical (managerial) level:
  knowledge management systems.

- Knowledge Work System (KWS).

  office automation systems.

- Office Automation Systems (OAS).

  At the level of knowledge:

- Transaction Processing Systems (TPS).

10 Operational Grade Systems Support Accounting and Control

For example, sales accounting, personnel accounting, accounting, material flow control. Systems at this level are data processing systems. An example of an element of a roadmap at an operational level is a recommended set of measures to improve the operation of a medical institution. However, at the current moment in time, this set of measures is not mandatory, but after 3–5 years it becomes mandatory, and subsequently it is included in the law of the subject of the federation or municipality as part of the mandatory requirements.

Another example of the operational level was the fulfillment of the UN and IAEA requirements for the decommissioning of equipment that uses Cesium-137, For example, in the United States, this requirement was supported by financial grants for organizations to replace equipment and was carried out with the participation of representatives of the New York City administration [4].

Knowledge-level systems ensure the automation of the development of new types of products, the creation and support of electronic archives, the extraction of information, new knowledge from electronic data storages (CAD, DataWarehousing, OLAP, Data Mining).

Tactical-level systems are designed to provide control, analysis, management, decision-making, and administrative actions for middle managers.

This level includes systems aimed at solving problems for which information requirements are not always clear. Answers to these questions often require new data, both external and internal, that cannot be obtained from existing operational level systems.

As an example of a roadmap element at a tactical level, registration and verification of mini X-ray machines in dental offices is mandatory since 2018. This is due to the fact that as a result of the accumulated statistics, the amount of such equipment in medical institutions began to make up a tangible value in% of the total amount of isotope-containing materials turnover and required the administration of the region's subject to introduce these requirements step by step (within 3 years).

Strategic-level systems are a tool to help top-level leaders and prepare strategic studies and long-term forecasts, both for city structures and for various external economic processes. An example of an element of a roadmap at a strategic level is the decision to mandate the use of electronic only X-ray images by 2021.

Thus, the conditions for the formation of a roadmap for the development of a geographically distributed medical information system is the analysis of quantitative and qualitative indicators of the ecosystem of infocommunication interaction in the field of medical services using isotope-containing materials.

The impulses for the inclusion of a particular series of measures in the Roadmap can be both the requirements of the Federal and regional levels, and the analysis of statistical indicators on the turnover of isotopic materials. Analysis of practice shows that the most optimal from the point of view of effectiveness are complexes of measures with short-term (up to 1 year) or medium-term planning (3–5 years).

When technological solutions are introduced with a period of more than 5 years, their efficiency indicator drops sharply, due to the fact that every three years Intel and AMD manufacturers release new processors, which is associated with the introduction of new technologies to the market. However, in the case of the operation of mass-use systems, the use of systems and software and hardware complexes created more than 15 years is observed.

11 Conclusions

The mathematical modeling allows at the practical level to carry out multi-parameter monitoring and control in the main critical areas. Graphically, the result of the work of the mathematical model is a volumetric landscape, which makes it possible to comprehensively assess the situation both in each of the city's districts and throughout the metropolis as a whole. The use of a qualitative assessment in parallel with a quantitative one allows the managing staff of the administration of a medical institution to obtain a more complete assessment of the situation in controlling the circulation of isotope-containing materials in the provision of medical services to the population. Requirements and recommendations for building a Roadmap for the development of geographically distributed medical information systems in the field of treatment of cancer patients are formulated.

References

1. Kuzovkova, T. A., Saliutina, T. Y., Kukharenko, E. G., & Sharavova, O.I. (2020). Mechanism of interconnected management of development of networks and platforms of the internet of things on the basis of evaluation of synergetic efficiency. In Wave Electronics and its Application in Information and Telecommunication Systems, WECONF 2020, 9131158. RU.
2. Gorodnichev, M. G., Kukharenko, E. G., Salutina, T. U., Moseva, M. S., & Kukharenko, A.M. (2019). Features of the development of information systems for working with blockchain technology. *Journal of Physics: Conference Series*. In *International Scientific Conference "Conference on Applied Physics, Information Technologies and Engineering - APITECH-2019"*. Krasnoyarsk Science and Technology City Hall of the Russian Union of Scientific and Engineering Associations; Polytechnical Institute of Siberian Federal University, 33039. RU.
3. Kukharenko, E. G., Korkunov, I. A., Gorodnichev, M. G., & Salutina, T. U. (2019). On the introduction of digital economics in the transport industry. In *Systems of Signals Generating and Processing in the Field of on Board Communications, SOSG 2019*, 8706797. RU.
4. Pecorella, R. F., & Stonecash, J. M. (2006). *Governing New York State* (5th ed.). SUNY Press.

Comprehensive Assessment of the Quality of Telecommunication Services of Software-Defined Networks

Igor Buzhin, Yuriy Mironov, Mikhail Gorodnichev, and Aleksandr Sheremetev

Abstract Mathematical models of the switch and controller of software-defined networks are built, which are the basis for the construction of wireless sensor networks. On the basis of these models, formulas have been derived for estimating time delays in telecommunications equipment of these networks. Also, the dependences of the time delays in the switch and the controller on the main parameters of the equipment, which have a major impact on the delays, are obtained. The results obtained can be used in the design of wireless sensor networks and the use of software-defined networks technology in conditions of various information impacts (with different input information flows) with a given level of service quality.

Keywords Software-defined networks (SDN) · Wireless sensor networks · Quality of services (QoS)

1 Introduction

The beginning of the XXI century was marked by a fairly widespread introduction of wireless sensor networks, which are the first self-organizing networks that began to be used on public communication networks in many countries of the world, including the Russian Federation. The emergence of the standards of the International Telecommunication Union, the successful implementation of pilot projects contributed to the

I. Buzhin · Y. Mironov (✉) · M. Gorodnichev · A. Sheremetev
Moscow Technical University of Communications and Informatics, Aviamotornaya St. 8A, 111024 Moscow, Russia
e-mail: i.b.mironov@mtuci.ru

I. Buzhin
e-mail: i.g.buzhin@mtuci.ru

M. Gorodnichev
e-mail: m.g.gorodnichev@mtuci.ru

A. Sheremetev
e-mail: a.v.sheremetev@mtuci.ru

E. Zaramenskikh and A. Fedorova (eds.), *Digitalization of Society, Economics and Management*, Lecture Notes in Information Systems and Organisation 53,
https://doi.org/10.1007/978-3-030-94252-6_15

fact that currently research is being carried out toward the creation and implementation of the concept of the Internet of Things. The concept of the Internet of Things, the technological basis of which in many of its applications became wireless sensor networks (WSS) [23], implies, first of all, a fundamental change in the quantitative characteristics of the network. The inclusion of things, both physical and virtual, in the client base of communication networks leads to the need to solve the problems of building communication networks, in which the number of network terminals will be in the trillions, in contrast to the existing traditional networks, the principles of which were guided by a billion-dollar client base. Technological progress made it possible to start creating flying networks, the Tactile Internet, using augmented reality to provide new telecommunication services, and creating ultra-dense networks with ultra-low delays, the so-called fifth-generation communication networks. One of the main directions of development in communication networks of the fifth generation is wireless sensor networks for unmanned vehicles (a car equipped with an automatic control system capable of moving from point A to point B without human intervention).

The large-scale introduction of wireless sensor networks to date and the need to collect information from them even when these networks are located in hard-to-reach areas have led to the need to simplify network management mechanisms and be independent of the physical characteristics of telecommunications equipment. These problems can be solved by the technology of software-defined networks (SDN/NFV) [1], which is based on the separation of the control function and the function of data transfer between different types of telecommunication equipment. The most important aspect of an SDN is logically centralized network management, which provides a global view of the topology and state of the managed network at both L2 and L3 levels.

At the same time, modern communication networks are influenced by various destabilizing factors—effects on the communication network, which lead to the failure of network elements. Under conditions of information impact, with sudden surges of the incoming load, large queues of packets (messages) can be formed, which must be processed by telecommunications equipment. In such conditions, it is necessary at the design stage of a communication network to assess the quality of telecommunication services to counter destructive information influences. The quality of telecommunication services is understood as a set of properties of a service, determined by the quality of network functioning, which characterize the ability to meet the needs of users. The quality of telecommunication services can be divided into two groups: Quality of Service and Network Performance. Service quality is a set of indicators that determine the degree of satisfaction of the user with the service provided to him. The quality of service is characterized by the properties of usability, security, availability, continuity, integrity, and security of the service. The quality of the network functioning determines the ability of the network to perform functions that provide communication between subscribers. It is characterized by the ability to handle traffic, the resources and capabilities of network objects, and reliability.

In terms of assessing the quality of service and the quality of functioning of communication networks built using the PCN technology, when providing information impact, mathematical models were obtained in works [4, 5]. These mathematical models do not provide for the possibility of a comprehensive calculation of the main indicators of the quality of service at all stages of the operation of telecommunications equipment in conditions of information impact.

Thus, when designing software-configurable networks under conditions of different information impact (with different input information flows), it is necessary to develop a methodology for a comprehensive assessment of the quality of telecommunication services of software-defined communication networks.

2 Concept of Software-Defined Networking

In modern telecommunication conditions, the explosive growth of traffic and a huge number of various network resources do not allow communication operators to build intelligent and self-organizing communication networks. The way out of this situation is SDN.

The main idea of the SDN is to separate the traffic transfer functions from the control functions (including the control of both the traffic itself and the devices carrying it). This idea allows us to increase the utilization of expensive network bandwidth from 40% to values that are close to 100%, and to solve the problem of a huge variety of network resources.

This approach provides for the complete separation of the data control layer (Control Plane) from the data transmission layer (Data Plane), which makes it possible to simplify and reduce the cost of network telecommunications equipment. The OpenFlow protocol allows the SDN software to interact with the SDN telecommunication equipment through open APIs (Application Programming Interface). SDN switches should simply forward frames from one port to another based on the switching table received from the controller. The SDN controller is also not engaged in building routes for each frame, but creates a switching table for streams of the same type of frames for a while, but the state of the network and the nature of traffic in it remain unchanged. The control of the SDN controller can also be subordinated to a higher-level controller, which makes it possible to build virtual networks of various levels.

According to [1], 3 levels are distinguished in the SDN architecture (Fig. 1). The application layer contains software that, when interacting with the SDN controller, form requirements for resources and include administration applications. This approach allows you to centralize the administration of all network resources in one place based on uniform network policies.

At the control level, the network control logic is implemented, which is carried out by the SDN controller, which is a software and hardware or software complex that provides the necessary resources for programming the SDN commutators.

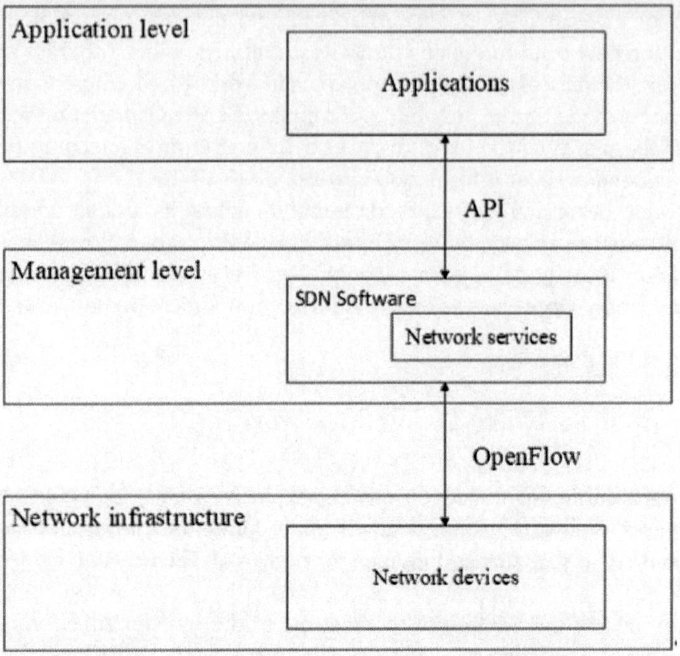

Fig. 1 Architecture SDN

The infrastructure or data layer represents the network infrastructure and consists of physical and virtual switches. SDN commutators are responsible for forwarding frames. Implementation of data buffers, priority parameters, and other parameters related to data transfer are vendor-specific. To implement the exchange of information between the control plane and the data plane, the OpenFlow open API is provided. Its main function is to provide interaction between the controller and the SDN commutators. The presence of programming interfaces allows the network administrator to create applications for network management. A network consisting of many devices from different manufacturers, thanks to the SDN controller, is presented to applications as one logical switch.

The implementation of the SDN architecture significantly simplifies the configuration and administration of the network, allows programming the network as a whole. SDN commutators are becoming much simpler and cheaper devices, the configuration and characteristics of the network can be changed in real time.

3 Methodology of Comprehensive Assessment of the Quality of Telecommunication Services of Software-Defined Networking

The separation of the control and data transmission level is solved within the SDN. Only the data transfer layer is implemented in the SDN commutators. Each SDN commutator has several input and output ports. The ports on a switch are connected to ports on another switch by physical links. The control port is connected to the SDN controller node—through this channel, OpenFlow messages are exchanged to control the switch.

The controller does not manage the network, it provides a programming interface (API) for management. Thus, in fact, the solution to network management problems is taken to the level of applications implemented on the basis of the network operating system API.

The SDN controller generates data on the state of all network resources and provides access to them for network management applications. These applications manage various aspects of the network, including topology building, routing decisions, and load balancing.

To implement this idea, an open protocol, OpenFlow, was developed to control network equipment, not targeting products of a particular vendor. With the help of these protocols, specialists themselves can determine and control which nodes, under what conditions and with what quality can interact in the network.

The switch is equipped with a set of flow tables that form a pipeline, which consists of one or more series-connected addressing tables. A packet arriving at one of the input ports of the switch is first processed (information is read from the packet header), then it enters the addressing pipeline. Sequential processing of the packet in the addressing tables begins. A packet is understood here as a bit string, from which two parts can be distinguished: the header and the payload. Operations performed on packets in the addressing tables do not change the packet load, but they can change its header.

The package header consists of several fields. Typically, these fields indicate the identifiers of the network protocols that must process the packet and the service information they use. In the process of passing a packet through the pipeline of addressing tables, service fields (metadata) can be added to the packet header, which are designed to transfer service information inside the pipeline, and are discarded when a packet arrives at one of the output ports of the switch. The composition and size of the service fields is determined by the technical characteristics of a particular SDN commutator. Thus, data transfer decisions are made based on streams, which are a combination of packet header fields.

The addressing table contains the flow records and instructions for applying actions to the packet. Stream records and relevant information from packet headers begin to match. If a match is found, then the corresponding action is performed on the package. Its result can be the removal of a packet from the switch, a transition to another (higher in number) addressing table, transmission to the controller through a secure OpenFlow channel, or sending a packet to the desired output port of the OpenFlow switch. If the switch cannot execute the instruction to apply the action to the packet, then the packet information is sent to the controller through the secure OpenFlow channel. If the information from the packet header does not match any of the flow records, then the packet is passed to the next addressing table.

The controller manages the contents of the addressing tables of the switches under its control. The OpenFlow protocol assumes that the main reason for this or that change in the contents of the switch tables is the controller's reaction to events from the network, and it suggests several types of notifications so that the switches can notify the controller about such events, as well as several types of commands with which the controller could enter modifications to the switch tables.

The switch processes every message received from the controller, with the option of generating a response if necessary. If the switch cannot fully process the message it receives from the controller, it must send an error message back to the controller. This can happen due to a switch reboot, QoS policy or if it is sent to a blocked or faulty port.

The OpenFlow protocol provides reliable message delivery and processing, but does not provide automatic delivery confirmations or orderly message processing. Message handling is provided for the primary connection and additional connections that use reliable data transfers, but is not supported on additional connections that use unreliable data transfers. Message delivery is guaranteed as long as the OpenFlow channel is active.

4 Methodology of Comprehensive Assessment of the Quality of Telecommunication Services of Software-Defined Networking

In [2], a mathematical model of the functioning of the SDN commutator and the SDN controller was built. Based on this model, we obtain formulas for estimating delays in telecommunication equipment of software-defined networks.

The quality of telecommunication services is a set of properties of a service, determined by the quality of the network's functioning, which characterize the ability to meet the needs of users. Ensuring the quality of telecommunications services is the goal of designing communications networks. One of the factors that determines quality of service (QoS) is Delay—the time it takes for a packet (message) after it has been sent to reach its destination. During the operation of the telecommunications equipment of the network, a switching delay (Switching Delay) is formed—the time it takes for a device that has received a packet (message) to start transmitting it to the next telecommunications device.

The model of functioning of the SDN commutator is a queuing network consisting of two parts (separate queuing systems): the first part is the input queue of the switch and a device for reading information from the packet header, the second part is the flow addressing tables. Two independent Poisson flows of claims of intensities λ_1 and λ_2 arrive at the input of the queuing network. These streams are numbered in descending order of order importance. At the end of the service, a customer is selected from the non-empty queue with the minimum number for the free server. Incoming claims with intensity λ_1 correspond to packets arriving at the control port of the switch (from the controller), claims with intensity λ_2 correspond to other packets arriving at the switch from external networks. The service times of claims of each of the flows are collectively independent and have an exponential distribution function. If all servers are busy, then the arriving customer waits in the storage, while the customers of both flow form a common queue. The first priority claims (1-claims or priority claims) include packets arriving at the SDN switch from the controller. They have relative priority compared to the second stream claims (2-claims, or non-priority claims). Then the average waiting time w1 of a priority claim in the first part of the switch operation model is estimated using formula (1):

$$w_1 = \frac{Q_1}{\lambda_1(1 - \pi_1)} \tag{1}$$

where Q_1 is the stationary average length of the queue of priority claims (packets arriving at the switch from the controller), π_1 is the probability of losing priority claims in the first part of the switch model.

The average waiting time w_2 for a non-priority claim is estimated using formula (2):

$$w_2 = \frac{Q_2}{\lambda_2(1 - \pi_1)} \tag{2}$$

where Q_2 is the stationary average length of the queue of non-priority claims (packets arriving at the switch from external networks).

The second part of the switch functioning model is a single-line queuing system, which receives a Poisson flow with intensity Λ_1 (the intensity of the output flow of the first part of the switch model). The processing of the packet with each record $i, i = \overline{1, S}$, and the execution of further actions on the packet will be represented by the server with an average time of matching the packet with the record about flows $1/\sigma$. Then the delay in the second part of the switch model is estimated as (3):

$$w_3 = \frac{S}{\sigma} \tag{3}$$

where S is the number of entries in the stream addressing table.

Then the total delay in the SDN commutator will be estimated using (4):

$$w = w_1 + w_2 + w_3 \tag{4}$$

The central place in the SDN architecture is occupied by the SDN controller. This device manages the contents of the flow addressing tables and lists of rules (actions) of its subordinate switches. Changes to the addressing tables of switches are based on the state of the network and messages received from the switches via the OpenFlow channel. We can construct a model for the functioning of the SDN controller without choosing a specific network operating system. The algorithm of functioning of the SDN controller described below does not depend on a specific network operating system and is common to all network operating systems. The network operating system will influence the choice of model inputs.

The controller receives messages from the OpenFlow channel from g commutators to the controller input. The controller recognizes all these messages and passes them on to the controller kernel, which decides what needs to be done in the appropriate situation. Next, a response to this message is formed, which will contain a list of actions to be performed by the controller. These actions can be: changing addressing tables, deleting or addressing a packet to another switch, etc. The choice of the appropriate action is made by the controller kernel from the action database, which is located on the controller. It contains all sorts of actions that the controller can choose. Further, the response is sent to the switch, where the mandatory performance of the actions specified in this response takes place.

The operation algorithm of the SDN controller can be described as a linear Queuing system (QS) with r waiting places ($r < \infty$), which receives a Poisson message flow via the OpenFlow channel from g switches. The service times of messages (claims) are independent, and the service time of each claim on any of the c servers is distributed exponentially with the parameter γ. Messages arriving in a crowded system (i.e., when all c servers and all r waiting places are occupied) are lost and are not returned to it again. The service device simulates the processor core of the SDN controller.

For the model of functioning of the SDN controller, the delay will be estimated by the stationary distribution of the time spent by messages in the model. Note that a message that is caught by the arrival of i other messages in the system immediately starts servicing if $i < c$, and waits for the start of service, the time required for servicing a fully loaded system $i - c + 1$ messages if $c \leq i < c + r$. With a fully loaded system, messages leave it in exponentially distributed times with the parameter $c\gamma$. Then the waiting time for the start of servicing a message that has found messages in the system $c + i$, $0 \leq i < r$ is distributed according to the Erlang $E_{i+1}(x)$ with the parameters $c\gamma$ and $i + 1$. Using the formula of total probability and taking into account that the distribution function of the stationary distribution $W_{con}(x)$ of the start time of waiting for the service of the message received in the system is conditional, we get:

$$W_{con}(x) = \frac{1}{1 - \pi_{con}}\left[\sum_{i=0}^{-1} p_i + \sum_{i=0}^{r-1} p_{c+i} E_{i+1}(x)\right] = \frac{1}{1 - \pi_{con}}\left[P_{w=0} + \sum_{i=0}^{r-1} p_{c+i} E_{i+1}(x)\right] \quad (5)$$

where p_i is the probability that there are i messages in the system at time t, $P_{w=0}$ is the probability of servicing a message without waiting in the queue, π_{con} is the probability of losing a message.

Moving on to the Laplace-Stieltjes transform:

$$\omega_{con}(s) = \int_0^\infty e^{-sx} dW_{con}(x) = \frac{1}{1-\pi_{con}}\left[P_{w=0} + c\gamma p_c \sum_{i=0}^{r-1} \frac{\lambda_{con}^i}{(s+c\gamma)^{i+1}}\right]$$
$$= \frac{1}{1-\pi_{con}}\left[P_{w=0} + c\gamma p_c \frac{1-\left(\frac{\lambda_{con}}{s+c\gamma}\right)^r}{s+c\gamma-\lambda_{con}}\right] \quad (6)$$

where λ_{con} is the intensity of messages arriving at the controller input.

Hence, taking into account the independence of the service time from the waiting time for the start of service, it follows that the stationary distribution $W_{con}(x)$ of the sojourn time in the system of a message received for service has the form (7):

$$\varphi_{con}(s) = \int_0^\infty e^{-sx} dW_{con}(x) = \frac{1}{1-\pi_{con}}\left[P_{w=0} + c\gamma p_c \frac{1-\left(\frac{\lambda_{con}}{s+c\gamma}\right)^r}{s+c\gamma-\lambda_{con}}\right]\frac{\gamma}{s+\gamma} \quad (7)$$

Stationary average waiting time for the start of service ω_{con}:

$$\omega_{con} = -\varphi'_{con}(0) = \frac{c\gamma - \left(\frac{\rho}{c}\right)^r\left[(r+1)c\gamma - r\lambda_{con}\right]}{(c\gamma-\lambda_{con})^2} \cdot \frac{p_c}{1-\pi_{con}}. \quad (8)$$

where $\rho = \lambda_{con}/\gamma$.

The stationary average time spent by a message in the system is calculated using the Little formula:

$$\varphi_{con} = \omega_{con} + \frac{1}{\gamma} \quad (9)$$

5 Analysis of the Dependences of Delays on the Parameters of Telecommunication Equipment

Based on the formulas obtained for evaluating the delays of telecommunications equipment in software-defined networks, we obtain graphs of the dependences of delays on the parameters of telecommunications equipment.

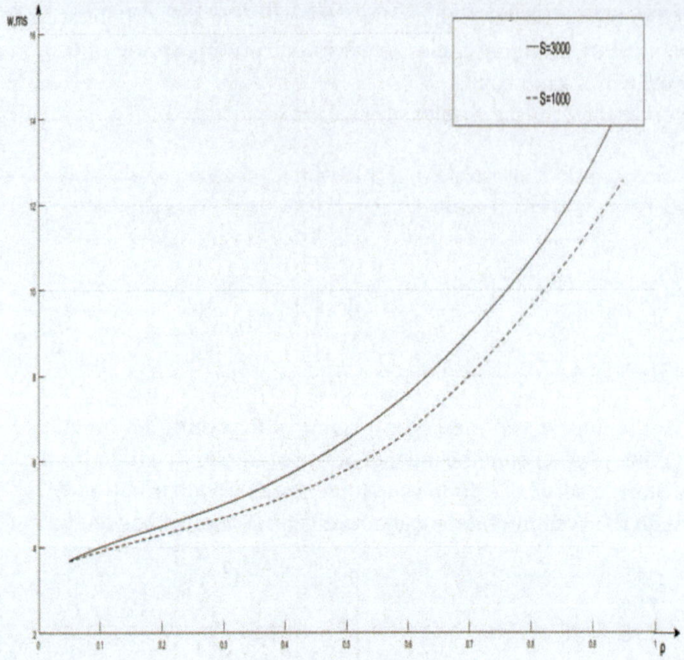

Fig. 2 The graph of the total delay w switch SDN from ρ

Based on formula (4), we construct a graph of the dependence (Fig. 2) of the total delay w on the parameter ρ, which is defined as the ratio of the intensity of the incoming flow to the intensity of packet processing.

The main influence on the delay in the SDN commutator is exerted by the intensity of the input stream, the intensity of processing the incoming packets and the number and number of entries in the addressing table. Parameter values for plotting the dependence (Fig. 2) are taken from datasheets [4, 5]. Based on Fig. 2, with an increase in the ratio of the intensity of the incoming flow to the intensity of packet processing, an increase in the total delay in the switch of the SDN occurs.

Based on formula (9), we will construct a graph of dependence (Fig. 3) (latency (average time φ_{con} of staying in the controller of the PMS) on the number of c cores of the controller processing processor.

The greatest influence on the delay in the SDN controller is exerted by its input queue, which is characterized by the average waiting time for the start of service (9), and the processor for processing messages and generating responses to requests from SDN commutators, which is characterized by the average message processing time.

Parameter values c for plotting the dependence (Fig. 3) are taken from datasheets [6]. Based on Fig. 3, with an increase in the number of logical cores of the message processor and the formation of responses to commutator requests, the time delay in the SDN controller decreases.

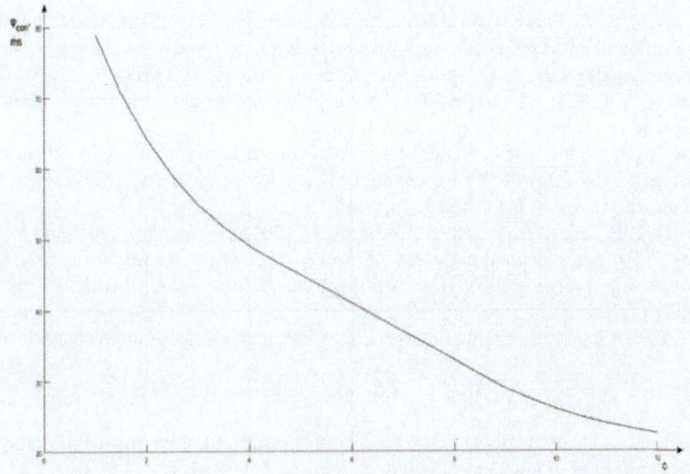

Fig. 3 The graph of the delay φ_{con} controller SDN from the number c of logical processor cores

6 Conclusion

In this article, formulas (4), (9) were obtained for estimating time delays in telecommunication equipment of wireless sensor networks using software-defined networks technology, namely, in the SDN commutator and the SDN controller.

The dependence of the time delay in the SDN commutator on the ratio of the intensity of the incoming flow to the intensity of packet processing was obtained. As a result, it was revealed that with an increase in the ratio of the intensity of the incoming flow to the intensity of packet processing, the overall delay in the commutator of the SDN increases.

Also, the dependence of the average time of stay of a message in the SDN controller on the number of logical cores of the packet processing processor and the formation of responses by the SDN commutator was obtained. As a result, it was revealed that with an increase in the number of logical cores of the message processor and the formation of responses to commutator requests, the time delay in the SDN controller decreases.

The results obtained can be used in the design of software-configurable networks in conditions of various information impact (with different input information flows) with a given level of service quality.

References

1. ONF TR-502: SDN Architecture. Open ONF TR-502: SDN Architecture [Electronic resource]. Open Networking Foundation. https://www.opennetworking.org/images/stories/downloads/sdn-resources/technical-reports/TR_SDN_ARCH_1.0_06062014.pdf.

2. Samouylov, K. E., Shalimov, I. A., Buzhin, I. G., & Mironov, Y. B. (2018). Model of functioning of telecommunication equipment for software configurated networks. *Modern Information Technologies and IT-Education, 14*(1). https://doi.org/10.25559/SITITO.14.201801.013-026.
3. Vishnevskiy, V. (2003). Theoretical foundations of computer network design. Moscow: The Technosphere (p. 512).
4. Altukhov, V., & Chemeritskiy, E. (2014). On real-time delay monitoring in software-defined networks. In *Porceedings 2014 International 'Science and Technologe Conference "Modern Networking Technologies (MoNeTec)"* (pp. 1–6).
5. Chemeritskiy, E., Smelyansky, R., & Zakharov, V. (2013). A formal model and verification problems for software defined networks. In *Proceedings of the 4-th International Workshop "Program Semantics, Specification and Verification: Theory and Applications"* (pp. 21–30). Yekaterinburg, Russia.
6. D-link. (2015). Gigabit Stackable Smart Managed Switches [Electronic resource]: Electronic text data.
7. HP. (2007). HP Performance Brief for External Audiences [Electronic resource]: Electronic text data.
8. OpenDaylight Controller:MD-SAL:FAQ [Electronic resource]//wiki.opendaylight.org. https://wiki.opendaylight.org/view/OpenDaylight_Controller:MD-SAL:FAQ.
9. ONF TR-539 OpenFlow Controller Benchmarking Methodologies [Electronic resource]. Open Network Foundation.. https://3vf60mmveq1g8vzn48q2o71a-wpengine.netdna-ssl.com/wp-content/uploads/2014/10/TR-539_OpenFlow_Controller_Benchmarking_Methodologies_v1.pdf.
10. Sherwood, R., Chan, M., Covington, A., Gibb, G., Flajslik, M., Handigol, N., Huang, T. -Y., Kazemian, P., Kobayashi, M., Naous, J., Seetharaman, S., Underhill, D., Yabe, T., Yap, K. -K., Yiakoumis, Y., Zeng, H., Appenzeller, G., Johari, R., McKeown, N., Parulkar, G. (2010). Carving research slices out of your production networks with OpenFlow. *SIGCOMM Computer Communication Review, 40*(1), 129–130.
11. Smeliansky, R. L., & Chemeritsky, E. V. (2014). On QoS management in SDN by multipath routing. SDN&NFV: The Next Generation of Computational Infrastructure: 2014 International Science and Technology Conference "Modern Networking Technologies (MoNeTec)": Proceedings (pp. 41–46). Russia: MAKS Press Moscow.
12. Buzhin, I. G., & Mironov, Y. B. (2019). Evaluation of delayed telecommunication equipment of software defined networks. SOSG 2019, Institute of Electrical and Electronics Engineers Inc. (p. 8706825). https://doi.org/10.1109/SOSG.2019.8706825.
13. Tsvetkov, V. K., Oreshkin, V. I., Buzhin, I. G., & Mironov, Y. B. (2019). Model of restoration of the communication network using the technology of software defined networks. ELCONRUS 2019, Institute of Electrical and Electronics Engineers Inc. (pp. 1559–1563). https://doi.org/10.1109/EIConRus.2019.8656723.
14. Shalimov, A., Zuikov, D., & Zimarina, D., et al. (2013). Advanced study of sdn/openflow controllers. 9th Central and Eastern European Software Engineering Conference in Russia, CEE-SECR 2013. ACM International Conference Proceeding Series. Moscow, Russian Federation. https://doi.org/10.1145/2556610.2556621.
15. Vladyko, A., Muthanna, A., & Kirichek, R. (2016). Comprehensive SDN testing based on model network. *Lecture Notes in Computer Science, 9870*, 539–549.
16. ITU-T Y.3300 Framework of software-defined networking [Electronic resource]. ITU. https://www.itu.int/rec/T-REC-Y.3300/en.
17. Kreutz, D. (2019). Software-defined networking: A comprehensive survey. In D. Kreutz, F. M. V. Ramos, P. E. Verissimo, C. E. Rothenberg, S. Azodomolky, S. Uhlig (Eds.), *Proceedings of the IEEE* (Vol. 103(1), pp.14–76). https://doi.org/10.1109/jproc.2014.2371999.
18. Zhao, Y., Iannone, L., & Riguidel, M. (2015). IEEE Conference on Network Function Virtualization and Software Defined Network, November 18–21, 2015. San Francisco, USA. https://doi.org/10.1109/NFV-SDN.2015.7387410.
19. OpenFlow Switch Specification version 1.3.0 [Electronic resource]. Open Network Foundation. https://www.opennetworking.org/. (date of the application: 09.02.2019).

20. Gude, N., Koponen, T., Pettit, J., Pfaff, B., Casado, M., & McKeown, N. (2008). ShenkerNOX: Towards an operating system for networks. *SIGCOMM Computer Communication Review, 38*(3), 105–110.
21. Smeliansky, R. (2014). SDN for network security. In *Proceedings of the 2014 International Science and Technology Conference "Modern Networking Technologies (MoNeTec)"*. SDN@NFV modern networking technologies. Макс Пресс Москва, Россия (pp. 155–159).
22. Kotani, D., Suzuki, K., & Shimonishi, H. (2012). A design and implementation of OpenFlow controller handling IP multicast with fast tree switching. In D. Kotani, K. Suzuki & H.Shimonishi (Eds.), *Proceedings of the IEEE/IPSJ International Symposium on Applications and the Internet (SAINT)*, Izmir, Turkey (16–20 July, pp. 60–67).

Application of M-polar Fuzzy Set Algorithm for Nontraditional Machining Process Selection

Madan Jagtap and Prasad Karande

Abstract Developed machining processes for hard materials are known as non-traditional machining (NTM) processes. The selection of the best NTM process in the manufacturing industry is a significant problem. In this paper, literature related to decision expert systems and data collected for NTM processes analyzed and an m-polar fuzzy set based selection of NTM processes methodology is developed. A conceptual design of the m-polar fuzzy set system is explained and implemented. Two problems are solved with the method. Problem solved by m-polar fuzzy set algebra is considering subgroups of parameters. The m-polar fuzzy set algorithm methodology is explained step by step. It gives nearly the same results as obtained in previous literature work for obtaining through cavities in metals and non-metals. It's observed m-polar fuzzy set can be used in the selection of the NTM process.

Keywords m-polar · Fuzzy set · Expert system · NTMPs

1 Introduction

In modern industry manufacturing practices, it is a daily job to machine materials with mechanical properties like toughness, hardness and higher strength. In sectors like automobile, tool and die making utilizes materials such as ceramics, titanium, composites and refractory alloys, which are difficult for creating accurate and complicated shapes. Complex shapes machining on tougher materials cannot be done with conventional machining processes identified for material removal in the form of a chip. Due to such limitations of traditional machining processes, change in manufacturing has been taking place since 1940. New tools and new forms of energy

M. Jagtap (✉)
Saraswati College of Engineering, Kharghar, Navi Mumbai 410210, India
e-mail: madan.jagtap@sce.edu

P. Karande
Veermata Jijabai Technological Institute, Matunga, Mumbai 400019, India

E. Zaramenskikh and A. Fedorova (eds.), *Digitalization of Society, Economics and Management*, Lecture Notes in Information Systems and Organisation 53,
https://doi.org/10.1007/978-3-030-94252-6_16

were utilized in the latest manufacturing era to achieve more sophisticated designs on complex machine materials [13].

NTM Processes have vague data. Every NTM Process requires the specific value of parameters as an optimum value. Tables 1, 2 and 3 explain NTM process data cognitively. Data describes the extent of process operations compared to its maximum limits. In Table 1 [10], various shape applications of NTM Processes are explained in a cognitive way, where the scale of various operations performed by NTM processes are divided into "Good" and "Fair", then with the eleven-point scale converted into quantitative values as per Table 5.

In Table 2 material application for metals, alloys and non-metals explained with respect to various NTM processes is explained in quantitative form with the help of eleven-point scale.

In Table 3 economics of different NTM processes are explained considering various costs like capital cost, tooling cost, power consumption cost, material removal rate efficiency, and tool wear cost.

In Table 4 various methods used for NTM process selection are discussed with various aspects like flexibility, computational time, programming complexity, decision-makers involvement and type of data used for the analysis.

Material applications of metals and alloys are explained by [6], where he relates various NTM Processes applications with metals and non-metals. The scale used to describe the applications is "Poor", "Fair" and "Good". Economics of NTM Processes is the essential factor during selection for suitable application. Yurdakul and Cogun [15] divides economics of NTM processes in Power consumption cost, Material removal rate efficiency, Capital cost, Tool wear and Tooling cost with scale "Very low", "low", "Medium" and "High". Table 5 shows eleven-point scale which can be used to convert linguistic variables into quantities.

Various methods are utilized in NTM processes selection. These methods have different Operational approaches, different performances and different outputs. Table 4 explained by Boral S. Genetic algorithm is having medium flexibility with numerical work. On the other hand, an artificial Neural Network is highly flexible with Numerical data output with high computational time. Simulated annealing with medium flexibility and medium computational time with numerical results. The expert system method is widely used due to its operational approach with medium flexibility and medium computational time with numerical and textual outputs considered in NTM process selection. Further, the Case-Based Research (CBR) method depends on similarity and takes low computational time with numerical and textual outcomes considered practical by several researchers.

The selection of NTM processes is a multi-criteria decision-making problem. Researchers are finding hybrid methods to get the exact selection process. Table 6 shows that the Authors are working on getting results from various MCDM techniques. They are achieving it quite often while implementing NTM processes. It is observed that most of the methods are not considering the uncertainty involved in the problem. Also, it comes to notice that these methods are not user-friendly, and implementing them requires technical knowledge of NTMPs. Expert systems like AHP based expert system, QFD based expert system, Hybrid method combination

Table 1 Shape application of NTMPs [10] conversion based on eleven-point scale [12]

	Holes				Through cavities		Surfacing		Through cutting	
Process	Precision small holes		Standard		Precision	Standard	Double contouring	Surface of revolution	Shallow	Deep
	Dia <0.025 mm	Dia >0.025 mm	L/D <20	L/D >20						
USM	–	–	0.665	0.335	0.665	0.665	0.335	–	0.335	–
AJM	–	–	0.50	0.335	0.335	0.50	–	–	0.665	–
ECM	–	–	0.665	0.665	0.50	0.665	0.665	0.50	0.665	0.665
CHM	0.50	0.50	–	–	0.335	0.50	–	–	0.665	–
EDM	–	–	0.665	0.50	0.665	0.665	0.50	–	0.335	–
EBM	0.665	0.665	0.50	0.335	0.335	0.335	–	–	–	–
LBM	0.665	0.665	0.50	0.335	0.335	0.335	–	–	0.665	0.50
PAM	–	–	0.50	–	0.335	0.335	–	0.335	0.665	0.665

Table 2 Material applications for metals and alloys [6] conversion based on eleven-point scale [12]

Process	Aluminum	Steel	Super alloy	Titanium	Refractory material	Ceramics	Plastic	Glass
USM	0.335	0.50	0.335	0.50	0.665	0.665	0.50	0.665
AJM	0.50	0.50	0.665	0.50	0.665	0.665	0.50	0.665
ECM	0.50	0.665	0.665	0.50	0.50	NA	NA	NA
CHM	0.665	0.665	0.50	0.50	0.335	0.335	0.335	0.50
EDM	0.50	0.665	0.665	0.665	0.665	NA	NA	NA
EBM	0.50	0.50	0.50	0.50	0.665	0.665	0.50	0.50
LBM	0.50	0.50	0.50	0.50	0.335	0.665	0.50	0.50
PAM	0.665	0.665	0.665	0.50	0.335	NA	NA	NA

Table 3 Economics of the various NTMPs [15] conversion based on eleven-point scale [12]

Process	Capital cost	Tooling cost	Power consumption cost	Material removal rate efficiency	Tool wear
USM	0.335	0.335	0.335	0.665	0.50
AJM	0.255	0.335	0.335	0.665	0.335
ECM	0.745	0.50	0.50	0.335	0.255
CHM	0.50	0.335	0.665	0.50	0.255
EDM	0.50	0.665	0.335	0.665	0.665
EBM	0.665	0.335	0.335	0.745	0.255
LBM	0.335	0.335	0.255	0.745	0.255
PAM	0.255	0.335	0.255	0.255	0.255

of AHP and TOPSIS, Decision tree-based expert system, Diagraph-based expert system and online knowledge-based fuzzy expert system are discussed to verify the selection methods implemented and to observe the limitations in the processes.

Chen [5] generalized the notion of bipolar fuzzy sets (FSs) to m-polar FSs. In a m-polar FS, the element's membership value ranges over $[0, 1]^m$ interval, representing all the m features of the element (Akram [1]). These FSs are fit for numerous real-life problems wherein information arrives from n agents ($n \geq 2$). The m-polar FSs have been largely used while modeling real-world problems which often involve multi-index, multi-object, multi-agent, multi-attribute, limits and/or uncertainty. These multipolar data further complicate the decision-making procedure in realistic scenarios thus initiating the multi-criteria decision-making (MCDM) problem. In resolving a MCDM task, the three preliminary steps to be followed include problem identification through determining the probable alternatives, assessment of alternatives depending on the condition provided by the decision-maker or decision-making experts and finally selection of the desired or best alternative. The m-polar FSs have been very effective tools in managing MCDM problems.

Table 4 Comparison of various methods for NTMPs Selections

	Flexibility	Computational time	Programming complexity	Decision maker's involvement	Type of data
Genetic algorithm	Medium (lack of learning ability)	High	High	High	Numerical
Artificial Neural network	High	High	Medium	Medium	Numerical
Simulated annealing	Medium	Medium	High	High	Numerical
Expert system	Medium	Medium	Medium	High	Both numerical and textual
CBR	High	Low	Low	Medium	Both numerical and textual

Table 5 Measure of NTM process selection attribute [12]

NTM selection attribute qualitative measure	Assigned value
Exceptionally low	0.0450
Extremely low	0.1350
Very low	0.2550
Low	0.3350
Below average	0.4100
Average	0.5000
Above average	0.5900
High	0.6650
Very high	0.7450
Extremely high	0.8650
Exceptionally high	0.9550

Research Gap

- Available expert systems for selecting non-traditional machining do not consider subgroup of variables for selection of best NTM process; the m-polar fuzzy set algorithm considers multipolar information (variables with subgroups).
- The m-polar fuzzy algorithm considers the percentage value of variables as input; it needs improved scaled information to the algorithm. Therefore, an eleven-point scale was used to present variables systematically.

Table 6 Existing non-traditional machining process selection systems with their limitations

Sr. No	Name of expert system	Selection method	Limitations	Author
1	Analytical Hierarchy process-based Expert System	The preference index value for the process	It is not made user friendly and needs technical knowledge of NTMPs in assigning priority values	[3]
2	Quality function deployment—based expert system	Overall scores obtained from weights of processes	It does not deal with multi-polar information	[4]
3	Multi-Attribute selection procedure-based expert system	It uses a combination of AHP and TOPSIS	It is not made user friendly, and the selection procedure is complex	[14]
4	Decision Tree-Based expert system	Depth-first search algorithm supported by utility functions	It does not deal with multi-polar information	[8]
5	A Diagraph- based expert system	Calculating the relative importance of different attributes affecting the NTMPs selection decision using pair-wise comparison matrices	It does not deal with multi-polar information	[7]
6	Online Knowledge-based Fuzzy Expert System	To calculate the outputs min–max method and weighted-centroid method are used in the system	It does not deal with multi-polar information	[14]
7	QFD-based NTM process selection framework	To automate the NTM process selection procedure with the help of graphical user interface and visual decision aid, Decision-making model in Visual BASIC 6.0	It does not deal with multi-polar information	[11]
8	PROMETHEE- GAIA method	It Used PROMETHEE-GAIA method, which is a visual aid to the decision engineers	It does not deal with multi-polar information	[9]

- The m-polar fuzzy set algorithm is used to solve various industry problems. However, it is not implemented for the selection of a non-traditional machining process.

2 Research Methodology

Research methodology followed to solve selection problem with the m-polar fuzzy set algorithm is explained below step by step.

Sr. No.	Steps to be followed [2]
1	Input A as Alternatives available
2	"P" as a input variable set
3	We are defining multipolar fuzzy soft relation R: A → P as per the alternatives and variables
4	The decision-maker requirement gives multipolar fuzzy subset Q over P, an optimal standard decision object
5	$\underline{R}(Q)$ and $R(Q)$ calculate multipolar soft, rough approximation operators
6	Evaluate choice set $C = \underline{R}(Q) \oplus R(Q)$
7	Select the optimal decision O_k

2.1 *Selection of a NTM Process for Non-metals to Obtain Through Cavities*

The selection of the NTM process to obtain through cavities in non-metals with the optimum cost is a decision-making problem. Since every process has different properties, the material for the application is essential for the non-traditional machining process. The number of factors that can be considered for selecting the good NTM process, based on the decision-maker's requirement such as good material, desirable through cavities and optimum cost. Suppose a person wants to select a non-traditional machining process for non-metals to achieve precision through cavities. There are four NTM alternatives available. The alternatives are $a_1 = $ USM, $a_2 = $ AJM, $a_3 = $ CHM, $a_4 = $ LBM. One can select the most suitable NTM process. The materials, through cavities and costs, are the variables for selecting a non-traditional machining process. In this case $A = \{a_1, a_2, a_3, a_4\}$ is set of four nontraditional machining processes under consideration and let $P = \{p_1, p_2, p_3\}$ set of parameters related to the nontraditional machining process in A, where,

"p_1" variable for the material,
"p_2" variable for the through Cavities,
"p_3" variable for the cost.

We present more features of these variables as follows:

- The "Material" of the nontraditional machining process includes Ceramics, Plastics, Glass.

Table 7 m-polar fuzzy linguistic decision matrix

R	p_1	p_2	p_3
a_1	(good, fair, good)	(good, good, poor)	(low, low, low)
a_2	(good, fair, good)	(poor, fair, poor)	(very low, low, low)
a_3	(poor, poor, fair)	(poor, fair, poor)	(medium, low, high)
a_4	(good, fair, fair)	(poor, poor, poor)	(low, low, very low)

- The "Through Cavities" of the Nontraditional machining process include Precision, Standard, rough.
- The "Cost" of the Nontraditional machining includes Capital cost, Tooling Cost, and Power Consumption cost.

Features of these variables are the "Material" of the NTM process including ceramics, plastics and glass. The "Through Cavities" of the NTM process include Precision, Standard and rough. Finally, the "Cost" of the NTM includes Capital cost, Tooling Cost and Power Consumption cost.

Suppose that Person explains the "Effective selection of non-traditional machining process" with 3-polar fuzzy soft relation R: A → P, as given below, Table 7 shows linguistic decision matrix for alternatives and parameters.

Table 8 gives eleven-point scale to convert linguistic variables into quantitative values, that can be used for writing decision matrix values in numbers.

Table 9 shows decision matrix for NTM process selection with numbers, combining Table 6 and Table 7.

Thus, R over A × P is 3-polar fuzzy soft relation, where material, through cavities and the cost of the operation are considered variables for the selection of NTM

Table 8 Quality scale for NTM process selection [12]

A qualitative measure of NTM selection attribute		Assigned value
Exceptionally low	Exceptionally poor	0.0450
Extremely low	Extremely poor	0.1350
Very low	Very poor	0.2550
low	Poor	0.3350
Below average	Below fair	0.4100
Average	Fair	0.5000
Above average	Above fair	0.5900
High	Good	0.6650
Very High	Very good	0.7450
Extremely high	Extremely good	0.8650
Exceptionally high	Exceptionally good	0.9550

Table 9 m-polar fuzzy decision matrix for NTM process selection

R	p_1	p_2	p_3
a_1	(0.665, 0.5, 0.665)	(0.665, 0.665, 0.335)	(0.335, 0.335, 0.335)
a_2	(0.665, 0.5, 0.665)	(0.335, 0.5, 0.335)	(0.255, 0.335, 0.335)
a_3	(0.335, 0.335, 0.5)	(0.335, 0.5, 0.335)	(0.5, 0.335, 0.665)
a_4	(0.665, 0.5, 0.5)	(0.335, 0.335, 0.335)	(0.335, 0.335, 0.255)

process. From the table, think "Material" of the non-traditional machining process $((a_1, p_1), 0.665, 0.5, 0.665)$ means that the non-traditional approach a_1 is suitable to the ceramics, fair to the plastics and good to the glass. Let us assume that the expert suggested the most favorable standard decision object Q, which can be shown as 3-polar fuzzy subset of R as follows:

$$Q = (p_1, 0.865, 0.745, 0.955), (p_2, 0.955, 0.745, 0.335), (p_3, 0.255, 0.335, 0.255).$$

From definition,

$\underline{Q_r}(a_1) = (0.665, 0.665, 0.665)$, $Q_r(a_1) = (0.335, 0.5, 0.335)$,
$\underline{Q_r}(a_2) = (0.745, 0.665, 0.665)$, $Q_r(a_2) = (0.665, 0.665, 0.335)$,
$\underline{Q_r}(a_3) = (0.5, 0.665, 0.335)$, $Q_r(a_3) = (0.665, 0.665, 0.5)$,
$\underline{Q_r}(a_4) = (0.665, 0.665, 0.665)$, $Q_r(a_4) = (0.665, 0.665, 0.745)$.

Now, 3-polar fuzzy soft rough approximation operators $\underline{R}(Q)$, $R(Q)$, respectively, are given by.

$\underline{R}(Q) = (a_1, 0.665, 0.665, 0.665),(a_2, 0.665, 0.665, 0.665),(a_3, 0.5, 0.665, 0.335),(a_4, 0.665, 0.665, 0.665)$,
$R(Q) = (a_1, 0.335, 0.5, 0.335),(a_2, 0.745, 0.665, 0.335),(a_3, 0.665, 0.665, 0.5),(a_4, 0.665, 0.665, 0.745)$.

These operators are very close to the decision alternatives y_n, $n = 1, 2, 3, 4$.

$\underline{R}(Q) \oplus R(Q) = (a_1, 0.7773, 0.8325, 0.7773),(a_2, 0.9146, 0.8878, 0.7773),(a_3, 0.8325, 0.8878, 0.6675),(a_4, 0.8878, 0.8878, 0.9146)$.

Thus, the Person will select the non-traditional process a_1 (USM) to obtain through cavities in non-metals because the most favorable decision in the choice set $\underline{R}(Q) \oplus R(Q)$ is a_1.

2.2 Selection of a NTM Process for Metals to Obtain Through Cavities

The selection of the NTM process for through cavities in non-metals with the optimum cost is a decision-making problem. Since every process has different properties, the material for the application is essential for the NTM. There are many factors to consider when selecting the right NTM process, whether we are looking for good material, desirable through cavities and optimum cost. Suppose a person wants to select a NTM process for non-metals to achieve precision through cavities. There are four alternatives in his mind. There are four non-traditional machining alternatives available. The alternatives are $a_1 = $ USM, $a_2 = $ AJM, $a_3 = $ CHM, $a_4 = $ LBM. One can select the most suitable NTM process. The materials, through cavities and costs, are the variables for selecting a NTM process. In this case $A = \{a_1, a_2, a_3, a_4\}$ is set of four nontraditional machining processes under consideration and let $P = \{p_1, p_2, p_3\}$ set of parameters related to the nontraditional machining process in A, where,

"p_1" variable for the material,
"p_2" variable for the through Cavities,
"p_3" variable for the cost.

We present more features of these variables as follows:

- The "Material" of the non-traditional machining process includes Aluminium, Steel, Titanium.
- The "Through Cavities" of the Nontraditional machining process include Precision, Standard, rough.
- The "Cost" of the Nontraditional machining includes Capital cost, Tooling Cost, and Power Consumption cost.

Suppose that Person explains the "Effective selection of nontraditional machining process" by forming a 3-polar fuzzy soft relation R: A → P, which is shown below,

Table 10 shows linguistic decision matrix for alternatives and parameters.

Table 11 gives eleven-point scale to convert linguistic variables into quantitative values, that can be used for writing decision matrix values in numbers.

Table 12 shows decision matrix for NTM process selection with numbers, combining Tables 10 and 11.

Table 10 Fuzzy Linguistic decision matrix

R	p_1	p_2	p_3
a_1	(poor, fair, fair)	(good, good, poor)	(low, low, low)
a_2	(fair, fair, fair)	(poor, fair, poor)	(very low, low, low)
a_3	(good, good, fair)	(poor, fair, poor)	(medium, low, high)
a_4	(fair, fair, fair)	(poor, poor, poor)	(low, low, very low)

Table 11 Qualitative measure for NTM process selection [12]

A qualitative measure of NTM selection attribute		Assigned value
Exceptionally low	Exceptionally poor	0.0450
Extremely low	Extremely poor	0.1350
Very low	Very poor	0.2550
low	Poor	0.3350
Below average	Below fair	0.4100
Average	Fair	0.5000
Above average	Above fair	0.5900
High	Good	0.6650
Very High	Very good	0.7450
Extremely high	Extremely good	0.8650
Exceptionally high	Exceptionally good	0.9550

Table 12 Decision matrix for NTM process selection

R	p_1	p_2	p_3
a_1	(0.335, 0.5, 0.50)	(0.665, 0.665, 0.335)	(0.335, 0.335, 0.335)
a_2	(0.50, 0.50, 0.50)	(0.335, 0.5, 0.335)	(0.255, 0.335, 0.335)
a_3	(0.665, 0.665, 0.50)	(0.335, 0.5, 0.335)	(0.5, 0.335, 0.665)
a_4	(0.50, 0.50, 0.50)	(0.335, 0.335, 0.335)	(0.335, 0.335, 0.255)

Thus, R over A × P is 3-polar fuzzy soft relation in which materials, through cavities and cost of the operation, are considered variables for the non-traditional machining process. From the table, think "Material" of the non-traditional machining process ((a_1, p_1), 0.335, 0.50, 0.50) means that the non-traditional approach a_1 is suitable to the ceramics, fair to the plastics and good to the glass. Let us assume that the expert suggested the most favorable standard decision object Q, which is a 3-polar fuzzy subset of R as follows:

$$Q = (p_1, 0.865, 0.745, 0.955), (p_2, 0.955, 0.745, 0.335), (p_3, 0.255, 0.335, 0.255).$$

From definition,

$$\underline{Q}_r\,(a_1) = (0.665, 0.665, 0.665),\ Q_r\,(a_1) = (0.665, 0.5, 0.5),$$
$$\underline{Q}_r\,(a_2) = (0.665, 0.665, 0.665),\ Q_r\,(a_2) = (0.665, 0.665, 0.5),$$
$$\underline{Q}_r\,(a_3) = (0.665, 0.665, 0.335),\ Q_r\,(a_3) = (0.665, 0.5, 0.5),$$
$$\underline{Q}_r\,(a_4) = (0.665, 0.665, 0.665),\ Q_r\,(a_4) = (0.665, 0.665, 0.5),$$

Now, 3-polar fuzzy soft rough approximation operators $\underline{R}(Q)$, $R(Q)$, respectively, are given by.

$\underline{R}(Q)$ = (a_1, 0.665, 0.665, 0.665),(a_2, 0.665, 0.665, 0.665),(a_3, 0.665, 0.665, 0.335),(a_4, 0.665, 0.665, 0.665),
$R(Q)$ = (a_1, 0.665, 0.5, 0.5),(a_2, 0.665, 0.665, 0.5),(a_3, 0.665, 0.5, 0.5),(a_4, 0.665, 0.665, 0.5).

These operators are very close to the decision alternatives y_n, n = 1, 2, 3, 4.

$\underline{R}(Q) \oplus R(Q)$ = (a_1, 0.8878, 0.8325, 0.8325),(a_2, 0.8878, 0.8878, 0.8325),(a_3, 0.8878, 0.8325, 0.8325),(a_4, 0.8878, 0.8878, 0.8325).

Thus, the Person will select the non-traditional process a_2 (AJM) to obtain through cavities in non-metals because the most favorable decision in the choice set $\underline{R}(Q) \oplus R(Q)$ is a_2.

3 Conclusion

A conceptual design of the multipolar fuzzy set is studied and implemented. Eleven-point scale is used to convert linguistic data of NTM processes compared to previous m-polar fuzzy set applications using data as a percentage of variables. Subgroups of variables are considered in the decision-making process. This approach helps solve the selection problem of the non-traditional machining process. Problem solved for non-metals resulted in the selection of USM as the best alternative. Problem solved for metals resulted in the selection of AJM as the best alternative. Previous work in this area shows the same results as obtained by the m-polar fuzzy set method. Further, this method is to be developed for exact uncertainty values in non-traditional machining processes.

1. References

1. Akram, M., Adeel A., Alcantud, J. C. R. (2019). Multi-criteria group decision-making using an m-polar hesitant fuzzy TOPSIS approach. *Symmetry, 11*(6), 795.
2. Akram, M., Ali, G., & Alshehri, N. O. (2017). A new multi-attribute decision-making method based on m-polar fuzzy soft rough sets. *Symmetry, 9*(11), 271.
3. Chakraborty, S., & Dey, S. (2006). Design of an analytic-hierarchy-process-based expert system for non-traditional machining process selection. *International Journal of Advanced Manufacturing Technology, 31*(5–6), 490–500.
4. Chakraborty, S., & Dey, S. (2007). QFD-based expert system for non-traditional machining processes selection. *Expert Systems with Applications, 32*(4), 1208–1217.
5. Chen, J., Li, S., Ma, S., & Wang, X., 2014. m–polar fuzzy sets: an extension of bipolar fuzzy sets. *The Scientific World Journal, 416530*, 8
6. Cogun, C. (1994). Computer-aided preliminary selection of non-traditional machining processes. *International Journal of Machine Tools & Manufacture, 34*, 315–326.
7. Chakladar, N. D., Das, R., & Chakraborty, S. (2009). A digraph-based expert system for non-traditional machining processes selection. *International Journal of Advanced Manufacturing Technology, 43*, 226–237.

8. Chandraseelan, E. R., Jehadeesan, R., & Raajenthiren, M. (2008). Web-based knowledge base system for selection of non-traditional machining processes. *Malaysian Journal of Computer Science, 21*, 45–56.
9. Karande, P., & Chakraborty, S. (2012). Application of PROMETHEE-GAIA method for non-traditional machining processes selection. *Management Science Letters, 2*, 2049–2060.
10. Mishra, P. K. (1997). Non-conventional Machining, The Institution of Engineers Text Book Series. New Delhi, India: Narosa Publishing House
11. Prasad, K., & Chakraborty, S. (2014). A decision-making model for non-traditional machining processes selection. *Decision Science Letters, 3*(4), 467–478.
12. Venkata Rao, R. (2008). Evaluating flexible manufacturing systems using a combined multiple attribute decision-making method. *International Journal of Production Research, 46*(7), 1975–1989.
13. Weller, E. J. (1983). *Non-traditional Machining Processes*. Society of Manufacturing Engineers, U.S.A.
14. Wong, S. V., & Hamouda, A. M. S. (2003). The development of an online knowledge-based expert system for machinability data selection. *Knowledge-Based Systems, 16*(4), 215–229.
15. Yurdakul, M., & Cogun, C. (2003). Development of a multi-attribute selection procedure for non-traditional machining processes. *Proceedings of the IMechE Part B: Journal of Engineering Engineering Manufacture, 217*, 993–1009.

The Principles of Forming a Data-Driven University Model Within the Cluster-Network Model of Innovative Development

Lyudmila Gadasina, Sergey Voitenko, and Lyudmila Vyunenko

Abstract The article is devoted to the problem of the formation of personnel competitive in the conditions of a post-industrial cluster-network model of innovative development. The authors develop an approach to constructing the cluster-network model based on new mechanisms for the collaboration of the Science, Industry and Government. The approach is implemented through the identification of the information, covering all the elements of the cluster-network model, significant for the analysis of human capital. An analysis of the prerequisites and the identification of conditions, criteria and methods that allow Universities to form personnel of a fundamentally new nature is performed. It made possible to develop a system of indicators for building a data-driven model describing the development of the University as the primary producer of human capital, in contrast to other participants in the collaboration being more the consumers of human resources. This gives opportunities and conditions for creating a data-driven educational environment management system for universities targeting at formatting human capital competitive in the new conditions.

Keywords Cluster-network model · Human capital · University · Data-driven system

1 Introduction

Social network communications, greatly increasing the speed and variety of exchanges, open up fundamentally wider opportunities for the development of the economy, society and human capital [1]. In the twenty-first century, economies with a single managing center can no longer cope with the growing massive online flows of economic information and are replaced by self-governing network systems built on horizontal connections and continuous approvals [2]. Such type of interactive

---

L. Gadasina · S. Voitenko · L. Vyunenko (✉)
St. Petersburg State University, 7–9, Universitetskaya nab., St Petersburg 199034, Russian Federation
e-mail: l.vyunenko@spbu.ru

E. Zaramenskikh and A. Fedorova (eds.), *Digitalization of Society, Economics and Management*, Lecture Notes in Information Systems and Organisation 53,
https://doi.org/10.1007/978-3-030-94252-6_17

network cooperation, called collaboration, is the main mechanism for the development of new economic systems, where network participants constantly exchange explicit and implicit knowledge, continuously reconcile decisions and coordinate actions [3]. New sources of growth emerge from the internal structural and balancing opportunities that arise in the course of collaboration. In this way, the formation of a Cluster-Network Model (CNM) of collective self-government is carried out, where ecosystems with a cluster structure acquire the ability of dynamic self-development without the participation of a hierarchical center. The main properties of the new model are its adaptability, emergence, development nonlinearity, self-organization and self-regulation, fractal repeatability and synergy [4].

Digital transformation, technology updates and global competition lead to the replacement of both hierarchical and market forms of interaction between economic entities with a new paradigm of network non-hierarchical order of interaction and cluster structure. The background for the changes were the diversification of production, nonlinear development of innovations, the emergence of a widespread online environment and multiform communication nodes around which global economic networks grow. The combination of these factors leads to the transformation of country and regional economies from a set of hierarchical structures into a complex system of cluster-network ecosystems that operate in the mode of collective creation and dissemination of innovations [5]. Note that the progressive development of integration and globalization processes is inevitably followed by a decline and a kind of rollback. Therefore, at certain stages of development, we can expect some weakening of the internationalization of the network economy, but the general vector of its development tends to grow [6].

Of all especially the regional clusters are the best basic structural units to meet the conditions of global digital reality [7]. The cluster is a complex adaptive system characterized by three analytical dimensions—special production agglomerations, special innovative ecosystems and special economic projects. Regional innovation clusters hold a central place among various types of business networks as new basic elements and a typical format for organizing production activities in the context of the transition of national economies to an innovative growth model. Of particular interest is the study of the dependence of the clusters' innovative capabilities on network synergistic effects arising from the collaboration of participants on the principles of a Triple Helix Model [8].

The phenomenon of the Triple Helix of University-Industry-Government relations, which first appeared in Silicon Valley, was later described as a special model of nonlinear and interactive collaboration—Triple Helix Model (THM), resembling linkages in a DNA chain. Collaboration of at least three functional different participants creates complex synergy and communication, which provides dynamic stability under conditions of uncertainty, allowing clusters to move to a higher level in self-development mode [9].

It is the University that begins to play a special role in the modern world, which becomes the center of inter-network relations at the national and supranational levels [10]. The University turns out to be the center of network connections and relations, often acting as their initiator within the framework of the classical model of a network society, according to [11]. The university in this new capacity has to carry out many new functions that did not exist earlier or, at best, were secondary. Interacting in the triad of University-Industry-Government relations, even a State University begins to work in many ways like a production corporation, simultaneously performing social functions, while maintaining the main purpose of its existence—science and education. In this aspect, the example of the University clearly demonstrates the tendency of expansion and intersection of functions of various actors of the Triple Helix Model, characteristic of the modern world [12].

In modern conditions of digital transformation, the data-driven approach is implemented primarily in Business, Finance and Industry. Examples are presented by SAP, Sberbank, Yandex, ID Finance, PJSC Gazpromneft and many others. In the work [13] authors showed that "organizations using big data and analytics within their innovation processes are 36% more likely to beat their competitors in terms of revenue growth and operating efficiency". Work [14] describes the application of data-driven business models by start-up firms. In [15], the cases of implementing data-driven business models in different companies are presented, as well as the framework of such a model.

Examples of using a data-driven control system in a school are known in the literature [16, 17] introduced in the conceptual framework for Data-Driven Decision Making (DDDM) for school. Paper [18] discusses the principal-agent theory to identify strengths and diagnose problems in current DDDM plans and to help devise policy options for plans for future. An empirical study of principals' DDDM practices identified the factors influencing DDDM using the theoretical frame of information use environments was carried out in [19]. In most studies, the school is considered as a consumer of new environmental requirements. A different approach is required by the University, which not only explores the needs of the modern market, but is itself the driving force behind its development, owing to scientific and innovative potential [20, 21].

2 Model Description

This paper explores the interactions of four cluster members—Government, Industry, University and Professional Community (ProfCommunity), considered in a generalized sense (Fig. 1).

The aim of the study is to describe the prerequisites and conditions for creating a system for managing the educational environment, which will provide the University with the formation of personnel competitive in the modern conditions of a post-industrial economic development with new mechanisms for the collaboration of the Government, Industry, Science and the University.

The approach is implemented through the study of information relevant to the analysis of human capital related to all elements of the CNM, and the identification of conditions, criteria and methods for the formation of personnel of a fundamentally

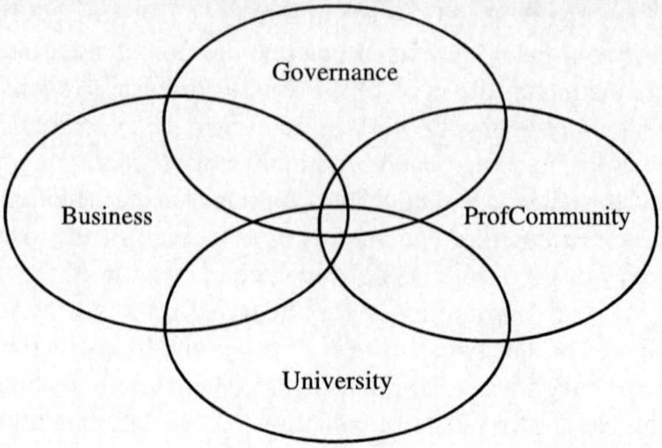

Fig. 1 Diagram of non-hierarchical network interaction of cluster members

new nature. It will allow developing a system of indicators for constructing a data-driven model for the development of the University as a major producer of human capital, unlike other participants in the collaboration, who are mainly consumers of human resources.

Since 2012, support for cluster initiatives has become a new instrument of Russian innovation policy. According to the results of the competitive selection, the "List of Pilot Programs for the Development of Innovative Territorial Clusters" included 25 cluster projects with high scientific and technical potential. Of these, 14 subsequently received the right to a state subsidy from the federal (33%), regional and local (14%) budgets, as well as from extra budgetary sources [22].

The effectiveness of cluster-network structures in Russia, depending on budgetary constraints, was studied in [23]. The typology of the regions and the system of indicators characterizing the regional cluster potential based on the assessment of the development of institutional sectors using the Triple Helix Model allowed the authors to identify four groups of regions with similar cluster potential indicators and draw conclusions about the prospects for regional innovative development (according to state statistics for 2013).

The work [24] presents a comparative analysis of the digital development of Russian regions based on open sources. Hierarchical clustering by standard indicators of state statistics (for 2014 and 2017) made it possible to identify four large groups of regions. The leading regions forming the first cluster (Moscow, Moscow obl., St. Petersburg, Tatarstan, Tyumen obl., Bashkortostan) can be compared in their level of digitalization with world leaders, while regions forming next two clusters are more comparable with the states of the Active Followers and Lagging Followers categories.

The system of indices developed in [23], based on an assessment of the development of institutions of power, science and business, which characterizes the cluster potential of a region, does not explicitly contain an index of digitalization. Nevertheless, all of the above-mentioned six leading regions are included in the group with the highest level of cluster potential identified in [23]. This is natural, since the level of digitalization of the region is both a necessary condition and a prerequisite for creating regional clusters.

An essential feature of the digitalization level indicator is that the digital disparity generated by the existing economic and social gap between the regions of Russia itself provides an opportunity to overcome it due to the fast and inexpensive scaling inherent in digital solutions and services. The issue of the comprehensive development of all Cluster-Network Model actors in order to level the economic and social disproportions of the regions requires additional research and the development of new approaches and methods.

One of the tasks of the national project "Science" of the Government of the Russian Federation for 2018–2024 [25] is to create a new form of networking in the form of a network of world-class Scientific and Educational Centers (SEC). In accordance with the Decree of the Government of the Russian Federation of April 30, 2019 [26], the first SECs in 2019 began operating in five pilot regions of the Russian Federation. In fact, they are developing within the framework of the Cluster-Network Model described above. The leaders of the Russian Academy of Sciences and the Ministry of Science and Higher Education emphasize the role of regional authorities, which should become active participants not only in the creation, but also in the functioning of world-class SEC, along with education sector and science. Industry and business representatives are also showing interest in this kind of regional collaboration.

Human capital in the Cluster-Network Model plays a key role due to the property of mixed globally local mobility, in contrast to globally circulating flows of financial and physical capitals, or social capital localized in a geographical area [27]. The predominant producer of human capital in this model is precisely the University, since its main goal—educational and scientific activity for training personnel, unlike other institutional structures. In this aspect, an urgent problem for the University is to develop new ways of forming human capital, effective in the modern conditions of the post-industrial economy with new mechanisms of cluster-network collaboration of the Government, Industry, Science and the Professional Community.

There are a number of original approaches to solving this problem. Some educational institutions, such as the French school of programming "Ecole 42" [28] and its Russian counterpart "School 21" [29], use only innovative methods—a problem-targeted approach to learning, the formation of the necessary skills through solving real problems, students' cooperation with each other and in active collaboration with employers.

Article 15 of the Federal Law "On Education in the Russian Federation" № 273-FZ, 29.12.2012 [30], provides a network form for students to master educational programs using the resources of several organizations, including foreign ones. It is positioned as the most promising area integrating science, education and industry in the field of personnel training. Student network-building activities in this sense are an important field of study for furthering understanding of academic collaboration and entrepreneurship.

Successful examples of the network approach are hybrid programs of the Novosibirsk State Technical University [31]. According to these programs, the Institute of Chemical Biophysics and Mathematics SB RAS provides a scientific and partially technological base for graduate departments. Another instance are industrial post-graduate studies at the MISIS National University of Science and Technology, where the University provides the training unit, and industrial partners participate in research, certification and diploma protection.

Some papers focus on Ph.D. students' participation in network-building activities understood as collaboration, mobility and support for commercialization from the university. The results of large-scale surveys at different European universities show that the majority of Ph.D. students are engaged in collaborations with external organizations, although they are on average interested in commercialization [32–34].

At the same time, general approaches to building a model for creating an educational environment that would allow the University to become a driver of human capital development within the framework of the CNM (Cluster-Network Model) have not been developed. The main difficulty here is not in adapting some foreign innovative initiatives, but in improving the competitive environment, encouraging collaboration and changing monopolistic structures. The solution to this problem is possible through the use of a strategic data-driven approach based on the operational analysis of actual big data, information and knowledge.

The proposed model of the educational environment based on a data-driven approach describes multidirectional interactive THM-type collaboration in a cluster University–ProfCommunity–Industry–Government. On the one hand, it is the basis for the development of strategic reengineering higher education process taking into account the needs of other cluster members. On the other hand, it allows revealing the opportunities for competitive development of Universities as suppliers of human capital for all elements of the network. The data-driven approach is implemented through the identification of information relevant for the analysis of human capital relating to all four elements of a CNM with new functions and collaboration mechanisms. It allows forming personnel of a fundamentally new nature, competitive in the new conditions, and helps the University to become a driver of human capital development in the context of digital transformation. In the classical approach of Schultz [35], human capital is considered as the potential ability of a person or group of people to generate income both through their innate abilities and talents, and through their education and competencies.

Changing the business models of companies leads to a change in the requirements for personnel from Business and Industry. This leads to the emergence of new trends in the development of HR technologies, such as HR branding—positioning the employer in the market, HR Digital—the transition of recruiting to the digital environment (using predictive analytics, machine learning, and artificial intelligence), Design Thinking—cognitive recruitment [36]. Some companies create corporate universities and training platforms, drawing on the potential of traditional educational institutions in the process of network interaction to meet their needs for staff competencies as quickly as possible [37].

The University forms such important elements of human capital as knowledge, skills and motivation. At the same time, the motivation increase is carried out also through the formation of knowledge and skills that are in demand in the labor market. On the other hand, the University, having scientific and innovative potential, can form such knowledge and skills that can become a driver for the industry, economics and other areas of activity development. Under these conditions, the University can create a system of knowledge formation by analyzing the needs of other elements of the Cluster-Network Model. Such a system will help to form knowledge that is not only in demand at the moment, but will also determine the development of the economy and other sectors included in the network model in the future.

The methodology of the data-driven approach suggests the possibility of combining several research methods without making an exclusive emphasis on qualitative or quantitative, the choice of a particular method is due to the nature of the available data.

For creating a data-driven system, it is necessary to determine the sources of data that characterize the interaction of elements in a CNM. Let us single out the attributes of CNM elements, which make it possible to analyze the current state and needs for human capital.

For Industry:

- Plans, goals, mission, values,
- strategy,
- technologies used,
- requirements for employees,
- company knowledge bases,
- corporate university programs.

For the Government:

- Government programs,
- development strategies,
- Federal State Educational Standards.

For Professional Community:

- Professional standards,
- Body of Knowledge, National standards and International standards,
- competency cards,
- research and practices,
- professional conferences.

For Universities:

- Curriculums,
- Educational Standards,
- course programs,
- educational technology,
- scientific capital,
- information technology,
- scientific events: academic conferences, workshops, discussion, etc.

The selected attributes are data sources for building a data-driven system. The allocation of significant information from the described sources by different methods, including semantic analysis, will make it possible to develop methods for analyzing the needs for human capital at present and in the future for Industry and the Government, as well as investigate the compliance of professional standards and business needs.

The professional community creates its own Body of Knowledge (BOK) and Professional Standards for different professional spheres. The Standards most fully reflect the requirements and development trends in these professional areas. In the field of software engineering, this standard is SWEBOK, in the field of IT process management—ITIL, COBIT, IT4IT, etc., in the field of data management—DMBOK, in the field of business process management—BPMBOK, in the field of project management—PMBOK and PRINCE, in areas of business analytics—BABOK, etc. All Standards are verified and updated on the basis of needs declared by business and government agencies. On the other hand, fundamental breakthrough scientific research carried out by the scientific community and universities allows not only the expansion and addition of existing Bodies of Knowledge, but also the formation of new ones.

An Industry as a consumer of human capital generates a request for hard & soft skills and knowledge, formalizing it through job advertisements. The role of the University's interaction with Industry in this aspect is to identify the current needs in skills and knowledge and to form broader knowledge and motivation among graduates through a promising vision of the development trends of science, economy and society.

Thus, the creation of a data-driven system is possible through the solution of the following tasks:

- Creation of a system for collecting and analyzing documents that are attributes of four entities: Government, Industry, Professional Communities, University.
- Identification of relevant information in terms of human capital.
- Creation of an indicator system for matching competencies of university graduates with the existing needs of companies based on an analysis of requirements for employees in the labor market.
- Creation of an indicator system for matching the competencies of university graduates with the company needs prospects.
- Creation of a system of indicators (quantitative and qualitative) and methods for conducting strategic reengineering of higher education process.
- Application of methods for the quantitative assessment of the educational programs' semantic significance.

The developed system allows constructing a University profile in terms of interaction with other CNM institutions in the framework of the regional cluster. Figure 2 shows a schematic diagram for such a profile:

- The University interacts with three elements of the network structure—the interaction is carried out in both directions (the up arrow indicates the impact of the University on other elements; the down arrow indicates the impact them on the University).

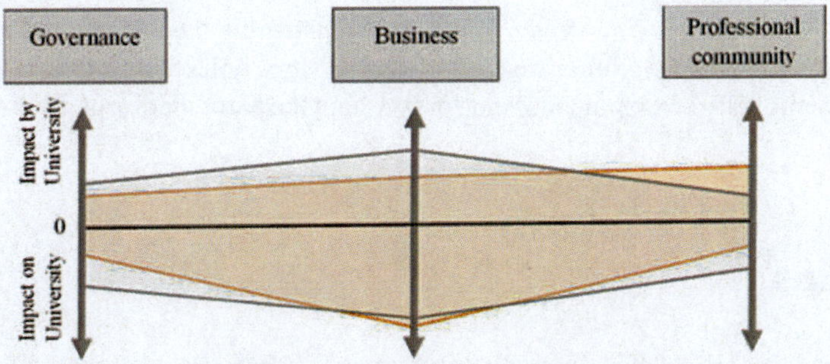

Fig. 2 A conceptual diagram for two universities portraits in the context of interaction with CNM elements within their cluster

- Each element of the network structure affects the formation of knowledge and skills—the University identifies the needs for human capital (the degree of impact is indicated by the distance from the zero level to the top line of the university profile).
- The University is influenced by the elements of the network structure—it forms the knowledge and skills that will be demanded in the future (the degree of impact is indicated by the distance from the zero level to the bottom line).

3 Conclusion

Digital transformation, technology upgrades and global competition determine the relevance of the national economies' transition to an innovative type of growth that is able to adapt the domestic economic environment to fundamental global changes. Digitalization and the widespread use of ICT give rise to the development of a new nonlinear, decentralized and interactive Cluster-Network Model of creating innovations. Both the creation of new ideas and knowledge and their transformation into innovations take place in the collective action mode of various institutional sectors, united on the Internet platforms into single ecosystems.

This gives opportunities and conditions for creating a data-driven educational environment management system for universities targeting at formatting human capital competitive in the new conditions. The goal is achieved through:

- Analysis of the interaction between the Government, Industry, Professional Community and the University based on a network model with horizontal connections. Each element of the network is viewed through a set of attributes related to human capital: needs, vision, prospects, etc.
- University positioning as a producer of human capital within the CNM.

The application of a data-driven approach to managing the educational environment for the formation of human capital by Universities will become one of the keys to the dynamic self-development of clusters without the participation of a hierarchical center.

References

1. Williamson, O.E. (2005). *Networks—Organizational Solutions to Future Challenges. Economics of Interfirm Networks*, pp. 3–27. Tübingen: Mohr Siebeck.
2. Castells, M. (2001). *The Internet Galaxy. Reflections on the Internet. Business and Society*, pp. 116–136. Oxford: Oxford University Press.
3. Man, A.-P. (2004). *The Network Economy: Strategy, Structure and Management*. Edward Elgar.
4. MacGregor, S.P., & Carleton T. (Eds.). (2012). *Sustaining Innovation. Collaboration Models for a Complex World*. New York: Springer. (2012).
5. Smorodinskaya, N. V. (2015). *Globalized Economy: From Hierarchies to a Network Order*. Institute of Economics RAS. (In Russ.).
6. Smirnov, E. N. (2020). The World Economy of Coronavirus: Search for Optimal Ways to Overcome the Consequences of the Crisis. *MGIMO Review of International Relations, 13*(3), 243–266. (In Russ.).
7. Russell, M. G., & Smorodinskaya, N. V. (2018). Leveraging complexity for ecosystemic innovation. *Technological Forecasting and Social Change, 136*, 114–131.
8. Smorodinskaya, N. V., & Katukov, D. D. (2019). When and why regional clusters become the basic link in the modern economy. *Baltic Region, 11*(3), 61–91. (In Russ.).
9. Etzkowitz, H., & Leydesdorff, L. (2000). The dynamics of innovation: From national systems and 'Mode 2' to a triple helix of university-industry-government relations. *Research Policy, 29*(2), 109–123.
10. Lebedeva, M. M. (2017). International political processes of integration of education. *Integratsiya obrazovaniya (Integration of Education), 21*(3), 385–394.
11. Castells, M. (1996, 1997, 1998). *The Information Age: Economy, Society and Culture* (Vol. I–III). Malden, MA; Oxford, UK: Blackwell.
12. Lebedeva M. M., Barabanov O. N. (2012). Global trends of universities' development and the transformation of the Russian educational policy. *Vestnik MGIMO Universiteta (MGIMO-University Bulletin), 6*, 265–279. (2012). (In Russ.).
13. Marshall, A., Mueck, S., & Shockley, R. (2015). How leading organizations use big data and analytics to innovate. *Strategy & Leadership, no, 43*, 32–39.
14. Hartmann, P. M., Zaki, M., Feldmann, N., & Neely, A. (2016). Capturing value from big data–a taxonomy of data-driven business models used by start-up firms. *International Journal of Operations & Production Management, 35*(10), 1382–1406.
15. Schaefer, D., Walker, J., & Flynn, J. (2017). A Data-Driven Business Model Framework for Value Capture in Industry 4.0. In *Advances in Manufacturing Technology. XXXI: Proceedings of the 15th International Conference on Manufacturing Research, Incorporating the 32nd National Conference on Manufacturing Research* (Vol. 6, p. 245). University of Greenwich, UK. IOS Press.
16. Halverson, R., Grigg, J., Prichett, R., & Thomas, C. (2007). The new instructional leadership: Creating data-driven instructional systems in school. *Journal of School Leadership, 17*(2), 159–194.
17. Mandinach, E. B., Honey, M., & Light, D. (2006). *A theoretical framework for data-driven decision making*. Annual meeting of the American Educational Research Association.
18. Wohlstetter, P., Datnow, A., & Park, V. (2008). Creating a system for data-driven decision-making: Applying the principal-agent framework. *School effectiveness and school improvement, 19*(3), 239–259.

19. Luo, M. (2008). Structural equation modeling for high school principals' data-driven decision making: An analysis of information use environments". *Educational Administration Quarterly, 5*(44), 603–634.
20. Philpott, K., Dooley, L., O'Reilly, C., & Lupton, G. (2011). The entrepreneurial university: Examining the underlying academic tensions. *Technovation, 31*(4), 161–170.
21. Sánchez-Barrioluengo, M. (2014). Articulating the 'three-missions' in Spanish universities. *Research Policy, 43*(10), 1760–1773.
22. Abashkin, V.L., Goland, M.Y., Gokhberg, L.M., Kutsenko, E.C., Rudnick, P.B., Shadrin, A.E.: Pilot innovative territorial clusters in the Russian Federation, M.: National Research University «Higher School of Economics» (2013).
23. Yolokhova, I. V., Kozonogova, E. V., & Dubrovskaya, Y. V. (2016). Russian Regions Typology Based on the Clusters Formation. *Bulletin of PNIPU. Socio-economic sciences, 4*, 160–171.
24. Gadasina, L., Voitenko, S., & Luukka, P. (2020). The Digital Diversity in Russian Regional Dynamics: Analysis by Machine Learning Methods. *Nordic Journal of Business, 69*(1), 7–20.
25. National Project "Science". Retrieved Sept. 29, 2020, from https://futurerussia.gov.ru/nauka.
26. Resolution of the Government of the Russian Federation of April 30, 2019 No. 537. Retrieved Sept. 29, 2020, from http://static.government.ru/media/acts/files/1201905080044.pdf.
27. Sölvell, Ö., Lindqvist, G., Ketels, C. (2003). *The Cluster Initiative Greenbook*. Stockholm: Ivory Tower.
28. Ecole 42. Disrupting Engineering Education. Retrieved Sept. 29, 2020, from https://www.42.us.org/.
29. School-21. Retrieved Sept. 29, 2020, from https://21-school.ru/.
30. On Education in the Russian Federation, N 273-FZ, from 29.12.2012 in the version of 02.12.2019. Retrieved Sept. 29, 2020, from http://zakon-ob-obrazovanii.ru/11.html.
31. Institute of Chemical Biology and Fundamental Medicine. Retrieved Sept. 29, 2020, from http://www.niboch.nsc.ru/doku.php/ru/education/esc.
32. Bienkowska, D., Klofsten, M. (2012). Creating entrepreneurial networks: academic entrepreneurship, mobility and collaboration during PhD education. *Higher Education, 64*, 207–222.
33. Gadasina, L., & Voitenko, S. (2017). Soft Skills of Developers in Software Engineering: View from the PhD Students' Side. *CEUR Workshop Proceedings, 1991*, 1–20.
34. Voitenko, S., Gadasina, L., & Sørensen, L. (2018). The need for soft skills for Ph.D.'s in software engineering. In *CEUR Workshop Proceedings* (Vol. 2256, pp. 13–22).
35. Schultz, T. W. (1958). The emerging economic scene and its relation to high school education. The high school in a new era, pp. 97–109.
36. Deloitte. (2018). The rise of the social enterprise. 2018 Deloitte Global Human Capital Trends. https://www2.deloitte.com/content/dam/Deloitte/at/Documents/human-capital/at-2018-deloitte-human-capital-trends.pdf
37. Bonomi, S., Za, S., De Marco, M., & Rossignoli, C. (2015). Knowledge sharing and value co-creation: designing a service system for fostering inter-generational cooperation. In *International Conference on Exploring Services Science* (pp. 25–35). Cham: Springer.

Principle of the Closest Profession for Creating Vector Vocational Guidance Tests

Vladimir Savelyev

Abstract This article presents the principle of the closest profession, which is a practical application of the principle of vector representation of professions, presented by the authors in the previous works. The latter postulates that any profession can be represented as a vector in the n-dimensional space of activity elements. This representation allows defining measures of similarity (for example, Euclidean distance) between different professions. The principle of the closest profession postulates that if with the help of some test, the vector of a person in the vector space of professions is determined, the Euclidean distances can be calculated from a person to all vectors of professions and the n-closest to him or her can be deduced. Such a test, which is called by the authors a vector test, in contrast to traditional vocational guidance methods, represents not just recommendations for a certain class of professions (for example, socionomic or technonomic), but an ordered list of professions recommended for the respondent to master. The paper presents a description of the algorithm for the development of vector vocational guidance tests, which consists of three stages—vectorization of professions, development of test materials, and assessment of the validity and reliability of the method. This algorithm was tested, which resulted in a screening vector questionnaire of professional preferences. An assessment of the retrospective validity of the questionnaire is presented. This questionnaire can serve as a confirmation of the efficiency of the principle of the closest profession for creating vocational guidance tests. However, additional research is required to substantiate its practical use.

Keywords Vocational guidance · Professional self-determination · Vocational guidance tests · Vector space of professions · Vector test

V. Savelyev (✉)
Ural Federal University, Yekaterinburg, Russia
e-mail: vladimir.savelev@urfu.ru

E. Zaramenskikh and A. Fedorova (eds.), *Digitalization of Society, Economics and Management*, Lecture Notes in Information Systems and Organisation 53,
https://doi.org/10.1007/978-3-030-94252-6_18

1 Introduction

As a result of the development of high technologies, the rate of appearance, disappearance, and change in the content of various professions has increased by many times. The increase in digital opportunities and professional mobility has led to the fact that people are faced with the choice of a profession not only before entering a university but throughout their lives. In these conditions, the development of new vocational guidance methods that meet the requirements of the rapidly changing world becomes especially urgent.

Vocational guidance tests are one of the methods of supporting professional self-determination. Traditionally, they are professional preference questionnaires or aptitude tests. Due to diagnostics, a person receives information about which classes of professions are closest to him or her. Examples of such tests are the Differential Diagnostic Questionnaire by Klimov [2] or the Test by Holland to determine the professional type of personality [5].

Back in the late 1980s, Gavrilov identified a fundamental problem that limits the possibilities of vocational guidance tests [1]. It concerns the problem of psychological classifications of professions on which the available tests are based. It lies in the fact that an attempt to describe all the diversity of the world of professions with the help of a small number of classes leads to a significant loss of information about their features, which are important from the point of view of vocational guidance.

Gavrilov proposed a modular approach to solving this problem. Within the framework of this approach, each profession is divided into separate elements of activity (modules), which are assigned a set of psychological traits. Gavrilov also described an algorithm for identifying such modules.

Gavrilov's ideas were developed in the works by Savelyev, who proposed to consider professions as vectors in the n-dimensional space of activity elements [4]. The values for each coordinate of the vector determine the degree to which these elements are inherent in a particular profession. This representation allows performing a number of mathematical operations on professions, including determining the degree of similarity between professions. According to the author, the vectorization of professions is a fairly good alternative to their classification.

Savelyev also proposed and tested two algorithms that can be used to perform vectorization. The first of them, described in the original study, involves expert evaluation of job descriptions, classification of individual labor functions according to a pre-selected criterion, and counting the number of labor functions of different classes.

The second one, described in an earlier work, involves the use of topic modeling methods for analyzing job descriptions [3]. Topic modeling is a set of methods for computer analysis of a large set of texts that determine the topics of these texts. A topic is a set of words that, with a certain frequency, occur together in a number of texts. For example, the words "ball, goalkeeper, referee" form the topic "football", and "jury, case, judge"—something related to jurisprudence. For each text, the belonging to a particular topic is determined. Formally, topics define the coordinate axes of some linear space, while each text is a vector in this space. This allows interpreting the results of the topic modeling of job descriptions as a set of vectors of professions defined in an n-dimensional vector space.

However, it remains unclear how exactly the principle of vector representation of professions can help in the development of vocational guidance tests. This work closes this gap. Another principle is proposed in it—the principle of closest professions, which will allow the development of such tests. The authors will also present the results of testing one screening vector questionnaire of professional preferences, which will illustrate the efficiency of the proposed principle.

2 Methods

To be able to use the principle of vector representation of professions for the development of vocational guidance tests, the following proposition is introduced: if the vector of a person is determined in the n-dimensional space of professions, then it is possible to calculate the Euclidean distances from a person to each of the professions and determine the k-closest to him or her. These professions will be recommended for further mastery. By analogy with the k-closest neighbor method used in machine learning, this provision is called the "principle of closest professions".

Thus, the test that determines that the vector of the respondent in n-dimensional space does not just indicate the priority class of professions—it displays an ordered list of professions that are more likely to suit this respondent. It is proposed to call such tests vector tests.

The development of such tests involves several stages.

At the first stage, it is required to vectorize professions, having received a vector space of professions. Of the two proposed vectorization algorithms, the priority is the one that uses topic modeling. It is the least labor-intensive and less error-prone than the expert one. However, it requires some training in machine learning from the researcher. The result of this stage will be a table with vectors of professions, as well as sets of words describing the coordinate of the vector (element of activity).

At the second stage, a question or a test task is developed for each element of the activity. This task should meet the criterion of apparent validity and quantify the degree to which the respondent's abilities/preferences correspond to this element of activity. For all questions/tasks, it is mandatory to establish a single dimension for scales with a quantitative assessment.

The third step is to determine the validity and reliability of the resulting test. Reliability can be assessed both by retesting and by determining the degree of internal consistency. However, the assessment of validity requires additional clarification.

In the psychological literature, it is common practice to assess convergent validity as an indicator of the overall validity of a test. The results of the new method are compared with the indicators of the old one, which measures the same psychological construct. However, in the authors' case, it is difficult due to the lack of similar tests.

Instead of assessing convergent validity, it is proposed to assess retrospective validity; namely, to see how accurately a given test can predict the profession in which the respondent is already working. An example of such an assessment is shown in the current study.

Due to the peculiarities and scope of this type of questionnaire, it makes no sense to perform standardization, since the main goal is to determine the pool of professions most suitable for the respondent. Standardization is necessary in order to obtain standards for comparing respondents in terms of the manifestation of one or another psychological trait.

The study presents the first results of testing this algorithm for the development of a vector questionnaire and is, in fact, a pilot one. The developed questionnaire is called the screening questionnaire of professional preferences. This study is limited only to assessing its retrospective validity. The general goal of the study is to determine the possibility and feasibility of developing a vocational guidance test according to the proposed algorithm.

The vector space for the development of this questionnaire was obtained by the authors by computer analysis of the descriptions of 431 basic groups of professions presented in the International Standard Classification of Occupations (MSKZ-08 or OKZ) using topic modeling. A specific method is Latent Dirichlet allocation (LDA).

Based on the results, the authors developed a screening questionnaire consisting of 17 questions.

To test this questionnaire, a sample of 222 people working in various specialties was taken. This sample is characterized by a bias toward highly qualified specialists and managers.

They were requested to complete the received questionnaire. The wording of the questionnaire was slightly changed—instead of asking them to indicate the desired profession, they were asked to assess how much their current profession includes this or that element. In addition, they had to indicate this profession in the questionnaire, which was subsequently assigned to one of the basic groups of professions in the OKZ.

The respondents' answers determined the vector of their current profession. Further, for each respondent, the Euclidean distances from the vector of their current profession to the vectors of professions in the OKZ were calculated. After that, the occupations of the OKZ were ordered in order of increasing distance from the smallest to the largest. Finally, in this series, the place (rank) occupied by the base group to which the respondent's profession belongs was determined. The lower the obtained rank was, the more accurately the respondent's current profession was determined by the test.

The ranks of the respondents' current occupation were used for further processing. A graph of accumulated frequencies was built, reflecting the number of subjects whose current profession rank is less than or equal to the given one. In addition, the first, second, and third quartiles were calculated by ranks, as well as the maximum rank in the sample.

The reliability was not assessed, since the purpose of the study was to test the very possibility of creating a vector questionnaire.

Microsoft Excel and the RStudio software development environment were used for data processing.

3 Results

Table 1 provides a description of the coordinate axes of the 17-dimensional vector space of professions, reflecting typical elements of activity. It is reminded that the authors obtained them as a result of LDA topic modeling, performed on job descriptions from the OKZ. Accordingly, the description is a set of words that define the topic.

It also provides wording for items on the screening questionnaire of professional preferences that correspond to each typical activity element.

General instruction for respondents:

- Assess how your real profession corresponds to the following statements (to assess the validity)
- Rate the extent to which what you would like to do corresponds to the following statements (to use the questionnaire).

The assessment is conducted on a six-point scale, where 1 is absolutely incorrect, and 6 is absolutely correct.

Table 2 provides examples of vectors of the three basic groups of specialties. In total, there are 431 vectors.

Please note that managers have the highest value along the T9 axis (organization, coordination, and control), doctors—along the T10 axis (treatment of diseases, receiving patients), and lawyers are distributed along three axes:

- T3—registration, recording, and paperwork; making reports; organization of information storage
- T4—research and experimentation; study of various objects and phenomena; expert judgment in any field
- T17—work in sales; consulting clients; acceptance of payment; organization of the sale and delivery of goods to the final recipient

Figure 1 shows a graph of accumulated frequencies. The abscissa shows the rank of the respondents' current profession. The ordinate is the number of subjects whose current profession rank is less than or equal to the given one. Thus, 17% of the subjects have the rank of their current profession less than or equal to 5. This means that for 17% of the subjects the test placed their own profession in the list of 5 professions closest to them.

The gray lines represent the 95% confidence interval.

Table 3 presents the quartiles according to the ranks of the base groups of the respondents' current professions.

Thus, for 25% of respondents, their own profession was in the top 9 of the closest, for 50%—in the top 25, for 75%—in the top 58. For all respondents, the rank of their basic professions was less than or equal to 290.

Table 1 Description of the coordinate axes of the vector space of professions obtained on the basis of the OKZ using LDA and the corresponding items of the questionnaire

No	Descriptions	Questionnaire items
T1[a]	Product, manufacture, use, form, fabric, clothing, machine, conformity, detail, glass	Making various products by hand; work with various materials: fabric, glass, wood, clay, etc
T2	Security, assistance, performance, rule, provision, compliance, implementation, definition, relevance, identification	Work in the field of security; ensuring that other people comply with various rules and regulations
T3	Information, maintenance, document, verification, accounting, provision, compilation, registration, receipt, storage	Registration, recording and paperwork; making reports; organization of information storage
T4	Conduct, analysis, development, research, method, definition, consultation, study, evaluation, report	Research and experimentation; study of various objects and phenomena; expert judgment in any field
T5	Repair, installation, service, tool, test, equipment, check, specification, component, device	Assembly, repair, and maintenance of technical systems; installation, testing, adjustment
T6	Products, animal, collection, species, production, operation, service, work, stock, planning	Working in the field of agriculture; growing plants and animals, taking care of trees, picking mushrooms and berries
T7	System, provision, purpose, development, data, problem, recommendation, transmission, network, communication	Work with computer systems; software development; work with data; maintenance of computer networks
T8	Equipment, operation, process, control, work, water, treatment, cleaning, sample, log	Work in the heavy and mining industries; control of machine tools and machines; production process control
T9	Organization, activity, leadership, control, personnel, planning, coordination, provision, implementation, use	Organization, coordination, and control of the activities of other people; drawing up plans, developing projects
T10	Patient, help, treatment, conduct, care, health, condition, disease, procedure, specialist	Treatment of diseases, reception of patients, provision of patient care, assistance in health matters
T11	Material, use, structure, building, placement, construction, site, measurement, stone, quality	Building; wall construction; roofing; finishing work
T12	Means, goal, place, movement, vessel, passenger, case, driving, way, loading	Work on sea, rail, or road transport
T13	Preparation, program, evaluation, conduct, student, maintenance, development, learning, event, child	Teaching children and adults; preparation of training programs; conducting classes; issuance and verification of educational assignments

(continued)

Table 1 (continued)

No	Descriptions	Questionnaire items
T14	Work, management, machine, control, processing, leather, coating, service, purpose, application	Work in the light industry; control of machines that produce paper products, fabrics, leather, and plastic
T15	Product, food, cooking, cleaning, washing, drink, take, mix, food, zone	Work in the food industry; preparing or serving food; cleaning and washing dishes
T16	Preparation, quality, creation, material, choice, image, object, performance, form, paper	Work in the field of media; writing articles and books; image production; creation and performance of musical works; work in a theater
T17	Customer, product, sale, service, receipt, condition, demand, decision, delivery, provision	Work in sales; consulting clients; acceptance of payment; organization of the sale and delivery of goods to the final recipient

[a]T—topic. One of the entities resulting from topic modeling, corresponding to the coordinate axis

Table 2 An example of vectors of three basic groups of professions

Coordinate	1120 Heads of institutions, organizations, and enterprises	2211 General practitioners	2611 Lawyers
T1	0.02	0.02	0.02
T2	0.03	0.04	0.07
T3	0.05	0.07	**0.13**
T4	0.05	0.06	**0.15**
T5	0.02	0.02	0.02
T6	0.02	0.06	0.04
T7	0.04	0.04	0.03
T8	0.02	0.03	0.04
T9	**0.47**	0.03	0.06
T10	0.02	**0.46**	0.03
T11	0.02	0.02	0.02
T12	0.02	0.03	0.07
T13	0.10	0.03	0.06
T14	0.02	0.02	0.02
T15	0.02	0.03	0.03
T16	0.02	0.02	0.09
T17	0.04	0.02	**0.13**

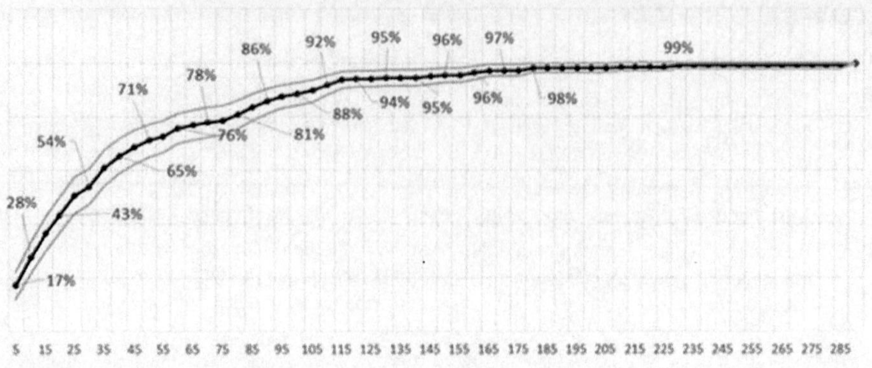

Fig. 1 A graph of accumulated frequencies

Table 3 Quartiles according to the ranks of the subjects' current professions

Indicator	Value
First quartile (25th percentile)	9.25
Second quartile (50th percentile)	25
Third quartile (75th percentile)	58
Maximum rank (100th percentile)	290

4 Discussion

It is reminded that the main goal of this study was to determine the possibility of developing a vocational guidance test based on the principle of vector representation of professions and the principle of the closest profession.

Based on the results of the first stage, a 17-dimensional vector space of professions was obtained. Moreover, each coordinate axis is fairly well interpreted from the point of view of the content of professional activity. Thus, the T9 axis clearly indicates managerial functions, while the T3 axis is connected with working with documents.

The optimal dimension of the space was chosen here by selecting and assessing the degree of interpretability of the resulting topics (coordinate axes). Thus, in the process of research, the authors have examined them in the range from 10-dimensional to 20-dimensional. 17-dimensional space appeared to be the most easily interpreted.

Topic modeling also enabled to vectorize 431 basic occupational groups from the OKZ, each of which received 17 coordinates. The examples were presented in Table 2.

The result of the second stage was a questionnaire consisting of 17 items. For each item, respondents needed to rate on a 6-point scale how much their current/desired profession includes the relevant activity.

At the third stage, the retrospective validity of the questionnaire was assessed by determining how much the questionnaire was able to predict the respondent's current occupation. The questionnaire showed acceptable accuracy—for 50% of the respondents, the base group of their current profession was included in the list of the 25 closest ones. Taking into account the examination of 431 base groups, this is a rather decent indicator. However, in the absence of accuracy standards for vector tests, it cannot be stated whether it is acceptable for practical use in vocational guidance work.

It is also noted that the sample of respondents was biased toward specialists with higher qualifications, which does not allow speaking about the applicability of this methodology for other groups of specialties.

Finally, the factors are noted that negatively affect the test accuracy indicators:

1. Insufficiently clear wording of questions
2. The expert's mistakes when correlating the current profession declared by the respondents to one of the basic groups of professions
3. Inconsistency of the descriptions of the basic groups of professions presented in the OKZ with the real professional activity of the respondents.

5 Conclusions

In this article, the principle of the closest professions was formulated. It is based on the principle of the vector representation of professions, and is as follows: if with the use of any test, one determines the vector of a person in the vector space of professions, the Euclidean distances can be calculated from a person to all vectors of professions and the n-closest to him or her can be deduced. Guided by this principle, the authors have developed an algorithm for creating vector questionnaires. Such questionnaires make it possible not only to recommend a particular class of profession for the respondents but also to display an ordered list of professions recommended for mastering.

The algorithm was tested by creating a screening test of professional preferences based on the 17-dimensional vector space of basic groups of professions presented in the International Standard Classification of Occupations (MSKZ-08 or OKZ).

It is noted that this is the first experience in creating such questionnaires nowadays. The methodology for their development needs further discussion and clarification. Especially the part that concerns the validity check—it is obvious that for this type of questionnaire the practice of assessing convergent validity using a similar methodology is not suitable. Therefore, in this article, the authors proposed a method for assessing retrospective validity, trying to determine how accurately the test "guesses" a person's current profession.

The screening questionnaire of professional preferences, created by the authors, cannot currently be used as a vocational guidance test due to sample bias. To get the possibility of its practical use, an extensive study on a representative sample is required. However, as a demonstration of the applicability of the principle of closest occupations for creating vocational guidance tests, it is applicable.

References

1. Gavrilov, V. E. (1987). Using a modular approach for the psychological classification of professions for vocational guidance. *Questions of Psychology, 1*, 111–117.
2. Klimov, E. A. (1995). Methodology "Differential-diagnostic questionnaire". In N.V. Kirshaeva & N.V. Ryabchikov (Eds.), *Psychology of personality: tests, questionnaires, methods.*
3. Savelyev, V. V. (2017). Application of topic modeling methods to professional standards to implement a modular approach to the classification of professions. *Pedagogical education in Russia, 3*, 22–28.
4. Savelyev, V. V. (2018). Profession as a vector in the n-dimensional space of activity elements. *Psychological Journal, 39*(5), 37–45.
5. Holland, J. L., Fritsche B. A., & Powell A. B. (1994). *SDS (self-directed search): Technical manual.* Odessa, FL: Psychological Assessment Resources.

Industry 4.0: Individual Perceptions About Its Nine Technologies

Francisco Diniz, Nelson Duarte, António Amaral, and Carla Pereira

Abstract Industry 4.0 is a trendy concept that everyone is talking about. However there are several concepts and technologies attached to Industry 4.0. The concept is considered as the most recent industrial revolution and takes us to the domains of automation, digitalization and information, among others. The concept is trendy, but sometimes firms and employees are not able to follow new trends. This paper summarizes a research on the concepts of industry 4.0 and the 9 technologies commonly associated to Industry 4.0 umbrella. Most of the literature recognizes it as something that can bring several benefits to firms. However, it is also pointed out, that the adoption of these technologies relies in several factors. In this paper the focus is the human factors. A group of 260 persons participated in a questionnaire where were asked about their perceptions on industry 4.0 and its technologies. The main objective was to find different responses to Industry 4.0 technologies, according to age, education level, gender or field of studies. In general, all the individuals present a similar approach. Main differences were found on Big Data, Augmented Reality and Simulation technologies.

Keywords Industry 4.0 · Technologies · I4.0 Profile

F. Diniz (✉)
CETRAD, UTAD, Vila Real, Portugal
e-mail: fdiniz@utad.pt

N. Duarte · A. Amaral · C. Pereira
CIICESI, ESTG, Politécnico Do Porto, Porto, Portugal

N. Duarte
IRIEM, Hong-Kong, China

A. Amaral
Departamento de Engenharia Mecânica, Instituto Superior de Engenharia Do Porto, Politécnico Do Porto, Porto, Portugal

C. Pereira
INESCTEC, Porto, Portugal

E. Zaramenskikh and A. Fedorova (eds.), *Digitalization of Society, Economics and Management*, Lecture Notes in Information Systems and Organisation 53,
https://doi.org/10.1007/978-3-030-94252-6_19

1 Introduction

In this new revolution—Industry 4.0 (I4.0) is leading us to the digital era: business models, production systems, smart and autonomous machines, augmented reality to support operators, smart products and services integration, big data analytics, value chain information—most of these activities are now being performed digitally.

According to Alcacér & Cruz-Machado (2019) [1] in 2011, the German government has brought into the world a new heading called Industry 4.0. This concept was assumed as the fourth industrial revolution because it is possible to identify four main industry changes throughout history [2].

"*Since I4.0 boom, the research community has experienced different approaches to I4.0 concept; however, the general society may be confused based on the lack of understanding on this area*" [1]. On one hand, it is clear that new (digital) technologies are in a way to increase productivity of modern organizations, on another hand a question arises: are our human resources fully committed with these new technologies? How open are we as human beings to accept, welcome and adapt to this new environment? The population, depending on the propensity to innovate, digital skills and the use of digital technology, varies considerably according to several factors, such as age, level of education, income, role in company among others.

Considering that the concept of I4.0 is composed by different technologies, and that not all of them are easy to understand by the overall population, this paper addresses this topic by intending to measure: how familiar are different groups of people with I4.0 and its technologies?

2 Industry 4.0 and Its Technologies

Some variations could be found in literature regarding I4.0 Technologies [7]. According to several authors [1, 5], it is generally accepted for successful implementation of I4.0, nine fundamental technologies are required to be the part of the entire system. I4.0 also brings increments in the development of automation, digitalization and digitization processes [4, 9], intelligent communication systems/technologies [5, 6] Cyber-physical systems [7, 8], among others.

The framework for Industry 4.0 might be presented as follows [1]:

- Internet of Things (IoT): A global system serving users worldwide with interconnected computer networks using Standard Internet Protocol. As individually distinguishable by the real world, the "things" can be anything like an object or a person.
- Augmented Reality: Augmented Reality increases the perception of reality by making use of artificial information about the environment, where the real world is fulfilled by its objects. It can help on closing some gaps, e.g., between product development and manufacturing operations, due to the ability to reproduce and

reuse digital information and enhance knowledge creation while supporting assembly operations.

- Big Data Analytics: Huge amount of (un)structured data from different types of sources that can come from interconnected and heterogeneous objects describes Big Data. Data collection or storage has no meaningful value, but the core characteristic of Big Data is to perform data analysis.
- Cloud: Cloud computing is an alternative technology for companies who intent to invest in IT outsourcing resources. The adoption of Cloud service has several advantages related to cost reduction, e.g., the direct and indirect costs on the removal of IT infrastructure from the organization.
- Cybersecurity: Cybersecurity is a high-level attribute of information security, and through the word "cyber" it spreads to apply also on industrial environments and IoT. Cybersecurity is a combination of technology and management protocols laying on protecting, detecting and responding to attacks.
- Simulation: Computer simulation is becoming a technology to better understand the dynamics of business systems. Simulation allows experiments for the validation of products, processes or systems design and configuration. Simulation modeling helps with cost reduction, decreases development cycles and increases product quality.
- Systems Integration (Vertical and Horizontal): Engineering, production, marketing, suppliers and supply chain operations, everything connected must create a collaborative scenario of systems integration, according to the information flow and considering the levels of automation. In I4.0 systems integration has two approaches: horizontal and vertical integrations.
- Additive Manufacturing: Additive Manufacturing is an enabling technology helping on the development of new products, new business models and new supply chains. A set of technologies that enables "3D printing" of physical objects form the collective term Additive Manufacturing. Products such as one-of-a-kind can be manufactured without the conventional surpluses, so it is a big advantage.
- Robotics: Robots with Artificial Intelligence increase the adaptability and flexibility of production systems that could facilitate the manufacturing of different products and consequently decrease its production costs reduction. Fully autonomous robots make their own decisions to perform tasks in constantly changeable environments with or without operator's interaction.

Recognizing the relevance of I4.0, as well as the benefits it can bring to firms [10–14] there are some dimensions to consider in the digitization process toward the I4.0 implementation [6]: (1) organization of work—new technologies need to rethink how the organization will operate; (2) human factors—new technologies require new competences and skills from the workers; (3) external environment—adoption of new technologies are dependent of the maturity where they are implemented. In this paper the focus is on the human factors dimension, that were already identified as a relevant factor by other authors [15, 16].

As stated by Kamble, Gunasekeran & Sharma (2018) "*the workforce lacks the adequate skills required to cope up with the upcoming automation and there is a lack of clarity in the standards for the implementation of industry 4.0 which has created ambiguity in many organizations*" [17]. For an effective and successful adoption of I4.0 "*A collaborative, explorative, and entrepreneurial mindset is a success factor that has to be established among a company's most important resource: the* employees" [14]. The same authors argue that managers should train and develop employees' competences on specific technologies of I4.0 (data analytics, IT, software, and human–machine interaction). Standing in line, new job profiles with novel requirements for training and education are expected to emerge, mostly referring to decreasing importance of manual labor, that will be replaced by workers with IT-skills [14, 18, 19]. Age, training and education factors are also pointed as factors to take into consideration [19].

Different authors also identified other differences, such as on the definition of I4.0 across academic disciplines, namely Operations Management, Industrial Engineering, Data Science, Operations Research and Control [20]. Differences on the adoption are also identified according to firms' size, business sector or role (user or provider) at I4.0 [14, 21]. Another relevant issue is related to SME, due to their typical style of management and short-term strategy that differs from their larger counterparts [13]. The same authors also conclude that "*despite the growing number of new tools and technologies, most of them are under-exploited, if not ignored by SMEs.*" Their study shows "*that the least expensive and least revolutionary technologies (simulation, cloud computing) are the most exploited in SMEs whereas those allowing profound business transformations (CPS, Machine-To-Machine, bigdata, collaborative robot) are still neglected by SMEs*" [13].

Considering the factors that are pointed out in the literature, some questions can be raised, namely: Is there any difference toward I4.0 Technologies according to gender? And according to the generation factor? Will the level of education or field of studies play a role on the openness to I4.0 Technologies on individuals? These are some questions that we will try to answer along this paper.

3 Methodology

The present paper results from a broader project aiming to identify specific characteristics among different generations. This project includes a multicultural team (Portugal, Poland and Latvia). The questionnaire was updated from a previous project. In the most recent version, in the Portuguese questionnaire, were added some questions in order to identify some issues related to I4.0.

The Portuguese survey was applied to 260 individuals, mainly by using the social networks. The main purpose for the inclusion of these items is related to the aim of this paper that is the identification of possible patterns among the respondents' characteristics (gender, generation, level of education and field of studies) with the nine technologies of I4.0.

In order to study the relationships, a statistical analysis was performed, using the SPSS Statistics software v.25, mainly using a crosstab's analysis.

The aim of the study was to explore the existence of specific patterns associated to specific characteristics. Therefore, the following research hypotheses were put forward:

$H_{1\text{ to }4}$: Is there any variable association between Gender (1); (Generation); (Level of Education (3); Field of Studies (4) and the Knowledge people claim to have about Industry 4.0?
$H_{5\text{ to }8}$: Is there a variable association between Gender (1); (Generation); (Level of Education (3); Field of Studies (4) and IOT.
$H_{9\text{ to}12}$: Is there a variable association between Gender (1); (Generation); (Level of Education (3); Field of Studies (4) and Augmented Reality.
$H_{13\text{ to }16}$: Is there a variable association between Gender (1); (Generation); (Level of Education (3); Field of Studies (4) and Big Data Analytics.
$H_{17\text{ to }20}$: Is there a variable association between Gender (1); (Generation); (Level of Education (3); Field of Studies (4) and Cloud.
$H_{21\text{ to }24}$: Is there a variable association between Gender (1); (Generation); (Level of Education (3); Field of Studies (4) and Cybersecurity.
$H_{25\text{ to }28}$: Is there a variable association between Gender (1); (Generation); (Level of Education (3); Field of Studies (4) and Simulation.
$H_{29\text{ to }32}$: Is there a variable association between Gender (1); (Generation); (Level of Education (3); Field of Studies (4) and Systems Integration.
$H_{33\text{ to }36}$: Is there a variable association between Gender (1); (Generation); (Level of Education (3); Field of Studies (4) and Additive Manufacturing.
$H_{37\text{ to }40}$: Is there a variable association between Gender (1); (Generation); (Level of Education (3); Field of Studies (4) and Robotics.

For the realization of the main objective of this study a diagnostic survey was applied using a Likert scale (from 0 to 5) and asked the respondents to mark a value within that range, in order to identify how comfortable they were with each one of the nine technologies of I4.0.

In order to explore variable association cross-tabulation tests will be performed based on the following hypothesis:

H_0: The variables are independent (do not exist variable association) vs.
H_1: The variables are dependent (exists association).

As stated in the literature, in order to analyze these hypotheses, one must run a χ^2 test. The decision will be taken according to the p-value obtained with the χ^2 test.

The survey was conducted from March to July 2020 through the social networks, in order to get the snowball effect.

4 Results

In this section the first figure being presented results from simple, but quite important analysis, in order to frame the subsequent analysis. Firstly, it is important to understand the perceptions that inquired individuals present about the basics of I4.0.

On a second stage it will be presented a brief characterization of the respondents, and after that, we will present some results in order to identify the existence of patterns among different groups of individuals and their perceptions about I4.0.

Considering the answers to those nine technologies the average figure (even being an average from a Likert scale) presents a result of 2.93 and a standard deviation of 1.24. Analyzing the frequencies from the Likert scale answers was verified that 30% of the respondents scored 4 out of 5 in a variable that combined into one of the nine technologies [(V1 + … + V9)/9]. Other curious but somehow expected results are the extremes: 4.6% of the respondents have no idea about I4.0 (scored 0), while 7.3% are fully committed, since they scored 5 out 5 in the nine technologies. At a first glance, the results seem to be positive, however, 62% of the respondents scored 3 or above. These first results suggest that further analysis might identify specific patterns, but this hypothesis will be explored later on.

When it comes to the technologies, at an individual level, the analysis shows that might be some differences toward the familiarization to each technology among respondents. First results are presented in Table 1.

From Table 1, where mean and mode for each technology is presented, it is possible to verify that the most familiar concept (among the nine technologies) is Cloud (the only technology with a mode of 5), followed by the concept of IoT, while the less familiar is Additive Manufacturing and Robotics.

These first results are in some way related and divergent to some findings from the literature review. For instance, Moeuf et al. [13] identified Cloud Computing and Simulation as the most frequent technologies in SMEs. Being Portugal a country where the overwhelming majority of firms are SMEs, Cloud technology seems to be aligned, but Simulation is one of the technologies with the lowest results.

Table 1 Mean and mode for each technology of I4.0

Technology	Mean	Mode
IoT	3.40	4
Augmented reality	2.89	3
Big data analytics	2.70	4
Cloud	3.71	5
Cybersecurity	3.18	4
Simulation	2.67	3
Systems integration	2.85	4
Additive manufacturing	2.42	3
Robotics	2.60	3

From the previous results it was not possible to disclose any pattern. But if we start to consider variables such as gender, age (or generation) or level of studies will we be able to find patterns? Those patterns might be interesting in order to identify the type of individuals and skills that are aligned with the employer's or project's requirements in terms of I4.0 Technologies. In order to explore these possibilities, it will be important to describe/characterize our group of respondents.

From the data available in Table 2, an overview of the respondents' profile could be seen. The main idea was to present a brief description from the respondents, in order to explore the patterns (and hypothesis) suggested in the previous chapters. Next, we will try to identify the existence of relations among some variables, according to the hypothesis and tests presented in the methodology section.

The first variable dependence test was related to I4.0 variable as a whole. At first was considered the variable that aggregates the nine technologies in order to find a possible variable association with gender, generation, education or field of studies. The results are as follows:

- cross-tabulation I4.0 vs Gender:

Table 2 Respondents' brief characterization

	%
Gender	
Male	48.1
Female	51.9
Generation	
Baby Boomer	0.4
Gen. X	20
Gen Y. (Millennial)	26.5
Gen Z	53.1
Education	
Basic School	3.8
High School	39.6
University Degree	36.9
Master or Doctorate	19.2
Missing	0.4
Field of Education	
Economics/Management	20.4
Social Sciences/Law	1.9
Tourism	0.4
STEM	33.1
Health	2.3
Others	8.8
Missing	33.1

The results observed and expected do not present a significant difference. By requiring the χ^2 test we got a p-value of 0.492. Since this result is higher than 0.05 it means that H_0 may not be rejected. So, the results suggest that on what regards I4.0 there are no differences between genders.

- cross-tabulation I4.0 vs Generation:

  The first test considering the 4 generations and the 6 levels of I4.0 (0 to 6) presented a result without statistical validity, since 37.5% of the cells presented a count of less than 5. In order to try a valid result, the levels of I4.0 were reduced from 6 to 3: [0 and 1 $\rightarrow$ 1; 2 and 3 $\rightarrow$ 2; 4 and 5 $\rightarrow$ 3]. After this reduction the test keeps without statistical validity. Looking to the results obtained were not identified unexpected patterns.
- cross-tabulation I4.0 vs Education:

  On what regards to Education the results are similar to those obtained in the Generation tests. There is no statistical validity, but there are no unexpected patterns identified so, does not make sense to readjust any variable.
- cross-tabulation I4.0 vs Field of Studies:

The first analysis of this relation presented a result without statistical validity. In this case were reduced both variables (I4.0 as in the previous ones, and the field of education to 3 categories: Economics and Management, STEM and others that now also aggregates Tourism, Health and Social Sciences/Law). The second test leaded to a statistical valid result, but with a p-value (on the χ^2 test) of 0.426—higher than 0.05 which means that H_0 may not be rejected. Anyway, there is a light tendency for a pattern: On the categories of Economics and Management and Others the number of cases in the lower levels of I4.0 is higher than the expected ones, and we got a lower (than the expected) count in the higher levels of I4.0. The opposite scenario was identified in the STEM category. Once again, these results originate from a detailed figures observation, rather than a statistical valid test.

The results from these analyses lead us to assume that with H_0 (variable independence) no rejection, one can assume that the familiarization with the concept of Industry 4.0 is not a particular characteristic of a specific group of people. It seems to be a concept that is equally known by different groups of people in this sample study.

The next step consists of similar analysis but this time considering each one of the nine technologies individually. In order to reduce the results without statistical validity, the levels of familiarization with these concepts were reduced from 6 to 3. In the category of generation considering that only one respondent was classified as baby-boomer, this generation was excluded from the analysis. In order to simplify the results are presented in the Table 3:

Comments:

IoT: No variable association.

Augmented Reality: It was identified a pattern: Generation Z are the ones that assume to be more familiar with this concept (p-value = 0.097).

Table 3 Results from the Cross-tabs among I4.0 Technologies and respondents' characteristics

Technology	Gender	Generation	Education	Field of Studies
IoT	H_0 Not Rejected	H_0 Not Rejected	H_0 Not Rejected	H_0 Not Rejected
Augmented Reality	H_0 Not Rejected	H_0 Rejected (10%)	Without statistical validity	H_0 Not Rejected
Big Data Analytics	H_0 Rejected (5%)	H_0 Not Rejected	Without statistical validity	H_0 Not Rejected
Cloud	H_0 Not Rejected	H_0 Not Rejected	H_0 Not Rejected	H_0 Not Rejected
Cybersecurity	H_0 Not Rejected	H_0 Not Rejected	H_0 Not Rejected	H_0 Not Rejected
Simulation	H_0 Not Rejected	H_0 Rejected (10%)	H_0 Not Rejected	H_0 Not Rejected
Systems Integration	H_0 Not Rejected	H_0 Rejected (5%)	H_0 Not Rejected	H_0 Not Rejected
Additive Manufacturing	H_0 Not Rejected	H_0 Not Rejected	H_0 Not Rejected	H_0 Not Rejected
Robotics	H_0 Not Rejected	H_0 Not Rejected	H_0 Not Rejected	H_0 Not Rejected

Big Data Analytics: Men are more familiar with this concept p-value = 0.038). Even without statistical validity there is an identified tendency to be more familiar to those with higher levels of education.

Cloud: No variable association.

Cybersecurity: No variable association.

Simulation: The younger generations (Y and Z) are more familiar with this technology.

Systems Integration: Y Generation (millennials) is the one that is more familiar with this concept (p-value = 0.030).

Additive Manufacturing: No variable association.

Robotics: No variable association.

The results obtained and presented in Table 3 are aligned with the results obtained on the Industry 4.0 variable as a whole. When the technologies are considered by themselves, in most cases the variable independence (no association) is the result. On those results with variable association, the most relevant is the Generation (or age). While younger people (Generation Z—born after 1994) are more familiar with the concept of Augmented Reality, the so-called Millennials (born between 1980 and 1994) are more familiar with Systems integration. Both (Y and Z) are comfortable with the Simulation concepts. On what regards Gender, men are more familiar with the Big Data concept?

5 Conclusion

As first conclusion in general it can be said that taking into consideration the results from this sample, there are no significative differences among the level of education or field of studies, towards I4.0 and its technologies. On what regards gender and generation some differences were identified? On gender it was verified that men are more comfortable with the concept of big data analytics than women. It was also identified that younger generations (Y and/or Z) are more confident in the following technologies: Augmented Reality, Simulation and Systems Integration.

A research developed in two large universities in Eastern Europe concluded that students from business, finance, economics, statistics, marketing and similar disciplines did not reject the inclusion of technical content (cloud computing, big data, social networks, cybersecurity) [22]. This result in some way justifies the results obtained in the field of studies analysis. Students, even those that are not in STEM, are aware and interested in the I4.0 Technologies.

Notwithstanding, the results point out a subliminal importance of technology embedding throughout generations which could produce expressive differences between perceptions and skills development among its members and generate difficulties to standardize the use of such technologies.

It is also important to point out that the digital transformation of society, industry and services, as well as in education field is in a development/transition phase which means that some of these previous results could vary through time. Therefore, in our view it will be important to measure these variables longitudinally toward picturing the tendencies and the degree of alignment between the perceptions and skills of people and the work requirements in the digitalized world.

Acknowledgements This work is supported by national funds, through the FCT—Portuguese Foundation for Science and Technology under the project UIDB/04011/2020.

References

1. Alcácer V., & Cruz-Machado, V. (2019). Scanning the industry 4.0: A literature review on technologies for manufacturing systems. *Engineering Science and Technology, an International Journal*, *22*(3).
2. Qin, J., Liu Y., & Grosvenor, R. (2016). A categorical framework of manufacturing for industry 4.0 and beyond. In *Procedia CIRP*, vol. 52.
3. Schlick, J., Stephan P., & Zühlke, D. (2012). 2020, Produktion Revolution, Auf dem Weg zur 4. Industriellen. In *IM information management und consulting* (pp. 26–33).
4. Lu, Y. (2017). Industry 4.0: A survey on technologies, applications and open research issues. *Journal of Industrial Information Integration.*
5. Salkin, C., Oner, M., Ustundag, A., & Cevikcan, E. (2018). A conceptual framework for industry 4.0. In A. Ustundag & Emre Cevikcan (Eds.), *Industry 4.0: Managing the digital transformation* (pp. 3–22). Springer International Publishing

6. Dalenogare, L., Benitez, G., Ayala, N., & Frank, A. (2018). The expected contribution of Industry 4.0 technologies for industrial performance. *International Journal of Production Economics, 204.*
7. Costa, M., Santos, L., Schaefer, J., Baierle, I., & Nara, E. (2019). Industry 4.0 technologies basic network identification. *Scientometrics, 121*(2).
8. Acatech. (2011). Cyber-physical systems driving force for innovation in mobility, health, energy and production acatech position paper. Springer.
9. Lasi, H., Fettke, P., Kemper, H., Feld, T., & Hoffmann, M. (2014). Industry 4.0. *Business & Information Systems Engineering.*
10. Brettel, M., Friederichsen, N., Keller, M., & Rosenberg, M. (2014). How virtualization, decentralization and network building change the manufacturing landscape. *International Journal of Mechanical Aerospace, Industrial and Mechatronics Engineering, 8*(1).
11. Ejsmont, K., Gladysz, B., Kluczek, A. (2020). Impact of industry 4.0 on sustainability-bibliometric literature review. *Sustainability (Switzerland), 12*(14).
12. Ghobakhloo, M. (2018). The future of manufacturing industry: a strategic roadmap toward Industry 4.0. *Journal of Manufacturing Technology Management, 29*(6).
13. Moeuf, A., Pellerin, R., Lamouri, S., Tamayo-Giraldo, S., & Barbaray, R. (2018). The industrial management of SMEs in the era of Industry 4.0. *International Journal of Production Research, 56*(3).
14. Müller, J., Kiel, D., & Voigt, K. (2018). What drives the implementation of Industry 4.0? The role of opportunities and challenges in the context of sustainability. *Sustainability, 10*(1).
15. Wei, Z., Song, X., & Wang, D. (2017). Manufacturing flexibility, business model design, and firm performance. *International Journal of Production Economics, 193.*
16. Ras, E., Wild, F., Stahl, C., & Baudet, A. (2017). Bridging the skills gap of workers in industry 4.0 by human performance augmentation tools—Challenges and roadmap. In *ACM international conference proceeding series*, vol. Part F128530.
17. Kamble, S., Gunasekaran, A., & Sharma, R. (2018). Analysis of the driving and dependence power of barriers to adopt industry 4.0 in Indian industry. *Computers in Industry, 101.*
18. Kubicek, B., & Korunka, C. (2017). The present and future of work: Some concluding remarks and reflections on upcoming trends. In *Job demands in a changing world of work: Impact on workers' health and performance and implications for research and practice.*
19. Dombrowski, U., & Wagner, T. (2014). Mental strain as field of action in the 4th industrial revolution. In *Procedia CIRP*, vol. 17.
20. Ivanov, D., Tang, C., Dolgui, A., Battini, D., & Das, A. (2020). Researchers' perspectives on Industry 4.0: multi-disciplinary analysis and opportunities for operations management. *International Journal of Production Research*, 1–24.
21. Sony, M., & Naik, S. (2019). Key ingredients for evaluating Industry 4.0 readiness for organizations: A literature review. *Benchmarking, 27*(7).
22. Bologa, R., Lupu, A., Boja, C., & Georgescu, T. (2017). Sustaining employability: A process for introducing cloud computing, big data, social networks, mobile programming and cybersecurity into academic curricula. *Sustainability, 9*(12).

Legal Regulation of Work in the Digital Economy: Protecting Employees from Psychosocial Risks

Alena Fedorova, Marina Chudinivskikh, and Ilona Polents

Abstract The emergence of new psychosocial risks at work and their impact on the employees' health and well-being under economy digitalization requires improved legal regulation of the labour sphere. In the digital economy, the distinction between working and rest time is blurring, creating new factors for work stress, including cyberstress. Employers are often not responsible for employees' stress having a negative impact on the physical and psychosocial well-being of the latter. The empirical basis of the study is the results of a sociological survey of respondents from several countries conducted in 2018 with a random sample of employees of different organizations. Comparative analysis of responses reveals the dominants, similarities and differences in the employees' perception of the work factors that affect their health and well-being. Most of the workers surveyed noted the negative impact of work on their self-felling. Among the main destructive factors, stress at work is dominant. It becomes obvious that protecting workers from work stress requires regulatory measures, the absence of which in many countries does not allow leaving this issue unattended. The authors consider the progressive foreign experience and relevant areas of Russian legislation improvement in the field of workers' health and well-being in the digital economy.

Keywords Digital transformation · Labour relations · Distance employees · Psychosocial risks · Workers' health and well-being · Right to disconnect

---

A. Fedorova (✉)
Ural Federal University, Mira str. 19, 620002 Yekaterinburg, Russian Federation
e-mail: a.e.fedorova@urfu.ru

M. Chudinivskikh
Ural State University of Economics, 8 Marta str., 62, 620144 Yekaterinburg, Russian Federation

I. Polents
University of West Bohemia, Plzen, Czech Republic

E. Zaramenskikh and A. Fedorova (eds.), *Digitalization of Society, Economics and Management*, Lecture Notes in Information Systems and Organisation 53,
https://doi.org/10.1007/978-3-030-94252-6_20

1 Introduction

The development of legislation should take into account the changes that are taking place in the economy. The last decade is the time of the boom of distance technology. The widespread use of the Internet and computer technology requires an adequate response of the legislation to emerging challenges. Today we have to admit the fact that Russian legislation so far weakly responds to new threats. The least protected in these conditions are distance workers [1].

The Institute of remote labour is relatively new to Russian law. Remote workers are not covered by traditional guarantees established by the Labour Code of the Russian Federation (in terms of overtime pay, night work, observance of the right to rest, etc.). Control in the field of labour protection of distance employees is practically absent, as well as it is especially difficult for them to prove that an accident occurred during work.

The fact that he is constantly included in the work also has a negative effect on the health of a remote employee. The reasons for this phenomenon are different: the desire to make more money, the difference in time zones, the need to maintain the smooth functioning of online services. Regardless of the reason, the boundaries between working time and rest time are blurred in the digital economy.

The urgent issue of legal regulation of the labour sphere remains the occurrence of psychosocial risks in the workplace and their impact on the employees' health. Russian workers are not protected by law from the effects of stress at the workplace. The employer is not liable for damage caused to the employee by stress associated with work [2]. The lack of proper legal regulation does not allow ignoring this issue.

In the past 20 years, standards have been emerging in European legislation that specify the protection of the employee's mental health. Thanks to the conclusion of the European framework agreements on harassment and violence at work, as well as on stress at work, the protection of employees from these psychosocial risks has been most developed [3]. One of the new types of stress is cyberstress stipulated by the rapid development of digital technologies and their implementation in the labour sphere. The problem of cyberstress today requires special attention of both researchers of psychosocial risks and lawmakers who are forming the legal and regulatory possibilities for managing issues of health promotion and well-being enhancement at work. Remote workers are especially susceptible to cyberstress due to the fact that they are often forced to go beyond the traditional regime of work and leisure. Therefore, legislative initiatives aimed at ensuring the right of workers to non-working hours are especially relevant for them. In a number of countries, these initiatives have already taken the form of legal acts, considered by the authors as an effective tool to reduce psychosocial risks for the employees' health and well-being.

2 Literature Review

Over the last decade governments in many nations enact statutes and regulations allowing employees the freedom to disengage from work activities beyond the official work hours (labeled “right to disconnect” codes) [4].

The right to disconnect can help protect the health of a remote worker. The concept of the right to disconnect began to be actively formed in the last ten years with the development of information and communication technologies and their implementation in management. From a legal point of view, the “right to disconnect” can be considered as the implementation of Art. 24 of the Universal Declaration of Human Rights, which states: “Everyone has the right to rest and leisure, including the right to a reasonable restriction on working hours and paid periodic leave”.

Foreign scholars are actively discussing the right to disconnect over the past few years both from the position of personnel management [5] and in the legal context [6]. The right is enshrined in French labour law as a result of studies on the impact of digital technology on labour. It is necessary to maintain a balance between work and personal life. The adoption of such a law is due to the need to adapt labour legislation to the digital economy. Without the right to disconnect, the risk of emotional and psychological overload, a feeling of constant fatigue, stress increases. The new French law, aimed at preventing professional burnout and preserving family relationships, requires companies with more than 50 employees to jointly with their employees include the issue of the right to disconnect in collective bargaining, determine and fix in the local act, at what hours employees have the right not to respond to business letters to avoid work interference in their privacy. If the employer has not included the right to disconnect in the Mandatory Annual Negotiation (MAN), a fine of about 4 thousand euros is imposed on him. The right to disconnect was also enshrined in Italian law. Senate Act No. 2233-B “Measures to safeguard non-entrepreneurial self-employment and measures to facilitate flexible articulation at times and places of subordinate employment” states that an employee’s rest time must be fixed in writing in an employment contract and described technical and organizational measures necessary to ensure that the employee is disconnected from the process equipment.

In Germany, the right to disconnect has not yet been enshrined in law, but in fact it is granted by leading concerns. So, Volkswagen refused to send corporate mail to employees in off hours. Another technological solution allows delaying the receipt of mail by an employee until the beginning of the next working day. A number of German companies block the distribution of electronic messages to employees who are on vacation or on sick leave [7, 8].

In 2018, a draft law was developed to amend the New York City Charter and the New York City Administrative Code for private employees who disconnect from emails in off hours. The bill is aimed at companies with more than 10 employees. It provides for a ban on requiring employees to respond to emails and text messages during the non-working hours. At the suggestion of US lawmakers, companies that violate these restrictions are expected to be fined [9].

Canada is another nation considering the after-hours communication from phones and computers outside office hours. The "Right to Disconnect Act" (2018) is aimed to "ensure that employee rest periods are respected by requiring employers to adopt an after-hour's disconnection policy." The bill includes fines for employers who fail to comply with the law. The legislation of South Korea seeks to ban companies from delivering work-related messages to their employees by telephone, text, social media, or mobile messaging after regular work hours. Cyberstress due to continual contact from work supervisors has developed into an increasingly important social issue in South Korea, a nation afflicted with a mix of its infamous workaholic culture and highly developed digital technology. A brief listing of other countries have voiced concern regarding work-life balance problems includes Japan, Spain, Philippines, Belgium, Luxembourg and the Netherlands [10–12].

It should be noted that for labour practices in most countries the right to disconnect is still a relatively new phenomenon. For instance, just a few scientific publications are devoted to this problem. Son and Chernova analyse the experience of several countries, including France, Germany and South Korea, in securing the right to disconnect in the legislation [13]. More often Russian researchers turn their attention to the problem of health promotion of workers in the context of digitalization of labour. Glukhov and Ponomareva consider transformations of Russian society and forming of new value orientations [14]. Fedorova et al. studies the transformation processes in labour relations and factors of the workplace that have a negative impact on the physical and psychosocial well-being of workers [15, 16]. Plutova and Kulkova suggest creating such a value system in a society that helps to formulate norms of healthy life and family traditions [17].

It is commonly known that the development of technology today is faster than the adaptation of human thought and just few people have adequate cultural and cognitive tools to keep up with the developments of technology [18]. The study presented in this article covers various aspects of the transformation of labour relations and working conditions, including changes related to the digitalization of the economy. The authors pay special attention to influence of the mentioned above transformational processes on physical and psychosocial well-being of workers, as well as the search for tools to reduce the negative impact of the high speed of introducing new, including digital, labour organization technologies.

3 Methodology

The research methodology covers the collection of primary data, their analysis and interpretation. The steps include composition of a questionnaire, pre-research, modification of a questionnaire, annual questionnaire study, data analysis and interpretation of the results.

The survey consists of a number of questions that the respondents had to answer in a set format. The questionnaire includes ordinal-polytomous and dichotomous closed-ended questions with the open-ended options in some of them. The questions were divided into six parts according to the problem area under investigation: (1) forms of employment relationship and wages, (2) changes in the organization's personnel policy, (3) forms of infringement committed by employers, (4) leadership decisions which are detrimental to employees' well-being, (5) sources of anxiety and threats at work, (6) personality. In 2018 the questionnaire was supplemented by questions regarding respondents' perceptions of the degree of influence of various intra-organizational factors on their well-being, and, therefore, on the state of their physical and psychological well-being.

In 2018 the survey was conducted in September–December and involved 690 employees in: Russian Federation—148, Czech Republic—130, Latvia—134, Pakistan—130, Kazakhstan—148. The majority work in service sector (30.2%); with the others being involved in manufacturing (14.4%) and energy production (6.9%), trade (11.4%), education (6.6%), construction (6.1%), finance (4.9%) and other sectors (19.5%). The aggregate sample of the respondents includes: 40.7%—qualified specialists; 20.8%—manual workers; 18.0%—line personnel; 11.5%—middle managers; 4.4%—top managers and 4.6%—trainees. The survey involved 47.7% of men and 52.3% of women. The age structure of the respondents can be divided into two groups consisting of young people up to 35 years old (51.0%), and the rest in the 36–50 age group (49.0%).

Despite the use of self-rated well-being at work in given surveys, its appropriateness is a potential limitation that imposes to be careful in case of cross-country comparisons. Because of its subjective nature, self-rated well-being at work may suffer from person-specific heterogeneity, so this evaluation could be downward biased for pessimistic individuals or could change across cultures. However, self-rated physical and emotional well-being closely links to objective conditions. Overall, it allows for a reliable evaluation of the general individual status and well-being at work: respondents, when assessing their condition in their workplaces, can account simultaneously for the different dimensions of labour relations.

The statements in this research are based on the use of descriptive statistical models (frequency, distribution, average) and detailed stochastical cross-tab and correlation analysis, supported by VORTEX software.

4 Results

Despite the fact that only 7.7% of Czech employees interviewed expressed concern about poor health in the workplace, two-thirds (66.2%) agreed that work had a negative impact on their health and well-being. It should be noted that respondents from all the countries agree with them: more than half note the presence of such an influence (Table 1).

The next question is intended to identify which factors of the working environment, according to the respondents, have an adverse effect on their physical well-being (Table 2).

Table 1 The responses given to the question: "Do you believe that your work has a negative impact on your health and wellbeing?", % of the respondents, 2018

Response options	Russian Federation	Czech Republic	Latvia	Pakistan	Kazakhstan
Yes	64.2	66.2	55.2	69.2	60.1
No	35.8	33.8	44.8	30.8	39.9

Table 2 The responses given to the question: "How exactly does your work affect your physical and psychological health?", % of the respondents, 2018

Response options	Russian Federation	Czech Republic	Latvia	Pakistan	Kazakhstan
My health deteriorates due to stress in the workplace	56.4	37.2	63.5	13.3	31.5
My health deteriorates due to the high working intensity	26.6	50.0	33.8	11.1	16.9
My health always deteriorates in the workplace	4.3	1.2	5.4	8.9	5.6
I suffer from sleep disorders/insomnia due to problems at work	24.5	18.4	28.4	7.8	27.0
Problems at work cause my overeating and/or obesity	10.6	10.5	13.5	16.7	28.1
Problems at work led to weight loss	2.1	0.0	1.4	4.4	1.1
I suffer from headaches due to problems at work	23.4	7.0	20.3	6.7	28.1
I have an occupational disease (injury) obtained at the workplace	3.2	0.0	8.1	5.5	7.9
I feel tired and exhausted at work	24.5	7.0	37.8	11.1	18.0
My work is the cause of my depression	13.8	0.0	12.2	11.1	12.4
I think that I am in a state of professional burnout	19.1	20.9	16.2	3.3	18.0
Other	2.1	3.5	4.1	0.0	1.1

More than half of the Russian respondents mention stress at work as one of the reasons for their health deterioration, and one in four mentions excessive work intensity. A quarter of the respondents complain about feeling tired and exhausted, insomnia and headaches; one in five is in a state of professional burnout, and one in seven suffers from depression. Unlike Russian respondents, half of the Czech employees surveyed attribute the deterioration of their physical well-being to excessive work intensity, and a little more than a third indicate high stress. The third most often mentioned factor is professional burnout, which was noted by every fifth respondent. It is also worth noting that insomnia is accompanied by overeating and obesity. The distribution of the responses is different for Latvian employees: the feeling of tiredness and emptiness is the top unfavourable factor. About a third of Latvian respondents indicated excessive work intensity, leading to deterioration in their physical well-being. Among the most commonly mentioned health effects are insomnia, headaches, overeating and obesity, as well as depression. Every sixth surveyed is in a state of professional burnout.

Despite the absence of pronounced patterns in the distribution of responses of Pakistani employees, it can be noted that overeating and obesity take the first place in the ranking of the adverse effects on employee health of certain social pollution factors. A little less than a third of those surveyed in Kazakhstan believe that the deterioration in their physical well-being is due to high stress at work. The most often mentioned consequences were headaches, overeating, obesity and insomnia. Almost every fifth Kazakh respondent suffers from professional burnout, feels exhausted and devastated and every eighth is depressed due to work.

5 Conclusion

Legislation in the health promotion and well-being of workers is a complex phenomenon. It is formed at the expense of labour, medical, administrative, criminal law. Table 3 summarizes the identified shortcomings and gaps in the legal regulation of workers health promotion and well-being increasing, as well as suggests measures to improve the regulatory framework.

In order to protect the employee from overload, it seems necessary to fix the norms in the Labour Code of the Russian Federation:

- establishing a prohibition for the employer to require the employee to complete production tasks during the non-working hours, including by sending electronic messages, using instant messengers;
- highlighting exceptional cases when the employer has the right to send messages to the employee during the off hours (for example, in the event of an industrial accident, fire);
- excluding the possibility of bringing the employee to disciplinary liability for non-performance of official duties upon receipt of such messages outside of work time.

Table 3 Problems and shortcomings of the Russian legal regulation of health promotion and well-being enhance of workers

Issues	Ways of solution
A number ILO Conventions are not ratified in Russia	Phased ratification of ILO Conventions
Complicated and controversial system of normative acts	Codification of legislation on the health and well-being of the population Revision of current regulatory acts of the Soviet period, assessment of the appropriateness of their replacement, cancellation or adaptation to modern conditions
Disproportion of administrative and criminal liability measures	Adoption of a new Code of Administrative Offenses The attribution of offenses that resulted in harm to health Systematization of fines and determination of their proportionality to consequences severity
Emerging new threats to worker health in a digital economy	Establish the employee rights to disconnect in the Labour Code Definition of organizational and technical measures for labour protection of remote workers

Thus, the improvement of Russian legislation in the field of health promotion and well-being enhance of workers should be carried out taking into account progressive foreign experience. Normative and legal regulation needs to be substantially revised by eliminating obsolete norms, codification and updating. The main vector of the development of legislation should be aimed at creating a system of joint responsibility of workers, employers and the state for the health of population and safe work.

References

1. Bikmetov, R. I. (2013). Features of ensuring the labor protection requirements of remote workers. Possible contradictions in the provision of social protection for remote workers injured as a result of injuries at work and occupational diseases. *Labor Law in Russia and Abroad, 3*, 48–49.
2. Vorontsov, D. I. (2018). Promising areas of stress management in the workplace: Legal and economic aspects. *Law and Economics, 2*, 67–72.
3. Protecting workers from psychosocial risks: European experience and its applicability in Russia. Part I: Protecting workers from work-related stress. *Labor Law, 7* (2014). Retrieved November 08, 2019, from https://www.top-personal.ru/lawissue.html?2400
4. Von Bergen, C. W., Bressler, M. S., & Proctor, T. L. (2019). On the grid 24/7/365 and the right to disconnect. *Employee Relations Law Journal, 45*(2), 3–20.
5. Chiuffo, F. (2019). The 'right to disconnect' or 'how to pull the plug on work'. Retrieved November 11, 2019, from https://ssrn.com/abstract=3422283 or http://dx.doi.org/10.2139/ssrn.3422283

6. Secunda, P. M. (2018). The employee right to disconnect. *Notre Dame Journal of International and Comparative Law, 8*(1), 1–34.
7. Hesselberth, P. (2017). Discourses on disconnectivity and the right to disconnect. *New Media & Society, 20*(5), 1994–2010.
8. Vasagar, J. (2013). Out of hours working banned by German labour ministry. Retrieved September 10, 2017, from https://www.telegraph.co.uk/news/worldnews/europe/germany/10276815/Out-of-hours-working-banned-by-German-labour-ministry.html
9. Private employees disconnecting from electronic communications during non-work hours. Retrieved November 8, 2019, from http://legistar.council.nyc.gov/LegislationDetail.aspx?ID=3458217&GUID=8930D471-5788-4AF4-B960-54620B2535F7&Options=ID%7CText%7C&Search=disconnect
10. Donini, F. R. T., & Annamaria, M. A. P. (2017). Janus and the trade union challenge of digital technology. *European Review of Labour and Research, 23*(2), 207–223.
11. Marcum, T., Cameron, E. A., & Versweyveld, L. (2018). Never off the clock: The legal implications of employees' after hours work. *Labor Law Journal, 73*(70), 75–84.
12. Derks, D., Van Duin, D., Tims, M., & Bakker, A. B. (2015). Smartphone use and work-home interference: The moderating role of social norms and employee work engagement. *Journal of Occupational & Organizational Psychology, 88*(1), 155–167.
13. Son, Kh. I., & Chernova, Zh. V. (2018). Mobile devices as a way to strike a balance between work and personal life: The flip side. *Public Opinion Monitoring: Economic and Social Change, 6*(148), 201–215.
14. Glukhov, V. V., & Ponomareva, O. Y. (2015). Effect of transformations of Russian society on forming of value orientation of today youth (On an example of Sverdlovskaya Region). *Journal of Advanced Research in Law and Economics, 6*(1), 88–95.
15. Fedorova, A., Katashinskikh, V. S., & Dvorakova, Z. (2016). Precarious labour relations as a factor of social pollution. *Economy of Region, 12*(3), 802–814.
16. Koropets, O., & Plutova, M. (2020). The impact of global risks of industry 4.0 on the psychological safety of workers: Content analysis on the internet. In *Proceedings of the 19th European Conference on Research Methodology for Business and Management Studies* (pp. 139–146).
17. Plutova, M. I., & Kulkova, I. A. (2020). The study of linkage quality of life indicators within regional demographic parameters. *Smart Innovation, Systems and Technologies, 138*, 316–325.
18. Fedorova, A., Ferrara, M., & Fierro, P. (2017). The general data protection regulation (GDPR): From static to dynamic compliance. *Law and Economics Yearly Review, 6*, 283–302.

Smart Working in Public Administration: Anti Pandemic Tool or Work Organization Model?

Marco De Marco, Francesco Marcone, and Danila Scarozza

Abstract This article focuses on the first outcomes due to the implementation of Smart Working (SW) before and after the COVID-19 emergency within Italian public administrations. Aware of describing a still ongoing situation, the authors adopt a deductive approach to analyse the Ministry of Economy and Finance case study in order to integrate the main indications obtained from current literature and regulatory framework. The implementation of SW within Italian public administration (both in ordinary conditions and in emergency conditions) is first described; then, the authors describe the main implications of SW. Particularly, the paper aims to investigate to answer the following questions: (i) what are the combination of the different elements affecting the configuration of SW? (ii) what are the outcomes of SW likely to be for smart workers, organizations and society? (iii) what are the impacts of Covid-19 pandemic disease on SW adoption?

Keywords Smart working · Public administration · Covid-19 · SW outcomes

1 Introduction

For several years, one of the most important assets of the government reform strategies is focused on "smartness" [1]. While there are many different perspectives on smart government, according to Gil-Garcia and colleagues [2, 3] smart government can be used to characterize activities that creatively invest in emergent technologies coupled with innovative strategies to achieve more agile and resilient government

M. De Marco
International Telematic University UNINETTUNO, 00186 Rome, Italy

F. Marcone
Ministry of Economy and Finance, 00187 Rome, Italy

D. Scarozza (✉)
Link Capus University, Via del Casale di S. Pio V, 44, 00165 Rome, Italy
e-mail: d.scarozza@unilink.it

E. Zaramenskikh and A. Fedorova (eds.), *Digitalization of Society, Economics and Management*, Lecture Notes in Information Systems and Organisation 53,
https://doi.org/10.1007/978-3-030-94252-6_21

structures and governance infrastructures. However, there is no consensus in terms of what this term includes and how it is related to innovation in the public sector.

It is generally accepted that today also governments operate in challenging and rapidly changing environments. The concept of innovation in the public sector has shifted from a value-based concept into a concrete goal with specific targets, including innovation as a specific performance objective for government administrators [4]. This shift requires that innovation be tied to specific goals and objectives within the organization and that the organizational structure supports the changes. Garicano and Heaton [5] found that while ICT investments were not strongly associated with improvements in relevant productivity measures when examined in isolation, when combined with complimentary organizational changes ICT investments were linked to increased productivity.

However, this debate about innovation in public sector organizations was over—and at the same time reinforced—with the outbreak of the coronavirus emergency. The pandemic has forced also public organizations to put in place mechanisms to keep working while ensuring the health and safety of workers. The COVID-19 emergency that we are facing today has provided the opportunity for many workers and public sector organizations to imagine the possibility of a different way of organizing work. The pandemic has brought out themes like "smart working", "agile working", "remote working", and "teleworking". Smart Working (SW) (or as they refer to it in Italy—"Agile Work" which is governed by Articles 18–23 of Law No. 81/2017) has recently been mentioned in various Decrees issued by the Italian Government during the COVID-19 emergency phase of the pandemic. It has been mentioned as a method of being able to continue to carry out the work performance, as a preference and even at times as compulsory, as a remote service which has proved to be a solution to reconcile the limitations due to the lockdown of travel and workplaces with the need to ensure services continuity. That said, it should be noted that what organizations have found themselves experiencing, often in an improvised (and forced) way, are basically measures for the prevention of contagion through a form of "Remote Working" (or "Teleworking"). This method of working lacks the characteristics of SW in Italy. True SW is characterized by the substantial freedom of choice on the part of the employee regarding the times and places of the work performance, as well as by the fact that the activity must be oriented and assessed on the basis of the achievement of production objectives, agreed with by the organization/employer (and not simply by making the worker available during office hours or by working an 8 h day). Therefore, it is evident that the development and diffusion of SW beyond the parameters of the current pandemic emergency, will require a radical change in the way the work is organized. There is the need to overcome the previous model and to introduce new ways of thinking in order to manage remote working groups in addition to identifying specific, measurable, realistic, and defined objectives over a certain time period. The implementation of proper SW, as the "new normal" work model, requires the preparation of radical organizational changes, and even more changes to work processes, procedures, and business planning.

Starting from these premises, in this paper we assume smart work (or smart working—SW) as one of the most important initiatives for building smart government. SW, in fact, refers to an alternative means of organizing work deploying a creative mix of emerging technologies and innovation, also in public sector organizations. Therefore, SW can be seen as an internal working process or working environment of smart government, which contributes to achieve a more efficient government and helps government employees enjoy higher quality of life. Previous studies show that applying emerging technologies to existing administrative processes, even to a relatively small degree, can have a substantial impact [5, 6]. Today, successful organizations are increasingly characterized by the ability to abandon now inappropriate working configurations [7] to support new organizational principles, new methods and tools through which work practices are accomplished [8]. The use of ICT provides an opportunity to be innovative in when we work, where we work and the way we work [9]. Specifically, there has been a noticeable diffusion among organizations of innovative ways of working and growing opportunities for their employees to perform work activities remotely, let them generally free to choose where (places) and when (time) carry out the assigned activities (spatial–temporal flexibility). This resulted in an increasing interest shown by both academics and practitioners towards different typologies of remote work arrangements, including telework, home-based telework, mobile work, virtual teams, and, more recently, smart work.

Specifically, SW has the potential to offer a wide range of individuals an alternative to traditional work arrangements. SW succeeds in modifying traditional work conditions and their natural environment, searching different and (till now) not totally and uniquely defined solutions, essentially grounded on a greater discretion in work activities and on a larger responsibility towards results workers are requested to provide. These two elements together are indeed believed to favour better performances by workers [10, 11]. This connection explains the increasing interest for SW, favouring the promotion of projects in the field [12–14].

Furthermore, over the last few years managers have started to acknowledge the potential advantages offered to both employees and organizations by SW. Howcroft and Taylor [15] point out the need for a significant change in the way people work. These changes are creating renewed interest in how work is conceptualized.

Also in the Italian public sector—especially after the adoption of the Law n.81/2017—Smart Working (SW) has emerged as a "new" way to define what is considered as an innovative approach to work organization and human resource management.

In this frame, this chapter proposes a conceptual model to better define SW. Furthermore, analysing the Italian Ministry of Economy and Finance case study the paper aims to investigate the nature and the dynamics of SW in order: (a) to offer a contribution to the debate on the workplaces' changes in response to the implementation of a SW project; (a) to offer a contribution to the debate on the workplaces' changes in response to Covid-19 emergency (b) to understand the effects of SW in terms of both work-life balance, individual performance and external benefits.

2 Smart Working: A Conceptual Framework

Technologies have changed (through enabling and/or constraining) HRM practices [15] bringing a new vocabulary to the HRM discourse [16]. In particular, changes in HRM and technologies [17, 18] have modified the geographical boundaries of HRM practices, distances in and between organizations have become shortened. Due to diverse technological advancements, organizations can offer their employees new ways of working by eliminating physical and time barriers and relying on such organizational forms as HRM shared services, virtual teams or SW.

Starting from these premises and focusing on SW in public sector, this paper was inspired by the following questions (Fig. 1): (i) what are the combination of the different elements affecting the configuration of SW? (ii) what are the outcomes of SW likely to be for smart workers, organizations, and society? (iii) what are the impacts of Covid-19 pandemic disease on SW adoption?

The context (of public organizations)

An important element for an effective SW implementation (not external to it, but part of the SW itself) is the context within which SW is adopted. SW could be seen as a system consisting of people, technology, organizations, and management practices related to human resource management. According to the principle of equifinality [19], the same final state may be reached from different initial conditions and HRM antecedents, in different ways, through different mechanisms. In order to better understand the relevance of SW and its functioning within public organizations, the context can be defined as the HRM context as the relevant external and internal conditions and elements. The external elements include societal values, the laws, the regulation and the labour market and the territorial level conditions within which the public organization has to work. There will be elements that are more directly under the organization's control but that are limited by previous managerial decisions and history, including the workforce characteristics. There will also be elements that are directly related to the administrative activities but are outside the direct remit of HRM, such as the management philosophy and the territorial features.

Focusing on SW, probably location has a major effect on how SW is understood and implemented, what practices have legitimacy and what the effects of those

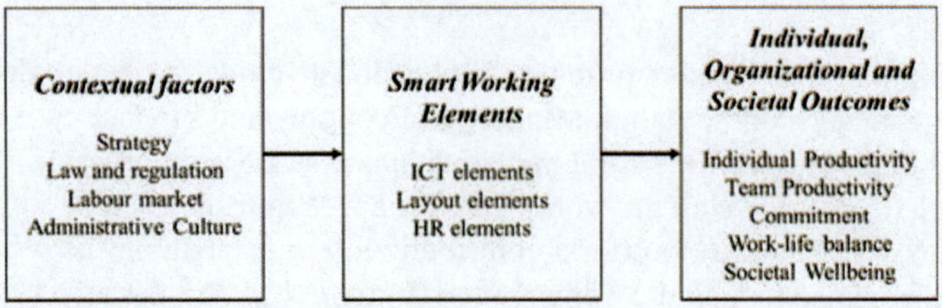

Fig. 1 The conceptual framework

practices are likely to be [20]. Countries have different SW regulations and practices because they are in different situations, have different cultures and different institutions. Specifically, governement and regulations play an important role for changing HRM practices and—consequently—SW [21]. In particular, regulations for the Italian context was one of the most important elements.

Starting from the Nineties, the telework was introduced in public administration as a form of distance work by Decree n.70/1999 providing information on both the features and the criteria in order to realize and use the teleworking stations. In 2012 another step was moved in the perspective of public organizations' modernization: the enactement of the decree n.221/2012 introduced the so-called "Telelavoro by default" inspired by what was done by the Obama government in the USA. Following this decree, public administrations were required to implement a plan for the telework adoption in which they had to specify "the modalities of realization and the possible activities for which the use of the telework was not possible". Despite these legislative interventions, Italy has not been able to make the best use of telework, which has been "trapped" by rigid rules. It has therefore become necessary to introduce new instruments of flexibility. In this direction, the Law for the Reform of the Public Administration (Madia Reform, law n.124/2015) on the one hand, provided suggestions for the strengthening of the telework adoption; on the other hand, promoted the adoption of SW. In addition, the law stated that in 2018 (3 years later the enactment of the law) flexible work tools should be used at least by 10% of public employees. The last step in the regulatory framework of SW in Italy is represented by the adoption of the Law n. 81/2017. The law defined SW as "a way to regulate the workers-organisation relationship, according to an agreement between the parties, also recurring to forms of organisation by stages, cycles and goals, without a defined timetable or place constraints working and the opportunity to use any technological tools to perform activities". Moreover, the Law (art. 18) stated that the main purpose of this new way to work is "both to increase competitiveness and to facilitate the balance of working and living times". The ratio of the Italian legislation is, on the one hand, to promote an improvement of the organizations' productivity and—on the other hand—to guarantee a better work-life balance to workers involved in the SW adoption [22]. Creating new rules with lightweight characteristics and obligations (for the worker and the employer), the SW law aims to stimulate a deep cultural change in the concept of work: the shift from "stamping the time-card" to work for goals, where the worker have large freedom to self-organize job as long as they meet the goals set at the due dates. The innovative part of the law is to configure SW as an organizational tool and not as a contractual type, with the aim of making it workable by all employees who carry out tasks that are compatible with SW.

However, even if the goal of introducing flexible ways of working within three years for at least 10% of employees on a voluntary basis was not yet achieved, at the beginning of the COVID-19 emergency, the pandemic has led to a significant acceleration in the use of SW, with simplified procedures and derogations from ordinary procedures. In particular, during the COVID-19 emergency, SW has become the standard work method for Italian Public Administrations. As part of the measures adopted by the Italian Government for the containment and management of the epidemiological emergency from COVID-19, the President of the Council of Ministers issued on March 1 2020 a Decree that intervenes on how to access SW, also confirmed by the Decree of 4 March 2020. As indicated in the Prime Minister Decree of 11 March 2020, it was recommended that organizations should make maximum use of agile working methods for activities that could be carried out at home, or remotely. According to the same Decree, "agile work" (or SW) is a mode of execution of subordinate employment relationships characterized by the absence of hourly or spatial constraints, as well as an organization by phases, cycles and objectives, established by an agreement between the organization and the employer.

Also, globalization will apply to SW too, since universal "good practice" will inevitably spread around the world [23], but there is little evidence that countries are becoming more alike in the way they conceive of and manage SW [24]. Some current problems characterizing Italian public administrations could impact the adoption of SW. One of the main issues of the Italian PA is the huge presence of elderly people working. Indeed, in 2015 less than 3 employees on 100 workers were younger than 30 years old and the average age was of 50.4 years [25]. One of the most important direct consequences is, for example, the closure towards innovation. Another critical aspect related to the Italian PA is the presence of corruption and the lack of transparency. In spite of the innovations introduced by the Madia Reform, such as the Freedom of Information Act (FOIA), the position covered by Italy in the international ranking of corruption is very disappointing. The causes of this positioning are that the FOIA needs time to be implemented properly and that the level of digitalization of Italian PA is still insufficient. Another problem is represented by the insufficient propensity to measure and evaluate the employees on their performances and by the inadequate planning: these are the bases of a culture that rewards the presence and not the actual effort destroying talents and productivity. Finally, due to the inadequate capability of Italian public administration to attract and retain valuable and highly qualified employees, it is more important than ever to understand what could attract people to the public service [26].

There may be debate about the balance between cultural differences and institutional differences [27], but together or independently culture and institutions will impact the SW/technology interface too.

The smart working elements

The development and diffusion of ICT, can support organizations in developing a SW system [28]. Previous literature has analysed how ICT has made work more portable and pervasive [29], there is not yet a comprehensive understanding the elements on which organizations should focus in case they want to adopt a SW organizational model.

According to the analysis developed by Mann [31], the three elements that can constitute a SW model are:

1. the ICT element: it is referred to the usage of ICT-based solutions. ICT solutions allow workers to share more easily files, information, data and ideas [31]. In

Table 1 Smart working elements

Elements	Dimension	References
ICT	Extent to which employees telework	Martínez-Sánchez et al. [33]
	Use of ICT personal devices and/or external ICT services	
HR	Extent to which employees can manage in a flexible way their working hours	Coenen and Kok [34]
	Change management actions implemented in the organization and new HRM practices/tools developed	
Layout	Adoption of initiatives of redesigning of the physical workspace for creating environments more flexible and oriented to collaboration	Elsbach and Pratt [35]

such a way, all employees can interact in real time in a flexible and effective way by contributing to a SW environment (software collaboration);

2. the HR element: this includes the innovations in the HR practices and in the organizational model (HR element). Changes in the HR practices can be introduced when a new organizational model is chosen, as SW is. Specifically, change management actions for managing the organizational models chosen can be applied by the organizations [32], such as training programmes, new communication plans, projects of cultural change, processes reorganization or a re-design of job role profiles.
3. the layout element: it is related to the reconfiguration of the workplace and of the office layout. According to some study, the strategy focused on the spatial reconfiguration of the office have an important role for the effecitiveness of a SW system. The attention to the layout can increase individual and team productivity and can allow workers to better their work-life balance. Therefore, particular office reconfigurations may lead to innovative ways of collaborating with others and thus simplifying the development of a SW model (Table 1).

Individual, Organizational and Societal Outcomes

SW has various impacts and consequences at different level: individual, organizational and societal. An understanding of these will help identify the values and motives that may support the promotion of this way of working.

At the individual level, a potential benefit of SW is represented by the opportunity for individual workers to establish an arrangement that is very personal and conducive to a superior quality of domestic life. SW can offer opportunities for people to improve their work-life balance more so than under traditional work conditions [35]. As a result, smart workers are often more motivated and enjoy better job satisfaction than conventional workers [36–38]. The positive perception of an improved work/life balance is recognized as one of the most important outcome of SW adoption. Other studies, suggested that smart workers are more committed since they worked longer hours than traditional employees, often without additional payment or remuneration for these extra hours [39–43]. One of the more sufficient potential benefits is increasing worker productivity that accrues from the practice of SW [44]. Organizations and businesses that have embraced telework have been able to increase output with the same number of staff, or reduce headcount and still provide the same level of service to their clients and customers.

Looking at the organizational level, SW must not be considered in isolation but rather placed in the overall context of existing and continuous business reorganization and change management environments. SW has the potential to become an integral, rather than an optional, way of working. Studies have shown SW can increase organizational productivity [45]. SW can reduce absenteeism and increase resilience, especially with decreased stress and anxiety levels and more control over working times and location [46, 47]. Another organizational impact of telework is the improvement it offers for services to citizens in a variety of ways. It can allow higher personalized responses to citizen demands without the need for a conventional base or office. This flexibility can fit into the ethos of how a PA operates and can lead to co-operative work across international boundaries and different time zones. SW implies also a rethiking of the control and supervision issues [45, 48]: the organisations need to difficult to trust unsupervised workers in a different manner. Moreover, the management of individual differences, and indeed similarities, between women and men and how they perceive their professional and domestic roles is an important issue when considering the adoption or development of SW. However, White et al. [49] maintained gender differences associated with frequency of working from home is insignificant, indicating a slightly lower proportion of females working from home at least once a week.

Finally, societal outcomes can be regarded also as long-term outcomes [49]. PA needs to create public value: since public organizations derive their legitimacy from society, HRM decisions and practices will have long-term benefits for the society.

In literature, there was a lack of interest in and evidence about the effects of SW adoption both on the community within which the organization operates and—more in general—on the society. Nevertheless, with the more recent development of notions such as sustainable HRM [50, 51] and corporate social responsibility [52] this is beginning to change. From a societal point of view, in fact, the magnitude of the impact of SW on environment, mobility and socioeconomic aspects is therefore relevant in order to determine whether a further encouragement of SW is useful and sustainable for the society as a whole [53]. SW can be seen as a way of offering environmental protection benefits by reducing, or eliminating, the commute to work leading to less fuel consumption and less CO_2 emissions, fewer traffic congestion problems and, savings in energy use in urban office spaces and buildings [54, 55]. Although these benefits are, to a certain extent, achievable with the correct understanding and strategies, the impact of SW on society continues to remain poorly understood [56]. SW also has the potential to bring about a more equitable distribution of economic activity throughout geographical areas and help redress the aggregation of economic activity in the main urban centres [57]. In addition, the spread of SW can assist in improving the economic and employment opportunities of underdeveloped areas [58].

3 Method

Since only limited empirical research on how PA deals with the adoption of SW [59] has been found an explorative approach has been chosen. Particularly, the research being reported in this paper involved the case study of Italian Ministry of Economy and Finance (MEF) in the adoption of SW since 2017. Other scholars used the case study approach to examine SW [60].

In this study, a single case is used, which is an appropriate way of establishing the field at the early stages of an emerging topic [61]. Moreover, the single case study approach is normally preferred when an inductive approach can be adopted, using theory to explain empirical observations and also to inform refinements and extension of the theory [62–64].

The case study presented in this paper aims to explore and to understand the configuration of SW and its outcomes at the individual, organizational and societal level.

According to our exploratory approach, we selected MEF as an exemplar case study [64], with unique circumstances. In particular, in MEF, the group project on SW begun to define the call and the way to implement SW prior both to the regulatory intervention by Italian legislation and the spread of the COVID-19 epidemic in Italy. In this setting, we analysed five different building blocks in order to understand both why and how SW has been adopted and what the outcomes obtained by a SW organizational model: (a) context; (b) ICT element; (c) layout element; (d) HR element; (e) SW outcomes.

The information gathered during this research relates to three different phases of the project called "Be MEF, Be Smart", which began in July 2017 and it is still ongoing in the new version "Be MEF, Be Smart 2.0". From a methodological point of view, data and information collection period is particularly significant for our analysis, since it allows us to better define the nature and the relevance of the collected information. The longitudinal approach used in the observation of the project development led to the analysis of context, groups, and individual dynamics, concerning the adoption of SW. To improve validity and reliability [64], of our findings and conclusions, we collected data from different sources. In relation to the four conceptual dimensions of analysis (ICT element, layout element, HR element and outcomes), a triangulation was carried out between documental information and interviews. The documents helped understanding the relevance given to the different phases and practices, the modes of interaction between actors and the technologies adopted for SW. Data have been collected by the "organization co-author" also through interviews and continuous information flows. All information gathered provided also evidence on both the process of internal communication and the role of people involved in trialing and adopting SW. The interviews were conducted with some of the key organizational actors involved in the SW adoption process. The interviews were conducted to ensure that the case study is "bounded" [64] and to guarantee that the conclusions of this study are based upon specific observations [65]. Thanks to a collaborative writing and analysis process between academics and organization co-author, the case study description has improved and the construct validity has increased [64].

4 The Case Study of the Ministry of Economy and Finance

The Ministry of Economy and Finance (MEF) carries out the tasks and responsibilities of the State in the fields of economic policy, financial policy, budgeting, and tax policies. Additionally, it carries out all activities related to the coordination of public spending and its oversight, planning of public investments, monitoring and oversight of public financial management, public debt management, and State stockholdings. MEF was created with the Bassanini reform which unified the economic ministers with the legislative decree n. 300 of 1999. In 2001 the Berlusconi II Cabinet applied the reform and the MEF was created with the merger of former ministries: the Ministry of Treasure, Budget and Economic Programming and the Ministry of Finances. MEF has a complex central structure derived from the merging of former ministries and from various modifications: main variations have been made with the legislative decree n. 173/2003, and the decree n. 227/2003. Finally, MEF was reorganized with the Presidential Decree n. 43/2008 which established offices in direct collaboration of the minister and proper departments. Today, MEF comprises the following departments: (i) Department of the Treasury (DT), (ii) State General Accounting Department (RGS), (iii) Department of Finance (DF), (iv) Department of General Administration, Personnel, and Services (DAG). MEF staff, consists of 5.599 women (55% of the total) and 4.586 men (45%). The 10.185 staff units are located throughout the country as follows: 4.863 in the central offices (47.75% of the total) and 5.322 in the peripheral offices (52.25%). Looking to the legal area, MEF staff consists of 523 managerial units and 9.662 units belonging to the three functional areas.

In this setting, in 2017, MEF launched a project to prepare the context for the development of a new way of working. Only in July 2017, the pilot started and the SW model became a reality in the organization. Starting from the pilot phase all the four Departments are involved in the SW project.

The project conducted by MEF represents one of the first SW initiatives at the central level of Italian PA.

4.1 *The Context for the Adoption of SW in MEF*

As stated before the context within the SW is adopted as one of the preliminary conditions to guarantee the effectiveness of the new working model. Looking at the internal context at the end of 2016 (October) MEF launched the project "Be MEF Be Smart" in order to define a roadmap and to create the "right internal context" for the adoption of SW itself. Specifically, the pilot phase started with a public call aimed to collect (voluntary) applications by workers for the SW project.

The project was realized following three main phases:

(1) the pilot phase (from July 2017 to January 2018)
(2) a second experimental phase (from February 2018 to March 2019)
(3) Be MEF Be Smart 2.0 (from March 2020 until today): this last phase was started in order to respond to the Covid 2019 emergency

MEF decided to develop the pilot phase following different steps:

- step 1: context analysis (October 2016)
- step 2: join the thematic table at the Department of Public function
- step 3: define the main characteristics of the SW project through the draft of a plan (duration, days of remote working, technological devices, recruitment criteria, etc.). Therefore, define the activities that cannot be worked remotely, identify yearly targets to reach the final objective of smart workers.
- step 4: create a MEF inter-departmental group (January 2017) including administrative members to support the start of experimentation. This group must analyse the macrostructure of the organization, map activities, processes, personnel and workers' needs (familiar or private);
- step 5: MEF policy document processing
- step 6: share and discuss the plan with trade unions (May–June 2017)
- step 7: start of the pilot phase (July 2017)
- step 8: provide a monitoring system (November 2017–January 2018) for both performance and productivity evaluation, identifying some relevant indicators based on features and functions of the selected department.

Although the difficulties of generating a standard cycle to implement SW, the paradigm proposed by MEF aims to become one of the best practice for other Italian public organizations.

4.2 *The Smart Working Elements in MEF*

From January 2017 the first pilot phase of SW started. Table 2 shows the percentage of workers who decided to take part in the SW project during the three different phases of the SW project in the several Departments. The total amount of people

Table 2 Smart workers involved in the project

Departments	I phase		II phase		III phase	
	Number	%	Number	%	Number	%
DT	29	13.3	55	15.4	1.194	13.0
RGS	96	44.0	132	37.0	4.776	52.0
DF	35	16.0	73	20.4	2.020	22.0
DAG	58	26.7	97	27.2	1.194	13.0

involved are 218 workers for the first phase, 357 in the second phase and 9.184 in the last phase.

The table shows a growth along the three phases, but the number of smart workers increases in a substantial way to manage the COVID emergency, involving 90% of total personnel. In order to complete the analysis related to the extent to which employees adopt SW a focus can be made on the category level. Similarly, Table 3 shows the number and the percentage of both managers and workers contractualized in the different professional Areas who decided to take part to the SW project along the three phases. The adoption trend of SW by managers in MEF seems to be very low in all the three phases.

Considering the absence of a supportive and mature digital infrastructure, MEF invested in the ICT element developing a digital environment able to complete the HR strategy of letting people work whenever and wherever they wanted. Thus, in addition to some investments in unified communication and collaboration tools, a mobile workspace (constituted by a laptop, a smartphone and an internet connection) has been made available to all employees. In the MEF worker indicated if he/she intend to use personal tools (laptop, smartphone, etc.) configured by the administration or tools directly provided by the administration. In both the cases MEF provided to every smart worker an informative note indicating general and specific risks related to the particular mode of execution of the activities, providing useful indications for the worker to make a conscious choice of the place where carry out the work activity.

Moreover, a set of cloud-based solutions has been developed in order to improve the performance and to ensure the smart workers the access to the shared documents. In this way, the working place is highly simplified, and human resource can focus on one task at a time and boost both their efficiency and effectiveness. Moreover, MEF ensured the access to several public platforms necessary to complete some activity (e.g. SICOGE is the platform used by PA to complete payments). In addition, using

Table 3 Category of people involved in the SW project

Category	I phase		II phase		III phase	
	Number	%	Number	%	Number	%
Managers	43	19.7	55	15.4	643	7.0
Area personnel	175	80.3	302	84.6	8541	93%

the smartphone workers are able to connect to the intranet and to use the mail as well as if in the office. In order to guarantee an effective interaction with their offices and a good performance, non-managerial workers must ensure, during the SW day, the contactability for at least 3 h (or for at least 1.5 h in the case of half a day), according to the time slots identified in the individual project.

The analysis of the HR element revealed that some new features have been introduced. Before to start with the second phase (the extension of the pilot phase), in fact, a new internal Regulation is adopted starting from the results obtained during the experimental phase. Firstly, the new internal document defines some key points for the adoption of SW. About workers' eligibility, the Regulation states that all the categories are suitable for SW initiatives both in the central and territorial structures. Moreover, the number of smart workers involved in the SW project is annually defined by the Head of DAG, according to the proposal received by the Departments. Moreover, several requirements are identified: in order to take part to the SW project, each worker have to respect the following requirements:

- the activities assigned to the employee can be relocated without the necessary physical presence in the workplace;
- the technological equipment used by the employee must be suitable for realizing the work outside the workplace,
- the employee must enjoy operational autonomy and must be able to organize the execution of work outside the workplace respecting both the assigned objectives and the organizational/functional needs of the office;
- the results of the activities assigned to the employee must be able to be monitored and assessed;
- the activities assigned to the employee are not among those, for which it is not possible the SW, due to the specific nature and methods of carrying out the tasks.

In addition, each worker has to present its application for taking part to the SW project consisting in an individual project. The individual project must be shared between the worker and his hierarchical superior in order to understand the real opportunity to present the application. The hierarchical superior approves the contents and methods of implementation, ensuring the alignment with the organizational needs of the structure. Moreover, the hierarchical superior checks the project proposal (Table 4) focusing the attention on both the activities involved in SW proposal (the suggested activities by the worker, in fact, must be included in those identified in the MEF annual statement) and the respect of several formal aspects (such as the lack of some causes for the exclusion from the SW project and the respect of the established deadline). After the approval is submitted both the individual project and the application are submitted to the Head of the general management structure, which also evaluates and approves the documents analysing the organizational and functional needs. The applications and the projects approved by each Department are sent to the Technical Assistance Secretariat through the Liaison Offices with the DAG.

Aiming to analyse these documents, to define the selection criteria, to select the applications and to monitor the activities carried out adopting SW, other three

Table 4 Individual project: contents

SW elements	Formal aspects
The process/sector of activity to be carried out in SW	Identification information of the employee
Aims of the project	Identification information of the office/service he/she belongs to
The technological equipment	Duration of the project
Methods of implementation Expected results	Timing of SW mode (number of days: from 1 to 6 per month)
Target	Contactability hours
Quantitative and/or qualitative indicators	Times for monitoring
Procedures for monitoring, verifying and evaluating the activity carried out	

"instruments" are introduced at the organizational level: the SW Commission, the technical group and the help desk.

The Commission is established with a statement by the Head DAG, in order to ensure the representation of all the Departments in the SW project. The main tasks assigned to the Commission are: the analysis of the individual projects, according to the criteria and principles set out in MEF internal regulation. When the applications for SW are higher than the quotas defined by the annual regulation approved by the Head of DAG, the Commission is called to select workers using departmental rankings; in order to select workers the Commission give priority to personnel who meet the following requirements: working fathers/mothers especially in the three years following the end of the maternity leave, parents of disabled children, or children with special needs. The departmental rankings are also defined taking into account the following conditions: situation of psycho/physical disability, or particular health conditions, single parent, care needs for minor children/family members, etc. Finally, the Commission provides suggestions and promotes changes to the internal regulation for SW, provides advisory opinions; approves the Annual Monitoring Report.

The technical group has been set up for supporting the implementation of SW. For each Department this technical office can be composed of a maximum of three officials and the main tasks of this group are the assistance to the SW Commission and the preparation of the document that collects the results of the monitoring activities. The adoption of SW, in fact, is subject to the assessment for both the organizational and individual performance evaluation. MEF progressively adjusts its internal monitoring and control systems, identifying suitable indicators in order to evaluate the efficiency, effectiveness and economy of the activities carried out using SW. However, SW does not vary the nature of the work agreement, the role of the employee in the administration and its workplace.

In order to provide more operational support, each Department designates one or more contact persons (managers) for SW: the main tasks assigned to the help desk are to ensure assistance and information, collecting the requests and sending them to the technical group for the analysis and the resolution of the problems.

Another important innovation at the organizational level is represented by the mapping of the activities carried out by each Department in order to identify which activities had to be excluded. In general, almost all activities were included except for those that: (i) require the physical presence (ii) require a constant and continuous relationship with the management. Some examples of excluded activities are: secretariats, protocol and archive, warehouse management, library management, etc.

Also, the procedures for monitoring, verifying and evaluating the activity carried out during SW represent an important element at the organizational level. MEF defines two different procedures for manager and employees. The managers, at the end of the SW period defined in the individual project, have to prepare a report synthesizing the results and any deviations from what has been set; after completing the managers send the report to the technical group. The workers, instead, during SW period, prepare (for each day) a document containing a summary of the activities they have carried out in the day. In addition, according to the timing defined in the individual project each worker complete a monitoring sheet for the identification of the activities, objectives, results and indicators used for the measurement of results; this document must be submitted to the hierarchical superior for the approval. At the end of the process, the technical group collect, analyse and elaborate the received reports in order to prepare the annual report for the Commission and for the analysis by the Head of DAG.

In addition, on HR element MEF realized also several training initiatives for supporting the change management process started through the adoption of a SW model. The general aim was to develop new competencies and capabilities necessary to efficiently and effectively accomplish the new tasks and activities connected to the new working model. Specifically, in terms of contents the training sessions are organized with the support of the Italian National School of Public Administration and they are focused on safety at work, on the use of technological tools and on the regulation developments.

Obviously, following the COVID-19 emergency, some change occurred for the HR elements analysed. Firstly, MEF approved the Directive n.2/2020 according to which SW has become the ordinary work model for carrying out the work activities. On the intranet was published the format for the request application for the SW, otherwise also the e-mail may be used for the request. Moreover, during pandemic, MEF guaranteed both the activities strictly related to the management of the emergency and the non-deferrable activities, adopting SW or personnel rotation in order to ensure a minimum contingent of personnel to be placed in charge of each office. For these activities personnel with managerial qualifications was preferred for their coordination role. Moreover, MEF adopted alternative solutions such as, for example, staff rotation, work leave period, or similar institutions, as well as holidays.

Finally—at the moment—no significant interventions are started on layout element.

4.3 Individual, Organizational and Societal Outcomes for MEF

The last phase, considering the COVID emergency, is still ongoing for this reason it is difficult to state the real outcomes of the SW project and to understand the real impacts of SW in times of crisis such as the current COVID-19 pandemic. However, it is possible to discuss the survey conducts at MEF at the end of the second experimental phase and after the third phase (after Covid emergency) and to evidence some preliminary outcomes from personal, organizational and society perspectives.

The survey is conducted as a part of the monitoring activity, in order understand the SW impacts (in terms of productivity, efficiency, organizational well-being, trust, sense of belonging and work-life balance) of both on staff and on the organization as a whole, verifying also the implementation of the objectives stated the law n. 124/2015 (art. 14). Moreover, through the survey MEF was able to identify potential corrections to be made to the internal policies, for a more effective implementation of the SW model. The surveys consisted of two different questionnaires: the first one for all the personnel and the second for the senior managers. The surveys were conducted on all the staff involved in SW, and it is structured into five sections: (i) personal information, (ii) professional information, (iii) ICT equipment, (iv) SW experiences, (v) conclusive assessment.

At the *individual level*, the surveys showed that perceived job flexibility, given a reasonable workweek, enables more employees to have work-family balance (personal and family benefit) and also enables employees to work longer hours before impacting work-family balance. Also at MEF perceived job flexibility should be significantly and positively related to work-family balance. Given a workweek of reasonable length, employees who perceive flexibility in the timing and location of work have less difficulty with work-family balance. In addition, employees with perceived flexibility in the timing and location of work can work longer hours before work-family balance becomes difficult. In particular, one possible benefit of SW has to do with a reduction in the stress associated with the daily commute. Flexplace also provides more options for where an employee might choose to live. One of the respondents, on this point, said the following:

> I work in Rome, but I live in Naples. This choice is influenced by economic reasons as well as family reasons. I strongly believe that also fathers are pillars in the development of a child's emotional well-being. So, I get up at 3.30 a.m. and my train leaves at 4.30 a.m. Thanks to SW I avoid travelling for so many hours and my productivity at work increases.

Smart workers at MEF, in fact, may choose to work from home or from other indoor/outdoor locations. In addition, the work at MEF, especially for senior managers is strongly influenced by the political moment. In a rigid work environment, during a political crisis, for example, could be extremely difficult simultaneously to meet the demands of work and family life because the work has to be done physically from the work location. By contrast, in a flexible work environment, an employee can work the same long number of hours, but intersperse several hours of quality family time each day. For this last reasons remain unclear the choice to use SW by MEF managers. Finally, our analysis reveals that the vast majority of smart workers (64%) are more than 51 years old in the second phase and between 51 and 60 (55%) during the third phase while young people are almost absent, a phenomenon which can easily be explained by the high number of employees seeking SW for medical pathologies, of course more frequent as the age increases.

At the *organizational level* the technology and, more in general, the role of the SW is one of the element supporting the digital transformation at MEF and in the public sector organizations. Since MEF can be classified as a large organization, it may have greater resources to support the technology required for flexplace. Moreover, with the SW adoption people are more aware of the use of digital technologies and the SW itself has became an opportunity in terms of organizational learning. Furthermore, at MEF the SW adoption is requiring a different stratification processes and procedures in order to maintain the alignment among objectives, behaviours and tools. Another implication is related to the culture and the philosophy at MEF. The organization that adopts SW also should move away from a "process-oriented" culture to a "results-oriented" culture, and performance evaluation systems must adapt to include more specifically measured objectives. Additionally, implementing SW should be possible to change the object of the evaluation moving from the physical presence to the obtained results presence. This new culture could discourage misbehaviours that are common in public institutions. By betting on trust and giving more responsibility to workers, it would be possible to distinguish valuable and willing people from lazybones and give everyone the rewards that thet deserve. Adopting a leaders' supportive behaviour based on trust has also a direct effect on feelings and emotions of employees and it is a way to create a work environment that enables employees to achieve organizational goals in public institutions [66]. Focusing on this point, respondents affirms:

> SW has been an opportunity to establish an existing working model in public administration based on the development of new technologies.
>
> I'm a senior manager and I observed an increase in productivity among my subordinates. This is due mainly to the greater responsibility.

The last, but not least, important aspect at the organizational level refers to the management of individual differences within MEF, especially the gender differences. As suggested from some scholars [67, 68], the analysis of the case study revealed that gender differences (Fig. 3) associated with adoption of SW could be significant, indicating a lower proportion of men adopting SW. Table 5 shows the number and the percentage of both women and men involved in the SW project along the three periods. The collected data reveals that SW is an important tool, especially for women.

Also, the overall satisfaction derived from the SW experience was revealed both for managers and for all the other personnel categories. In particular, as shown in the next Figs. 2 and 3, the satisfaction was measured before and after COVID-19 emergency.

Table 5 Distribution of smart workers by gender

Category	I phase		II phase		III phase	
	Number	%	Number	%	Number	%
Men	87	40	135	38	3.949	43
Women	131	60	222	62	5.235	57

Fig. 2 SW experience—overall satisfaction before COVID-19 emergency

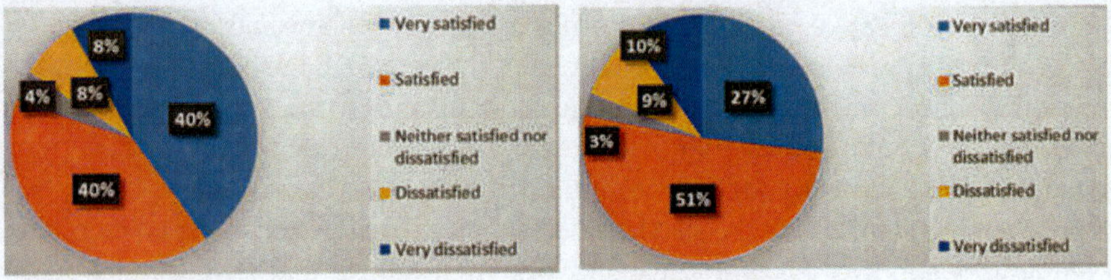

Fig. 3 SW experience—overall satisfaction after COVID-19 emergency

The results of the surveys showed no relevant differences in the perception about SW before the pandemic. On the contrary, an evidence is particular relevant in the data collected after the Covid-19 emergency. In this second survey, in fact, the level of senior managers who declared to be very satisfied in lower than the percentage of employess in the functional areas.

Finally, outcomes at the societal level are not yet evaluated because the project (and the pandemic!) is still ongoing. However, it is possible to discuss about the expectations of MEF on this level. Of course, looking at the environmental consequences and sustainability of SW, the experience conducted at MEF should moderate private car use reducing environmental and socio-economic impacts of mobility on society. Congestion, air pollution, noise, the increase in time loss due to traffic and externalities linked to up-and downstream processes are the most well-known transport-related externalities. Roma results, in fact, the city where the number of smart wokers is higher than in other cities. More in general, through the adoption of SW, MEF could provide a significant externalities saving.

Furthermore, the introduction of SW in the public sector would imply an additional investment on the digitalization of processes and practices. It has been proven by several researches that the creation of e-government reduces corruption and enhances transparency [69–71].

The adoption of SW would produce positive economic effects also on the national budget. The private companies that adopted these methodologies demonstrated how the application of SW enabled them to save money and to improve productivity. The savings deriving from only the reduction of the required spaces could be between 1 and 3 billion Euro. Adopting SW, it is possible to increase efficiency without reducing the number of workers, to improve productivity and, consequently, the quality of the services. Furthermore, extending SW to public employees is a way to avoid creating further discrimination and to improve the relationship between politics, public opinion and social parts.

5 Conclusions and Next Steps

SW represents a journey at both organizational and national level and this journey has only just begun. Starting from the assumption that there is not a unique path for developing a SW, but a set of potential paths that have to be designed taking into account the characteristics of the organization investing in SW, this study highlights some considerations regarding the context, the elements and the outcomes characterizing a SW model.

In particular, the analyzed case study help to understand that there are a number of pre-requisites for SW adoption and implementation in an organization. The main reasons for which an organization invests in SW tend to shape and being shaped by the investments accomplished in SW elements [60]. However, SW is not only a way to reduce costs: there is the need to go beyond the SW elements (ICT, layout and HR) analyzed in this paper and to focus on the core beliefs and culture of the organization as the underpinning factor that makes an organization "smart".

Moreover, MEF case study suggests it is better to proceed through a gradual developmental process in order to identify the most effective solutions for creating value both for people and the organization. The adoption of SW can be seen as a change management process. For this reason, the design and the implementation of a SW model should be followed by the monitoring activities.

However, during last year, SW it is become a common practice due to the Covid-19 emergency. In MEF the percentage of personnel involved in SW before the pandemic was 4% of the total, this percentage there was a shift from the 4% of the personnel before the pandemic, this percentage has grown exponentially reaching the 90% during pandemic. Consequently, we have to analyse the phenomenon in all its complexity without attaching any ready-made labels, because we are on the brink of a radical change in the concept of work. It is not easy to understand the differences between SW, agile work or telework—especially during crisis times. We understand SW as a way of providing flexibility as to where and when we work. In other words, work can be performed in a wide variety of places and at times that are not necessarily the same as office hours. Probably, this has little to do with how MEF experiencing it during the lockdown. This recent experience is closer to remote work but one piece of the puzzle is missing, and public administration—in general—are responsible for that piece. Before Covid, just a few public organizations in Italy had introduced limited forms of flexibility. Even if many challenges have risen to the surface, MEF had the opportunity to deal with this emergency with a SW framework. The positive impact of SW on productivity, employee wellbeing and the balance between work and personal life appears to be the same both before and after Covid-19. These positive results were due more to the presence of procedures and tools to implement and to manage SW. SW did not fail the test in MEF but with a form of SW that is not an emergency measure, in the future we could see a paradigm shift where the focus is on results and objectives rather than on the time actually spent in the workplace. Much will depend on the context and on how results can be measured in each sector of activity. Last but not least, in MEF there should be a focus on re-designing organization's layout: it is important that there is a balance in how the spaces in the organization are managed, they should be liveable and take into account security and cleanliness. There has to be the right mix between working in the office, at home or in the variety of other spaces available. Redesigning infrastructure and office layout will be one of the main topics for the organization of the future.

In conclusion, despite SW was studied in literature from using different perspectives, this chapter provides an important approach to how conceptualize and operationalize SW concept in public administration. The application of this conceptual framework, in fact, is important from a practical viewpoint when introducing SW in organization as planners and implementers will consider the readiness to adopt, the SW options available and how their impact will be assessed before the implementation occurs.

Future research could better determine the nature of strategy, organizational structure and culture patterns during the adoption of a SW model. This case study showed that MEF begin implementing SW with a small group of smart workers and anticipate scaling their efforts; future research could identify core factors that need to be considered during institutional scaling. Examples of such issues could include physical and technical infrastructure needs and the continued use of incentives to facilitate workers' adoption.

Finally, as with many exploratory studies, several limitations should be taken into account. First, the results are derived from a single organization operating in the public sector. It is thus not possible to predict the extent to which the results can be found in other public organizations adopting a SW model in Italy. No attempt are be made, in this research phase, to generalize the obtained results to the wider Italian public sector. On this point, a next step of the research is to increase the number of case in order to compare different approaches for adopting SW.

References

1. Buchanan, T., Sainter, P., & Saunders, G. (2013). Factors affecting faculty use of learning technologies: Implications for models of technology adoption. *Journal of Computing in Higher Education, 25*, 1–11.
2. Gil-Garcia, J. C. R., Helbig, N., & Adegboyega, O. (2014). Being smart: Emerging technologies and innovation in the public sector. *Government Information Quarterly, 31*, 11-I8.
3. Gil-Garcia, J. R. (2012). Towards a smart state? Inter-agency collaboration, information integration, and beyond. *Information Polity, 17*, 269–280.
4. Reddick, C. G. (2009). The adoption of centralized customer service systems: A survey of local governments. *Government Information Quarterly, 26*, 219–226.
5. Garicano, L., & Heaton, P. (2010). Information technology, organization, and productivity in the public sector: Evidence from police departments. *Journal of Labor Economics, 28*, 167–201.
6. Jin, G. Z., & Lee, J. (2013). *Inspection technology, detection and compliance: Evidence from Florida restaurant inspections*. National Bureau of Economic Research, w18939.
7. Morgan, J. (2014). *The future of work: Attract new talent, build better leaders, and create a competitive organization*. Wiley.
8. Birkinshaw, J., Hamel, G., & Mol, M. (2008). Management Innovation. *Academy of Management Review, 33*, 25–845.
9. Hamel, G. (2012). *What matters now: How to win in a world of relentless change, ferocious competition, and unstoppable innovation*. Jossey-Bass.
10. Harvey, D. (2010). *The enigma and capital: And the crises of capitalism*. Profile Books.
11. Haines, V. Y., III., & Stoge, S. (2012). Performance management effectiveness: Practices or context? *The International Journal of Human Resource Management, 2*, 1158–1175.
12. Wood, S., Van Veldhoven, M., Croon, M., & De Menezes, L. M. (2012). Enriched job design, high involvement management and organizational performance: The mediating roles of job satisfaction and well-being. *Human Relations, 65*, 419.
13. Clapperton, G., & Vanhoutte, P. (2014). *The smarter working manifesto*. Sunmakers Eldamar.
14. Iacono, G. (2013). *Smart knowledge working*. Digitpub.
15. Howcroft, D., & Taylor, P. (2014). Plus ca change, plus la meme chose?—Researching and theorising 'new' new technologies. *New Technology, Work and Employment, 29*, 1–8.
16. Stone, D. L., Deadrick, D. L., Lukaszewski, K. M., & Johnson, R. (2015). The influence of technology on the future of human resource management. *Human Resource Management Review, 25*, 216–231.
17. Bondarouk, T., & Brewster, C. (2016). Conceptualising the future of HRM and technology research. *The International Journal of Human Resource Management, 27*, 2652–2671.
18. Kiesler, S., Siegel, J., & McGuire, T. W. (1984). Social psychological aspects of computer mediated communication. *American Psychologist, 39*, 1123–1134.
19. Martin, G., & Cerdin, J. L. (2014). Employer branding and career theory: New directions for research. In P. R. Sparrow, H. Scullion, & I. Tarique (Eds.), *Strategic talent management: Contemporary issues in international context* (pp. 151–176). Cambridge University Press.
20. Von Bertalanffy, L. (1969). *General systems theory*. George Braziller.
21. Brewster, C., & Mayrhofer, W. (2012). *Handbook of research on comparative HRM*. Edward Elgar.
22. Jackson, S. E., Schuler, R. S., & Jiang, K. (2014). An aspirational framework for strategic human resource management. *The Academy of Management Annals, 8*, 1–56.
23. Capobianco, M. (2017). Il lavoro agile tra proposte di legge e accordi di fatto. Lo stato di attuazione dello smart working in Italia e nell'U.E.
24. Cooke, W. N. (2003). *Multinational companies and global human resource management strategies*. Quorum Books.
25. Gooderham, P. N., & Nordhaug, O. (2011). One European model of HRM? Cranet empirical contributions. *Human Resource Management Review, 21*, 27–36.
26. Aran. (2015). Dati statistici: Occupati nella PA per classi di anzianità e genere.

27. Lewis, G. B., & Frank, S. A. (2002). Who wants to work for the government? *Public Administration Review, 62*, 395–404.
28. Aycan, Z., Kanungo, R., Mendonca, M., Yu, K., Deller, J., Stahl, G., & Kurshid, A. (2000). Impact of culture on human resource management practices: A 10-country comparison. *Applied Psychology, 49*, 192–221.
29. Ahuja, M. K., Chudoba, K. M., Kacmar, C. J., McKnight, D. H., & George, J. F. (2007). IT road warriors: Balancing work-family conflict, job autonomy, and work overload to mitigate turnover intentions. *MIS Quarterly, 31*, 1–17.
30. Yoo, Y., Henfridsson, O., & Lyytinen, K. (2010). Research commentary—The new organizing logic of digital innovation: An agenda for information systems research. *Information Systems Research, 21*, 724–735.
31. Mann, J. (2012). Transform the workplace with focus on bricks, behaviors and bits, Gartner Report No. G0021229.
32. Chudoba, K. M., Wynn, E., Lu, M., & Watson-Manheim, M. B. (2005). How virtual are we? Measuring virtuality and understanding its impact on a global organisation. *Information Systems Journal, 15*, 279–306.
33. Martínez-Sánchez, A., Pérez-Pérez, M., De Luis, Carnicer, P., Vela, & Jiménez, M. J. (2007). Telework, human resource flexibility and firm performance. *New Technology, Work and Employment, 22*, 208–223.
34. Coenen, M., & Kok, R. A. W. (2014). Workplace flexibility and new product development performance. *European Management Journal, 32*, 564–576.
35. Elsbach, K. D., & Pratt, M. G. (2007). The physical environment in organizations. *Academy of Management Annals, 1*, 181–224.
36. Duxbury, L. E., & Higgins, C. A. (2002). Telework: A primer for the millennium introduction. In C. L. Cooper & J. R. Burke (Eds.), *The new world of work: Challenges and opportunities* (pp. 157–200). Sage Publications.
37. Spillman, R. D., & Markham, F. B. (1997). Telecommuting: Acceptance, adoption and application. *Journal of Computer Information Systems, 37*, 8–12.
38. Himmelsbach, V. (1998). Working at home given top marks by employees. *Computing Canada, 24*, 29.
39. James, P. (2004). *Is teleworking sustainable?—An analysis of its economic, environmental and social impacts.* SUSTEL, Sustainable Telework.
40. Huws, U., Robinson, W. B., & Robinson, S. (1990). *Telework towards the elusive office.* Wiley.
41. Michelson, W. (2000). Home-based employment and quality of life: A time-use analysis. In E. Diener & D. R. Rahtz (Eds.), *Advances in quality of life theory and research* (pp. 183–203). Kluwer.
42. Hill, E. J., Hawkins, A. J., Ferris, M., & Weitzman, M. (2001). Finding an extra day a week: The positive influence of perceived job flexibility on work and family life balance. *Family Relations, 50*, 49–58.
43. Duxbury, L. E., & Higgins, C. A. (2002). Work-life balance in the new millennium: Where are we?: Where do we need to go? *Canadian Policy Research Networks.*
44. Peters, P., Wetzels, C., & Tijdens, K. (2008). Telework: Timesaving or time-consuming? An investigation into actual working hours. *The Journal of Interdisciplinary Economics, 20*, 421–422
45. Ruth, S., & Chaudhry, I. (2008). Telework: A productivity paradox? Internet computing. *IEEE, 12*, 87–90
46. Baruch, Y. (2000). Teleworking: Benefits and pitfalls as perceived by professionals and managers. *New technology, work and employment, 15*, 34–49.
47. Costa, G., Åkerstedt, T., Nachreiner, F., Baltieri, F., Carvalhais, J., & Folkard, S. (2004). Flexible working hours, health, and well-being in Europe: Some considerations from a SALTSA project. *Chronobiology International, 21*, 831–844.
48. Olsen, K. M., & Dahl, S. Å. (2010). Working time: implications for sickness absence and the work–family balance. *International Journal of Social Welfare, 19*, 45–53.

49. White, P., Christodoulou, G., Mackett, R., Titheridge, H., Thoreau, R., & Polak, J. (2010). The impacts of teleworking on sustainability and travel. In T. Manzi, K. Lucas, T. L. Jones & J. Allen (Eds.), *Social sustainability in urban areas: Communities, connectivity and the urban fabric* (pp. 141–154). Earthscan Publications Ltd.
50. Bondarouk, T. V. (2014). *Orchestrating the e-HRM symphony*. Twente University Press.
51. Ehnert, I., & Harry, W. (2012). Recent developments and future prospects on sustainable human resource management: Introduction to the special issue. *Management Revue, 23*, 221–238.
52. Taylor, S., Osland, J., & Egri, C. P. (2012). Guest editors' introduction: Introduction to HRM's role in sustainability: Systems, strategies, and practices. *Human Resource Management, 51*, 789–798.
53. Lindgreen, A., & Swaen, V. (2010). Corporate social responsibility. *International journal of management reviews, 12*, 1–7.
54. Van Lier, T., De Witte, A., & Macharis, C. (2012). The impact of telework on transport externalities: The case of Brussels Capital Region. *Procedia-Social and Behavioral Sciences*, 54, 240–250.
55. Verbeke, A., Schulz, R., Greidanus, N., & Hambley, L. (2008). *Growing the virtual workplace: The integrative value proposition for telework*. Edward Elgar Publishing.
56. Nidumolu, R., Prahalad, C. K., & Rangaswami, M. R. (2009). Why sustainability is now the key driver of innovation. *Harvard Business Review, 87*(9), 56–64.
57. Glaister, S. (2008). Alternative view: Homeworking won't stem rising car use. In T. Dwelly & A. Lake (Eds.), *Can homeworking save the planet? How homes can become workspaces in a low carbon economy* (pp. 80–85). The Smith Institute
58. Callanan, T. A. (1999). *New ways of living and working: Teleworking in Ireland*. Department of Enterprise Trade and Employment, Report of the National Advisory Council on Teleworking.
59. Forgacs, T. (2010). Empirical research findings on telework: Management experiences and attitudes. *Business and Economic Horizons, 1*, 6–13.
60. Eom, S-J., Choi, N., & Sung, W. (2016). The use of smart work in government: Empirical analysis of Korean experiences. *Government Information Quarterly, 33*(3), 562–571.
61. Gastaldi, L., Corso, M., Raguseo, E., Neirotti, P., Paolucci, E., & Martini, A. (2014, September). Smart working: Rethinking work practices to leverage employees' innovation potential. In *Proceedings of the 15th International CINet Conference, Operating Innovation—Innovating Operations*, Budapest
62. Eisenhardt, K. M. (1989). Building theories from case study research. *Academy of Management Review, 14*, 532–550.
63. Berry, A., Loughton, E., & Otley, D. (1991). Control in a financial services company (RIF): A case study. *Management Accounting Research, 2*, 109–139.
64. Otley, D. T., & Berry, A. J. (1994). Case study research in management accounting and control. *Management Accounting Research, 5*, 45–65.
65. Yin, R. K. (2009). *Case study research: Design and methods*. Sage Publications.
66. Maxwell, J. A. (2012). *Qualitative research design: An interactive approach*. Sage
67. Wijewardena, N., Samaratunge, R., & Härtel, C. (2014). Creating better employees through positive leadership behavior in the public sector. *International Journal of Public Administration, 37*, 288–298.
68. Posig, M., & Kickul, J. (2004). Work-role expectations and work family conflict: Gender differences in emotional exhaustion. *Women in Management Review 19*, 373–386
69. Walker, E., & Webster, B. (2004). Gender issues in home-based businesses. *Women in Management Review, 19*, 404–412
70. Zhao, X., & Xu, H. D. (2015). E-government and corruption: A longitudinal analysis of countries. *International Journal of Public Administration, 38*, 410–421.
71. Anderson, J. (2007). Solving China's rebalancing puzzle. *Finance and Development, 44*, 32–35.
72. Georges, G., Glynn-Burke, T., & McGrat, A. (2013). *Improving the local landscape for innovation: Mechanics, partners, and clusters*. Ash Center for Democratic Governance and Innovation, Harvard Kennedy School.
73. Hartog, K. L., Solimene, A., & Tufani, G. (2015). *The smart working book*. Seedble.

74. Cameron, E., & Green, M. (2012). *Making sense of change management: A complete guide to the models tools and techniques of organisational change.* Kogan Page Publishers.
75. Flynn, G. (1995). Warning: Your best ideas may work against you. *Personnel Journal 74*, 76–99
76. Cho, Y. H., Choi, B.D. (2004). E-government to combat corruption: The case of Seoul Metropolitan Government. *International Journal of Public Administration, 27*, 719–735.

Digital Transformation of Health Service in Turkey by Hybrid-Delphi Method

Hüseyin Ataş, Selim Gündüz, and Esra Karakaş

Abstract Among the education, health and justice services, which are among the basic public services in the world, education has been the best service that adapts to the current era in the digital sense. However, with the Covid-19 pandemic, it has been seen that basic health services should also be digitized. In this study, what kind of health care services can be offered as online Hybrid Delphi technique was investigated by health professionals for both conservation and effective resource management in Turkey. The Hybrid Delphi technique is a combined version of the strengths of group decision making techniques. In the research, an expert group consisting of doctors with at least 5 years of working experience in the public sector was formed. matters which are not in agreement and consensus on what kind of online health services may be offered in Turkey were determined. In addition, the benefits of online healthcare and concerns over ethics have also been raised. Our findings have shown that some special treatment and examination processes can be done online. However, there is no necessary legal and physical infrastructure in Turkey. In Turkey, there is a need for legislation to be presented to online health services online.

Keywords Online health service · Hybrid Delphi · Digitalization

1 Introduction

Education, which is accepted as one of the basic public services all over the world, has become the best service that adapts to our era in the digital sense. It cannot be said that digital transformation has been achieved in education and training all over the world, but a lot of progress has been made in the digital transformation of education/training services in developed countries and many developing countries.

H. Ataş (✉)
Adiyaman University Vocational School of Social Sciences, Adiyaman 02040, Turkey
e-mail: hatas@adiyaman.edu.tr

S. Gündüz · E. Karakaş
Adana Alparslan Türkeş Science and Technology University, Adana 01250, Turkey

E. Zaramenskikh and A. Fedorova (eds.), *Digitalization of Society, Economics and Management*, Lecture Notes in Information Systems and Organisation 53,
https://doi.org/10.1007/978-3-030-94252-6_22

Technological developments should also be used in other public services. It is important to determine what online public services can be that will provide effective resource use and fast service for citizens. During the Covid-19 pandemic period, all resources especially in the field of health are devoted to fighting the virus. Because of this, it has become more important to provide some health care services online. With the ability to provide some healthcare services online, the workload of healthcare professionals would be reduced, as well as citizens and healthcare professionals could be protected from viral epidemics.

However, online health services (OHS) have both positive and negative aspects for patients and physicians. Nonetheless, there are more positive aspects of online healthcare for patients. For example, online healthcare means better access to doctors for patients, more personalized care services, and less costs. Of course, online healthcare is not a suitable method for all diseases. For Turkey, it is necessary to determine which health services can be offered online and to estimate the possible problems that may be encountered in the provision of online health services.

In this study, it has been investigated how digital transformation could occur in health services in Turkey. The opinions of specialist medical doctors who have at least 5 years of experience in their field were consulted. By asking doctors who can provide the service, inferences have been about how the transition to online health services can be. In this aspect, it is an original study that explores different options for the delivery of health care for Turkey.

1.1 Literature

Online healthcare is defined as the provision of healthcare services such as health information and medical consultations via the Internet [1, 2]. Digitalization in the health sector changes the communication, roles and relationships between doctors and patient. In recent years, the role of patients has started to change from passive, addicted to active-informed and responsible participant [3, 4].

Although providing healthcare services via the Internet is gaining popularity around the world, experimental research in this area is very limited. Mou and Cohen [5] discussed the relationship between trust and intention to accept e-health services. Chen et al. [6] found that patients receiving online health services have a positive effect on their health status. Zhang et al. [2] revealed that satisfaction with traditional health services, in other words, offline healthcare services, is an obstacle to the spread of online health services [2].

The application of OHS started to be seen in the USA in the 1990s. Net Clinic is one of the first and most important organizations providing online health services. The Net Clinic portal provides fee-based medical advice as well as free services. Empirical studies have also been carried out on customer loyalty in online health services, which are becoming increasingly popular in the world. Gummerus [7] stated the variables of service quality, trust and satisfaction as determinants of customer addiction in an online health service. Powell et al. [8] investigated the pros and cons of online health services in the UK.

OHS is also implemented in China. Kuang [9] argued that OHS in China increases the service quality of physicians and provides additional financial income to physicians. OHS is a service area that is increasing day by day in Israel. The online healthcare industry, especially with its chronic diseases, is constantly growing [10]. In a field study conducted in Israel, it was found that 59% of citizens over the age of 45 who use internet have benefited from e-health services at least once [11]. It is advocated that online health services in the UK should be developed in an evolutionary, not revolutionary way, for the benefit of the community [12]. The rate of beneficiaries of e-health consultancy services in England was 37% in 2005 and 68% in 2009 [13].

1.2 Ethical and Legal Concerns in eHealth Services

There is no national or international legal legislation regulating the use of online-based health services.

Protecting patients and patient information is one of the biggest concerns in OHS. Although there are many studies in the e-health literature that support reaching patients through the internet, there is also another approach that argues that these practices do not comply with medical ethics, and are ethically and legally problematic. Some of these studies are listed below:

- Damayanti et al. [14] argues that the use of OHS is a major public health issue;
- Yeung [15] argues that medical ethics should be adhered to in OHS practices, and that e-health principles should be developed with experts in informatics, health services and medicine;
- Kugelmass [16] stated that healthcare workers providing OHS may engage in discriminatory and unethical behavior;
- Burgess et al. [17] argues that OHS may be a public health issue;
- Ananny and Crawford [18] noted that online health care can lead to problems that will last for years due to ethical problems;
- Hall and McGraw [19] state that there are privacy and security risks related to OHS, and that there are no controls and laws regarding the collection and use of sensitive personal information.

2 Method

Delphi technique is an effective method when the experts whose opinions are to be taken are far from each other and it is costly to come together [20]. Selecting the expert group in Delphi applications according to their knowledge and experience ensures that selected people care about the work and feel privileged [21]. Delphi technique is essentially a survey method, but it differs from other surveys in terms of preparation and implementation. The difference of this application from questionnaires is that it is applied to people who are experts in various subjects [22]. Today, it is used in a wide variety of fields to address complex issues in a holistic manner, to collect opinions on the issue, and to determine the priority and order of importance of the relevant components.

Delphi technique is considered as both a positivist/quantitative and interpretive/qualitative technique [23]. Delphi technique can also be considered as a hybrid research technique in this respect. Although it is a positivist and quantitative technique, it is advocated that qualitative reliability studies, not quantitative validity, should be used to measure the meticulousness of the method [24].

Delphi, which is a consensus-building technique, also allows to systematically obtain expert opinions on a problem. In Delphi technique, it is aimed that experts and groups who look at a problem from different angles can easily explain their opinions without coming face to face and update their opinions by being aware of the feedback of other experts. It enables individuals in an expert group to communicate effectively in order to overcome technical or complex problems [25]. Also, Graham et al. [26] states that Delphi technique is one of the "best practices" in determining treatment protocols in areas where consensus is needed and in hospitals.

With the Delphi technique, the same questionnaire is applied consecutively to the individuals in a group to clarify their views [27]. The first survey [28] in the application is prepared by the moderator team. It is essential that the respondents choose their own answers without contacting each other. It is tried to find common points between the different views obtained from the study and the views are converged. The primary assumption in this technique is that the consensus provided by a group is a better guide than individual ideas [29, 30].

Following the implementation of Delphi surveys, the responses of the experts are analyzed statistically and shared with the experts in an explanatory way. Surveys are applied in the form of consecutive rounds throughout the Delphi application. The results of each questionnaire are shared with the expert group by making relevant analyzes and trends regarding the relevant opinion are conveyed. Individuals in the expert group reconsider their views according to the results communicated to them. Controlled feedback makes it easier to reach consensus.

The group of experts where the technique is applied is also called Delphi panel. In the selection of panel members, there should be expertise in the relevant problem. Panel members should have the depth to respond to the research subject with their experiences and qualifications [31]. There is no agreed number regarding the number of expert groups that the Delphi technique will be applied to. Delphi technique can be applied to groups of more than 100 people. Van De and Delbecq [32] state that Delphi application can be carried out with an expert group of 10–15 people. It is recommended that the ideal group size is between 10 and 20, and it should be 7 if the minimum is [31]. In practice, if the number of participants is low, representation on the subject at hand may decrease. In cases where the number of participants is high, there may be an increase in the time taken for data collection and low response rates.

The Delphi technique is a tool that attempts to capture the common knowledge and experience of a specific group of experts in order to improve decision processes. In this study, the Hybrid Delphi technique, a combined version of the strengths of group decision-making techniques, was used. Hybrid Delphi is a different version of Delphi technique. The Hybrid Delphi technique has been developed by combining the strengths of multiple decision techniques that enable professional groups to consensus, generate solutions, and predict. The effort to develop hybrid new techniques by combining the strengths of multi-group decision-making techniques is actually something that is highly tried in the field of health research. There are many studies in the literature where brainstorming, focus group technique, nominal group technique, and Delphi techniques are hybridized in pairs [31, 33–36].

Landeta et al. [37] put forward the Hybrid Delphi technique by combining the strengths of the focus group interview, nominal grouping and Delphi technique. Hybrid Delphi consists of roughly two stages. The first stage is carried out face-to-face, and the examination, which is applied in focus group and nominal group experiments, aims to make a comprehensive and in-depth exploration of dairy. The second stage aims to access and predict milk consensus ideas to the problem concerned by applying classical Delphi.

3 Findings

The applications in the study will be carried out in two stages in accordance with the Hybrid Delphi application. In the first application phase of the study, an exploratory focus group meeting will be held first with various physicians selected by determining a concrete criterion. In the second stage, the benefits and possible handicaps of online health services will be estimated with the e-Delphi application and the areas where it can be applied will be discussed.

A panel team of 9 medical doctors was formed for this technique, which was carried out with a group of experts with sufficient knowledge and experience on the subject. Since determining the experts to be selected as Delphi panel members will directly affect the application success of the technique, it is important to determine the criteria concretely. In this study, the criteria of working as a doctor for at least five years in the public sector was applied for the selection of specialists, and a heterogeneous distribution was observed in the selection of specialists. Exploratory talks were held in August 2020. The 1st round survey was conducted in October 2020 and the 2nd round Delphi survey was conducted in November 2020.

"In which healthcare services do you think digital tools can be used and what are their benefits?" The answers to the question can be categorized and listed as follows:

- OHS protect patients and physicians from contagious infections;
- the OHS is beneficial for patients who have been previously examined and followed up;
- symptom inquiries and preventive health services can be done remotely;

- OHS will reduce the workload in hospitals;
- in OHS, it can be questioned whether the patient should have an online or physical examination according to the triage code;
- OHS provide savings to the state.
- OHS will reduce the workload of family doctors.

Panelists were asked to respond to the 18-item statement pool created to get their opinions about the positive aspects of digital transformation in healthcare services as "1 = Strongly Disagree, 2 = Disagree, 3 = Neither Agree Neither Disagree, 4 = Agree, 5 = Strongly Agree". Analyzes of the responses in both the 1st and the 2nd round are presented in Table 1. The table includes the arithmetic mean ($\overline{x}$), standard deviation (ss) and interquartile distance values (IQR) and the percentage distribution of the responses given to the expressions.

"12. E-health services will reduce the workload of family doctors." It is the most agreed statement at the end of the 2nd round ($\overline{x}$ = 4.11; ss = 1.05). Statements 1, 3, 7, 8, 9, 10 and 12 are also the opinions agreed upon. "17. Providing e-health services to pediatric and geriatric patients provides psychological satisfaction and rapid results." It is the statement with the greatest difference of opinion on the article numbered 17 ($\overline{x}$ = 2.44; ss = 1.13). There is a high difference of opinion on the 13th and 15th statements.

"What kind of a path should be followed for digital transformation in health services? What are the negative aspects of digital transformation in healthcare?" The answers to the question can be categorized and listed as follows.

1. Legal infrastructure should be established in order to provide OHS.
2. It is not possible to be treated without taking the patient's history and physical examination.
3. Developing legal legislation on e-health enables healthcare operators to invest in this area.
4. The development of legal legislation on e-health creates new employment areas and additional income opportunities for physicians and healthcare professionals.
5. Ethical protocols and guidelines for e-health practices should be developed.

The panelists were asked to respond to the 9-item statement pool, which was created to get their opinions about the negative aspects of digital transformation in health services, as "1 = Strongly Disagree, 2 = Disagree, 3 = Neither Agree Neither Disagree, 4 = Agree, 5 = Strongly Agree". Analyzes of the responses in both the 1st and the 2nd round are presented in Table 2. The table includes the arithmetic mean ($\overline{x}$), standard deviation (ss) and interquartile distance values (IQR) and the percentage distribution of the responses given to the expressions.

"1.5 E-health service points can be piloted for efficiency tests in certain cities with platforms to be established in the family medicine center." It was the statement that agreed with the highest score on the statement ($\overline{x}$ = 4.67; ss = 0.71). The statements numbered 1, 3, 4, 6, 8 are also the expressions on which agreement is reached. "1.2 E-health is against medical ethics." It is an expression that is in dispute over

Table 1 Statements on the positive aspects of digital transformation in healthcare

Expressions	1st Round			2nd Round					
	$\overline{x}$	SS	IQR	$\overline{x}$	SS	IQR	Frequency (%)		
							1–2	3	4–5
1. E-health services protect patients and doctors from contagious infections	4.00	0.94	1.25	3.89	1.17	2.00	22.2	0.0	77.8
2. E-health services contribute to the efficient use of resources	3.90	0.57	0.25	3.22	1.20	1.50	22.2	33.3	44.4
3. E-health service is beneficial for patients who have been previously examined and followed up	4.10	0.74	1.25	4.00	1.00	1.50	11.1	11.1	77.8
4. Diabetes, diabetes and blood pressure patients can be monitored and controlled online	3.60	0.84	1.00	3.44	1.13	2.00	22.2	33.3	44.4
5. Online treatment protocols can be developed and applied for all diseases that do not require examination	3.90	0.99	2.00	3.33	1.41	3.00	44.4	11.1	44.4
6. Vaccination and pregnancy follow-up can be done online by family doctors	3.80	1.03	2.00	3.33	1.22	1.50	22.2	22.2	55.6
7. Symptom inquiries can be done remotely	3.30	1.34	2.25	3.56	1.59	3.00	22.2	11.1	66.7
8. E-health service will reduce the workload in hospitals	4.00	1.05	2.00	3.78	1.09	1.50	22.2	0.0	77.8
9. In e-health services, the triage code can be determined and the patient's need for online or physical examination can be questioned accordingly	3.70	1.16	1.25	3.67	1.00	1.00	22.2	0.0	77.8
10. Preventive health services can be provided online	4.00	0.82	2.00	4.00	0.87	2.00	0.0	33.3	66.7
11. E-health services provide savings to the public	3.00	1.63	3.25	3.78	1.20	2.50	22.2	11.1	66.7
12. E-health services will reduce the workload of family doctors	4.00	0.82	2.00	4.11	1.05	1.50	11.1	11.1	77.8
13. E-health services can be applied to patients with psychiatric and psychological problems	3.00	1.41	2.25	2.78	1.30	2.50	44.4	11.1	44.4
14. Radiology units can provide online services when the patient's history and symptoms are known	3.20	1.32	1.50	3.56	1.33	3.00	33.3	11.1	55.5
15. Preliminary examinations can be done online for all diseases that do not require blood tests	2.80	1.62	3.25	2.89	1.27	2.00	44.4	22.2	33.3

(continued)

Table 1 (continued)

Expressions	1st Round			2nd Round					
	$\overline{x}$	SS	IQR	$\overline{x}$	SS	IQR	Frequency (%)		
							1–2	3	4–5
16. E-health and pre-examination and counseling services reduce the number of applications to health units and physicians in primary care	3.50	1.43	1.75	3.89	0.93	1.00	11.1	11.1	77.8
17. Providing e-health services to pediatric and geriatric patients offers psychological satisfaction and rapid results	2.50	1.27	3.00	2.44	1.13	2.00	55.5	22.2	22.2
18. E-health services facilitate rapid diagnosis based on disease history through anamnesis	2.90	1.52	2.50	3.00	1.32	2.00	44.4	11.1	44.4

Table 2 Statements and actions to be taken regarding the negative aspects of digital transformation in healthcare

Expressions	1st Round			2nd Round					
	$\overline{x}$	SS	IQR	$\overline{x}$	SS	IQR	Frequency (%)		
							1–2	3	4–5
1.1 Legal infrastructure should be established in order to provide e-health services	4.20	1.32	1.25	3.78	1.39	2.00	22.2	0.0	77.8
1.2 E-health is against medical ethics	2.80	1.03	1.00	2.33	1.22	1.50	66.6	22.2	11.1
1.3 Remote examination and consultation is not an efficient and effective option	3.60	1.65	3.25	3.11	1.36	2.50	55.6	22.2	22.2
1.4 It is essential to see, touch and examine the patient. It is not possible to be treated without taking the patient's history and physical examination	4.00	1.25	2.25	3.89	1.36	2.50	22.2	22.2	55.6
1.5 E-health service points can be piloted for efficiency tests in certain cities with platforms to be established in the family medicine center	4.30	.0.68	1.00	4.67	0.71	0.50	0.0	11.1	88.9
1.6 Developing legal legislation regarding e-health enables healthcare operators to invest in this area	4.10	0.57	0.25	3.89	1.27	1.50	11.1	11.1	77.8
1.7 The development of legal legislation on e-health creates new employment areas and additional income opportunities for physicians and healthcare professionals	4.00	0.67	0.50	3.00	1.22	2.00	22.2	33.3	44.4
1.8 Ethical protocols and guidelines for e-health practices should be developed	4.50	0.71	1.00	4.11	1.36	1.50	11.1	11.1	77.8
1.9 E-health services have the potential to be a public health problem	2.90	1.20	2.00	3.11	1.27	2.50	44.4	22.2	33.3

the expression ($\overline{x} = 2.33$; ss $= 1.22$). Doctors consider online healthcare not to be against medical ethics.

4 Conclusion

Turkey is in need of legal regulations in order to provide online health services online. During the pandemic period, it is necessary to benefit from digital tools at the maximum level in order to provide effective public resources, especially health services.

The online submission of health services in Turkey is expected to create a situation in favor of both the Doctor and patient. online without breach of medical ethics by doctors on health care services, as developed in Turkey will protect doctors and health workers from viral threats. It will also be possible for citizens to access health services faster.

Our findings have shown that some special treatment and examination processes can be done online. However, there is no necessary legal and physical infrastructure in Turkey. First of all, legal and physical infrastructure should be developed in order to provide online health services. Afterwards, services that can be offered remotely should be analyzed and planned more comprehensively.

References

1. Castrén, J., Huttunen, T., & Kunttu, K. (2008). Users and non users of web based health advice service among Finnish university students chronic conditions and self reported health status (a cross sectional study). *BMC Medical Informatics and Decision Making, 8*(1:1 8).
2. Zhang, X., Guo, X., Lai, K. H., Yin, C., & Meng, F. (2017). From offline healthcare to online health service: The role of offline healthcare satisfaction and habits. *Journal of Electronic Commerce Research, 18*(2), 138–154.
3. Kessler, S. H., & Schmidt-Weitmann, S. (2019). Diseases and emotions: An automated content analysis of health narratives in ınquiries to an online health consultation service. *Health Communication*, 1–10.https://doi.org/10.1080/10410236.2019.1673950
4. Meinzer, D. C. (2019). *Die Arzt-Patient-Beziehung in einer digitalisierten Welt [The doctor-patient relationship in a digitized world]*. Springer.
5. Mou, J., & Cohen, J. F. (2014). A longitudinal study of trust and perceived usefulness in consumer acceptance of an eservice: The case of online health services. In *The 2014 Pacific Asia Conference on Information Systems*.
6. Chen, J.-F., Wu, L.-L., Chou, S.-C., & Chang, C.-H. (2014). Online social support for weight control and improved quality of life. In *The 2014 Pacific Asia Conference on Information Systems* (Vol. 19, pp. 1–12).
7. Gummerus, J., Liljander, V., Pura, M., & Van Riel, A. (2004). Customer loyalty to content-based web sites: The case of an online health-care service. *Journal of Services Marketing, 18*(3), 175–186. https://doi.org/10.1108/08876040410536486
8. Powell, J., Inglis, N., Ronnie, J., & Large, S. (2011). The characteristics and motivations of online health information seekers: Cross-sectional survey and qualitative interview study. *Journal of Medical Internet Research, 13*(1), 1–10. https://doi.org/10.2196/jmir.1600

9. Kuang, J., Kuang, L., & Yan, Z. (2018). The impact of penetration rate of online health service on service quality and price: Evidence from online health communities. *ACM International Conference Proceeding Series*. https://doi.org/10.1145/3265689.3265720
10. Mano, R. S. (2016). Chronic disease and use of online health information and online health services. *Journal of Hospital Administration, 5*(4), 55. https://doi.org/10.5430/jha.v5n4p55
11. Crotty, B. H., & Slack, W. V. (2016). Designing online health services for patients. *Israel Journal of Health Policy Research, 5*(1), 4–6. https://doi.org/10.1186/s13584-016-0082-7
12. Powell, J., Inglis, N., Ronnie, J., & Large, S. (2011b). The characteristics and motivations of online health information seekers: Cross-sectional survey and qualitative interview study. *Journal of Medical Internet Research, 13*(1), 1–11. https://doi.org/10.2196/jmir.1600
13. Dutton, W. H., Helsper, E. J., & Gerber, M. M. (2009). *Oxford Internet Survey.* The Internet in Britain 2009. https://www.webcitation.org/5qhaRndTy
14. Damayanti, F. N., Rejeki, S., Absori;, & Wardiono, K. (2020). Ethical and legal issues in the use of TPN. *SOEPRA Jurnal Hukum Kesehatan, 6*(1), 15–23
15. Yeung, K. (2017). 'Hypernudge': Big data as a mode of regulation by design. *Information Communication and Society, 20*(1), 118–136.
16. Kugelmass, H. (2019). "Just the Type with whom I Like to Work": Two correspondence field experiments in an online mental health care market. *Society and Mental Health, 9*(3), 350–365. https://doi.org/10.1177/2156869318755213
17. Burgess V. D. (2008). Patient race and physicians' decisions to prescribe opioids for chronic low back pain. *Social Science and Medicine, 67*(11), 1852–1860.
18. Ananny, M., & Crawford, K. (2018). Seeing without knowing: Limitations of the transparency ideal and its application to algorithmic accountability. *New Media and Society, 20*, 973–989.
19. Hall, J. L., & McGraw, D. (2014). For telehealth to succeed, privacy and security risks must be identified and addressed. *Health Affairs, 33*(2), 216–221. https://doi.org/10.1377/hlthaff.2013.0997
20. Turoff, M., & Hiltz, S. R. (2001). *Computer based Delphi processes*. Kingsley.
21. Pollard, R., & Tamlin, M. (1995). The use of expert teachers to improve education. *Education, 116*(1), 3–9.
22. İçöz, O. (2005). *Turizm Ekonomisi* (3. baskı). Turhan Kitabevi.
23. Hasson, F., & Keeney, S. (2011). Enhancing rigour in the Delphi technique research. *Techno logical Forecasting and Social Change, 78*(9), 1695–1704. https://doi.org/10.1016/j.techfore.2011.04.005
24. Hanafin, S. (2004). *Review of literature on the Delphi Technique*. National Children's Office. https://doi.org/10.1177/0013164404266386
25. Linstone, H., & Turoff, M. (1975). *Introduction the Delphi method: Techniques and applications*. Addison-Wesley Publishing Company.
26. Graham, B., Regehr, G., & Wright, J. G. (2003). Delphi as a method to establish consensus for diagnostic criteria. *Journal of Clinical Epidemiology, 56*(12), 1150–1156.
27. Gündüz, S., Ataş, H., & Elkovan, C. G. (2020). *Çoklu Karar Verme Teknikleri* (1. baskı). Gazi Kitabevi.
28. Rubenfeld, G. D., & Rhodes, A. (2014). How many intensive care beds are enough? *Intensive Care Medicine, 40*(3), 451–452. https://doi.org/10.1007/s00134-014-3215-x
29. Tübitak. (2001). *Teknoloji Öngörüsü ve Ülke Örnekleri Çalışma Raporu, 01/03*. Bilim ve Teknoloji Politikaları Dairesi Başkanlığı Politika Strateji Çalışmaları TÜBİTAK BTP.
30. Yavuz, M. C. (2007). *Uluslararası Destinasyon Markası Oluşturulmasında Kimlik Geliştirme Süreci: Adana Örneği* [Ç.Ü. Sosyal Bilimler Enstitüsü]. https://doi.org/10.23943/9781400889877
31. Şahin, A. E. (2001). Eğitim araştırmalarında delphi tekniği ve kullanımı. *Hacettepe Üniversitesi Eğitim Fakültesi Dergisi, 20*(20), 215–220.
32. Van De, A., & Delbecq, A. L. (1971). Nominal versus interacting group processes for committee decision-making effectiveness. *Academy of Management Journal, 14*(2), 203–212. https://doi.org/10.5465/255307

33. Barry, M. L., Steyn, H., & Brent, A. (2008). Determining the most important factors for sustainable energy technology selection in Africa: Application of the Focus Group Technique. In *PICMET 2008 Proceedings* (pp. 27–31).
34. Cook, S. P., & Birrell, M. (2007). Defining an occupational therapy intervention for people with psychosis. *British Journal of Occupational Therapy, 70*(3), 96–106.
35. Duggan, E. W., & Thachenkary, C. S. (2004). Integrating nominal group technique and joint application development for improved systems requirements determination. *Information and Management Amsterdam, 41*(4), 399–411.
36. Garjón, F. J., Aza, M., Elfau, M., Aller, A. I., Buisán, M. J., & Celaya, C. (2008). Indicadores de calidad de prescripción seleccionados mediante una técnica de consenso. *An. Pediatr, 69*(4), 329–334.
37. Landeta, J., Barrutia, J., & Lertxundi, A. (2011). Hybrid Delphi: A methodology to facilitate contribution from experts in professional contexts. *Technological Forecasting and Social Change, 78*(9), 1629–1641. https://doi.org/10.1016/j.techfore.2011.03.009

The Evolving Role of Pharmacies in the Digital Transformation Era: A Case Study from Italy

Marta Musso, Roberta Pinna, Pier Paolo Carrus, Eleonora Veglianti, and Elisabetta Magnaghi

Abstract The aim of the study is to explore how the implementation of a teleconsultation diagnostic solution carried out with pharmacies is able to improve quality and access of care and which are its impacts on the health service ecosystem. The method adopted is an explorative case study, preceded by a rapid theoretical focus on telehealth facilitated by information technologies and telemedicine tools. The case study refers to the project concerning teleconsultation diagnostic for heart diseases. The project, developed in Italy, involves a growing number of pharmacy and hospitals. The technology is based on real-time teleconsultation platform able to support clinicians with the telepresence of a specialist, offering different types of exams in pharmacy within the whole Italian territory. The adoption of the real-time telemedicine solution when supported by the appropriate organization design, can promote new care models, encouraging a rational and effective use of resources. In this context, a noticeable change in the role of pharmacies has been observed and provision of the services have been evaluated. The study has a normative value and its indications can be extended also in other clinical contexts that require operator-dependent diagnostic techniques.

Keywords Telehealth · Telepharmacy · Digitalization · Healthcare system

1 Introduction

Access, equity, quality and cost-effectiveness are key issues facing health care in both developed and less economically developed countries. Information and Communication Technology (ICT) have great potential to address some of the challenges faced by countries in providing adequate and equal access to healthcare services, primary

M. Musso · R. Pinna · P. P. Carrus
Department of Economics and Management, University of Cagliari, 09124 Cagliari, Italy

E. Veglianti (✉) · E. Magnaghi
FGES, Université Catholique de Lille, 59800 Lille, France
e-mail: eleonora.veglianti@univ-catholille.fr

E. Zaramenskikh and A. Fedorova (eds.), *Digitalization of Society, Economics and Management*, Lecture Notes in Information Systems and Organisation 53,
https://doi.org/10.1007/978-3-030-94252-6_23

prevention, early diagnosis, appropriate therapy [1, 2]. Starting from these reasons, recently the national and local governments in the world are doing pressure on health care organizations in reconfiguring their service delivery processes by the use of technology solutions in order to improve public health and health service delivery. In order to improve the citizens help and the economic and social sustainability of treating such diseases, the World Health Organization (WHO) points out the need to adopt new business models, based on innovative tools and active participation of all actors involved in health service. In the current pandemic emergency, Italy was found unprepared to manage lockdown with chronic disease, due to limited availability and diffusion of large-scale telemedicine solution. Telehealth, (the provision of care at a distance), is a key component in future integrated care and it is particularly oriented to sustain such transformation, by enabling new relationship between patients and health professionals. An increasingly solid evidence base is emerging indicating that telehealth can be used effectively to respond to the growing call for improved care, in particular for those with chronic conditions or cardiologic diseases prevention. The Italian Ministry of Health has identified telehealth as one of the essential components of the reorganization of health services focused on citizens and able to facilitate access to health services on national territory. The goal is to redesign the organization of the network of services, especially in order to strengthen the territorial scope of assistance. Technological innovation can contribute to a reorganization of healthcare, in particular by supporting the shift of healthcare from hospital to territory. Moreover, usage of telemedicine applications will help optimize the costs of healthcare in the long term. While literature provides clear evidence to support the integration of these services in clinical practice, it also points out areas that currently lack substantial evidence and the need for future research. One of these areas is the evaluation of telemedicine services in new health care organizational models that involve novel roles for advanced practitioners, such as pharmacists. The structure of the NHS is shifting with the result that services need to be reconfigured to fit new models of care where Pharmacists are an integral part of the health care team and are more accessible health care professionals. This accessibility allows them to perform more patient care activities, including counselling, medication management and preventive care. In the last decade, scholars [3] point out that pharmacists have begun to take on more active roles in the management of chronic diseases such as anticoagulation, diabetes and hypertension management. A strategy that allows pharmacists to expand the reach of their interventions even further in an efficient manner is through the utilization of telemedicine. In the literature, there are example of clinical pharmacist services delivered by telemedicine technology [4, 5] that demonstrated the potential benefits for patients from utilization of remote clinical pharmacist services. This is supported by evidence from currently implemented outpatient-based physician telemedicine services. However, despite the growing popularity of practice models with pharmacists remotely providing clinical care via telemedicine technologies, there has been no comprehensive systematic assessment of the overall impact of these services on patient outcomes. For example, primary prevention, early diagnosis, appropriate therapy and also patient education become important in the clinical disease. Telemedicine allows pharmacists to extend the reach of clinical interventions, connecting them with patients and providers [6]. In light of these considerations the aim of this paper is firstly to explore which are the impacts of clinical pharmacist interventions on the health service, when delivered using telemedicine. Secondly, the research wanted to evaluate the organizational impact linked to the opportunities of the telehealth ecosystem. In particular, by adopting an empirical case study, our study aims at describing the clinical pharmacist service delivered via telemedicine. Moreover, the study is focused on the heart failure chronic disease who would be able to co-produce their health conditions by an innovative interaction model with the telemedicine system. The rest of the paper is organized as follows. First, the theoretical background of the study is explained along with a review of relevant literature. Next, the research methodology employed is detailed. Finally, we provide a summary of the key findings and discuss the implications for practitioners.

2 Theoretical Background

2.1 Telehealth, Quality of Care and Accessibility

EHealth encompasses all applications of ICT towards supporting and interconnecting health service processes and health system actors, both at the local level and remotely. E-Health applications are the most appropriate technologies in order to improve the quality and safety of healthcare delivery with the use of up-to-date healthcare information and communication technology to meet the need of citizens, patients, healthcare professionals, and healthcare providers [7–10].

Telehealth can be understood as a specific domain of the more comprehensive concept of eHealth, with the aim to realize care integration. Telemedicine, a term coined in the 1970s, which literally means "healing at distance", signifies the use of ICT to improve patient outcomes by increasing access to care and medical information. Recognizing that there isn't one definitive definition of telemedicine, the WHO has adopted the following broad description: "The delivery of health care service, where distance is a critical factor, by health care professionals using information and communication technologies, for the exchange of valid information for diagnosis, treatment and prevention of disease and injuries, research and evaluation, and for the continuing of health care providers, all in the interests of advancing the health of individuals and their communities". Four important elements belong to telemedicine:

1. Its purpose is to provide clinical support.
2. It is intended to overcome geographical barriers connecting users who are not in the same location.
3. It involves the use of a growing variety of applications and services using two-way video, email, smart phones, wireless tools and other forms of telecommunications technology.
4. Its goal is to improve health outcomes.

Telehealth services come in many different forms. They usually can be divided into two types based on the timing of the interaction between patient and health professional. The first type is store and forward (asynchronous), when telemedicine involves the exchange of pre-recorded data between two or more individuals at different times; and the second is real time (synchronous) when telemedicine requires the involved individuals to be simultaneously present for immediate exchange of information.

Thus, introducing telehealth implies some change for organizations. Several benefits of telehealth digitalization have been well documented in literature [11, 12]. The literature [13] reports that while telemedicine offers great opportunities in general, in terms of improving the efficiency of healthcare organizations, it could be even more beneficial for regions with limited infrastructure, where access to specialized professionals is too difficult. In particular, telemedicine can aid communities traditionally underserved—those in rural or remote areas with few health services and staff—because it overcomes distance and time barriers between health care providers and patients [14]. By increasing the accessibility of medical care telemedicine can enable patients to seek treatment earlier and adhere better to their prescribed treatments and improve the quality of life for patients with chronic conditions [15]. Telemedicine has been advocated in situations where the health professional on duty has little or no access to expert help; it is able to offer remote physician access to otherwise unavailable specialist opinions, providing reassurance to both doctors and patients [16]. Telemedicine also provides opportunities by opening up new channels for communication and facilitates cross-site and inter-country collaboration and networking. Furthermore, it also provides opportunities for learning and professional development by enabling the dissemination of information and the remote training of health care professionals. Telehealth is not a separate medical specialty and has the potential to increase quality and access to healthcare to lower cost [17, 18]. One of the positive benefits of building high speed networks is that they allow for real-time monitoring and interaction with patients without requiring their physical presence at a care centre. For instance, this technology can support the delivery of specialized services in a timely fashion for remote populations, facilitate access to education for clinicians, and save travel costs for patients and professionals.

2.2 *Telemedicine and the New Role of Pharmacies*

The role of pharmacists in telemedicine models was first documented in the early 2000s and since then the literature showing the impact of these models has been expanding. Pharmacists have played a critical role in improving access to clinical pharmacy services in rural areas. However, pharmacists are frequently referred to as the most underutilized healthcare professionals [19]. Due to easy accessibility, pharmacies are the first point of contact in the healthcare system in many developed and developing countries [20, 21]. Pharmacists are qualified health professionals, capable of assisting with many of the challenges that currently exist in the healthcare system, including physician shortages and high readmission rates. While pharmacists are not often the sole providers in decision-making in patient care, they often serve as patient care team members and facilitators of communication between other healthcare providers, and also between healthcare providers and patients. In the last decade, pharmacists have begun to take on more active roles in the management of chronic diseases such as diabetes, hypertension, and anticoagulation management. They have also taken a lead role in transitions of care, with the goal of improving patient adherence and preventing adverse drug events (ADEs) after discharge to prevent rehospitalization. A strategy that allows pharmacists to expand the reach of their interventions even further in an efficient manner is through the utilization of telemedicine. The telepharmacy may be defined as "the delivery of pharmaceutical care to outpatients at a distance through the use of telecommunication and other advanced technology" [16, 22]. Telepharmacy services are not a new concept but the pandemic emergency has increased the need to adopt telemedicine service, including telepharmacy. Telepharmacy embracing heterogeneous interventions which involve the pharmacist in more professional activities: drug therapy monitoring, order review and dispensing, patient counselling and monitoring, provision of clinical service medication therapy management, automated dispensing systems and the chronic disease management [23]. Different studies showed the potential benefit from utilization of remote clinical pharmacist services. For example, in the rural communities context, telepharmacy represents a unique and innovative way to deliver a full service with potential benefits in terms of enhancement of the access to care, short waiting list, results quickly available, time and cost saving, services provided in a professional setting by a healthcare professional [19, 24]. In particular, telepharmacy can offer new ways to manage cardiovascular patients by connecting healthcare team members and clinical specialists to provide consultations in settings where specialty services are unavailable. Through the use of telemedicine pharmacists can now expand their activities and provide remote clinical services in the outpatient or ambulatory care setting with benefit for patients and their managing physicians.

3 Methodology

A case study [25] has been conducted to explore the research question of this study. As Rogers [26] states: "data about the innovation process are obtained by synthesizing the recallable perceptions of key actors in the innovation process, written records of the organization adopting, and other data sources". The case under consideration is a telehealth project—the HTN platform and Pharmacy of Services—developed between a technology provider, the University and pharmacies focused on providing services for cardiovascular diseases prevention.

Data have been collected through internal documentation, protocols and in-depth interviews, which have been coded following literature indications integrated with a thematic analysis. In the following sections of the paragraph, the case description is presented followed by the description of the main results.

Data included in the internal documentations have been elaborated obtaining regarding the project diffusion and its effectivity.

The interviewees included clinical pharmacist the medical staff and technology providers involved in the project. Interviews lasted two hours, they have been tape-recorded with the consent of respondents and a verbatim transcript has been made. The data obtained from the interviews were triangulated with those collected using other methods, including field observation and official documentation, regional laws, archives, historical data and organizational plans provided directly by the organization, scientific journals and local newspapers. Although the number of interviews may be considered small, they were related to the key roles that the respondents had in the planning and development of this innovation. They give indeed a high level of reliability and validity to the research findings and they have been very suitable to explore how the different actors collaborated to provide the service and evaluate the impacts of the telehealth solution on the service network.

Interview schemas were elaborated from the literature. A different schema was prepared for clinicians and the technology provider. The interview schema for the clinical pharmacist and the medical doctor was divided into two parts. The first part comprised questions about motivations and the effects of telehealth on clinical practice and on the new relationships between professionals. The second part of the interview covered insights about the organizational impacts as well as the conditions that would facilitate telehealth integration into clinical work and the new role of the pharmacies. Finally, were interviewed technologies providers. Questions addressed about the characteristic of the platform and their opinion about the key conditions for successful telehealth implementation and their impact on the health service provision through different devices. In addition, information about the different collaborative action was asked to investigate how this service has been coproduced and value has been co-created between actors.

4 Results and Discussion

4.1 The Project Description

The case study considered concerned the telehealth HTN and Pharmacies of service project developed in Italy since 2013 with the aim to introduce telemedicine service in pharmacy spread all over the country.

The project has been authorized by Ministerial Decree No. 153 of 2009 designing a Pharmacy that can legitimately:

- provide health facilities in terms of "services for public health".
- provide clients with advice on health behaviour and needs.

As part of the Pharmacy of Services, a collaboration agreement has been settled with Universities for the realization of the project "Telemedicine in the primary and secondary prevention of cardiovascular diseases". The project concerns distance reporting from the authorized specialist centre (electrocardiograms, blood pressure monitoring, cardiac holter monitoring), allowing the detection of numerous anomalies, including cases of red code sent to the emergency centre. Agreements with several ASL (Local Health Institutions) have been activated to control value of the PT-INR in the pharmacy. Pharmacies, indeed, duly trained and equipped with software capable of interfacing with the relevant TAO centres, can take care of the patient with oral anticoagulant therapy, detecting the value of the PT, transmitting it to the Center and receiving from the same doctor possible adjustment of therapy. The technology which supports the project consists mainly in a platform developed by HTN—(Health Telematic Network), in collaboration with healthcare professionals, operational structure of the Service Center and users. From the synthesis of this work the Smart Telemedicine Platform has been created; it is an advanced Health Care software platform whose TelMed, Video Web and TelMed Wireless Solutions are tool used to build and deliver all HTN Telemedicine Services. The peculiarities of SmartTelemedicine Platform are linked to:

- clinical innovation (in terms of providing early diagnosis, remote control, follow-up and decision support),
- technological innovation (linked to the use of automatic learning techniques integrated with ontological reasoning; techniques that, applied in real time to the raw data provided by the sensor infrastructure, allow the recognition of a wide range of human activities and situations of clinics risk),
- market innovation (represented by the possibility of acquiring multiple information within the home and/or on the move and being able to correlate it with the user's clinical history).

In particular, the services provided by the telemedicine platform with the pharmacies concern a wide range of health facilities referred to prevention.

The HTN Virtual Hospital telemedicine makes the equipment available for Pharmacies:

- teleelectrocardiography
- registration of dynamic electrocardiograms according to Holter
- telemonitoring of home arterial pressure
- holter telemonitoring 24 h of arterial pressure
- assessment of lung capacity by self-spirometry
- telemonitoring of blood oxygen saturation percentage.

HTN telemedicine provides to the pharmacy involved in the project functioning as "spoke" unit, devices such as multi-specialist teleconsultation, remote reporting, instrumental home telemonitoring of the main vital parameters, prolonged home monitoring for patients suffering from chronic diseases. All the clinical-instrumental services are provided in real time, 24 h a day, through the service centre of excellence as tertiary hospital which serves as the "hub" unit, using the most modern telecommunication technologies (smartphone, tablet, internet) and the advanced "Smart-Telemedicine Platform". A Personal Health Record (Personal Health Record) is generated for each user, with informed consent.

The pharmacist is assigned a password that allows him to access the user's personal health record on the web, to view health data and physiological parameters and to print the reports of the various instrumental surveys whose signals the platform have collected.

Thus, this technology allows echocardiographic exams to be performed remotely, without physical interaction between the patient and the specialist. The specialist can guide the clinical pharmacist close to the patient during the execution of the analysis, visualizing in real time the video streaming from the echography and from the camera recording the examination.

4.2 *The Impact of the HTN Telemedicine and Pharmacy of Services Project*

All the interviewees agree that telehealth was perceived as a powerful tool to improve health services for citizens and improve access to care. The above-described project allowed to enjoy several benefits, some of which are more difficult to be assessed in terms of money, although equally relevant. In addition, thanks to the growing number of pharmacies involved in the project it has been possible to observe an increasing number of examinations carried out, with a consequent considerable impact on disease prevention. As it can be seen from Fig. 1, throughout 2018, the Services Pharmacy Network that provides HTN telemedicine services has grown by 22% compared to 2017 (the 2017 increase over 2016 was 21%). The network currently has 4,008 pharmacies (+4% compared to 30 September 2018).

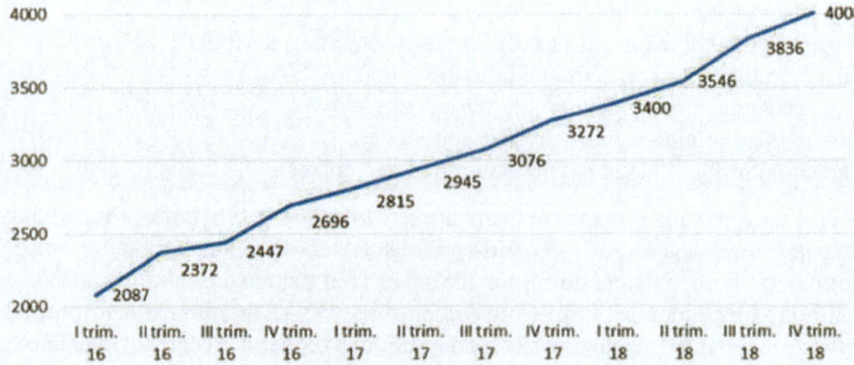

Fig. 1 Pharmacies network using HTN telemedicine

As one of the managers of the project states, given the growing number of activities a huge change in the role of pharmacy is approaching:

> we have to say that there is an increase in the number of requests, including an increase in the number of pharmacies participating in these health services, which means that the role of the pharmacy, as well as the dispensation of the drug, it is becoming most of all presiding over the territory for health services. This is for us a fundamental purpose, because only in this way the pharmacy will succeed itself also as a tool for primary prevention. However, in addition to raising the professional value of the pharmacy, the Htn system opens up different scenarios as far as profitability of pharmacies is concerned.

It is worth mentioning that there is a constant increasing tendency to perform examination in pharmacy thanks to the technology provided by HTN telemedicine (see Fig. 2). It should be noted that the final balance for the second quarter of 2018 closed with a total of 19,742 s-level services provided, marking an increase of 66% compared to the same period of 2017. The total number of services provided in the first half of 2018 was 43,439, an increase of 58% compared to the first half of 2017 (27,480 benefits) and equivalent to 66% of the total benefits paid in 2017 (65.511).

In 2018, a total of 99,923 services were delivered, with an increase of 53% compared to 2017 (65,511 performances). The increase in benefits paid in 2017 compared to 2016 was 51%. In the 2016–2018 three-year period, a total of 208,955 services were provided. In particular, in the second quarter of 2018 10,486 electrocardiograms were performed (+66% compared to the second quarter of 2017), 5,001 holter monitors (+67% compared to the second quarter of 2017) and 4,255 blood pressure monitoring in the 24 h—ABPM (+63% compared to the second quarter 2017). The most relevant consequence has been that: (1) for electrocardiograms, in 2018, a total of 5.136 anomalies were found (8.07% of users); (2) for Holter monitoring, in 2018, a total of 3,314 anomalies (17.02% of users) were found, of which

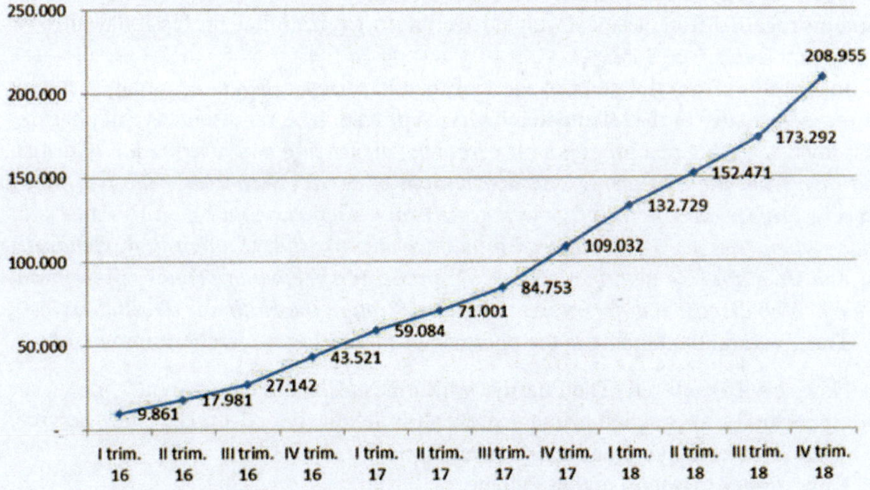

Fig. 2 Number of health examinations developed in pharmacies

352 judged serious (1.81% of users); (3) for arterial pressure monitoring in 2018, a total of 6,497 anomalies were detected (38.59% of users), whose 1,109 with high sisto-diastolic values (6.59% of users) and 2,607 with high heart rate values (15.48% of users).

These results highlight the changing role of pharmacies as spokes unit to augment the presence of the health public service improving the access to care for population spread all over the country. Telehealth can be viewed as an efficient means to perform follow-up visits in order to improve continuity of care and reduce the wait times for patients who do need subspecialty care visits. As it can be observed from the results, the telemedicine project can also allow for better emergency management. An accurate, priority-aware management procedure starting from the pharmacies can reduce significantly the time to diagnosis for urgent cases: "*It is possible in this way to obtain a rapid and efficient evaluation of critical situations where it might be necessary to transfer the patient to a specialized centre, such as the tertiary hospital*". (*medical doctor states*).

In addition, the technology provider argues that: "thanks to the use of a single Telemedicine platform (SmartTelemedicine) HTN can guarantee uniformity in the collection of health data, uniformity of equipment of hospital-type electro-medical equipment by every pharmacy, uniformity in the provision of specialist teleconsultation professional services and telemedical report. Moreover, HTN provide with a single shared database in full compliance with privacy regulations".

Thus, another important consideration can be assessed referring to the validity and comparability of data deriving from the HTN and Pharmacy of Service project. The homogeneity of tools and methodologies in the collection of results, can make improvement in the monitoring levels and cost efficiency of examination given the immediate availability of data. It also makes it possible to reach higher level of service quality during chronic disease monitoring.

Because of the thematic analysis on the interview relevant benefit emerged. These benefits regard different aspects related to clinic, organizational, professional and cost efficiency levels (see Table 1).

In addition, from the point of view of the pharmacy, relevant advantages can be observed because of the telemedicine service provision. A representative of pharmacist says: "*Finding resources not only from the dispensing and distribution of drugs, but also from the dispensing and distribution of services, enhances the pharmacy from a professional point of view but also raises the economic performance that today often trudges. If we succeed in making it clear that through high standards (which we elaborate with the ISS) we act in the perspective of primary prevention, we can also discuss a different remuneration through the National Health Service*".

Thus, several benefits from the pharmacies point of view can be summarized:

- New services offered (The Pharmacy becomes a "health care provider").
- Opportunity to practice primary prevention (extensive coverage, quick service, short referral delivery and user convenience.
- Opportunity to obtain higher income.
- Possible committed clients (through Electronic Health Record).

Table 1 Telehealth advantages on service

Access to care	Facilitated access to specialized services in underserved region and all over the country Time reduction to diagnosis for urgent cases management Reduced errors in diagnosis
Professional	Valorizing professional competence exchange Development and update knowledge Multi-disciplinary/multi-centred exchanges Facilitates communication with peers, and access to a second opinion
Organizational	Creating new organizational models (hub and spoke model)
Cost efficiency for health system	Potential to save costs for patients and transfer facilitation Cost efficiency deriving from improvement in disease prevention and emergency management

- Possible image improvement for the Pharmacist (quality service and expertise).

The results show also important insights about the collaborative and interactional approach between actors that the whole project had. The different actors involved (such as the pharmacies, the technology provider, the Universities and the hospital all together with patients) had to exchange a wide range of information and collaborate constantly to build the solution and to deliver the telepharmacy service. With the HTN telemedicine, created in collaboration with Promofarma, the Pharmacy of Services therefore affirms its important role in the prevention of cardiovascular diseases. Indeed, the ability to network across the entire country is confirmed, thanks to the quality of the diagnostic services provided and the convenience for the patient to avoid long waiting queues in other types of medical-health facilities.

The strength of HTN lies in the way they work and the constant interaction with the ServiceCenter making it possible for them to focus on the critical management issues that come up from time to time. The software solutions are developed according to indications and to working requirements that come from pharmacies, professionals, universities and even patient, working needs we come across every day. Information and needs to be exploited are indicated by the operators of the call's centres, by specialists and by the different types of clients. So basically, the solution is developed together with the network (the technology provider).

5 Conclusions

This paper presents the preliminary results of the impacts of an important telehealth project involving pharmacies, public health institutions and the HTN provider covering the whole Italian territory. It has been possible to highlight benefits referring to different level as access to care for the population, professional and organizational.

Implications in terms of public healthcare strategies can be introduced. In particular, if policymakers are desirous of improving patient care quality and cost reduction, then the promotion of sustainable health systems is important. This suggests an urgent need for care provided at the prime point of need, favouring services through the territory or in the community whenever possible. It also points to a need for improved coordination, partnership working and integration in the delivery of health promotion, public health and social care services. This can be achieved by public healthcare sector adopting e new organizational model of service delivery in order to improve the quality of clinical practice. In this organizational design, pharmacists will continue to play a critical role in the provision of healthcare services, and they have the opportunity to explore and embrace novel paradigm to continue to provide high-quality patient care and pharmacy services. Future studies should investigate the cost-effectiveness of these services to provide further evidence to support continued implementation.

References

1. Palozzi, G., Binci, D., & Appolloni, A. (2017). E-health and co-production: Critical drivers for chronic diseases management. In *Service Business Model Innovation in Healthcare and Hospital Management* (pp. 269–296). Springer, Cham.
2. Rossignoli, C., Zardini, A., & Benettollo, P. (2014). The process of digitalisation in radiology as a lever for organisational change: the case of the academic integrated hospital of Verona. In G. Phillips-Wren, S. Carlsson, A. Respício & P. Brézillon (Eds.), *DSS 2.0—Supporting Decision Making with New Technologies* (Vol. 261, pp. 24–35). IOS Press, London.
3. Niznik, J. D., He, H., & Kane-Gill, S. L. (2018). Impact of clinical pharmacist services delivered via telemedicine in the outpatient or ambulatory care setting: A systematic review. *Research in Social and Administrative Pharmacy, 14*(8), 707–717.
4. Alsabbagh, M. W., Lemstra, M., Eurich, D., Wilson, T. W., Robertson, P., & Blackburn, D. F. (2012). Pharmacist intervention in cardiac rehabilitation: A randomized controlled trial. *Journal of cardiopulmonary rehabilitation and prevention, 32*(6), 394–399.
5. Wu, J. Y., Leung, W. Y., Chang, S., Lee, B., Zee, B., Tong, P. C., & Chan, J. C. (2006). Effectiveness of telephone counselling by a pharmacist in reducing mortality in patients receiving polypharmacy: Randomised controlled trial. *BMJ, 333*(7567), 522.
6. Carter, E. L., Nunlee-Bland, G., & Callender, C. (2011). A patient-centric, provider-assisted diabetes telehealth self-management intervention for urban minorities. In *Perspectives in health information management/AHIMA, American health information management association, 8 Adler-Milstein and Bates.*
7. Vitacca, M., Mazzù, M., & Scalvini, S. (2009). Socio-technical and organizational challenges to wider e-health implementation. *Chronic Respiratory Disease, 6*(2), 91–97.
8. Ferretti, M., Favalli, F., & Zangrandi, A. (2014). Impact of a logistic improvement in an hospital pharmacy: Effects on the economics of a healthcare organization. *International Journal of Engineering, Science and Technology, 6*(3), 85–95.
9. Torre, T. (2016). Information technologies and quality management. towards a new ıdea of quality. In *Information and Communication Technologies in Organizations and Society* (Vol. 15, pp. 191–204). Springer.
10. Bacigalupe, G., & Askari, S. F. (2013). E-health innovations, collaboration and healthcare disparities: Developing criteria for culturally competent evaluation. *American Psycological Association, 31*(3).

11. Ossebaard, H. C., & Van Gemert-Pijnen, L. (2016). eHealth and quality in health care: implementation time. *International Journal for Quality in Health Care, 28*(3), 415–419; Davis, P., Howard, R., & Brockway, P. (2001). An evaluation of telehealth in the provision of rheumatologic consults to a remote area. *The Journal of Rheumatology, 28*(8), 1910–1913.
12. Froelich, W., et al. (2009). Case report: An example of international telemedicine success. *Journal of Telemedicine and Telecare, 15*(4), 208–210.
13. El-Miedany, Y. (2017). Telehealth and telemedicine: How the digital era is changing standard health care. *Smart Homecare Technology and Telehealth, 4*, 43–51.
14. Sorrentino, M., De Marco, M., & Rossignoli, C. (2016). Health care co-production: Co-creation of value in flexible boundary spheres. In *International Conference on Exploring Services Science* (pp. 649–659). Springer, Cham.
15. Pinna, R., Carrus, P. P., & Musso, M. (2016). Excellence in healthcare: Telemedicine project in an Italian region. In *19° Toulon-Verona Conference "Excellence in Services Conference Proceedings.*
16. Grant, B., Morgan, J. G, McCrossan, B. A., Crealey, E.G., Sands, A., Craig, B., & Casey, A. F. (2010). Remote diagnosis of congenital heart disease: the impact of telemedicine. *Archives of Disease in Childhood, 95*(4), 276–280.
17. George, P. P., Molina, J. A., & Cheah, J., et al. (2010). The evolving role of the community pharmacist in chronic disease management—A literature review. *Annals Academy of Medicine Singapore*, 861–867.
18. Gilardi, S., Guglielmetti, C., Marsilio, M., & Sorrentino, M. (2016). Co-production in healthcare: moving patient engagement towards a managerial approach. In *Co-production in the Public Sector* (pp. 77–95). Springer, Cham.
19. Rotta, I., Salgado, T. M., Silva, M. L., Correr, C. J., & Fernandez-Llimos, F. (2015). Effectiveness of clinical pharmacy services: An overview of systematic reviews (2000–2010). *International Journal of Clinical Pharmacy, 37*(5), 687–697. https://doi.org/10.1007/s11096-015-0137-9
20. Perdew, C., Erickson, K., & Litke, J. (2017). Innovative models for providing clinical pharmacy services to remote locations using clinical video telehealth. *American Journal of Health-System Pharmacy.*
21. Pinna, R., Carrus, P. P., & Musso, M. (2016). Excellence in healthcare: Telemedicine project in an Italian region. In *19° Toulon Verona Conference "Excellence in Services" Conference Proceedings.*
22. Heinzelmann, P. J., Lugn, N. E., & Kvedar, J. C. (2005). Telemedicine in the future. *Journal of Telemedicine and Telecare, 11*(8), 384–390.
23. Bynum, A., Hopkins, D., Thomas, A., Copeland, N., & Irwin, C. (2001). The effect of telepharmacy counseling on metered-dose inhaler technique among adolescents with asthma in rural Arkansas. *Telemedicine Journal and E-Health., 7*(3), 207–217.
24. Ossebaard, H. C., & Van Gemert-Pijnen, L. (2016). eHealth and quality in health care: Implementation time. *International Journal for Quality in Health Care, 28*(3), 415–419.
25. Yin, R. K. (2014). *Case study research: Design and methods*, 5th ed. Thousand Oaks.
26. Kapoor, K. K., Dwivedi, Y. K., & Williams, M. D. (2014). Rogers' innovation adoption attributes: A systematic review and synthesis of existing research. *Information Systems Management, 31*(1), 74–91.

Digital HRM and Hotel Business: A Global Bibliometric Analysis

Khaled Ghazy and Alena Fedorova

Abstract As digital human resource management is taking great significance in scholarly discussions, studies around this field are on the growth. Digital technology develops many industries in several concerns, consequently making it eligible for investigation and debate. Bibliometric analysis of digital HRM publications conducted using the Scopus database. The research is limited to the significant works related to digital HRM in the section of (Social Sciences, Business, Management, Accounting, Economics, Econometrics, Finance, and Arts & Humanities). After preprocessing the data, the analysis explored the thematic development of the topic considering coauthorship between the countries and co-occurrences of keywords using the VOSviewer software for visualizing the data. After that, a specific analysis has conducted to identify the status of digital HRM in the hotel business context. The results present an overview of previous studies that revealed challenges and main trends in the hotel digital HRM. Finally, this research contributes to digital HRM literature and makes recommendations for future studies.

Keywords Digitalization · Human resource management · Hotel business · Bibliometric analysis

1 Introduction

The highly competitive market forces organizations to continuously improve their products, develop their resources, and keep up with everything new to survive in the industry [1, 2]. The digital transformation improves many industries in concerns such as enhancing productivity, enhancing market accessibility, and reducing costs [3, 4].

Moreover, digital economy developments provide international platforms, enable collaborations, and support among firms over the world. It cannot be easy to digitalize

K. Ghazy · A. Fedorova (✉)
Ural Federal University, Mira Street, 620102 Yekaterinburg, Russian Federation
e-mail: a.e.fedorova@urfu.ru

E. Zaramenskikh and A. Fedorova (eds.), *Digitalization of Society, Economics and Management*, Lecture Notes in Information Systems and Organisation 53,
https://doi.org/10.1007/978-3-030-94252-6_24

all the economy sectors, but with the lack of digitalization, it will be hard to step toward the world economy [5].

According to Evseeva et al. [2], digital human resources is recently considered a new covenant for the human resource market. It should be placed in a new strategic level of management. Firms have to encourage their employees to eliminate concerns toward technology and global integration. Besides, in recent years, internet development enabled organizations to adopt various technological applications on human resources, which led to positive consequences such as accelerate the processes and give an enjoyable experience for employees and customers [6].

Ahmed [7] mentioned that businesses have to manage rapid development in digital human resources. The marketplace requires new skills, knowledge, and personnel abilities. Furthermore, with the highly integrated digital HR network, all the operations are easy to access by HRM, managers, and employees [8]. Therefore, development requires a new kind of organization and management to deal with unpredictable global economy changes.

In the hotel business context, digital HRM is essential, and it is helping many organizations achieve the desired development. The hotel business is a crucial sector for the economy and a labor-intensive industry where the human element is an integral part of the organization [9]. Likewise, digital technology has influenced many businesses such as retail business and transportation; it also affected the hotel business, such as Foursquare, Airbnb, and Traveloka.com, which offer low prices [10].

However, digital HRM is extensively adopted in the hotel business nowadays. Studies are rare, and hotels have many challenges, such as taking advantage of innovation and responding to the changing environment [11].

2 Research Method

According to Benckendorff and Zehrer [12], bibliometrics is a statistical research method of publication that provides quantitative perception into academic literature. The data collected can be analyzed from the database to indicate publication growth in the research field. Bibliometrics can perform many approaches, such as co-citation, citation-analysis, and author keywords [13].

2.1 Data Sources and Search Strategy

The data was collected using the Scopus database on October 11, 2020, and other search engines such as Google scholar. The central theme was a review article in the title and abstract that involved digital human resources. Due to the enormous amount of digital HR documents, the analysis limits to such sections as (Social Sciences, Business, Management, Accounting, Economics, Econometrics, Finance, Arts, and Humanities). The search question string used was: TITLE-ABS KEY (digital AND human AND resource AND management) AND (LIMIT-TO (SUBJAREA, "SOCI") OR LIMIT TO (SUBJAREA,"BUSI") OR LIMIT TO (SUBJAREA, "ARTS"). The query string's output was 702 documents. VOSviewer, a software tool, was used for bibliometric mapping and visualizing the documents.

3 Results and Discussion

3.1 *Digital HRM Overview*

Figure 1 illustrates a total of 642 research articles published for a ten-year period. From 2010 to 2012, the publication rate was almost stable between 19 and 21 documents every year. At the beginning of 2013, a sharp increase in digital HRM research publications is indicated, which refers to the authors' interest in this field of study. The annual publication increased gradually until it reached the peak point in 2019 at 149 documents, which is expected since our life has engaged with digital developments.

VOSviewer reveals co-authorship between the countries of the research activity of the digital HRM. The findings of co-authorship displayed the top countries where the most common scientific cooperation on digital HRM ordered as following: the United States (51 links), UK (47 links), Germany (34 links), Italy (32 links), Sweden (32 links), China (27 links), Finland (21 links), Japan (19 links), Russia (18 links), Switzerland (17 links) and others.

A total of 5448 author keywords were verified, among which 1255 (23%) were used only twice, 627 keywords (11.5%) were used thrice. After re-interchangeable marking Single terms and congeneric phrases, 319 keywords reached the threshold of 5 occurrences as a minimum for the mapping in VOSviewer.

The findings showed that human resource management was the most frequently identified item with 265 occurrences and 1360 links to other keywords (Fig. 3). We also noticed the use of common keywords such as 'digital storage' (89 occurrences, 526 links), 'knowledge management' (62 occurrences, 327 links), and 'online training' (40 occurrences, 265 links). In addition, we noted some attributes, methods,

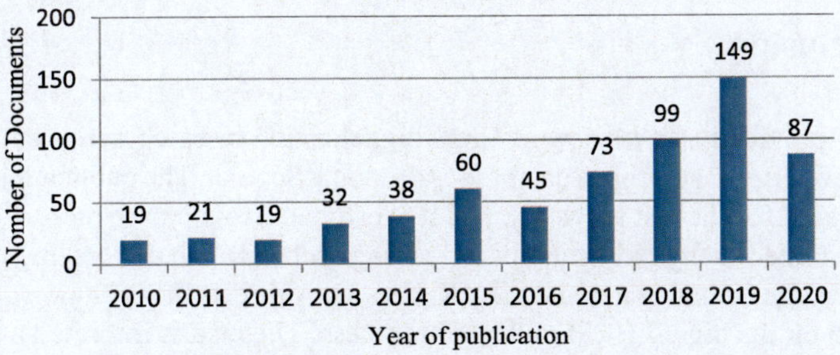

Fig. 1 The digital HRM annual publications from 2010 to 2020 in the Scopus database

and configurations used for naming the Digital HRM, such as Electronic Human Resource Management (e-HRM), electronic-HRM, eHRM, and digital HR management (d-HRM). Likewise, for e-learning, online training, and others, several words were used.

3.2 *Digital HRM in the Hotel Business*

A cross-analysis of applications showed that currently, only 11 works submitted are simultaneously matched the digital HRM in the Hotel Business, which allows us to conclude the potential opportunities and prospects for further research in this field. These documents address issues of digitalization in different areas related to the HRM in the hotels. The majority of the studies have been performed in Asia (Table 1). Several studies, on the one hand, examined the impact of the digital HRM on hotel performance such as ([10, 14, 15]), and on the other, some studies investigated the digital HRM patterns and practices in the hotels such as [16, 17, 18]. In addition, an integrated model to conduct a sustainable digital transformation is suggested, which includes reconfiguring resources such as digital leadership capabilities, digital market capabilities, and digital technology capabilities [11]. At the same time, digitalization provides organizations with extra capabilities to hire talented candidates and affect organizational effectiveness. Therefore, digitalization is now a priority in any organization strategy agenda [11, 19].

Nevertheless, digital HRM is adopted in the hotel business extensively nowadays as well as researches pointed out the inevitability of digital HRM and its essential and benefits. The case studies are rare in the context of the hotel business; researches are scattered and limited at one or two functions of d-HRM such as (recruitment and selection), and deep discussion is narrow from a strategic perspective ([9, 10, 16, 17, 18, 19]. Besides, the hotel business needs to take initiatives to deal with rapid market changes and benefit from information technology [11]. The analysis formalized an overview of the organizations' digital HRM status and addressed the hotel's challenges related to HRM digitalization, which require further research.

4 Conclusion

This study provided an overview of HRM digitalization research trends on publications retrieved from the Scopus database and Google Scholar. The publication growth has been rapid for the last ten years, and it is estimated to increase more. The analysis has revealed many publications and strong global collaborations in countries, for example, the United States and the UK. This study directs the evolution of themes in research on the digital HRM and hotel business. The results indicate an increase

Table 1 List of researches on the digital HRM in the hotel business and their central themes

Author(s)	Central theme	Description	Country
Sun et al. [9]	Infomationization and HRM	The authors explored the effect of information technology on the hotel human resources management	China
Choochote and Chochiang [16]	Digital HRM patterns of hotel business	The study presents the pattern of the digital human resources management (d-HRM) of the hotel business	Thailand
Pandey and Kumar [10]	Hotel performance and d-HRM	The authors investigated the impact of the contents of d-HRM on hotel performance	India
Saha and Pandita [20]	Digital HRM, gamification, and employee engagement	The study presented the hotel companies' initiatives by adopting gamification as a tool to obtain employee engagement	India
Pandey and Kumar [10]	Digital HRM practices of the hotel business	An empirical investigation into the factors influencing d-HRM Practices in Hotel Industry	India
Jooss et al. [17]	Digital innovation of HRM practices	the study evaluated the degree of digital innovation of HR practices in the hotel industry	Ireland
Morsy and El Demerdash [18]	The application of d-HRM in hotels and travel agents	Investigating the status of the d-HRM application in hotels and travel Agents, and examining the challenges facing d-HRM application	Egypt
Rady and Ebraheem [15]	The use of electronic human resource management	Assessing electronic human resource management of travel agencies and hotels and its impact on hotel performance	Egypt

(continued)

Table 1 (continued)

Author(s)	Central theme	Description	Country
Kataria et al. [14]	Digital HR and employee performance	Exploring d-HRM use as a contingency factor in the relationship between High-Performance HR practices (HPHRPs) and Employee Performance in the hotel industry	India
Prihanto and Kurniasari [11]	Sustainable digital transformation	The study examined an integrated model for the hotel industry leaders' ability to reconfigure resources to conduct sustainable digital transformation	Indonesia
Johnson et al. [19]	E-HRM and artificial intelligence for talent acquisition	The study discussed how e-recruiting and e-selection, and AI tools to help hospitality and tourism organizations improve recruiting and selection outcomes	USA

in discussions around the topic of the. Thus, the bibliometric analysis revealed challenges and main trends in hotel digital HRM studies and identified promising areas for further work.

References

1. Jatobá, M., Santos, J., Gutierriz, I., Moscon, D., Fernandes, P., & Teixeira, J. (2019). Evolution of artificial intelligence research in human resources. *Procedia Computer Science, 164*, 137–142.
2. Evseeva, O., Kalchenko, O., Evseeva, S., & Plis, K. (2019). Instruments of human resource management based on the digital technologies in Russia. In *International Conference on Digital Technologies in Logistics and Infrastructure (ICDTLI 2019)*. Atlantis Press.
3. OECD. (2014). The digital economy, new business models and key features. In *Addressing the tax challenges of the digital economy*. Paris: s.l.: OECD Publishing.
4. Agbozo, E. (2020). A bibliometric perspective of digital economy research in Russia. *In Digital transformation and new challenges* (pp. 25–36) https://doi.org/10.1007/978-3-030-43993-4_3.
5. Bulturbayevich, M., & Jurayevich, M. (2020). The impact of the digital economy on economic growth. *International Journal of Business, Law, and Education, 1*(1), 4–7.
6. Fenech, R., Baguant, P., & Ivanov, D. (2019). The changing role of human resource management in an era of digital transformation. *Journal of Management Information and Decision Sciences, 22*(2), 1–10.
7. Ahmed, M. (2019).E-HRM practices and its impact on organizational performance: A study on the manufacturing industry in Bangladesh. *European Journal of Business and Management, 11*(6), 50–60. ISSN 2222-1905 (Paper) (Online) https://doi.org/10.7176/EJBM.

8. Tripathi, R., & Kushwaha, P. (2017). *A study on innovative practices in digital human resource management. national seminar on digital transformation of business in India: Opportunities and challenges*. IMS Unison University.
9. Sun, H., Han, B., & Yu, C. (2015). Research and application on human resource management information system in China First-class hotels. In *International Conference on Education Technology, Management and Humanities Science (ETMHS 2015)*. Atlantis Press.
10. Pandey, A., & Kumar, M. S. S. (2017). A study on E-HRM practices in hotel industry in New Delhi. *Vindhya International Journal of Management & Research (VIJMR), 3*(1), 2395–2059. Available at: https://web.archive.org/web/20180422122310id. https://vijmr.org/papers/VIJMR031701.pdf.
11. Prihanto, J., & Kurniasari, F. (2019). Sustainable digital transformation in the hospitality industry: A study of the hotel industry in Indonesia. In *International Conference on Organizational Innovation (ICOI 19)*. Atlantis Press.
12. Benckendorff, P., & Zehrer, A. (2013). A network analysis of tourism research. *Annals of Tourism Research 43*, 121–149.
13. De Bellis, N. (2009). *Bibliometrics and citation analysis: From the science citation index to cybermetrics*. Scarecrow Press, Lanham, MD. https://lib.ugent.be/catalog/rug01:001668507.
14. Kataria, A., Arora, A., & Kataria, A. (2018). Shaping employee performance through E-HRM: Evidence from the hotel industry of India. In *The 4th International Conference on eLearning for Knowledge-Based Society* (pp. 21–25).
15. Rady, A., & Wahab, H. A. (2018). Assessing electronic human resource management of travel agencies and hotels in Minia Governorate. *Minia Journal of Tourism and Hospitality Research MJTHR, 3*(1), 19–46. Available at: https://journals.ekb.eg/article_139605_391a72f49b8a0cd6938c0cd0d48e69c6.pdf
16. Choochote, K., & Chochiang, K. (2015). Electronic human resource management (e-hrm) of hotel business in Phuket. *International Journal of Advanced Computer Science and Applications, 6*(4), 73–78.
17. Jooss, S., Burbach, R., & Street, C. (2017). Assessing the degree of human resource innovation: An exploratory analysis of Irish hotel corporations. *Electronic HRM in the Smart Era* (pp. 33–57). Emerald Publishing Limited.
18. Morsy, N., & El Demerdash, J. M. (2017). Investigating the potential use of E-HRM: the context of Egyptian hotels and travel agents. *Journal of Tourism Research, 16*(1), 81–86. Available at: http://jotr.eu/images/T151617PDF/V16.pdf#page=82
19. Johnson, R., Stone, D., & Lukaszewski, K. (2020). The benefits of eHRM and AI for talent acquisition. *Journal of Tourism Futures*. https://doi.org/10.1108/JTF-02-2020-0013.
20. Saha, M., & Pandita, D. (2017). Digitalizing human resources through gamification for employee engagement. *ELK Asia Pacific Journals, 4*.
21. Strohmeier, S. (2006). Coping with contradictory consequences of e-HRM. In *Proceedings of the First Academic Workshop on e-HRM Research* (pp. 25–26).

Digitalization and Executive Education: A Czech Case

Zuzana Dvorakova

Abstract Digital transformation of education remains a protean concept attracting attention from practitioners and researchers. Higher education institutions are undergoing a digital transformation to recruit and retain students to balance their work and study duties. During the last decades, business schools are increasingly uncoupled from practice and losing real value. The critical concern covers executive education, as it means to get revenues, reputations, and higher rankings, mainly for business schools. The paper aims to digitalize education focusing on specifics regarding executive education, demonstrating the situation in the Czech case. Methods use bibliographic analysis of publications, one focus group with Czech lecturers, and two unstructured interviews with top managers. Findings from secondary sources reveal that universities see the digital transformation of learning as a challenge, but few have successfully integrated executive education with online approaches. Some designers believe in applying a project-based approach, business-driven action learning, learning combined with coaching, and individualized online courses based on interactive platforms.

Keywords Digitalization · University · Executive education

1 Introduction

Digital transformation remains a protean concept attracting growing attention from practitioners and researchers. It refers to evolving an organization's foundational practices to serve customers better and operate streamlined processes using technology and data. Digitalization covers strategic, organizational, technological, and cultural changes that require commitment and involvement of top management [1].

In the context of Industry 4.0, higher education institutions (HEIs) confront digital opportunities and threats. No traditional student exists as he/she strives to balance

Z. Dvorakova (✉)
University of Chemistry and Technology Prague, Technická 5, Prague 6, 166 28 Prague, Czech Republic
e-mail: Zuzana3.Dvorakova@vscht.cz

E. Zaramenskikh and A. Fedorova (eds.), *Digitalization of Society, Economics and Management*, Lecture Notes in Information Systems and Organisation 53,
https://doi.org/10.1007/978-3-030-94252-6_25

study, work, family, and leisure time. Students receive incredible opportunities—they can choose between public or private universities, full-time or part-time enrollment, on-campus versus online courses. Universities strive to differentiate their services and optimize resources to achieve competitiveness [2]. They are undergoing a digital transformation to recruit and retain students by using social media, websites, and e-marketing, to measure institutional success exploiting their big data, digitalize library sources, and inform students by mobile apps about events and news.

Global education competitors' pressure becomes crucial for business schools when they aspire to combine research with managerial relevance. Debates on business schools' relevance in addressing business needs consider that academic research is not applicable to practice. However, value-adding benefits to practice are best completed when academia fights the seductive tendency to submit to the client's immediate demands [3]. Tushman et al. [4] believe that business schools are increasingly uncoupled from practice, losing real value for the business, negatively affecting the quality of teaching and institutional legitimacy. Such critical opinions are crucial for the future in terms of executive education, often seen as flagships demonstrating contributions to research and managerial practice. Management and executive education proliferated since the 1990s, primarily because of the financial crisis at the end of the first decade of the new millennium. The growing number of corporate academies is accompanied by growing criticism of direction, relevance, and effectiveness of higher education institutions' management training. Corporate training and development programs assessed as innovative provided learning at the time of need, embedded in a work context, and delivered in rapid "bite-sized pieces" [5]. The Executive Education Futures report, published in 2018, states that the most widely used executive education delivers the in-house academy (60%), followed by consulting firms (51%) and online providers (46%), and fewer than a third of organizations (28%) use business schools [6]. Lifelong learning for corporate managers signifies a big business, and higher education institutions take only a tiny portion of the whole market [7]. However, executive education means for business schools to get revenues, reputations, and higher rankings announcing about how they successfully compete and gain knowledge of and exposure to specific industries, companies, and executives [8].

The paper aims at digitalization with a focus on executive education, demonstrating the situation in the Czech case. The intention stands to discover the role of digitalization in higher education and approaches to executive education.

2 Methods

The methods enable a triangular analysis. The research begins with investigating secondary sources, mainly papers from the Web of Science published in 2000–2020. The qualitative methods use one focus group and two in-depth unstructured interviews.

The focus group was held with eight university lecturers in September 2020. It provided information for Study 1. The group represented a typical staff structure consisting of:

- two senior lecturers (women) and two senior lecturers (men),
- two associate professors (men)
- one associate professor and one professor (women),
- aged 40–49: two persons, 50–59: three, and 60+ three.

The interviews were with top managers/owners, the first one in November and the second one in December 2020. Their results assisted in writing two narrative cases.

The selected methods reflect that digital education influences all actors at universities in institutional requirements deeply rooted in history, culture, values, political and economic conditions. Based on the bibliometric analysis, a need for an innovative approach to executive education emerges due to the fast-moving competitiveness in the education market and dynamics in online education. Therefore, the research applies an interpretative group of methods that reveal the state-of-art in executive education to open questions for the future.

3 Findings

3.1 Analysis of Bibliographic Data

The analysis of bibliographic data in digital transformation and executive education enables one to overview the publication scope and the profile in the last two decades. We retrieved 18 271 bibliographic records that matched the query in database search in 2000–2020: records from the Web of Science databases count for 6 476 and Scopus 11 795. The structure of bibliographic records shows Table 1. It documents an impressive increase in the searched topics in the period 2018–2020. The Web of Science database outlines the development of promising directions in several areas,

Table 1 Bibliographic records by the query in the Web of Science and Scopus (2000–2020)

Query	Web of science 2000–2020	Web of science 2018–2020	Scopus 2000–2020	Scopus 2018–2020
"Digital transformation"	2 838	2 350	5 108	4 265
"Digital transformation" AND "Education"	375	318	577	493
"Digital transformation" AND "University"	173	149	445	384
"Executive education"	220	53	431	92
Total	3 606	2 870	6 561	5 234

Source Author [accessed on 2021/01/18]

mostly in management, business, computer science (information systems and theory methods), education and educational research, and economics.

According to the number of publications in the period 2018–2020, the first five countries show Table 2.

The number of references dealt with the most analyzed topics increase during the last twenty years, as shown in Table 3. It demonstrates that organizations look at digital transformation in education and digital transformation at universities with a steadily rising potential for improving processes and services.

The amount of literature on various sciences does not allow conducting a complete analysis of all of them. So, desk research limits findings on the most significant works, considering the citation index related to digital transformation and education, digital transformation and university, and executive education.

Table 2 Number of publications in the first five countries plus the CR in the Web of science (2018–2020)

Query	Ranking of countries by the number of publications (the number of publications)					
	1	2	3	4	5	CR
"Digital transformation"	Germany (379)	Russia (317)	USA (208)	Spain (184)	England (154)	(23)
"Digital transformation" AND "Education"	Russia (68)	Germany (60)	Spain (39)	USA (29)	Portugal (28)	(5)
"Digital transformation" AND "University"	Russia (40)	Germany (23)	Spain (20)	USA (10)	Portugal, Italy (9)	(1)
"Executive education"	USA (74)	England (33)	France (18)	Australia (11)	Scotland (9)	(2)

Source Author [accessed on 2021/01/18]

Table 3 Number of publications according to publication years in the Web of Science (2000–2020)

Query	2000	2005	2010	2015	2016	2017	2018	2019	2020
"Digital transformation"	–	5	7	43	110	258	543	941	866
"Digital transformation" AND "Education"	–	–	–	6	14	33	69	128	121
"Digital transformation" AND "University"	–	–	–	1	6	15	26	69	54
"Executive education"	4	5	11	17	17	31	20	14	19

Source Author [accessed on 2021/01/18]

3.2 Theoretical Grounds

Digital transformation can define as the use of new digital technologies, such as mobile, artificial intelligence, cloud, blockchain, and the Internet of things technologies, enabling significant business improvements, augmenting customer experience, streamlining operations, or creating new business models [9]. It belongs to existing trends that build challenges and offer potential solutions as they affect organizational processes, workforce, and culture. Zhu et al. [10] argue that an innovation diffusion based on technology determines characteristics, like a relative advantage, compatibility, costs, security concern, and contextual factors defined by technology competence, organization size, competitive pressure, and partner readiness. They recommend that the designers of any organization's digital transformation consider the aspects mentioned above, plus the economic and regulatory factors.

However, to understand digital transformation, we need to embrace ideas and concepts from multiple disciplines and acknowledge digital technologies' role in transforming organizations and social relationships [11]. It is a part of open innovation, a widely used concept in business, academia, and policymaking [12]. It accepts that digital technologies create disturbances generating strategic responses from organizations to shift their value creation process, master the structural changes, and restrict organizational barriers that hinder digitalization results [13].

Universities presently undertake the transition from conventional teaching based on transferring knowledge through lecturing and printed texts toward approaches based on project management, action learning, and interaction with digital tools [14]. University libraries face similar challenges as educators. Digitalization, the Internet, social networks, and other technologies push them to diversify their services and cooperate with other departments and institutions in favor, e.g., to promote open data, open access, curating data, and others [15]. Benavides et al. [16] analyze characteristics of the digital transformation in higher education institutions (HEIs) and detect nineteen papers from 1980 to 2019 as relevant to the theme of universities' digitalization process. They conclude that the process stands as an emerging field. However, no proposal of the university's digital transformation has a holistic dimension, although using digital technologies is one of the decisive factors for mastering transnational collaboration among HEIs [16]. Business schools were among the first HEIs that implemented online teaching, but few have successfully integrated executive education with online approaches [17].

The market for learning and development is growing speedily, and classroom learning becomes no primary concern due to the COVID-19. The pandemic creates a critical moment of opportunity for reshaping HEIs with implementation, development, and diffusion of digital technologies [18] and innovative thinking that the pandemic can positively affect the integral digital transformation in the future [19]. As an alternative, digital education converts to significantly influence the university's growth as lifelong learning is upward, and HEIs can utilize new opportunities by offering online courses. However, universities' ability to use digital technologies effectively in education, research, and organizing processes determines contextual factors, as documented, e.g., in Spain and Mexico [20].

Attention must apply to executive development programs as they changed significantly since their introduction in the early twentieth century and are still considered an efficient practice for emerging organizational leaders [21]. Across all sectors, demand for developing the top talents nurtures. From 1945 to 1970, the US universities' role in providing executive education was to act according to their societal obligations and develop potential top executives' cultural, symbolic, and social capital by offering the new leaders norms and values that characterized the managerial capitalism [22]. Innes-Taylor, Yamazaki, and Inoue [23] believe that executive education attracts global leaders by the latest education on leadership, strategy, critical thinking, and technology learned together with culturally diverse participants.

Leaders must engage themselves in constant learning processes that combine technical and financial topics and soft skills needed for self-awareness [24]. According to George et al. [25], achieving business results is a long-term outcome of authentic leadership when anybody learns from their experiences and develops self-awareness through persistence and courage self-exploration. A top-tier US university went through changes in an open-enrollment senior executive program for ten years, and program staff believes that an innovative curriculum integrates adult learning and human resource development theory with executive education [26]. The study of 222 executives and senior leaders about the effects of executive learning and development reports that it has positive, quantifiable implications for business performance and organizational effectiveness [27]. However, companies often get a meager return on their investment due to several reasons:

1. Business schools are not flexible enough to teach soft skills vital for today's success.
2. Employers do not offer attractive incentives to retain people, and learners cannot apply classroom lessons to their jobs [28].
3. Digitalization of education in general, not only executive education, should lead to individualized online courses and interactive platforms.

Top management career patterns of globalized companies are deeply rooted in national culture and parent-country employers. International HRM discusses convergence and divergence factors influencing career management and is used for third-country and host-country nationals, arguing that globalization generates a new managerial elite with specific characteristics and career tracks [29]. A piece of evidence signaling such a trend supports two surveys. The first one was done by Davoine and Ravasi [30], who analyzed data about biographies and careers of 916 top managers employed by 111 companies located in France, Germany, Great Britain, and Switzerland. They argue that the national models of career paths erode due to the growing influx of highly educated migrants in the pool of top managers, but this process occurs very slowly regardless of the business internationalization. The second one from Gentry et al. [31] asked 763 participants of leadership development programs from seven different countries (China/Hong Kong, Egypt, India, Singapore, Spain, the United Kingdom, and the United States) their expectations and needs.

They conclude that leaders face similar challenges across countries, and the leadership competencies for becoming successful in all countries primarily cover leading employees, resourcefulness, and change management. They believe that executive education goes through cultural convergence around the world.

Business schools and others interested in the executive education debate whether strategic management can teach or be a part of executive education to future leaders. The concern lies in the problem of how individuals learn strategic thinking. It appears that project-based learning combined with business action learning match job requirements in a highly flexible environment. Goldman [32] investigates the different ways how executives acquire their expertise in strategic thinking. She believes that such a process typically takes more than a decade. An obstacle traditionally exists in dividing responsibilities among organizational units for talent management. Corporate boards have usually left leadership planning and development to their CEOs and human resources departments. Cohn, Khurana, and Reeves [33] recommend that the board of directors and senior executives acutely participate in finding and growing talent. Line managers should accept as a precious source of future leaders based on their contributions to the business performance. In the talent management system, HR departments must create and facilitate HR practices, but the business units must take responsibility for development activities, and the board ultimately needs to oversee the system. One possibility seems to be an integrated service-learning program when participants send in teams to developing countries to work in cross-sector partnerships with NGOs, social entrepreneurs, or international organizations to facilitate learning in six areas: responsible mind-set, ethical literacy, cultural intelligence, global mind-set, self-development, and community building [34].

Based on the desk analysis, approaches to executive education can summarize in the following:

- a project-based approach,
- business driven action learning as a part of management development programs [35],
- individualized learning experience that combines learning and coaching,
- individualized online courses and interactive platforms.

Reid et al. [36] suggest including into an executive education program:

- learning knowledge at a macro-level and doing at a micro-level,
- sharing know-how in pre-determined context-free influences and going to the self-determined context-specific environment,
- providing impersonal access to many subject experts and caring through personal access to one process professional,
- directly taking participants out of themselves and indirectly taking each of them into him/herself,
- giving critical feedback centered on normative standards and offering supportive feedback focused on personalized traits.

3.3 Qualitative Research

Study 1. The focus group comprehends the digitization of education as an online education in which a safe and proven platform is available for the university. The employer allows online teaching and consultations only utilizing MS Teams and doing the course administration, such as informing students, providing materials and testing, by Moodle, eventually the university e-learning system. They see the perspective in video recordings of lectures for regularly repeated subjects with many students, creating test databases for home practice and examinations, and a greater connection between teaching and library databases to prepare textbooks and write articles.

Due to the COVID-19, the number of hours devoted to the online course preparation has increased, as has the scope of individual consultation hours. The subjects with 25 or more students can only lecture online since spring 2020. After more than ten months of online education, there is a noticeable loss of personal contacts, and students lose social skills for teamwork. It becomes evident that self-discipline is essential for teachers regarding whether and how they use teaching and publishing time. On the part of students, the concern is their motivation to learn and not circumvent their knowledge evaluation requirements. Instead, they seem to be predominantly trying to abuse online teaching freedom, passively and formally joining online lectures and exercises, and technical ICT problems are a common excuse for anonymity (with the camera closed and the microphone turned off). The requirements regarding knowledge are gradually decreasing. It turns out that they do not have developed communication skills, such as an appropriate self-presentation or a written style.

From the beginning of online teaching, the university provided technical support and training for lecturers on providing distance education. Students have access to the high-speed Internet at the university and dormitories, but in the days of the COVID-19 provisions, Czech students are mostly outside these areas.

They perceive the improvement of the quality of online teaching if it can apply blending learning. However, subjects that have been standardized for a long time need to be digitally refined to a professional level, i.e., equipped with audio–video aids replacing printed texts. Teachers see several opportunities in distance learning; they notice that they can provide their subjects regardless of time and space, i.e., in the regime 24/7. Some of them, mostly workers 50+ , see the risks in the non-ergonomic arrangement of their home workplace, intensifying musculoskeletal disorders, and rising or deepening eye caries.

Teachers with a background in business at managerial positions, eventually cooperating on a long-term basis as business consultants, are competent to create and participate in executive education. They believe in combining academic knowledge, which is systemic and oriented toward long-term horizons, with expectations of what and how to teach in an unknown environment. Three lecturers participated in MBA programs or corporate programs for senior managers. They assume that university executive education creates a challenge for cooperation between a university and business after the pandemic. They consider it necessary to offer the program in English, be multinational, and use action learning through team projects. They prefer full-time teaching, especially training soft skills. One obstacle exists if a Czech university can attract enough applicants. They believe that attractiveness will depend on lecturers known for their business results and having international experience.

Narrative case 1. Pavel, 57, managing partner, a multinational consultancy firm specialized in human resource development. The headquarters stands in Portugal, and subsidiaries are in seven European countries and five outside Europe. The consultancy focuses on corporate training and development, coaching, appraisal interviews, and designing competency models. Each subsidiary can rely on support from the headquarters and utilize international know-how in soft skills. The Czech branch provides services to clients located in the CR, Slovakia, and partly German-speaking countries.

Pavel has been cooperating with Czech universities since the early 1990s in teaching full-time students, in MBA programs, and HR Academies. It compares the approaches and the content of teaching at universities with corporate practice, for which he trains and coaches employees, senior, and top managers. Even though, no experience with an executive education program at a Czech university, he is slightly optimistic that Czech universities, which have a position up to 500th in the QS rating, can become attractive for corporate clients in the CEE region networks know-how of local specifics. He sees the main challenge in how well universities master such a program's marketing and convinces CEOs and HR directors of its benefits. Large Czech companies and branches of multinational enterprises primarily use their corporate university and career development systems. They look at business schools in the Central and Eastern European regions with skepticism regarding their business knowledge across borders. Based on his long-term cooperation with universities and knowledge of the corporate environment, he is ready to prepare teaching aids for executive education, train (traditionally or online), and provide individual consultations in soft skills. In online education, its clients prefer ZOOM or Google Meet because they have technical complications or encounter limited MS Teams functionality when participants are outside of the organizing institution.

Narrative case 2. Karel, 58, is the director and owner of a dairy industry's trading company, producing conventional and organic food. For more than ten years, he was the managing director of a medium-sized dairy and the managing director of a company engaged in processing secondary raw materials in the dairy sector. Since 2001, he focuses on production and trade in the food industry and HRM of small and medium-sized companies. He completed education for coaching, emphasizing human resources, civic issues, primary and pre-school education. He is also active in promoting Czech producers' business interests in the Arab world as a consultant and direct trade.

Karel has been cooperating with universities since 2003 in educating students in managing small and medium-sized manufacturing companies in the dairy industry. From a practical point of view, he tries to simulate the management of small and medium-sized companies. The emphasis places on executive education regarding skills necessary for expanding opportunities for business partners, subordinates, and consumers who have some relationship to the company's operations. The principle of his coaching and motivation to work is: "the wider the knowledge, skills, abilities, overview, and education of the business partner and employees, the greater the mutual opportunity because it creates more space for" joint profit." The implementation of the principle mentioned above means sharing the advantage achieved, eventually, moving forward, and spreading joint combined efforts to a greater good breadth. Universities' role in society as irreplaceable institutions, according to him, is that mediate learners' orientation in a dynamically changing environment teaches changes in perception and negotiation. He witnesses that companies often have very balanced technical equipment based on digitalization, but their human capital is directed unilaterally to short-term profit. He sees the future executive education as to how to transfer global knowledge by blended learning and developing soft skills, which have proven to be timeless for sustainable development, protection of achieved material values, and respect for life diversity. He tends to trust Czech universities, especially those rated by the international community among the top 500 QS ratings. However, time will prove whether they can prepare and implement executive education capable of withstanding the growing competition among HEIs.

4 Conclusion

Universities strive to differentiate their services and optimize resources to achieve competitiveness in the global education market. They move from traditional teaching toward approaches based on project management, action learning, and interaction with digital tools. The challenge for them exists in how to design and provide executive education. Corporate boards have usually left leadership planning and development to their CEOs and human resources departments when preferring corporate academies and consultancy firms instead of universities. Any other concern includes how and what to learn the future leaders. Globalized business means that leaders face similar challenges regardless of the country, and leadership competencies are converging, primarily stressing to lead employees, ensure resources and manage changes. Executive education requires developing strategic thinking and soft skills. Effective teaching methods become project-based learning, action learning, individualized learning combined with coaching and providing individualized courses, in person or blended learning. In the CR, executive education designed by a Czech university is at the beginning. Credibility for its mastering is seen in university position in QS ratings and closed cooperation with business.

References

1. Matt, C., Hess, T., & Benlian, A. (2015). Digital transformation strategies. *Business & Information Systems Engineering, 57*(5), 339–343.
2. Fedorova, A., Koropets, O., Kacane, I., Eremenko, G., & Ovchinnikov, A. (2020). Digitalization of educational and managerial processes in higher school: Challenges faced by academic staff. In B. L. G. Chova, A. L. Martinez & I. C. Torres (Eds.), *INTED Proceedings (INTED2020), International Academy of Technology, Education and Development* (pp. 3449–3455).
3. Paton, S., Chia, R., & Burt, G. (2014). Relevance or "relevate"? How university business schools can add value through reflexively learning from strategic partnerships with business. *Management Learning, 45*(3), 267–288.
4. Tushman, M. L., O'Reilly, C. A., Fenollosa, A., Kleinbaum, A. M., & McGrath, D. (2007). Relevance and rigor: Executive education as a lever in shaping practice and research. *Academy of Management Learning & Education, 6*(3), 345–362.
5. Armstrong, S. J., & Sadler-Smith, E. (2008). Learning on demand, at your own pace, in rapid bite-sized chunks: The future shape of management development? *Academy of Management Learning & Education, 7*(4), 571–586.
6. CARRINGTONCRISP. Retrieved November 23, 2020, from https://www.carringtoncrisp.com/intelligence/executive-education-futures.
7. Maranville, S., & Uecker, W. (2008). Lifelong learning for managers. The business of executive education. A case study of a small university providers. In C. Wankel, R. DeFillippi (Eds.), *University and corporate innovations in lifelong learning (research in management education and development)* (pp. 213–236). Information Age Publishing, Charlotte, NC.
8. Doh, J. P., & Stumpf, S. A. (2007). Executive education: A view from the top. *Academy of Management Learning & Education, 6*(3), 388–400.
9. Warner, K. S. R., & Wager, M. (2019). Building dynamic capabilities for digital transformation: An ongoing process of strategic renewal. *Long Range Planning, 52*(3), 326–349.
10. Zhu, K., Dong, S. T., Xu, S. X., & Kraemer, K. L. (2006). Innovation diffusion in global contexts: Determinants of post-adoption digital transformation of European companies. *European Journal of Information Systems, 15*(6), 601–616.
11. Nambisan, S., Wright, M., & Feldman, M. (2019) The digital transformation of innovation and entrepreneurship: Progress, challenges and key themes. *Research Policy, 48*(8), 103773.
12. Bogers, M., Chesbrough, H., & Moedas, C. (2018). Open innovations: Research, practices, and policies. *California Management Research, 60*(2), 5–16.
13. Vial, G. (2019). Understanding digital transformation: A review and a research. *Journal of Strategic Information Systems, 28*(2), 118–144.
14. Moreira, M. A. (2018). Towards the digital university: Where are we and where are we going? *Ried-Revista Iberoamericana de Educacion a Distancia, 21*(2), 25–30.
15. Varela-Prado, C., & Baiget, T. (2012). The future of academic libraries: Uncertainties, opportunities, and challenges. *Investigacion Bibliotecologiga, 26*(56), 115–135.
16. Benavides, L. M. C., Tamayo Arias, J. A., Arango Serna, M. D., Branch Bedoya, J. W., & Burgos, D. (2020). Digital transformation in higher education institutions: a systematic literature review. *Sensors 20*, 3291.
17. Caniglia, G., Luederitz, C., Gross, M., Muhr, M., John, B., Keeler, L. W., von Wehrden, H., Laubichler, M., Wiek, A., & Lang, D. (2017). Transnational collaboration for sustainability in higher education: Lessons from a systematic review. *Journal of Cleaner Production, 168*, 764–779.
18. Jacobson, D., Chapman, R., Ye, C., & Van Os, J. (2017). A project-based approach to executive education. *Decision Sciences Journal of Innovative Education, 15*(1), 42–61.
19. Sa, M. J., & Serpa, S. (2020). The Covid-19 pandemic as an opportunity to foster the sustainable development of teaching in higher education. *Sustainability, 12*(20), 8525.
20. Garcia-Penalvo, F. J., & Corell, A. (2020). The Covid-19: The enzyme of the digital transformation of teaching or the reflection of a methodological and competence crisis in higher education? *Campus Virtuales, 9*(2), 83–98.

21. Rodriguez-Abitia, G., Martinez-Perez, S., Ramirez-Montoya, M. S., & Loper-Caudana, E. (2020). Digital gap in universities and challenges for quality education: A diagnostic study in Mexico and Spain. *Sustainability, 12*(21), 9069.
22. Wuestenwald, T. (2016). Adult learning in executive development programs. *Adult Learning, 27*(2), 68–75.
23. Amdam, R. P. (2020). Creating the new executive: postwar executive education and socialization into the managerial elite. *Management & Organizational History SI.*
24. Innes-Taylor, A. R., Yamazaki, A. K., & Inoue, M. (2019). Leadership and communication in diverse environments for global top executives: a survey of executive education at international business schools. In *2019 IEEE International Professional Communication Conference (ProComm)* (pp. 206–210). IEEE, Aachen, Germany.
25. Hogan, R., & Warrenfeltz, R. (2003). Educating the modern manager. *Academy of Management Learning & Education, 2*(1), 74–84.
26. George, B., Sims, P., McLean, A.N., & Mayer, D. (2007). Discovering your authentic leadership. *Harvard Business Review, 85*(2), 129.
27. Yorks, L., Beechler, S., & Ciporen, R. (2007). Enhancing the impact of an open-enrollment executive program through assessment. *Academy of Management Learning & Education, 6*(3), 310–320.
28. Akrofi, S. (2016). Evaluating the effects of executive learning and development on organizational performance: Implications for developing senior manager and executive capabilities. *International Journal of Training and Development, 20*(3), 177–199.
29. Moldoveanu, M., & Narayandas, D. (2019). The future of leadership development. *Harvard Business Review 97*(2), 40.
30. Poór, J., Engle, A. D., Kovács, I. É., Morley, M. J., Kerekes, K., Slavic, A., Berber, N., Juhász, T., Zaharie, M., Legnerová, K., Dvořáková, Z., Stor, M., Suchodolski, A., Buzády, Z., & Abdrazakova, A. (2020). Multinationals and the evolving contours of their human management practices in Central and Eastern Europe and the former Soviet Union. *Employee Relations, 42*(3), 582–608.
31. Davoine, E., & Ravasi, C. (2013). The relative stability of national career patterns in European top management careers in the age of globalisation: A comparative study in France/Germany/Great Britain and Switzerland. *European Management Journal, 31*(2), 152–163.
32. Gentry, W. A., Eckert, R. H., Munusamy, V. P., Stawiski, S. A., & Martin, J. L. (2014). The needs of participants in leadership development programs: A qualitative and quantitative cross-country investigation. *Journal of Leadership & Organizational Studies, 21*(1), 83–101.
33. Goldman, E. F. (2007). Strategic thinking at the top. *MIT Sloan Management Review, 48*(4), 75.
34. Cohn, J. M., Khurana, R., & Reeves, L. (2005). Growing talent as if your business depended on it. *Harvard Business Review, 83*(10), 62.
35. Pless, N. M., Maak, T., & Stahl, G. K. (2011). Developing responsible global leaders through international service-learning programs: The Ulysses experience. *Academy of Management Learning & Education, 10*(2), 237–260.
36. Robertson, J., & Bell, D. (2017). Safe or unsafe? The paradox of action learning. *Action Learning, 14*(2), 185–196.

The Challenges of Digitalization of the Teaching/Learning Process During Covid-19

Dzintra Iliško, Ilze Kačāne, and Jeļena Badjanova

Abstract At present teachers are facing a number of challenges caused by the reform processes in education that require acquisition of new competencies. Digital competence, that includes both technical skills needed to manage the software and cognitive skills that are related to education, has been gradually introduced in the curricula over the past decade. Teachers' digital competence includes the ability to use technologies efficiently, developing digital content and inspiring students to work in a digital environment. This also requires a wider conceptualization of digital competence in the context of re-conceptualization of flexible learning. The methodology employed in this study is three focus group interviews with forty-three teachers of comprehensive and vocational schools in Latvia on their experience in integrating digital technologies into the remote teaching process during the emergency situation due to coronavirus disease COVID-19 from March until June 2020. The study focuses on digital transformations in education process at schools in Latvia and is aimed at exploring difficulties and challenges faced by teachers while ensuring remote teaching/learning process. COVID-19 was a big push towards the introduction and wider usage of technologies into education process that also greatly impacted the level of pressure and stress experienced by educators due to the demand to adapt to urgent and swift shift.

Keywords Digital competence · Digital society · Transformation of education system

D. Iliško (✉) · I. Kačāne · J. Badjanova
Daugavpils University, Vienības iela 13, Daugavpils LV-5401, Latvia
e-mail: dzintra.ilisko@du.lv

I. Kačāne
e-mail: ilze.kacane@du.lv

J. Badjanova
e-mail: jelena.badjanova@du.lv

E. Zaramenskikh and A. Fedorova (eds.), *Digitalization of Society, Economics and Management*, Lecture Notes in Information Systems and Organisation 53,
https://doi.org/10.1007/978-3-030-94252-6_26

1 Introduction

Digital competence is one of the EU priorities highlighted in many strategic European and national policy documents and is seen as crucial for accelerating human progress, developing knowledge (digital) societies, transprofessionalism, as well as for ensuring qualitative, inclusive, accessible, equitable quality education. [1–6] In the framework of transforming reality of a digital economy in the EU it has been stated that 98% of workplaces require employees to have basic digital skills [7]. Digital competence includes such areas as information and data literacy (evaluation of digital content, managing content data, interacting via digital technologies, engaging through digital technologies), digital content creation (developing digital content, copyright issues), safety (protecting personal data and well-being), problem solving (solving technical problems, using digital devices creatively) [8–10].

As an aggregate of knowledge, skills and attitudes digital competence is necessary for a responsible use of digital technologies in education [11]. Being a transversal skill that needs to be upgraded throughout one's lifetime, it envisages a confident and multiform employment of technologies for solving teaching/learning problems at school [12], as well as contributes to the processes of designing digital content for enhancing pupils' learning in e-environment [13]. Integration of technologies, tools and digital content as part of whole class, group and individual student allows teachers to involve learners in a collaborative problem-based learning and deal with complex real-life questions in digital learning ecosystems which promote "diversified, hybrid, fertile and dynamic learning environments" [14].

The need for digitization of the education process has been defined in Latvia's long-term strategic document "Latvia's Sustainable Development Strategy until 2030" [15]. It has also been emphasized in the framework of the reform project "Competency Based Curriculum" or Skola2030 (2016–2021)-oriented towards modernization of education and implemented by the National Centre for Education. The project focusses on strengthening the importance of interdisciplinarity, transversal skills (including digital and media transversal competence, mathematics and ICT, etc. [16]), and mutual cooperation among teachers in planning a learning process. Currently, Skola2030 defines such transversal competencies as critical thinking, problem solving, entrepreneurship, self-directed learning, cooperation, citizenship competence, and digital skills, thus, digitalization of a teaching/learning process has been declared a focal point of a competency-based approach in education [17].

The long-awaited transformation towards digitization was accelerated by coronavirus disease COVID-19 when the situation changed drastically over few weeks. Following the global tendencies regarding the possibility to limit the spread of COVID-19, on March 12, 2020, the emergency situation was announced in Latvia [18] and the decision was adopted to suspend in-class learning in all educational institutions, as well as all kind of teaching/learning processes outside the educational institutions and to provide teaching/learning remotely [19]. Ministry of Education and Science of Latvia (MES) initially suggested appointing a 2-week distance learning period from March 23 up to April 6, 2020 (after spring holidays), which later was prolonged till July 31, allowing the learners who were getting ready for national or qualification examinations to have face-to-face consultations with their teachers after the emergency situation was cancelled, i.e. from June 10, 2020 [20].

According to the survey data on self-perception of digital literacy [21], 30% of teachers have a high level of digital skills, while 30% have a medium level of knowledge, and 30% of teachers have low level of digital literacy. Although MES acknowledged the need to improve teachers' digital skills, this rapid "turning-point" has been a challenge for them.

On July 28, 2020, the Cabinet of Ministers of Latvia confirmed the amendments to the regulations offered by MES regulating the epidemiological security measures taken for limiting COVID-19, allowing to return to in-class studies when starting a new academic year, on September 1, 2020 [22], which among teachers raised positive hopes that they could return to their usual pre-crisis classroom space. However, there still remains a question whether such returning to the "old normal" is in general possible under the new conditions, or whether today the improvement of contemporary teachers' professional qualification is more urgently required than before not only by the reform of education system (the case of Latvia), but also, and especially markedly, by the radical changes in functioning and communication mechanisms of the world. The aim of the study is to explore difficulties and challenges faced by teachers while ensuring remote teaching/learning process under the COVID-19 circumstances.

2 Methodology

To obtain in-depth understanding of the issue from purposely selected group of individuals the research methodology was based on the qualitative research approach. The challenges of digitalization of the teaching/learning process and difficulties faced by teachers while ensuring remote teaching/learning process were explored via three focus group interviews with comprehensive and vocational school teachers in Latvia. The study took place in August–September, 2020 in response to the global COVID-19 pandemic and was oriented towards the investigation of the ways it fostered digital transformations in education process at schools. In total, forty-three teachers participated in focus group interviews. Two focus group interviews were carried out virtually and one took place in a real-life classroom environment. Among the participants 80% were female and 20%—male respondents. Majority of them (90%) were from urban schools and 10%—from rural schools. The interviewees represented the age group from 30 to 45. Three of the participants were involved in the school administrative work. The key themes that emerged from the focus group interviews with teachers are as follows: the access to and use of ICTs, teachers' professional development and digital competence, teachers' emotional well-being.

3 Research Findings

During the emergency situation due to coronavirus disease COVID-19, learner-centred educational strategy was applied in teaching/learning process revealing the need for re-conceptualization of flexible pedagogy [23]. The pandemic paved the way for the implementation of a self-directed learning process challenging learners to develop their motivation, become more independent, self-disciplined, self-confident and aim-oriented [24]. According to the study on implementation of remote teaching/learning during the first two weeks of emergency situation due to COVID-19 pandemic in Latvia [25], pupils' reactions were polarised: from complete satisfaction with a self-directed learning process at home to frustration having resulted from their inability to perform well without teachers' directed teaching and complete lack of socialization opportunities with their peers at school. Based on the survey, teachers (86%) reported they had managed to continue teaching reasonably well and were devoted to designing interdisciplinary tasks and new digital materials to avoid a fragmentation of a learning process. However, by the end of the study year, as the focus group discussions testified to, teachers' optimism deteriorated.

3.1 The Access to and Use of ICTs

Trying to resolve the problem of ensuring a remote teaching/learning process during a crisis situation, each learner's individual situation (access to Internet and smart equipment) was assessed via a questionnaire survey carried out in 625 out of 702 basic and secondary education institutions by MES. The outcomes of the survey allowed concluding that learners' families, especially low income and large families, are not adequately equipped with computer technologies: about 3% or 5000 learners in Latvia didn't have either a computer or a smartphone with internet connection available at home, thus, they couldn't adequately participate in the remote teaching/learning process. Learners were gradually supplied with smart devices (smartphones and tablets) by involving state institutions, local governments and private partners in this work.

However, the capacity of schools to ensure the remote teaching/learning process was also different. The teachers from schools that are digitally well-equipped and who have been trained to use digital technologies confirmed that it was relatively easy for them to continue teaching remotely, whereas the teachers from schools without a strong digitalization policy found it much more difficult to make a transition to an online environment: "At the beginning I experienced a complete shock how to deal with a new situation, but gradually, with the assistance of the ICT teacher, I learned a number of useful technologies for my work." Some teachers reported the lack of technologies or having very outdated equipment thus they were required to individually obtain new devices.

All participants stated that among the crucial aspects were accessibility of ICTs and students' autonomy—skills to set goals, manage time, and avoid distractions. Contemporary learners are "digital natives" whose life revolves around media [26, p. 12, 27]; by handling digital devices since their very birth, the use of digital technologies has become normality for them, however due to lack of direct contact the notion of "indoor child" [28, p. 15] becomes relevant. The teachers were of the same opinion that since their early childhood contemporary learners have been surrounded by different kind of devices, however they have been unequally equipped. The teachers who were dealing with children from disadvantaged and large families had to find an individual approach to ensure their inclusion into the learning process: "I came to realize that there are children who do not have a regular access to internet and who do not have proper technologies to joint online learning environment." Children from well-to-do families also needed an individual approach as they "do not integrate technologies in a meaningful way as well." Not all pupils were motivated for a self-directed learning: "There are evident differences in capacities of students in their resilience and motivation for a self-directed learning."

Initially, schools provided weekly teaching materials and hand-outs for the families who were not able to participate in a remote learning process due to the lack of necessary equipment. Since availability of digital technologies constituted an issue for some pupils a viable solution to rent the equipment with the support of stakeholders was found by schools. Almost all teachers pointed to inequalities implicit in the process of implementing a remote learning and indicated that local municipalities provided the necessary support in solving this issue: "They involved multiple stakeholders in providing necessary technological support for pupils from the disadvantaged families to carry out their homework."

The teachers had to adapt digitally flexible approaches that were suitable for a new online teaching/learning environment. They mentioned diverse digital channels and platforms used for creating a digital content, as well as in teaching their pupils and their own learning process when attending online courses or training. They referred to multiple internet sites for finding and selecting digital sources and after assessing the appropriateness of the material they also ensured that the usage of ICTs has added value. The teachers used both internet-based synchronous and asynchronous activities in organizing their teaching but always relying on the learner's own responsibility: "We as teachers have to trust pupils to organize their learning environment themselves in a more self-directed way."

Many teachers admitted that it was also important to provide timely and accurate feedback and support for their learners in developing personalized learning. In addition, the teachers had to be sensitive to the needs of their learners: "I tried to organize flexible learning schedule, and also displayed high levels of empathy, care and understanding." While transiting to an online teaching/learning process, the teachers simultaneously had to facilitate relationships with learners in online settings. According to the teachers, the most efficient was a mixed type of teaching that combined both live teaching and teacher-guided discussion and activities that didn't require a teacher's presence online, i.e. online tasks and a teacher's generated material. Still, a teacher's presence, on-going communication and reflective feedback provided learners with a general sense of the meaning and purpose.

During the months of the emergency situation, the teachers had to undertake the role of a designer of a teaching process and a creator of new online materials; they needed to accept the role of the evaluator of the pupil's learning experience and a role of a mediator and communicator with pupils' parents. Evident differences have been observed in the amount of support pupils received from their families and in capacities of schools to support children while learning remotely.

3.2 Teachers' Professional Development and Digital Competence

A day after the announcement of the emergency situation, MES published several possible variants of implementing a teaching/learning process remotely, pointing out that the communication with parents and pupils should also take place via the online platforms available at the education institution (e-class, Mykoob.lv, WhatsApp, e-mail, etc.), if this is also possible for a family [29]. To ensure a reliable connectivity for study purposes, file and synchronization platforms GoogleDrive, DropBox, educational portals eduspace.lv, classflow.com, e-class, mykoob.lv, soma.lv, uzdevumi.lv, etc., were offered. The teachers simultaneously had to develop teaching materials in the form they would be accessible also to learners who did not have Internet or smart equipment. Consequently, apart from basic knowledge acquired during studies in the higher education institution, innovative and new competences, skills and abilities, being in little demand or passive until now were urgently required.

The interviewed teachers emphasized their participation in a great number of professional development activities. Among various workshops, the teachers mentioned mastering ICT skills and experimenting with web-based activities, which allowed them to learn the ways of how to integrate technologies and tools into the teaching/learning process. Among the newly acquired online networks, there were the following tools and platforms mentioned: WhatsApp groups, Zoom, Cisco Webex, Moodle, Google Classroom, Microsoft Office 365 Teams, Mykoob, Google Docs, etc.

Learning innovative technologies has been a serious challenge for the teachers who used to work in a traditional environment: "For me the process of acquiring teaching/learning technologies is quite slow and difficult. I have to invest a lot of time that is accompanied with extra stress and immense dosage of patience. But I understand that there is no chance to stay in the past, I need to move forward." Those teachers who previously had not felt a necessity of integrating ICTs in their work were forced to accept the format of remote teaching/learning. In order to improve their digital competence, they had to master the technologies in a very compressed time frame. The teachers needed more time to reflect on and to adjust to technology-based learning approaches. All who participated in focus group interviews acknowledged that currently schools are undergoing extensive digital transformations in order to meet the needs of the younger generation and the digitalized future. They also admitted that this is more complicated for the older teachers to meet this challenge.

3.3 Teachers' Emotional Well-Being

Emotional wellbeing is an important aspect in teachers' personal and professional lives [29]. A great number of researchers discuss well-being as a vital component of teacher's daily performance and everyday work [30–32]. The concept of well-being includes not only coping with negative emotions, but satisfaction with life, working conditions, purpose in life and the meaningfulness of taken actions. Teachers' self-efficacy is linked to their wellbeing, therefore support for maintaining balance and mental well-being should be provided and defensive strategies adopted [33, 34].

The disruption caused by the COVID-19 influenced teachers' daily routine, emotional well-being, personal safety and health, consequently, teachers' performance, and student outcomes. Restrictions imposed by the government affected the availability of and access to safe and quality services. Social isolation, mobility restrictions, instability in employment and financial income impacted teachers' emotional well-being resulting in the increased feeling of frustration.

The interviewed administrators of schools commented that the teachers experienced enormous double or even triple workload during the lockdown in the months of the emergency situation: "Teachers were engaged in preparing lessons, giving feedback, answering queries from students and parents and fulfilling many other duties that have caused enormous burn-out among teachers." The teachers had to work in new circumstances that caused the increased level of stress and anxiety among the teachers; this left a negative impact on their socio-emotional well-being. Schools were required to enhance a school-wide well-being policy by enchaining positive emotions and relationships in order to decrease teachers' burnout and depression which was impacting teachers' performance and consequently was affecting relationships with learners and their families.

School administrators also emphasized the crucial importance of providing the necessary support for the teaching staff: "It is particularly essential to listen to the needs of teachers, their perspectives by providing a space to voice difficulties and opportunities in relation to implementing remote teaching process. It is important to provide teachers with the opportunities to express their anxiety and worries in order to find viable solutions." The teachers confirmed they are in acute need for emotional support in dealing with uncertain situations. According to the teachers from the focus groups, their workload increased up to extra 15–20 h per week. While providing emotional support to their pupils and their families, the teachers had to overcome their own anxiety and stress. The teachers were striving to schedule the time for their own children who were left neglected and suffered emotional detachment. During the focus group interviews, they complained about their inability to manage work and family balance that left impact not only on their own but all family members' emotional well-being. Extra working hours during the emergency situation made it hard to stay mindful, therefore practice of mindfulness to reduce stress and obtain emotional calmness was necessary.

4 Conclusion

The comprehensiveness and accuracy of the obtained data was reached by careful disclosure of the meaning and essence of the issue of study derived from the analyses of focus group interviews with the teachers. The teachers' experience may be regarded as authentic since they were sharing their experience with each other and the researchers allowed every teacher's voice to emerge, thus creating "heteroglossia not only by collaborating together but also by juxtaposing and interacting with pedagogies of places and cultural artifacts." [35, pp. 14–15] The participants were engaged in the study as co-researchers to produce a reflective journey about their experience of the use of ICTs during remote teaching/learning process.

The COVID-19 brought a huge challenge to education and highlighted the digital deficit and issues in education in regards to teachers' skills, attitudes and actual preparedness. Through the remote teaching/learning process, the global pandemic has speeded up digitalization in Latvia's schools. Although the government of Latvia issued the regulations for schools to make a transition to a remote teaching almost overnight, the teachers needed time to address the availability of ICTs, make a decision on the preferred online networks or platforms and master them, design digital contents, carry out students' assessment, and support learners' emotional well-being. Listed among the top competencies of the twenty-first century, a transversal digital competence has been in acute need to master other competencies such as communication, language skills and others.

Under the COVID-19 circumstances when to provide equal opportunities for all learners without creating a risk of not participating in the learning process became especially essential, it was much easier to shift to a new reality for those educators who had already mastered the use of modern technologies. Technologies strengthened their position in the field of education. Many teachers, however, faced problems not only due to the issues related to learners' personal/domestic circumstances (e.g. poor internet connection, parents' socio-economic status to afford devices), insufficient pedagogical skills of work with modern technologies, but also to their own psychological and emotional preparedness to carry out the expected tasks. The carried out research revealed that measures need to be taken to ensure equal access to ICTs, improvement of digital competence for the teachers enabling them to create the digital content, ensuring the teachers' well-being.

After the months of remote teaching almost all schools have figured out their ways of providing the education process. Technically equipped online environment serves as a catalyst for the teachers to experiment and to reflect on their current practices in order to meet the needs of a contemporary generation. Higher education establishments need to invest time in the teachers' professional development by providing advanced technology and psychological training.

5 Discussion

Teachers are the major players in the education process and the key in reaching education goals. When the global pandemic hit Latvia the education system was not prepared for the urgent and swift shift in the teaching/learning process. Teachers were left by themselves in decision-making related to problem solving, especially in the first weeks of the emergency situation. A successful integration of ICTs in teaching/learning process largely depended on the teachers' knowledge, skills, and psychological factors and needs (perception, motivation, attitudes). Since the beginning of the pandemic, they have been mastering a number of important competencies, including their digital skills; however, their emotional well-being due to the rising level of anxiety has been affected. The teachers had to perform multitasking and synchronous work at the level unprecedented before by undertaking the functions of learners' mentors, counsellors, and coaches, thus by investing time in work and supporting the well-being of their pupils outside work hours they sacrificed their own well-being. Integration of ICTs into the teaching process enhanced learning opportunities largely based on the teachers' enthusiasm.

Changes and obstacles are inevitable elements of school communities that need to be perceived as opportunities for growth. Current aims and tasks of the reform processes in Latvia's education system were speeded up by the pandemic and it forced the teachers to update their ICT knowledge and transversal skills in a more compressed time. Although hardships like the COVID-19 pandemic make the teachers feel anxious, they can also contribute to a long-term growth. Responding to required changes and unexpected situations with flexibility and adaptability improves the teachers' coping ability. Learning how to function outside one's comfort zone is a healthy and functional way of living and working. This challenge has made the teachers learn new strategies of adaptation and flexibility, which might increase their coping ability in the future, and equipped them with experience in and knowledge on regaining courage, confidence, resilience, creativity in a rapidly changing contemporary world.

Digital transformation of education in general and digitalization of higher education in specific is of great importance: "it is obvious that the ongoing digitalization of higher education on the one hand simplifies and automates the performance of certain work functions of academic staff, and on the other hand presents new requirements for the personal and professional competencies of the teacher." [36, p. 3450] In addition, the teachers' professional development programmes should include subjects providing future teachers with more advanced technology and psychological training. Developing tools for adaptation to the changing needs of learners is recommended to become a part of educators' routine.

On the national level, it is recommended to elaborate a model of psychological and pedagogical support, e.g. a substitute or supply teacher system (the case of Canada) to prevent the teachers' emotional burnout syndrome. This would allow replacing an employed teacher upon a request when needed for a definite number of days per a study year to recover his/her emotional well-being. The ability to have paid days off when physically, emotionally and mentally drained and unable to perform work duties properly, would provide a support system that would result in higher teaching quality. Acknowledging one's personal limits as well as possibilities can provide the teachers with a degree of protection from feeling vulnerable at work. The ability to develop growth mindset will allow the teachers to be self-compassionate when they go through ups and downs while facing changes in education. Being present and mindful are important means for keeping things in perspective.

References

1. EC: EUROPE 2020. (2010). *A strategy for smart, sustainable and inclusive growth.* EUR-Lex Homepage. https://eur-lex.europa.eu/legal-content/en/ALL/?uri=CELEX%3A52010DC2020.
2. UNESCO. (2011). *UNESCO ICT competency framework for teachers.* UNESCO Homepage. Retrieved October 07, 2020, from https://unesdoc.unesco.org/ark:/48223/pf0000213475.
3. UNESCO. (2018). *UNESCO ICT competency framework for teachers.* UNESCO Homepage. Retrieved October 07, 2020, From https://unesdoc.unesco.org/ark:/48223/pf0000265721.
4. UN. (2015). *Resolution adopted by the general assembly on 25 September 2015. Transforming our world: The 2030 agenda for sustainable development*. UN Homepage. Retrieved September 12, 2020, from https://www.un.org/ga/search/view_doc.asp?symbol=A/RES/70/1&Lang=E.
5. EC. (2018). *Communication on the digital education action plan.* The European Union Homepage. Retrieved October 05, 2020, from https://ec.europa.eu/education/education-in-the-eu/digital-education-action-plan_en.
6. CSCC. (2012). *NAP2020: National development plan for 2014–2020.* CSCC Homepage. Retrieved September 52, 2020, from https://www.pkc.gov.lv/lv/attistibas-planosana-latvija/nacionalais-attistibas-plans/nap2020.
7. EC. (2017). ICT for work: Digital skills in the workplace. *DG Communications Networks, Content & Technology*. The European Union Homepage. Retrieved September 23, 2020, from https://ec.europa.eu/digital-single-market/en/news/ict-work-digital-skills-workplace.
8. EU. (2020). *The digital competence framework 2.0.* The European Union Homepage. Retrieved October 05, 2020, from https://ec.europa.eu/jrc/en/digcomp/digital-competence-framework.
9. Ferrari, A. (2013). DIGCOMP: A framework for developing and understanding digital competence in Europe Luxembourg. In Y. Punie, & B. N. Brečko (Eds.), *Publications office of the European Union* . The European Union Homepage. Retrieved September 27, 2020, from https://publications.jrc.ec.europa.eu/repository/bitstream/JRC83167/lb-na-26035-enn.pdf. https://doi.org/10.2788/52966.
10. Falloon, G. (2020). From digital literacy to digital competence: The teacher digital competency (TDC) framework. *Educational Technology Research and Development, 68*, 2449–2472. https://doi.org/10.1007/s11423-020-09767-4
11. Tigelaar, D. E., Dolmans, D. H., Wolfhagen, I. H., & Van der Vleuten, C. P. (2004). The development and validation of a framework for teaching competencies in higher education. *Higher Education, 48*, 253–268. https://doi.org/10.1023/B:HIGH.0000034318.74275.e4
12. Borthwick, A., & Hansen, R. (2017). Digital literacy in teacher education. Are teacher educators competent? *Journal of Digital Learning in Teacher Education, 33*(2), 46–48. https://doi.org/10.1080/21532974.2017.1291249.

13. Dexter, S., Doering, A., & Riedel, E. (2006). Content area specific technology integration: A model for educating teachers. *Journal of Technology and Teacher Education, 14*(2), 325–345.
14. Dias-Trindade, S., & Moreira, J. A. (2020). Assessment of high school teachers' on their digital competences. *magis, Revista Internacional de Investigación en Educación, 13*, 1–21. https://doi.org/10.11144/Javeriana.m13.ahst.
15. Saeima. (2010). *Sustainable Development Strategy of Latvia until 2030*. CSCC Homepage. Retrieved September 25, 2020, from https://www.pkc.gov.lv/sites/default/files/inline-files/LIAS_2030_en_0.pdf.
16. Catlaks, G. (2016). Kompetencēs balstīta vispārējā izglītības satura ieviešana standartu un programmu izstrādē mācību priekšmetus ļaus integrēt un apvienot. Retrieved October 11, 2020, from http://www.kimijas-sk.lv/index.php/viedokli/item/1166-jauna-macibu-satura-reforma-lausmacibu-prieksmetus-apvienot.
17. Skola2030 Homepage. Retrieved October 10, 2020, from https://www.skola2030.lv/lv.
18. Cabinet of Ministers. (2020). Republic of Latvia Cabinet Order No. 103 Adopted 12 March 2020 Regarding Declaration of the Emergency Situation. Likumi Homepage. Retrieved September 29, 2020, from https://likumi.lv/ta/en/en/id/313191-regarding-declaration-of-the-emergency-situation.
19. MK: Grozījumi Ministru kabineta 2020. gada 12. marta rīkojumā Nr. 103 Par ārkārtējās situācijas izsludināšanu. Ministru kabineta rīkojums Nr. 105. Ministru kabineta noteikumi Nr. 105, 2020. gada 14. marts. Likumi Homepage. Retrieved September 29, 2020, from https://likumi.lv/ta/id/313216-grozijumi-ministru-kabineta-2020-gada-12-marta-rikojuma-nr-103-par-arkartejas-situacijas-izsludinasanu.
20. MK. (2020). Epidemioloģiskās drošības pasākumi Covid-19 infekcijas izplatības ierobežošanai. Ministru kabineta noteikumi Nr. 360, 2020. gada 9. jūnijs. Likumi Homepage. Retrieved September 30, 2020, from https://likumi.lv/ta/id/315304-epidemiologiskas-drosibas-pasakumi-covid-19-infekcijas-izplatibas-ierobezosanai.
21. Šuplinska. (2020). Attālinātās mācības ir milzīgs grūdiens tehnoloģiju ienākšanai izglītībā. TVNET Homepage. Retrieved September 09, 2020, from https://www.tvnet.lv/6971671/suplinska-attalinatas-macibas-ir-milzigs-grudiens-tehnologiju-ienaksanai-izglitiba.
22. MK. (2020). Grozījumi Ministru kabineta. gada 9. jūnija noteikumos Nr. 360 Epidemioloģiskās drošības pasākumi Covid-19 infekcijas izplatības ierobežošanai. Ministru kabineta noteikumi Nr. 460, 2020. gada 28. jūlijs. Likumi Homepage. Retrievd September 30, 2020, from https://likumi.lv/ta/id/316384-grozijumi-ministru-kabineta-2020-gada-9-junija-noteikumos-nr-360-epidemiologiskas-drosibas-pasakumi-covid-19-infekcijas-izplati.
23. Huang, R. H., Liu, D. J., Tlili, A., Yang, J. F., & Wang, H. H. (2020). *Handbook on facilitating flexible learning during educational disruption: The Chinese experience in maintaining undisrupted learning in COVID-19 outbreak*. Smart Learning Institute of Beijing Normal University.
24. Muižniece, A. (2020). Izglītība Covid-19 ēnā. Ir. Ir Homepage, Retrieved September 20, 2020, from https://ir.lv/2020/04/15/izglitiba-covid-19-ena/.
25. IZM, Eriduo. (2020). Attālināto mācību pirmās 2 nedēļas. IZM un Edurio aptauju rezultāti. Edurio Homepage Retrieved October 17, 2020, from https://home.edurio.com/izm-attalinato-macibu-rezultati.
26. Sharma, M. (2017). Teacher in a digital era. *Global Journal of Computer Science and Technology: Interdisciplinary, 17*(3), 10–14.
27. Underwood, J. D. M., & Farrington-Flint, L. (2015). *Learning and the E-generation*. West Sussex, Wiley Blackwell.
28. Rubene, Z. (2016). Tehnoloģiju integrēšana izglītībā – izaicinājumi un iespējas izglītībā. Tagad. Latviešu valodas aģentūras (LVA) zinātniski metodisks izdevums, 1(10), 4–8. Retrieved August 29, 2020, from http://www.telerehabilitation.lv/sites/default/files/Tagad_10_16.pdf.
29. IZM. (2020). *Rīki un iespējas mācību nodrošināšanai attālināti*. MES Homepage. Retrieved October 17, 2020, from https://www.izm.gov.lv/lv/aktualitates/3960-riki-un-iespejas-macibu-nodrosinasanai-attalinati.

30. Fernández-Berrocal, P., Gutiérrez-Cobo, M. J., Rodriguez-Corrales, J., & Cabello, R. (2017). Teachers' affective well-being and teaching experience: The protective role of perceived emotional intelligence. *Frontiers in Psychology, 8*. https://doi.org/10.3389/fpsyg.2017.02227.
31. Biron, C., & Karanika, M. (2013). Process evaluation for organizational stress and well-being interventions: Implications for theory, method, and practice. *International Journal of Stress Management, 21*, 85–111. https://doi.org/10.1037/a0033227
32. van Wingerden, J., Bakker, A. B., & Derks, D. (2017). The longitudinal impact of a job crafting intervention. *European Journal of Work Organizational Psychology, 26*(1), 107–119. https://doi.org/10.1080/1359432X.2016.1224233
33. Ryff, C. D. (2014). Psychological well-being revisited: Advances in the science and practice of eudaimonia. *Psychotherapy and Psychosomatic, 83*(1), 10–28. https://doi.org/10.1159/000353263
34. Ryan, R. M., & Huta, V. (2009). Wellness as healthy functioning or wellness as happiness: The importance of eudaimonic thinking (response to the Kashdan et al. and Waterman discussion). *The Journal of Positive Psychology, 4*(3), 202–204. https://doi.org/10.1080/17439760902844285
35. Norris, J., & Sawyer, R. D. (2012). Towards a dialogical methodology. In J. Norris, R. D. Sawyer, & D. Lund (Eds.), *Duoethnography: dialogic methods for social, health, and educational research* (pp. 9–39). Walnut Creek, Left Coast Press.
36. Fedorova, A., Koropets, O., Kacane I., Eremenko, G., & Ovchinnikov A. (2020). Digitalization of educational and managerial processes in higher school: Challenges faced by academic staff. In *14th International Technology, Education and Development Conference, INTED2020 Proceedings* (pp. 3449–3455). Valencia, Spain. https://doi.org/10.21125/inted.2020.0978.

Research on the Level of Soft Skills of the Digital Generation

Elena Vasilieva

Abstract In the context of constant changes, modern organizations need exactly the π-shaped specialists, whose competence is based on professional specialization, breadth of knowledge in various fields, as well as empathy and cooperation skills. The relevance of modern companies in soft skills of employees is emphasized. It is on them that the emphasis should be placed in the educational programs of universities. However, there are number of problems with the perception of information material by young people. The purpose of the study is to determine the competencies that currently need the most development among university students. The results of testing students' soft skills using the methods of assessment of emotional competence (COMET), evaluation of VSQ values and social Pattern Variables (Social Pattern Variables), psychological testing MBTI, analysis of creative types and self-assessment of emotional intelligence EQ Hall are presented. The students showed a fairly high level of emotional self-awareness, creativity, practical emotional intelligence, and communication skills. But they lack self-confidence, imagination, and distal vision, which is important for achieving goals, creative ideas, and innovation. Repeated testing showed that the introduction of design thinking into the educational process allowed students to develop soft skills. So, the rationale for the use of design thinking for the formation of soft skills of specialists is given. The main areas of application of design thinking are identified—when creating an innovative product that is in demand by the consumer (Design Service); for improving the organization's processes and in team building (Employee Experience Management); for personal growth and creativity development "Neuro Design Thinking". The author draws attention to the fact that at present, when managing personnel, it is necessary to analyze and competently plan the employee's path in the company—"Employee Experience". The role of project work during design sessions in obtaining skills of integrative thinking and teamwork skills is emphasized. A project-based approach to training based on design thinking will improve the quality of training, reduce the GAP between the requirements of the labor market and the level of training of university graduates, simplify and speed up the process of adapting young professionals to the

E. Vasilieva (✉)
Financial University Under the Government of the Russian Federation, Moscow 125993, Russia
e-mail: evvasileva@fa.ru

E. Zaramenskikh and A. Fedorova (eds.), *Digitalization of Society, Economics and Management*, Lecture Notes in Information Systems and Organisation 53,
https://doi.org/10.1007/978-3-030-94252-6_27

workplace, prepare full-fledged members of self-organizing project teams, DevOps teams and flexible organizations.

Keywords π-shaped qualifications · Competencies · Flexible skills · Staff training · Human-centered design · Project training · Design thinking · Group work · Creativity

1 Introduction

Student of the future, what is he like? The old methods are getting worse for the students who come to universities today. Today, the word "digital" and related terms and concepts have taken a leading position in our lives. Increasingly, we are faced with various concepts and aspects of the modern digital economy, such as Digital Economy, Digital Transformation, Digital Mindset, Digital Skill, Digital Etiquette, and others. Digital Mindset is a set of habits and approaches to work that allows you to anticipate additional opportunities for the organization and successfully implement them. When applied to modern business, Digital Mindset means understanding how modern technologies, and their use, can help simplify organizational structures and business processes; how to apply this understanding in an organization and derive additional business benefits from it. A person with digital thinking is able to trust the decisions of the machine, quickly delve into the essence of endless streams of information, be able to adapt to changing technologies, etc.

The digital generation, which spends most of its time at the computer, becoming dependent on gadgets, finds it difficult to connect with people in face-to-face communication. There is a social phenomenon of human consciousness, which develops primarily through interaction with other people. The social nature of information is that it is "a reflection of the display of our considerations", as it was defined by the famous scientist Chernavsky [1]. In fact, through information, there is an exchange of acquired, stored in a materialized form of experience. Collective thinking in the information society grows wiser as a person grows older, but faster than the intelligence of one person [2].

The changed style of perception of information material by young people makes it necessary to pay attention to the change of traditional educational technologies. However, there are a number of problems that are not unique to young people.

Constantly being in the information noise, people stop storing a lot of data in their memory, which means that they are less likely to resort to creating associative links between new and existing information, negating their ability to think, logic. And, as a result, they lose their learning skills. The availability of information and the wealth of expert opinions on almost all issues in the Internet environment affects the fact that people do not need to predict possible developments or make forecasts themselves. Accordingly, they lose the ability to form their own vision of the future. And a person without distal vision experiences difficulties in determining the goal. Getting used to getting easy results in his cognitive activity, he becomes not tolerant of failures and risks. And all this, in general, will not work in the best way for the economy, for civilization as a whole.

We are what we watch. But a new problem of our time has already clearly identified itself: visual images have replaced systematic and analytical thinking. Primitive content, which abounds in social networks and online entertainment resources, is easier to perceive, and therefore it is not necessary to make efforts not just to thoughtlessly consume information, but to try to make sense of it.

The situation is complicated by the fact that soft skills cannot be taught in theory by reading a solid volume or watching a video clip. They are developed only through social interaction, in practice. In addition, the skill is developed only in the process of repeated repetition. Therefore, the university, as the main platform for the formation of a worldview and style of thinking, must necessarily place a significant emphasis in its educational programs on the regularity of seminars in which soft skills are mastered.

2 Hard and Soft Skills

Most jobs require different combinations of "hard" skills and "soft" skills. In the workplace today, employees need to process huge amounts of information, be able to manage both virtual assistants and remote teams. Thanks to virtual technologies, the information age, where the economy was dominated by knowledge workers using computer and other electronic devices in sectors such as research, finance, consulting, information technology, etc., created, high-speed Internet and end-to-end technologies, a completely different paradigm. In the list of required competencies by 2020, published at the World Economic Forum in 2016 [3] in the first place are: cognitive abilities and creativity, active learning, emotional intelligence, and the ability to communicate with others, the ability to comprehensively solve problems and critical thinking.

"Hard skills" work in a given context. They are measurable and transferable in the learning process. However, the most important problem is how to form soft skills or competencies in specialists that are necessary in working in an uncertain environment with inaccurate task formulation, as well as allow them to adapt to a changing environment and constantly develop. "Soft skills", such as emotional intelligence, time management, and leadership, are not related to a specific type of activity, but to the ability to effectively build relationships with colleagues, clients, and partners.

Organizations in the new, transforming environment are more likely to benefit from "image-based" professionals, where empathy and collaborative skills are another foundation of their competence [4, 5].

According to Leonard-Barton [6], in the metaphor of "T-shaped" qualification, the top of the letter "T", its horizontal line, is a deep and broad knowledge and skills of a specialist in various fields, and the vertical characterizes his narrow professional specialization, the depth of expertise within his own competence. In the IDEO lab, their specialists are called "T-people", where the horizontal line from the letter "T" is the breadth of their knowledge in various fields, and the vertical line is their specialization [4]. Today, it is more correct to talk about the need for a "π-shaped" competence of specialists [5]. A modern specialist needs professional competencies and soft skills, and especially empathy and willingness to cooperate. Interpersonal competencies are manifested through the ability to express their own and understand other people's feelings and emotions (self-empathy and empathy), serve as the basis for achieving common goals in the course of joint activities [7].

There is no recipe that clearly states how many people and with what level of Soft Skills should work in the company for it to be successful. One thing remains true: the team must have the ability to develop behavioral patterns and thinking styles to ensure the success of the common cause.

Back in the 1960s, Dr. Claire William Graves, an American psychologist who developed the concept of spiral dynamics, changed the way people understand human values. In terms of the "double helix", he reflected the dynamics of development not only of the organization as a system, but also emphasized the importance of changing the range of values of each of its employees. Target memes, like DNA codes, form a worldview, a certain level of psychological existence, a belief structure, and a person's way of thinking [8, 9]. And this worldview changes in the course of life, under the influence of the views of other people, in the process of gaining experience and knowledge about this world. According to Graves [8]: "The value system of managers determines many of the decisions that management will make, and the value system of employees largely determines the reaction that management decisions will make." In order for people's value system to be formed from the correct codes, it is necessary to make every effort to develop empathy, emotional intelligence, creativity, communication, and other soft skills at all stages of their life, and especially during their studies at the university, including based on the methodology of design thinking.

The University is an important base for the formation of the worldview of young people. The transition of a university graduate to the status of a full-fledged employee is one of the most important stages of his life. And here it is important to correctly and timely assess the potential of each student in order to choose the right trajectory for his professional and personal development.

3 The Results of the Survey of Graduate Students

There are many approaches to the system of assessing the readiness of a university graduate for real work, but more and more popular are the measures of his emotional mood, ability to interpersonal communication, creativity, attitude to life in society. In order to understand how bad or good our students are with soft skills, in the period 2019–2020, we tested the undergraduates of the Business Informatics department of the Financial University. A total of 53 people participated in the study. The average age is from 20 to 22 years. The tests used the methods of assessment of emotional competence (COMET), assessment of VSQ values and social pattern variables (Social Pattern Variables), psychological testing MBTI, analysis of creative types of creative types and self-assessment of emotional intelligence EQ Hall. All tests are available on the relevant resources for free. The results are shown in Figs. 1, 2, 3 and 4. It should be noted that a group of first-year students of BI20 passed the test in 2020 and just started studying on our educational program. The BI19 group was tested in the 1st year and repeated in the second year, close to the end of their studies at our university. This group was the first to study and apply the design thinking approach throughout their Master's studies in various disciplines, with warm-ups held at seminars, and tasks aimed at developing soft skills—empathy, collaboration, creativity, and so on. A group of second-year students (BI18) was tested in 2019 by the end of the training. In their training program, the emphasis on soft skills was not so pronounced. This was reflected in the final assessments of competencies.

The emotional competence assessment methodology allows you to conduct a self-assessment using the 360° feedback tool, based on the COMET methodology. This questionnaire is based on many years of research by Patrick E. K. Merlevede, Denis Bridoux, and others, which they lead to the books "7 Steps to Emotional Intelligence" [10] and "Mastering Mentoring & Coaching with Emotional Intelligence" [11]. You can take the test on the website JobEQ.net [12]. In the same place, the site presents a range of points calculated based on the results of the responses of the people who have already answered, who make up the control group (red zone). The average value of the degree of competence that make up the red zone is the typical responses of 66% of the total number of people tested. Note that most of the group consists of

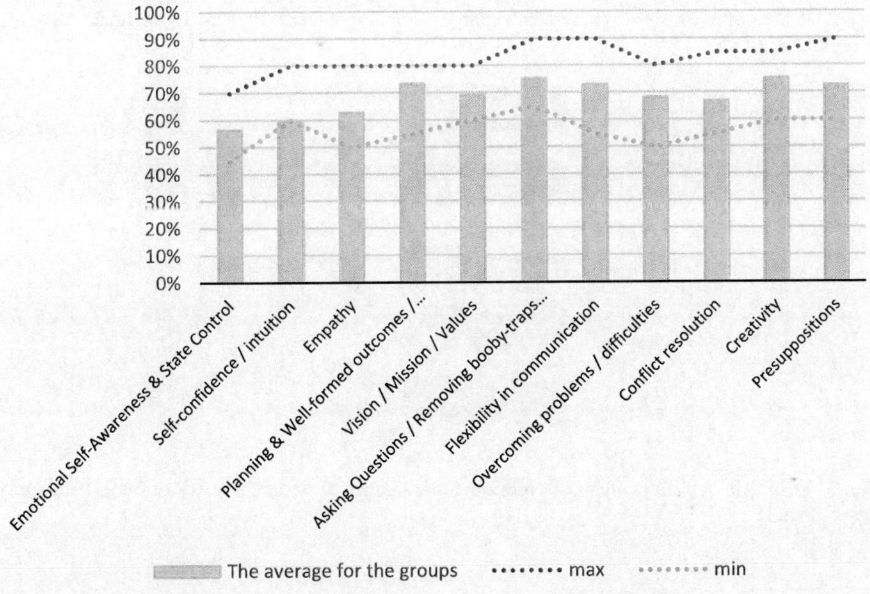

Fig. 1 Results of the self-assessment of emotional competencies of undergraduates on the COMET questionnaire

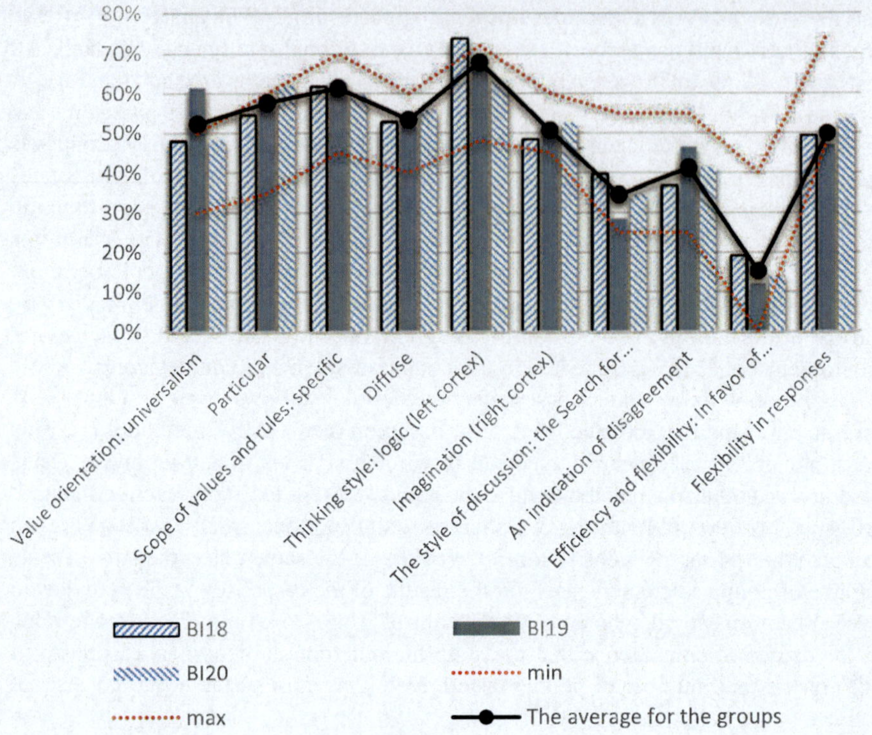

Fig. 2 Results of measurement of typical variables of undergraduates on the VSQ Section 2: "Social Pattern Variables"

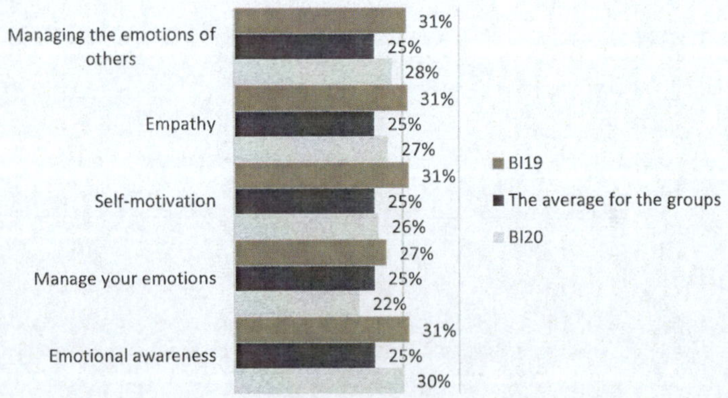

Fig. 3 Results of self-assessment of emotional intelligence of undergraduates of the 1st and 2nd years of study

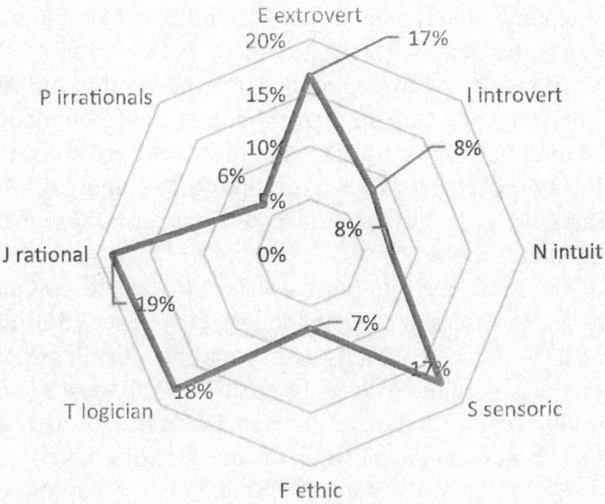

Fig. 4 Myers-Briggs personality type test results (MBTI): 16 Myers-Briggs personality types (MBTI)—total

citizens of Belgium, where jobEQ researchers tested more than 70,000 people [13]. The obtained self-assessment is compared with the responses of the control group. According to the developers of this questionnaire, people who get 17% points lower than the control group have the lowest degree of competence, and 17% higher—the highest. A score that falls in the center of the red zone indicates an "average" level of competence. Note that people with high emotional intelligence experience less stress, are healthier, work better, and generally have a higher quality of life.

Undergraduates on average showed a high level of emotional self-awareness, creativity, practical emotional intelligence and are able to communicate and negotiate with others.

The level of "Emotional Self-Awareness & State Control"—shows the maturity of awareness of one's own emotions and emotional choices. A person with this competence can name the emotions that they are experiencing, can deal with this emotion (for example, find out what a message about a negative emotion is, and deal with it), and even consciously choose what emotional state to be in.

Practical emotional intelligence ("Presuppositions") is the ability to adapt to the surrounding conditions and create your own psychological space. In everyday life, this ability is extremely in demand, because it helps to make a choice.

People who have received high scores for the Creativity competence are open to new experiences and new ideas, are attuned to different ways of realizing their dreams, and are always eager to learn.

Communication between people is an art, and it can be hindered by various misunderstandings. A person who has received a high score for the competence "Asking Questions/Removing booby-traps from Communication" has the skills to ask the necessary questions to smooth out the roughness in communication, takes adequate precautions to minimize any misunderstandings.

Experience is subjective, and the perception of the external environment changes depending on how we talk about it with other people. A person who is flexible in communication (competence “Flexibility in Communication”) can adapt to the style of his interlocutor.

Although the average value for the groups of students in the category Self-confidence and trust in their intuition (“Self-confidence/Intuition”) coincided with the minimum value (the lower border of the red zone, in Fig. 1, is a series of “Min”). But in the category of positive thinking (“Planning & Well-formed outcomes/Positive Thinking”), the guys approached the upper border of the red zone (in Fig. 1, this is the “Max” row).

The Jobeq website presents The Value Systems Questionnaire (VSQ), based on the value assessment methodology [14]. The VSQ questionnaire is based on two models—Graves’ value systems of spiral dynamics [8, 9] and Talcott Parsons’ understanding of cultural diversity [15]. The VSQ test contains various questions about personal values and social patterns. In this test, from the point of view of this book, the second section is interesting, the questions of which make it possible to create a set of “Social Pattern Variables” (“Social Pattern Variables”). This set reflects the social patterns or patterns of values and thinking styles used in specific social situations. The results of testing of undergraduates are shown in Fig. 2.

The boundaries of the red zone were drawn up by the authors of the test based on the responses of 933 respondents [13] Behavioral patterns, values, and thinking styles are grouped by 10 variables into 5 pairs of related patterns—“Pattern variables” according to the value orientation of the American sociologist Talcott Parsons [15]. Each pair represents the polar types of people’s behavior in a situation or their choice to get out of it.

1. To determine the value orientation (Type of Value-Orientation: Universal—Particular), Parsons has identified a pair of standard variables: universalism and particularism. This set of variables measures whether someone accepts the rules as absolute (and obeys those rules) or retains some freedom and claims the right to judge themselves independently of generally accepted norms. As you can see in Fig. 2, most of our respondents assess the situation based on personal rules, and not on generally accepted norms. Moreover, the answers of undergraduates approach the upper limit of the red zone.
2. The “Scope of values and rules: Specific - Diffuse” set of variables measures whether someone sets clear boundaries or not. If the boundaries are clear (specific), then the actions within the boundary can be direct (even to the point of absurdity), precise, and synchronized. These are the principles that most of the Master’s students who took part in the survey adhere to. If someone sees the boundaries blurred, what happens in one context will also be perceived as interfering with other contexts.
3. In the set of “Thinking Style” (Left Brain—Logic and Right Brain—Creativity), the answers allow you to distinguish the style of thinking: logic, which is responsible for the Roger Sperry’ theory of left hemisphere of the brain, and imagination (right hemisphere). Our testing has shown that most of our students prioritize reasoning and analysis over images and inspiration. It can also be noted that it would be useful for them to develop imagination, distal vision, as

a basis for goal-setting and striving to achieve goals, the ability to be creative and think outside the box.

4. Variables of the "Discussion Style" set (at ease with conflict: Match-Mismatch) describes the extent to which one person is looking for matches (patterns, correlations, etc.), and the other, on the contrary, defending their position, looking for exceptions, counterexamples, etc. A person with developed skills in finding agreement will try to avoid conflict, while not having such skills will feel at ease during the conflict and may consider this a normal stage in making a decision. According to the test results, the adherents of one or the other style were about equal on average to obtain estimates fall in the middle of the red zone.
5. Variables of the set "Efficiency & Flexibility" allow you to evaluate the perception of meetings. And it also summarizes how flexibly people responded to questions related to the other 8 variables mentioned in this section. Here, the number of responses near the lower border of the red zone was obtained by a large margin. Most likely, this result is due to the fact that our respondents were less likely to choose a combination of possible answers than the control group participants, and they stuck to the same position.

Strong emotional intelligence suggests that you can manage to some extent not only your own emotions, but also the emotions of others. And that can quickly turn into a problem [16].

The term "emotional intelligence" first appeared in a publication by the American psychologists P. Salovey and J. R. R. Tolkien. Mayer in 1990, and became popular after the publication of the book of the same name by the scientific journalist Daniel Goleman in 1995. Emotional Intelligence (Emotional Intelligence or Emotional Quotient) is the ability to recognize and understand the emotions, intentions, motivations, desires of your own and other people and manage them.

Goleman included the concept of "emotional intelligence" in the composition of social intelligence, highlighting the 4 main components: Self-awareness (understanding your emotions); self-control, including adaptability, optimism, and commitment; social perception (empathy plus organizational perception); relationship building skills (authority, coaching and mentoring skills, teamwork, ability to inspire and resolve conflicts).

Strong self-awareness and self-control in a situation of confrontation will allow you to control your mood, extinguish the initial impulses and anxiety in a conversation with other people, not to let the experience drown out the ability to think. A highly developed sense of empathy, which is part of social perception, will allow you to see the situation from the other person's point of view, and you will be able to present your arguments so that they feel that you are listening to them and taking their interests into account.

This will help to avoid unnecessary disappointments. The ability to build relationships determines the manner of behavior in conflicts. According to Goleman, emotional intelligence develops with the acquisition of life experience and qualities that allow you to achieve excellent results in work, and most importantly, it is the basis of leadership.

Hall's EQ Emotional Intelligence self-assessment test is available at: psytests.org. The questionnaire consists of 30 questions, the results are combined in 5 groups:

1. Emotional awareness is the awareness and understanding of your emotions, the constant replenishment of your own vocabulary of emotions. People with high emotional awareness are more aware of their inner state than others.
2. Managing your emotions is emotional responsiveness, emotional flexibility, in other words-arbitrary management of your emotions.
3. Self-motivation-managing your behavior by managing your emotions.
4. Empathy is the understanding of other people's emotions, the ability to empathize with the current emotional state of another person, as well as the willingness to provide support. This is the ability to understand the state of a person by facial expressions, gestures, shades of speech, posture.
5. Managing the emotions of others—the ability to influence the emotional state of other people.

The results of the self-assessment of emotional intelligence of undergraduates 1 (BI20) and 2 (BI19) years of study in 2020 are shown in Fig. 3. First-year students of the BI20 group need to learn empathy, the skills to manage the emotions of others, but especially their own. The best performance was demonstrated by second-year students (BI19), and this was influenced by the fact that they engaged in design thinking in three training modules in various academic disciplines on a regular basis. Although at the beginning of their training, the scores of this group when testing soft skills were much lower.

We also note the results of the conducted testing for creative types. The test of the Creative Types project is posted on the portal: https://mycreativetype.com. The author of the content is Carolyn Gregoire, author of articles in such publications as Scientific American, TIME, Harvard Business Review and Huffington Post, devoted to research on the inner life of people: from psychedelic research to Neuroesthetics and Vedic meditation. She is also the co-author of "Wired to Create: Unravelling the Mysteries of the Creative Mind" [17]. Based on psychological research, the test evaluates the main habits and tendencies of the respondent—how he thinks, how he acts, how he sees the world. This should help you better understand how creative this person is. You can gain a deeper understanding of motivations, as well as an understanding of how to maximize your natural abilities and solve your problems.

The results of the testing of undergraduates of the 1st and 2nd years of study in the direction of "Business Informatics" are as follows. As can be seen from the results, the competence of the Maker (creator) prevails—26%, Innovators—22%, but few Thinkers (8%), Dreamers (7%), Producers (7%), and Visionaries (4%). Therefore, it is important to develop these students' creative skills and entrepreneurial abilities by applying non-standard teaching methods, including active ways of learning through the development of new ideas, the generation and testing of new techno-projects, the study of trends and their understanding to find open opportunities for creating new unexpected products and services, the emancipation of thought and the inclusion of imagination.

Many Western companies apply the MBTI test for employment. In the name of the test, the abbreviation of the Myers-Briggs Type Indicator typology is hidden, for which the term "socionics" is also often used. The essence of the MBTI psychological testing system is that, by measuring unique combinations of personal factors of a person, it is possible to predict his propensity for a certain type of activity, the style of his actions, the nature of decisions, and other features that allow him to feel comfortable and confident. For what purpose, 4 scales (descriptors) were invented, according to which the personality is studied:

- orientation of consciousness (introversion-extroversion),
- orientation in a situation (common sense-intuition)
- the basis of decision-making (logos-pathos)
- the method of preparing decisions (rationality-irrationality).

The test is posted on the portal: https://4brain.ru/blog/). The test identifies 16 personality types (you can learn more about them in the book "Creative You" by Goldstein and Kroeger [18].

If we consider in more detail the division of respondents by 16 personality types according to Myers-Briggs (MBTI), we get this picture (see Fig. 4). The group of undergraduates is dominated by rationals (19%, of which 47% are women), logicians (18%, only 42% of them are women), extroverts and sensorics (17% each, half men and women). Less (8%) represented irrationals, introverts (for both types—half men and women) and intuits (60% of them—women), as well as ethics (7%, 83%—women).

It is interesting to compare the results of the group of undergraduates of the BI19 group with the BI18 group. Among the former, there were more extroverts (19% vs. 15%), intuitives (10% vs. 4%), ethicists (10% vs. 2%), irrationals (8% vs. 4%), and fewer introverts (6% vs. 10%), logicians (15% vs. 23%), rationals (17% vs. 21%), and sensorists (15% vs. 21%). At the seminars, most of the time which involved interactive activities, it was the BI19 group that perceived game mechanics better in the classroom, and was open to any active forms, creativity. The group of undergraduates of BI18 was not ready for any activities, preferring lectures and working at the computer. However, in this group there was a more cohesive team, the homework was clearly distributed among the classmates. Each student of the group was ready to support the other (developed sensory skills).

But in general, the results of the survey of undergraduates cannot be called brilliant. This confirms the fact that it is necessary to develop soft skills, and the best platform for this is schools and universities, as long as young people are ready to learn something new and are open to change. Then, and in a more mature age, the ability to adapt, flexible behavior, and personal growth will be quite strong.

4 How to Teach Soft Skills?

The forced transition of educational institutions to remote work in the context of the pandemic has added to the experience of teachers and teachers. At a revolutionary pace, education was changing and becoming overgrown with new experiences, successful cases and disillusionment with methods that seemed so perfect until recently. I cannot speak authoritatively about the school, because I believe that it has not just its own specifics, but a much more complex base for research, but there is good news for professional education. To date, we have accumulated a sufficient baggage of methods of many scientists, teachers, and facilitators who have been engaged in various times in research in the field of organizing group interaction, conducting brainstorming sessions and business games, strategic sessions and trainings. Many of these achievements were included in the arsenal of the new approach "Design Thinking".

Thinking is a cognitive activity of a person. Thus, the definition of design thinking combines our perception of creativity from the term "Design" and a systematic approach—from the word "Thinking".

The design thinking processes are based on the principles of Human-Centered Design (HCD). Each of the stages is supported by a set of tools and techniques that allow you to analyze the problem in a multidisciplinary team of specialists.

Three important principles-empathy (the ability to look at the world through the eyes of other people), an interdisciplinary approach to problem solving (involving designers, psychologists, marketers) and the organization of communication in the development of innovations between different stakeholders (consumers, manufacturers, partners, etc.)—distinguish design thinking from other schools that deal with solving inventive problems and organizing strategic sessions to solve the problems of the organization.

The key steps of design thinking are built through the following processes: Empathize, Define (Point-of-View), Ideate, Choice, Prototype, Test.

The design thinking approach is currently developing in three directions—the methodology for researching and improving the customer experience (Service Design), the basis for team building and corporate culture growth (as part of Employee Experience Management), and Neuro Design Thinking (see Fig. 5).

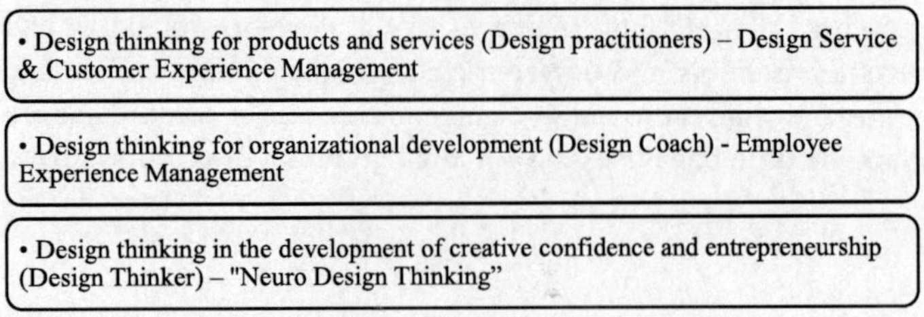

Fig. 5 Directions of application of design thinking

Two megatrends—digitalization and service orientation-make the transformation of the business model a major strategic priority for many leaders [19]. Design thinking for products and services, or more often today you can find the term "service design" (Design Service)—this is a way of studying the deep needs of customers, allowing companies to be on the wave with their consumers, providing their needs throughout life.

However, the basis for change is a comprehensive program of organizational change. That is why design thinking is currently developing in two other areas - Design Thinking for organizational development (Employee XM) and Neuro Design Thinking. They are aimed to promote the development of creative abilities, to develop different styles of thinking at the level of a person and in the space of the entire personnel landscape of the organization.

A modern manager understands that the working environment and human-oriented business processes create a good psychological climate, which determines how an employee will be able to solve tasks, get business results, show and be focused on developing their talents. That is, everything that we put into the concept of Employee Experience. Thus, by implementing the design thinking approach in its activities, SAP builds relationships with employees in such a way that the employee becomes a partner, a part of the company's system. Thus, the focus is not so much "on the role of the employee in the life of the company, but on the role of the company in the life of the employee" [20].

Design Thinking is implemented as part of the management process in international companies AirBnb, Healthcare, Procter & Gamble and Philips Electronic, IBM, General Electric, Apple, Facebook, Coca-Cola, Samsung, Phillips, Barclays and Virgin Group. Many Russian companies, especially those whose activities are related to the provision of services, often use various tools of design thinking to identify and solve problems of data security, customer comfort, search for new forms of cooperation with partners and develop their business strategy. These are, for example, Sberbank, Raiffeisenbank, Promsvyazbank, Alfa-Bank. The results of design research are implemented on the portals of the Moscow Government, in the services of the Moscow Metro, the state Corporation "Rosatom", the company "TELE2", etc.

Herman Gref, head of Sber, considers the staff as internal customers, thereby emphasizing the importance of creating a favorable impression of employees ("Employee Experience") for obtaining successful results in their work.

The Design Thinking approach aims to develop a person's creative abilities through rules of thumb and experience, emotional intelligence, and recognition of the value of other people's opinions. The ideas that formed the basis of the approach were formulated at various times by foreign and Russian scientists and thinkers, including G. Simon, G. Altshuller, G. P. Shchedrovitsky, N. P. Bekhtereva, N. Yu. Khryashcheva, M. Mikalko, E. de Bono, S. Blank, etc.

Anything that goes beyond a specific judgment, a set of ready-made answers, and already standard cases requires integrative thinking. To solve a non-standard (unconventional) problem, a person must be able to think in several projections, see simple facts, but also be able to reveal a deep meaning, catch metaphors, relying on imagination. This is the basis that is important for the world of Volatile, Uncertain, Complex and Ambiguous or VUCA, where it is necessary to "take into account the unpredictable" People with integrative thinking know how to expand the scope of issues related to the problem [4, 21]. They abandon "no, and/or" in favor of other bundles of words "and/yes and", "how else?" and phrases, and, therefore, in favor of other understandings and judgments, learning to hear each other and negotiate.

Discoveries in the fields of neurophysiology, cognitive psychology, and behavioral economics allowed design thinkers to quickly introduce new methods of social work and test them directly in the "field" conditions. Many researchers and practitioners have published articles on the implementation of design thinking as a working research tool and as a creative methodology [4, 5, 21–24].

Integrative thinking skills during a design session are essential and help the team go beyond the obvious solutions, leverage collective creativity, and discover new and unexpected areas to explore. Talents, skills, and experience are combined. People try to think multidimensional. At different stages, different styles of thinking are included. The problem is considered in several projections. The search for patterns in the studied phenomena, events, and processes develops system thinking. People learn to ask the right questions and are not afraid of not being heard. They get used to taking other people's opinions as the basis for their ideas. In metaphors and light displays of insight, the design thinker is able to capture innovation. The process of constant discussion and focus on the main thing trains you to put together a harmonious whole from the parts.

The portfolio of tools included in a clearly described design solution structure helps guide the creative team to effectively use their cognitive abilities, which ultimately allows them to find a breakthrough innovative solution.

As a project-based learning technology, design thinking changes the roles of students and teachers: students become active participants in the research process, and teachers direct this process, rather than broadcasting ready-made information. Students know that there are no ready-made solutions, but there are tools for self-learning and further decision-making, so you can only count on yourself and your friends. The implementation of cases together forms the project consciousness of the group, teaches to organize and direct collective co-creativity, to use practical thinking and to recognize the opinions of other people.

5 Conclusion

1. Digitalization has influenced the change in human thinking. On the one hand, the younger generation learns technology more easily and adapts faster to changing conditions. But dependence on gadgets and the Internet has reduced communication skills, information perception and learning abilities. The ability to distal vision, system, and analytical thinking are lost. However, in the new transforming conditions, modern organizations more than ever need the π-shaped specialists, where their competence is based on professional specialization,

breadth of knowledge in various fields, as well as empathy and cooperation skills.
2. The educational programs of universities should provide for a mandatory shift toward the formation of soft skills. Moreover, seminars in which soft skills are mastered should be held regularly throughout the entire training period.
3. The test results of the students showed that they have a fairly high level of emotional self-awareness, creativity, practical emotional intelligence, and communication skills. But they lack self-confidence and imagination, distal vision, which is important for achieving goals, creative ideas, and innovation. Repeated testing showed that the introduction of design thinking into the educational process allowed students to develop soft skills.
4. The philosophy of design thinking is built around project work in a multidisciplinary team and building communication between participants, interdisciplinary knowledge exchange, iterative processes, and reflection. Let's just say that DM is, first of all, a project-based learning method focused on working in a group.

In general, the project approach to training based on design thinking and case methodology will improve the quality of training of specialists, reduce the gap between the requirements of the labor market and the level of training of university graduates. This will also speed up the process of adapting young professionals to the workplace and to the DevOps teams.

References

1. Chernavsky, D. (2001). *Synergetics and information: Dynamic theory of information*. Nauka.
2. Slavin, B. B. (2013). *The Epoch of Collective reason: On the role of information in society and on the communicative nature of man*. Lenand.
3. Chapter 1. *The future of jobs and skills*. Report. Retrieved November 21, 2021, from http://reports.weforum.org/future-of-jobs-2016/.
4. Brown, T. (2009). *Change by design: How design thinking transforms organizations and inspires innovation*. HarperCollins Business.
5. Levrik, M., Link, P., & Leifer, L. (2019). *Design thinking from insight to new products and markets*. Peter
6. Leonard-Barton, D. (1996). *Wellsprings of knowledge: Building and sustaining the sources of innovation*. Harvard Business School Press.
7. Sanchez, A. V., Ruiz, M. P., other. (2008). *Competence-based learning. A proposal for the assessment of generic competences*. University of Deusto.
8. Graves, C. W. (2004). *Levels of human existence*. Example Product Manufacturer.
9. Ben, D., & Cowan, K. (2005). *Spiral dynamics: Mastering values, leadership and change*. Wiley-Blackwell.
10. Merlevede, P. (2001). *7 Steps to emotional intelligence*. Crown House Publishing.
11. Merlevede, P., Bridoux, D., & Wilkinson-Carr, S. (2004). *Mastering mentoring & coaching with emotional intelligence*. Crown House Publishing.
12. COMET questionnaire—emotional competencies. Retrieved October 11, 2020, from https://jobeq.com/

13. Merlevede, P. *Face validity of the value systems questionnaire*. Retrieved January 1, 2021, from https://jobeq.com/articles/VSQfaceValidity.pdf
14. Value systems testing & cultural research. Retrieved October 11, 2020, from https://jobeq.com/
15. Parsons, T. (1978). *Action theory and the human condition*. Free Press.
16. Goleman, D. (2005). *Emotional intelligence: Why it can matter more than IQ?* Bantam Books.
17. Kaufman, S. B., & Gregoire C. (2015). *Wired to create: Unravelling the mysteries of the creative mind*. TarcherPerigee.
18. Goldstein, D. B., & Kroeger, O. (2013). *Creative you: Using your personality type to thrive*. Atria Books/Beyond Words.
19. Linz, C., Muller-Stewens, G., & Zimmermann, A. (2017). *Radical business model transformation: Gaining the competitive edge in a disruptive world*. Kogan Page.
20. Bordugova, T. *Employee experience—Employee path in the company. How to attract, engage and retain the most talented*. Retrieved November 21, 2020, from http://hrdocs.ru/poleznaya-informacziya/employee-experience-put-sotrudnika
21. Kelley, T., & Kelley, D. (2013). *Creative confidence unleashing the creative potential within us all*. Crown Business.
22. Liedtka, J., & Ogilvie, T. (2011). *Designing for growth: A design thinking toolkit for managers*. Columbia University Press.
23. Clark, T., Osterwalder, A., & Pigneur, Y. (2012). *Business model you: A one-page method for reinventing your career*. Wiley.
24. Vasilieva, E. (2018). Developing the creative abilities and competencies of future digital professionals. *Automatic Documentation and Mathematical Linguistics, 52*(5), 248–256.

The Vision of Students of Their Professional Activities in the Industry 4.0

Olga Koropets, Irina Detkova, Alexandra Leontyeva, and Alexander Ovchinnikov

Abstract The active spread of digital technologies and the development of artificial intelligence have led to the transformation of the world of work and to the replacement of not only physical, but also mental work tasks. Requirements for the competencies and psychological characteristics of future workers in helping professions have changed. There is a need to improve the training system in higher educational institutions in order to prepare students for professional activities in the context of technological changes. Students' vision of the threats and opportunities of Industry 4.0 for professional activities, awareness of technological innovations and attention to the development of digital competencies form their ability to adapt to changing working conditions. The article presents the results of a narrative analysis of the vision of the professional activity of future specialists in the field of psychology and social work, studying at the university of the Russian Federation. The students' vision about changes in the requirements for professional competencies of a psychologist and a social worker in connection with digitalization and robotization of labor were analyzed. Four groups of respondents were identified with different views on the Industry 4.0 threats to future professional activities. The results of the study show that the majority of students studying helping professions are not sufficiently informed about innovative processes in their professional sphere and have a low level of readiness to develop the necessary competencies, which poses a threat to their well-being in the future workplace.

Keywords The fourth industrial revolution · Helping professions · Students · Workers well-being · Digital technologies

O. Koropets (✉) · A. Ovchinnikov
Ural Federal University, Yekaterinburg, Russian Federation
e-mail: o.a.koropets@urfu.ru

I. Detkova · A. Leontyeva
Adyghe State University, Maykop, Russian Federation

E. Zaramenskikh and A. Fedorova (eds.), *Digitalization of Society, Economics and Management*, Lecture Notes in Information Systems and Organisation 53,
https://doi.org/10.1007/978-3-030-94252-6_28

1 Introduction

The fourth industrial revolution is accompanied by the active introduction of digital technologies in all spheres of human life, including the professional sphere. The spread of artificial intelligence, machine learning, cloud computing, and digital platforms has transformed the world of work. The digitalization of the economy has contributed to the formation of new types of employment that can help to level the existing gender inequality in the labor market [1]. There are new requirements for the employee, related both to the need to develop new competencies and to rethink the concepts of career development and employment. New technologies constantly change those skills that graduates may need for work in the future, and that leads to changes in the labor market. For example, employment in the services sector has increased significantly in Australia, with expansion of health and social care, retail, scientific and technical services, while in the manufacturing industry, which has been the main employment sector for a long time, there is a significant decline [2]. A systematic review of the literature reveals that core competencies for Industry 4.0 include multiple skills, including self-organization, proactivity, interdisciplinarity, innovation, adaptability, flexibility, and self-management skills, as well as knowledge, for example, in the field of information and communication technologies [3]. In the near future, a person will need to learn how to interact and share the workspace and compete in the labor market, not only with other people, but also with robots [4]. Experts predict the disappearance of a number of professions. Frey and Osborne identified occupations with high, medium, and low risk of extinction, depending on the likelihood of their computerization [5]. Technological unemployment, polarization, and precarization of employment are possible threats to the well-being of various categories of workers [6]. Young specialists, including graduates of higher educational institutions, are primarily at risk. Negative tendencies in the employment of young specialists, for example, unemployment, performance of work that does not correspond to the level, and profile of professional training, low wages, are already recorded in the Russian Federation [7]. According to monitoring data, the most in demand are graduates who have completed engineering and medical training, the least in demand are graduates who have received humanitarian and creative specialties [8]. The actively developing digitalization of labor can exacerbate these trends. At the same time, the new labor economy needs innovative human capital [8], and in this connection the issue of effective and high-quality training of workers for Industry 4.0 becomes relevant [9]. It is necessary to improve the training system both in educational institutions and in production so that people can work with new technologies, including artificial intelligence.

The opinion is quite widespread that machines will never be able to match the intellectual potential of people, so the risk of digitalization for creative and helping professions, in which human-to-human communication is important, is low. However, today the key direction in the development of artificial intelligence is the replacement of mental rather than physical tasks. There are programs for speech and image recognition, machine translation, and automatic text creation, for example, for short journalistic articles and legal contracts, medical expert systems for the analysis and diagnosis of patient pathologies. Computers are already making music and art [10]. The fourth industrial revolution is launching fundamental changes in helping professions such as elderly care service. According to Frennert, social technology and digitalization are not only information technology, but also organizational changes and new work processes. Therefore, care managers should strive to be digital fluent and stay up to date with the latest innovations in care. However, a Swedish study found that home care staff lacked digital skills [11].

In recent years, the use of humanoid robots in the field of educational and clinical psychology has begun, for example, the humanoid robot NAO was used in the treatment of cognitive disorders and dementia center of the Italian health service. The robot performed certain tasks from the usual protocol of the memory training program. As a result, patients who interacted with the robot were diagnosed with significant improvements: the indicators of visual perception and prosaic memory increased, therapeutic behavior enhanced, in some cases the symptoms of depression reduced, and speech fluency improved [12]. Social robots are a promising technology to help psychologists identify and treat neurocognitive disorders in the elderly [13]. The possibility of using humanoid robots to interview children has been explored in a number of studies. The experiment of interest is which assessed the effectiveness of the use of the humanoid robot Kaspar by teacher-psychologist to interview ten primary school students about the video they watched before the interview [14]. Thus, the opinion that the helping professions are not influenced by Industry 4.0. is highly exaggerating.

In the context of the fourth industrial revolution, the main task is the timely adaptation of the employee to the changing conditions of the organizational, social, and economic environment. Measures must be taken in order to protect employees who have lost their jobs due to automation, as well as young professionals who cannot find employment in their specialty sphere. Transformation of systems of additional education, advanced training, and retraining of personnel have an important role [15]. It is also necessary to expand the range of consulting services to prepare young professionals for future careers [16]. In this connection, the issues of students' preparedness for professional activity in the context of its transformation are gaining relevance. Of particular interest is the study of the subjective reflection of threats, arising with Industry 4.0, by future specialists. Threats associated with the fourth industrial revolution can be classified as probabilistic threats, their occurrence is possible and predictable in the near future. An important task of ensuring the well-being of potential workers in conditions of Industry 4.0 is the formation of a high degree of readiness to face threats, based on awareness and knowledge of possible remedies.

The purpose of the study is to identify the ideas of students studying in helping professions about professional activities in the context of Industry 4.0.

2 Method

The study involved full-time students studying in the directions: "Psychology and Social Pedagogy" and "Social Work" on the basis of the Adygeya State University, located in the Russian Federation. In total, 41 people took part in the study on a voluntary basis: 10 young men and 31 ladies aged 19 to 21 years old, students of the second, third, and fourth years of full-time education. A small sample size is acceptable for qualitative research. The authors used the narrative interview technique, which was created and developed within the framework of a qualitative approach in the social sciences. The use of narrative texts is widespread in psychology and sociology; narratives are seen as knowledge that represents the social reality of the narrator [17]. Both specially created stories and any fragment of oral or written text can act as a narrative. The advantages of the method include its versatility and ease of use, as well as the possibility of qualitative data analysis and the multidimensionality of the material for interpretation. The obvious disadvantages of the method are its subjectivity, dependence on the volume and quality of the data obtained, and large time costs for collecting and summarizing data.

The study used written narrative interview, since an audio recording on a dictaphone can block the respondent's will to share his thoughts and reduce the quality of the material received [18]. As a narrative impulse, the respondents were asked to describe their ideas about their future work (profession) in the context of the fourth industrial revolution, their thoughts, feelings, and possible actions in the professional future, as well as possible threats (risks) for career in conditions of Industry 4.0 that seem most likely to them. The authors used open, axial, and selective coding of narrative passages. As a result of coding, was selected a central category—"Students' readiness for professional activity in the conditions of Industry 4.0". The methodological basis of the study was the concept of D. Bar Tal, which shows that people, when forming attitude, are trying to fulfill their need for security and minimize the threat, selectively collecting information about security and avoiding information that, according to their opinion, indicates the danger. Therefore, it is difficult for people to change or correct their beliefs, even taking into account new important information [19]. The authors of the article identified the following thematic cores, which are indicators for assessing preparedness for professional activity in the context of technological changes:

- assessment of the situation as threatening or safe;
- assessment of external and internal resources for protection against Industry 4.0 threats;
- awareness of innovative processes in the professional activities of a psychologist and social worker.

3 Research Results

A qualitative comparison of narratives was carried out in order to identify the similarities and differences in students' opinions about their future professional activities. As a result of processing the narratives, four groups of respondents with different types of ideas about professional activity in the context of technological changes were identified.

The first group includes the respondents who deny the threat of Industry 4.0 to their professional activities. The respondents of the first group (29.27%) assessed the situation as safe for their professional future in the field of psychology and social work. The analysis of the situation was based on ideas about the immutability of the professions of a psychologist, social worker or social teacher, or a partial change in their functions in the distant future. Assessment of external and internal resources for protection against possible threats was not carried out. Information about possible threats was either completely ignored, or the danger was minimized. For example, Anastasia (19 years old, 2nd year student, name changed) writes: "At the moment, as far as I know, Industry 4.0 practically does not affect the professional activities of psychologists and social workers. I think that in the near future the professional activity of a psychologist and social worker will not change. In 10 years, the replacement of employees with robots may begin. But I think that qualified employees will still be needed, since robots cannot replace living people in this profession. I don't know yet how these changes will affect me personally." The most common statement for the respondents of this group is as follows: "Smart machines are not needed for my specialty, since they will never replace real human labor. The robot will not be able, in my opinion, to understand people's emotions, empathize and reflect feelings." The respondents of the first group demonstrated a low awareness of innovative processes in their professional activities and a low willingness to master new technologies and methods of work. Potential changes in professional activities were linked exclusively by the respondents with the use of Internet resources to find the information a specialist needs and with online consulting. The respondents of this group emphasized their unwillingness to work in online consulting, although they did not completely deny some of the positive aspects of using modern means of communication. So, Inna (21 years old, 4th year student, name changed) writes: "I would not want such specialties as psychologist and social worker to switch to online work, nothing replaces personal communication with clients. More efficient work is done personally with the client, rather than via the Internet. But, perhaps, with the introduction of different technologies in these professions, the performance of these specialists will be able to reach a new level, and more opportunities will appear."

The second group—respondents who admit a threat to the professional activities of others.

The respondents in the second group (9.76%) were characterized by depersonalization and stigmatization of the threat. The respondents were aware of the possible threats of Industry 4.0 for society in general and its individual groups, primarily for workers of other professional groups and future generations. The respondents pointed to such potential threats as staff cuts in organizations, unemployment, increased psychosocial risks in the workplace, and deterioration in health due to extended computer hours. In this regard, it was noted that the demand for psychologists in the future will only increase. So, Maria (21 years old, 4th year student, name changed) points: "I believe that the profession of a psychologist and social teacher is the profession of the future, since more and more often we come across people who need help of these specialists." The narratives demonstrated the confidence that specialists would face the main difficulties in the distant future. Among the respondents of the second group, planning of possible future activities was carried out mainly on the basis of knowledge about technologies and methods of work that currently exist. Like the first group of respondents, they emphasized the advantages of offline communication and dialogue with the person. As an example, consider a fragment from the narrative of Svetlana (20 years old, 2nd year student, name changed): "This will all happen gradually. In two or three generations, robots will be everywhere. Someone will say that it is more convenient this way, but this is only at first. Unfortunately, nothing can be changed. For example, a client comes to a psychologist, and in front of him sits a robot (without a soul and without emotions) and everything is somehow different. In 10 years, I think, we will not have this, but I suppose that it will slowly begin in developed countries and cities with a population of over one million. In 50 years, everything will be different. I do not think that this will somehow affect me, because our generation is unlikely to face Industry 4.0, but in 100 years there will definitely be changes." Thus, the respondents of this group viewed their future workplace as safe from the point of view of possible threats associated with technological progress, and demonstrated an average degree of awareness of innovative processes in professional activity.

The third group—respondents who exaggerate the threat of Industry 4.0 to their professional activities.

The respondents of the third group (31.7%) assessed the situation at future workplaces as unsafe for themselves, experienced strong anxiety, focused on the threats of the fourth industrial revolution, demonstrated confusion and uncertainty about the relevance of their professional activities in the future. For example, Oksana (20 years old, 3rd year student, name changed) writes: "Industry 4.0 today greatly influences the professional activities of psychologists and social workers. The influence occurs both from the positive and from the negative side. And in my opinion, most of all from a negative one, as psychologists cannot fully help their clients. In other words, live communication comes to naught. But in the work of a psychologist and social worker, communication is the main thing. I am afraid to imagine how the professional activity of a psychologist and social worker will change in the near future and in 10 years. I think that these professions will soon cease to be necessary. Robots will become psychologists and social workers. I can assume that all these changes can affect me negatively. If distance learning was difficult for me, then I don't know what will happen next." The respondents of this group are concerned about both the professional future within the chosen specialty and the future in the labor sphere in general. For example, Alexandra (20 years old, 3rd year student, name changed) reasons as follows: "I think that robots will soon replace many professions, including our future profession. And soon there will be no such work. People will need any kind of work to survive, not live." Students do not assess resources of protection against threats, the need to adapt to new conditions is perceived as a forced measure. Denis (19 years old, 2nd year student, name has been changed) notes: "In 10 years, the human profession of a social worker may disappear. Robots will replace the people in this post. Perhaps the profession of a human psychologist will still be relevant. If I choose the profession of a social worker, in the future I may lose my job, I will have to adjust to the new living conditions, change my activity." Awareness of innovations in the professional sphere is at an average level, readiness for professional activity in the conditions of Industry 4.0 is below average.

The fourth group—respondents who adequately assess the threat for their professional activities.

The respondents of the fourth group (29.27%) revealed an average or high level of awareness of technological innovations. The narratives of the respondents analyzed both the opportunities and threats of the fourth industrial revolution. For example, Anna (21 years old, 4th year student, name changed) writes: "In the future, on the one hand, psychologists will have more opportunities to communicate with their clients via the Internet, and on the other hand, these specialties require personal communication with clients. During the consultation, the person feels most comfortable if the environment facilitates it. During a face-to-face consultation, this environment is created by a psychologist. In the process of online consulting, this environment is created by the client himself, as he wants it to be. He does not need to be distracted by various trivia, since most often a person applies for a consultation from home, where he feels most calm and protected. I believe that whatever kind of consulting it is - face-to-face or online, the main thing is that it helps the client." The respondents of the fourth group are focused on the development of new competencies that are in demand in Industry 4.0, are ready to study throughout their careers. So, Vadim (19 years old, 2nd year student, name changed) notes: "Special attention should be paid to such skills as: communication, flexibility and adaptability, capability to learn and digital skills. Like everyone else, I will have a turning point in the professional sense, and like for everyone else, there is a lot to learn for me! But this is not new for the teaching profession! The specific of pedagogical activity, whether it is a teacher-psychologist or a teacher, does not stand still throughout the entire professional path." The respondents of the fourth group showed willingness develop and improve within the framework of their specialty, while alternative employment options were practically not considered. The respondents of this group are already working on improving their own professional competencies, describing detailed plans for professional development, and also considering the personal qualities necessary for successful adaptation to Industry 4.0.

4 Discussion of the Results

The respondents of the first and second groups have differences in assessing the situation, but there are no differences in assessing the need to use resources of protection. As a result, they have the formed illusion of the safety of professional activities during the fourth industrial revolution. Such picture reduces the level of preparedness to face possible threats.

On the contrary, the respondents of the third and fourth groups have similarities in assessing threats; however, there are differences in terms of assessing resources of protection. Pupils from the third group showed ignorance of ways to protect themselves from the threats of Industry 4.0, as a result, a low readiness to face the threat is formed. The fourth group respondents demonstrated beliefs in their own ability to cope with changes in working conditions. They showed a high awareness of possible changes in professional activity, described in detail the ways of possible professional development. As a result, pupils formed ideas about the opportunities and threats of Industry 4.0 and a high readiness for professional activity throughout the technological changes.

The results of the study confirm the results of other studies, in particular, the study of visions of the psychological safety of professional activities of students studying in the direction "Personnel Management" [20]. Comparison of research results shows that students studying helping professions tend to exaggerate the threats to Industry 4.0 and less willing to adapt to changes in their professional activities.

The negative attitude of the majority of students studying helping professions to online counseling is alarming. Perhaps this is due to the lack of practice and bias associated with the negative experience of forced online education during the coronavirus pandemic. These attitudes do not coincide with the opinions of practicing psychologists. In particular, a survey conducted with Italian psychologists showed that most psychologists rate online counseling positively, but have questions regarding ethical and legal issues regarding online methods. It is noteworthy that some of the specialists have already used online technologies in working with clients [21].

Differences in visions can be explained both by the personality traits of students and by different levels of awareness of innovative processes in professional activity and society in general, as well as by differences in the quality and content of education in a higher educational institution.

5 Conclusion

The study showed that the respondents' visions of professional activity in the context of Industry 4.0 are heterogeneous. Only 29% of respondents are inclined to adequately assess possible threats to professional activity associated with the fourth industrial revolution, and their response methods are based on the choice of optimal resources for protection. Unfortunately, there is a fairly large number of respondents (first and second groups) who underestimate or completely deny possible threats, which indicates the presence of distortion of information, or low awareness of innovative processes in professional activity. The students' ideas about the future professional activity need correction, otherwise the respondents will have difficulties in adapting to changing working conditions. Thus, the majority of respondents have a low and medium level of awareness of innovative processes in the professional sphere and a low level of readiness to develop the necessary competencies, which poses a threat to the well-being of future psychologists and social workers. While awareness of technological innovation, focus on the development of soft and digital competencies, a readiness for continuous learning, timely assessment of the risks and threats of Industry 4.0 are important to ensure a high level of employee well-being in future workplaces. The study has practical value due to the need to form adequate perception of technological changes in professional activities among students studying helping professions. Industry 4.0 is inevitable, it can save people from routine exhausting work, and therefore, a deliberate strategy of adaptation to changes and results of this revolution is vital. Such strategy must enable young specialists to realize their abilities and expand competencies in a comfortable psychological environment. The prospect of further research is the study of the personal characteristics of students with different types of responses to threats to professional activity in the context of the fourth industrial revolution.

Acknowledgements The study was funded by RFBR, project number 20-010-00952.

References

1. Pesha, A. V., & Tonkikh, N. V. (2020). Digitalization of the economy and remote employment of women: An analysis of the situation and development prospects. In D. Solovev, V. Savaley, A. Bekker, & V. Petukhov (Eds.), *Proceeding of the International Science and Technology Conference "FarEastCon 2019"* (Vol. 172, pp. 557–568). Smart Innovation, Systems and Technologies. Springer.
2. Torii, K., & O'Connell, M. (2017). *Preparing young people for the future of work*. Mitchell Institute Policy Paper. Mitchell Institute.
3. Kipper, L. M., Iepsen, S., Dal Forno, A. J., Frozza, R., Furstenau, L., Agnes, J., & Cossul, D. (2021). Scientific mapping to identify competencies required by industry 4.0. *Technology in Society, 64*, 101454.
4. Rojas, R. A., Ruiz Garcia, M. A., Wehrle, E., & Vidonim R. (2019). A variational approach to minimum-jerk trajectories for psychological safety in collaborative assembly stations. *IEEE Robotics and Automation Letters, 4*(2), 823–829.
5. Frey, C. B., & Osborne, M. A. (2017). The future of employment: How susceptible are jobs to computerisation? *Technological Forecasting and Social Change, 114*, 254–280.
6. Menshikova, M., Fedorova, A., & Gatti, M. (2020). Introducing smart-working in the conditions of digital business transformation: Analysis of an employee's experience. In B. E. Zaramenskikh & A. Fedorova (Eds.), *Digital transformation and new challenges—Digitalization of society, economics, management and education, DSEME 2018* (Vol. 40, pp. 59–71). Lecture Notes in Information Systems and Organisation. Springer.

7. Bulatova, G. A. (2020). Graduate employment of higher education institutions: Analytical review of statistical data and research materials. *Economics Profession Business, 3*, 14–20.
8. Lysenko, E., & Yaroshenko, A. (2020). Using theory of generation for attraction and retention of young professionals. In *Proceedings of 16th European Conference on Management, Leadership and Governance* (pp. 138–148). Academic Conferences International Limited.
9. Li, G., Hou, Y., & Wu, A. (2017). Fourth industrial revolution: Technological drivers, impacts and coping methods. *Chinese Geographical Science, 4*, 626–637.
10. Ernst, E., Merola, R., & Samaan, D. (2019). Economics of artificial intelligence: Implications for the future of work. *IZA Journal of Labor Policy, 9*(1). Retrieved August 11, 2020, from https://content.sciendo.com/view/journals/izajolp/9/1/article-20190004.xml
11. Frennert, S. (2018). Lost in digitalization? Municipality employment of welfare technologies. *Disability and Rehabilitation: Assistive Technology, 14*(6), 635–642.
12. Pino, O., Palestra, G., Trevino, R., & De Carolis, B. (2020). The humanoid robot NAO as trainer in a memory program for elderly people with mild cognitive impairment. *International Journal of Social Robotics, 12*(1), 21–33.
13. Cormons, L., Poulet, C., Pellier, D., Pesty, S., & Fiorino, H. (2020). Testing social robot acceptance: What if you could be assessed for dementia by a robot? A pilot study. In *Proceedings of the 6th International Conference on Mechatronics and Robotics Engineering (ICMRE)* (pp. 92–98).
14. Krakosta, E., Dautenhahn, K., Syrdal, D. S., Wood, L. J., & Robins, B. (2019). Using the humanoid robot Kaspar in a Greek school environment to support children with Autism spectrum condition. *Paladyn, Journal of Behavioral Robotics, 10*(1), 298–317.
15. Kulkova, I. A., Plutova, M. I., & Kuryachaya, E. A. (2019). The effectiveness assessment of health care provider's additional professional training. *IOP Conference Series: Earth and Environmental Science, 272*(3), 032212. IOP Publishing.
16. Lent, R. W. (2018). Future of work in the digital world: Preparing for instability and opportunity. *The Career Development Quarterly, 66*(3), 205–219.
17. Franzosi, R. (1998). Narrative analysis—Or why (and how) sociologists should be interested in narrative. *Annual Review of Sociology, 24*(1), 517–554.
18. Anderson, C., & Kirkpatrick, S. (2016). Narrative interviewing. *International Journal of Clinical Pharmacy, 38*(3), 631–634.
19. Bar-Tal, D., & Jacobson, D. (1998). A psychological perspective on security. *Applied Psychology, 47*(1), 59–71.
20. Koropets, O. A. (2020). Students' ideas about the psychological safety of the professional activity. World of Science. *Pedagogy and Psychology, 6*(8). Retrieved December 25, 2020, https://mir-nauki.com/PDF/19PSMN620.pdf (in Russian)
21. Cipolletta, S., & Mocellin, D. (2018). Online counseling: An exploratory survey of Italian psychologists' attitudes towards new ways of interaction. *Psychotherapy Research, 28*(6), 909–924.

The Impact of Digital Supply Chain on Operational a Case Study on Cruise Sector

Roberta Pinna, Eleonora Veglianti, Marta Musso, and Marco De Marco

Abstract In the last decade, the cruise sector operates in a dynamic and highly competitive environment requiring more flexible and resilient organizations. With the Fourth Industrial Revolution, many companies in the cruise sector recognize the importance of innovative digital technologies for their business. Digital Supply Chain describes an organizational change process leading to the application and implementation of digital technology in order to achieve effective and efficient flows of products, services and information, to provide maximum value to the customer. This study explores the potential of cloud-based B2B integration brokerage solution in order to improve efficiency and collaboration in extended enterprise processes, by enabling a multiformat and multi-protocol data exchange management. The paper uses primary data obtained through in-depth semi-structured interview with an executive staff from a cruise company operating in the Mediterranean region. Research findings unveil the strategy of a cruise company's supply chain and the operational performance with the use of digital technologies.

Keywords Cruise sector · Digital supply chain · Integration

1 Introduction

The cruise sector operates in a dynamic and highly competitive environment requiring more flexible and resilient organizations [1]. Factors like large lot sizes, increasingly distant destinations, just in time deliveries, global sourcing, worldwide operations, make cruise supply chain management more complex than in the past. Indeed, quality,

R. Pinna · M. Musso
Department of Economics and Management, University of Cagliari, 09124 Cagliari, Italy

E. Veglianti (✉)
FGES, Université Catholique de Lille, 59800 Lille, France
e-mail: eleonora.veglianti@univ-catholille.fr

M. De Marco
Department of Economics, International Telematic University Uninettuno, 00186 Rome, Italy

E. Zaramenskikh and A. Fedorova (eds.), *Digitalization of Society, Economics and Management*, Lecture Notes in Information Systems and Organisation 53,
https://doi.org/10.1007/978-3-030-94252-6_29

service innovation, and customer focus are today's key factors in terms of competitiveness. In the cruise sector, the final consumer is the cruiser who wants good quality food, fit for consumption as well as safe. At the same time, the cruiser demands product diversity and convenience. This onboard service quality is supported by the company's supply chain, which is responsible for the on-time replenishment of ships and the availability of supplies on board [2]. Keeping the food quality moving on the supply chain is very important for cruiser ship as the cost of replacing a missed order is very high. Given the nature of the tourism product offered by the cruise industry today, the supply chain function is crucial as an integral part of the service to the consumer. Therefore, it is required an efficient and well-organized supply chain. These competitive dimensions must be delivered in most cases simultaneously and always at the lowest costs attainable. Researchers and practitioners have pointed out the need for the companies to redesign their networks through a close integrated relationship between firms and their supply chain partners [3, 4]. However, only recently, with the increase of global competition, the improvement of inter-organizational processes has become a high priority [5]. Supply chain managers and professionals look at the integration as a possible strategy of creating strategic partnerships to improve supply chain performance and to achieve cost reduction and to decrease lead time. The rapid technological progress in the more recent past has opened a range of new business potentials and opportunities [6–8]. Trends and new catchwords such as digitalization, the internet of things (IoT), the internet of services (IoS) and the cyber-physical systems (CPS) are becoming more and more relevant. In such high competitive context characterized by "time compression", the digitalization of supply chain processes is considered one of the most strategic answers due to its power to provide timely, accurate and reliable information and it has been recognized as a critical factor in the improvement of supply chain management [9, 10]. Today, many supply chains are transforming from a static sequence to a dynamic and interconnected system—the digital supply network—that can be a more readily incorporated ecosystem partners and it can evolve to a more optimal state over time. Digital supply networks (DSN) integrate information from many different sources and locations to drive the physical act of production and distribution. Best practice examples suggest that digital platforms play a critical role in managing supply chain activities and partnerships that generate performance gains for firms. DSNs allow businesses to create new sources of revenue by providing new and faster access to markets. They can also support the production of smart products, enable more informed decisions, and allow systems to adapt and learn from the world around them, driving more flexible processes. Although some authors point out the need to improve the efficiency of the supply chain that is a new competitive advantage for cruise company [2] and the benefits of digital supply chain management [11], there is still limited academic investigation on how and why digital technology can create performance gains for cruise companies in a Supply Chain Management (SCM) context.

In this study, we concentrate our attention on the cruise sector, where the role of suppliers and the relationship with them is crucial. Consequently, the main research questions are: What is the importance of digitalization in ensuring an efficient supply chain? What improvements can the implementation of the web-based system bring in terms of visibility, velocity, accuracy and coordination? Which efficiencies can be gained with such a technology?

In the present paper, the role played by digital technologies in the supply chain integration is investigated. It is hypothesized that information technology capability of third-party logistics providers improves performance in the chain, and it becomes a fundamental factor in a strategic B2B relationship.

The article is structured as follows. Section 2 presents the theoretical background of the paper. Section 3 introduces the methodology and the approach used to verify how procurement process digitalization promotes the integration between members of supply chain and which benefits originate for each member. Then, Sect. 4 discusses the managerial implications of the findings. Finally, Sect. 5 concludes analysing the limitations and presenting inputs for further researches.

2 Literature Review

2.1 Supply Chain Integration

Supply Chain (SC) is a process that includes all the activities ranging from the identification of a customer need through product selection, negotiation with suppliers, payment, storage, distribution and redistribution. It is a set of three or more entities directly involved in the upstream and downstream flows of products, services, finances, and information from a source to a customer. SCM therefore, refers to upstream and downstream relationships with suppliers and customers in order to deliver the best customer value at the lowest cost [12]. This network has some major actors who determine the efficiency and the effectiveness of the network [13]. The SCM definition shows the importance of integration of internal processes within a company and effectively linking them with the external operations of suppliers, customers and other members. For instance, some scholars define the Supply Chain Integration (SCI) as "the degree to which a firm can strategically collaborate with its supply chain partners and collaboratively manage the intra and inter organization processes to achieve an efficient flows of products and services, information, money and decisions with the objective of providing maximum value to customers at low cost and high speed" [3]. The definition points out the multidimensionality of the SCI construct, that includes three dimensions, internal integration, customer integration and supplier integration [14]. The management of these dimensions requires the internal and external processes synchronization to meet customers' requirements [5]. Suppliers are very crucial for cruise supply chain as they are the initial stage. Thus, the food and beverage offering is an important part of the onboard experience [15, 16], and while it constitutes a majority of the supplies loaded for the duration of the week, other, various supplies also need to find their way on board [2]. All these supplies uniquely contribute to the support of the high-quality onboard service delivery. They have to provide the demanded quantity in the required quality, at the right place and at the agreed time. To see this, one need only to look at the variety of food offered to passengers on board. A cruise line cannot offer such variety and guarantee, for example, fresh products to thousands of consumers around the world without taking into consideration the strategic importance of SCM. For instance, for 1.200 passengers to be served, over ten dining venues are required. Moreover, considering that a typical cruise in the Mediterranean lasts ten days, massive amount of food and beverage is required to satisfy the passengers. Some researchers, for example, pointed out that the complexity of the cruise supply chain derives from some characteristics of the cruise supply chain itself, as maintaining a large global deployment to achieve the required service quality for the cruiser, a long term planning and a centralized communication infrastructure as well as the ability to source high variety of suppliers in large quantities or the short time window available for replenishment [17]. Therefore, all these features require coordination in planning the supply chain. The just in time procedure is needed as the stock out is not acceptable and missed shipment increases the cost rapidly. Others refer to the need of controlling and guarantying the food quality in the supply chain by using time-dependent quality information [18]. Authors believe that investment in the food chain design are important both for improving logistics performance and for persevering the food quality, in order to have the right products to be delivered at the right price, at the agreed time and with the demanded quality. Sharing real-time information facilitates seamless services, ensures cost-efficient passage at sea, reduces transaction costs and risks, and can improve operations across the entire SC. Supply chain integration refers to joint planning and strategic information sharing and collaboration between a focal firm and its upstream suppliers and downstream customers in managing a collaborative and synchronized process in order to meet customer needs [19]. Integration is the degree to which members along the supply chain collaborate and work together to manage intra and inter-organizational processes for higher performance and profitability while meeting the demands of the customer. In this way, it is possible to improve the decision making and to get all the component of the chain interacting in a more efficient manner. The result is a stronger supply chain visibility as well as the identification of bottlenecks. The principal elements of an integrated supply chain model can be characterized by cooperation, collaboration, information sharing, trust, partnership, shared technology as well as a fundamental shift away from managing individual functional processes to integrated chains of processes [20, 21]. Firms integrating their information and material flow would lead to optimal management of the supply chain. It involves the alignment of business functions internally within a firm and with its supply chain partners to reduce costs and to increase customer value as well as the overall performance across the supply chain for all partners. Central to collaboration is the mutual sharing of large information among supply chain members [22]. Numerous researchers have found that when the components of the chain communicate and share information they are more likely to improve the quality of their products or services; to reduce the cycle time; to decrease the costs of protecting against opportunistic behaviour and to increase the cost savings through greater product design and operational efficiencies [23, 24].

Integration and coordination within a supply chain are a strategic response to the challenges that arise from these dependencies. Benefits from coordination of supply chain activities are well-documented in the literature. There is higher attention in academic research, in a variety of disciplines, on coordination in supply chains, particularly addressing the potential coordination mechanisms available to eliminate sub-optimization within supply chains. Similarly, there is a growing interest in industry to better understand supply chain coordination its mechanisms that are available to assist the supply chain manager. For instance, authors surveyed the literature on supply chain integration and proposed information sharing and coordination among supply chain members as the primary drivers of supply chain performance [25].

2.2 *Digital Supply Chain*

Behind the great potential of the digital supply chain (DSC) lies the so-called Industry 4.0 or fourth industrial revolution. In this scenario, digitization is about companies orienting themselves to the customer through e-commerce, digital marketing, social media, and the customer experience. The overall result of this digital revolution is a modern, digitalized supply chain that can be distinguished from traditional supply chains in manifold aspects. Digitalized supply chains are significantly different in terms of shape and multidimensional network structures which are replacing the simple linear structures [26, 27]. They offer entirely new levels of visibility and flexibility [28]. Moreover, they increasingly rely on automated processes and activities [29, 30]. The DSC is characterized by the strategic and operative exchange of information between entities in the ecosystem, including firms and their suppliers, employees, and customers. Integration is a central key within Industry 4.0 paradigm. In other words, being a firm 4.0 means to integrate those activities and actors of the value chain. The business goal of the digital supply chain is to deliver the right product into the customer's hands as quickly as possible—but also to do so in a responsible and reliable manner, while increasing efficiency and cutting costs through automation. A critical element will be the evolution of traditional supply chains towards a connected, smart, and highly efficient supply chain ecosystem. Appropriate information models are needed to collect, store and deliver information in supply chains. This often requires the development of platforms and the integration among multiple platforms. This ecosystem will be based on a full implementation of a wide range of information technologies, for example the enterprise resource planning (ERP), the radio frequency identification (RFID) and the electronic data interchange (EDI). The implementation of these technologies can integrate and coordinate material, information and financial flows among supply chain actors including suppliers, companies, retailers and final users [31].

Today, the supply chain is a series of largely discrete steps taken through marketing, product development, manufacturing, and distribution, to reach finally the hands of the customer. Digitization brings down those walls, and the chain becomes a completely integrated ecosystem that is fully transparent to all the players involved—from suppliers to customers. Efficient integration and management of suppliers is a critical building block in the digital supply chain ecosystem. The digitization of many traditional aspects of procurement is already under way, as companies use a variety of big data tools and techniques to be more connected with suppliers, to aid the planning process, to improve sourcing, to actively manage supplier risk and to encourage the collaboration. DSC establishes the swift from manual transactions to digitalized information flows in both intrafirm and interfirm operations. Therefore, technology offers companies the option of reducing internal management costs, increasing efficiency through digitalization or sustaining competitiveness by digitalizing external networks.

For instance, the development of collaborative cloud-based platforms allows companies to increase the amount of information sharing in the supply chain and to reduce the complexity of information sharing and communication with their supply chain members. Thus, a firm can provide real-time information and it can interact with supply chain stakeholders fully and quickly. By integrating data across the entire supply chain, in real time and often without human intervention, delivery lead times can be significantly decreased, and freight and inventory management optimized [32, 33].

Therefore, the benefits and value drivers of digitalization for supply chains are considerable. Some scholars [34] point out that the key motivation for supply chain integration is the efficiency associated with minimizing governance costs, including the costs of exchange with other ecosystem participants and with those within the individual organization. Information technology-based cost savings enable a higher amount of information to be processed more accurately and frequently from different sources around the world [35]. Moreover, when properly automated, these information flows eliminate the need for manual data entry and, thus, there is less possibility of having human error [36]. Other benefits of DSC include the reduction of product or service costs, the creation of competitive advantage and barriers to competition, the decrease of supply chain lead times and the increase of flexibility in supply chain design.

3 Methodology

A case study was conducted in order to explore the hypotheses of the research. The case-study approach is an empirical inquiry used to investigate situations where little is known about a peculiar phenomenon and when the research is exploratory [37, 38]. Moreover, the case study research is the most popular qualitative method as well as the most well-established and published approach in information systems research and in other social sciences, particularly in the business and management field [39]. The case considered is the development of Purchase Order Integration project (P:O:INT.) of a leading cruise company Costa Crociere S.p.A. The data analysed mainly consist of primary data collected through qualitative explorative and semi-structured interviews. Secondary data—such as reports, and other material provided by the service provider or retrieved on thc web—were also used. Seven face to face qualitative interviews were conducted to supply chain managers and service provider staff. When available, we asked for and received additional documentations. During the interviews, we focused on issues related to information on general practice in SCM including the company's competitive strategies and the procurement process flow. We investigated the type of IT deployed and how such is shared within the company as well as with suppliers. We examined which kind of information are shared, such as the planning, the demand and the supply. Then, we probed on issues regarding collaborations from various aspects: relationship with partners as well as suppliers and joint performance measurement. Although the number of interviews may be considered relatively small, they were related to the key role that the respondents had in the planning and development of e-services. They provide a high level of reliability and validity to the research findings. Through our reference to the data were carefully analysed by following the general strategy of theoretical orientation of the case study [38].

3.1 The Study Context

Costa Crociere is the Europe's most relevant cruise company and in the last 60 years, it offers the best of the Italian hospitality, gastronomy and entertainment worldwide ensuring high quality services in leisure sector. Costa Crociere S.p.A. is the largest Italian cruise operator, it owns the following brands: Costa Crociere, AIDA Cruises and Iberocruceros. Costa Crociere S.p.A. belongs to Carnival Corporation & plc—the global cruise company leader in the industry. The supply chain management for the company is very complex because it has to manage a fleet of 15 ships, about 55 home ports, 73.000 annual purchase orders, 13.000 items and more than 500 suppliers involved in five continents. The cruise supply chain manages two main activities: food, beverage and hotel and technical operations. For this study food, beverage and hotel products are considered that involved all the procurement activities in order to provide hotel service aboard ships. Being generally of high value, these items arrive via road transport or express parcel delivery service for consolidation at the cruise company's warehouse. Before introducing the new platform, the absence of an integrated logistic process with suppliers created inefficiencies because the information exchange with the suppliers was unstructured (i.e. telephone calls, faxes of variation, emails). These involved high transaction costs and a high risk of error, low rapidity and accuracy of the order confirmation management, longer time communications with suppliers regarding the order change management and the relevant tracking. To overcome the above-mentioned criticalities, Costa Crociere decided to digitalize the logistic process through the implementation of the software called *web Tesi net Supply* of P.O.INT.—Purchase Order INTegration in 2011, with the following objectives: to provide a uniform system for the administrative management of the suppliers; to support the control of procurement expenditure; to allow the logistics activities dematerialization process; to reduce the lead time and to improve the services of the ships; to increase the supplier ability in terms of performance monitoring and of a better collaboration resulting in mutual advantages. Based on these objectives, the procurement department of Costa Cruise Operations area expressed to its service provider TESISQUARE the need to develop a single Web-based system. The latter is opened to suppliers and can manage the whole process linked to food, beverage and hotel products purchase orders to be sent to suppliers. Therefore, the basic idea was to adopt technique, tools and infrastructures web-based IT system opened to suppliers and able to manage the physical and information flows from the publication to the delivery in the port. It is a cloud-based B2B integration brokerage solution that improves efficiency and collaboration in extended enterprise processes, by enabling a multiformat and multi-protocol data exchange management. It is the first EDI platform in Italy in terms of active relationship, volumes of flows and documents exchange in compliance with the most important national and international standards. The EDI service allows users to manage standard and non-standard messages, while exchanging different types of business documents in the network. The new solution was intended to enable the exceptions and anomalies associated with the orders typical of Costa's business, such as tolerances relating to the supply quantities or the issue of supplementary orders for "exceptional" requests from the ship, to be highlighted and managed in the best possible way. Moreover, the platform increases data accuracy, the efficiency and the speed of business transactions and it supports the rationalization and simplification of data flow generation and control.

4 Main Findings and Discussion

Based on the interviews done to the managers of the company and on the reports analysed, the main benefits are the following:

- The process efficacy increased, as a consequence of the purchase order integration that optimizes the communication among ships, the procurement office and suppliers; the elimination of not value-added activities, a greater efficiency in order transmission as well as the reduction of non-compliance management time and more accurate tracking orders.
- The adoption of electronic invoicing system creates a reduction of transmission time/costs, physical space for storage and time to search for documents.
- The Integration Brokerage decreases paper documents and their physical storage costs. Moreover, there is a reduction of business data flow acquisition inside legacy system and data entry costs related to working time and input error.
- The digitalization of all the logistics activities that affected various areas of the work organization increases autonomy, flexibility and productivity.
- The enhancement of the service quality in the ships, thanks the ability to manage the exceptions in the procurement process.
- The improvement of a win–win approach with suppliers.

For almost the interviews, one of the most immediate benefits is the greater efficacy in the logistic process of order confirmation. The information system plays a strategic role in terms of managing the supply chain in such a complex global operation because all these supplies need to be delivered to the ship on a continuous basis. Such an operation requires an integrated system that can handle the continuous flow of information as well as keep a good uptime record. The procurement personnel have to efficiently track it, process it, consolidate it, get it to the ship and receive it and, finally, pay the bills. As a logistics supervisor says: "*Manually, the activities were done but with a high risk of error, low rapidity and accuracy of the order confirmation management, more long-time communications with supplier*". The respondents report that they modified their supply chain during the Web-system implementation. With the web-based system the ship transmits to the Supply chain office the procurement application; after the relevant completion in the Costa ERP, the purchase orders of the Cruise Operations area are published in real time so that the suppliers can receive a prompt notification via email. Then, by accessing to the portal, suppliers are able to immediately indicate any proposals of order changes with reference to the delivery date and/or to the quantity. TESI SCM automatically checks that the order confirmation meets the tolerance thresholds and highlights any exceptions that—if accepted—are shared with the other ships; moreover, the procedure supports Costa in managing critical issues resulting from delivery date changes. As a Supply Chain System Director says: "*The P.O.Int. project has been a breakthrough in the performances of the Procurement processes in the Food & Beverage area: from a paper-based management with more than 70,000 documents per year to the possibility to accurately analyse the procurement exceptions by increasing the level of service delivered to our fleet. Moreover, it was required to manage the exceptions to the standard process, typical of the Costa activity, such as tolerances concerning the procurement quantity or issues of additional orders for "exceptional" requirements and requests coming from the ship*".

One of the main impacts of digitalization on the organization of work is higher flexibility, which influences how workers interact and communicate with each other and with suppliers. Digitalization and technological innovation lead employers to deal with the development of more flexible ways of performing tasks. This point was mentioned by one of Costa Crociere manager: "*Digitalisation and change in the organization work resulted in greater productivity. The digitalization of the activities reduced manual work in the procurement tasks, transforming paperwork into electronic software systems and then changes hither to labour intense tasks to work-flow and IT supported processes*". From the point of view of economic theory, enhanced flexibility can be regarded as a change in the intra- and inter-organization coordination costs. With higher level of digitization, the company is increasing the extent to which they conduct both internal and external supply chain activities in a fully electronic environment.

Significant concern is that the adoption of an integrated logistic process implies a much higher degree of exchangeability of data and of automation in the information exchange. Hence, the relationship and collaboration with suppliers and service provider are very important in the logistic innovation process. Therefore, the findings suggest that web-based supply chain applications provide information capabilities that result in valuable business benefits, namely a more efficient planning and replenishment, better on-time delivery performance, a reduction of coordination costs with suppliers. In this way, it is possible to improve the coordination of supply chain activities, the material requirements and the planning roles and responsibilities. As a logistic manager explains: "*by sharing information, suppliers and the company increase supply chain visibility, allowing them to perform supply chain activities efficiently with effectively satisfy items requirements. Indeed, with better visibility, company can manipulate its operations to achieve economies of scale, coordinate inventory replenishment and optimize deliveries to ships. In this way it was possible to increase the efficacy of about 25%*". This suggests that strategic buyer–supplier relationships help foster collaborative behaviour that facilitates joint planning and processes beyond the levels reached in less intensive trading relationships. In other words, when suppliers are involved in supply management processes, contributions to higher quality, greater sharing of cost savings and reduced time to market are more easily attained.

Moreover, the solution has been successfully deployed with all current suppliers in the Food & Beverage area; subsequently, it has proven to be suitable for the downstream integration in the billing management process: the supplier attaches the invoice in pdf format to the PO published in TESI SCM; the Costa OCR (Optical Character Recognition) software automatically processes this document that, after a verification by the Finance operator, entered into the accounting system, ready to be paid. The process is then completed in "substitutive storage" through a completely "paperless" cycle. This shows that the development of strategic buyer–supplier relationship focuses on initiatives that improve superior characteristics among the supply chain members and create a *win–win* situation for buyer and supplier firms. As a Finance & Supply Chain System Director explains: "*the digitalization of Supply Chain generates a value-added partnership where both parties interact and negotiate the best agreement. This collaboration is formalized through a partnership. In this way, the suppliers and service provider contribute to improve the logistic process and also serve as a basis for knowledge sharing. Offering a multiply supplier platform allows the company to have a better control on B2B relations. Moreover, with reference to the suppliers, the partnership increases their ability of monitoring performance and a better collaboration results in mutual advantages that can be extended to other processes. The invoice web integration system allowed to increase the efficiency of the Finance and Supply chain department of about 20% and a reduction of 50% of posting lead time*". Therefore, the findings provide evidence that building collaborative relationships with suppliers allows company to achieve superior financial and business performance.

5 Conclusion and Limitations

This paper presents preliminary results of a case study on the adoption of a Web-based system open to suppliers in the cruise sector. The interest in this specific sector derives from the fact that the cruise industry is in a continuously developing phase as well as the management of its supply chain is characterized by high complexity. In particular, the study examined whether the digital supply chain management has a positive impact on the operational performance of companies. Our study provides theoretical and empirical evidence on the strength of using IT system open to suppliers and it also discusses the impact on the minimization of transaction costs thanks to: a better coordination of economic activities, higher efficiency of logistics process and of manual work. One of the main impacts from Industry 4.0 is the increasing need to integrate data and processes from outside the company. From a technological perspective, a digital supply chain becomes highly interconnected and collaborative at the global level. An integrative Web-based supply chain system provides information capabilities that result in valuable business benefits, namely: a more efficient planning and replenishment, better on-time delivery performance, less coordination costs with suppliers as well as more availability of items. This is in line with some previous scientific investigations [19, 28, 40–42]. To sum up, our study provides evidence on the utility of an integrated supply chain in order to achieve effective and efficient flows of products and services, information, money and decisions as well as to give maximum value to the customer. Moreover, this paper shows interesting insights on innovations in supply chain contributing to the debate on how digital transformation is changing the way companies compete, create value and engage with their business partners and customers. While this article makes significant contributions to research and practice, there are some limitations that present opportunities for future researches. We only conducted in depth interviews in one cruise company and we can only claim that the results of this work are generalizable to companies that operate in the cruise sector. Future researches may extend the study by collecting data from various cruise companies and their suppliers. In addition, next papers could deal with multi-level analysis comparing cruise companies in different countries.

References

1. Feibert, D. C., Hansen, M. S., & Jacobsen, P.: An integrated process and digitalization perspective on the shipping supply chain—A literature review. In *2017 IEEE International Conference on Industrial Engineering and Engineering Management (IEEM)*, pp. 1352–1356.
2. Véronneau, S., Roy, J., & Beaulieu, M. (2015). Cruise ship suppliers: A field study of the supplier relationship characteristics in a service supply chain. *Tourism Management Perspectives, 16*, 76–84.
3. Flynn, B. B., Huo, B., & Zhao, X. (2010). The impact of supply chain integration on performance: A contingency and configuration approach. *Journal of Operations Management, 28*, 58–71.

4. Za, S., Marzo, F., De Marco, M., & Cavallari, M.: Agent based simulation of trust dynamics in dependence networks. In *International Conference on Exploring Services Science*, vol. February, pp. 243–252. Springer, Cham.
5. Zhao, X., Huo, B., Flynn, B. B., & Yeunga, J. H. Y. (2008). The impact of power and relationship commitment on the integration between manufacturers and customers in a supply chain. *Journal of Operations Management, 26*(3), 368–388.
6. Ganotakis, P., Hsieh, W. L., & Love, J. H. (2013). Information systems, inter-functional collaboration and innovation in Taiwanese high-tech manufacturing firms. *Production Planning & Control, 24*, 837–850.
7. Gunasekaran, A., & Ngai, E. W. T. (2004). Information systems in supply chain integration and management. *European Journal of Operational Research, 159*, 269–295.
8. Depaoli, P., & Za, S.: Towards the redesign of e-Business maturity models for SMEs. In *Designing organizational systems* (pp. 285–300). Springer.
9. Gupta, U. G., & Capen, M. (1996). An empirical investigation of the contribution of iS to manufacturing productivity. *Information and Management, 31*(4), 227–233.
10. Koh, S. C. L., & Saad, S. M. (2006). Managing uncertainty in ERP-controlled manufacturing environments in SMEs. *International Journal of Production Economics, 101*(1), 109–127.
11. Vaggelas, G. K., & Lagoudis, I. N.: Analysing the supply chain strategy of the cruise industry: the case of a small cruise company. *Presented: International Association of Maritime Economists*, Lisbona, 1–17 July 2010.
12. Li, G., Yang, H., Sun, L., & Sohal, A. S. (2009). The Impact of IT implementation on supply chain integration and performance. *International Journal of Production Economics, 120*, 125–138.
13. Alfalla-Luque, R., Medina-Lopez, C., & Dey, P. K. (2013). Supply chain integration framework using literature review. *Production Planning & Control, 24*(8–9), 800–817.
14. Wantao, Y.: The effect of IT-enabled supply chain integration on performance. *Production Planning & Control. The Management of Operations, 26*, 945–957.
15. Erkoc, M., Iakovou, E. T., & Spaulding, A. E. (2005). Multi-stage onboard inventory management policies for food and beverage items in cruise liner operations. *Journal of Food Engineering, 70*(3), 269–279.
16. Qu, H., & Ping, E. W. Y. (1999). A service performance model of Hong Kong cruise travelers' motivation factors and satisfaction. *Tourism Management., 20*(2), 237–244.
17. Véronneau, S., & Roy, J. (2009). RFID benefits, costs, and possibilities: The economical analysis of RFID deployment in a cruise corporation global service supply chain. *International Journal of Production Economics, 122*(2), 692–702.
18. Aramyan, L. H., Oude Lansink, G. J. M., van der Vorst, G. A. J., & van Kooten, O.: Performance measurement in agri-food supply chains: A case study. *Supply Chain Management*, *12*(4). Emerald.
19. Yu, W. (2015). The effect of IT-enabled supply chain integration on performance. *Production Planning & Control, 26*(12), 945–957.
20. Chubachi, I. S., & Junior, W. R. G. (2016). Integration in the chain: A case study on the collaboration in the chain of a resale company of parts for industrial equipment. *Independent Journal of Management & Production, 7*(5), 662–677.
21. Garo, W. R., Jr., & Guimarães, M. R. N. (2018). Competitive priorities and strategic alignment as mediators in the relationship between companies in the Brazilian automotive supply chain. *South African Journal of Industrial Engineering, 29*(1), 184–194.
22. Cooper, M. C., Lambert, D. M., & Pagh, J. D. (1997). Supply chain management: More than a new name for logistics. *The International Journal of Logistics Management, 8*(1), 1–14.
23. Paulraj, A., & Chen, I. J. (2007). Strategic buyer–supplier relationships, information technology and external logistics integration. *Journal of Supply Chain Management, 43*(2), 2–14.
24. Giunipero, L., Handfield, R. B., & Eltantawy, R. (2006). Supply management's evolution: Key skill sets for the supply manager of the future. *International Journal of Operations & Production Management, 26*(7), 822–844.

25. Sahin, F., & Robinson, E. P. (2002). Flow coordination and information sharing in supply chains: Review, implications, and directions for future research. *Decision sciences, 33*(4), 505–536.
26. Hearnshaw, E. J., & Wilson, M. M. (2013). A complex network approach to supply chain network theory. *International Journal of Operations & Production Management, 33*(4), 442–469.
27. Stevens, G. C., & Johnson, M. (2016). Integrating the supply chain... 25 years on. *International Journal of Physical Distribution & Logistics Management, 46*(1), 19–42.
28. Chengalur-Smith, I., Duchessi, P., & Gil-Garcia, J. R. (2012). Information sharing and business systems leveraging in supply chains: An empirical investigation of one web-based application. *Information & Management, 49*(1), 58–67.
29. Wu, L., Yue, X., Jin, A., & Yen, D. C. (2016). Smart supply chain management: A review and implications for future research. *The International Journal of Logistics Management, 27*(2), 395–417.
30. Alicke, K., Rexhausen, D., & Seyfert, A.: Supply chain 4.0 in consumer goods. Mckinsey & Company.
31. Prajogo, D., & Olhager, J. (2012). Supply chain integration and performance: The effects of long-term relationships, information technology and sharing, and logistics integration. *International Journal of Production Economics, 135*(1), 514–522.
32. Vickery, S. K., Jayaram, J., Droge, C., & Calantone, R. (2003). The effects of an integrative supply chain strategy on customer service and financial performance: An analysis of direct versus indirect relationships. *Journal of Operations Management, 21*, 523–539.
33. Brettel, M., Friederichsen, N., Keller, M., & Rosenberg, M.: How virtualization, decentralization and network building change the manufacturing landscape: An industry 4.0 perspective. *International Journal of Mechanical, Industrial Science and Engineering, 8*(1), 37–44.
34. Santos, F. M., & Eisenhardt, K. M. (2005). Organizational boundaries and theories of organization. *Organization Science, 16*(5), 491–508.
35. Neubert, G., Ouzrout, Y., & Bouras, A. (2004). Collaboration and integration through information technologies in supply chains. *International Journal of Technology Management, 28*, 2.
36. La Londe, B. J., & Masters, J. M. (1994). Emerging logistics strategies: Blueprints for the next century. *International Journal of Physical Distribution & Logistics Management, 24*(7), 35–47.
37. Eisenhardt, K. M. (1989). Building theories from case study research. *Academy of management review, 14*(4), 532–550.
38. Yin, R. K. (2013). Validity and generalization in future case study evaluations. *Evaluation, 19*(3), 321–332.
39. Recker, J.: *Scientific research in information systems: A beginner's guide.* Springer Science & Business Media.
40. Vendrell-Herrero, F., Bustinza, O. F., Parry, G., & Georgantzis, N. (2017). Servitization, digitization and supply chain interdependency. *Industrial Marketing Management, 60*, 69–81.
41. Presutti, W. D., Jr. (2003). Supply management and e-procurement: Creating value added in the supply chain. *Industrial marketing management, 32*(3), 219–226.
42. Hasan, M. (2013). Sustainable supply chain management practices and operational performance. *American Journal of Industrial and Business Management, 3*(1), 42.

Discretion and Continuity of Psychological Space

Andrey Khudyakov

Abstract The problem of discreteness—continuity of sensory space, and as a consequence—of psychological space is considered. Different models used in psychophysics, different interpretation of the threshold problem in psychology, as well as different threshold theories lead to ambiguous understanding of this problem. Our model of psychological measurement is based on the concept of "generalized image" (GI). By definition, GI is a dynamic system that is in a continuous process of self-formation. This process can be represented as a continuous series of acts of comparison of the predicted state of the GI with the current one. As a result of such acts of comparison, a certain "measuring space" arises, in which further forecast of the state of the GI is carried out. Each stimulus set corresponds to a certain stable set of subjective characteristics (the main characteristics of the mental image of the stimulus set), which basically determine the psychological assessment of the stimulus. We call this stable set of subjective characteristics the quasi-objective scale. In the process of measurement, incentives are distributed along this scale in accordance with the degree of representation in them of certain subjective characteristics.

Keywords Psychological space · Discreteness · Continuity · Quasi-objective scales · Sensory space

1 Introduction

From the dichotomy of the "yes–no" comparison result, it follows the conclusion about the discreteness of the psychological space in which this operation is performed. But the comparison processes are multiple and dynamic. They underlie the continuous self-formation of the generalized image (GI). This multiplicity is superimposed on the discrete psychological space of the "single instantaneous cut" and thus creates a continuous psychological space of the generalized image, both external and internal. The external psychological space is defined here as the space in

A. Khudyakov (✉)
Herzen State Pedagogical University of Russia (Herzen University), 48 Moika river embankments, Saint Petersburg 191186, Russian Federation

E. Zaramenskikh and A. Fedorova (eds.), *Digitalization of Society, Economics and Management*, Lecture Notes in Information Systems and Organisation 53,
https://doi.org/10.1007/978-3-030-94252-6_30

which decisions determining activity are made. On the other hand, making managerial decisions requires a certain discreteness of information necessary for this. Namely, the discreteness of the external psychological space is imposed by the tasks of activity solved in it.

Therefore, on the one hand, the evaluation field is built on a discrete physical-sensory space in what the Bouguer-Weber law is performed, and on the other hand, this field itself is continuous. The discontinuities are observed in the space of stimuli, in the psychological space each point is inextricably bound to its adjacent points, i.e. it is always possible to find infinitely small *a* and *b*, in order to perform inequality $|E\text{-}a| \leq b$. For example, the theory of signal detection operates in the decision-making space, which conceals the discreteness of the physical-sensory space, while Stevens' neuroquantum theory, on the contrary, was built in the continuous model.

The attitude to the threshold problem determines the researcher's view of the structure of the sensory space. Supporters of Fechner's views consider sensory space as a discrete formation, reflecting the discreteness of mental processes. Opponents consider the sensory space to be continuous, from which the conclusion follows about the continuity of the psyche as a whole.

The problem of the discreteness and continuity of the psyche is associated with the structure of sensory space because it represents an "input" whereby information is perceived by the psyche. Incoming information can be "quantified" at the input (the difference threshold can be considered as a "mental quantum"), as follows from Fechner's threshold model, or perceived continuously, as follows from models that do not recognize the presence of a threshold as a theoretical construct. It follows from the Fechner model that the psyche is essentially discrete, and its observed continuity is determined by processes of a sufficiently high level of organization. The opposite conclusion can be drawn from the model of its opponents: the psyche is initially continuous, and sometimes the observed discreteness in its work is determined by the situation provoking the work of corresponding mental processes of a sufficiently high level of organization.

2 Method

The idea of discreteness of mental space goes back to the model of Fechner's sensory space, which, based on the Bouguer-Weber law, postulated the presence of the JND (just-noticeable difference) as an indivisible "quantum" of sensory space. The development of other models (Stevens, Zabrodin, Khudyakov) led to a revision of the attitude to the Bouguer-Weber law in psychology. But F. Clicks encourages not to exclude this law from psychology, and claims that it is quite valid in cases of one-dimensional psychophysical dimensions. That is, in the case of explicit psychophysical correlates.

G. Ekman from the logarithmic type of connection between the Thurston model's scale ("law of comparative judgments") and the scale based on the data of the direct method of relationship evaluation made a conclusion about the execution in the "psychological space" of the relation similar to the Bouguer-Weber law for sensory space.

3 Research Results

The Bouguer-Weber law establishes a constant relationship between the magnitude of the stimulus affecting the psyche and the value of the JND corresponding to this value of the stimulus: $e/R = k$, where e is the value of the JND (the value of the change in the stimulus $R1$-R, which causes a change in sensation), R is the initial the intensity of the stimulus, k is a certain constant. It follows from this relation that $e = kR$. But the JND has its own subjective analogue s. s can be interpreted in this context as a certain zone of uncertainty, i.e. a zone of "accumulation of sensory change" which is not noticed until the value of the stimulus reaches R_1. In a continuous subjective space, this zone is represented by a point. However, each point in the theoretical model corresponds in the experimental model to a "confidence interval" determined by the measurement error. The confidence interval can serve as an estimate of the value of s, which in turn is somehow related to the value of the sensation E caused by the influencing stimulus $s = f(E)$.

In a measurement experiment, both e and s can be assessed by the standard deviation d of subjective assessments of the stimulus value.

Thus, $d = f(E)$ and $d = kR$.

Consequently, from this experimentally established relationship, one can obtain the form of the psychophysical law $E = g(R)$, where g is the inverse function of f, that is, the equation $E = k_1 g(d)$ represents the form of the psychophysical law accurate to the constant k_1.

This seemingly obvious conclusion is well tested in psychophysical studies of the relationships between explicit psychophysical correlates, in which the physical stimulus can be measured at least on a scale of intervals. In cases where physical correlates cannot be established or measured, the resulting relationship becomes less obvious. Provided that the Bouguer-Weber law is fulfilled, the $R = f(E)$ correlation makes it possible to reconstruct the physical scale if it is impossible to obtain the physical scale by direct measurements. We will call such a reconstructed scale "quasi-objective". The quasi-objective scale provides a quantitative representation in the sensory space of those objective characteristics of stimuli, which mainly determine subjective assessments, but cannot always be directly measured by objective (physical) methods [1].

The above reasoning was related to the classical psychophysical dimensions within the framework of the sensory space model. In the transition to the model of "psychological measuring space" we can no longer talk about the Bouguer-Weber law, but only about its possible analogue. Especially since so far many psychophysicists have denied the possibility of excluding the subject of psychophysics from the sensory space.

Our model of psychological measurement is based on the concept of "generalized image" (GI). By definition, GI is a dynamic system that is in a continuous process of self-formation. This process can be represented as a continuous series of acts of comparison of the predicted state of the GI with the current one. As a result of such acts of comparison, a certain "measuring space" arises, in which further forecast of the state of the GI is carried out.

The success of our existence indicates that our interaction with the environment is sufficiently adequate. The basis of any interaction is prediction, thus, comparison, and therefore measurement. It is the success of our existence that makes it possible to assume the invariance of the measuring space to the "external field of meanings". "Measuring space" will be called an intermediate working construct between the "external field of meanings" and the GI. The "field of meanings" is the entire subjective–objective environment, the interaction with which determines the activity. As a result of the latter, self-formation of the GI occurs.

Previously, we showed the possibility of constructing psychological metric scales (intervals and ratios) for measuring stimuli that do not have a physical metric, based on direct methods of assessment. It follows from this that the psychological measurement space can be regarded as a continuous metric space of real numbers with the metric $d = |x–y|$ (in the multidimensional case as a Euclidean space of the corresponding dimension). In this space, all operations applicable to real numbers are allowed.

In the measurement process in this space, a subjective standard is formed on the basis of self-instruction and self-criterion, the comparison of the image of the stimulus with which determines the evaluation of this stimulus. In this case, the image of the stimulus is not identical to its prototype. It can be represented as a function $F(S, I, P)$, where S is a stimulus; I—instruction (the whole experimental situation); P is the personality of the subject.

Each stimulus set corresponds to a certain stable set of subjective characteristics (the main characteristics of the mental image of the stimulus set), which basically determine the psychological assessment of the stimulus. We call this stable set of subjective characteristics the quasi-objective scale. In the process of measurement, incentives are distributed along this scale in accordance with the degree of representation in them of certain subjective characteristics. In the case of psychophysical measurements of "simple" stimuli by simple evaluation criteria, quasi-objective scales represent psychophysical correlates of physical parameters of stimuli. But even in these rather "simple" cases, the observed correspondence is far from being an identity. In the case of psychometric measurements, when it is fundamentally impossible to measure the characteristics of stimuli in a physical scale, the resulting psychological (psychometric) scales "get lost in the ether" and lose the physical basis familiar to a psychophysicist.

Nevertheless, it would be interesting to arrange the stimuli on a scale of "primary" subjective characteristics, on which psychological assessments on more complex (integral) criteria are based. For example, when measuring the handwriting aesthetics (a classic example of a psychometric measurement), the integral assessment is a combination of assessments according to more specific criteria—the inclination of letters, ornateness, line thickness, etc. However, the assessment for all particular and integral criteria may be based on one set of "primary" subjective characteristics. This hypothetical set is, in our opinion, a quasi-objective scale.

4 Discussion

In a basis of a method of construction of a quasi-objective scale, we have put an assumption that in psychological space the relationship between size of an influencing stimulus and a zone of uncertainty of perception of change of this size is carried out similar to the Bouguer-Weber law for sensory space.

$$r/R = k \tag{1}$$

r is the zone of uncertainty in the assessment of the stimulus.

This zone is determined not only by the physical significance of the barely noticeable change in the stimulus, but also by the error in the psychological measurement of this stimulus.

$$r = k_1 e \tag{2}$$

where e is the error of psychological measurement, which determines the psychological zone of uncertainty; k_I—proportionality coefficient [2].

In turn, e is a function of the value of the estimate E:

$$\begin{aligned} e &= f(E) \text{ or} \\ E &= f^{-1}(e) = F\left(kR/k_1\right) \end{aligned} \tag{3}$$

This ratio makes it possible to construct a quasi-objective scale based on the values of e.

In psychological measurements, it is difficult to expect an explicit manifestation of the alleged pattern due to the many factors affecting the error. In addition to the desired uncertainty e, the total error s includes errors d caused by factors that are not directly related to the subject of measurement, but which violate its "ideal" course; d'—random errors:

$$s = e + d + d' \tag{4}$$

Therefore, if it is possible to isolate from n estimates of stimuli a set of at least m estimates ($m < n$), in which the desired regularity is traced (monotonic dependence of the value of e on the value of the estimate E), then one can expect to determine the remaining "correct" values of e by approximating the dependence by m points. Of course, the closer m is to n, the more confidence in the correctness of the established pattern.

Assuming that the "genuine" dependencies are "concealed" behind a large measurement error and that they can be restored using approximation, we make a rather strong statement. The stronger the statement, the easier it is to refute it, therefore, if, as a result of further analysis of the experimental data, this statement does not stand up to criticism, we will have to part with the idea of constructing a quasi-objective scale. We are deliberately taking this risk.

The quasi-objective scales constructed in the above way leave us within the framework of this particular experience. This makes it impossible to compare the results of different experiments. In order to overcome this disadvantage, we applied a linear transformation to the constructed quasi-objective scales, which we used earlier when constructing the scales of intervals and ratios:

$$y = (b_2 - b_1)(x - a_1)/(a_2 - a_1) + b_1 \tag{5}$$

where x is the scale value of the original scale; y – scale value of the new scale; a_2, a_1—minimum and maximum values of the original scale; b_2, b_1—the minimum and maximum values of the new scale, $b_2 = 10$, $b_1 = 0$ were chosen.

We used the concept of a quasi-objective scale to build a model of the space of the results of psychophysical measurement. This model seems to be in the following form.

The subject in the context of the measurement experiment forms a subjective standard of the "ideal stimulus". As a result of comparison with this standard, the stimuli are located in the measuring psychological space along an axis, which is determined by a quasi-objective scale. The closer the stimulus is on this axis to the standard, the higher its subjective assessment. Ideally, when the stimulus coincides with the reference, this estimate reaches its maximum. Of course, we mean images of stimuli, and not the stimuli themselves as such. Therefore, this subjective axis is an "inverted" quasi-objective scale—the maximum of the axis coincides with the minimum of the quasi-objective scale and vice versa. Further, we will call this axis in subjective space the quasi-objective scale proper.

With this insight, we built a "framework" for the measurement space. Next, we are interested in how the estimates of stimuli will behave in this space. Obviously, the evaluation of a stimulus depends on the location of the stimulus on a quasi-objective scale. If we denote the coordinate of the stimulus position by s, and the value of the estimate by E, then $E = f(s)$. It can be assumed that this function reaches its maximum when the stimulus coincides with the standard ($s = 0$); with increasing s, the value of the estimate decreases and asymptotically tends to zero. We cannot indicate the exact position on the quasi-objective scale that would most likely determine the zero value of the stimulus. The assumption of asymptotic tendency to zero with increasing argument excludes the representation of the desired function in a linear form.

5 Conclusion

Let us consider possible cases of the behavior of the derivative dE/ds. If the derivative is equal to 0, then this means that the assessment does not depend on the position of the stimulus on the scale, or that all the stimuli were in the same place on the scale, that is, either the measurement experiment did not work out for us, or the subjects did not distinguish between stimuli according to a given evaluation criterion—"everything looks the same". We will consider these cases as special. Further, if the derivative is constant, then we get a linear estimation function. We have already rejected this case. We use a fairly popular model dE/ds = kE, where k is a constant. The solution to this differential equation will be the ratio:

$$\begin{aligned} \ln(E) &= ks + k_1 \text{ or} \\ E &= e^{ks} e^{k1} = pe^{ks} \end{aligned} \tag{6}$$

where p is some constant. When $s = 0, p = E$, that is, the value of p coincides with the assessment of the standard, therefore, with the maximum possible assessment in this case. Since with increasing s E decreases, then $k < 0$. When $|k|=1/s$, $E = p/e^1$, it follows from this that the value of k determines the range of measurement of the value of estimates—the larger k is in absolute value, the narrower this range. Thereby, we defined the psychological meaning of integration constants.

References

1. Khudyakov A. I. (2016). Psychology of psychological dimensions (471 pp.). Palmarium Academic Publishing. AP LAMBERT Academic Publishing GmbH & Co. KG.
2. Faltermeier E.A., & Khudyakov A. I. (2017). Experimental bases for constructing psychological metric scales (171 pp.). Palmarium Academic Publishing. AP LAMBERT Academic Publishing GmbH & Co. KG.
3. Stevens, S. S. (1957). On the psychophysical law. *Psychological Review, 64*(3), 153–181.
4. Stevens, S. S. (2017). *Psychophysics: Introduction to its perceptual, neural and social prospects*. Routledge.
5. Khudyakov, A. I. (2016). Psychology of psychological dimensions. Palmarium Academic Publishing. AP LAMBERT Academic Publishing GmbH & Co. KG.
6. Klix, F. (1962). Elementaranalysen zur psychophysik der raumwahrnehmung. Berlin.
7. Ekman, P., & Friesen, W. V. (1971). Constants across cultures in the face and emotion. *Journal of Personality and Social Psychology, 17*(2), 124–129.
8. Geissler, H. G., & Puffe, M. (1983). The inferential basis of classification: From perceptual to memory code systems. *Advances in Psychology, 11*, 87–124.
9. Geissler, H. G. (1989). Psychophysical law: The need for more than one level of explanation. *Behavioral and Brain Sciences, 12*(2), 274–275.
10. Geissler, H. G., Schebera, F. U., & Kompass, R. (1999). Ultra-precise quantal timing: Evidence from simultaneity thresholds in long-range apparent movement. *Perception & Psychophysics, 61*(4), 707–726.

Professional Deformation of Staff Under the Digital Economy

Elena Gasparovich and Ekaterina Uskova

Abstract In the article, the authors focus on the study of personnel in the context of the digital economy. The influence of professional deformation of personnel, which prevents the formation of a demanded employee in the digital economy, was studied using the example of salespeople of retail chains. It is assumed that digitalization leads to the emergence of multitasking, lack of time and constant control, which are additional stress factors that exacerbate professional deformation. To conduct an empirical study the following methods were used: "The level of emotional burnout" by V. V. Boyko, R. Cattell 16 Personality Factors Test, "The level of subjective control" by J. Rotter (LSC test), the method of pictorial associations by S. Rosenzweig. We identified two groups of network sellers with pronounced symptoms of professional deformation in the digital economy: experimental and control. The experimental group revealed the existence of a set of personal deformations: egocentrism, neuroticism, impatience. The sources of these deformations in the course of the personality adaptation to the peculiarities of professional activity have been determined. One of the main manifestations of the professional deformation of these workers is the internal locus control, the tendency to control everyone around, to be responsible for everything, to assume the role of a "resolver of difficulties" with low indicators of communication competence. A list of measures that allow the development and implementation of preventive response technologies in the organization's management are proposed, the use of which will ensure the controllability of personnel deformation.

Keywords Professional deformation · The level of subjective control · Emotional burnout · Digitalization of the economy

E. Gasparovich (✉) · E. Uskova
Ural Federal University, Yekaterinburg, Russia

E. Uskova
e-mail: e.v.uskova@urfu.ru

E. Zaramenskikh and A. Fedorova (eds.), *Digitalization of Society, Economics and Management*, Lecture Notes in Information Systems and Organisation 53,
https://doi.org/10.1007/978-3-030-94252-6_31

1 Introduction

The transition to the digital economy requires a gradual change in approaches to the management of all contingents of enterprise personnel, and the upholding of personnel training processes for the transition period. This also applies to retail chains, where the effectiveness of activities primarily depends on the personnel, their preparedness and readiness to quickly and at a modern level to carry out professional activities.

The digital economy requires a highly dynamic workforce. These are people who must be ready for change and continuously learn. The personnel that will be in demand must have a certain set of competencies: critical and analytical thinking, willingness to work in a multicultural environment, openness to joint activities in distributed mobile teams and a willingness to propose new creative solutions for the tasks of a new economy. The quality of the personnel working in the contact zone should be considered as an important factor in the development of the digital economy, which can both accelerate or slow down the processes of digitalization of all areas of professional activity of organizations.

Digitalization and the emergence of modern technologies require constant improvement of all categories of personnel. Retail chain employees must be prepared for the need to constantly learn and work under time pressure. The staff of modern retail chains must be ready to work not only with people, but also to work with a computer. All operations that are performed in reality are duplicated in a computer program. This requires the ability to simultaneously work with people and technology, which was previously impossible. Accordingly, one and the same person at the same time period performs many completely different operations. In addition, the quality performance of these operations requires ongoing training, which is often carried out directly on the job, without interrupting work. In addition, modern technologies allow constant control over the quality of employees' work, which is carried out using audio and video recording of their work, which is also an additional stress factor. It is obvious that working in such conditions requires special skills from people and their constant improvement. Not surprisingly, fatigue and burnout are a direct result of working in such harsh conditions.

Salespeople of retail chains belong to a group of professions where the "human factor" is decisive for professional success. Work in the contact zone "man-man" requires the use of internal reserves, "strain" adaptation mechanisms [7]. Over time, in such professions, people burn out, their work efficiency decreases, and professional deformations are formed. Managing these processes is an important task for the management of retail chains wishing to remain competitive in the current requirements of the digital economy.

Studying the problem of the impact of professional deformations of modern enterprises employees and the development of new technologies for personnel management is becoming an urgent task in the context of the digitalization of the economy. The purpose of this article is to study the above problem using the example of salespeople in a trading network. This contingent of employees has to work in constant contact with people, often overly emotional and sometimes unfriendly; at the same time, their work requires a readiness to act in the face of pressure from the requirements of the trading network and administration.

As a result, professional deformation manifests itself in negative changes in behavior in professional activity: at the beginning, the style of communication changes subtly, a formal attitude toward the performance of functional duties is manifested. After that, the structure of the skill changes, and finally, new formations appear in the personality of the employee himself. These transformations entail changes in the negative side of the professional capabilities of the individual and his inclinations [10, 20]. As professionalization progresses, the success of an activity begins to be determined by an ensemble of professionally important qualities that have been "exploited" for years. Some of them are gradually transformed into professionally undesirable qualities. At the same time, professional accentuations are gradually developing—excessively expressed qualities and their combinations, which negatively affect the activity and behavior of a specialist. Some functionally neutral personality traits, developing, can be transformed into professional negative qualities. The result of all these psychological metamorphoses is the deformation of the specialist's personality [15]. With an extreme degree of professional deformation, which is already called professional degradation, a person changes his moral value orientations, becomes professionally untenable (19).

The study in order to identify the impact of professional deformation on the formation of personnel in the context of digitalization of the economy was conducted on the basis of "Element-Trade" LLC in Ekaterinburg, which sells food products.

Research objectives:

1. To identify the impact of professional deformation on the staff of retail chains (category: seller) in the context of the digitalization of the economy.
2. Investigate the level of emotional burnout among the salespeople of the retail chain, its influence on the professional deformation of personnel and, on this basis, form two surveyed groups of salespeople (experimental and control).
3. To identify other social and psychological characteristics of the personality of the network sellers, which affect professional deformation.
4. To study the level of subjectiveness in two surveyed groups of sellers.
5. To identify the style of behavior of salespeople and determine the level of adaptation to the social environment.

The hypothesis of our research: there is a negative impact of professional deformation on the formation of personnel in the context of the digitalization of the economy, which requires a separate study and solution of the indicated problem based on the attraction of the potential of personnel management practice.

To test this hypothesis, we consider it possible to use a number of psychological tests: "The level of emotional burnout" V. V. by Boyko [4], Cattell 16 Personality Factors Test, "The level of subjective control" by J. Rotter (LSC test) [2], the technique of risky associations by S. Rosenzweig [16]. The data obtained from these tests will help to answer the questions posed.

The number of personnel who took part in the study is 142 people, which is a sufficient number of subjects for the study [9]. The age of the subjects was from 22 to 48 years old. Personnel survey was carried out during working hours. The age of the subjects was from 22 to 48 years old. Gender of the subjects: men 38%, women 62%. The work experience of the subjects was from 5 to 8 years. All subjects are mid-level personnel.

Research methods are: theoretical (analysis, generalization of scientific literature on the research problem); practical: testing, inter-view.

The structure of the article includes: Introduction with an indication of relevance, theoretical validity of the article. Materials and Methods with a description of the main directions of research and statistical data on the research problem. Results of research and Discussion on the problems of professional deformation of trade network employees (sellers) in the digital economy. Conclusion based on the study.

2 Literature Review

Research shows that the performance of professional activities causes the emergence of deformed personal properties under the influence of psychogenic influences [1, 6]. At the stage of professionalization in many types of professions, the development of professional destruction takes place [20].

In modern literature, to determine the destructive influence of professional activity on the personality of a specialist, the terms "personality deformation", "professional deformation" are used. The professional deformation of the personality of a specialist in the most general form can be defined as a change in the qualities and properties of a person under the influence of his performance of professional activities [14]. This phenomenon was first described in the 1960s in the USA in order to study the effectiveness of professions depending on the social environment. H. J. Freundenberger got its definition—a "characteristic of the psychological state of healthy people who are in an intense and close contact with customers in an emotionally laden, saturated atmosphere at giving them professional help" [5]. In domestic studies, professional deformation within the framework of the teaching profession began to be studied by A. K. Markova, N. V. Kuzmina [10, 11] in the context of the study of the professional activity of the master of industrial training. We find the study of the term "professional deformation" in the works of O. Polyakova [13].

Based on research in this area, the following provisions can be listed.

First, in the socionomic professions of the "person - person" system, the phenomenon of professional deformation is revealed. "The communicative practices of representatives of socionomic professions and their perception of the client determine the most pronounced and typical professional deformations that create risks for clients and the social environment, and therefore require a set of measures for timely diagnosis and prevention" [18].

Secondly, as professionalization progresses, a set of personal qualities is determined, which are intensively "exploited". Some of them, as a rule, due to interaction with people, become dominant character traits and negatively affect professional activity. At the same time, some functionally neutral qualities are gradually transformed into professionally negative personality traits. The personality under the influence of the profession undergoes significant changes.

Thirdly, professions of the "person – person" type are most susceptible to professional deformations. According to S. P. Beznosov, this happens due to the fact that communication with another person necessarily includes his reverse impact on the subject of the given labor [3].

Fourthly, the constant performance of one and the same professional activity leads to the appearance of professional fatigue, the emergence of psychological barriers, the impoverishment of the repertoire of ways to perform activities, the loss of professional skills and abilities, and a decrease in work ability. When work becomes a labor service or just a source of money, apathy often seizes the person. Emotionally, such an individual is characterized not only by indifference and disinterest, but also by the irritability that is caused by both clients and colleagues. The amplitude of a person's emotional reactions in this state ranges from indifference and dissatisfaction to despair and aggressiveness. He loses the ability to distinguish the impulses of the psychological reality of other people. All this is destructive for the person himself, but is compensated by other mental structures so as not to be reflected in other people, clients. As a result, professional deformation manifests itself in negative changes in behavior in professional activity: at the beginning, the communication style changes subtly, a formal attitude toward the performance of functional duties is manifested. After that, the structure of the skill changes, and finally, new formations appear in the personality of the employee himself. These transformations entail changes in the negative side of the professional capabilities of the individual and his inclinations [10, 20]. As professionalization progresses, the success of activity begins to be determined by an ensemble of professionally important qualities that have been "exploited" for years. Some of them are gradually transformed into professionally undesirable qualities. At the same time, professional accentuations are gradually developing—overly expressed qualities and their combinations, which negatively affect the activity and behavior of a specialist. Some functionally neutral personality traits, developing, can be transformed into professional negative qualities. The result of all these psychological metamorphoses is the deformation of the specialist's personality [15]. With an extreme degree of professional deformation, which is already called professional degradation, a person changes his moral value orientations, becomes professionally untenable [19].

3 Research Methodology

For the study, a diagnostic toolkit was developed, which included the following tests and methods. First, the methodology for diagnosing the level of emotional burnout by V. V. Boyko. Secondly, R. Kettell's test for diagnostics of personality traits suffering from occupational deformation. Thirdly, the methodology "The level of subjective control" by J. Rotter (adapted for research in the professional environment by E.F. Bazhina, S.A. Golynkina, A.M. Etkind). Fourthly, S. Rosenzweig's method of drawing frustration.

Methodology for diagnosing the level of emotional burnout by V. V. Boyko.

Purpose of the method: Revealing the severity of the components of "burnout" as a strategy of defensive behavior among representatives of communicative professions.

Application of the technique: In individual and group examination in combination with other techniques for the diagnosis of personality traits. Each of the three components of "burnout" (voltage, resistance, exhaustion) is diagnosed by 4 signs that form the corresponding scales. This technique provides a detailed picture of the burnout syndrome. The score for each symptom is expressed in the range from 0 to 30 points. The technique identifies the leading symptoms of burnout (according to the appropriate scales). It measures quite different phenomena—such as reactions to external and internal factors, methods of psychological defense, the state of the nervous system. Quantitative indicators determine the degree of formation of each of the "burnout" phases. The dominant symptoms are diagnosed (in individual phases and in general), it is determined by what factors they are caused (professional environment or subjective-personal characteristics). The results of diagnostics using this technique provide the basis for further work to reduce the "risk factors" of burnout in the professional environment and work with personnel. Survey: Working with a methodology form, self-assessment of the severity of symptoms by calculating points and comparing them with the key.

R. Kettell's test, for the diagnosis of personality traits suffering from occupational deformation.

Purpose of the methodology: R. Cattell's questionnaire is a multidimensional methodology that assesses the properties of a normal personality, it describes the personality structure of a person, identifies personality problems, helps to find corrective mechanisms for solving personality problems.

Application of the methodology: The basis of the R. Cattell test is the "theory of personality traits", while the personality is described by a set of primary personality traits that determine its inner content and behavior. The person being tested falls into a ready-made coordinate system, and their properties are measured and compared with predetermined properties. R. Cattell's 16-factor personality questionnaire is a method of an objective experimental psychological research of personality, its express diagnostics. This is a standardized questionnaire that includes 187 judgments, divided into 16 groups—scales that measure various polar personality traits. Each of the scales assesses a separate personality trait in standard points. The sum of the points obtained on each scale is converted into scores on a 10-point scale. The maximum score is 10 points, the average value is 5.5 points. Extreme grades—1 and 10 points—are rare in practice, they correspond to extreme, accentuated personality traits. Judgments, instructions, application procedure, methods of obtaining, presentation of results and conclusions are unchanged and apply in all cases of testing. With the help of tests by methods of factor analysis, factors that characterize the general properties of a person are revealed. In the text of the document of the package "Personality" (Kettell's questionnaire PF-16), scales of assessments of each of the personality traits of an adult are given. The results of testing in the Cattell PF-16 computer questionnaire are presented quantitatively for each investigated personality trait of an adult, as well as in the form of a graph and qualitative interpretation.

Methodology "The level of subjective control" by J. Rotter (adapted for research in a professional environment Bazhina E. F., Golynkina S. A., Etkind A. M).

Purpose of the technique: The technique is a modified version of the questionnaire of the American psychologist J. Rotter. With its help, it is possible to assess the level of subjective control over various situations, in other words, to determine the degree of responsibility of a person for his actions and his life.

Application of the methodology: Personnel differ in how they explain the causes of events that are significant to themselves and where they localize control over them. There are two polar types of such localization: external (external locus) and internal (internal locus). The first type manifests itself when a person believes that what is happening to him does not depend on him, but is the result of external causes (for example, chance or intervention of other people). In the second case, a person interprets significant events as the result of his own efforts. Considering the two polar types of localization, it should be remembered that each person has a different level of subjective control over significant situations. The locus of control of a particular personality is more or less universal in relation to different types of events that he has to face, both in case of success and in case of failure. In general, people with an external locus of control are more inherent in conformal and compliant behavior, they prefer to work in a group, are more often passive, dependent, anxious and unsure of themselves. People with an internal locus are more active, independent in work, they more often have a positive self-esteem, which is associated with a pronounced self-confidence and tolerance toward other people. Thus, the degree of internality of each person is associated with his attitude to his own development and personal growth. The LSC questionnaire consists of 44 proposition statements concerning externality-internality in interpersonal (industrial and family) relations, as well as in relation to one's own health.

S. Rosenzweig's technique of drawing frustration.

Purpose of the methodology: it is designed to study reactions to failure and ways to get out of situations that impede activity or satisfaction of personality needs.

Application of the technique: The technique consists of 24 schematic contour drawings, which depict two or more people engaged in an unfinished conversation. The situations depicted in the figures can be divided into two main groups: situations of "obstacles", situations of "blame" (there is a relationship between the groups of situations). Drawings are presented to the subject. It is assumed that "being responsible for the other", the subject will more easily, more reliably express his opinion and will show typical reactions for him out of conflict situations. The researcher notes the total time of the experiment. The test can be applied both individually and in groups. But unlike a group study, an individual study uses another important technique: they ask to read the written answers aloud. The experimenter notes the peculiarities of intonation, etc., which can help in clarifying the content of the answer (for example, a sarcastic tone of voice). In addition, the subject may be asked questions about very short or ambiguous answers (this is also necessary for counting). Sometimes it happens that the subject misunderstands a particular situation, and, although such errors in themselves are significant for a qualitative interpretation, nevertheless, after the necessary explanation, a new answer should be received from him. The survey should be conducted as carefully as possible, so that the questions do not contain additional information.

4 Results and Discussion

The study made it possible to analyze and come to the following conclusions. At the first stage of the study, the diagnosis of the level of emotional burnout according to the method of V. V. Boyko identified the results and identified the preliminary four groups. In the first group, 16% of the subjects did not have emotional burnout, and, accordingly, there was not a single phase of it. These people are relatively emotionally "healthy", they like work in trade, they like the team of employees, and professional duties, and the rhythm of work. Basically, this group includes relatively young employees (up to 36 years old), with or with a little work experience in this place. This is the first group of subjects without professional burnout.

All other participants in the experiment (88%) showed one or another phase of emotional burnout. Of these, in the second group, 24% of the subjects developed the "tension" phase. It can be assumed that, although they are experiencing traumatic circumstances at the workplace, the phases of exhaustion and residence did not come; Probably, these subjects are satisfied with their professional activities, although they experience a slight feeling of anxiety, but for some reason they cannot or do not want to change their place of work or profession. Since the very characteristics of the phase, as well as its symptomatology, are implicitly expressed, we also assigned these employees to the first group, conditionally not having burnout.

In the third group, 24% of the subjects developed the "resistance" phase. This suggests that they show an inadequate emotional response, emotional and moral disorientation, the expansion of the spheres of saving emotions, the reduction of professional duties in the performance of their activities. Such workers are characterized by: low emotionality, rigidity, dominance of stereotypes in behavior toward people, manifestation of a functional approach. It can be assumed that this part of the salespeople developed a feeling of fatigue, awareness of failure, reduced interest in work, which affects its effectiveness. They pay less attention to customers, do not try to solve problems, conflicts are possible.

In the fourth group, 36% of the subjects developed the "exhaustion" phase. For salespeople with a pronounced phase of exhaustion, symptoms such as emotional restraint, a tendency to accumulate affect, and irritability are characteristic. At the same time, indifference is expressed to most of the events taking place around a person (politics, health, including one's own; love, etc.). As can be seen from the results, the exhaustion phase, namely the prevailing symptoms of this phase, has higher rates compared to other phases. In addition, the exhaustion phase is characterized by the formation of psychosomatic diseases. It can be assumed that these people

Table 1 The results of a study of personality traits suffering from professional deformation using the R. Cattell test

Results according to R. Cattell scales (average score)	C	N	G	H	Q3	F1	F2	F3
Control group	0.5	10.0	6.5	9.5	6.0	4.0	11.5	8.5
Experi-mental group	11.0	3.5	2.5	3.0	11.5	8.0	7.0	5.0

experience long-term exposure to stressors at work, as a result of which they have become cynical, insensitive to work and to their customers. The reasons for this may be heavy workload, loss of interest in their work, disappointment in it.

At the second stage of the study, on the basis of the data obtained during the first stage, the features of the manifestations of professional deformations in sellers were identified separately in two groups. The first group "without deformities" served as a control to monitor the difference in the manifestation of symptoms. The rest of the participants were assigned to the experimental group (with different levels of deformation). Diagnostics of personality traits suffering from professional deformation was carried out on the basis of generalization of the data obtained using the R. Cattell test. As a result of the study, C (emotional stability—instability), N (straightforwardness—diplomacy), G (susceptibility to feelings—high normality), H (indecision—courage), Q3 (low—high self-control) were identified as the main significant factors.), and additional factors Fl (anxiety), F2 (extroversion—introversion), F3 (sensitivity—reactive balance). For the seller's work, professionally significant qualities are: emotional stability, high normality of behavior, courage, diplomacy, self-control, anxiety, extraversion, and reactive balance. The peaks for these factors in "–"or "+" confirm professional burnout [17].

The results of a study of personality traits suffering from occupational deformity using the R. Kettell test are presented in Table 1.

Consider the indicators in the experimental group. 80% of employees with a burnout rate have pronounced peaks in: high control over their emotions and behavior; high anxiety, average adaptability, dissatisfaction with what has been achieved. An emotional approach to events and people is expressed. Sensitivity, fragile emotionality, sensitivity to events are observed. They establish and maintain average contacts. Difficulties in making a decision are observed.

In the control group of employees, there are no clearly expressed and unambiguous indicators for the above factors. These employees demonstrate poise, stability, cheerfulness, decisiveness, enterprise, a tendency to not notice details; expressed social courage, activity, readiness to deal with unfamiliar circumstances and people; determined by the propensity to take risks, disinhibited-femininity, the tendency to hold on freely. Most of these employees demonstrate calmness and politeness.

At the third stage of the study, we used the technique of J. Rotter R. (LSC test), adapted for research in the professional environment by Bazhina E. F., Golynkina S. A., Etkind A. M., to investigate the level of subjective control.

The results according to the method of J. Rotter in Table 2.

Table 2 The results according to the method of J. Rotter

Investigated features	Control group	Experimental group
Level of subjective control	26%—low values on the scale of "internality" 67%—average values on the scale "internality" 7%—high values on the scale of "internality"	3%—low values on the scale of "internality" 10%—average values on the scale "internality" 87%—high values on the scale "internality"

The data obtained allow us to assert that in the experimental group there is a pronounced responsibility and high control of professional events, with a pronounced understanding. It can be assumed that employees with deformations, due to the need to control everything and be responsible for everything in life, should have an extremely heightened sense of anxiety, both situational and personal, and there should be a number of emotional disorders, such as feeling of guilty, if the control is not successful, dissatisfaction with oneself is possible, etc.

In the experimental group on the scale of "internality" in the area of achievement, as well as in the area of failure, high "stens" were found. This indicates a pronounced motivation to achieve high social goals and a high level of aspirations. The explanation lies in a kind of "flight into work", an attempt to avoid deformations, which reduces the overall level of anxiety. However, high "stens" on the scale of failure indicate a developed sense of subjective control in relation to negative events and situations, which manifests itself in a tendency to blame oneself for various professional failures, troubles, and suffering.

There is no such uniformity in the control group.

At the fourth stage of the study, to identify the style of behavior of salespeople and determine the level of adaptation to the social environment, S. Rosenzweig's method of drawing associations was used. Selected results of the study by the method of S. Rosenzweig are presented in Table 3.

In the experimental group, the indicators of the coefficient of "group conformity" are below the normal level, which allows us to assert that the level of adaptability of sellers to the social environment is low, and the problems of adaptation give rise to problems of communication with people. High indicators in the direction of "reaction

Table 3 The results of the average values of reactions to frustrating situations in the experimental group according to the method of S. Rosenzweig

Parameters	0-D	E-D	N-P	General	%
E	–	–	–	6.58	27.42
I	–	–	–	8.95	39.29
M	–	–	–	7.82	33.29
General	6.0	5.35	12.73		
%	25.0	21.9	53.04		

I", i.e. most sellers in a frustrating situation tend to adapt, twist, or deny responsibility, looking for justifying circumstances. This is an assimilative type of conflict behavior, that is, denial or suppression of the conflict. Probably the presence of such defenses as rationalization, intellectualization, annulment, sublimation. Rationalistic discrediting of the goal, self-deception, and overestimation of what is available can be viewed as a neurotic symptom, the desire to maintain peace at any cost, not to succumb to a nervous breakdown.

In addition, the salespeople of the experimental group are prone to excessive initiative unjustified by the interests of the case, the desire to rely on their own strength when trying to get out of difficult situations. In this case, it can be interpreted as the presence of a hidden inferiority complex, self-doubt, and a desire to prove to oneself and others the opposite. In a situation of frustration, the main defenses are identification and overcompensation. The behavior is characterized by stubbornness and lack of flexibility. Another obvious tendency is selective passivity, staying in anticipation of such a development of circumstances, when everything will be settled by itself, without their personal intervention in the course of events; characterized by withdrawal reactions, indecision, avoidance of activity.

In the control group, they are inclined to show initiative, the desire to rely on general strength when trying to get out of difficult situations. Another obvious trend is activity, personal interest in resolving professional issues in a positive aspect. Typical behavioral reactions, such as: determination, purposefulness, manifestation of will.

5 Discussion

The results of the study led to the following conclusions. The influence of professional deformation on the staff of retail chains (category: seller) in the context of the digitalization of the economy is revealed).

During an additional conversation with subjects of the third and fourth groups (who showed the phases of "resistance" and "exhaustion") turned out that all of them have more than five years of work experience and would like to change the type of their professional activity. They characterize their work as "nervous" and "endless", they say that "they do not see a person in a person", but perceive him as "an irritant that needs to be quickly served". Moreover, employees who fall into the first and second groups do not give this kind of assessment either to their work or to their clients. This gave us grounds to single out the third and fourth last groups of employees as having professional deformation, with vivid symptoms of emotional burnout. Matyushkina E.Y. also noted the relationship between professional burnout and work experience in a study of call center workers, however, no significant correlation was found between these parameters; professional burnout, according to the author, is more likely associated with a lack of intrinsic motivation [12].

Thus, according to the diagnostic methodology of the "Level of subjective control" by J. Rotter, in general, employees with professional deformity have a strongly pronounced internal locus of control, which indicates a high level of subjective control over any significant events. In the control group, this trend is absent.

The results of the study led to the following conclusions. The influence of professional deformation on the staff of retail chains (category: seller) in the context of the digitalization of the economy is revealed. The identity and differences between the socio-psychological characteristics of the personality of network sellers with high and low levels of emotional burnout was established, affecting the professional deformation of personnel in the context of the digitalization of the economy.

Professional deformation is presented as a process and a by-product of professional activity in working with people. It has a negative impact on staff from among the sellers of retail chains in the context of the digitalization of the economy.

Practical research has shown that about 88% of the subjects show symptoms of burnout, this indicates a manifested professional deformation.

By the nature of their professional activities, sellers of a trading network have to deal with different types of buyers. At the same time, sellers experience a great stressful load, they constantly need to communicate with a large number of buyers, which leads to fatigue and loss of interest in their professional activities, cynicism, and emotional detachment. The leading symptom of burnout in this sample is the reduction of professional responsibilities.

In the context of the professional environment of network sellers, one can find the existence of a set of personal deformations: egocentrism, neuroticism, impatience. The origins of these deformations are in the process of adaptation of the individual to the peculiarities of professional activity. One of the main manifestations of the professional deformation of these specialists is the internal locus control, the tendency to control everyone around, to be responsible for everything, to assume the role of a "resolver of difficulties" with low indicators of communication competence.

In a situation of frustration, the sellers of the trading network choose such behavior strategies as (1) taking responsibility for resolving the situation; (2) a strategy of waiting, in which everything will be resolved somehow, avoiding solving the problem, avoiding the situation. The first strategy is obviously not constructive, but testifies to the desire to turn on, with the inability to keep the tension in a difficult situation. The second strategy can be flawed for the reason that professional activity requires constant stress from salespeople and solving complex problems, because they are the face of the organization. Therefore, such a behavior strategy is often taken for laziness, unwillingness to work. This creates a bad reputation for sellers.

6 Conclusion

Studying the phenomenology of professional deformation of salespeople in a retail network is an important part of organizational work, which allows monitoring the state of the company's personnel. For the sellers of the trading network, it manifests itself in the fact that he does not see the buyer, his main task is to instrumentally fulfill his duties.

The prospect of studying the problem is the use of the results of practical research to develop preventive measures in order to reduce the impact of professional deformation of staff, which prevents the formation of demanded employees in the digital economy.

The practical significance of the study lies in the timely response and preventive work with personnel, which will maintain the company's image at a sufficiently high level. As part of the digitalization of modern society, it is necessary to develop and implement preventive response technologies in the management of the organization, the use of which will ensure controllability of personnel deformation, increase their competitiveness and form the demanded meta-competencies of the modern digital professional community.

Among such preventive technologies, we offer the following:

1. Reducing the number of work shifts per month and compiling a flexible work schedule that would take into account the interests and needs of employees;
2. The ability to take a day off at your own expense when necessary;
3. Creating a comfortable and positive working atmosphere, decorating the interiors of working rooms with the possibility of choosing colors and designs by the staff;
4. Creation of a working microclimate focused on support and mutual assistance;
5. The opportunity to visit the gym, pool or participate in other sports sections at the expense of the employer. [See, for example, [8], p. 204]

All these and other similar activities will reduce the risks of burnout as one of the components of professional deformation.

We believe that the results of our research can serve to analyze the level of professional burnout in socionomic professions (work with people) among employees, to prevent such conditions and take measures to eliminate them in a timely manner. The proposed methodology, which consists of 4 types of tests, can be refined and improved, which will require further theoretical and practical research.

References

1. Aleksandrovsky, Y. A. (2017). Psychogeny in extreme conditions. 142 p. Medicine.
2. Bazhin, E. F., Golynkina, E. A., & Etkind, A. M. (1984). Method of researching the level of subjective control. *Psychology zhurn, 3*, 152–162.
3. Beznosov, S. P. (2014). Professional personality deformation (114 p.). Rech, SPb.
4. Boyko, V. V. (2013). Burnout syndrome in professional communication (32 p.). Madam, SPb.
5. Freundenberger, H. J. (1974). Staff burnout. *Journal of Social Issues, 30*(1), 159–165.
6. Gindikin, V. Ya., & Gurieva, V. A. (2017). Personal pathology (62 p.). Triada-X.
7. Greenberg, J. (2014). Stress management (166 p.). Peter, SPb.
8. Ivanovic, T., Ivancevic, S., & Maricic, M. (2020). The relationship between recruiter burnout, work engagement and turnover intention: Evidence from Serbia. *Engineering Economics, 31*(2), 197–210. Retrieved April 06, 2021, from https://doi.org/10.5755/j01.ee.31.2.24100
9. Kulikov, L. V. (1995). Psychological research: method, recommendations for conducting. (122 p.). SPb.

10. Kuzmina, N. V. (2019). Professionalism of the personality of the teacher and master of industrial training (152 pp.).
11. Markova, A. K. (1996). Psychology of professionalism (312 pp.).
12. Matyushkina, E. Ya. (2017). Factors of professional burnout of specialists (on the example of contact center workers). *Consultative Psychology and Psychotherapy, 25*(4), 42–58. Retrieved April 06, 2021, from https://doi.org/10.17759/cpp.2017250404
13. Polyakova, O. (2014). Category «Proofessional deformation» in psychology third annual international conference «Early childhood care and education». *Procedia—Social and Behavioral Sciences, 146*, 279–282. Retrieved April 06, 2021, from https://doi.org/10.1016/j.sbspro.2014.08.129
14. Dushkova, B. A., Smirnova B. A., & Korolev A. V. (Eds.). (2013). Psychology of labor, professional, informational and organizational activity: dictionary, 2nd edn. Add. and revised. (141 pp.). Academic project, M. Business book.
15. Ronginskaya, T. I. (2016). Burnout syndrome in social professions. *Psychological Journal, 23*(3), 85–95.
16. Rosenzweig, S. (1945). The picture-association method and its application in a study of reactions to frustration. *Journal of Personality, 14*(1), 3–23.
17. Shtroo, V. A. (2018). Defense mechanisms: From personality to group. *Questions of psychology., 4*, 54–61.
18. Temnova, L. V., Faiman, N. S. (2019). Professional deformations in socionic professions. *RUDN Journal of Sociology, 19*(1), 7–19. Retrieved April 06, 2021, from https://doi.org/10.22363/2313-2272-2019-19-1-7-19
19. Varfolomeeva, T. P.: Professional deformation of workers involved in socialy-dependent occupations. *Scientific Bulletin, 4*(5), 46–48. Samara.
20. Zeer, E. F. (2019). Psychology of vocational education (115 pp.). Yurayt.